ALSO BY **SUSAN HERTOG**

. . .

Anne Morrow Lindbergh: Her Life

DANGEROUS
AMBITION

SUSAN HERTOG

BALLANTINE BOOKS
NEW YORK

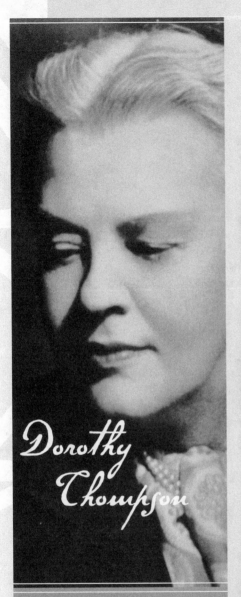

DANGEROUS AMBITION

Dorothy Thompson

NEW WOMEN IN SEARCH OF LOVE AND POWER

and Rebecca West

Published in the United States by Ballantine Books,
an imprint of The Random House Publishing Group,
a division of Random House, Inc., New York.

BALLANTINE and colophon are registered
trademarks of Random House, Inc.

Photo and text permissions credits are located beginning on page 479.

LIBRARY OF CONGRESS CATALOGING-IN-PUBLICATION DATA
Hertog, Susan.
Dangerous ambition : Rebecca West and Dorothy Thompson :
new women in search of love and power / Susan Hertog.
p.   cm.
  Includes bibliographical references and index.
  ISBN 978-0-345-45986-2 (hardcover : alk. paper) —
ISBN 978-0-345-52943-5 (ebook)
1. West, Rebecca, 1892–1983.   2. West, Rebecca, 1892–1983—
Relations with men.   3. Women authors, English—20th century—
Biography.   4. Women journalists—Great Britain—Biography.
5. Thompson, Dorothy, 1893–1961.   6. Thompson, Dorothy,
1893–1961—Relations with men.   7. Women authors, American—
20th century—Biography.   8. Women journalists—United States—
Biography.   I. Title.
PR6045.E8Z68 2011
828'.91209—dc23
[B]   2011035119

Printed in the United States of America on acid-free paper

www.ballantinebooks.com

9 8 7 6 5 4 3 2 1

FIRST EDITION

Book design by Barbara M. Bachman

To my children

Allison

Justin

David

Only part of us is sane: only part of us loves pleasure and the longer day of happiness, wants to live to our nineties and die in peace, in a house that we built, that shall shelter those who come after us. The other half of us is nearly mad. It prefers the disagreeable to the agreeable, loves pain and its darker night despair, and wants to die in a catastrophe that will set back life to its beginnings and leave nothing of our house save its blackened foundations.

—REBECCA WEST, *Black Lamb and Grey Falcon,* 1941

I love life because I am conscious of my existence in an order which is sublime. My "reason to live" is to strive to recognize, accept, cooperate, and serve that order, and thus help to fulfill the law of Nature, Creation, God. And since that order encompasses my death, in organic nature, the acceptance gives me sufficient "reason to die." Over and over again these days, we hear the phrase, "The world is in chaos." But "the world" is *not* in chaos. . . . Men are in chaos.

—DOROTHY THOMPSON, *The Courage to Be Happy,* 1957

CONTENTS

INTRODUCTION

> The attributes of True Womanhood, by which
> a woman judged herself and was judged by her
> husband, her neighbors, and society, could
> be divided into four cardinal virtues—piety,
> purity, submissiveness and domesticity. Put
> them all together and they spelled mother,
> daughter, sister, wife—woman. Without them
> no matter whether there was fame, achievement
> or wealth, all was ashes. With them she was
> promised happiness and power.
>
> —BARBARA WELTER,
> "The Cult of True Womanhood, 1820–1860," 1966

Born in the age of Victoria on opposite sides of the Atlantic, Rebecca West, an Englishwoman of Scots-Irish ancestry, and Dorothy Thompson, an American with English and Scottish roots, were brilliant and ambitious women whose driving sense of personal mission pierced the norms of conventional womanhood to achieve professional success and unprecedented fame at a time when female accomplishment was thwarted and demonized. Thompson, the rebellious daughter of a fundamentalist Methodist preacher, insatiably curious and hungry for experience, craved the excitement of foreign travel and the peripatetic life of a journalist. Later, as an influential commentator with a preacher's penchant for fire and brimstone, she gained domestic and international fame as one of the first to decry appeasement toward ruthless fascist regimes that threatened the annihilation of Western democracies.

West, the self-educated daughter of a notorious huckster and polemicist, was a precocious teenager who became a formidable journalist and literary critic before the age of twenty. By thirty, she was a biographer, novelist, and literary theorist, and by fifty, an eminent historian and international journalist. By the time her life was over, West was an international literary icon; her legacy informs twenty-first-century thinking.

But even as their professional lives prospered, their personal relationships shattered. Pioneering feminists, they broke the rules before new ones were invented. They loved and married men as ambitious as themselves and as incapable of enduring relationships, ultimately finding shards of joy in family and friendship, and, if not fulfillment, satisfaction in their work.

Feminists say that the Victorian era began in 1837 and ended in the mid-1960s with the social upheaval of the booming generation that came of age after the Second World War. These women, born in the 1890s and living through most of the twentieth century, prove it true. The cult of true womanhood hovered over their lives, clouding their desires and ambitions with guilt and, at times, turning them into social pariahs. They may be admired for their tenacity and their accomplishments but not envied for the choices they made within the historical moment in which they lived. They can be held responsible for their insensitive and destructive impulses, but they also deserve to be understood.

Victorian women, it may be assumed, were no less lusty or determined than contemporary ones, but they had no prototypes, no social institutions, and no ethical scaffolding that permitted them to ascend and flourish. The double standards that the American and British societies into which Thompson and West were born upheld made duplicity inevitable. Beneath the smooth veneer of propriety, which was both punitive and unforgiving to women, men were permitted the luxury of straying. If women dipped below the surface into that forbidden male realm, they were castigated and denounced as evil or diseased. Yet, both men and women were prisoners of this ethic. Since divorce and out-of-wedlock birth, especially in England, carried a burden of social stigma unimaginable today, men who chose adultery were treacherous by necessity. They, too, must be held responsible and must be understood.

REBECCA WOULD WRITE, tongue in cheek, that she admired biographers because they had the courage of a Canute. Which is to say she didn't admire them at all. Canute, the Viking king who conquered England in the eleventh century, impressed his subjects by asking his courtiers to carry him to the edge of the Atlantic. Sitting at the ocean's shore, he would raise his arms and command the waters to ebb and flow to demonstrate the majesty of his power.

Furthermore, she would write, it was impossible for biographers to know anything beyond the bare facts about the details of their subjects' intimate lives or subjective experience. She was right. Arrogance and unadulterated conjecture are part of the game. But it is a fascinating game that requires intense and far-ranging research from a myriad of vantage points, the discerning of patterns, and the synthesizing of the chaos of experience into a comprehensible, meaningful, and entertaining narrative that captures the essence of an individual. I have had the utter gall to think I can understand and link *two* lives—women who were bound by friendship, a consonant social and political vision, and the commonality of fame, marriage, and motherhood. It is, of course, an impossible task that I have undertaken, and I submit the fruits of my labor with great humility.

Nonetheless, I justify my efforts in my belief that the lives of these women are important, not only in and of themselves, but because they are emblematic of female consciousness at a time of great social and moral upheaval and escalating scientific discovery—when psychological survival required the redefinition of one's relationship to oneself, society, and the universe, both physical and divine. Few were up to the task, and the trajectory of most lives was an exercise in experimentation, frustration, and failure. Thompson and West, however, had the extraordinary advantage of raw intelligence, along with the desire to make a difference in the world.

To understand these women and their men in the context of the social and political forces that determined the thrust and contour of their lives, and to draw lessons relevant to our lives and times, is the end toward which I have written this book.

Susan Hertog
August 2011

DANGEROUS
AMBITION

GEMINI

One spoke of Berlin as one speaks of a highly
desirable woman. . . . Everyone wanted her. . . .
[The] man who had Berlin owned the world.

—CARL ZUCKMAYER

BERLIN, 1925

Still in her dressing gown, Dorothy leaned against the balustrade, devouring the heat of the midday sun. For a woman devoted to the life of the mind, she seemed to swallow her pleasures whole. Two stories up on a tree-lined street not far from town, her sprawling flat was her "bird's nest" of respite from the din of a city reinventing itself.

In the distance she could see bridges and skyscrapers of glass and steel towering above the trolley cars and automobiles; she could hear the screech of trains as they pulled into the new triangle junction like clockwork. The grandeur of technology made human life seem small and weak, lost in the body of a great machine pushing Germany with astonishing speed toward a future beyond anyone's imagination. Dorothy couldn't decide if it was paradise or purgatory—a benediction to human creativity or the desecration of all the values she held dear. She saw herself as a country girl. As a child growing up in rural upstate New York, Dorothy had found comfort and sustenance in the exquisite beauty of full-blown trees and grassy meadows laced with summer blooms.

This flat was to have been the first real home she would share with her husband, Joseph Bard. She had hunted for months to find the perfect location, had handpicked each piece of furniture, and had had the chairs and sofas upholstered in brocades and velvets to lend warmth to the otherwise undistinguished rooms. It was to be their office by day and their salon by night—a quiet place to think and write, yet grand enough to entertain notables, colleagues, and friends as they swept in and out of town. Charmed by the scene outside the windows, Dorothy followed the play of light as it filtered through the trees. This home, she had believed, would be the symbol of their commitment to marriage.

Dorothy Thompson and Joseph Bard in Vienna in 1923

After the morning rush to finish her stories for the *New York Evening Post*, there was nothing she liked more than to watch the children play on the lawns of the Tiergarten below. Their laughter and song were irrepressible; their joy made her nostalgic and sad. As a child she had played with the same innocence, climbing trees with the boys and diving in the pond until darkness and exhaustion overtook her. By now she had hoped to have children of her own, but once again she found herself alone. There was a familiarity about her loneliness that had grown strangely comfortable. After her mother had died when Dorothy was eight, she had learned the depth of her strength and the value of independence. She held it close, as insurance against turbulent times.

Pink-skinned and radiant as she turned her face to catch the sun, Dorothy looked younger than her thirty-two years. Yet her eyes were shrouded in pain. She was still mourning the death of her marriage. Her raven-haired Semitic "prince" had left her for another woman the pre-

vious spring. At first she thought it was just another one of his fanciful flings, but once she realized that he was not coming back, she had
been nearly suicidal with grief. Joseph had fallen in love with a wealthy
young art student in London, whom he apparently found more attractive and sensitive than Dorothy. Eileen Agar, said Joseph to their
friends, understood his needs and loved him deeply without wanting to
possess him.

For the moment, Dorothy's despair eclipsed her unparalleled success
as a foreign correspondent. There had been a few other female journalists who had risen to the top, but most had been relegated to the so-called
women's pages. Her guts and drive, along with her fluency in German,
had earned her a post as a special reporter in Vienna responsible for covering all of central Europe, and now, as the first female head of a news
bureau, permanently stationed in Berlin, she was celebrated for her integrity in a distinguished coterie of men. But Dorothy saw her work as
shallow and impotent—a superficial record of daily flux that had no impact on the course of events. Joseph was to have been her savior, the
sensitive poet/philosopher who was, like her preacher father, too good
for the tawdry universe of common men. Joseph's ambition to write a
philosophical history of Europe had given her life purpose and meaning,
a reason to keep writing. He was to be the literary genius who would
profit from the financial good fortune engendered by her ceaseless hard
work. In the end, though, Joseph had used her; he had sucked her energy,
her idealism, and her bank account dry. She was bitter, but more than
that, she felt rejected and emotionally drained. She chastised herself for
playing his fool.

Before him, she had written to a friend, she had lived the solitary life
of a wildcat, ready to pounce on the next big story, scavenge a revolution, and feed on the carcasses of people and events. She had relished the
competition, the rush of the hunt, and the momentary flush of the limelight. But having known the comfort of loving companionship, and the
promise of a home and family, she would never look at the world in the
same way again. Her innocence, she had written, had been irrevocably
lost. He had taken a chaste girl and made her both a woman and a man
with his bestial sexuality, and had then discarded her. She had been willing to do anything to keep his love, but now she realized it had been an
illusion. There was nothing to do but bury herself in her work.

Her afternoon, like every other, would be full of diversions—perhaps a meeting with a foreign dignitary, a politician on the rise, a well-informed friend. Dorothy was willing to talk with anyone—radicals, refugees, spies, disillusioned republicans; for the price of a hearty lunch or dinner, she could seduce them into passing on information and eye-witness accounts. After her morning of writing articles, and editing her local stringers for the American taste in news, she would go to her small office in the center of town and, without the luxury of secretaries or a full-time staff, plan her stories for the next day's news. She covered eight countries besides Germany—Austria, Czechoslovakia, Albania, Hungary, Romania, Yugoslavia, Turkey, and Greece.

Preparing herself for the afternoon was an arduous task, and yet it was tempered by a touch of relief because she could mask herself in the folds of couture. It was a strange fancy for a woman of serious inclination, but she knew that her voluptuous body was an asset to enhance. Dorothy liked men; she needed to feel desirable and attractive, yet also appreciated for her fertile mind. After Joseph had left, she consulted with Sigmund Freud, and she had taken his advice seriously. "Buy a new wardrobe and change the color of your lipstick," he had said. Optimistic by nature, and disciplined as a reporter at feigning nonchalance, Dorothy knew Freud was right. She indulged her penchant for brightly colored clothes, trimmed with ribbons and floppy bows. The semblance of *bon vivance* cheered her even as it disguised her grief.

Standing at her bedroom closet, still half full of Joseph's clothes, she plucked out two suits like flowers in a garden. Should she wear the royal blue wool with the matching straw cloche, or the yellow linen with the silk ascot blouse? As much as she wanted to bring the sunlight with her, the blue wool would take her into the evening hours when Berlin would awaken with clubs and cafés, theaters and films, concerts, jazz bands, and nudie shows. To drown her sadness, she had thrown herself into the nightlife of the city. She drank too much, ate too much, and perhaps, as those close to her whispered, had taken on lovers for a moment's respite and physical warmth.

On the bus ride from Händelstrasse into town, a mile and a half away, she braced herself for the onslaught of crowds and noise. The population of greater Berlin had soared to nearly four million, doubling since the start of the war. Émigrés from all over Europe and Russia flooded the city's sidewalks, while trolleys, cars, and buses fought for space honking their way through the thoroughfares. There were con men in tango trousers and garish coats and stock market winners in horn-rimmed glasses and flat-backed Bolshevik haircuts. Intellectuals and artists walked alongside one-legged beggars maimed in the war and well-heeled matrons flaunting the wealth of their industrialist husbands. Slavic, Latinate, and Teutonic tongues rang through the streets, and the smell of shashliks and blintzes intermingled with wurst as Dorothy's bus passed the open-air cafés.

The despair that had hovered over Berlin after the war had given way to gaiety and optimism. Commerce with the United Kingdom and the United States—along with generous Allied loans—had bolstered an economy on the verge of collapse. The Weimar government had thrust Germany into unprecedented poverty and hyperinflation, but now the Rentenmark was up, unemployment was down, dresses had risen to the upper stratum of the knee, and long hair was cropped to a chin-length bob. Women had been liberated not only from their corsets but from household work as well. Typing in offices during the day, they shimmied all night in clubs and bars. No longer expected just to marry and bear children, some even went to university. But the social and political enfranchisement of the "New Woman" struck fear in the heart of the male culture; everything from unemployment to moral laxity was blamed on the liberation of women. Like the Communists and the Jews, they were considered traitors to the new republic.

AS DOROTHY EXITED THE BUS, she ran into her colleague John Gunther, a blue-eyed, sandy-haired Chicagoan with the jovial air of indomitable youth. He was always graceful and lithe, but today he was practically pirouetting in the street. "Rebecca's in town!" he shouted.

"Why?" Dorothy asked.

"To see me!" he answered.

"Bring her to my flat tonight! I'm having a party!" she yelled. "Eight o'clock." Too far down the street to be heard, he vigorously nodded his head.

John Gunther and Rebecca West had been lovers for two years; they had met during her first trip to America in 1923. He had been one of many men who had courted her that fall—among them, Max Beaverbrook, a wealthy industrialist and newspaper magnate, and Charlie Chaplin, the Hollywood celebrity of comic satire. Rebecca believed she was doomed to attract the wrong kind of lovers—dominating, posses-sive, and callous. She no longer trusted her instincts toward men. She needed their strength and protection too much, and those who were will-ing to pay her price expected total dedication in return. Her abandon-ment by her father in childhood had taught her that dependence on men was a suicidal impulse. She, her mother, and her sisters had lived in pov-erty and shame.

John had remained a loyal friend and lover to Rebecca, and while they both realized that they had no future together, they adored each other's style and looks. He was as tall and fair as she was dark and petite, as disciplined and scholarly as she was volatile and imaginative, as soft-spoken and sensitive as she was brash and intolerant. But they shared a chemistry and respect that seemed to sustain them. His gentility and ad-miration for her talent and ambition was a salve to the wounds inflicted by the many egocentric men she had known.

As Dorothy walked to the small office she kept on Motzstrasse, she remembered the first time she had met Rebecca, shortly after she arrived in London in 1921, a fledgling reporter hustling for freelance assign-ments from the International News Service. Making her way through the Fleet Street labyrinth, cultivating connections and scavenging for leads, Dorothy had met H. G. Wells and Rebecca at a London party. H.G., already an author of wealth and fame for his scientific fantasies and romantic novels, was accompanied by his precocious, sylphlike mis-tress, twenty-six years his junior. Rebecca, despite her youth, had already published several books of her own, including a literary biography of Henry James, and had earned a reputation as an outspoken foe of the political establishment. She was becoming notorious as a literary critic; her scathing analysis spared no one, regardless of his or her public stand-ing or reputation. George Bernard Shaw, Arnold Bennett, and even H. G. Wells had been fodder. In fact, that was how she had met Wells. Unintimidated by his universal acclaim, she challenged his characteriza-tion of women and his distorted views on marriage. It wasn't long after their first meeting that Wells's steel-blue eyes, radiant sensuality, and penetrating mind evoked Rebecca's passionate love.

Dorothy knew that Rebecca and H.G. had been lovers, but she sus-pected it was a stormy relationship. He was a married man with two chil-dren, and Rebecca had not been his only young mistress. At first their clandestine romance suited their wild, rebellious natures; they called each other "Jaguar" and "Panther," jungle cats who made their own rules on instinct. But by 1923 word had gotten around that they had broken up; after their child was born they learned that perhaps they weren't so wild after all. In London, Dorothy had met Rebecca's so-called nephew, Anthony, the alleged son of her dead sister who had left him in her care; he was about eight years old at the time and had come home from school for the summer holiday. After spending four years in Europe and having so many experiences, Dorothy wondered how this literary wunderkind would appear through the prism of her own rapid success and newfound prestige.

Dorothy walked faster as she imbibed the rhythm of the city. She had come to understand Berlin and to learn it was a city one had to revere. It seemed to her like a natural force that moved according to Darwinian law. It could gobble you up, grind you to a pulp, and spit you out, if you didn't have the stamina to endure its abuse. But Dorothy found it as exhilarating as it was frightening; it was a city where dreams could come true for a person of talent. Charlatans and poseurs didn't stand a chance, nor did the weak-willed and cowardly. She had come here as a journalist with an established reputation, but Joseph, an intellectual with literary aspirations, had been repelled by Berlin's capricious cruelty.

At a time when two-thirds of the city's young male population had been killed or maimed, the emphasis was "now" and the password was "progress." And yet, it was exactly this disillusion that had made cultural fermentation possible; Berlin had become the new artistic capital of Europe. The signs were everywhere—in the architecture, the paintings, the novels, the dramas, the music, and the films. New art forms arose in the ashes of the old. Expressionism and Dadaism, obsessed with the meaninglessness of life, legitimized torture, murder, sickness, and decay. In reaction, the Germans flocked to American films—big musical extravaganzas with elaborate costumes and lighthearted dance, even as German cinema remained conservative and introspective.

It was the theater, however, deemed to be in its "golden age," that allured Dorothy. Its haunting immediacy was an anodyne to her sadness. She would often attend three or four nights a week. The plays of Ernst Toller and Bertolt Brecht were full of postwar disappointment and gloom, but the young playwright Carl Zuckmayer saw the hope of resurrection of society through the individual. His humanism, expressed in lyrical prose, lifted her to a higher sphere of comprehension, much as her father's sermons had done when she was a child. Like Dorothy, Zuck-mayer was intrigued by the relationship between man and the divine, the tension between the individual and transcendent social and moral truths. And Zuckmayer had the courage to question the status quo: the coun-try's rampant militarism and frightening cultural propensity toward blind obedience.

Before the theater, Dorothy would often stop by the Hotel Adlon to have drinks with her colleagues at the bar. With its sprawling marble lobby, bronze statues, and cathedral ceiling, the Art Deco hotel attracted rich tourists who came to Berlin to buy silver and crystal in its bright new shops, hoping to have a foretaste of the country's future. Because few natives could afford the Adlon's prices, British and American journalists saw it as a refuge from the war-ravaged crowds of the city. It was a place to exchange information and share one's views, and you could always count on a poker game, day or night. This famed watering hole drew old-timers, including Raymond Swing, London correspondent for Philadelphia's *Public Ledger;* George Seldes and Floyd Gibbons of the *Chicago Tribune;* Marcel Fodor of the *Manchester Guardian;* and Claud Cockburn of the London *Times;* and newcomers, such as William Shirer and Vincent Sheenan with the *Chicago Tribune;* John Gunther, Edgar Mowrer, and Paul Mowrer of the *Chicago Daily News;* and Seldes's as-sistant, Sigrid Schultz. Of course the regulars showed up every night, but one never knew who else would be passing through. Berlin had be-come the nexus for journalists moving west toward Paris and London, and east toward Prague, Budapest, and Moscow. In Europe, where jour-nalists were perceived as a de facto intelligence arm of their govern-ments, American correspondents were seen as dangerous "buzzards" who preyed on the carrion of people and events. Feared by officials, do-mestic and foreign, they were kept at bay, forced to stalk weak-livered informants who forked the flesh of their compatriots. While the alien status of the foreign press forged an esprit de corps among Dorothy's colleagues, there was an underlying current of competition. The ethic of getting it right and getting it first prevailed even among friends, and hon-est conversation had its bounds. Everyone played by the rules of the game, but each could count on others for cash, food, lodging, and moral support in times of trouble.

They didn't know it, but they were the pioneers of modern journal-ism; these men and women had been assigned to Berlin just as the nature of foreign correspondence had changed. Journalists were given unprecedented latitude by the large urban newspapers competing for readers; they were expected to bring historical and personal perspective to the facts, stirring up controversy that imbued the news with the glamour of entertainment. While many of her colleagues traveled constantly, Dorothy had run out of steam after her abandonment by Joseph. She was sick of reporting, and after the emotional upheaval of the past year, she felt ugly, old, and tired. She told a friend that she wanted to be someone in her own country; she wanted to write something important and enduring, such as novels and other books. Professionally, she wanted to be "something no other woman has been yet." And yet, a new doubt had taken hold. Could she ever commit herself to a man, but remain true to herself? Her ambition was beginning to frighten her.

When the theater was over and it was still too early to go home, Dorothy would frequently join the city's café life, just warming up. She had always needed people, and now, without Joseph, she craved company more than ever. At night, Berlin, with its loose morals and iconoclastic art, seemed like a city outside Germany—an island unto itself. It drew nothing from the land, covering it up with asphalt and bricks, and had shed the national mores and costumes. The avant-garde intellectuals prided themselves on being the aristocratic arbiters of beauty and truth. What they said in the cafés in the evening would be echoed by the intelligentsia in pubs all over the world—London, Paris, New York, and Rio. Within that elite, each clan and circle had its own turf and haunt. Academics, poets, and novelists of all stripes discussed the literary landscape or played chess on well-frequented balconies.

Dorothy would often stay late, only to rise before dawn. On this night, however, her late-afternoon and evening rituals fell by the wayside as she transformed her home into a salon. Dorothy hurried back to Händelstrasse, checking in on the caterer and florist. Dorothy's salon had become an institution in Berlin, celebrated for its good food and wine and as a gathering place for local and foreign intellectuals and officials—but it also had a self-serving purpose: It gathered people who could expand her base and inform her work. Dorothy "picked them for their brains," and they would attempt to do the same.

Like a performer preparing for the stage, Dorothy molded the curl in her bob so that her toast-colored hair swept across her forehead and fell in a perfect wave over her right ear. It was true that her face was a bit too wide, but with touches of makeup under her blue-green eyes, and the illusion of hollows on her rouged cheeks, she could look passingly attractive. She stopped for a moment, as she often did, to assess the degree of her feminine appeal. Her belly was flaccid, and her breasts were too full for the flapper fashion, but she was proud of her strong, sturdy body, softened by the curve of her breasts and hips.

Her pink satin dress slid easily over her powdered skin. If she was to tie her magenta sash low and loose around her waist, the full-length hem would elongate her torso and hide the fullness of her ankles. Her long, slender fingers, still adorned with Joseph's ring, would give her, at least, an image of elegance.

As the sun dropped low through the summer trees, she arranged the flowers and the chairs. Tonight the crowd would be larger than usual— too large to seat in the dining room. Her Biedermeier tables, normally overflowing with books and papers, were covered in linen to serve as a buffet. It was important that she review her guest list and her questions, and to remember not to drink too much. She needed to keep her wits about her. The political tide was turning again; antidemocratic sentiment against the fledgling Weimar Republic had dwindled with the economic gain. But its pillars were becoming increasingly unstable with internecine quarrels among leftist groups and the conservative elements that vied for power.

Sigrid Schultz was among the first to arrive. Though she was outwardly civil, Sigrid saw Dorothy as an intruder on her turf. Soon Sigrid would move to the position of chief of the European desk for the *Chicago Tribune,* replacing George Seldes. Blond and petite with delicate features and Clara Bow lips, she courted government officials with a style and grace atypical of American journalists. Also arriving early were Dorothy's friends, colleagues, and neighbors from one floor below, Edgar and Lilian Mowrer. American journalists who had just relocated from Mussolini's Rome, where foreign journalists had been virtually disenfranchised with the passage of a press law that required all reporters to register with the Fascist Journalists' Association, the Mowrers found Berlin's intellectual and cultural fertility refreshing. Despite being a working reporter, Lilian would later say that Dorothy's parties were boring if you were a woman; Dorothy believed that most wives lacked intellectual luster and chose to live in cocoons of domesticity. They were often pushed to the sidelines while she lavished attention on their influential spouses.

Encircled by men, Dorothy talked feverishly about political events and trends. But when her friend arrived on the arm of John Gunther, the whole atmosphere changed. Girlishly slender with black curly hair and wide, dark eyes that seemed to penetrate everything, Rebecca cut a captivating figure in her long, flowing chiffon dress. Her toga-like clothes radiated sensuality subdued by classical restraint. She, like Dorothy, had learned the power of feminine wile. But Rebecca had taken the insight further. Just as she believed that art raised the human spirit to a higher realm, so she believed that the artfully dressed enhanced the dignity and influence of their social presence. She swept into a room like a trained actress, harnessing every aspect of her being in service to her task.

Dorothy was perceptive; she saw Rebecca in a way that others did not. Despite her friend's casual air and sympathetic smile, Dorothy saw callousness in her face and a touch of pain around her eyes that hadn't been evident four years earlier. Rebecca seemed to wear the scars of battle. Gone were the unself-conscious innocence and humility she had feigned in the company of Wells. Since the two women last met, Rebecca had written articles and books acclaimed by publishers on both sides of the Atlantic. During her American tour in 1923, when Rebecca realized just how attractive and renowned she was, she had become supremely confident of her literary gifts. She had ridden her celebrity from the East Coast to West, attracting an entourage of admirers and reporters. But there was an emptiness just below the surface that Dorothy detected was akin to her own.

Dorothy moved toward Rebecca with outstretched arms, and ushered her and John toward the male assemblage. Taking a cigarette out of her purse, while ten arms raced to light her smoke, Rebecca inhaled the ambience along with the smoke, beginning in earnest to ask questions.

Capable of conversing in two languages—English and French—Rebecca spoke clearly with Americans and her compatriots, as well as with the French ambassador to Berlin, Pierre de Margerie. Dorothy helped her to understand the German. "Was there violence in the streets among fascists, Communists, and republicans? Could the republic really survive? Did they take the National Socialists' racial policies seriously? How did the influx of foreigners and the Russian presence affect the artistic and intellectual complexion of the city?" The intensity in her voice demanded thoughtful answers.

Claud Cockburn, a left-leaning correspondent for *The Times* known for his skill and conviction, answered first. The military had never accepted the surrender of the civil authorities to the Allies and the Treaty of Versailles. They felt stabbed in the back by politicians after four years of sustaining so many losses. Everyone knew that the Germans were defying the treaty with their buildup of military forces and training; nothing had changed, especially now that Field Marshal Hindenburg was in charge. Some of the military sought to bring back the monarchy, and others were eager to align with the fascists. *Mein Kampf,* written by Adolf Hitler—that Austrian painter turned revolutionary—had laid out a plan to resurrect the Prussian empire. Inflation and unemployment had made people desperate for work and eager to accept his vision for prosperity and power as a practical alternative to the chaos of Weimar. No, Cockburn was certain that even now, Germany was still a substantial threat.

The French ambassador concurred that the Germans could not be trusted—they would do it all again, if given the chance. Yet, two years earlier, Margerie, representing the French premier, had tried to make a secret trade with Weimar. The French economy was in a state of collapse, and they had hoped to reestablish ties with the Germans and simultaneously settle war reparations. Their attempt to circumvent their allies, however, was doomed to failure. The survival of the economies of France and Germany was ultimately dependent on the goodwill and support of Britain and America. Pragmatic issues aside, Margerie believed that the Germans deserved everything taken from them at Versailles. France had paid its pound of flesh, more so than any other Ally. Its young male population was wiped out, proportionately more than the British, the Russians, or the Americans. The Germans had bombed its cities, ravaged its farmland, and ruined its steel industry. France would never tolerate another war, and he believed that the League of Nations was an idealistic dream—peace with Germany could never endure.

Dorothy was certain Margerie was right. The surest road to war was government instability. If the republic were to survive, it would have to morph into a hybrid organism, at once democratic and repressive. It was already showing signs of moving in that direction. The violence in the streets had abated only after the government had been forced to quell

Communist infiltration and military demonstrations by force. And the Jews were viewed with increasing suspicion. Journalists, novelists, theater producers, poets, eminent professionals, industrialists, and financiers—they had influence beyond their numbers. They had even gained powerful political positions in the Reichstag, the cabinet, and in state governments, making them prime targets for scapegoating by those who blamed their corrupting influence for German defeat. But even as Dorothy slandered the German government, she admitted, perhaps thinking of Joseph, that the Jews exacerbated the threat of social disorder; the sexuality at the heart of Freudian theory, the economic egalitarianism of Marx, and even Einstein's theory of relativity contributed to the fear that German culture was being contaminated by alien blood. At this point, her friend Carl Zuckmayer, who was married to a Jew, scoffed at the discussion of racist policies; Jews, like all of us, are first and foremost Germans, he said. They had fought heroically beside their compatriots throughout the war.

Dorothy then offered the American perspective, a cigarette carelessly hanging from her lips. Unlike the French and other western European nations such as Belgium and Italy, whose economies were devastated by the Germans, the United States had been willing to trade with the Germans because the country could afford to be generous. America's geographical isolation and its modicum of human losses in the war made European political issues seem a bit abstract. Besides, there was a new treaty in the offing called the Rhineland Pact, which would guarantee the borders between Germany, Belgium, and France, and Germany would soon join the League of Nations. Didn't its bylaws guarantee national sovereignty and borders? Surely the executive council and the general assembly would demand German compliance. One must view the German government as distinct from its people, she asserted. It was true that their government sought dominance and power, but she was certain that the German people, with their distinguished cultural and philosophical traditions, would never bend to mindless tyranny. The French ambassador, shocked at Dorothy's naïveté, shook his head and muttered under his breath. It was obvious to him that her love of the German culture was clouding her vision.

In consonance with the French, Rebecca offered a darker perspective. The German strain of militarism would not tolerate democracy or peace, and the league would be powerless to stop them. But militarism didn't belong to Germany alone. Greed, lust for power, and gratuitous evil, she believed, were integral to human nature, and war was an inevitable chapter in the history of nations.

As the sky grew dark, and the Tiergarten grew silent, the circle of women, assembled in self-defense, began moving toward their spouses, hoping to be privy to their conversation. Politely breaking away, Dorothy signaled the waiters to lay the buffet. Dorothy was known for her rapacious appetite and her gourmet tastes, and she loved the opportunity to spoil her guests. Luscious meats, puddings, and vegetables adorned the table in quantities those with lesser expense accounts had rarely known. Rebecca, Dorothy would find, loved food almost as much as she, and while they balanced their plates on their knees, they caught up with each other's lives.

Not at all shy, Rebecca might have asked Dorothy why her husband was out of town. Dorothy, not quick enough to dodge her foil, might have dropped her jovial mask. In asking the question, Rebecca would disarm herself, opening the way for Dorothy's counterpoint. Are you still seeing Wells? Their stories, shortened to fit the moment, perhaps continued into dessert.

Two "actresses," hurt, alone, and hungry for a friend, paused to commiserate. Their rebellious youth over, these "wildcats" had mellowed with time. Neither ever articulated what drew them together or why love seemed to have passed them both by; perhaps they sensed that the sadness they shared was rooted so deep, that they dared not try.

PART
1

BECOMING REBECCA

When winds and showers raged around,
Faithful unto my side you stayed.
Why, now in time of sunny dawn,
Why should your faith so sudden fade.

—CICELY FAIRFIELD, age eight

LONDON, 1901

In late October 1901, Charles Fairfield abandoned his wife, Isabella, and their three daughters in the dark of night. Cicely was eight years old; her eldest sister, Letitia, called Lettie, was sixteen; and Winifred, or Winnie, was thirteen. Isabella, forty-eight years old and with nothing but memories of a thwarted music career, was left penniless. Charles had gambled away their money, absconded with their hidden cash, and left them not only to dig themselves out of debt, but also to bear the shame of penury and social ostracism. Neither his wife nor his family would see Charles alive again.

Those were the facts. The myths came later, and as time passed they kept on changing, depending on Cicely's turn of mind and emotional needs. She was too young to feel anything but sadness and confusion, but her instinct was that she had lost a kindred soul—a piece of herself. Through the years, she would see her father as a person who meant everything and nothing—a principled thinker and a skilled polemicist, an ideal man and a role model, and someone whose perfidy infected the sinews of her life with feverous distortions and unbearable pain. While she would search for him in her relationships with men, in her own way, she set out to become him.

As a woman in her seventies, still trying to make sense of an event that had occurred more than six decades earlier, Rebecca, née Cicely Fairfield, a skilled storyteller with a penchant for molding the contours of her past to her own ends, recounted the story of her father's leaving with the romantic nostalgia of a nineteenth-century child in her book *The Fountain Overflows.*

She tells of awakening with her sisters in their second-story bedroom on a bright and cloudless Saturday morning on the cusp of fall to the sound of windblown trees. As the girls teased and chattered, preparing for a day that was certain to bring adventure after a humdrum week of homework and school, their mother barged into their room wild-eyed and trembling, letter in hand. In a tragic tone using biblical prose, Rebecca relates her mother's heartbreaking shock as she read aloud her father's words declaring his sudden and hasty departure. She describes a family shattered by confusion and grief—her mother on the brink of a breakdown and her older sisters trying to console her and soothe their baby sister's fears.

Cicely (Rebecca West) being fed blackberries by her sister Winnie, while Lettie, lower left, and cousins look on, circa 1898

But the reality of the Fairfield family could not have been more different. The marriage of Isabella and Charles had not been amicable for years. In fact, the conception of Cicely had been a failed attempt at reconciliation. They no longer slept in the same bed or shared the same room. Isabella, anticipating her husband's eventual departure, had not informed him of the value of a piece of family art, in the hopes that its sale might cover their debt. But, in fact, Charles's leaving forced her to sell their furniture and the one remnant of her youthful aspiration—her beloved piano.

Within weeks, Isabella moved the family back to her native Edinburgh and her mother's home.

The marriage of Isabella Campbell Mackenzie and Charles Fairfield in 1883 had begun well enough. Aboard a ship sailing from Britain to exotic, sun-drenched Melbourne in Australia, they caught each other's eye as Isabella played the piano one evening after dinner in the salon. Dark-eyed, delicate, and wistful with auburn hair and porcelain skin, Isabella had long slender fingers that scaled the keyboard with the skill and nuance that attested to a deep spiritual appreciation of music. Thirty years old, on a family goodwill mission to help her ailing brother, Isabella was pleased to be striking out on her own, after too many years of disappointing lovers and the looming prospect of spinsterhood. The dark-haired and handsome Charles Fairfield, a forty-one-year-old Irishman, harnessed to the charitable task of taking an orphaned boy to his relatives abroad, feigned a love of music to charm the gifted pianist. He seemed a man without a past, or at least with one sketchy enough to evoke an air of mystery.

Three months later they were engaged, and, despite the groom's atheist inclination, they married in December 1883 in an Anglican church whose rose-stoned spire punctuated the broad Australian sky. Later, Rebecca would describe it as a marriage of "loneliness to loneliness."

Charles, a gifted cartoonist, had secured his first job in Australia drawing for a Melbourne newspaper called *The Argus*. But his freelance articles proved superior to his caricatures, and he was offered a post as a social, political, and economic commentator with a regular column. Isabella and Charles settled into a small home in St. Kilda, a suburb of Melbourne, near the soft blue sea they had come to love. For two years they lived an idyllic life, wrote Rebecca, touched by the magic of their storybook house and the brilliant Australian sun that streaked the sky indigo and red as evening drew near. Earning a reputation as a fine cook and housekeeper, Isabella spent her evenings with her husband's colleagues and public officials whose views spanned the political spectrum, from socialists to Tory Conservatives to anarchists like Charles. While she didn't relish the constant intrusion and relentless debate, Isabella knew it was her duty to keep her silence.

Born in Edinburgh in 1853, when married women could neither vote nor own property, Isabella assumed a mask of submission. Careful never to publicly contradict her husband, she was bound to his will by law. But she could no longer hold her tongue as Charles's career as a journalist went sour. Now a practiced orator as well as a columnist, he espoused radical views that alienated his readers and compelled his editor to let him go. With Charles out of work and Isabella no longer silent, the magic of their early years was gone. Grown sick with worry, and pregnant with their third child, Isabella implored Charles to take her home.

Perhaps it was amid the wrenching chaos of their move back to Britain that Isabella learned the true story of Charles's past, which she later told in whispers to her eldest daughter, Letitia. Until then, Charles had perpetuated a labyrinthine legend worthy of the storyteller he had become. According to him, he had joined the Royal Artillery as an ensign and traveled the world from Canada to Austria, dutifully serving his country until deciding to emigrate to America to fight in the Civil War. Once the war ended, or so he said, he had married a woman in Virginia and fathered a son, then left them to travel west to the woodlands of Colorado. There he had earned his living in a sawmill, biding his time until circumstances provided release in the form of an orphaned boy in need of an escort to Australia. This history was pure fiction, a convoluted attempt of a convicted thief to cover his tracks.

The real story, uncovered recently by a British scholar, revealed that Charles had indeed served in the Royal Rifle Brigade. But the details depict a man deeply flawed and deceptive. Between the ages of seventeen and twenty-four, he was posted in Malta and Ontario, and was known to gamble and act in burlesque theater. Lonely and aimless, he went back to his mother's home in London, where he joined the Royal United Service Institute, a think tank that provided companionship and intellectual colloquia, and functioned as a military library and repository of coins and medals.

Charles Fairfield in his Royal Rifle Brigade uniform, circa 1868

In the summer of 1868, having just returned from a disappointing jaunt to America, Charles must have become desperate. The discrepancy between his instinctive sense of intellectual superiority and his lack of social stature and career success prompted him to pursue a plan that would both taint and taunt him for the rest of his life. Dressed for an evening in the West End of London, Charles entered the RUSI and obtained the librarian's key. Beginning in late July and ending seven weeks later on September 22, Charles stole four hundred coins and medals, as well as original copies of Samuel Coleridge's letters, from its cabinets and drawers, each time stashing them in a hatbox that he blithely carried out through the front door. Seemingly without thought to the repercussions or moral implications of his acts, he proceeded to sell the purloined goods to pawnbrokers and goldsmiths throughout the city, leaving a paper trail of receipts and checks.

Once the administrators discovered that the items were missing, the police easily traced the crime back to him. One evening, when Charles returned to the institution, sporting on his watch chain the finest of the stolen gold coins, he was arrested. In court, his solicitor's plea that Charles had a "disordered mind" was rejected. Medical officers of the court believed that Charles understood the moral implications of his theft, and he was sentenced to five years of hard labor in a penal institution.

In prison, Charles's health quickly deteriorated. He had been diagnosed and treated for syphilis while he was in the army, and in the course of physical and psychological testing, prison physicians also discerned a strain of hereditary insanity. Sometime between 1871 and 1872, increasingly weak and malnourished, he was transferred to the Woking Invalid Prison, which functioned both as a hospital and a penitentiary. Charles served his prison term for four years, and then returned to his mother's home in London on a year's probation.

Charles was now a gaunt thirty-six-year-old, but as handsome as ever. The five years between the end of his prison term and his voyage to Melbourne remain undocumented. It is possible, since Isabella confirmed that he arrived at the dock in Melbourne with a young boy for whom he was responsible, that during these years Charles had returned to America and married, or went directly west to Colorado, where the opportunity to go to Australia was fatefully thrust upon him. It is also possible that the young boy he escorted to relatives was his own son. At this point in time, his whereabouts during these years remain a mystery. But both his marriage to Isabella and their return to England in 1892 are undisputed.

BY THE TIME Cicely was born on December 21, 1892, the Fairfields lived in a shabby Victorian house in Richmond upon Thames, at the outer edges of southwest London. Once neoclassical palaces situated on the hill, the homes were now carved-up tenements inhabited by the nouveaux riches, mostly upwardly mobile industrialists with a taste for the aristocratic charm of a genteel past. Yet, without efficient trams and trains, Richmond upon Thames had failed to attract more than a handful of residents willing to commute the ten miles into London proper.

The Sleeping Warrior, *a drawing of Cicely Isabel*
at age six by Charles Fairfield

But to those such as the Fairfields, who could not afford to live close to town, the two-story homes that dipped below the hill were more than adequate. Their squalor was assuaged by access to three thousand acres of unspoiled public parkland. The family took pleasure in ascending the terrace overlooking the valley above the Thames, which flowed westward toward Windsor.

These family outings ended after Cicely's father left. Later she realized it was her memories of the Richmond parkland and its natural beauty, the magic of her mother's music and her father's words, that made life tolerable and could rescue her from "madness," her recurring metaphor for rage and depression. One thing is certain: The departure of Charles Fairfield was the defining moment of Cicely's life. In a memoir published more than fifty years later, she said through the voice of her protagonist, "I had a glorious father; I had no father at all." But her protestations aside, he was the central force that determined her attitude toward men, intimacy, marriage, parenthood, human nature, and women's rights. She vowed to never trust or depend on any man.

With his compulsive gambling and unbridled philandering, Charles seemed to harbor a perverse delight in disappointing those who trusted him. He viewed people and events through a veil of indifference, she recalled, often so absorbed in himself that he was cruel and insensitive to those he loved. Throughout her life, Rebecca used him as a foil to define who she was and who she wasn't, as the progenitor of her literary talent and guts as well as her frailties of mood and character, and the primal cause of her sense of victimhood. Her forever-absent father remained a kaleidoscope of personalities intertwined with her own.

After a failed attempt to start a business in South Africa, Charles returned to England within the year, scrambling to make a living copying documents in Liverpool. No one knew where he was or why he left. Perhaps someone was blackmailing him about his criminal past, or maybe his failure at life for the second time proved too much to bear. When he returned, it was his eldest daughter, Lettie, with whom he corresponded, and whom he considered his lifeline to home. Five years after his nighttime escape, Charles died in 1906 in the back room of a filthy boarding-house, bereft of possessions; he had even hocked his watch to eat. When Lettie went to England to bring him home to Scotland for burial, she found a note he had scrawled on a piece of paper before he died, telling Isabella that he loved her and their daughters. Lettie would also find letters from young women with whom he had had sexual liaisons. In addition to the regimental medal Charles left behind in Richmond, these were the only tangible relics of his existence.

Once the Fairfields found lodgings of their own in Edinburgh, Cicely was sent to George Watson's Ladies' College—a private day school with high academic standards, run by a family friend. There she studied music, mathematics, art, Latin, French, and German, but her nose for hypocrisy and her aversion to social etiquette rankled her teachers and alienated her peers. Obviously poor and without social rank, she and her family lived in isolation. A bout with tuberculosis that required her to leave school became a grand opportunity to read and study whatever she wished—classical, medieval, and Enlightenment philosophy and literature. She had a hungry, inquisitive mind, and the long therapeutic walks the doctors prescribed revived her body and fostered her fearlessness. In

1907, at the age of fourteen, Cicely, who inherited her father's gift for polemics, had a letter published in *The Scotsman,* signed in her own name. It was an argument for female suffrage and women's rights. Appalled by her mother's poverty, her inability to influence social policy, and her dependency on the financial support of wealthier family and friends, Cicely became a socialist, following her sisters into the suffrage movement, becoming, even then, a spokesperson for its cause. It was a theme that would filter through her novels and essays.

Cicely as a schoolgirl

IN 1901, WHILE EIGHT-YEAR-OLD Cicely was mourning the abandonment by her father, a thirty-five-year-old journalist and science fiction novelist living in northwest London named H. G. Wells published an essay entitled "Anticipations of the Reaction of Mechanical and Scientific Progress upon Human Life and Thought," which presciently captured the emerging zeitgeist. Scientific progress, he believed, would necessitate the reform of social institutions, enlighten the mind, and liberate the human spirit from church doctrine and traditional values. Machines would hasten the dissemination of information, lead to new forms of travel, and enable the improved transport of goods and services. These, in turn, would create an affluent middle class capable of purchasing these products, restructuring the flow of money and the distribution of political power. Now the "lowborn," men such as Wells, could acquire aristocratic manners and status, and influence the course of public opinion.

Born in 1866 in Bromley, Kent, Herbert George "Bert" Wells was the youngest son of a gardener, Joseph, and a ladies' maid, Sarah, employed at a large country home in Sussex called Uppark. They were married in 1853, but shortly afterward Sarah knew she had made a mistake: Joe was an undisciplined scoundrel with a penchant for women, a distaste for work, and a wanderlust that kept him away from home. When her boys were young, Sarah took full responsibility for their family business as well as for maintaining the household. But as soon as Bert turned thirteen, she placed him as an apprentice draper, threw her husband out, and sold the shop. Tired, emotionally disheartened, and desperate to live out her years in equanimity, Sarah returned to domestic service at Uppark. It was a simple life where the role of a lowborn woman seemed consonant with natural law. Content to walk the underground tunnels from her lady's kitchen to the servants' quarters, she never questioned the superiority of her mistress or her own place as a handmaiden to her needs.

Bert, however, seemed destined to be a supreme disappointment. As aimless and rebellious as his father and too clever by far to accept Sarah's unexamined existence, Bert was a constant reminder of her renegade husband and her failed marriage. Trapped in a world antithetical to his nature, Bert refused to become a slave to skills he neither valued nor mastered. While his brothers thrived as tradesmen, Bert was dismissed after his trial tenure. When Bert arrived at Uppark, seeking comfort from his mother, he instead evoked her contempt and resentment. His discharge embarrassed Sarah. Frustrated by her son's failure to meet her expectations and confounded by his turn of mind, she simply turned away.

Tolerated but shunned at Uppark as a misfit, Bert found solace in the "mystery" and "splendor" of its undulating meadows covered in wildflowers, and its gleaming canopies of natural forest. A massive Georgian colonial with panoramic views to the sea, it would always be a "precious sapphire" in his memory, representing the very essence of beauty. It would also remain the symbol of upper-class living that would dominate his imagination, pervade his work, and color his social perceptions. This vision of unearned wealth would become the crux of the conflict between his notions of social justice and his desire for an elegant and leisured creative life.

Nonetheless, at Uppark young Bert could sequester himself in the abundantly furnished library, finding solitude and intellectual substance for long stretches of unobserved time. Left on his own, much like Cicely, he had the leisure to gorge on reading biology, classical and Enlightenment philosophy, and literature. It was here, and in the warmth of his paternal uncle's home near Eton, that his mind exploded with ideas. The cool rationality of science lifted him above the flux of human frailty, and the great works of literature and philosophy stirred his imagination and fired his ambition to study and write. During this time he wrote several short stories and reformulated his knowledge of biology and chemistry into the embryonic cells that would mature into his science fiction novels.

His uncle, a successful merchant, was the first person to take him seriously and to understand his potential. He offered him a place in his home and the means to attend grammar school, where he studied chemistry and physics. Bert had planned to become a certified teacher at a normal school upon graduation from grammar school, but his mother, too simpleminded to understand his desire to study and hoping to tame his rebellious bent, once again ensnared him in her provincial web, binding Bert to a four-year contract with an itinerant draper who sailed the islands of the South Seas. Once at sea, fearing that his academic career had come to an end and knowing that he could not break free of his contract without the promise of another position, Bert wrote to the headmaster of his grammar school, begging him for employment. While waiting for a reply, he managed to keep his sanity by reading the science and philosophy textbooks he had packed in his bag. Miraculously, his headmaster offered him a post as an assistant teacher, and after one year of service, Bert sailed for England and returned to his uncle's home. Proving his talent as a teacher, Bert was awarded a scholarship to a normal school and prepared to enter university in London.

During the five years he had lived in his paternal uncle's home as a family member, he had fallen in love with his doe-eyed and delicate cousin, Isabel Mary Wells, who physically and temperamentally resembled his mother. She became the Venus of his adolescent dreams and ignited his desire in a way he would never experience again. Now back home with his professional plans settled, he was ready to ask for Isabel's hand. In 1891 they married with his uncle's blessing, but the fulfillment of his boyhood lust would remain a fantasy; Isabel had little appetite for sex, according to Bert, and saw it as an intrusion on her clockwork life of studied convention. Perhaps, however, few women could have satisfied his voracious desires. Furthermore, his mind was bursting with knowledge and ideas, and he came to believe that his beautiful and uneducated wife, much like his mother, could never understand him. Within a year of their marriage, he began a clandestine relationship with one of his tutorial students, a clever and ambitious woman named Amy Catherine Robbins, whose determined countenance and stalwart attitude seemed the antithesis to that of his submissive, complacent wife. Amy not only adored him, she was bright enough to converse about the ideas he valued most—science, theology, moral philosophy, and politics. Bert initiated a court divorce, most likely on the grounds of nonconsummation and his flagrant adultery, and married Amy in 1895. She proved to be a warm maternal figure who loved him unconditionally, in a way that his mother never could. As the daughter of a wealthy family, Amy was able to attend school without the worry of planning a lucrative career. Although the wealthier classes were active in the movement toward female suffrage and women's rights, Amy was willing to sacrifice her desire to teach and write in order to help Bert to pursue his career. She concluded that she could make a more substantial literary contribution by tending to the needs of her brilliant husband.

With Amy acting as his housekeeper and his secretary, Bert was able to produce several works, including *The Time Machine* (1895), *The Island of Dr. Moreau* (1896), *The Invisible Man* (1897), and *The War of the Worlds* (1898), earning him unprecedented sums of money and a reputation as a talented science fiction novelist with reformist views. Despite his public image, Bert, now the eminent H. G. Wells, lacked confidence that could be bolstered only by controlling every aspect of his personal life. He demanded that Amy play the role of "mother" and conversed with her in baby talk, making it clear that he would not tolerate any impulse toward autonomy. Displeased with both of her Christian names, H.G. decided to call her "Jane." In a sense, his wife became his artifact— Galatea to his Pygmalion.

So needy was he of her sole attention that after their first son, George

Philip ("Gip"), was born in 1901, he left home at the age of thirty-four on his bicycle for two months without explanation. After Jane gave birth to their second son, Frank, two years later, H.G. lost interest in her as a sexual partner. Jane was more conventional than he had anticipated, and while she was uncommonly educated, he was increasingly aware she was no match for his genius and no longer able to grasp his ideas. Ironically, Jane's submission to his will was a double-edged sword; the control he exercised had sucked her vitality, making her intellectually flabby and self-absorbed. H.G. made Jane a proposition she dared not refuse: He would never divorce her, and their home would remain the center of his life, but she must give him the freedom to have affairs with other women and to come and go as he pleased. Unable to express his gratitude and devotion for fear of losing her, and too self-absorbed to encourage her desire for a life of letters, H.G. chained her to him. Shrewd enough to know that divorce would make her and their sons social pariahs, and loving him passionately despite his flaws, she surrendered to his terms.

In effect, he was straddling two fantasies: a home with a perfect mother/wife, and the prospect of a sexual and intellectual companion whom he would call his "lover-shadow"—the embodiment of all his romantic longings. All H.G.'s lovers would become reflections of his own light—shadowy moons to his sun—and idealized projections of his needs and desires.

Jane and H.G. lived divided lives. In public, Jane was the wealthy, meticulously groomed wife of a famous author, but privately, she wrote stories and poems expressing her desire for romance and happiness much akin to her husband's. At home H.G. was an indulged and protected child, enjoying the simple pleasures of walking, cycling, and reading; as the internationally acclaimed essayist and novelist, he swaggered onto the public stage with confident self-possession. Jane's writing, posthumously published in 1928 by H.G. in a collection entitled *The Book of Catherine Wells*, was the poignantly sad musings of an unfulfilled woman desperately longing for release. Her poems and stories are riddled with violent rebellion and the desire for suicide. They serve as testimony to Wells's aberrant notions of love, to Jane's weakness for money and status, and to the macabre norms of Victorian and Edwardian society. While H.G. would remain unaware of Jane's true desires until her death, it is clear that the arrangement he had fashioned with her was destructive and perverse.

H.G.'s memories of his childhood poverty, along with his growing vision of the individual as the rightful arbiter of his own ethos, drew him toward the Fabian Society, an organization founded in 1884 and dedicated to establishing a socialist state in Britain within the existing political structure. By the time H.G. became an active member in 1903, the Fabians were entrenched in the Labour Party and had become inflexible in their methods and views. Impatient and aggressive by nature and unwilling to ride the slow wave of reform, H.G. preached a militant form of government upheaval. As radical in his views as he was rigid, yet lacking leadership skills and a practical knowledge of public policy, Wells was condemned and marginalized. To make matters worse, his blatant espousal of women's rights and "free love" attracted the affection of many of the members' wives. The men were eager to engineer his downfall.

Among the regular attendees of the meetings were the New Zealand–born industrialist William Pember Reeves and his feminist wife, Maud. While Maud was entranced by the sexual magnetism of Wells, her daughter Amber was to become the youngest of his conquests. In her late teens when they first met, Amber seemed the quintessential liberated woman. Taught by her parents to follow her conscience rather than the dicta of convention, she was a vivacious, rebellious, and strong-willed feminist who sought the companionship of older men and women.

As brainy as she was beautiful, Amber was accepted at Cambridge at a time when only the most gifted women gained entry, especially into the male dominion of classical science. She was now nearly twenty, with striking red hair and a womanly body. Twice her age and flattered by her feelings of attraction toward him, H.G. was overjoyed to take her as his mistress. In an attempt to avoid scandal, he whisked her off to the remote French village of Le Torquet, where they set up house. Isolated from their family and friends, they were totally dependent on each other's good faith, but their clandestine rendezvous fell short of their imagined ideal. Nonetheless, two years later, when Amber found that she was pregnant, she was totally unperturbed; she relished the knowledge that she was carrying the great H. G. Wells's baby.

But Wells soon grew irritable and verbally abusive. Denouncing her as a half-wit intellectual who didn't understand the implications of her views, he berated her for her inability to care for a mature man. Unwilling to keep house or indulge his needs, Amber became a burden that siphoned H.G.'s creative energy. More and more often he sought refuge in England in the efficiently run home he shared with Jane.

When H.G. returned to the French villa after one of his cross-Channel trips, Amber confronted him. A quarrel ensued, after which H.G. gave her an ultimatum. He told her that unless she was willing to carry the stigma of unwed motherhood alone, she should return home and marry her besotted former boyfriend, Rivers Blanco White. Maliciously, he used the conventions he despised to twist Amber toward his own ends. Enraged that his proposal was tantamount to social prostitution, Amber, not as independent as she had imagined, nonetheless acquiesced. In December 1909, she gave birth to their daughter, and H.G., unscathed, resumed his normal, if deeply unsatisfying, life.

As was to become his pattern, H.G. wrote an autobiographical novel as a vehicle for catharsis. *Ann Veronica*, about his affair with a young suffragist, clearly recognizable as Amber, was published in 1909. A social treatise under the guise of fiction, his book implied that female sexual desire existed apart from wife and motherhood, and that extramarital sex was neither low nor sinful. To think otherwise was to succumb to Christian "propaganda" that denied the polygamous nature of humanity and thwarted its generic betterment. In 1911, he published another novel, *The New Machiavelli*, that elaborated upon and affirmed these views. But these fictional accounts had no correlation to reality. H.G. was inclined to experience the same fits of fancy as Cicely; in his letters to Amber, as well as in documented accounts of their relationship by friends, he expressed neither regret nor sadness about casting Amber and their baby out. She had become a potential cog in the wheel of his literary ambition, a burden and an embarrassment. He was, in short, happy to be rid of her.

MEANWHILE, THE FAIRFIELDS had moved from Edinburgh to Hampstead Garden, a London suburb. It was a planned and subsidized community in which the houses were arranged in neighborhoods, separate yet contiguous, according to socioeconomic status. Planners ensured that each of the homes had a backyard, garden, and trees, in the hopes of nurturing a love of natural beauty and imbuing even the poor with the pride of landownership. Isabella had grasped that moving her daughters to a government-supported home in Hampstead would raise their station without depleting their funds.

While the Fairfields' house, Fairliehope, was situated among the poorest, the move enabled Isabella to keep her family together. Letitia had been awarded a scholarship to medical school in London, and Hampstead Garden had easy access to the train. Winifred, as clever and gifted as either of her sisters, would choose to attend a normal school and become a teacher, a career consonant with her gentle, modest nature and her family's need for immediate income. Cicely, on the other hand, was eccentric and contrary in her aspirations: She hoped to become a stage actress—a relatively "naughty" thing to do. To become a legitimate actress at the turn of the century was to enter a competitive universe, in which one either succeeded or was compelled to earn money performing in the "girly reviews."

In the forty years that preceded the maturity of the Fairfield sisters, the number of working women in the British marketplace increased by 300 to 400 percent. The same factors of industrialization and urbanization that had affected the employment of men, along with the rise of socialism and women's suffrage, drew women toward professions once beyond their sphere. English drama was becoming popular, and a career in the theater became a coveted option. New companies funded and managed by female entrepreneurs cropped up in reaction to traditional male-dominated companies that feared the "feminization" of theater.

It is quite possible that Cicely's impulse to act was rooted in her passion for social reform, but the Academy of Dramatic Art, which she entered in 1910, was a training ground for classical actors. Within the first year, however, Cicely realized that she was neither beautiful nor talented enough to succeed. Her irregular features—that is, her broad brow and receding chin—robbed her of the idealized countenance of English heroines, and her emotional volatility ultimately proved resistant to discipline. Yet her experience at the academy helped her develop her oratorical skills and gain the confidence to speak in the public arena. Ready to turn her energy toward prose, Cicely filled in for a friend who was writing theater reviews. The discipline of the printed page fused self-control with a creative latitude she had not found on the stage.

By this time, Cicely's initial vision of the suffragist movement as the means through which to right the wrongs of her mother's betrayal had waned. Its leaders had become too autocratic, and she had outgrown its narrow social and political platform. Spurred by the enlightened influence of Britain's renowned social philosopher John Stuart Mill, the first generation of nineteenth-century suffragists had succeeded in effecting female enfranchisement for unmarried women—the rights of those who were married were subsumed by their husbands' votes—in most aspects of municipal governance. But by the turn of the century, the mantle had fallen on the second generation; the movement had become fractious and weak, despite its efforts to consolidate into the national organization NUWSS (National Union of Women's Suffrage Societies). Moreover, violence against suffragists by ordinary citizens and government police was rampant, both on the streets and in jail. Cicely, who had no taste for formal protest, except as a passionate observer and commentator, would later write, "This callousness should teach suffragettes two lessons. Firstly, that they cannot win their cause by mere virtuosic exhibitions of courage. Courage requires an audience of heroes. . . . The second lesson is one for men. It never seems to strike men that a party which renounced the principle of liberty, when dealing with women, might renounce them dealing with men."

Concomitant with the rise of feminist theater was the proliferation of feminist journals. Cicely's devil-may-care suffragist friend Dora Marsden, "the most exquisite beauty of person," founded a magazine called *The Freewoman* in 1911 and asked her to join the staff as its literary editor. It was devoted, as H.G. would say, to causes that ladies should never espouse—free love, auto- and homoeroticism, celibacy, and economic independence. Cicely, who would call *The Freewoman* more humanist than feminist—after all, its message aimed to liberate men from the burdens of patriarchy as much as women—sought to develop a serious literary focus that would illuminate and probe the status quo. Using her critiques of the essays and books of antifeminist and antisocialist authors as a forum for crystallizing her personal vision, she confronted the social injustices and hypocrisy of Edwardian England, still steeped in the vestiges of the Victorian ethos and only beginning to marshal the political will toward social reform. In bold and persuasive prose, she held sacred social institutions and mores to the light of reason—sexuality, marriage, motherhood, the Christian church, the rights of the poor, and the oppression of women—and systematically analyzed their validity. She viewed marriage as the only nursery for children; happiness within an indissoluble union was the birthright of every child. Yet a marriage of incompatible minds, she believed, eroded the well-being of the child, at the very center of the Trinity. In this case, she asserted, divorce was not an option; divorce was a duty. When the 1912 Royal Commission on Divorce bill was proposed in Parliament, Cicely saw it as a watershed moment in social reform.

Moreover, she believed that the structure of marriage should become consonant with the realities of female potential. Cicely worried that the institution had become a means of oppressing women and rendering them impotent. Contemptuous of parasitic and submissive women, Cicely reprimanded the women of England for surrendering their creativity, intelligence, physical strength, and independence to men. In the upper classes, she wrote, ladies pursued bodily and material self-indulgence, and engaged in mindless social rituals to pass the time. The relentless childbearing of lower-class women, to whom information about birth control was inaccessible or incomprehensible, as well as their incessant household drudgery, rendered their lives no better than that of field animals. This contempt for domesticity would stay with her for most of her life; the mindlessness of housekeeping siphoned the creativity of artistic women, the new aristocracy of intellectual elites.

While many of her articles on socialism, feminism, and women's education, rights, and economic oppression were compatible with her mother's and sisters' privately held views, Cicely, fearful that her public diatribes would threaten the social acceptance of her upwardly mobile family, assumed a nom de plume. She chose the name Rebecca West, a defiant, freethinking, anti-establishment character in Henrik Ibsen's play *Rosmersholm,* about illicit love. Through the mouthpiece of his Rebecca West, Ibsen asserts his belief that the individual can prevail without legal or religious sanction. While human nature is subject to sin and corruption, he implies, love is the vehicle through which one might achieve salvation. Cicely would carry Ibsen's idea one step further; as Rebecca West she would deem literature itself a means of spiritual liberation and salvation.

Later, Cicely would dismiss her choice of nom de plume as pure whimsy. Yet, consciously or not, Cicely assumed the name of a fearless, irreverent rebel—the intellectual firebrand she sought to become. Ironically, the flagrant amorality of Ibsen's Rebecca West at the beginning of the story reveals the dangers inherent in challenging the underpinnings of tradition-bound views and presaged Rebecca's own dalliance with men who had little capacity for self-reflection or understanding of the pain they inflicted on those around them. For Cicely, Ibsen's play hit upon some essential truths.

Rebecca at age nineteen, in 1911,
at the Royal Academy of Dramatic Art

Within her first year at *The Freewoman*, Rebecca, not yet twenty, had earned a reputation as a savage critic eager to attack the eminent literary figures of the day. After denouncing George Bernard Shaw and Arnold Bennett as superficial—Shaw as a pompous prose stylist with little understanding of male-female relationships, and Bennett, the esteemed novelist, as a gluttonous, whimpering male chauvinist—she set her sights on dethroning Wells. In 1912, when Wells published his novel *Marriage,* reflecting perhaps his relationship with Jane, Rebecca wrote a shattering two-thousand-word critique that caught his attention. It was as if his book, with its stereotypical characters and views, rolled the entire social pretense she struggled against into one huge hypocritical ball. All her work, it seemed, had prepared her for this moment. She asserted that Wells's feminism smacked of self-deception and that his view of marriage, despite his hearty proclamations to the contrary, was "sinfully" mired in patriarchal disdain. Rebecca wrote that his fictional representation of the "normal" woman, Marjorie—submissive, acquisitive, and soul sucking—was content to barter her husband's passion for science for the sake of "sideboards and prestige." While "Mr. Wells sees Marjorie as a scoundrel," she wrote, "he accepts her scoundrelism as the normal condition of women." The weak sort of "Marjories," she believed, would become prostitutes and beggars, while the strong "Marjories" would develop decency, courage, and tenacity. In short, Rebecca took a Darwinian stance toward women, in the hopes that it would foster the survival of the fittest and strengthen the moral fiber of coming generations.

Wells, a regular reader and sometime contributor to *The Freewoman,* was apparently intrigued by the remarks of this sassy young journalist. He invited her to visit him and Jane at their country home, Easton Glebe, in Essex. A redbrick Georgian colonial on several wooded acres, it was a paltry facsimile of H.G.'s beloved Uppark, but to Rebecca, the house must have seemed like a mansion. As she rang the bell of its white-pillared entrance, she would have noted that his self-deception ran deep; this dyed-in-the-wool socialist had upper-crust pretensions. Jane, an attractive and delicate woman of nearly forty, was gracious and hospitable. Wells, at forty-six, cut a middle-aged figure. No longer the lean ascetic of his youth, H.G. had grown corpulent feasting on the fruits of his success. His small physique and flabby torso were flanked by truncated arms and perched on tiny feet. While his manner was effete and his voice high-pitched, his prominent forehead, penetrating blue eyes, and fiery intellect, Rebecca would say, gave him the swaggering "walk of the matador into the center of the arena when he is going to fight the bull to the finish." Only fifteen years younger than Rebecca's dead father, he must have seemed, despite his fleshy wrappings, much like Charles Fairfield, if not in achievement, then in potential and ambition. His intellectual confidence, insatiable curiosity, verbal acuity, and ability to analyze and synthesize ideas, along with his innate creativity and well-developed imagination, made him a reasonable successor to the man who had deserted her—the protective male figure who had robbed her of intellectual and emotional affirmation at the time she needed it most. In fact, Wells had met Charles Fairfield, a rabid antisocialist, at the Fabian Society when Charles had skillfully debated George Bernard Shaw. It was said that Fairfield was among the very few capable of presenting an articulate and logical case against socialism.

Wells was pleased to find that this slim, sturdy nineteen-year-old with a dark complexion and black hair exhibited the same vitality and wit he admired in her writing. He was so taken with this "enfant terrible" that he spoke to Rebecca for five hours, filling her mind with his immense vitality and hunger for ideas. Jane, by now outwardly reconciled to her husband's fascination with bright young women, faded into the background, enabling them to converse uninterrupted by the domestic routine and the bustle of a household occupied by their two active sons. While Rebecca was grateful for her time alone with H.G., she was puzzled by Jane's persona. Conventionally coiffed and dressed, with a birdlike voice and manner, Jane seemed unduly withdrawn and submissive—altogether too revering and apologetic toward her husband. Rebecca wondered what she was like beneath her poker face. Was she his adorable and adoring "soul-sucking" Marjorie?

By the time the afternoon was over, the young writer was thoroughly captivated by the loquacious master of literature and philosophy. His powerful intellect and riveting eyes transformed the misshapen Wells into an irresistibly attractive Lothario.

After Rebecca left, Wells would comment, "She had a fine broad brow and dark expressive eyes; she had a big soft mouth and a small chin; she talked well and she had evidently read voraciously—with an excellent memory. We argued and she stood up to my opinions very stoutly but very reasonably. I had never met anything quite like her before, and I doubt if there ever was anything like her before. Or ever will be." Perhaps because he was struggling with his own literary and psychological restlessness, he could discern the signs of mental embattlement. Her facial expressions, he noted, exuded countervailing impulses—dark and light, expansive and concentrated, sensual and intellectual. In short, Wells was awestruck by this luscious-mouthed prodigy who he hoped had a sexual appetite as voracious as his own.

Besides the immediate physical chemistry between them, there was a deeper affinity, based perhaps on the core emotional void in their youth. Neither West nor Wells had a childhood that was psychologically or economically sound. To use Rebecca's metaphor in explanation, neither had been the central figure in the family trinity that was each person's birthright. It was this unconscious kinship of mind and heart that drew them together.

During the weeks subsequent to their meeting, Wells and West exchanged a series of notes, but their relationship, to Rebecca's dismay, seemed hopelessly mired in cerebral esoterica. As much as they found comity in notions of social policy, institutional reform, and the role of education and reason in the liberation of men and women, Rebecca wanted more.

She had read his novels about an older man's affair with a young suffragist, and had probably heard gossip about Amber Reeves, but perhaps she didn't understand how close H.G. had come to ruin. Possibly, as well, she was naïve enough to think that she would be the one who could make him stay, who could fold his mind inside her own, satisfy his sexual needs, and give him the courage to relinquish his hold on his marriage to Jane.

Wells would grace the Fairfield home in Hampstead with a spontaneous two-and-a-half-hour social call, impressing even Isabella with his magnanimous mind and paternal interest in her young daughter's career. After this visit, Rebecca and H.G. began to see each other frequently at his flat in London on Church Street and at a hotel in town. Their relationship, it seemed, had become intimate. In February 1913, he wrote Rebecca this letter:

You're a very compelling person. I suppose I shall have to do what you want me to do. But anyhow I mean to help you all I can in your great adventure.

You consider me an entirely generous and sympathetic brother in all your arrangements.

I'll help you all I can and I'll take the risk of its being known about. . . .

H.G., it seems, was back to living two lives, and Rebecca had the newfound luxury of a lover and a mentor. The course of her writing career had changed as well. In 1912, Dora Marsden had appointed Rebecca the assistant editor of *The Freewoman*. Both women had taken great pleasure in the magazine's acerbic iconoclasm and delighted in the controversy their writing evoked. Both cared desperately that it should survive, and as partners, they did their best to raise funds. With further backing, *The New Freewoman* came into being in 1913. But when it became clear that this venture was no longer viable, Rebecca started writing for the radical socialist journal *The Clarion*. A broad-spectrum publication with a less specialized readership, the weekly offered her more space and latitude in which to present her views. The price she paid, however, was rigidly enforced deadlines; while Rebecca's productivity increased, her articles lacked her personal style. When in April 1913 the women's suffrage amendment to the franchise bill was about to be defeated by anti-suffragist members of the Conservative Party, the Conservative and Unionist Women's Franchise Association (CUWFA), initially run by the same woman who had supported *The New Freewoman*, Millicent Fawcett, flew into action. Although it was successful in its effort to back pro-suffragist Conservative candidates, it turned the political arena into a war between the sexes. In effect, Rebecca's cause célèbre took on personal implications.

Quite suddenly, Wells dropped Rebecca. She instinctively believed it was Jane's doing; a young woman like Rebecca, unlike Wells's middle-aged mistresses of high social status, could offer Jane nothing but embarrassment. Devastated, Rebecca sank into a deep depression. Perhaps it seems facile to connect her loss of H.G. to the abrupt abandonment by her father, but Rebecca would always espouse Freud's theory of unconscious responses that fan out from a traumatic core connecting one's past to one's present. She would always be torn between her intellect and her emotions; by her rare ability for rational analysis and the ungovernable impulses of her psyche. The fact remains that Rebecca fell ill with bronchitis and took to her bed for two months without the energy or desire for social interchange or creative work. Finally, in May 1913, she consented to travel with her mother to Spain. Immersed in the warm earthiness of Spanish culture, Rebecca regained her perspective, if not her optimism. During this time she wrote autobiographical fiction, addressing, in part, the validity of suicide. The lyrical quality of her prose reemerged as she combined social and cultural analysis with philosophic inquiry.

When Rebecca returned to London, Wells invited her to "come and talk" at his new flat at 52 Saint James Court, a residential mews on the border of Knightsbridge and Mayfair. Wells, still wary of another involvement with a young, volatile woman, agreed to maintain a casual friendship. It was a blow from which Rebecca believed she would never recover. Upon leaving his flat, she wrote this letter:

Dear H.G.

During the next few days I shall either put a bullet through my head or commit something more shattering to myself than death. . . .

You've always been unconsciously hostile to me and I have tried to conciliate you by hacking away at my love for you, cutting it down to the little thing that was the most you wanted. I am always at a loss when I meet hostility, because I can love and I can do practically nothing else. I was the wrong sort of person for you to have to do with. You want a world of people falling over each other like puppies, people to quarrel and play with, people who rage and ache instead of people who burn. You can't conceive a person resenting the humiliation of an emotional failure so much that they twice tried to kill themselves: that seems silly to you. I can't conceive of a person who runs about lighting bonfires and yet nourishes a dislike of flame: that seems silly to me.

You've literally ruined me. I'm burned down to my foundations. I may build myself again or I may not. . . .

I would give my whole life to feel your arms round me again. . . .

Don't leave me utterly alone. If I live write to me now and then. You like me enough for that. At least I pretend to myself you do.

A perceptive and astute analysis of her own and H.G.'s character, her letter, nonetheless, did not evoke the hoped-for response. Wells's return letter was detached and dismissive: "How can I be your friend to this accompaniment? I don't see that I can be of use or help to you at all. You have my entire sympathy, but until we can meet on a reasonable basis, goodbye."

Rebecca did not take her life, and when her Spanish stories were published in the spring of 1913, in the resurrected monthly *The New Freewoman*, Wells's reaction was effusive. Apparently, her profound disappointment precipitated a degree of emotional objectivity heretofore inaccessible; through this rational lens she could use her own experience to begin to deduce universal axioms of human experience. She had gained confidence, and, at least on paper, the capacity to discern the absurd from the real. Her sense of humor and appreciation of beauty emerged as never before, raising her status among critics to the footing of the eminent literary journalists of the day: Shaw, Chesterton, and Wells.

In July, Wells wrote her a letter: "You are as wise as God when you write—at times—and then you are a tortured, untidy . . . little disaster of a girl who can't even manage the most elementary trick of her sex. You are like a beautiful voice singing out in a darkened room into which one grasps and finds nothing."

This was, to say the least, a left-handed compliment. And yet, Wells recognized Rebecca's crystalline voice and implied that its beauty deserved carnal substance. One senses that the feminine "trick" to which he referred was her inability to give sexual and emotional comfort, without which, in his view, her intellectual and aesthetic vision was rendered impotent.

No one is certain how their rapprochement occurred, but Rebecca and H.G. began meeting again in London. Rebecca had made her point; she was an independent agent, with the courage and stamina to stand on her own. It was H.G., now, who was overcome with desire and willing to chance the potential stain of a libelous affair. Within months of the publication of Rebecca's stories, their relationship resumed with new intensity. And by November 1913, after only two sexual encounters, twenty-year-old Rebecca found herself pregnant.

H.G. had warned her that she would have to spend Christmas without him; he would return home to Easton Glebe to be with his wife and children. The celebration of Christmas, despite Rebecca's avowed agnosticism, was a ritual integral to her childhood memories and an affirmation of life she could not ignore. Sworn to secrecy by H.G., she decided not to go home to Fairliehope, fearing that in a gush of holiday joy, she would reveal her condition to her sisters. Instead she went to the beautiful country home of her friends and mentors, Violet Hunt and Ford Madox Ford. Violet and Ford had introduced her to the London literary world. Confident that her talent augured great success, they lovingly took her into their home. Persuaded by H.G. that she would never spend another Christmas without him, Rebecca reveled in the knowledge that she was carrying the child of the eminent writer.

Ironically, shortly before becoming pregnant, Rebecca had published an article condemning out-of-wedlock birth as damaging to the psyches of the "bastard" child and the unwed mother. Often deemed "loose" or, worse, "feeble-minded," lower-class and impoverished single mothers were incarcerated in workhouses to prevent them from being "menaces" to society. In Rebecca's mind, H.G. was the only thing between her and the workhouse; the only thing between Rebecca and motherhood was the dangerous option of an abortion. While abortion was prevalent among those who could afford it, its illegality made it subject to quackery. H.G. tried to convince her that she would come to no harm, but she vehemently refused to risk disease and death at the hands of an unlicensed doctor. Reluctantly, H.G. accepted Rebecca's decision on the grounds that he was wealthy enough to provide for her and her baby. He had come to believe that he had finally found the woman of his dreams—the companion lover who had constantly eluded him. Rebecca, unlike Amber, was truly brilliant and precocious, and he was convinced that she could handle the responsibility. And she was deeply in love with him.

H.G. would always call the conception an "accident," a spontaneous ejaculation caused by a valet's unexpected knock on the door of his rented rooms. But the question remains: How could these remarkably sophisticated and knowledgeable advocates of birth control use the most unreliable form of contraception? By 1913, thanks to government pressure by eugenics advocates who feared that the lower classes would inherit the world, even the poorest and least educated women of the working class were adopting more effective methods—the pessary, a soluble vaginal suppository that blocked semen from entering the womb; a vinegar, water, and herbal douche during the supposedly "safe" period two weeks into the menstrual cycle; a penile sheath that caught the sperm (a method that H.G. passionately opposed); or a cervical cap that blocked the semen from entering the uterus. While none of these methods was infallible, and they were advocated by the church and state for use only by married women, surely Rebecca and H.G. had access to sources that would have accommodated their needs. One may conclude that Rebecca, probably a virgin, trusted H.G.—an eminent scientific mind and an experienced lover. And he, quite simply, thought he could get away with it.

They saw themselves not only as lovers, but also as "confederates"—intellectual equals with common goals toward social reform. They would survive as "outsiders" preying upon the complacency and hypocrisy of social mores and laws. "Jaguar" and "Panther" were names not only symbolic of their relationship to each other and society; they were integral to their identity as individuals. Even as a child, Rebecca admired the independence, fire, and dignity of cats. The metaphor of Englishwomen as "lions" fighting against the enslavement of matrimony and motherhood was a call to battle in her early days at *The Freewoman*. A cat, through Rebecca's eyes, was an amalgam of extremes—innate self-reliance and the profound need for affection on its own terms. For his part, H.G. had always seen himself as an alien creature, belonging to no social or economic class. The instinctive pounce of the jaguar was consonant with his notion that espousing the natural lessons of primitive amorality would reveal the need for social change. To H.G., the panther was both an able huntress and a velvety feline creature whose comradeship held the promise of domestic comfort and stability.

Yet, as proved earlier when he threw Amber and their child to the wind, H.G. could tolerate neither the potential of personal and family stain, nor the prospect of professional damage. With Jane's help, he secured the domestic services of a family friend, Mrs. Townshend, and rented Rebecca a flat in Kensington.

Rebecca, isolated and lonely by choice, wanting to spare her family the stigma of her illicit affair and illegitimate child, was dependent upon Wells for money and comfort, and she continued to try desperately to hold on to his promise of marriage. What she didn't know was that he was simultaneously reassuring Jane that she would always remain at the center of his life. Despite H.G.'s uncanny ability to compartmentalize his emotions, he, too, was deeply in love and determined to stand by Rebecca during her pregnancy. Breathlessly, he moved among his three homes, visiting her twice a week at her flat in Kensington. He warned her not to give her address to anyone and to maintain the "legend" that she was a married woman, Mrs. West, whose husband, a cinematographer, traveled widely but required a separate bedroom in which to write. He told her that she must take care of him, sexually and emotionally, and provide a comfortable and orderly home in which he could work. Buoyed by his love for her and confident that he would make her his wife, Rebecca, against her deepest instincts, did her best to comply.

H.G. had convinced himself, and tried to persuade her, that the birth of their child would change nothing between them. They would continue to write, take long leisurely walks, and share domestic pleasures. And with judicious evasion, he promised Rebecca that eventually their relationship would be sanctified by marriage. In the meantime, however, he prepared her for the periods of separation intrinsic to his "double life," and compelled her to make sudden and frequent moves to new locations so as not to arouse suspicion. Plotting complex logistics for simple train rides to and from London in order to conceal her condition and their intimacy, he would concoct tactics that bordered on farcical. Rebecca was beginning to wonder if her lover was, in fact, paranoid.

H.G. would require Rebecca to endure four more moves. From Kensington, she moved to Hunstanton, north of London, where they took long walks together and wrote—he his new novel, *The Research Magnificent,* and she her articles. And in March 1914, H.G. settled Rebecca in Leigh-on-Sea, an unpretentious resort town on the southeast coast of England, unattractive to anyone of social standing. It was there she hid during her final months of confinement. While H.G., now forty-seven and often ill, kept up his social engagements, Rebecca endured loneliness that was slowly turning into rage. In an ugly late Victorian villa ironically named Brig-y-Don, attended by a midwife and sedated with chloroform, she gave birth to a son on August 4, 1914—the same day that England declared war on Germany. His name, chosen by H.G., was Anthony Panther West. Rebecca felt robbed of the glory of his birth by her own and H.G.'s preoccupation with war, and yet all thoughts of giving him up for adoption melted at the peril the war foreboded. She wanted to hold him close and protect the fragile innocence of her newborn son.

Hearing the news of Anthony's birth, H.G. wrote to Rebecca, "I am radiant this morning. With difficulty I refrain from giving people large tips. I am so delighted I have a manchild in the world—of yours. I will get the world tidy for him. . . . I keep on thinking of your dear, dear, dear grave sweet beloved face on your pillow and you and it. I do most tremendous love you Panther." H.G. was convinced that Anthony would grow to be a "great man." It was his fourth attempt at self-realization through an heir, and it was his hope that the child of his beautiful and brilliant "Panther" would be a genius like himself.

Determined to disseminate his views and in constant need of money to maintain his residences, H.G. spent less time on books and more on articles for newspapers and magazines. Nonetheless, he managed to visit Rebecca every two or three days, and wrote to her regularly when they were separated. Between visits, H.G., who had taken a trip to Russia, was working on a series of articles about the war, but Rebecca, shocked by the war's reality, felt helpless and irrelevant. Jealously coveting a meaningful role in the war effort, she fantasized about joining the Red Cross or becoming a foreign correspondent. She eased her guilt by writing commentaries on the unsung heroines who worked at the home front. As mates and mothers, she wrote, women could be a refuge of comfort and morality to their men and children. H.G. encouraged her to stay at home and prepare her "Citizen for the Age of Peace."

In truth, Rebecca needed little persuasion. She had fallen in love with Anthony, delighting in watching him sleep and suckle. The simple rhythm of her days by his side calmed and soothed her. At first, her mother, thrilled by the birth of her first grandchild, had come to visit, but Rebecca's refusal to bring him "home" to Fairliehope because of her mother's loathing of Wells—whom she blamed for the "reckless" accident—curtailed her desire to visit. Nonetheless, Rebecca's sisters, Winnie and Lettie, sustained their interest, visiting her often and proudly lauding the robust health of her "little cub."

But as the autumn days grew colder, and the prospect of spending months indoors became visceral, Rebecca, once again, sank into depression. H.G. had tried to anticipate her boredom with domesticity by introducing her to Walter Lippmann, the editor of an embryonic American publication called *The New Republic*, dedicated to analyzing public policy and trends in literature and the arts. Lippmann, who saw Wells as the prophet of a new age of hope and adventure, agreed to appoint Rebecca as a contributing editor. Soon she was busy writing social and literary commentary, but it was only a minor diversion from her underlying resentment of H.G.'s frequent absences, her social isolation, and her constant bouts with respiratory infection. Furthermore, competent servants were difficult to find and retain during wartime, and food rationing made giving Anthony a healthy diet nearly impossible.

In an attempt to placate her unhappiness, H.G. moved Rebecca and Anthony to a rented farmhouse in Braughing, a Hertfordshire village thirty miles north of London. The move did little to ameliorate Rebecca's sense of isolation, but H.G. hoped that the efficiency of the trains would enable him to visit her and Anthony more often. Rebecca found her articles for *The New Republic* barely satisfying, but Americans and Englishmen alike found them bold and incisive, and hailed the genius of her literary critiques.

While Hertfordshire proved more accessible to her friends than Leigh-on-Sea, Rebecca received few visitors. She longed for the excitement of theater and concerts and the literary fertility of London. At the end of July 1915, she moved into a large furnished villa at Hatch End, Pinner, a medieval town, once the property of the archbishops of Canterbury, now the home of landscape gardeners, artists, and artisans. Now that Rebecca was too close to the city proper for his comfort, Wells fabricated a new twist to her identity. She was to present herself as Mrs. West, the wife of a roving journalist and the caretaker of her nephew Anthony, the child of her sister who had died in childbirth.

Despite H.G.'s declarations of eternal love, Rebecca began to loathe her domestic quarantine and was becoming disgusted with incompetent servants who stole her money and threatened to expose her relationship with H.G. In truth, he was beginning to have his doubts, as well. When H.G. had decided to support her and permit her to keep the baby, he had thought she was a strong and courageous soul mate with whom he could change the course of history. But now, as with Amber, he was finding that she was emotionally volatile and cared too much for social regard and too little for making him a comfortable home. He resented that most of the time they were surrounded by servants or her sisters, and that except for furtive overnight stays in rented rooms in London they were hardly alone. He wanted to "detach us lovers a little more from the nursery," and to take her away to a romantic island where, he fantasized, they could live an idyllic life. In fact, they were finding that they were too much alike, though neither would have admitted it. Each found the source of their troubles in the character of the other: Both were emotionally needy and demanding, and both were willing to sacrifice their relationships to pursue their work. While they took great pleasure in each other's bodies and minds, they were too competitive to be compatible.

Unbeknownst to Rebecca, Wells had already been unfaithful; even as she had lain in her birth bed suckling their child, he had seduced the raven-haired and brilliant young mistress of Maxim Gorky, Moura Budberg, on his trip to Russia at the start of the war. While she had not suspected his infidelity, Rebecca was beginning to resent the relatively opulent lifestyle of Jane and his sons at Easton Glebe, and wondered if she would ever marry H.G.

By the summer of 1916, Rebecca had taken her career into her own hands. In 1916, she published an appreciative study of Henry James, with whom Wells had an antagonistic relationship. Running counter to Wells's denigration of this self-exiled American novelist, she defended the quality and relevance of James's social perceptions and his extraordinary ability to draw his characters with realistic precision yet infuse them with transcendent significance. In this literary spat with Wells, who had deprecated James as a myopic purveyor of solipsistic art, Rebecca declared that the principles of "criticism must break down when it comes to masterpieces." It was she who would now decide what was worthy.

In 1918, Rebecca published her first novella, *The Return of the Soldier,* an exposé of the deleterious effect of social conformity on one's capacity to live an authentic life. Rebecca continued to write articles and essays for the *Daily News* and the *Daily Chronicle* in London, and *The New Republic* in Washington, and was beginning to divine that in the not-too-distant future, she might become financially independent. And yet, she wrote to a friend, life was passing her by. She rarely saw "the great man," and while her sisters and friends had rallied to her side, she said: "I am in the most miserable state. Everything emotional that has kept me going through the worries and hardships of the last three or four years has suddenly failed me. It is nobody's fault . . . but my life is empty and I am possessed by a terrifying sense that I am growing old, and there will be no more peacocks and sunsets in the world." At the age of twenty-four, sobered by experience, Rebecca believed that her youth was over.

CHAPTER 2

BECOMING DOROTHY

I'm the child of a King,
the child of a King.
With Jesus, my Savior
I'm the child of a King.

—HATTIE E. BUELL,
"The Child of a King," a Methodist hymn

HAMBURG, NEW YORK, 1902

The week before Easter was a crescendo of excitement. The parsonage bustled with preparation for the Sunday feast and the white-spired church across the lawn rang with music and song. To eight-year-old Dorothy, the works of man and the works of God seemed in perfect harmony. The long winter in western New York State was over, and the earth cracked with new life; the snow had melted and young shoots of flowers rose through the mud. The Thompson family, disciplined by ritual, personal and public, prepared for the bittersweet celebration of Christ's resurrection. While her father, a preacher in the Methodist church, composed his sermon and chose his excerpts from the scripture and psalms, her mother, Margaret Grierson Thompson, cleaned the house, baked the pies, and colored the eggs for the annual roll and hunt. Dorothy, her brother, Willard, six, and sister, Peggy, four, helped their mother in the kitchen, while the oft visiting Grandma Grierson, a large, dark-haired, dark-eyed matron embittered by her abandonment by her "black Scot" husband, provided a running commentary on her daughter's incompetence. She was working too hard, she said. The children's manners needed improvement, the food was impossible, the furniture needed polishing, and she was too subservient to the needs of her husband, whose income wouldn't support a church mouse. Dorothy was irritated by the familiar dance, but no one could kill the joy of Easter with the cut of words. Preparations finally ended on Thursday, and when the Thompsons turned down the oil lamps that evening, they knelt in gratitude to their Maker, and went to sleep.

But something happened between Thursday and Saturday that Dorothy could not understand. Grandma Grierson had taken the reins, while her mother, suddenly and mysteriously ill, lay in her bedclothes in the upstairs room. On Saturday afternoon, her brother and sister were whisked off to a neighbor's house, while Dorothy played in the parsonage garden, listening to the sounds of the choir rehearsing.

She loved the poetry of the cants and scriptures, and took pleasure in memorizing passage and phrase. As the shadows lengthened and she sang along in harmony with the sweet choir voices, her father suddenly took her by surprise. Later, she would recall, "He took my hand and we walked up and down . . . and I said that the night which was falling was dark without a star in the sky and Father said in a voice like a groan that it was the darkest night he had ever known. That was all he said except, after a little while, that my mother wanted to see me."

"I was afraid," Dorothy remembered, "though how could I be afraid of Mama?" But when she saw her mother in bed, "her lovely eyes sunk in pools the color of bruises, smoke-dark hair like a mourning wreath spread on the white pillow, her head moving restlessly, white hands on the white coverlet restless, plucking and plucking at its threads," she knew her instincts were right.

"Hello, Mama," Dorothy said, trying to shield herself from despair by imagining her as just another dying parishioner whom she routinely visited with her father. "I touched her hand and recoiled because it was icy cold, but she held mine and spoke rapidly as though she had no time."

"You are the oldest," Margaret said. "Promise me you will always care for your little sister and your father."

The reality of her mother's words cut through Dorothy's pretense. "Oh, Mama," was all she could say.

Her mother was dead by Easter morning. Given that immutable fact, perhaps it was fortunate that the day focused on the ascension of Christ. Her father told her, along with her brother and sister, "Your mother is with the angels," but Dorothy was not consoled.

The Easter morning service went on as usual, and her father stood at the altar decorated with white lilies beside the cross. With complete faith in the benevolence of God, Peter Thompson might have commented during his sermon that God had a plan for Jesus and for all of humanity. But when the corpse was laid out for the neighbors in the good front parlor, Dorothy felt nothing but sadness. "I ran out of the room with screaming silent in my throat. Father followed me. . . . He was not mad at me. He held me very tight."

"Your mother has a new life," her father said, "a beautiful new life." Yet, as he spoke, he broke into tears and Dorothy, for the first time, permitted herself to cry.

Dorothy tried to convince herself that all would be the same, but she would soon notice that the parishioners would treat her differently: She was a motherless child in a town blessed with young married couples and their children.

A rumor prevailed that Margaret had died in childbirth, but Dorothy soon learned the truth. Margaret had been pregnant, but Dorothy's grandmother believed that her already overburdened daughter should not bear another child. Without the knowledge or consent of Margaret, or so she said, Grandma Grierson precipitated a miscarriage by giving her an herbal concoction, most likely of savin and pennyroyal tea. Margaret began to hemorrhage, and Peter, worried, wanted to call the doctor. Grandma Grierson initially refused, trying to avoid a confrontation. By the time she consented, the physician, ignorant of the cause, "plugged the flow, sealing in the poisons." Within forty-eight hours, a severe blood infection ravaged her body.

All abortions, either surgical or induced by pill or herb, were illegal, except to save the mother's life. It was estimated, however, that there were two million abortions a year in the United States at this time, and that Dorothy's mother was one among those who died of "home remedy" concoctions. It is likely that Margaret Grierson could not afford a physician-supervised abortion. Her mother must have convinced her of the efficacy of the procedure, which she kept quiet knowing that her preacher husband would have seen any attempt to terminate a pregnancy as a sin. It is also likely that despite her mother's attempt to protect her from moral stain, Margaret knew exactly what was about to transpire.

Motives, methods, and medical details aside, the cold fact remained that Dorothy's mother was dead. But the more the townspeople pitied

Dorothy, the more she resolved to carry out her promise to her mother. It was apparent, even to her, that she was capable, smart, strong, and determined. It was an easy slide into the role of housemaid and caretaker. From that time on, it was Dorothy who greeted her father at the door, took his coat and his muffler, and brought him his slippers. It was she who stoked the fire and brewed his tea, and made their dinner and helped her brother and sister with their homework. While Peter Thompson praised his "child-wife," he was wise enough to understand that he was robbing Dorothy of her childhood.

The Thompson family after
Margaret Grierson Thompson's death, 1901—
Willard, Rev. Peter Thompson, Peggy, and Dorothy

Peter asked his sister, Elizabeth "Lizzie" Hill, a widow with ten grown children of her own, to come to Hamburg to care for his family. Lizzie Hill was a straitlaced, conventional matron, "crackling with starch and reeking of cleanliness," Dorothy's sister, Peggy, would later say. She had a simple commonsense philosophy of life: "No troubles, physical or mental . . . could not be cured by a dose of castor oil, a good cup of tea, and faith." Aunt Lizzie ruled the parsonage with an instinctive mix of discipline and unconditional love, and Dorothy flourished under her steady hand. Shortly after Lizzie arrived, Peter sailed home to England to feel once again the cool winds of the wild moors of his childhood.

Peter Thompson was born in 1870 in the northern English county of

Durham, just south of the Scottish border. When his father, a feckless drunkard, abandoned his family, Peter had been a burden to his relatives, shuttled about from home to home like extra baggage. But in 1888 at the age of eighteen, Peter, a sensitive, frail young man, found his calling within the fold of the burgeoning Methodist church. Leaving his Anglican roots behind, he became a circuit rider among the pious poor and the miners of southwest Wales. The Methodist church, an offshoot of Anglicanism, assured individual salvation through the body of Christ, asserted the perfectibility of mankind, and emphasized Bible study, secular education, and social activism. Interested in the Americanization of Methodism, and encouraged by his elder brother who had emigrated several years earlier, Peter sailed to New York City in 1890. The revolution in steamboat and railway technology enabled Peter Thompson, much as it had Charles Fairfield, to cross oceans and continents cheaply and efficiently. He railed across the state and sailed down Lake Erie to the port city of Buffalo. The countryside was lush and fertile, and a preponderance of immigrants from England and Germany gave the city and its outlying land a European quality. Attracted to the vibrancy and beauty of northwestern New York, Peter nonetheless planned to return to Wales to resume his work. That is, until he met Margaret Grierson on a visit to Pittsburgh.

Margaret, a delicate, dark-haired Scot, was the eighteen-year-old daughter of coarse, uneducated, and radically conservative working-class immigrants. Drawn to each other's sensitivity and idealism, Peter and Margaret informed their families of their intent to marry, only to evoke heated hostility from both. Peter's family opposed the Griersons on grounds that they were déclassé, while the proud salt-of-the-earth Scots were rankled by the effete pretensions of a poet preacher who would doom their daughter to a life of threadbare poverty governed by the will of a powerful church. Against their parents' wishes, Peter and Margaret married in 1892, choosing to accept a post in Lancaster, New York, eleven miles east of Buffalo.

On July 9, 1893, their first child was born. Dorothea Celene, heavenly "gift of God," became the first Thompson or Grierson to be a citizen of the United States. Dorothy would always love American ideals, but her British bloodline gave her the clarity and perspective of one who was at once a bona fide native and a rightful critic. Her British parents wore their European manner and dress as a badge of distinction. In keeping with the philosophy of the Methodist church, they believed that their poverty was a blessing; that God had released them from concern with material possessions, so that they could revel in important things—their family, the church, the camaraderie of neighbors and friends, the beauty and glory of nature, and the power of serving mankind through good works and prayer.

Dorothy was convinced that God walked in the room with her father. Her love for him crystallized her love of God, her "King." While she discerned early that he was not a gifted preacher, her father's passionate recitation of scripture, homily, and prayer became her floodgate to language and a love of words. It was around the kitchen table during one of her father's early morning sessions reading the book of Job with his children that Dorothy came to feel the magic of words. She felt as though she had "fallen in love" with literature. For the first time, she "suddenly discovered that the words [she] was obediently and absently attending were beautiful." The sounds "rose and fell like a powerful melody like the greatest, strongest hymn [she] had ever heard." For Dorothy, the story of Job captured both her helplessness and her power. While largely unarticulated, it would be this understanding of salvation through faith that would sustain Dorothy through the vicissitudes of her life. The process of self-examination and reconciliation to God's will would continue to feed her optimism and fuel her strength.

Buttressed by biblical parable, embraced by the warmth and solidarity of her home, Dorothy was confident she would become a writer. After her mother's death, she became a voracious reader of American and British novels: science fiction, poetry, nature studies, history, and allegories.

Dorothy's life, much like Rebecca's, could be divided into two parts: before and after her parent died. Her childhood before her mother's death, she wrote, was "idyllic." The town of Hamburg, fifteen miles south of Buffalo, once open farmland, had become the prototype of small-town America, replete with Main Street shops, quaint Victorian hotels, and "mansions" dressed in prissy lace curtains, Brussels carpets, and oak- and walnut-paneled walls. The people of Hamburg, nonetheless, exuded simplicity. The fundamental values of the community, its atmosphere of trust and mutuality, and its long open stretches of unfenced gardens and lawns, gave Dorothy the freedom to test the limits of her feisty, rebellious nature. These memories would always define Dorothy's vision of "home."

But the people of Hamburg had their own prejudices, which would strongly influence Dorothy's views in the years to come. "I was exposed to the notion that English were best, Germans next best, and Irish, Poles and Eyetalians not good at all. . . . All of them were Roman Catholics and Papists which was a terrible thing to be." The pope, she surmised, "had horns and a tail," and seemed to have precipitated the poverty that surrounded her. Her father would also add that God was always hard on the Jews because they were the "chosen people" who should have known better. But within the Thompson household, Dorothy would say, prejudice had no place.

Aunt Lizzie's presence enabled the children to move beyond tragedy, giving them the courage to go on with their lives after their mother's death. After two years, however, it became obvious to everyone, including Peter Thompson, that his sister could not stay forever—he needed the reliable hand of a partner and a wife. The spinsters of Hamburg swarmed around the sweet, gentle preacher, but none more so than Eliza Maria Abbott, the pianist at the Methodist church. The homely daughter of one of the wealthiest families in Hamburg, Miss Abbott had reached the grand age of forty without developing one iota of sensitivity, generosity, or charm.

Peter Thompson's decision to marry Eliza Abbott was a practical acquiescence to financial security and domestic necessity. Dorothy and the other children were convinced that he could not possibly love her; she was so different from their vivacious, beautiful, and loving mother.

In August 1903, Dorothy, now ten years old, grudgingly walked down the aisle, strewing sweet peas in the path of the withered and hideous oncoming bride. To Miss Abbott's horror, Dorothy suddenly broke loose, somersaulting down the aisle with her bloomers exposed to those assembled for the solemn occasion. It was clear from the beginning that the new Mrs. Thompson had an allergy to children. Critical, sharp-tongued, and repressive, she ruled the house like a divinely ordained matriarch. Almost immediately, there was antipathy between Dorothy and her stepmother. Dorothy felt persecuted, emotionally abused, and degraded by the woman's constant ridicule and, to her amazement, her father meekly deferred to his wife, rarely lifting his voice to protect her. Feeling betrayed and abandoned by her beloved father, who seemed to have bartered her well-being for money and companionship, Dorothy lost faith in the strength of her once flawless minister to the "King."

Dorothy Thompson in grammar school, age twelve

As might be expected, Dorothy grew spiteful and rebellious, pushing her stepmother to the brink of a breakdown. But Eliza knew that the frail preacher would cave to her demand, and her demand was simple: Dorothy had to be sent away.

Her father's cowardice set Dorothy free from the muddled mores of small-town New York and enabled her to discover the landscape of fertile Midwest America. Continuing her father's journey west twenty years later, Dorothy boarded the Erie Railroad and rode down the line through

Pennsylvania and Michigan to the great port city at the base of Lake Michigan—Chicago, Illinois. Living in the midst of this hodgepodge of eastern European immigrants, corporate millionaires, lumber processing plants, and working-class insurgents, were Peter Thompson's sisters Margaret Heming and Hetty Thompson. The former was a widow and the latter a spinster—both were more than happy to give comfort to their motherless and alienated twelve-year-old niece.

Sensing the fertility and range of Dorothy's mind, they sent her to Lewis Institute, a private secondary school and two-year junior college for the "poor but proud." "Aunt" and "Auntie," as she called them, delighted in introducing her to the theater, ballet, music, and art exhibitions, and taught her to cultivate her "feminine" virtues, rearranging her hair and dressing her in attractive clothing. "Also they kept telling me I was pretty. I can't tell you what a difference it made in my young life, and in my relations with everybody."

The change in Dorothy's attitude was evident to all who knew her when she traveled home for the holidays. She carried herself with a new-found dignity, as if she were privileged and beautiful. The reality mattered less than the perception; her self-pride evoked the admiration of others.

The academic and cultural advantages of private education in a diverse, avant-garde city gave her an air of ethereal sophistication at once amusing and intimidating to her friends. Even her father began to acknowledge that Dorothy's rebellion had morphed into a substantive independence that was difficult to counter or control. Dorothy had learned to trust her judgment and to break the rules when she deemed them unjust. At school she had become a skilled debater, and she demanded rational interchange at home. Never again would she choose to live at the parsonage.

Dorothy was disappointed when she was turned down by the Seven Sisters schools, yet at the same time she felt fortunate to be among the 3.8 percent of college-age women who had the privilege of attending any institute of higher learning. Lacking a practical alternative, in the fall of 1912 Dorothy returned to western New York to attend Syracuse University. A socially progressive institution that gave scholarships to children of the Methodist clergy, Syracuse encouraged the uneducated and the disenfranchised poor to pursue social and political activism against economic injustice. At school, she was known as extroverted

Dorothy at her junior college graduation in 1912

and gregarious—as one who needed the company of people to truly shine. Dorothy quickly gained a reputation for intellectual intensity; her good-natured laughter could easily turn caustic when she felt unfairly challenged or thwarted by circumstance. She was and would remain prone to sudden outbursts of tears and affection. Interested in boys, she nonetheless found them boring, preferring instead the company of women. "Passionate attachments" among independent and ambitious women were deemed acceptable at the time, extending even to declarations of love.

She chose her alignments carefully. Eighteen-year-old Dorothy and the thirty-year-old Syracuse dean of women, Jean Marie Richards, became "real friends." Richards was a Boston-born beauty—"the epitome of all worldliness, elegance, culture, and refinement," according to Dorothy. Her exquisite diction, her mastery of the French language and culture, and her passion for literature evoked Dorothy's adoration. A professor of literature, Richards would keep Dorothy after class, tutoring her on the essentials of good writing and affirming her "capacity to meet life." Sitting by the fireside nursing pots of tea, the professor and the student became ardent friends in a relationship that seemed to transcend intellectual exchange. Despite her Chicago-bred aura of confidence, Dorothy harbored feelings of extreme self-doubt and craved the encouragement of kindred minds, not to mention the warmth of maternal bodies.

But by senior year, the harsh realities of economic self-sufficiency dominated Dorothy's mind. Honoring her promise to her mother, she knew she needed to save money for her sister's and brother's college educations. Her father, always the man of faith, articulated the connection between spirituality and reality. If she worked at something she instinctively valued, money would be an inevitable by-product. After graduating cum laude, she found a job at the Buffalo headquarters of the women's suffrage movement. At least for the moment, passion and practicality merged.

Her mother's death had taught her about the vulnerability of women, and while she never believed that her mother had played a submissive role, Dorothy wanted to make certain that American women had an equal hand in determining social and political law. Nearly seventy years earlier, west-central New York had been a hotbed of rebellion. The first women's rights convention was held in Seneca Falls, one hundred miles east of Buffalo, and the hometown of Elizabeth Cady Stanton, who, with Lucretia Mott, formulated the Declaration of Sentiments, patterned on the Declaration of Independence. But by 1914, New York State had become vehemently resistant to female enfranchisement. Dorothy, eager for the challenge, volunteered her services. For a short time she functioned as an envelope-licking clerk, but as her verbal talents and fiery temperament became better known, she was sent on the road as a spokesperson and event coordinator—an "organizer." Hustling mayors to endorse her soapbox sideshow, she stumped every town in western New York—six thousand square miles of territory—stirring the local townspeople with feminist propaganda. Her job, according to headquarters, was to "make people love [her]" and to cater to the interests of men as well as women.

Unfortunately, the efforts of Dorothy and her colleagues were to go down in defeat. In order to become the law of the land, that is, a constitutional amendment, the bill had to be passed by two-thirds of both houses of Congress and ratified by three-fourths of the states. Among the most populous states, New York was crucial to its passage. Nonetheless, in January 1915, the bill failed to pass in the House. The Nineteenth Amendment, guaranteeing the enfranchisement of women, was not ratified until 1920.

But Dorothy had learned that the anti-suffragist propaganda that she was up against could be venomous. Much like Rebecca and her British colleagues, American suffragettes were kicked, abused, dragged, and jailed. Often accused of being "unnatural," unfeminine, homosexual, and man hating, they were treated like social pariahs. Driven by common frustrations and ends, the American and British suffragist movements had formed the International Council of Women, through which they exchanged ideas, experiences, strategy, and literature, often traveling across the Atlantic to inspire one another.

On the circuit, Dorothy met Gertrude Franchot Tone, who was to become her mentor, spiritual guide, and confidante. The daughter of a New York state senator and the wife of a wealthy businessman, who, it was said, owned "half of Niagara Falls," Gertrude was a radical feminist who bemoaned her womanhood and her moment in time. Older and more experienced than Dorothy, Gertrude seemed to have offered her more than friendship—she was among those women whose maternal warmth filled her deep emotional void.

While she was disheartened by the failure of her efforts and, much like Rebecca, beginning to find one-issue politics a self-limiting platform for broad-spectrum social reform, Dorothy's compassion for the uneducated, socially alienated, and foreign-born poor was stoked by her suffrage tour. For the first time she met working-class and immigrant women with political views of all types—anarchists, socialists, progressives. They joined together with students and intellectuals and aging dowagers to work for voting rights for women. Dorothy wanted to bring her past full circle, integrating small-town values with the economic and cultural opportunities of big-city living. She joined the National Social Unit Organization, headquartered in Cincinnati, whose mission was to empower, educate, and raise the standard of living for the urban poor.

Deeming herself a "modern woman," and caught up in the contemporary notion that the touchstones for all one's beliefs were science and reason, she had convinced herself that her father's God was fossilized and irrelevant. But the Methodist social and moral ethic continued to be an enduring source of inspiration. In 1918 American idealism seemed trumped by the atrocities of the Great War, but it flowed through Dorothy like mother's milk.

Despite her exalted ideals and devotion to her work, Dorothy's experience was disappointing on many planes. Between the summer of 1918 when she arrived in Cincinnati and the end of the following year, she became disillusioned with the idea that any one person could make a difference. Human nature was not quite as malleable as she had thought, and good faith was not sufficient to effect social reform.

Her disillusionment was heightened by the sting of unrequited love. Wilbur Phillips, the brain behind the National Social Unit Organization, stirred her fantasies of sexuality and marriage by consenting to a rendezvous. For Dorothy, who was now twenty-five, this was just the beginning; Phillips was the first man she had ever loved. He seemed to fuse the spirit's soulful dedication with a palpable joy of physical pleasure. While Dorothy longed for a union no less fulsome than the flawless sacrament between her father, the gentle preacher, and her mother, his vibrant, sensual, devoted Scot, Dorothy and Phillip's fantasy of creating a new life together was thwarted by practical matters. To marry Dorothy, Phillips would have to divorce his wife and renounce his mission to serve the poor, casting himself into penury. And Dorothy was still the preacher's daughter, wedded, almost in spite of herself, to the sacred bonds of marital fidelity.

Dorothy wrote to her college friend Ruth Hoople that she saw something prescient in its failure; as though "something of the kind was fated to happen to me . . . from the very beginning." Much like Rebecca, Dorothy feared that she would never find happiness with a man.

Wretched with sadness and disappointment, but having fulfilled her obligations to her brother and sister, Dorothy left Cincinnati determined to pursue her childhood dream of becoming a writer. Later she would say that she became a journalist by accident, but it was her lust for experience, her intellectual curiosity, her European roots, and perhaps her need to prove her worth in a male-dominated profession that drew her to England in the hopes of becoming a foreign correspondent. On June 19,

1920, shortly before her twenty-seventh birthday, Dorothy and her beloved friend Barbara de Porte, a Russian-born Jew who had served with her as a suffragette and as a social worker, sailed for England. With portfolios in hand, their goal was to gain credentials as freelance reporters and to make their way across Europe to witness the aftermath of the revolution in Russia. Idealistic socialists, they, like many others, hoped that the new Bolshevik government presaged the just society of the future.

Dorothy wrote that after the war, there was only one thing that

> still kindled our hopes and aspirations. . . . That was Russia, symbol formerly of the blackest reaction in our minds. . . . The Russian Revolution . . . seemed the only bright light on the horizon. Here, it seemed to us, something was unfolding which had the grandeur of the doings of days and nights, the elemental force of nature itself, sweeping away the old and outworn, and creating in blood a whole, great new order of things.

Conceived to create a classless, warless society, Bolshevism appealed to the exhausted people of Europe who felt victimized by nationalism and capitalism. But the slow and painful process of bringing the Bolshevik society into place, racked as Russia was at the time by internecine social and political conflict, impelled Lenin to break with the Allies and make a separate peace with Germany. To quell the raging civil war, Lenin tightened the reins on social and political freedom. Little did Dorothy know that the new order was much like the old. By 1920, Lenin had replaced one repressive regime with another.

In a rare gesture of encouragement, Dorothy's father traveled down from Buffalo to New York City to see her off. After giving her his blessings, he left her with a humorous twist of wisdom: "Since you are obliged to earn your own living, it will not always be possible for you to remain a lady. But I pray you, Dorothy—please promise me, that you will always remain a gentleman."

From the moment Dorothy walked up the gangplank of the SS *Finland,* her survival instincts surfaced with intensity—she simply could not and would not fail. Charming a group of Zionists on board with her open-minded curiosity, she closely observed their culture and customs and listened intently to their views. By the time she arrived in England, she had an invitation to an international Zionist conference and the raw material for the first article she would present to the London bureau at the International News Service, the syndicate that served newspapers in the United States. While her article was rejected, she made a deal that she would write "on space," releasing them from any obligation to buy her stories. Dorothy found London to be a marvelous city of great beauty and culture, home to some of the most interesting writers of the time—H. G. Wells, Rebecca West, Frederick and Emmeline Pethick-Lawrence, and H. N. Brailsford, contributor to *The Nation*. By August, she was sufficiently plugged in to Anglo-Irish politics to observe what was tantamount to a civil war, becoming the last correspondent to interview a Sinn Féin revolutionary before his death in a unionist prison.

This time syndicate editors touted her efforts, paying her sufficiently so that she could travel to Italy to witness a general strike that heralded the coming of a political coup by Benito Mussolini. She believed she had arrived at a crucial moment when "democracy, socialism, nationalism were all assuming new, strange forms." She would call it "luck," but it was much more than that: Her friend Barbara de Porte would later say that Dorothy would do anything to get the job done, no matter how difficult or how little she was paid.

Dorothy had gone to Europe with $150 in her pocket, feeling she had nothing to lose. But five months later, when she left Rome for Paris in November 1920, the International News Service was ready to take her seriously. She also garnered work from the American Red Cross, which agreed to send her to Vienna and Budapest to write articles for U.S. newspapers and magazines.

Her "inside track" on the revolution in Rome earned her enough money to go to Vienna. But once there, she heard rumors that monarchists were about to reinstate the king in Hungary, who was currently en route through Switzerland to Budapest. Stalking the king on his journey home, Dorothy snared the only audience and interview with him. Within two years, she had earned a reputation in the trade for a remarkable nose for news; in 1921, the Curtis Publishing Company offered her a job as their Vienna and Balkan correspondent for Philadelphia's *Public Ledger*. "For the first time since leaving home," she later wrote to a friend, "I had a salary." Her father had been right that passion would bring monetary sustenance, but the victory was all hers.

Yet her personal life was at odds with her professional success. While she had mastered the techniques of her craft, love still eluded her. She longed for a meaningful liaison with a man, but the fact was that she resisted it—when it came down to a choice between a romantic suitor and the possibility of scooping a rival, she always chose the latter. In Rome she had literally left a lover in the shadows to pursue the movements of the Hungarian king. When Barbara de Porte, her sensitive, empathetic, and idealistic companion, sailed home to marry Meir Grossman, the right-hand man of militant Zionist Vladimir Jabotinsky, she was crushed. It was clear that Dorothy was truly on her own.

It has been said that she felt Barbara betrayed her; some chalk it up to Dorothy's lesbian desire. But while that could never be refuted or confirmed, shortly thereafter she embarked upon an intimate friendship with author and journalist Rose Wilder Lane, the daughter of novelist Laura Ingalls Wilder, who wrote the Little House books. Recently divorced, Rose was wrapped in a cloud of pessimism. Her irrepressible joie de vivre, curiosity, and lust for adventure made her a perfect confidante for Dorothy at the moment of her disappointment with Barbara. For Rose, Dorothy was an anodyne to her sadness: "There has never been anyone like you for clearing away this muddle in which I struggle to live, for somehow giving me fresh air, and light, and the freedom to be." Dorothy could only deduce that Rose was in love with her. On holiday, they walked for miles, even in the rain, on the banks of the Loire. While Dorothy was less passionate than Rose, she knew she had found a lifelong friend.

Back in Paris, Dorothy wrote an article on the Russian civil war for the *Public Ledger* that came to the attention of Paul Mowrer, the chief of the Paris bureau of the *Chicago Daily News*. Impressed with her work, intelligence, and drive, he suggested that she leave the competitive maelstrom of Paris to report from another city, one less inundated with reporters and more representative of European political ferment. And Dorothy knew exactly where she wanted to go—her ten days in Vienna before she had gone to Rome had convinced her that the Austrian capital was as fascinating as it was "heartbreaking."

Once again she made a deal that would barter her credentials for a risky future. The editor of the *Public Ledger* in Paris reluctantly agreed to give Dorothy the title of "special correspondent" without a salary or promise of advancement. Eager to nourish her dreams of becoming a novelist, Dorothy consented. Before leaving, she wrote to a friend, "I believe being happy doesn't count. . . . Getting somewhere does. . . . My dear, only fools and cows are happy."

To ensure that she wouldn't starve, Dorothy shuttled between Vienna and Budapest, where she wrote articles for the American Red Cross. As usual, she guarded her freedom. Central Europe was feverish with revolutions and riots, and she loved the paroxysms of the political fray.

In 1921, Dorothy wrote, Vienna, shattered by the Treaty of Versailles, was suffering from the loss of the empire. Once the capital of central Europe, it was suffocating from political, economic, and cultural strangulation, unable to feed or house its two million residents or the four million others who populated its rural western townships. It had become slumlike, perfumed with "good strong coffee," "bad sour wine," and the smell of kraut and lilac. As in postwar Berlin, a social ennui had taken hold, which bred moral anarchy along with great experimentation in art, theater, and music.

Dorothy lived in the city's student neighborhood, where rents were cheap and political ideas festered. As a freelance reporter, she had to work harder and smarter and faster than correspondents on salary. The fact that she was a woman meant nothing; the rules were the same. But she learned fast and her German became fluent, if not always grammatical.

On one of her weekly jaunts to Budapest, Dorothy had met Marcel Fodor, the correspondent assigned to Vienna and Budapest by the *Manchester Guardian*. It was one of those chance encounters that later seem "fated." It was he whose knowledge and generosity would launch Dorothy's career in central Europe, and it was he who would introduce her to a man who would turn every thought into a riddle and every certainty into a question.

Fodor was taken with Dorothy's pink-skinned radiance and genuine manner; Dorothy, in turn, was impressed by his knowledge and expertise, and touched by his unselfish generosity. Dorothy had found a friend and a mentor; Marcel had found a colleague worthy of his time and akin to his activist, optimistic nature. Quickly, they became invaluable to each other's work, ". . . he as a news-collector," Dorothy wrote, "and I as a news-analyzer and presenter."

After the fall of the Hapsburg Empire, Hungary, like Austria, had been shaken to the core. Autonomous, economically progressive, and secure for more than half a century, Hungary had been reduced to one-third of its size after the war. Food was scarce, strikes were rampant, and political chaos bred anarchy and resentment. Dorothy wrote, "Nowhere are capital and labor farther apart; nowhere is the Jewish question more strained. . . . Here is a nation whose social structure has been more violently assailed than that of any European country except Russia."

Fascinated by the country's political flux, Dorothy sat in the lobby of the Ritz Hotel in Budapest in the spring of 1921 listening intently to the observations of Marcel Fodor and sounding her views against his tutored ear. Consumed in conversation, plotting her next set of moves like a seasoned chess player, Dorothy looked up to see a young man approaching their table. A Budapest native with grand ambitions, Joseph Bard cultivated connections with journalists of repute in his native city. Fodor stood up to greet him, and Joseph, a man of studied manners, bowed to kiss Dorothy's hand. Catching his dark, deep-set eyes, she felt as though she were hit by "a thunder bolt." It was love, said one of her friends, "not only at first sight but at a glance. . . . There was no turning back thereafter."

Twenty-eight years old and still a virgin, Dorothy was ripe for an erotic encounter, and Joseph, as intuitive as he was clever, sensed the intensity of her response. That same evening, Dorothy and Joseph dined at the home of his mentor, Professor Rusztem Vámbéry, an eminent legal scholar and criminologist who also served as a counselor at the British delegation in Budapest.

Joseph, neither a virgin nor a man of conservative tastes, was the son of a Jewish father and a piously Catholic Croatian mother. At thirty years old, he could boast of both academic accomplishment and practical experience, having served in the Hungarian army during the Great War and been educated as a lawyer at the Sorbonne; he was a linguist who fancied himself a philosopher/historian. Joseph was biding his time, working as a freelance journalist for Reuters and the Associated Press until he found the right opportunity to continue his "real work"— a sweeping treatise on the metaphysics of Europe, which he had begun to write in three languages simultaneously.

Dorothy thought he looked like an Egyptian prince. "His hair lay on his head like burnished wings and his body was smooth, his limbs slender. . . . Something emanated from him. . . . Not desire, exactly, not so . . . centered. Tenderness . . . beauty . . . one felt always shy before it. A little blinded." Dorothy felt humbled by his beauty and eroticism; he seemed more than a man—a prince with a touch of divinity. It is interesting to note that Dorothy still craved the element of godliness in men, despite her disillusionment with her preacher father and his fossilized views. The hope, the ideal of salvation through love, was something she truly could not let go.

Unlike the slow burn of Dorothy's affair with Wilbur Phillips, she and Joseph became lovers within days. Later she wrote to him: "Your charm for me is essentially an erotic one." The racial and cultural gap between them meant little to Dorothy. She wanted to begin a new era in her life—"something imaginative, kindling, kind, strong, passionate, clean-cutting, well-holding . . . creative companionship: inner loyalty." Her platonic relationships with Phillips and Fodor had expanded her mind and soothed her loneliness, but her friendship with Bard mingled body and spirit. She hoped, perhaps, that it had the depth to endure.

Joseph zealously pursued Dorothy, and his near desperation frightened her. Almost from the beginning, he begged her to marry him. His profound loneliness, hatred of Budapest, and possessive sexuality threatened her sense of autonomy and integrity. And yet, she wrote to a friend, "He is a gentle and remote soul, interested in abstract philosophy. He does not crush my personality." But doubt and fear mingled with uncertainty. Dorothy knew that Joseph loved her, but she questioned his capacity for fidelity and commitment. His actions seemed to belie his words. An "accomplished flirt," he thought nothing of engaging in frivolous sex; it was "a national pastime in Hungary," he told her. For Dorothy, the quintessential idealist for whom marriage was inviolate, Joseph's philandering was difficult to swallow; no one, not even her friends, was beyond seduction. She, the preacher's daughter, had given herself to him wholeheartedly, and he, always the rebellious renegade, acted on impulse rather than principle. Dorothy saw him as a manipulator—a real Svengali.

For nearly two years, Dorothy continued to work as usual—meeting with Fodor, writing articles, and traveling wherever events took her. In the summer of 1922, after she agreed to assume a post for a colleague on a five-month leave in Berlin, Joseph wrote her a letter from Budapest: "Back again in this hot and smelly town and longing and perishing more than ever to hold my Stormy Spring in my arms. How long still? When, Darling, when?"

Dorothy was at the height of her beauty. Those whom she befriended, such as Phyllis Bottome, a psychologist, found her "radiantly pretty"; John Gunther, a reporter she met in Vienna, described her as "all woman"—voluptuous and feminine; and Carl Zuckermayer, a Viennese playwright, saw her as radiant and energetic, with her shiny brown hair and her lovely blue eyes. To Zuckerman she was the very essence of spring (and decidedly not stormy). Dorothy's lust for knowledge and experience enhanced her beauty and peppered it with confidence. She was beautiful, twenty-nine, and free, but she knew Joseph would not wait forever.

Dorothy had written to her friend Rose Wilder Lane, confiding that she valued her freedom more than anything. She wondered if she was pathologically selfish; she cared more about herself than anyone else.

Sometimes I want love . . . the surrounding kindliness and sympathy of someone who loves you more than he loves anything or anybody in the world. And I desperately need to love someone who needs me . . . a home . . . some course to my life . . . some stability in the compass. But then, at other times, my heart sits in me and bleeds like a thing in chains. . . . I know if I marry, I'll never take risks again in the same way. I'll never start off across the world with nothing in my pocket again, and be able to say, "well it's my own life, isn't it?"

Dorothy seethed with foreboding. She had despised her life after her mother's death when she was emotionally dependent upon people who could not or would not understand her. What if Joseph wasn't up to the task? Worse, what if she wasn't? Conventional expectations meant nothing to her. She questioned her aptitude for wife- or motherhood. "If I had [children]," she wrote, "they wouldn't be very nice."

Yet, Dorothy knew she could be happy only if she were connected to an ideal beyond herself. She struggled with the great social issues of the day—women's rights and roles after enfranchisement—but she concluded that "the relations between men and women will take years to resolve," as she wrote to her friend Gertrude Tone.

> *Oh, Gertrude, will any loving man realize that to be lonely, to be in-secure, but to be free; to make one's friendships where and as one will, without artificial restraint; to violate never the integrity of one's own spirit; to give oneself because one wishes to give and never because of habit or custom—to give oneself generously, but never to be owned— will* any *loving man believe that any loving woman can count these things greater than love?*

In the end, Dorothy decided to leave it to the "gods"; they had always been good to her.

In multiple letters, Joseph implored Dorothy to make a decision. "I have humbled myself before you; I have eaten dust. . . . I have had very little love in my life. . . . Tell me how much love you really feel for me. . . ."

In April 1923, Dorothea Celene Thompson married Joseph Bard in the town hall of Budapest, across the Danube from the Royal Palace. As distinguished architecturally as any of the public edifices in Budapest, with its majestic spire, turrets, and carved stone entries, it nonetheless lacked the sanctity of a church. One might imagine that Dorothy would have preferred to pass through the magnificent archways of Budapest's Inner City Church on her way to the altar. As she took her vows, the moment must have been tinged with sadness—her father was dead, her siblings were a continent away, and she was tarnishing the Thompson heritage by marrying not only an atheist, but a Jew. While there are no extant descriptions of the civil ceremony or the subsequent celebration, one might imagine Joseph in a dapper three-piece suit and Dorothy dressed in a shade of green that played off her honey-brown hair and her sea-blue eyes.

In an unsent letter, one of many composed in the loneliness of the night, she wrote, "I have in me the capacity to be deeply faithful to one man. . . . What I want is to . . . build a life with him which shall have breadth, depth, creative quality, dignity, beauty and inner loyalty." In short, she wanted what she sought for herself within the bond of marriage.

All her friends applauded Dorothy's decision. They found Joseph charming, amusing, generous, and brilliantly articulate. Only one of them disagreed: "[Joseph was] not an unkindly soul, the equivalent of a hairdresser with a naïve passion for fancy vests," said Rebecca West.

As usual, Rebecca had cut a slice of truth. Like a peacock in plume, Joseph strutted about, tail high, during their honeymoon. Before it was over, just to make certain he hadn't lost his allure, he had seduced a young "hen" right under Dorothy's cocksure nose.

For two years, according to Dorothy, they lived in "perfect bliss," in a capacious flat with a commanding view of the Belvedere Palace on Prinz-Eugen-Strasse in Vienna. There, she slogged "ahead at Journalism," while Joseph immersed himself in the unfamiliar luxury of devoting all his time to his mammoth project, *The Mind of Europe,* a historical and philosophical analysis of the evolution of the underpinnings of European social and political thought. "Delirious with love, I was delirious with youth and love together," Dorothy wrote, "and yet in the midst of it that blackness over my heart, that certainty of apprehension: This man will let me down; I shall break my heart over this." But she brushed her doubts away as a primitive pessimism, linked, possibly, to her father's betrayal.

At first it seemed as if Joseph was making progress on his book. He holed himself away from domestic noise, writing diligently with little distraction. But discipline was not Joseph's strong suit, and he soon grew restless. While Dorothy had confidence in his intellect, she began to treat him like a prodigal son, planning his day with schedules and chores to curb his wanderlust. But the more Joseph needed structure, the more he pulled away. He began to disappear, unannounced, on "research" expeditions. It would not be the last time Dorothy imposed control by remodeling men in her own image, but she was certain of her ethical absolutes—and disciplined hard work was one of them.

Finally, it had reached a point, Dorothy later told him, that she and Joseph "had so little time together. The work piled up, piled up. And in free moments, staleness. Why? I used to come to you, thinking you would say 'we will go to the country for a weekend.' Thinking you would make the plans. Never any. The work pulled me away and when I was there you went away."

Nonetheless, Dorothy was confident that their fractured marriage would heal as soon as Joseph became a "success." But Joseph's restlessness would reveal itself in unexpected ways, the nature of which changes according to who tells the story. Dorothy's straitlaced fundamentalism shattered in the face of her desperate desire for love. She would have done anything to make him stay, including blaspheming every precept of marital sex she held sacred. And Joseph knew it. He feigned disgust at Dorothy's friends' sexual practices and toys, and Dorothy raged at his attempts to throw her "back into a semi-homosexual state of adolescence by Budapest eroticism." His "tricks," which evoked "infantile narcissism," robbed her of the womanly satisfaction she had felt in his arms. Ménage à trois? Serial sex? It is difficult to know. But Dorothy was hurt by Joseph's constant cracks about her feminine attractiveness and allusions to homosexuality, even as she began to sense his own.

As usual, fantasy trumped reality. If only she could hang on despite his assaults. But by the time Dorothy was offered a post in Berlin in late 1924 by the *Public Ledger,* as the first female head of a news bureau in central Europe, she and Joseph were living apart. Hiding their break from her colleagues became a major effort; deluding herself became exhausting. She told everyone that Joseph hated Berlin and that his work was keeping him in Vienna. But privately Dorothy was flooded by self-hatred and despair.

She marshaled her friends for support and insight. Rose Wilder Lane urged her to come immediately to Paris to be by her side. Gertrude Tone, unfazed but nonetheless empathetic, took the occasion to discourse on the inferior morality of men. But it was her Viennese friend Eugenia Schwarzwald—social reformer, *salonnière,* and mentor—who confirmed her worst nightmare: Joseph had fallen in love with another woman.

It wasn't just a tryst. Dorothy could have handled that. Joseph had met a woman who offered him wealth, comfort, and understanding the likes of which he had never known with Dorothy. A while back, in a hotel in Munich, he had asked Dorothy, "If I have a friend with whom I can work, and talk, who suits my peculiar temperament—would you mind? You always said you didn't care so long as you didn't know about it." She agreed, saying, "If you find the woman you describe, then go to her, because she is the wife/woman/friend you want." But the abstract was easier to accept than the reality. With little finesse and less conscience, Joseph had been leading a double life. Fearful of confrontation and hesitant to make a complete break with Dorothy, he hid behind the maternal apron strings of her friend and mentor Eugenia Schwarzwald. Joseph confided in Genia that he had been unhappy with Dorothy for a very long time. Dorothy's efforts to control him were emasculating; she seemed to believe he could "starch his prick" on demand. Dorothy deplored his tactics almost as much as his betrayal. Joseph's duplicity revealed his true character—or lack of it. Dorothy wrote to him: "And on top of that you *planned* to go on leading a double life, using my love, trust, and work, using my youth."

Like a preacher whipped into fevered attestation, Dorothy spewed out her moral venom: She had tortured herself in journalism to support him; worked herself to death to pay his bills; and tried to make him comfortable and satisfied, while he used her youth, money, and inexhaustible goodwill to betray her.

Yet, as was the case with Dorothy's father, Joseph's cowardice actually served as an awakening. Having been shaken free from her delusion, this time Dorothy was dead set on destroying Joseph's. Sitting at her Biedermeier desk in their flat on the Händelstrasse, the flat that would have been their home, she gazed through windows to the Tiergarten and beyond. Shaken by his treachery into rational insight, Dorothy wrote him a letter, withholding nothing. He was looking outside himself instead of within, she told him. His fractured fiction and nonfiction writing had flashes of brilliance but were, in the end, vacuous and cheap. He understood nothing about Eros, love, or the psychology of women, and his lack of insight would make any relationship or creative work a failure. Freedom from her was an excuse for running away from himself.

Dorothy struggled to lift the failure of her marriage to Joseph above the mundane rage of a cheated woman. She put her own and his psychology aside, probing the core of femininity, forming a theory, and evaluating herself within its framework: "A real woman can be two things to a man metaphysically speaking: a Martha or a Mary: Heavenly or Earthly Love. I should have preferred to be Mary. There is more beauty in me, more rest, more <u>quiet</u> strength, more poise than you have ever known."

Joseph's new love, Eileen Agar, saw life as a coalescence of impulse, fantasy, and chaos. There were no moral absolutes; no valid religious or philosophical doctrine; no forbidden ground; no fixed image of men or women. Eileen was a bohemian twenty-five-year-old who was studying (against her parents' wishes) at the Slade School of Fine Art in London, an avant-garde and experimental institution outside the periphery of traditional painting and sculpture. Delicately beautiful, calm, and introverted, yet free and open-minded, Eileen was the antithesis of Dorothy. Noting that her family and friends had warned her of Joseph's "Byronic" reputation, Eileen nonetheless found his soft, clear voice, his simple language and playful, affectionate manner "irresistible." The problem was that she, too, was married. But Joseph, whom she deemed far wiser and more experienced than herself, told her that both their spouses would get over it. Joseph told Eileen that Dorothy had been so busy working that she scarcely noticed his presence when he was around.

Through Joseph's eyes, one can see that Dorothy, too, had a hand in their failure. To him she was nothing more than a glorified schoolmarm motivated by some abstract notion of love, but unable to translate her feelings into warmth and understanding. Totally absorbed in her work, Dorothy made him feel like an accoutrement, a pretty boy, she could fondle or flaunt, but just as readily ignore. Eileen believed she could heal Joseph's childhood pain and sexual impotence, and in the process liberate his mind. Argentinean by birth, Eileen believed that Joseph was cursed with the European neurosis of over-intellectualism—"his head [was] overfed and his heart starved."

Joseph found the perfect rationale for initiating a divorce when Dorothy, in his absence, turned to her American colleague Floyd Gibbons for physical and sexual comfort. This romantic development was all Joseph needed to finally explode with pseudo indignity, justifying his own perfidy by hers.

Hysterical with grief and shame, Dorothy, nonetheless, could not let him go. As much as she condemned him, she was willing to make him a deal. Unable to reconcile her guilt at having defied every standard of Christian virtue, only to court degradation and failure, she begged him to sustain their social charade. She would stay married to him on any terms he would offer. Joseph refused.

During 1925 and 1926, Dorothy would write Joseph hundreds of letters, some sent and some tucked away in a drawer, ceaselessly analyzing what had gone wrong and what each might have done to deter failure. Her "suffering for [him] and through [him]," she wrote, felt like a "crucifixion"—a slow, painful death of goodness and innocence. She even contemplated suicide.

While Dorothy was convinced that she would always love Joseph in a creative way more than she could any other man, in December 1926, after three and a half years of marriage, she agreed to set him free. Dorothy wrote to Eileen: "I am sending this boy of mine back to you. I mean, I am letting him go. He wants to so much! You can do a great deal for him now, and believe me, dear Eileen, he is worth doing something for. Beauty is in him, and goodness."

"Curious," she wrote to Joseph, "how I believed in our marriage. As in God."

CHAPTER 3

THE TRINITY

In the trinity of the man, the woman and the
child, the child is the most important person.

—REBECCA WEST, *The Clarion*, 1912

HERTFORDSHIRE, JUNE 1917

It was the summer of 1917, and "Mrs. West" and her "nephew" Anthony huddled together in the upstairs bedroom of their rambling farmhouse in Hertfordshire, as German bombs plummeted to earth with terrifying force. The old casement windows rattled in the din of enemy fire that set the sky ablaze with light. While Anthony sobbed inconsolably in her arms, Rebecca cursed H.G. along with her womanhood. One might imagine her slipping into reveries of lost autonomy. She had fashioned her life to abjure the suffering her mother had endured, and yet there she was, without emotional or financial security, bound to the needs of a three-year-old child.

Also into its third year, the war that should have been over in months was spiraling out of control like a mindless machine hell-bent on destruction. Allied commanders had come and gone, governments had risen only to fall, and while the British and French had made modest gains on the western front, casualties were high and morale was low. America had finally joined the Allies, and the infusion of money, manpower, and munitions that it brought provoked a German air offensive more brutal and reckless than before. Day and night, planes bombed civilian targets in and around London, leaving human and physical devastation in their wake.

Anthony loved his "Auntie Panther"; he liked to stroke her dark brown hair and to cuddle into her soft warm breast, but her gaze was always cool and distant, as if her mind was someplace else. As for his Uncle "Wellsie," he was endless fun, making up stories and silly games, engaging his attention fully and wholeheartedly as his "auntie" never could. That is, when he came around, and by 1917 he was coming around less and less. Consumed by anger, Rebecca refused to give H.G. comfort or soothe the hunger of his incessant desire. He had begun to prefer the dull equanimity of Jane to the fiery pounce of his once welcoming Panther. The desolation of war had snapped Rebecca's mind, along with the bonds of their less-than-sacred trinity.

After a night of bombing, she and Anthony would find craters less than a half mile from their home and cows lying dead in the nearby fields. One morning, said Rebecca, she had found the carcass of her cat. It was then that she decided to send Anthony away to boarding school.

Nearly forty years later, Anthony would describe his feelings of betrayal in a semiautobiographical novel, *Heritage*. According to him, without the least forewarning, Auntie Panther packed his bags and shuttled him onto a train to London. Throughout her life, with as much anger as indignity, Rebecca would justify her decision: It was a necessity precipitated by war and their economic survival; she had sent him to a handpicked Montessori school run by her friend and suited to his temperament; she had spent a week with him in London, shopping for clothes and placating his fears. But the veracity of Anthony's account doesn't matter—his sense of abandonment and rejection would pursue him endlessly. Forever he would cast himself in the role of victim, viewing every woman, but most of all his mother, as a malicious and manipulative perpetrator. Later he would write that Wellsie's absences and Auntie Panther's self-absorption were "a classic set-up for inducing emotional mal-nutrition, and all the distortions and hallucinations that go with it."

It is fair to say that Rebecca's decision to send Anthony away at the age of three was self-serving. Her love for H.G. had already waned; she wanted to be free to travel and write, to become financially independent, and to rejoin the literary circles in London. To begin, she needed time and solitude. No doubt she also feared for Anthony's safety, but, as with her stories about the abandonment by her father, the determining factor was a spin of the wheel, depending upon her state of mind and her needs at the moment. In sum, there was no evidence that her cat had died.

In September 1917, when the bombs were falling, Rebecca's first novel, *The Return of the Soldier,* had been accepted by *The Century Magazine* for serialization. It is possible that this offer, and the hope that it presaged success in a new genre, further steeled her mind against keeping Anthony at home. The short novel was critically acclaimed in England and America. She was touted for her elegant and artful prose, as well as for her psychological insight. Based on a news account of a traumatized amnesiac who had lost his inhibitions along with his memory, Rebecca's debut novel was at once a love story between a shell-shocked gentleman soldier and the working-class lover of his youth, and social commentary on the idle rich and the pitiful necessity of sustaining their aristocratic pretensions. Its themes would resonate throughout her work.

Filtering through the voices of her semiautobiographical characters is evidence of the intellectual currency of Rebecca's time: Freudian theory, which had as many critics as converts, pervaded European culture as a pseudoscientific tool to explain human emotions and behavior. The "cure" in essence was a valuable form of fiction, agreeable to both analyst and analysand. It was Freud as well who had invented the epithet "shell shock" to describe the mental disturbances of soldiers exposed to prolonged fighting on the French-German front. Although Rebecca would deny that she had read Freud at that time, her voracious desire to analyze male-female relations would make it likely that psychoanalytic theory, in any form, would seep into her consciousness.

The most poignant message slips off the tongue of the novel's female narrator. She says, "When one is an adult, one must raise to one's lips the wine of the truth heedless that it is not sweet like milk but draws the mouth with its strength, and celebrate communion with reality, or else walk forever queer and small like a dwarf." "Truth," in this context, is the inevitable tension between individual desire and prevailing social conventions. Despite the profundity of her insight, Rebecca's personal "communion with reality" was yet to come.

Spurred by the success of her first novel and released from the care of Anthony, Rebecca became more ambitious than ever. Within three months, she had finished half of a new novel called *The Judge.* Like a scientist examining a specimen under a microscope, she was determined to dissect her relationship with Wells. Drawing upon her childhood in Edinburgh and her experience as an unwed mother, she told the story of a young, naïve suffragist who falls in love with a handsome and worldly sailor, only to be caught in the hellish quagmire of his family relations. The plot moves toward the sailor's murder of his illegitimate brother and the suicide of their brokenhearted mother. Trapped in the emotional patterns of their childhoods and caught in the grip of a mysterious force, her protagonists surrender to the pull of "destiny." An omnipotent power, Rebecca implies, guides their fate, and they dangle like puppets at the whim and mercy of invisible hands. For the first time, she sought to understand the human condition in the context of a higher law. While Rebecca eschewed the notion of an anthropomorphic God, she could not deny the existence of an inscrutable force.

Her female protagonist concludes that "Every mother is a judge who sentences the children for the sins of the father." Perhaps it is an apologetic nod, written in tranquillity, to explain the universal reasons for Anthony's suffering. But it is also a vision of humanity caught in the current of ungovernable forces that exonerates her personal guilt.

It is interesting to note that despite Rebecca's urgent desire to resurrect her career, it took her five years to complete this novel. She did not seem to know how to resolve its psychological, social, and spiritual dilemmas until the death of her own mother in 1921. Her mother's illness, after a slow deterioration from Graves' disease, seemed to Rebecca a form of crucifixion that intensified her lifelong contempt for the self-punitive doctrines of Christianity. Yet, simultaneously, she longed to find spiritual solace in a godless world.

While *The Judge* was greeted by mixed reviews, it was recognized by the literary icons of the day. Virginia Woolf, among those who believed that Rebecca's critical brilliance weakened her characters and preempted her fiction, deemed *The Judge* "a stout, generous, lively, voluminous novel" that she could not finish reading because it "burst like an overstuffed sausage." H.G. hated its unwieldy structure. He called it "an ill-conceived sprawl of a book with a faked hero and a faked climax, an aimless waste of your powers." Perhaps it was H.G.'s revenge, in the guise of a literary critique, for Rebecca's public denunciation. Her friends would call his comments cruel and sadistic. Her knife cut both ways.

As if in response to the failure of her novel, in the years that followed Rebecca's own literary reviews became increasingly vitriolic. She began to write for *The Egoist*, an iconoclastic literary review and the newest iteration of *The Freewoman*, in 1918, and in *The New Republic*, an American left-of-center magazine. By 1922, Rebecca had finished fifty-five two-thousand-word critiques of 136 novels. More than ever, she attacked the literary icons of her time. She had come to believe that most of her female contemporaries were writing the best work, although the establishment deemed their efforts "minor fiction." Their work had not risen to the level of that of their male counterparts, she asserted, because editorial prejudice and social mores prevented them from fulfilling their potential. Female authors, she said, in concert with Virginia Woolf, were often judged according to their conformity to the traditional patriarchal values of English literature.

In 1919, with money saved from her own earnings, supplemented by H.G.'s stipends for Anthony, Rebecca was finally able to leave the countryside for a flat in London at Queen's Gate in South Kensington. Once a string of multistoried homesteads with classic white pillars and elegant façades, these mansions had been converted into one-story flats leased at moderate cost. Now happily situated within a short distance of London center and her literary friends, Rebecca brought Anthony home, enrolling him in a nearby day school.

This was a time of reconciliation between Rebecca and H.G.; he admired her feisty struggle for independence and she, now somewhat free of his grip, allowed herself to be vulnerable again. His desire for her seemed to heighten when she needed him least. Anthony was delighted to be at home with his "auntie" and to revel once again in "Wellsie's" stories and games. Before taking Rebecca out for the evening, H.G. would wrap his five-year-old offspring in the folds of his imagination, magically transporting him beyond the bounds of ordinary life. These fantastical voyages were etched in Anthony's mind like dreams he could later conjure for his own literary inspiration.

At the age of seven, however, Anthony was, to use his word, "pitched" into his first conventional preparatory boarding school for boys, St. Piran's at Maidenhead, twenty-five miles west of London and run by a friend of H.G.'s, who would turn out to be an incompetent drunk. Anthony felt abandoned for the second time. Once at school, which he would describe as the "sort of place in which the inconvenient, the unwanted, and the illegitimate middle class child was . . . dumped," he had to fabricate a story that he "didn't believe and couldn't possibly defend." Like a blind man whose survival depended on things he could not see, Anthony had sharpened his skills of perception to remain vigilant against loss or deception of any kind. Even before he left, Anthony sensed that his "auntie's" anger at "Wellsie" for his flings with women proved that they were more than friends.

By the next academic year, Anthony, the target of ruthless interrogations by his classmates, confronted Rebecca about his parentage. She admitted that he was the biological son of her and Wells, but made Anthony promise that he would never share his knowledge with anyone until he was grown up. The family's story, she told him, was one ordinary people wouldn't understand, and she and Wells would get into "terrible trouble," if it were known.

Perhaps it was momentary sympathy that moved her to tell her son the truth, but it was a reflexive action that imposed a burden on eight-year-old Anthony that even she, at thirty, could barely carry. To her amazement, and to Anthony's psychological ruin, he guarded her secret for many years. Rebecca's sister Lettie, in on the secret from the beginning, would relate a vignette that would become a family heirloom. Shortly after Rebecca had told Anthony that he was her son, Aunt Lettie took Anthony to the beach. According to the story, Anthony climbed to the top of a tall sand dune and, raising his arms to the sky, screamed at the top of his lungs: "She's my mother! She's my mother!" As Lettie watched her nephew squeal with joy, she could feel only great sadness. She pitied the child for all the pain he had felt, and the prospects of his future tainted with illegitimacy.

Sadly, Anthony's moment of ecstasy would not last. Once back at school, sworn to secrecy, he barely managed to hang on to his sanity. While Anthony sought consolation from his aunts and their knowing friends, his parents' relationship began to unravel. Plagued by what would later be diagnosed as diabetes, H.G. had become increasingly volatile; Rebecca never knew which aspect of her lover would come to her door or move his hand as he wrote her letters.

AS ANTHONY HAD SURMISED, Rebecca had suspected, and Jane knew, H.G. had had several affairs with women during their time together. The first was with Moura Budberg, the seductively beautiful secretary of Maxim Gorky, whom H.G. had first met on a trip to Russia in 1914 after Anthony was born. His other paramour was Margaret Sanger, the brash and fiery leader of the birth control movement in America, whom he had met on a trip to the States in 1921. To him both represented the essence of the New Woman—an independent sexual being who craved neither long-term commitment nor the sacrament of marriage. When he returned to England in the fall of 1921, exhausted from his tour and on the brink of physical and emotional breakdown, H.G. begged Rebecca to remain his lover, and she, unaware of his tryst with Sanger, consented.

His entreaties aside, it was clear to H.G. that he and Rebecca were drifting apart. Probing the reasons for their rift, he wrote: "It seems to me that almost fundamental in this trouble is something I should call *Drive.* . . . It is a race against death. . . . You, I don't think, have Drive as I have."

Rebecca's new independence cut both ways. While she was more admirable and less dependent, she was also more difficult to harness and control than she had been in the past. Quite simply, he was hurt, and the only way the "great man" could pump himself up was by depicting Rebecca as a female dilettante. She quickly caught on, hacking away at his lofty pedestal of existential angst. While H.G. had found the reasons for their demise in their diverging degrees of intensity and style, Rebecca attacked him at the root. She deemed him intolerably selfish and maliciously cruel—a mindless vehicle of suffering and pain. Later she would recite her litany of grievances for a prospective biographer: "He treated me with the sharpest cruelty imaginable for those horrible years that he humiliated me. . . . He overworked me and refused to allow me to rest when I was ill. . . . He has cheated me of all but one child . . . his perpetual irascibility ruined my nerves . . . he isolated me and drove away my friends." Furthermore, she said, H.G. had deprived her and Anthony of material comfort, while supporting Jane and their sons in lavish style.

H.G. was beginning to believe that he had loved an illusion of Rebecca and not the woman herself. In early 1922, he wrote, "I do love some sort of Rebecca West who isn't like this, I love her passionately now, a wise, kind & admirable love. But she's a dream. . . . I'd rather be with her & work with her than spend my time in any other way. . . . It is [a] tragedy that we are not together."

He feared letting Rebecca go—she was young, vibrant, beautiful, and prolific, a rising star in the London literary scene just as his creativity and health were on the wane. He reminded her that he had loved her mind before he had loved her body, and he was certain that he would never find a more brilliant woman or a more satisfying lover, no matter how long he lived.

But whereas H.G. was conflicted about their relationship, Rebecca knew it was doomed. There was another triangle, another trinity, with H.G.'s wife at its center. The primacy of H.G.'s relationship with Jane and their sons made it impossible for Rebecca to see a future for her with him. Rebecca saw Jane as a duplicitous gold-digging woman who was using her husband for her own material and social ends. Jane, she observed, found sadistic pleasure in knowing that H.G.'s naïve young lovers would inevitably fall on the proverbial ash heap. And Rebecca surmised that Jane had encouraged H.G.'s lust for women to ease the burden of his consuming demands and to liberate her from home and domesticity. Jane's sadomasochism found release in punishing her husband's lovers and siphoning H.G.'s funds while basking in his glory.

Rebecca and H. G. Wells, circa 1923

But H.G. seemed blind to the dark side of Jane; he saw her as the only loyal and self-sacrificing woman in his life—a "Virgin Mary" of pure and unwavering character who, by sweetening his life with domestic tranquillity and order, enabled him to bring his work to fruition. It was this dichotomy between Virgin Mother and sexual slave, Rebecca believed, that would ultimately destroy them.

H.G.'s visits to Rebecca from Easton Glebe and his London flat had grown less frequent, and by the spring of 1923, sensing the looming prospect of defeat, he desperately sought Rebecca's compassion while simultaneously offering her an easy way out.

Lonely, ill, and disheartened, he revealed that his sure-footed strength and veneer of confidence were nothing more than self-made fiction. Poignantly he wrote,

> *I'm not really a Jaguar or a Pusted or a Fido or any of the dear things I have loved to pretend to be. I am a man who has had the dearest most wonderful love & has requited it ill. . . . And if the Jaguar you created vanishes, there remains a man you don't understand who cares for you & worships you, as well as insulting & raging & beating at you. . . . We may have learnt a mutual consideration, but it is foolish to make promises. We shall love and we shall jar. You say the love isn't [worth] the torment of the discord. Leave it at that.*

For a short time, H.G.'s humility, perhaps as he had intended, lured Rebecca back. But later that spring, when his unbalanced Austrian mistress, yet another lover about whom Rebecca had been ignorant, attempted suicide in his London flat, she no longer felt a trace of loyalty. H.G.'s insatiable thirst for sexual satisfaction, which threatened to ruin Rebecca's hard-won reputation, compounded by his resistance to leaving Jane, made it absolutely clear that they could have no future.

Shortly thereafter, Rebecca gave H.G. an ultimatum—one she would later say was actually a ploy to bring their relationship to an end. Knowing that he would never consent, Rebecca demanded that they marry or permanently separate. H.G. snidely replied, "I don't think it just for you to turn on me this growing mania of yours about the injustice of my treatment of you in not murdering Jane. . . . I can do no more than I have done." In another letter he wrote, "Will you ask yourself if you love me, & if you do, will you do this for me, will you try to make a common life for us possible?"

Rebecca, however, was making plans to go to the States. Just before she left for New York, Rebecca, H.G., and Anthony took their last "family" vacation together in Swanage, a seaside resort on the southeast coast of Dorset. But their holiday was marred when Anthony, now age nine, started acting out; their time together was a cruel reminder of the family he would never have. While H.G., along with her sisters, had long predicted that Anthony's sensitivity and intelligence would ignite his rage, Rebecca refused to acknowledge that his behavior was anything but normal. "Rebecca was always making excuses for Anthony," her sister Winnie's daughter would later say.

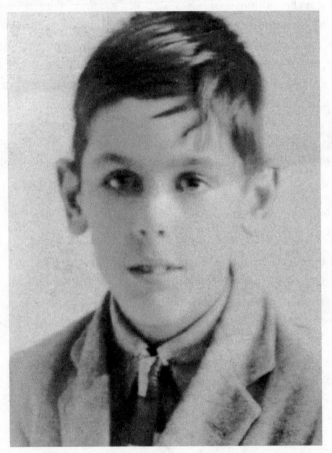

Anthony West, age eight, 1922

In truth, H.G. and Rebecca were still deeply in love, but the same feelings of kinship that had brought them together were tearing them apart. Each had been emotionally crippled by parental desertion, and in its wake a subsequent loss of faith in human nature and social justice had emerged.

These losses had impelled them to ask the impossible of each other: to sacrifice their ambition for the sake of their union. Yet neither Rebecca nor H.G. could put anyone else's needs above her or his own, including those of their suffering child. Ironically, their professed iconoclasm was an intellectual smoke screen that veiled their need for social legitimacy. No matter how many times they told themselves and each other that intellectuals were the true aristocrats, each craved the pedigree possessed only by the highborn. When the ideal lover each had sought revealed his or her frailty, their love became nothing more than an abstraction.

By traveling alone to America, Rebecca would violate their unwritten contract. Heretofore, it was H.G. who had traveled so far for so long, always leaving Anthony behind. Now it was she who was planning a five-month tour through the States, hoping to reap the fruits of her literary renown and widen the swath of her influence. Anthony adopted his usual stoicism when he returned to St. Piran's. Yet his letter to his mother before she left resonated with the sadness and worry of one who perpetually feared abandonment. After wishing her a good voyage, he wrote, "I shall miss you so much, so hurry up and come back. Don't forget to send me your address. I will write as often as I can."

THE GREAT WAR had initiated a second industrial revolution in England; the new technology that had enabled an Allied victory, as H.G. had predicted, also revolutionized land and sea transport, enabling passenger ships to offer the kind of luxuries once exclusively enjoyed by wealthy aristocrats. These mammoth seagoing vessels had become the dukedom of celebrities who had made their fame and fortune in radio, print media, and the cinema. Rebecca was among them.

She departed from Southampton on October 20, 1923, and six days later, her ship glided up New York harbor. It was "gorgeous," she wrote to her sister Winnie.

Miles and miles of shore covered with low dock buildings—incredibly strange erections of a Robot civilisation—then this cluster of sky-scrapers, white and slim like lilies. The Statue of Liberty is a washout—she gets her stays at the same place as Queen Mary! I was

*met by Mrs. Lamont + my publisher's publicity agent + my London
literary agent. . . . I then had a hectic day. Two hours with reporters—
five of them—during which one or two of them tried to make me say
something unwise. One published an impertinent interview.*

When asked if she was a literary protégée of Mr. Wells, Rebecca
quickly changed the subject.

Her defiant air and unpretentious beauty evoked the interest of many
journalists. The same high brow, flashing black eyes, and soft childlike
mouth that exuded both innocence and lust that had captivated Wells ten
years earlier seemed to enthrall the press.

Although H.G. had warned her that the American clubwomen—
a national network of straitlaced, leisured upper- and middle-class women
whose mission was to educate themselves and their communities—
would be on her tail for their illicit affair, Rebecca was shocked by the
vehemence of their anger and their zealous resolve to have her deported.
Fearing their fury and the intrusion of the press, she rarely went out to the
theater or cinema in New York, except with friends she knew she could
trust. Yet having been isolated by necessity for so many years, even with
these constraints Rebecca felt like a nun released from a convent.

Beyond the threat of moral harassment, Rebecca's entry into New
York society had its satisfactions. She cultivated a coterie of loyal friends
who would protect her from the onslaught of negative press and people.
She was drawn to Fannie Hurst, an American-born novelist of international repute—a "Jewess of the most opulent oriental type"—whose
fierce independence and insatiable ambition were akin to her own. Fannie's cool rationality toward men and sex was a salve to Rebecca's emotional anguish. In an effort to assuage the storm of public attack by
clubwomen, Fannie held a party in Rebecca's honor, to which she invited
her literary friends. There Rebecca met Emanie Sachs, an aspiring novelist and short-story writer, along with another American feminist, Doris
Stevens, whose book she had reviewed the previous year in the British
journal *Time and Tide*. While Emanie proved to be a kindhearted soul
prone to depression, Doris's optimism boosted Rebecca's spirits and nurtured her courage to carry on.

Despite H.G.'s efforts to preempt Rebecca's arrival in New York by
corresponding with his literary associates and friends, maligning her as a

feminist poseur who had sapped his mind and milked him dry, the tide was beginning to turn in her favor. A chance meeting with Alexander Woollcott, radio commentator, drama critic, and literary superstar of the Algonquin Round Table, would become pivotal to Rebecca's success in the States. Taken with Rebecca's beauty, wit, and brilliance, the owl-eyed, bloated, and irascible journalist became her self-appointed mentor and devotee. His efforts to introduce her to luminaries such as Irita Van Doren, the literary editor of the *New York Herald Tribune,* were invaluable in sustaining and funding her tour. Van Doren, one of the few female editors of a major New York newspaper, offered Rebecca a freelance position as a literary critic that would evolve into a long-term contract. In much the same way that Marcel Fodor had launched Dorothy Thompson's career in central Europe, Woollcott propelled Rebecca into the limelight, teaching her the nuances of American protocol and culture. And, like Dorothy, Rebecca would be eternally grateful for her mentor's devotion and goodwill.

But the thoughts she shared in public belied her true impressions of America in 1923. She wrote to Sinclair Lewis, the celebrated author of *Main Street,* a satiric portrait of American greed and social hypocrisy, "I love America and I loathe it." She loved its land, lakes, and rivers but loathed its phony materialist culture. Later she would tell a prospective biographer that she had hated America on her first visit. There was too much drinking and vacuous talk, she said. No one conversed about ideas. It certainly was not a place to bring up a child. Yet the honesty of her letter to Winnie, shortly after her arrival, rivaled none. Expressing, not for the first time, a profound strain of misogyny, she wrote:

I have been in three places now—New York, Springfield (Mass.)— and here [Philadelphia]—everywhere the women are hideous and beyond all belief slovenly. . . . Their utter and complete lack of sex attraction is simply terrifying. Not that it matters—for the men seem entirely lacking in virility. . . . The mechanical side of life here— telephones, taxis, trolleys—but a pale humanity falters along in the midst of it. . . . They are slow in speech, slow in movement, slow in thought.

Rebecca was beginning to realize that she herself was highly attractive, and by sheer coincidence H.G. would serve as minister to his own downfall. He had introduced her to Max Beaverbrook five years earlier in London. Max, now Lord Beaverbrook, was a Canadian-born industrialist who had owned a utilities, cement, and steel conglomerate and had settled in England in 1910 in the wake of claims of corporate corruption made against him by the Canadian government. By the time Rebecca met him, Max had spent four years as an MP in the House of Commons and owned several newspapers, including the *Daily Express* and the *Evening Standard*, and had a sizable share in a film and cinema chain. He had earned the epithet of "press lord," one who wielded influence over millions of people in the street as well as many in high government office. After he had read the *New York Times* interview and learned that Rebecca was in New York without H.G., Max sent out a search party of employees to find her. By Christmas, they were sharing a bed. Captivated by his erudite mind, his photographic memory, and clever wit, Rebecca found that he reminded her of H.G. and her father. Max made her feel uniquely desirable and was as facile in bed as he was in conversation. They would often fall into fits of laughter, which cheered her after ten years of living under the cloud of H.G.'s pessimism and abuse. Smitten by his charm and sartorial elegance, and impressed by his international clout and social connections, she hoped that they could make a stable life together. Once again, she put her future into the hands of a married man, assuming that she, above all others, could lure him away from his wife and children.

It didn't take more than a couple of weeks, however, for Max to begin treating Rebecca like a sexual plaything, coming and going as he pleased. Paralyzed by disappointment, and even more troubled by her consistently poor judgment about men, she fell ill with influenza and bronchitis, delaying the remainder of her tour for at least a month. She was beginning to think that she was "hounded by a malevolent fate." Perhaps there was something "evil" inside her, she thought, which condemned her to a lonely, loveless life.

But on a tour of Chicago her faith was restored when she met John Gunther, a twenty-two-year-old reporter for the *Chicago Daily News*. His tall, lean physique, angular face, and blond, blue-eyed heartland good looks made him seem like "a gothic angel." John not only represented a break with stereotype, but he satisfied her desire to bask in the naïveté and energy of a younger man. An aspiring novelist, John shared some of his fiction with the renowned literary diva; with her usual lack of finesse, she promptly advised him to stick to journalism. Within a year, they would become lovers.

Rebecca's last stop in the States was Los Angeles. In April 1924, it was a burgeoning media and financial center, surrounded by verdant canyons and wildflower-strewn valleys. To Rebecca, the city was a dream. In Hollywood, where she overdosed on vainglorious film actors, Rebecca became the lover of Charlie Chaplin. Once again H.G. had been an unwitting instrument of further estrangement, having introduced them in London three years earlier. Although Rebecca had been warned of Chaplin's penchant for intellectual women, not to mention nubile girls, she was beguiled by his romantic, lusty nature and his worldwide influence. Before Rebecca left for London, Chaplin flew to New York to see her. Years later, she would laughingly tell of their spontaneous break-in to the Central Park boathouse after dark. As they made love in a rowboat on the lake, it capsized, and, soaking wet, they walked sheepishly through the streets back to her hotel. While she would always mourn the years she had wasted with H.G., and her self-delusory affair with Max, Rebecca saw her relationship with Charlie as a casual fling to be enjoyed and stashed in the vault of her memory.

IF ONLY SHE COULD put H.G. behind her, but they were inextricably tied to each other through their son. After Rebecca returned to London in May 1924, she and H.G. resumed their lovemaking. But even as she lay in his welcoming arms, her rejection by Max continued to haunt her. She sent him letters in the hope of reconciliation, but he made it clear that he had never taken her seriously. As in the early days of her relationship with H.G., the realization that she had been underestimated by a lover she admired plunged her into suicidal despair. In a letter to Fannie Hurst, she wrote, "If it wasn't for Anthony, I really would kill myself. Not talking for effect. I feel so dirty, so fouled, so infected." Rebecca's desire for men who were powerful, rich, and inaccessible was becoming apparent, even to her.

She was beginning to feel that something was terribly wrong. The "evil" that stalked her, human or divine, had the power to destroy her; she wrestled with a stranger she could not see. But still holding on to the idea that the "evil" was external, she continued to cast blame on others. Much like the biblical Joseph, disowned and alone in a hostile desert, she would never be certain if the demon was within or the moral tests of a vengeful God. Whether she was the perpetrator or the victim, Rebecca knew she must conquer the "evil" to survive.

Giving up on Max, and sick of dangling on the string of recalcitrant lovers, she point-blank refused to see H.G. again. The act of inflicting pain on him soothed her. In a sense, she turned his "not murdering Jane" back on him, acting as though killing their relationship would end her pain. Rebecca had been rewarded for this behavior before, reminding him of her importance in his life. But now she was ready to leave him behind. Throughout Rebecca's late summer holiday with Anthony in Austria, H.G. wrote her plaintive and imploring letters, lamenting the loss of his one true love and begging her to return to him. Steadfast in her decision to leave him, Rebecca evoked his revenge. Using Anthony as his weapon, he threatened to remove their son from her care. But H.G. must have realized that his loss of Rebecca should not be avenged by inflicting damage on their son, and soon he renounced his claim.

In September 1924, before H.G. left for the south of France with his newly appointed "body slave," Odette Keun, a self-sacrificing, love-hungry ex-nun who had immigrated to France from Russia after the war, he apologized for his rash statement, promising that they would find "some way of dealing with the boy."

But "the boy" had noticed a change in his mother after she returned from the States, one he neither liked nor understood. Her emotional distance was compounded by a newfound strain of vanity. He would often catch her examining herself in the mirror in expensive clothes that smacked of Park Avenue and her rising fame. Ignorant of her disappointment with Max and her intent to make a permanent break with his father, Anthony interpreted her preening as a form of self-aggrandizement he had heretofore seen only onstage. And, in part, he was right. During her six months in America, she had carved her beauty into a stony persona—a mask through which she could observe others with impunity. Unknown to him, his mother's narcissism was her link to sanity; the figure in the mirror was the only thing between her and the "madness" she feared. She had spent her youth fencing with icons, and now she sought to become one.

Portrait of Rebecca West, circa 1926

BETWEEN 1924 AND her second trip to America two years later, Rebecca began to write a series of short stories based on her impressions of society and small-town culture. Her evolving understanding of human nature and male-female relations would become evident in a story she published in 1928 in *The Saturday Evening Post*, "There Is No Conversation." The female protagonist describes Rebecca's inscrutable state of mind best: "I have told you there is no conversation; that no one listens to what the other one says. But it appears that the inter-silence of the universe is more profound even than this. It appears that even the different parts of the same person do not converse among themselves."

But once again, her intellectual epiphany outraced her emotions. She had diagnosed the problem without effecting the cure.

During another trip to New York in the fall of 1926, she had had an affair with a banker she had met in Los Angeles two years earlier. While he didn't evoke the passion she had felt toward H.G. or Max, or possess their literary knowledge or expertise, his love of poetry and his adequate wealth held the promise of something "real and lasting." Best of all, he seemed to need her as much as she needed him. But two months later, in January 1927, when she returned to Los Angeles intending to marry him, she learned that he had a terminal illness—instead of becoming his wife, she became his nurse. Within weeks, he was dead.

Rebecca's affair with Max, whose quest for lovers, she decided, although he vehemently disagreed, was a symptom of his impotence, along with her tryst with Charlie Chaplin, who would later claim that their encounter had precipitated his sexual ruin, impelled her to seek psychoanalysis. Troubled by the pattern of making men feel impotent, self-delusory or not, Rebecca retreated to Florence, Italy, during the spring and early summer of 1927. There she planned to write a novel called *Sunflower*, in order to examine her affairs with Wells and Beaverbrook as paradigms for male-female relations. But she sensed that the integrity of the book rested on her unresolved feelings toward her father. To achieve resolution, and with it, literary potency, she hired an American lay analyst working in London, Mary Wilshire, whose intuitive gifts and knowledge of Freudian theory Rebecca hoped might enable her to uncover the mysteries of her childhood. Through intensive sessions with Wilshire, long-repressed memories of sexual violation by her father came to light that had tainted her vision of her mother, herself, and the value of women. She remembered that her father had exposed his penis through the slats of her crib when she was a child and later attempted to put the tip of his penis into her mouth, and then her vagina. When Rebecca had summoned her mother for consolation, she recalled, she treated her vaginal sores with mustard plaster, an act Rebecca interpreted as a heartless punishment for her complicit violation by her father. Her father's over-arching power, as cruel as it was exciting, evoked feelings of desire and loathing. She remembered fantasizing that if only they had been "animals we would be free to enjoy each other." Just as her father's absence had augured abandonment, infusing separation with existential fear, his presence followed her everywhere, twisting every relationship into a dirty and sordid ménage à trois. She believed that she had finally disrobed the demon that haunted her.

An absurd flight of imagination, a self-serving rationale, or a sliver of recaptured past, these "memories" gave Rebecca relief of her fear of "lurking evil." Whether the agreed-upon narrative between her and the therapist would be a lasting salve to her hurt was unclear. Yet her paranoia and misogyny are classic symptoms of women who have been sexually abused.

Later in 1927, H.G. suffered a loss he could never have predicted. After a three-year affair with Odette Keun that had turned sour when he had resumed relations with Moura Budberg in London, he returned to Easton Glebe to find that his wife's chronic indigestion was, in fact, the final stages of stomach cancer. Anthony would later write that Jane's death was not in his father's script. She was his rock—the one who had always smoothed things over, paid the bills, and made the only home he could rely upon. He was the one who was supposed to die first, leaving her with the money and luxury that she wanted and deserved. He mourned his inability to tell her how important she was as his friend and helpmate, how he appreciated the way she had given her sons and all of them a home and had sacrificed her own sexual and emotional liberation for his, permitting him to live out his literary life. He resolved to make things up to Rebecca and their son. H.G. invited Anthony to spend time with his half brothers, Gip and Frank, and their wives, openly acknowledging his parentage. And he finally offered Rebecca the social legitimacy she had always craved; he asked her to marry him. She declined, but not out of spite or revenge, she would say. She was no longer willing to live in the vortex of his emotional storms, nor bear the burden of his infidelity or his impulse to destroy himself and those he loved. She simply turned away.

When the law changed in 1928, permitting unmarried women to adopt their offspring, Rebecca filed papers to make Anthony her legal son. While at first H.G. agreed to renounce his paternal rights, he soon reneged, counterfiling documents to prove Rebecca's maternal incompetence. Ultimately the judge ruled in Rebecca's favor, but not until H.G. negotiated visiting rights and a voice in determining the course of Anthony's education.

But Anthony, like his mother and Jane, was to become a victim of his father's imagination—an idealized receptacle of H.G.'s unfulfilled dreams that would deny Anthony his individuality. Overwhelmed with subconscious guilt for his very existence, Anthony could not exorcise the demons of his own self-hatred. Although he was innately clever and immensely fluent in his native tongue, to his father's disappointment Anthony could master neither Latin grammar nor the principles of science and mathematics required for entry into Oxford University. Caught in the crossfire of his parents' fury, Anthony killed the "mock family" they had made. Now eighteen years old, Anthony would have the final word.

Dear Mr. Wells (or should I say dear father)

I think my mother is very well equipped to control my future without your help. Why you consider that you have any interest in the matter I can't think; you've treated mother like dirt ever since I was born and you have almost entirely neglected me—£100 per annum for my education, food, board, clothing, munificent—you only came to see me to get Panther when I was small and now you have the impertinence to imagine that you can take me from her. And listen, little sadist sweetheart, not only are you wrong but you've made me realize what a little wart you are. Telling me how wonderfully you've done for me! But for public scandal you would have given me the works as you did to Ann Reeves and all the other poor creatures that have been fools enough to believe in you.

I think your [sic] an ace wart and, God, how I loathe you.

Your loving son,
Anthony P. West

CHAPTER 4

RESURRECTION

> Marriage is the triumph of imagination over
> intelligence. Second marriage is the triumph of
> hope over experience.
>
> —OSCAR WILDE

BERLIN, JULY 6, 1927

Joseph Bard was finally out of Dorothy's life. Her beautiful raven-haired "prince" who once filled her days with purpose and passion had been nothing more than a grand illusion. Once again, betrayal had set her free. Her father had succumbed to the wishes of his domineering second wife, and Joseph had denied her the dignity of an honest parting. In the end, both men were shadows, images behind a gossamer screen.

The Hungarian document delivered in the morning mail to Dorothy's Berlin apartment, marked with the seal of a nation in tatters, seemed a fitting end to a marriage doomed by perfidy and delusion. And while she mourned the death of their union as deeply as she had mourned the death of her father's beneficent God, her faith in life and the Christian ethic remained unshakable. Her consuming despair had waned—the prospect of suicide, which she had contemplated, defied everything she held dear. Human suffering, she had learned at her father's knee, bred new life, more vital and creative than before.

Her spiritual courage resonated through her life, according to her friend Vincent "Jimmy" Sheean, a young journalist she had met in Vienna. "It was a vitally important element in Dorothy's greatness that she could always step over corpses and go on, steadily, resolutely, right to the end, with her head held very high indeed."

Three days out of wedlock, and Dorothy was ready to celebrate. It was Saturday, July 9, 1927, her thirty-fourth birthday, and summer had arrived with a vengeance after a cool, wet spring. Her flat on Händelstrasse overlooking the lavish lawns and glades of the Tiergarten no longer seemed the sarcophagus of a failed affair. It was alive with friends and colleagues, animated with conversation and seething with ideas.

A salon of sorts in the grand French and German tradition, at once subversive and eminently proper— unguarded inquiry robed in silk— Dorothy's party was a vehicle of dissemination and fiery exchange. No matter how personal the celebration at Händelstrasse 9, it was not private—"private" was not in Dorothy's lexicon. She called herself a "first rate peripatetic brain picker" with the taste, energy, and good sense to spot sources of quality information. If she were to make her long-desired leap from reporting to interpretive journalism, her contacts would be essential to her success.

Despite feeling robbed of her girlish "innocence," Dorothy still appeared the peaches-and-cream essence of American youth. Yet her social sophistication was evident everywhere; she knew how to set her stage and place her props. Her balconied drawing room exuded its usual Viennese charm, her food was plentiful and elegantly prepared, her French and German wines were among the best, and her vases were laden with dramatically posed and artfully arranged summer blooms.

Her birthday guests included men and women from central Europe, along with her American colleagues and friends. The guest of honor was the ousted prime minister of the Republic of Hungary, Count Karolyi, cattle millionaire turned statesman, whom Dorothy admired for his steadfast integrity in the face of overwhelming opposition. Her friend Countess Dorothy von Moltke and her dashing and defiant son Helmuth added spice and perspective to the trilingual conversation.

Dorothy's American guests included Lilian Mowrer, neighbor, confidante, news reporter, and the wife of Edgar Mowrer, the Berlin correspondent for the *Chicago Daily News;* Dorothy's assistant, H. R. "Knick" Knickerbocker, doctoral student cum journalist; and her newest bright "star," Sinclair Lewis. The previous afternoon, as usual, Dorothy had gone to the weekly tea hosted by the German foreign minister, Gustav Stresemann, where she met Lewis. That evening, Knick had chauffeured Lewis around town, stopping in at the Adlon where Dorothy and her colleagues were engaged in their ritual of booze and blasphemy. Lewis, newly arrived from Paris, was in the midst of a drunken sprawl through Europe in search of distraction and oblivion. His wife, Grace Hegger, was in love with another man, and his newly published novel, *Elmer Gantry*, an exposé of "orgiastic" moral corruption among the clergy, had been targeted by the church. He made it a habit of getting out of town when one of his books was published; he detested reviews and feared confrontation, personal or literary. All of this, of course, had been unknown to Dorothy as she sat sipping her lager, Lewis by her side, at the sleek lacquered bar overlooking the Adlon's cathedral-like lobby.

But it wasn't Lewis's literary reputation that intrigued Dorothy, although that might have sufficed; it was his ineffable sadness, and what she would call the Christ-like weight of his visceral suffering. He was built like an ostrich, six feet tall with a short torso set on long, spindly legs; his head was crowned with a tuft of copper-penny hair that heightened the red of his acne-scarred face. Hiding his hurt behind his intellect, Lewis seemed entombed in mottled stone, yet the purity of his soul, Dorothy would say, shone through his ice-blue eyes, transforming him into a luminescent figure. At once strikingly smart and deeply humble, a serious thinker and a quick-witted clown, Lewis, Dorothy was certain, would be part of her life, or at least a guest at her birthday party.

As she introduced Lewis to her guests, their eyebrows lifted in immediate recognition. His semiautobiographical novel, *Main Street* (1920), a satiric take on Midwestern provincialism and social pretension, had been hailed a masterpiece, and *Babbitt* (1922), a scathing look at how small-town mores and institutions suffocate authentic impulse and creativity, was deemed equally ingenious and provocative. He was, in essence, one of the most acclaimed English-language authors of the time.

Sobered up for the occasion, and looking dapper as he twirled his cane in his Savile Row tie and three-piece suit, he charmed everyone, including Dorothy. As the guests queued for coffee and dessert, Lewis pushed Dorothy into a corner and asked her to marry him. Assuming he could not be serious, Dorothy coyly replied, "I don't even know you, Mr. Lewis." Unperturbed, he vowed to ask her to marry him every time he saw her, in public or private, relenting only when she said "Yes."

Despite protestations to the contrary, after two years of grieving over Joseph's betrayal, Dorothy was flattered by the advances of this celebrated man of letters. In truth, she had felt an immediate kinship. She, too, had suffered "pretty brutally," she later wrote, "but suddenly I wanted to say: Let's stop suffering. Suddenly I felt oddly gay." There had been no divine thunderbolt when they had met, as there had been with Bard, but Lewis was a proven entity, not a wishy-washy novice still tied by his umbilical cord to his wife and mother. And, it occurred to her, at least in passing, that this uncomely suitor would tend not to stray.

Yet, Dorothy still believed that she would never love anyone as she had loved Joseph. He had been her first lover, her cultural and philosophical lodestar, her artistic and political mentor, and her friend as well as her husband. While everything with Joseph had ineluctably turned sour, Dorothy believed in the ideal of marriage; it was an heirloom of her Methodist childhood to value family, community, and nationhood above her paltry personal desires. Her task was to find a man she trusted. She believed that with the right one, she could make marriage work. The prospect of a future with a loving and amusing companion seemed more than attractive.

Dorothy did not know that Lewis was married or that his wife of thirteen years had come to loathe him. He was not much of a husband or a father, Grace believed; he was just one thing—a writer. A wellborn editor at *Vogue* when they met, Grace was a woman who was used to living in high style. At first, Lewis had enjoyed indulging his beautiful wife, but he soon came to see her as a domineering parasite, incapable of understanding his work, his emotional needs, or his desire for freedom and solitude. Their son, Wells, named in honor of Lewis's literary idol, H.G., was approaching his teen years. A handsome, blond-haired child who resembled his mother, Wells grated on Lewis's nerves with his incessant demands and sullen nature. Grace, convinced that Lewis was incorrigible, had fallen in love with a Spanish count named Telesforo Casanova who gave her the sexual and emotional intimacy she craved. "Red" Lewis, the carrot-topped guy who never had a girl growing up, was alone again; he was deeply hurt that Grace was leaving him for another man—he had always considered himself morally superior to his acquisitive, social-climbing wife.

At forty-two years old, Lewis was a profoundly lonely man for whom writing was his sole lifeline—a way out and above the eternal quagmire of human relationships. A best-selling author of international renown, he was a shell of a person, he would later admit; everything good about him went into his books. The people in his life became the raw data of his allegorical satire; their frailties reflected the social maladies and distortions of postwar America as he saw them. As a craftsman, he combined keen observation with profound substance. No matter how acute his insights, however, they could not assuage his loneliness.

Red was raised in Sauk Centre, a prairie town in central Minnesota, where he was honored for his brilliance yet emasculated by his domineering physician father and ridiculed by his peers. All his young life, even at Yale, he had been riddled with self-doubt that had brought him to the edge of impotence and plunged him into alcoholism. Grace had been the first woman to penetrate his ugly façade to his intellectual core; she gave him the confidence he needed to affirm his manhood and pursue his dream of writing fiction. Both Dorothy and Red had sought partners who they believed would fill their emptiness, yet each lacked the tools of true reciprocity. Dorothy's marriage to Joseph was an idealized union based on sexual desire and delusions of cultivating a home and family with an infamous gigolo. Lewis's marriage to Grace was equally fanciful, born of emotional deprivation and social rejection.

But this time, perhaps, it would be different. Red needed to be saved from himself, and Dorothy liked nothing more than rescuing lost souls.

Hal, as Dorothy now called him, a diminutive of Harry, his given name, was constantly courting her. And, to her surprise, she found that she enjoyed his company. He evoked her long-repressed playful side with his childlike imagination and uncensored antics. When he was fired up, his flair for mimicry and outrageous banter made him funnier than any man she knew. Dorothy wrote to her sister Peggy, "When I was beginning to live a little again . . . suddenly the gods decided to be kind to me, and I met the man, who, I think, I have been looking subconsciously for all my life."

For weeks Hal had kept his marriage secret; he didn't want to scare Dorothy away until he was certain that she cared. To assuage her fears and show his sincerity, he cabled his wife and his publisher, Harcourt, Brace, and Company, that he would remain in Europe for several months. He promised to secure a small flat in Berlin and to go to the U.S. Embassy in Paris to inquire about a divorce.

The American colony in Berlin was abuzz with rumors, but no one dared to expose the Lewis-Thompson affair to the press. Dorothy's colleague Sigrid Schultz, as jealous as she was competitive, broke ranks with Dorothy's more loyal associates by advising her editor at the *Chicago Tribune* that he should tell his Paris correspondent to keep tabs on Lewis and to send a reporter to Reno, Nevada, to watch for signs of a quickie divorce in the works. The flamboyant couple was easily observed; they took no pains to cover their tracks. Throughout July, they walked nearly every street and boulevard in Berlin, talking and laughing with careless nonchalance. Sexual relations had not become an issue; the couple had not yet made love. It must have been a relief to Dorothy, after Bard, not to compete for sexual favors.

Despite Hal's daily declarations of love, Dorothy was painfully aware that words easily masked intentions. She decided to offer him a "business deal." Rumors of a workers' revolution in Vienna required her to fly to Austria immediately. He could join her, she told him, on one condition. He must write a series of articles on the rioting for the *Public Ledger*. It was, in effect, a test of his commitment. They both knew that Lewis's byline on a reportorial piece within her domain would be tantamount to a public declaration of love. The absurdity of linking his name to a political report at the apex of his career could mean nothing else. Lewis was either serious or not; Dorothy would not risk social embarrassment again.

Hal consented.

The articles completed and the promise fulfilled, Dorothy no longer doubted Lewis's intent. It was time to give him the reins. The *Ledger* owed her a vacation and she agreed to go with him on a walking tour. Dorothy gave Hal carte blanche in charting their route, and he chose to walk in the countryside he loved more than any other, Shropshire and Cornwall on the west coast of England.

Rambling was not only one of his favorite pastimes, it was one at which he was truly gifted. His lean physique and frenetic stride were perfectly suited to the task. Dorothy, newly svelte to meet the rigor of her lover's sport, was a serious walker, but she could hardly keep up with him. With fierce determination, he would walk up and down hills, through woodlands and fields, for hours on end, and then, without warning, throw himself to the ground on a grassy knoll and amuse himself and Dorothy by fabricating stories about the cows that grazed in the fields. He could rattle on for hours, without pause, composing a novel or a couple of plays. To Dorothy's surprise, however, there were times when he was completely silent, in a state of entranced contemplation unthinkable when he was wrestling with the demands of ordinary life. Never did he feel more at peace with himself, healthier, more compassionate, clearheaded, or calm than when he was on a walking tour.

In a self-portrait he wrote alluding to that miraculous August, Hal would berate himself as a "dull fellow," with little imagination or he wouldn't need the "new streets, new hills, new faces." He needed to move, to engage in experience, no matter how gainful or foolish, to spur his imagination and grease his creativity. Rebecca, who had met him earlier in the 1920s at a dinner party with H.G., had reviewed his book *Elmer Gantry*, which seemed to skim the surface of experience: "If he would sit still so that life could make any deep impression on him, if he would attach himself to the human tradition by occasionally reading a book, which would set him a standard of profundity, he could give his genius a chance."

As Rebecca had written in *The Strange Necessity*, the wellspring of fiction rose from within, fed by self-reflection, memory, emotion recollected, and the habit of meticulous observation. "Genius" might have its own rules, but H.G., Lewis's literary hero, held solitude inviolate. Rebecca shared this credo, and ultimately it was the source of their undoing. Certainly Lewis had the habit of observation, but he had neither the gift of self-reflection nor an objective grasp of his emotions. Both required placid solitude, of which he was incapable.

Dorothy, like Lewis, was always at her best in the company of others. But Hal, Dorothy observed, took it a step further—he needed an audience in order to shine. Although he would say that his own integrity was the sole touchstone of his work, the affirmation of his peers, his publisher, and the reading public was essential to the sustenance of his creative will. Dorothy sensed that loving him would require her to constantly approve of him.

When one of Dorothy's colleagues, a Communist correspondent, arranged that she be invited to Moscow for the tenth anniversary of the Bolshevik Revolution, Hal decided to remain in Berlin because he was writing again. But after several weeks, his old sense of loneliness and futility set in. Missing her terribly, Hal flew to Moscow in secret. By the time he arrived at the station, however, the news had leaked; Lewis was greeted like a celebrity by a slew of reporters, several Russian writers, and an official brass band. When a reporter asked him why he had come, he replied, "To see Dorothy." Disturbed by his lack of interest in commemorating the revolution, the reporter repeated his question. "Dorothy . . . just Dorothy," Lewis declared.

As he had been in Vienna, Hal was an invaluable asset to Dorothy's work—his ability to analyze, hone, and articulate his observations was extraordinary. Dorothy had never pushed against such a brilliant mind.

With Hal as her mentor, Dorothy took her narrative style to a new level. The stories she filed from Moscow to her editors at the *Public Ledger* and the *New York Evening Post* were deemed the best that she had ever written. As H.G. had done for Rebecca, Hal promoted Dorothy's work to editors in the States. In the hopes of securing her a book contract, he wrote to his publisher, asking that he give her articles a serious reading. Soon thereafter, Alfred Harcourt signed Dorothy on. All at once she was certain that Hal was a man she could not live without.

Finally, the "creative marriage" she had always hoped for was within reach. Hal was the first man to take pleasure in enabling her career without envy or rancor, and Dorothy believed that with her by his side, Hal's best work was yet to come. As far as Hal was concerned, Dorothy made him feel like a man, and after a long period of self-degradation he permitted himself to feel optimistic again.

There was only one hurdle to their happiness. Hal was still legally married. A New York state divorce was nearly impossible to get. One partner, most commonly the woman, would have to prove that her husband's "cruel and inhuman" behavior had profoundly impaired her health, or that he had irrevocably deserted her. Like Hal and Grace, most couples were compelled to go to Reno, Nevada, which in competition with the state of Idaho, had dropped its residency requirements for divorce to six weeks. But until then Dorothy and Hal, now publicly recognized as a couple, would engage in Berlin's social life.

These past two months together had opened a window onto Hal's frailties as well as his brilliance, loyalty, and charm. Dorothy had come to see glimpses of his alcohol addiction—too much to drink at the Adlon bar or a local café spawning talk too loose, too loud and vulgar. Of course, she had heard rumors from colleagues and friends that he could easily turn abusive, but in her company, he had never been hurtful or out of control. So she hadn't been ready for what was about to unfold.

While it was clear to Dorothy that Hal was ill at ease with her journalist friends, she nonetheless arranged that he be invited to all their parties. One evening in September 1927, Dorothy stood by her window waiting for Hal to escort her to a dance. She was dressed in "the little Lanvin taffeta " frock, and had spent the afternoon having her hair and nails done. Hal was to come at 7:45. At 8:30 he phoned. His voice was thick. "I'm shot," he said. "Come here, Darling."

Dorothy went to his flat, only to find him lying in his underwear, dead drunk on his bed. Enraged, she shook him and threatened to leave. "No, no," he said. "Stay here. . . . I will die if you go." She took off her dress and collapsed into tears; everything they had dreamed of—their country house in New England, their travels, and the baby she wanted— evaporated in the perfume of Hal's brandy-drenched breath.

I saw all this and thought, I will get up and go. Somehow I will re- construct my life. There is still work. . . . And I knew that there was not even that. I saw that being a woman has got to me, at last, too. I saw that if Hal goes now, I am finished. I cannot live by myself, for myself. All my heart cried out this is my man, the one man, and he has come too late! Nothing left for me but to become brittle or to rot. All the time Hal was making love to me. Feebly, but tenderly. I kissed his breast, and he yearned toward me. I wished I could lift him up and carry him to a high hill, where wind would be blowing.

After their lovemaking, she began to cry. Hal sat on the side of the bed.

Suddenly he looked at me. His eyes were like red moons. He started to whimper. "I cannot ruin your life. . . . You are wholly good . . . wholly good. Get up—you mustn't stay here—get dressed," he said. "I will take you home. Tomorrow I will go away. . . . You will never see me again. I am finished. You must never have any- thing to do with me again."

I was dressed now. "Hal," I said, "I will go. But don't think that you can just walk off and free me of you. Wherever you go, I will be with you, in you, and you with me, in me. And if you are finished, I am finished, too. [But] . . . if you don't give up spirits, I cannot marry you. We must separate. But that's no solution for me either. You're my man. I'm thirty-three years old [Dorothy al- ways cut a year off her age], and I've been married once, and I've had lovers, but it was all a search for you. I won't get over this." He held me so closely. So dearly. I said, "Oh, Hal, you'll get over this! It *will* be all right."

Something vital to the relationship had changed; Dorothy had inex- tricably tied her happiness to his, becoming responsible for both their lives. As she had with Joseph, Dorothy convinced herself that her life meant nothing without his genius. Her mission, her duty, was to take care of him so that his voice could enlighten the world.

Dorothy was beginning to see that their plan for a quiet life was an illusion. His self-indulgent slips into alcoholic stupor, his innate impatience and irritability, his incessant wanderlust for new places and quest for new people, would preclude the reality of a stable and nurturing home. On Christmas Day, 1927, Dorothy wrote a sonnet for Hal—light and graceful, but riddled with sadness:

> *I know you fondly dream to settle down*
> *With me, in some profoundly static spot,*
>
> *Beside a river, not too near a town;*
> *But will we stay there? Answer: We will not.*
>
> *Old wanderlusts will all these plans unravel;*
> *Take me, and this, and be prepared to travel.*

Hal and Grace, with some bitterness on his part in light of her betrayal, had agreed to obtain a divorce. Knowing that Hal was working on a novel, Grace generously offered, with self-serving eagerness, to go to Reno as soon as their son, Wells, went back to school at the turn of the year. She informed him that perhaps by April they would be free to remarry.

Dorothy made immediate plans to facilitate their freedom. She prepared to sell her flat on Händelstrasse, and she chose a successor at the *Public Ledger.* Her assistant Knick, a serious journalist, lacked her clout but matched her in energy, discipline, and will to succeed. By chronicling the implosion of the Weimar Republic and the dangers inherent in the rise of Hitler's Nazi Party, the twenty-nine-year-old Knick was to become the perfect heir to her career as a foreign correspondent in central Europe. (He went on to win the Pulitzer Prize for Correspondence in 1931 and wrote books until his untimely death in 1949.)

Dorothy and Hal decided to marry in London as soon as his divorce was granted. England, in fact, all of Great Britain—Scotland, Ireland, and Wales—felt like home to Dorothy. It was the ancestral land of her mother and father. To Hal, England always seemed the only "real" country in all of Europe. It was, he believed, an ancient land of unsurpassed beauty and majestic culture, with a lust for language and literature—including his novels—that exceeded anything he had known in the States. In the meantime, they would spend the next three months in Italy to seek respite from the blustery winter in Berlin and rest before the feverish summer that loomed ahead. When she was younger, Dorothy might have called her new marriage "destiny," but time had taught her that what often appeared to be an end point was merely the beginning of a labyrinth.

Dorothy and Hal in early 1928 sailing to Italy

Dorothy and Hal found refuge as guests of friends in the same *dipendenza* on Cape Posillipo where the infamous Marxist Maxim Gorky had hidden and hosted visits from his secretary and mistress, Moura Budberg, after his self-exile from Russia. Moura, it may be remembered, had become the object of Rebecca's loathing when she became the mistress of H.G., even as their newborn son lay suckling at Rebecca's breast.

But in the winter of 1928, Dorothy and Hal found neither happiness nor respite. Their cottage, set on a small piece of land on forty acres, had a salon, a kitchen, four bedrooms, and a glass veranda overlooking Naples and the sea. Hoping to find harmony by adhering to a strict schedule, they awakened at seven o'clock each morning to begin to write. Hal was deep into his novel *Dodsworth* and Dorothy was finishing her first book, an adaptation of her Russian articles. But Hal was drinking again and his verbal abuse became unbearable, especially when they were in the company of friends. The magnificent gardens that lay at their doorstep and the view of Mount Vesuvius in the distance could not quell her fears of marrying him. Both of them wanted so much to love each other, but they wondered if love was even possible after so many disappointments. For the first time, their relationship was tinged with dishonesty. They soothed themselves by acting out a romantic charade, ironically, much like one Lewis might have scorned in one of his novels.

By mid-March, the American press was alerted to Grace's presence in Reno. Lewis's critics called him a cad and a fool who had blighted America with his books and now sought to stain the sanctity of marriage. A month later, Grace was granted a divorce on the grounds of "incompatibility and desertion." Hal immediately left for London to establish his brief but necessary residency for marriage. He drew up the agreed-upon guest list, sent out the invitations, and bought a $2,000 caravan (trailer) that they intended to hitch to a car for their honeymoon trip through the English countryside.

On May 14, 1928, at noon, Dorothea Celene Thompson and Harry Sinclair Lewis were married in a civil ceremony at St. Martin's Registry on Henrietta Street, witnessed by his British publisher Jonathan Cape and his wife. Dorothy was dressed in a blue calf-length chemise of lace and silk over a white ruffled blouse and matching lace skirt. She wore a large silk hat with a turned-down brim and held a bouquet of lilies, daisies, and daffodils. Hal, hatless, wore a blue serge pinstriped three-piece suit, adorned with a flower from Dorothy's bouquet, and held a long silver-tipped black cane. As they walked toward the Savoy Chapel, the only church that would marry divorcees, a dozen photographers snapped their picture. Dorothy could not quite fathom that her vows on Henrietta Street had swept her irretrievably into Hal's circle of fame. No longer was she Dorothy Thompson, foreign correspondent, admired within a narrow sphere of colleagues and diplomats. She was Mrs. Sinclair Lewis, wife of an internationally renowned author, as notorious as he was acclaimed.

At the chapel, they recited vows according to the Anglican tradition before Reverend Hugh Chapman, who blessed their union in the presence of God and the church. Unfortunately, the reverend began shouting "at the top of his lungs to drown out the starlings who were making an ungodly racket on the Thames embankment," said one attendee. Chapman then turned to address the groom. In perhaps a harbinger of events to come, he entreated Lewis to write books that men "go to for strength when they are in despair." Reverend Chapman could not have known how profoundly he had touched the spiritual nexus that held Dorothy and Hal together. As the bride and groom stepped out of the darkened chamber, arm in arm, into the light of early spring, the joy of the moment merely obscured the demons that lingered.

A photo taken as they emerged to greet their guests shows Hal bowed in reverence. Head buried into his stiff shirt collar, he glances sideways at the camera as if embarrassed by the public nature of their sacred vows. The words of his deceased churchgoing parents and the lessons from the scriptures he had studied as a young man must have echoed in his thoughts. He had consented to a church wedding ostensibly to please Dorothy, but it was he who had wanted a "real" Christian wedding in the hopes that the sacraments and the discipline they implied would lend him the strength to endure, despite his fear that his crippled heart lacked the courage to love.

Dorothy, however, was steady and poised, head held high and smiling. Their union had been blessed by a Protestant minister in a manner that would have pleased her father and ameliorated the blasphemy of having previously married a Jew. She was ready to go forward; despite

Dorothy and Hal's wedding in London, May 14, 1928

his frailties and her own, they had entered the marriage covenant in good faith.

The luncheon at the Savoy was a true celebration. Party personae fully in place, the newlyweds entertained their guests. Dorothy, a seasoned hostess, graciously attended their family and friends, while Hal, as usual, played the clever clown. Removing manifold notes from his breast pocket, he made a toast to his bride in the form of a monologue with much the same exalted hyperbole as one might address a convocation of jute merchants on the state of the trade in the British Empire. The guests, it was said, were laughing in the aisles. Among them were British and American friends and literary figures. But one who declined to share the merriment was Dorothy's friend Rebecca West. She would be out of town, she explained when declining the invitation, but later she commented that she would not have come anyway.

Rebecca's distaste for Lewis was not solely literary—she admired his humor, his craftsmanship, and his distinctly American vitality. It was his character she quarreled with; a notorious drunk with a repulsive demeanor, he had slobbered kisses up and down her arm the first evening they met, and mistreated a young female acquaintance for whom she had great respect. Rebecca knew trouble when she saw it. Red Lewis was simply not good enough for her friend.

Perhaps Lewis's loneliness, hidden beneath a cascade of words, along with his dependency on women, under which lay a tinge of misogyny, seemed hauntingly familiar. Perhaps he reminded Rebecca of the silver-tongued philanderer who continued to be her nemesis, Lewis's Lord of Satire, H. G. Wells.

PART 2

CHAPTER 5

DESCENT

Descend, so that you may ascend.

—SAINT AUGUSTINE, *The Confessions of St. Augustine*

AUGUST 1927

At thirty-five, Rebecca was no longer the swan that sailed the room. Less Tchaikovsky than Stravinsky, she held her head high and moved with purpose, though her movements were sharp and rapid and her mind roiled in dissonance. She appeared nervous and exhausted. Her romantic alliances continued to breed bitterness.

After six weeks in Agay on the Côte d'Azur, where she had soaked in the primal pleasures of the sea, Rebecca arrived in Paris hungry for the elixir of literature and art. Her visit was to be a curative for the sensual indulgences of body and mind, or so she would later write.

Rebecca adored Paris, as much for its pride in its past as for its postwar embrace of immigrants and their cultures. She felt comfortable and unfettered amid its ethic of the individual and cultivation of style. Unlike Londoners, whose city was unscathed and whose three million compatriots had died on foreign soil, Parisians mourned not only their six million who had died on the front, but also those who had died inside homes in a city that had endured countless enemy bombs. Their sense of loss was visceral. Paris reveled in the pleasures of "now" and the promise of a future tamed by technology. World War I had devastated 20 percent of the military age male population and with it the illusions of divine justice and moral absolutes. And in response, Paris, like Berlin, had become a cauldron of ideas—political, aesthetic, and moral. Nothing was sacred; nothing was forbidden.

After a long day of touring the city, wandering through its wide boulevards and tree-lined side streets, and foraging through her favorite bookshop, she donned the couture of a late summer night to attend a soiree at a friend's home. It was there that Rebecca met a Spanish duke—attractive, landed, and sexually wild. Later, he would make passionate love to her, while she spun fantasies of a future free of British restraint and fossilized tradition. But when Rebecca returned to see him two weeks later, her lover unleashed a tirade of abuse, more hideous and perverse than she could have ever imagined.

Once back in London, pleased for the moment to wrap herself in the safety of its cocoon, she met a man who appeared the quintessence of English gentility. He ardently pursued her, undaunted by her refusal to marry him. Tired of his badgering and desirous of a quiet, settled life, Rebecca finally succumbed to betrothal. His conquest complete, the gentleman turned savage—gratuitously sadistic in a manner that was hauntingly familiar. She wrote to her friend Fannie Hurst, "I am thinking of making a marriage blanc. . . . There are no material advantages but it will mean peace from this kind of extraordinary humiliation." She was certain that "the source of my troubles have not been touched by psychoanalysis." Her masochistic relationship with men went beyond her relationship with her father, Rebecca would imply; there was a visceral specter that threatened to destroy her. "I am entirely convinced now that there is an external force working against me. I have been down into myself in the analysis so deeply that this isn't a superficial point of view. I am going to live so far as possible utterly and absolutely alone from now on, because simply and straightly I believe that if I don't I am going to get killed." Is it possible that this "visceral specter" was the same strain of hereditary mental illness that had stalked her father into the grave?

By 1927, Rebecca wasn't the only one who felt she was walking with the specter of death. Her fundamental distrust of human nature was consonant with the political landscape. Russia under Stalin had become a tyrannical imperialist state, and a virulent form of European nationalism had arisen in response. The fear of an international uprising of workers, purportedly commandeered by Jews, revived a medieval strain of anti-Semitism that threatened the lives of thirteen million people across the Continent. Mussolini's Fascist stranglehold on Italy, along with the dissolution of the Weimar Republic and rise of the Nazi Party in Germany, augured the descent of moral darkness.

In January 1928, Rebecca withdrew to her room in Onslow Gardens in search of solace. As a woman who spoke as well as she wrote, with far-ranging knowledge and the courage to make her opinions known, she was deemed the most fascinating female in town. But despite her "dazzling" brilliance, maturity, and calm, she had, once again, lost faith in life. As a young woman she had despaired that she would never find love; now she feared that love itself was an illusion.

Anthony, thirteen years old and now a student at St. Piran's, was in a sanatorium convalescing from an illness diagnosed as tuberculosis. Rebecca had been called by the headmaster of St. Piran's several weeks earlier informing her that Anthony had developed a lingering cough after returning from the Christmas holidays. Subsequently diagnosed with tuberculosis, Anthony was transferred to a sanatorium to convalesce. Suddenly propelled into crisis mode, Rebecca found old feelings of resentment resurfacing. Neither capable nor desirous of nurturing him, she felt cheated of time and work. In anger she wrote a letter to a friend damning her child for being sick again. Although H.G. was verbally sympathetic, he was, as usual, critical of Rebecca and unresponsive to Anthony; he offered her no respite from her responsibility. Life had treated her, along with everyone else, like a dog, she often complained.

Rebecca's Onslow Gardens flat in South Kensington, which she had chosen for its wide vista and breadth of light, was nonetheless dull and gloomy in winter. Its décor of soft green and ivory flooded the flat with the promise of spring, but the "corpse" of winter remained ubiquitous. Sitting at her desk, she wrote draft upon draft of an essay into her notebooks, an act of self-discovery that was slowly evolving into a treatise on the metaphysics of art. She wanted to understand what motivated her to seek knowledge and release through writing. Throughout the winter, between hospital visits to Anthony, she fleshed out her ideas with personal observations, scientific analogies, and profiles of artists and their work. Scholar and novelist, critic and artist, she formulated a first-person narrative both imaginary and real, using her mind as a prism through which to gain insight into human nature. She wanted, needed, a sustaining belief that would affirm the value of her life—in sum, she sought a reason to go on living.

When the weather finally turned warmer, Rebecca carried her typewriter onto the broad balcony overlooking the communal garden. Moving in accord with the rhythms of nature, inspired by the push of slender shoots through the thawing soil, she worked like a demon to complete her work.

The first part of her essay related the techniques of behavioral science to the realm of art making, while incorporating a semiautobiographical narrative to sweeten the text. She engaged the reader in a pseudo-Socratic journey toward "truth," in the process of which she held the literary icons of the day up to the light of her sacrosanct principles: stylistic charm, lack of sentimentality, the fusion of mind and subject, and the discernment and interpretation of patterns of behavior.

Harnessing Freudian theory to unravel the secrets of the creative mind, Rebecca portrayed the soul as a battlefield of impulses: Eros and Thanatos, the will to live and the will to die. Only art could touch the essence, she wrote, and bring about a harmony of opposites. Great art, she explained, depends upon the complexity of the conflict and its resolution. In a wild leap of Freudian analogy, Rebecca linked the ecstasy of sexual orgasm with the transcendent excitation of art.

The artistic process, she concluded, was double pronged; the artist must tear down the existing order with his unique perceptions, and then restore cultural equilibrium by integrating the new with the old. And only the art critic, the self-appointed voice of reason, could discern artistic integrity and distinguish poseur from genius, histrionics from authentic probing of the heart. Not one voice alone but a choral symphony of critiques would ultimately reveal the truth.

Yet even as Rebecca portrayed the critic as the priestess of artistic salvation, she lacked the virtue to obey her own dogma. While H.G. sought reprisals by vying for Anthony's affection and loyalty, she continued to use her own writing, and her readers, as a way to settle the score with him. Her spiritual quest would soon morph into a vicious mode of revenge.

Through the prism of her Freudian metaphor, Rebecca examined the legacy of male icons who had influenced the course of modern literature. She chose to begin with Wells. Sandwiched between odes to his genius and exhortations of gratitude for having borne witness to his greatness, she attacked the quality of his prose in a metaphor that smacked of sexual castration:

The only thing against Uncle Wells was that he did so love to shut himself up in the drawing room and put out all the lights except the lamp with the pink silk shade, and sit down at the piano and have a lovely time warbling in too fruity a tenor. . . . You know perfectly well what I mean: the passages where his prose suddenly loses its firmness and begins to shake like blanc-mange.

When the complete essay was published as a book entitled *The Strange Necessity* in July 1928, H.G. sent her three letters, the last of which explodes with contempt:

So is this book a sham. It is a beautiful voice & a keen & sensitive mind doing "Big thinks" to the utmost of its ability—which is nil. God gave you all the gifts needed for a fine & precious artist & he left out humility. And humility in the artist is what charity is in the saint. There my dear Pussy is some more stuff for your little behind. You sit down on it & think.

Rebecca's analogy between art and love seems to ring true. Just as great art is a complex battlefield, so is great love. Despite its acrimony, born of psychic kinship and the compulsion to create, there can be no doubt that the love between Rebecca and H.G. was profound. Their parting had been as impassioned and labyrinthine as their love, and their scheme of revenge just as clever.

After recovering from his yearlong illness, a viral infection misdiagnosed as tuberculosis (a fact that H.G. never ceased to blame on Rebecca's poor judgment), Anthony was enrolled in Stowe School in September 1929. A secondary school, established by J. F. Roxburgh six years earlier on the magnificent grounds of an eighteenth-century mansion, Stowe aimed to liberate boys from the rules, rituals, and curriculum of nineteenth-century public schools. While retaining standards of academic excellence grounded in Christian values, it permitted its students relative freedom and offered a broad range of subjects beyond book learning. An artful amalgamation of old and new, its curriculum included traditional subjects, along with modern literature, nature study, drawing, painting, music, and photography. For Rebecca, it seemed that the vision of the school, filled with boys whose vitality was honored while simultaneously disciplined through sport, was not only consistent with her own beliefs but with Anthony's artistic and freewheeling nature.

Soon, however, Rebecca's hopes were dashed. "Freedom" translated into lack of supervision. Despite Roxburgh's reforms, the older boys, who were still mired in their fathers' rituals of demeaning and "enslaving" lower classmen, abused Anthony. Bullied, as well, by a punitive housemaster, Anthony, who was never able to stand up to authority, grew terribly unhappy. Moreover, the loose structure of academic life exacerbated rather than moderated his recalcitrance.

After Anthony's first semester at Stowe, H.G., appalled by their son's academic standing, wrote a letter to Rebecca: "It means we have neglected the formal education of our exceptionally brilliant boy so that he figures as a backward one." He noted that Anthony was over fifteen and yet had failed to learn the basics of science. Moreover, he dismissed the headmaster's suggestion that Anthony had a "block" against Latin as absurd. Anthony, he concluded, must simply work harder.

Rebecca retorted, "I am afraid you've got the facts about Anthony's education rather dark in your mind. The trouble started, of course, at St. Piran's [the school that H.G. had initially chosen for Anthony] where he learned nothing." Despite tutoring him in Latin during every holiday from school, she wrote, every master who taught him had concluded that he had a block. It was not a matter of pushing him to study; it was a matter of accepting his limitations.

Apparently, Anthony was not the descendant of a genius that H.G. wished him to be. But as Rebecca would say throughout her life, his limitations were grounded in something deeper: a psychological chasm between her and H.G. and the burden of his illegitimacy. As much as she could not bear H.G.'s accusation of neglect, she could not admit that Anthony was also the victim of her own self-absorption. As usual, she would blame Anthony's failure to meet scholastic expectations on H.G.

While Rebecca made it clear to her friends exactly how she felt about Anthony's prospects, later she would make it part of the "official" record. After H.G.'s death, she would write to one of his biographers, Gordon Ray, that Anthony was not brilliant at all; he required tutors in almost every subject. "He was in fact almost ineducable, but his sophisticated comments and command of language were always remarkable, also his power to draw and paint." H.G. had mistaken Anthony's mastery of spoken English for "brilliance," she implied.

Rebecca's belief that Anthony was a lost cause, although not spoken aloud at the time, fanned the animosity between her and H.G. and intensified Anthony's sense of illegitimacy, along with his rage against Rebecca. H.G.'s perception of him as an extension of himself was both a blessing and a curse. While Anthony felt that he was a constant disappointment to his father, he could hang on to the hope that success was in reach. Unlike Rebecca, who unabashedly articulated her lack of faith in human nature and blithely voiced her assessment of H.G. and everyone else, H.G. hid behind a mask of optimism that belied his personal sense of futility and profound distrust of individual integrity. His obsession with work as the sole mode of justification for life could not permit the possibility of failure. His son could and must succeed.

Each of them was as vulnerable yet impervious as the other, and neither could see Anthony as he truly was: a boy whose intelligence did not rise to genius, paralyzed by divided loyalties and self-doubt. Hope, always more attractive than despair, pushed Anthony into his father's arms. Sadly for Rebecca, Anthony was pulling away from her and finding solace with H.G. and his half brothers at Easton Glebe.

Rebecca felt threatened by the intensity of their alliance. Rejection was *her* prerogative, the birthright stolen by her feckless father. Despite her ambivalence toward Anthony, it was clear that he belonged to her. She alone had tended and nurtured him; for all intents and purposes, H.G. had refused to have anything to do with him until Jane's death two years earlier. Jealous and uncertain of her son's allegiance, she called her attorney to request that he draw up adoption papers. Now that the law had changed to permit single women to adopt their children, Rebecca was eager to gain full control.

To make matters worse, for the first time Rebecca's professional reputation had been tarnished. *The Strange Necessity* was trashed not only by H.G. but by critics on both sides of the Atlantic. As she read the reviews on her balcony overlooking the garden, covered with blooms withering in the late summer sun, she could only believe that the demons were conspiring against her. Her paranoia, while neurotic, found confirmation in the cruelty of her reviewers, who took issue with her imperious style. She wrote to her American mentor and admirer Alexander Woollcott that the attacks were expressions of personal vendettas by those who saw her as a social butterfly incapable of serious thought and analysis.

Even her friends and family were disappointed by the ruthlessness of her analyses. Her British friend and mentor S. K. Ratcliffe deemed her book hard to navigate and unworthy of her, or her readers', effort. Her sister Winnie, Rebecca's literary barometer since childhood, concurred.

Hugh Walpole of *The New York Times*, among the few who had given her an evenhanded review, sent a personal letter explaining the critical backlash. Established authors, he wrote, did not count her qualified to evaluate their books. Despite her prominence and intellectual courage, she was still considered a literary novice. He reminded her that she had published only four books, most of which were difficult to understand. Walpole's words would have the force of revelation. His cool assessment succeeded where H.G.'s heated contempt had failed. Rebecca set out to redeem her reputation by writing about what she knew best: the inevitable animosity between men and women.

Turning the aesthetic theory of her essay into practice, she studied the dynamic of love under a microscope, in the hope that the inherent tension between the sexes would reveal its secrets. For this, Rebecca chose to compose another novel, later saying that "Fiction and poetry are the only way one can stop time and give an account of an experience and nail it down so that it lasts forever." The book, *Harriet Hume: A London Fantasy*, studied the possibility of harmony between the sexes. Psychologically pivotal among all her novels, it is a semiautobiographical narrative that unmasked her profound longing for the unconditional love of a man.

Rebecca created an allegorical house of mirrors that heightened and distorted the flaws and virtues of the sexes. Like an impressionist painting, awash with light, it lovingly sets the beauty of London's parks, gardens, and bridges into the context of its bustling commercial and political life. Drawing upon her sexual encounters, originating with her father and including her affairs with Wells and Beaverbrook and subsequent entanglements with vengeful men, Rebecca studied the amorality of male power and its counterforce, the instinctive machinations of feminine guile. At least on paper, she had figured out why she and perhaps all women were the victims of male rage and desecration. Even her harshest critic, H.G., believed that she had succeeded in demystifying the conflicting visions of male and female that necessarily led to resentment and disillusion.

After reading the book, he wrote her a letter on September 13, 1929: "It's more your stuff than anything you have ever written hitherto. You've got your distinctive fantasy and humour into it and it gives play

for just the peculiar intricate wittiness which is one of your most delightful and inimitable characteristics. . . . It's a joy to praise you unreservedly. Homage and admiration." He suggested that she read Jung's
explanation of the relationship between the animus and the anima, twin
projections of male-female ideals based on childhood fantasies of their
parents. Had she taken his advice and read Jung, Rebecca would have
been appalled by Jung's misogyny, not to mention H.G.'s. In short, wrote
Jung, men are rational; women, Eros, are slaves to opinion. As it was, she
discerned the gist of H.G.'s intent, intuiting that his praise was a disguised slur on her capacity to write a good book.

If *The Strange Necessity* had given her a raison d'être, *Harriet Hume*
gave her a literary mode. In *The Judge*, Rebecca had acknowledged an
invisible force that dangled humanity like puppets on strings; through
Harriet Hume, Rebecca had become the puppeteer. Her novel confirmed
that as an artist she must contemplate the eternal, but as a woman she
must be Machiavellian if she was to survive.

A YEAR AFTER *Harriet Hume* was published, life seemed to imitate
art. Rebecca was introduced to a man so sensitive, kind, and cultured that
he melted her fear of male domination—a man who appeared to be a
harmony of opposites. Henry Andrews was a thirty-five-year-old Oxford graduate whose mastery of seven European languages, charm, and
equanimity made him a unique asset to the powerful international merchant bank run by its namesake, Baron Kurt von Schröder, a moneyed
right-wing German who would become an early supporter of Hitler.
Dubbed Schroders' "European ambassador" and a trusted member of its
managerial triumvirate, Henry exuded an air of well-honed elegance.
Rebecca and Henry were invited to a dinner party by their mutual friend
Vera Brittain, whose husband, George Catlin, was a classmate of Henry's. Vera knew that Henry was an avid, almost obsessive, admirer of
Rebecca's work; he had read her novella *The Return of the Soldier* six
times. Rebecca admired Vera as a writer of extraordinary generosity and
integrity; she assured Rebecca that Henry was exactly what he appeared
to be—an English gentleman of impeccable character. His unfortunate
incarceration by the Germans during the war, she said, had bred moral
strength and heightened sensitivity.

Unbeknownst to Rebecca, Vera had understated both his gifts and his past. Henry had been a student of nineteen on holiday in Hamburg when he was captured as a British spy. Suddenly denied what he loved most—books and scholarship—he was determined not to lose his academic grounding. Throughout the Great War, Henry conducted a veritable university within the walls of the detention camp, where many of his fellow prisoners gathered to study literature and philosophy, exchange research papers, and debate ethical and literary perspectives.

Professorial in demeanor and meticulously groomed in a three-piece suit and tie, Henry spoke with erudition and propriety. After dinner, Henry sat on a velvet cushion at Rebecca's feet, a form of reverence and humility that was foreign to her experience. Immediately, he made her feel at ease. For two hours, they spoke of her work, classical literature, art, and architecture. When the conversation turned to France, they discovered a common passion for its diversity of culture, its museums and cathedrals, its unparalleled food, and its glorious coastline. The evening was crowned by Rebecca's confession that the beauty of the carving of Christ and his apostles over the portal of the Basilica of Saint Mary Magdalene in Vézelay had evoked a spiritual, quasi-religious response in her, and miraculously he concurred.

With Henry, she easily shed her veil of reason; she wasn't afraid to speak of divine mysteries and the meaning with which they imbued her daily life. It was rare for this daughter of the Enlightenment, this Christian agnostic, this radical devotee of secular humanism, to reveal her awe of Christian symbolism, except through the voices of her fictional characters, yet there she was, with a near stranger unmasking the inner secrets of her heart. Within the space of hours, Henry had gained her trust. That evening he walked her home, and the next morning, and many mornings thereafter, he sent her flowers and visited her at her flat.

Rebecca came to enjoy Henry's company; he was grounded and practical, yet intellectually sophisticated, funny, and kind. He was simply the most stable and generous man she had ever known, and his "bluer than blue" eyes embraced her with warmth. Like Max Beaverbrook, he loved women and had a "knack of making you feel the only woman in the world." Unlike H.G.'s, Henry's intellect was a vehicle for tender exchange, not a battle arena or a game of chess. Best of all, Henry was not famous, powerful, or married, and he saw love not as a means of conquest but as a source of affirmation and empowerment.

Physically, however, Rebecca had to admit that he was less than attractive. A tall, thin, plain-faced man whose head had "sides but no back," Henry, she quipped, was handsome "from the neck down." Henry fascinated her friends, who were quick to nickname him the "Elk," but his singularly restrained and slow responses made them worry that he was not an intellectual match for Rebecca. Consoled by the fact that Rebecca cared for him, they had to assume that Henry was smart and sincere. Soon they were to learn that his way of conversing was the result of a childhood soccer injury that had left him deaf in one ear.

Furthermore, Rebecca's friends were amused that Henry addressed her as Rebecca Cicely (her given name), as though she were at once a famous author and an endearing child whose future was full of unfathomed possibility. Intuitively, Henry seemed to know what she needed. Although he was a year younger than she, Henry assumed a paternal stance; he was a father—a protector, a passionate lover, and an intelligent and sympathetic friend.

When Anthony returned to Stowe in January 1930, Rebecca left for her semiannual monthlong stay in New York. Since her first trip to the States in 1923, she had been writing book reviews for Irita Van Doren at the *Herald Tribune,* and had later signed a contract with *The Bookman,* a literary magazine published in America and Britain, to write social and cultural commentary, profiles of contemporary authors, and essays on British, American, and European theater, art, architecture, and literature. Provocative by design, her essays were a potpourri of science, psychology, sociology, and philosophy brewed into digestible and entertaining narratives, at once light-handed, ironic, and profound.

Upon Rebecca's return to London in mid-February, her relationship with Henry deepened. She found him to be not only a wonderful companion, but a welcome buffer to the increasing contention between her and H.G. and Anthony. Still seething with anger for his lot in life, Anthony assumed the role of victim—a stance that Rebecca had come to realize was not entirely his fault. And Rebecca's intimacy with Henry seemed to add to Anthony's troubles.

With Henry's encouragement, Rebecca spent several weeks in Paris imbibing the beauty of its museums and cathedrals. She then made her way south on the new luxurious Blue Train line, a Pullman replete with sitting/sleeping rooms decorated like the finest French ships with metalwork, lacquer, and state-of-the-art lighting and ventilation. Then she took a hired car and headed east on the winding golden coast road carved into the Hyères cliffs toward the ancient Provence town of Agay. She arrived on May 1, 1930, in "high season" after the rains of March and April had passed, and the weather had turned sunny and warm. Nestled between the red overhanging cliffs and the volcanic rocky coves and beaches of the bay was her favorite retreat, Villa Mysto. It was a vibrant community of painters and writers, including Guy de Maupassant, Jean Aicard, and Rebecca's contemporaries Maurice Donnay and Antoine de Saint-Exupéry, whose homes lined the narrow streets along short, steep, donkey-sized steps that ascended the foothills. She relished both the camaraderie and the solitude; the informal tête-à-têtes with friends undisturbed by the sound of telephones and radios; the raw beauty of the light and the turquoise sea. Each morning she would sit on the balcony drinking her coffee, perusing the newspaper, and letting her mind and imagination run free.

After a short visit to Villa Mysto, Henry, occupied by his work for the German bank Shröders in Europe, suggested that Rebecca remain until she completed her book *Ending in Earnest,* a compendium of her essays published in *The Bookman.* As he had promised Rebecca before she had left, Henry had visited Anthony at Stowe, overseeing his progress and cultivating a rapport. He told Rebecca that Anthony seemed to be doing well, and that he had spoken kindly of her. Henry's adoration seemed to grow in her absence; he wrote her lovesick letters several times a week, and, when his emotions overflowed, sent her ardent telegrams, calling her his "loving delight." Rebecca, as well, seemed increasingly fond of him; unbridled passion and its dangers had lost their allure.

When she returned in mid-June to London, Henry met her at the station, declaring they were about to embark on a new beginning. Rebecca had agreed to marry him. She wrote to her friend S. K. Ratcliffe that Henry had been a wonderful friend throughout Anthony's illness and had helped her deal with H.G.'s vengeful courtroom threats during her efforts to adopt him. "If I had no happiness to look forward to I would want the wedding as a sign of gratitude to Henry for what his feeling for me during the last year has done to build me up." For her, Henry's kindness had made the difference between "heaven and hell."

Rebecca did, nonetheless, communicate her doubts about marrying Henry to her sister Winnie. At Rebecca's request, she and Winnie spent a weekend alone in a rented cottage at Leigh-on-Sea to discuss her concerns. The main issue was that she really didn't love him. At least, not in the way she had loved H.G. or Max. She felt sorry for Henry, and he had been such a good friend, especially during her troubled times with Anthony. And perhaps it could be argued that at this stage in her life, she needed a friend more than a lover. Apparently Winnie, now a decade-long veteran at the game of marriage and the mother of two, touted the value of friendship.

Winnie and Lettie were relieved, not only for themselves, but in memory of their mother "who adored her baby so." They were pleased that their troubled, often wayward, sister was about to settle down with a man they could understand—a solid, conventional, job-holding Englishman who obviously cared for her and Anthony.

Some would speculate that her betrothal to a banker was a betrayal of her socialist ideology—that Henry was emblematic of the ruthless international capitalist machine she had always despised. Those who could not discern the quality of Henry's character, or his passion for scholarship, assumed that Rebecca's motive was mercenary. But Henry was far from rich; in fact, he was nearly broke when they met. His stock market speculations after the war had collapsed along with the economy, forcing him to live solely on his salary. His inheritance from his uncle Ernest, who had supported him and his family after his father's death, was years off, and although his uncle promised him financial help when he and Rebecca married, his offer was less than they had hoped for.

A façade of English gentility consonant with their intellectual and aesthetic sensibilities was important to Henry and Rebecca's view of themselves as "outsiders"—it was part of what brought them together. Born in Scotland into poverty, Rebecca inherited not only her father's mind and disposition but his lost dreams of landed aristocracy—the feudal grange in Ireland that his mother had forfeited after his father's death. Henry, too, felt cheated of his family's fortune. He had been born in Burma to a family of Scottish origins with a Jewish strain; his grandfather had married a Jewish woman in the early 1900s. Henry's father, Lewis, had been a prosperous importer-exporter who had provided a comfortable home and fine education to his two sons, Henry and Ernest. But much like Rebecca's father, Lewis Andrews had died penniless, leaving his wife, Mary, and their children with a taste for luxury they could no longer afford. Rather than choosing a poor but independent path of survival like that of Isabella Fairfield, however, Henry's mother chose to become dependent on the less-than-generous support of her husband's brother Ernest. For both Rebecca and Henry, deprived of the emotional presence of their fathers, the semblance of stability and wealth seemed a necessity. The young Rebecca had been wedded to the ideal of economic parity and had denigrated H.G. for his material lust; now in middle age, she was determined to get her due.

Much like Dorothy, Rebecca had contrived an image of emotional independence that concealed her loneliness, and much like Hal Lewis, Henry had suffered the anguish of the unloved. Echoing the words of Dorothy upon meeting Hal, Rebecca would later write: "I have never known anybody so isolated as Henry. . . . I have never known anybody who struck me at once as so uncared for."

Rebecca was finally able to care for someone and be generous with her money. Her economic self-sufficiency permitted her to relieve Henry of their financial burdens; she told him that she would be pleased to pool their funds. Nonetheless, she was convinced that the rarity of their arrangement might embarrass him if it were to be made public. Tight-lipped among her family and friends, as well as with reporters who pursued her romantic entanglements as doggedly as her career, she conceded that perception would have to trump reality.

As his mother's marriage to Henry became a certainty, Anthony grew increasingly hostile and rebellious; Rebecca worried that he would have a breakdown—a perception that would prove prescient. She artfully planned their fall wedding to take place after Anthony's return to school, but Rebecca thought it proper to inform H.G. of her plans. Their prior meetings and conversations, primarily concerning Anthony's schooling and their visitation rights, had always been tinged with rancor and resentment. H.G. had recently returned to London from Grasse, France, having spent four years in the care of the good-hearted Odette Keun. Now he hoped to extricate himself from this increasingly demanding and debilitating mistress. The arrangement had been tolerable while Jane was alive, but after she died in 1927, Odette was no longer willing to dangle at his mercy. She wanted him to marry her.

Later, H.G. would write in the postscript to his autobiography that most of his affairs were the equivalent of fishing expeditions. The "fish," however, were central to his life. He simply could not live alone. He liked his women smart and emotionally starved; he considered self-assertion tantamount to betrayal. In truth, he needed a womb, not a woman; someone who could comfort, protect, and sexually satisfy him—in his words, a "body slave." Odette, like Rebecca, wouldn't play by his rules. Like Jane, Odette had sacrificed her own career for his, but when she asked for more, he, as usual, had turned away.

Moura Budberg had been the rare exception. Solid and independent to the core, she was as Machiavellian as she was seductive. When H.G. had met her sixteen years earlier in Moscow at the outbreak of the war, Moura was rumored to have been a double agent who had manipulated H.G., still reaping the royalties of his best-selling books, to fill the coffers of her Bolshevik informants. He didn't care; his love for her transcended pride. Inaccessible, mysterious, above the petty concerns of other women, Moura offered him love without strings. Unbeknownst to Odette or Rebecca, Moura was coming back to him, willing, for the first time, to share his home and his bed, if not his name.

H.G. would later record, "[Rebecca] invited herself to tea with me one day. . . . She told me she was going to marry. I thought it was a sisterly thing to come and tell me and it warmed my heart to her. She married and she married very happily. . . . He is an able business man; he admires her unreservedly, and she can live with him without the perpetual friction of antagonistic mental disposition and conflicting literary ambition." Rebecca appeared unusually calm and mellow, he wrote, and he had expressed his good wishes. Sitting together in his spacious flat overlooking Paddington Gardens, they seemed to have finally found friendship. For the moment, each was poised on the precipice of a new life.

In a surprising move for an agnostic iconoclast, yet strangely consistent with Rebecca's lifelong search for social legitimacy, she decided to marry Henry in a small country church at Abinger, Surrey, where her cousin Sir Henry Denny was parson. Since neither she nor Henry believed in Christian doctrine, it puzzled their friends that they chose to have a traditional Anglican ceremony. One friend wrote to Rebecca that she had expected her to marry on impulse in a registrar's office, or be kidnapped by a deranged suitor and forced into wedlock. After receiving permission from Henry's mother and uncle Ernest (a formality Rebecca reluctantly observed) and visiting Lettie and Winnie, the couple made their final plans.

Rebecca West and Henry Andrews's wedding, November 1, 1930

On November 1, 1930, a date chosen because it was easy to remember, Rebecca married Henry. Dressed in the muted colors of late fall, she wore a honey-beige velvet dress. Her matching cloche hat covered a myriad of sins—her notoriously unruly hair and perhaps a head full of untamed thoughts and manifold fears. Carrying loosely bound stalks of winter lilies and red anemones, she seemed to canter down the aisle, as if the draft she was about to imbibe was best done quickly. Escorted by her elder sister, Lettie, Rebecca met her groom at the altar. Henry, dressed in a handmade three-piece suit, exuded an air of propriety and humility that impressed observers as "the proper backdrop" for this restive journalist and author.

Like an ill-cast actress, beautifully costumed in the fashion of the day, Rebecca walked onto a perfectly rendered country-church stage. Intoning the same solemn vows as Dorothy had made to Hal two and a half years earlier, Rebecca promised herself to Henry in the presence of Christ—with two unconventional, some might say blasphemous, omissions in the scripture. Rebecca refused to say "obey" as part of her marriage covenant, and Henry, perhaps at her behest, substituted "share" for "endow" when he pledged his bride his worldly goods. Unlike Dorothy, who wholeheartedly embraced the rituals of her Protestant tradition, Rebecca used them as a means to an end. Much like Hal, Rebecca wanted to do it "right" in the hope that propriety would breed authenticity. She liked her perfectly tailored groom, as much as she could like any man; she needed his friendship and adoration and craved the stability and security their covenant would provide. She vowed to make their marriage work, as much for him as for herself.

After the ceremony, Rebecca and Henry walked together up the aisle to the applause of their family and friends. Those in attendance found Rebecca happier and more radiant than they'd ever seen her.

By the time the wedding party and guests left the church to dine at the rectory, dusk was falling. The evening air was unusually mild and calm for early November, and the rain fell lightly on Rebecca's shoulders. At least for the moment, the autumnal wind similar to the one that had augured her father's abandonment a quarter of a century earlier had abated; the serenity seemed an omen of a new beginning.

The next day, as Rebecca and Henry packed for their honeymoon, a violent squall swept through Britain.

CHAPTER 6

RENAISSANCE

Show me a woman married to an artist who can
succeed in her marriage without making a
full-time profession out of it. Oh, Jesus, God!

—DOROTHY THOMPSON

LONDON, MAY 1928

It was a divine spring—lush, wet, and prosperous. The stock markets soared, optimism reigned, and the West was convinced that diplomacy had rendered warfare obsolete.

Dorothy knew better. Experience had taught her that Weimar Germany was in tatters, the Nazi Party was gaining strength, and Stalin's Russia was a ruthless autocracy. Nationalism was rampant, and Europe was a tinderbox. But she preferred not to think about it. She would let nothing intrude on her happiness. All her doubts were locked away, all warnings eschewed. She could recite a litany of blessings: Her husband was one of the most celebrated novelists in America and Europe; she was wealthy, secure, and loved beyond imagining. Finally, she had a cause worthy of her dedication; finally, she knew who she was.

Hal was Dorothy's oracle of wisdom, and it was her role to serve him. Before God and the church he had made his covenant, and through her faith and will, she would carry them both up to Mount Moriah. Her father had been her vicar of Christ and Bard had been her Jewish deliverer, until he betrayed her. Hal was her second chance to live a good Christian life.

Dorothy preferred not to think about a lot of things as she prepared for their honeymoon—Hal's alcoholism, the future of her career, and her desire for a child and a real home—these thoughts were swallowed up in the sheer frenzy with which she worked. Work had always been her panacea, and Dorothy attacked the domestic challenges of a three-month trip in a caravan along the English Channel coast with the same fervor as she had her reportage. Within a week, she had organized everything, including a contract for a series of articles Hal would write for the *New York Herald Tribune* called "The Babbitts of Britain." The articles would virtually pay for their trip.

"What can you carry in a caravan?" she asked herself in her honeymoon diary. A fridge stocked with American-cut steak, bacon, butter, fruits, and vegetables, and a larder full of cakes, ginger cookies, jam and honey, canned goods, and wine. They would need, of course, cups, plates, and knives and forks, a stove, bedding, lamps, a variety of clothing. But perhaps, most important, the caravan would carry two typewriters, paper, lots of books (forty!), and cigarettes. "In short," she writes, "everything which a civilized human being wants, if his wife knows how to cook."

Dorothy and Hal on their "caravan honeymoon" in July 1928

These words heralded the role she coveted: helpmate to a genius. To Dorothy it seemed the natural order of things. But why? Others as gifted as she had chosen otherwise. She had to look no further than Rebecca, who had cast off the stranglehold of H.G., even before she knew she could earn a living. Was it self-disdain or naïveté? The fallout of Methodist-inspired faith or just plain idealism? It was probably a mixture of all these. Her friends would call it neurotic; she would call it Christian virtue. Everyone, however, was alarmed by the intensity of her dedication and her anticipation of bliss.

Rebecca and Dorothy were equally controlling, but unlike Rebecca, Dorothy's demeanor was neither Machiavellian nor punitive. Perhaps too "modern" to admit it, Dorothy derived her inspiration from the power of God. In his name she would strive, against all odds, to do the impossible: She would take Hal to the covenantal mountaintop on her back, if necessary; Dorothy would be the divine spirit who would sanctify their marriage and their lives.

Like the honey in their larder, their trip began sweetly. Rumbling along in their little Chrysler at fifteen miles an hour (so that the china wouldn't break) hauling their three-thousand-pound caravan behind them, Dorothy and Hal traveled south from London toward the coast. Wanting to please him, and knowing that a church reference was a surefire way to win a smile, Dorothy turned to Hal and said, "You are . . . a bread pudding . . . made of the divine host." And then, "That's a compliment no one ever made anyone before."

Within days they would meet their first two Babbitts, narrow-minded cousins of Hal's, Midwestern blowhards who had never quite gotten over the American Revolution—they had chosen to return to the fatherland. The presence of two Yankees wanting to justify their self-exile evoked from Hal an accommodating discourse on the inferiority of American life and culture. Recording the raw data of their encounter in her diary for Hal to polish into magazine prose, Dorothy exposed the hypocrisy of these tradesmen, who denigrated Americans for fabricating their past, while producing copies of British antiques.

As they made their way west from Sussex to Dorset in their caravan, Dorothy wrote detailed descriptions of the late medieval architecture of the southern towns and the magnificence of the parks, estates, and seascapes, along with a running commentary on British social customs, fashions, legal codes, and school systems. She made it clear that while she appreciated Old World manners and ethics, she abhorred English class distinctions, attitudes toward women, anti-intellectualism, and anti-Americanism.

On rainy days, Dorothy and Hal would sit or lie in bed reading and writing, but when the weather was sunny and warm, they would sit on the steps of the caravan and write. Between articles, Hal worked on *Dodsworth* and Dorothy edited her pieces on Russia for publication as a book. But seeping through the cracks of her diary was evidence of the unraveling of their marriage. When Hal was not writing, he had begun to drink again, and his outbursts were as abusive as before. He was as insensitive to her needs as he was sensitive to his own. Volatile, angry, and emotionally inept, he was jealous of her admirers and contemptuous of her work. He would rage without warning and think nothing of deserting her in public places.

Dorothy was sad but, above all, scared, perhaps as much by Hal's temper as her own misjudgment and self-deception. How could she have thought it would work? Nothing, nothing, could ameliorate her pain—food, wine, the hospitality of friends, were mere distractions. By the time they returned to London, their "holy union" had become a sham.

She wrote in her diary on August 2, 1928: "Bad temper is the most destructive of human faults. It supplants trust with fear; it poisons love; it breeds aversion or indifference; it sterilizes emotion. Unless he stops taking me on or casting me off as the mood suits him I shall eventually cease to love H."

But she did love him—or perhaps the ideal he had represented when they married. Loving him, she had always known, implied sacrifice; she, after all, was totally unimportant, and Hal was a man of genius.

After returning to Berlin to retrieve their belongings, they sailed for America on the *Hamburg*, arriving in New York on August 28, 1928. In an attempt, perhaps, to fasten their union to a place and a community, they had rented two floors of a house at 37 West Tenth Street, sight unseen, before they had left London. The brownstone, just west of Fifth Avenue, was neither as aristocratic as the Federal style mansions that bordered Washington Square nor as paltry as the multifamily tenement buildings to the west that housed the Irish-Italian longshoremen and saloon keepers. The social radicalism of the war years had waned, but West Tenth Street was still a place attractive to artists, writers, and socialists—people who eschewed the "Babbittry" of mindless capitalism and the oppression of its social institutions. Flanked on one side by artist studios and on the other by the nineteenth-century Episcopal Church of the Ascension, 37 West Tenth Street was a respectable address suited to those who took their individuality, work, and politics seriously. Dorothy and Hal sensed they would feel comfortable in the neighborhood's smoky clubs and artists' saloons, which were not much different from the cafés in Paris or Berlin. They wanted to be accepted, even applauded, for being exactly who they were without the burden of social pretense.

In a way, the setting proved too comfortable, at least for Hal. Liquor, despite Prohibition, was easy to come by. He drank on impulse from the time he woke up until way past dinner. The chaos in their home, which ran according to Hal's whim, was exasperating to the housekeeper and butler—a couple that Dorothy had brought from Berlin—but most of all to Dorothy herself, for whom order and social amenity were integral to life. She was in control of nothing. Hal hated to leave the house, refused to plan ahead, and invited whomever he pleased at the last minute for dinner without consulting Dorothy or the staff. Socially, Hal was a Venus flytrap, imprisoning his favorite people of the moment until they were forced to lie to gain their freedom. He would then invite unsuspecting others to replace them, often leaving for a nap in the middle of dinner, expecting Dorothy to feed, cajole, and entertain his guests.

Dorothy wanted more. She had married a famous writer and lived in the largest and most exciting city in America, yet she was chained to their apartment like an indentured servant to a drunken madman.

After nine years abroad, Dorothy found New York crass, shrill, and boring. The reputation and influence she had cultivated in Europe meant nothing in the States. The arrogance of the literati was unbearable; the Algonquin Group and their acolytes dismissed her as a mere literary appendage without distinction of her own. The only thing that sustained her was her idyllic fantasy of living with Hal in the country home they dreamed of buying.

For Dorothy, "home" was a place that was peaceful and unspoiled. She had grown up at a time when small-town living was both unsullied and secure. Hamburg, New York, was not only bricks and mortar on a swath of land; it was a community and a way of life. Hal must have felt the same, but his memories were more painful because his outsized intellect and misshapen body had made him an outcast in his hometown of Sauk Centre. Just as Rebecca and Henry had first searched for legitimacy in order to reclaim their past, Dorothy and Hal needed to reconstruct the childhood landscape that seemed to have betrayed them.

They drove deep into the New England countryside to find a home, but after a month of searching, they had begun to lose hope. Scavenging their minds for leads, they remembered that Mr. Connett, the man who had rented them their Tenth Street apartment, was living in a town called Pomfret, in eastern Vermont. Hoping for guidance from this old New Englander, they found their way to his home. An elderly man who lived alone, Connett was delighted to see them and took pleasure in showing them around. Within fifteen minutes, Dorothy and Hal had offered to buy his house, and by dinnertime the papers had been signed. It seemed like a miracle—Kismet—Mr. Connett, a widower, had wanted to retire to Florida, and they had found the "perfect" home.

Dorothy would call it Twin Farms, the name given to it by two brothers a half century earlier. Farmers, these men had built two houses on opposite sides of a small fertile valley. Their land encompassed more than three hundred acres of pasture, rock, valley, and stream, akin to the terrain Dorothy and Hal had loved to hike in western England. The two houses faced each other through the stark winter landscape; in the fullness of summer, they would be enclaves to themselves.

Built in 1796, at the height of optimism for the founding of the new republic, the main house was an archetypal New England farmhouse, recently electrified, yet architecturally untouched. Its clean lines and sloping roof remained true to its roots, and perhaps, most important to Dorothy and Hal, spiritually pure. Whatever their differences, the Lewises were romantic, idealistic, and hungry for the myth that was America. They purchased their piece of it for $10,000.

Naïve about the endless costs related to homeownership, they spoke of the cheapness of it all and their plans for renovating the smaller home on the far side of the hill into a guest house. Despite the carpentry and masonry bills, all Hal could think about was what a wonderful home they would have come the following year. Dorothy bought furnishings, planted the gardens, and hired servants. By late spring they would be ready to move in. It was the place they had dreamed of when they had first decided to marry, although it reflected something they sensed about themselves and each other: Their "lovely place" was two homes separated by a valley.

The winter in New York proved more stressful and less satisfying than they anticipated. Although *Dodsworth* was selling in the tens of thousands and being hailed as the best Sinclair Lewis novel ever written, Hal was not pleased with his publisher, Alfred Harcourt. He felt he deserved a compendium of his works and was miffed that the recognition of his extraordinary success had been denied him. While Hal may have been right, nothing could have ameliorated his unhappiness. Dorothy missed her job, her influence, and her colleagues in Berlin, and no matter how she tried to help him, she could not fill his emptiness. Ironically, Hal condemned her for not having written anything in a year, and Dorothy felt betrayed by her virtue.

By February, both she and Hal were physically and emotionally exhausted. "[Hal] had been drinking terribly again," she wrote in her diary; and in a last-ditch effort to break his cycle, she reluctantly agreed to accompany him on a fishing trip to Florida. "My heart is heavy and rebellious," she wrote. "My God—Florida mud flats, and all next summer in Vermont! Not one enjoyable dinner party the whole winter; not one evening at the opera; not one concert, not a single human relationship— Can't bear it. I *won't* bear it. I had rather go on and work in someone's kitchen than lead this sort of life, chased, pursued, harassed by fear's fear."

Like Rebecca's, her fear was rooted in her past. Trapped in a childhood delusion that she must obey her husband's will, regardless of its validity or her own desire to do so, she would do anything to preserve her marriage. One might say that this fear of confrontation had killed her mother, forcing her to undergo a secret abortion. In effect, Dorothy was defying the very principle of female self-determination that she had spent her suffragette youth defending.

She recited, once more, a litany of self-degradation. Her life was nothing next to Hal's genius; he deserved the sacrifice to which she was committed. This time, however, it brought no solace. During her marriage to Joseph Bard, she had cultivated a core of strength to which she could retreat for sustenance and perspective. While her impulse was either to leave Hal or die with him, she had to find another way. Dorothy could not tolerate the thought that she had failed again. She would feel like an apostate, a hypocrite—a fraud.

She decided to carve a niche for herself as an American journalist, using the skills she had gained in her ten years as a foreign correspondent. She would gather information, write articles, and go on lecture tours. The articles might not pay much, but she could get a thousand dollars for each lecture. This way, she could maintain her marriage, at least nominally, until she decided what to do or until her professional career took off.

Dorothy knew exactly what she wanted out of life. "I want to understand all manner of things better," she wrote in her diary. "I know I have good taste & a good head. My creative gifts are negligible. But I should like to contribute to a clearer and deeper understanding of the things I understand. My gifts are pre-eminently social." She craved human relationships and she wanted a home that would be a "center of life and illumination." Her gifts were recording and interpretation, she wrote, and her interest lay in the "humanities," politics, literature of ideas, economics, and "the attributes of civilized living—cooking, house-furnishing—manners." Her passion was "creative men," without whom, she wrote, she was "stultified and rendered sterile."

Dorothy would come to the conclusion that Hal wasn't worth giving up her life for, and besides, she wrote, "I can really do nothing for him. He is like a vampire—he absorbs all my energy, all my beauty . . . all the things I prize in the world, all beautiful civilized manners and forms, he violates. . . . I am inexpressibly weary and sore. I want to get away, somewhere forever."

Dorothy went to Florida with Hal, as he wished, hoping that long walks in the sea air and fishing with his friends might jolt him out of his alcoholic languor, renew his will, and restore his drive to write again. Dorothy would stay for a few days and then leave, traveling first to Pittsburgh to visit Rose Wilder Lane and then north to Canada to gather information on the social and criminal effects of Prohibition for articles commissioned by Curtis newspapers.

These pieces would be a professional turning point for Dorothy when they were published in June. Syndicated throughout the States, they initiated a cascade of requests for articles and lectures about Russia, Germany, art, theater, and European politics. Hal had tutored her on her prose style and had introduced her to an editor of *The Saturday Evening Post*, Thomas Costain. His efforts paid off when Costain requested that Dorothy write some articles for them. Hal was thrilled. This was the Dorothy he had fallen in love with, not the Dorothy who was paralyzed by his failings. He was overwhelmingly proud: The *Post* was the highest paying periodical in the country.

Hal's trip to Florida had steadied his mind, and their summer together at Twin Farms, teeming with visitors, alleviated his profound loneliness. He was wrestling with a mammoth, multigenerational novel on the American labor movement that many—including Dorothy—believed was over his head.

After the first isolated, debilitating winter of their marriage, Dorothy was thrilled to welcome those who arrived at Twin Farms to augment Hal's research, men who she must have thought would be useful to her work as well: Clarence Darrow, a labor and criminal lawyer; Carl Van Doren, biographer and brother-in-law of editor Irita; Ben Stolberg, the Far Left labor journalist; and Francis Perkins, who would later join Franklin D. Roosevelt's cabinet as secretary of labor. Dorothy also assembled a cadre of her foreign correspondent buddies. John Gunther and Floyd Gibbons were preoccupied with family and work, but Jimmy Sheean, the brilliant young journalist whom she had adoringly taken under her wing in Vienna, was still unmarried. Now trying his hand at fiction, he welcomed the prospect of spending ten quiet days in the New England countryside. Jimmy had a way of melting Dorothy and Hal's differences; Hal saw him as the gifted young writer he himself had been twenty years earlier, and took pleasure in prodding him to do his best. Dorothy, six and a half years Jimmy's senior, adored him like a mother but also relished the multifaceted quality and precision of his mind. Jimmy took long walks in the woods with Hal, and spoke with Dorothy for hours over coffee and beer, discussing the rise of fascism and its threat to the survival of democracy in Europe.

Jimmy fell in love with the bucolic beauty and the ebb and flow of quietude and stimulation at Twin Farms. The Lewises fell in love with Jimmy. They asked him to "stay more or less forever."

It had been a fruitful summer. Hal's *Dodsworth* continued to sell widely, and several of his short stories, published in *Cosmopolitan,* were bringing in substantial fees. Unsophisticated about money and risk averse even during the boom of the twenties, they luckily had not invested in the stock market. When the crash came, they were blissfully immune. Then Dorothy learned that she was pregnant.

She should have been delighted by the prospect of motherhood, and yet she was frightened. Wasn't this the baby she had always wanted? The child that her marriage to Joseph had nearly cheated her of? Perhaps she feared she was too old at thirty-six to carry a normal child to term. Most babies were born to women in their early twenties. Theoretically, both she and her child faced certain risk. Her own mother had been twenty-one when Dorothy was born. By the age of twenty-five, her mother, Margaret Grierson Thompson, had given birth to three children, and by twenty-nine, she was dead. Dorothy had helped to raise her brother and sister, but this was her child—an irrevocable responsibility. Perhaps its birth might tighten the bond between her and Hal. Perhaps this would be the linchpin that would keep them together—the blood knot that would draw energy from each of them and propel them forward. Or maybe, it would drive them further apart; Hal's relationship with his son Wells did not augur well. Abortion, however, was out of the question. She resolved to marshal all her strength to keep the baby and hold their marriage together—there was still a piece of her that wanted to believe she was chosen to save Hal from the darkness.

By November 1929, she was nearly three months pregnant and profoundly lonely. She spent most of her days in the duplex on Tenth Street, once again a prisoner of Hal's drunken whims. Her friends were scattered—Rose Wilder Lane had gone back home to the Ozarks, Gertrude Tone was divorced and in hiding, and Rebecca was not only busy writing—rumor had it that she had a new lover.

When Dorothy left Europe, her friendship with Rebecca fell dormant. Too proud to relay her sadness and disappointment, too worried that she would bring shame on Hal in literary circles abroad, Dorothy chose silence. Rebecca, too, was ashamed. Anthony, now fifteen years old, was failing at school, and she was quarreling with H.G. about who was the more neglectful parent. Except for Henry and her most intimate friends, Rebecca had shut down all communication. Their ships—Dorothy's and Rebecca's—had literally passed on the Atlantic. Dorothy was in Europe when Rebecca was making her reputation in the States, and Dorothy came home to New York after Rebecca's love affair with America, and its men, had withered. Transatlantic phone calls and letters did not provide the warmth and commiseration Dorothy craved. She would have to rely on friends closer to home for comfort and support.

But even that wasn't sufficient. Clearly depressed, Dorothy sought consolation through Freud's newest form of therapy—psychodynamic theater in which both the players and the audience acted out their neuroses. It was a throwback, perhaps, to the classical forms of dramatic catharsis. But the play, at least for Dorothy, was not the "thing."

Before learning of her pregnancy, Dorothy had begun to drink—one might say that she came by it naturally; her father had been an alcoholic, just as his father was before him. Perhaps that's why he had sought the discipline of the church. Yet, it was out of character for Dorothy to succumb. Perhaps it was an attempt to get into bed with the enemy, so to speak—to know her husband's disease as intimately as she knew him. Or perhaps it was a cry for help, for if Dorothy were to become sick and in need of sympathy, she might reverse their roles and regain control. In short, it appeared that she was breaking down in order to break free.

Whatever the reason, drinking had become an obsession of Dorothy's, to the point that one of her male friends forbade her to drink in his favorite saloon. Dorothy gravitated to places where alcoholic writers were de rigueur. Buttressed by her growing reputation, she once again approached the Algonquin Group, fraternizing with Hal's acquaintances—Alexander Woollcott, Heyward Broun, and Harold Ross, the same men who six years before had become facilitators of Rebecca's career. Dorothy's discussions with the prolific writers in the group heightened her sense of frustration and paralysis. She was desperate to get away from Hal—when he wasn't pretending to write his labor novel, he would spend hours on the telephone talking to his bootlegger. Determined to stop her suicidal slide, and eager to earn money for her child's future, she convinced her agent to book her a speaking tour through the Midwest.

But the illusion of professional and personal independence did not relieve her loneliness. Riding on trains that sloshed her belly from side to side and sleeping in hotel rooms in Terre Haute, Grand Rapids, and Detroit, all left her fearing a miscarriage and feeling that she was far away from the life that she should have been living. She longed for the comfort of her husband, that is, the husband Hal might have been, and her work at the crux of political events in Europe. She felt like a second-rate hack, dependent on information siphoned from her friends overseas.

After a month on the road, Dorothy was pleased to come home. But she hadn't counted on Hal's incorrigible restlessness. Perhaps afraid that fatherhood would once again pen him in, he told Dorothy that he needed to return to the "one-and-only earthly edition of paradise" where he had lived as a young man: Monterey, California. He argued that he had to go to Reno, anyway, to petition the lowering of his alimony to Grace, but the truth was that he might have done that by legal proxy. Hal presented the trip as a fait accompli, and she, under the circumstances, was reluctant to refuse. They would leave in February, he announced, and stay the winter.

Monterey was as magnificent as Hal remembered. On a peninsula jutting out toward the Pacific, protected from its fierce winds by rocky cliffs, the city of Monterey faced the bay harbor. Its white sandy beaches, bordered by scrubby dunes that gave way to three forested mountain ranges, bestowed a singular beauty, rivaled, perhaps, only by the Côte d'Azure. By the time of their arrival, the economy of the city was in a state of transition. While the fishing industry still flourished, tourism had taken hold. The population on the peninsula had doubled during the previous ten years, and tennis, golf, polo, and gambling thrived in the expansive Del Monte Resort on Pebble Beach. Hal was drinking, and liquor flowed unrestrained through the highways that cut southward along the coast, making Monterey "the Queen of the Watering Holes" on the Pacific. Dorothy, perhaps longing for the man whose body had once conquered her loneliness, wrote to Joseph Bard and described the area as "Ponce de Leon's country . . . rejuvenating for the body and degenerating to the mind."

Dorothy had found them "the most delightful little house," she wrote to a friend. "It has a writing room for Hal, a little sitting room, and dining room & kitchen, two charming bedrooms, and a lovely garden full of roses, mimosa, blossoming quinces, forget-me-nots, and narcissus, etc." She loved their neighbors and the "crowd at Pebble Beach & Carmel," but she and Hal were alone most of the time.

However, Dorothy's enchantment with Monterey faded quickly. In the social notices in the local newspaper, Hal, as Dorothy might have predicted, had become an object of derision. Despite the fact that they dined at the finest homes of the rich and fashionable, she was certain that their hosts ridiculed him behind his back. Both literary star and court jester—amusing in a bizarre kind of way with his rhyming ditties and ad-lib imitations, Hal was earning a less-than-stellar reputation.

Dorothy was ashamed. She was ashamed of him, and as his pregnant wife, ashamed of being seen as his appendage. To them she was Mrs. Sinclair Lewis, Hal's subordinate without a mind of her own. She couldn't help but observe how far she had dropped in public esteem since returning from Europe, where reporters had lined up to interview her. She vowed to reclaim her independence.

Dorothy left Monterey two weeks before Hal to visit her friend Rose

Wilder Lane, now at home on her farm in Mansfield, Missouri. She needed Rose's tenderness and strength to carry her through her pregnancy.

When Hal returned to New York in April, instead of coming straight home he took a room at the Lafayette Hotel on East Fourth Street, seeking the solitude that would permit him to write, yet just a short walk from home. But he was still drinking heavily, and the labor novel had fizzled. Dorothy and the staff were relieved to have him out of their way, but in the evenings when Hal came home, he still drained the lifeblood of the house. He and Dorothy were constantly at odds, attacking each other about anything and nothing.

In May, eight months pregnant, Dorothy began to plot her escape. Jimmy Sheean, who had become their neighbor on West Fourth Street, was both her confidant and a witness to the disintegration of their marriage. One evening when Hal, as usual, had passed out in the bedroom, Dorothy begged Jimmy to take her to the Roosevelt Hotel where she could hide until the birth of her child. But as she set down her suitcase in the hotel lobby to sign the register, she realized how her stealthy exit, once made public, would ruin Hal's reputation. She put down the pen, apologized to the clerk, and taxied home.

The parties on Tenth Street resumed without respite, often beginning at five in the afternoon and lasting through Hal's naps into the night. Dorothy, literally fighting for her sanity, countered his guests with friends of her own. On the evening of June 19, 1930, the sitting room and the adjacent dining room were overflowing with devotees of Dorothy. It was a dinner in honor of H. R. Knickerbocker, the young man she had chosen to assume her post in Berlin when she had left to marry Hal, and his pretty redheaded bride, Laura. Hal, who must have had his own source of liquor, was staggering drunk, while the others revolved around the punch bowl, filled with tea and juice lightly laced with liqueurs. Dorothy relished the tenor of the evening, reminiscent of her gatherings on Händelstrasse in Berlin. Her guests argued incessantly about politics and told stories of their adventures, hilariously abortive and unexpectedly grand. By two in the morning, Dorothy, exhausted and huge with child, was mercifully left alone to sleep. But by four, her labor pains were coming hard and fast. She pleaded with Hal, still hopelessly drunk, to take her up to the Woman's Hospital on 110th Street. After a phone call to her doctor, he finally consented. Their baby, Michael Lewis, was born before dawn.

She and Hal had been sure that they were having a girl, but Michael was not a disappointment. Dorothy adored her blue-eyed baby with his fuzz of golden red hair. The only peeve had been the boredom of gestation and the humiliation of birth. "A woman must be gravid, like an animal, until the unseen forces command the delivery," she told Jimmy the next morning. The human womb was no different from that of a cow or a horse. "This is barbarous and utterly unworthy of those wise and great men who rule our universe," she teased. Radiant in her pink silk nightie, she bellowed, "I protest!" She and Jimmy broke into laughter and Dorothy rang for the nurse. In an imperious tone, she roared, "Bring in the child."

CHAPTER 7

A COLD WIND

A cold wind blew past me. . . . I felt my bowels
as a moving snake, my skin seemed to slip and
then writhe back to where it had been. Then
there was the sense—almost the sound—of the
rent veil.

—REBECCA WEST, *A Letter to a Grandfather*

LONDON, 1931

It had been twenty years since Rebecca had abandoned the stage for
her pen, but she was still the mistress of self-imagery; she could play any
role required with panache and pageantry. But at the ripe old age of
thirty-eight, she was a bluestocking all the way. Fortunately, Rebecca
had married the right man. Henry was an art aficionado who shared her
desire for social legitimacy and material comfort. Moved by a common
vision of the way life ought to be, Rebecca and Henry worked hard to
support their desire for status and luxury. True to their vows, they were
partners who had left old prototypes behind. They pooled their money,
shared expenses, and nourished each other's independence.

While Rebecca remained in London, Henry resumed his ambassado-
rial role for Schroders bank, traveling to Germany and throughout the
Continent, often for weeks at a time. They spent many nights apart, yet
their warm, chatty letters chronicling their daily lives dispelled their
loneliness. When Henry was in London, they enjoyed each other's
company—laughing and chiding, walking and dining, attending the theater and the cinema, visiting museums and reveling in the quiet beauty of
the home that Rebecca had crafted. They were not only lovers, but

friends; they called themselves "Ric and Rac," bound like the canine brothers in a French comic strip. A far cry from the wild and rebellious Jaguar and Panther, Henry and Rebecca were domesticated and loyal creatures seemingly content with a conventional upper-middle-class home life. The essential male-female contention she had experienced with H.G. dissipated in the face of their common humanity. They needed and trusted each other. Henry was the problem solver, the rock, the nurturer; Rebecca was the spiritual and intellectual force that infused their lives with meaning.

Henry was profoundly grateful. In July 1931, only eight months into their marriage, he redrafted his will, leaving all his money to Rebecca upon his death, requesting only that she support his mother. A letter accompanied the will, which would remain unopened until the appointed time:

No words can express what I owe to you. All the best that life gave me until I met you, all generous thoughts and efforts, seemed to find their true value in whatever ability they gave me to understand you and to love you. If ever you should feel lonely or disheartened I hope you will recall how when I was lonely your work recalled me to the ideals and enthusiasm of my youth and gave me a strength not to compromise. Your Ric

Rebecca had earned her freedom; Henry's love permitted her to craft her days, choose her friends, and work as hard and as long as she pleased. Yet, their posh London lifestyle required that she pay a price more dear than expected. She wrote to her American friend and mentor Alexander Woollcott that "she [had] sold herself into bondage" for £20 ($100) a week writing two six-hundred-word columns called I Said to Me for the *New York American.* Well endowed with Rebecca's fine eye for details, her columns were conversational musings on contemporary lifestyle, social issues, and culture, along with a smattering of observations on the European political scene. Self-reflective and thoughtful but rarely profound, the columns afforded her little satisfaction beyond the hope that they would finance her fiction. To augment her income, this once radical socialist agreed to write a weekly literary column for the *Daily Telegraph,* an established Conservative Party organ. For fifteen guineas, or about $76, Rebecca had orchestrated her own triumph of money over politics.

She wrote to her sister Winnie in February 1931 that she was writing her columns and overseeing the renovation of their new Mayfair flat at 15 Orchard Court, which was exhausting. She had never worked so hard in her life.

"I must say," Rebecca said, "[it is] as lovely a flat as I have ever seen. . . . It is, full of light, not like this dark hole." Several months earlier, Rebecca had moved out of Onslow Gardens to a flat at 94 Queen's Gate. Onslow, she wrote, had been barely large enough for her and Henry, let alone Anthony. Besides, she wanted another servant. She was going "mad," she wrote.

Finally, in March, after four months of renovation, the long wait was over. The flat, perched on the top floor of a steel and concrete five-story high-rise, built on the ruins of eighteenth-century mansions, was akin to the lofty apartments on Park Avenue that looked out over Central Park and the East River in Manhattan. One observer remarked that "the whole of London, from Piccadilly to St. Paul's, roll[ed] away from the windows, a glorious panorama of roof and spire angles sheathed in a dove-blue mist."

Much like Onslow Gardens, the interior was a study in green—sea green, apple green, silver green—with a touch of seashell peach. But Onslow paled to the grandeur of the new décor. The carpets were thick and lush, the curtains were billowy taffeta and flowing brocade, and the glass-topped mahogany tables and silvered mirrors refracted the skylight, giving the rooms the feel of a garden sanctuary in the midst of an urban wilderness. A concrete symbol of her aesthetic vision, the flat's furnishings were a finely tuned synthesis of old and new.

Rebecca's move to Mayfair was transforming. If the depth of her sacrifice measured her desire for the visible accoutrements of wealth, then her flat was a psychic necessity. Having weighed the comforts of the moment against her serious literary goals for the future, Rebecca had chosen the former. She was willing to become a hack journalist and to write reviews for a Tory newspaper in order to live in the style of a Park Avenue matron—a pretension she had once loathed. She was radiantly happy. Gone was the darkness that had followed her since youth; she was clear, uncluttered, and quick to laugh.

Before he returned to school in October 1931, Anthony, now seventeen, stayed in the new Mayfair flat. Its majesty, so alien to their past, confirmed everything he had come to believe about his mother; her self-indulgence, vanity, and lust for the material had found its voice in their home. To compound his disgust, the stranger who was his mother's husband siphoned her attention, leaving him to vie for tidbits of affection. Anthony felt like an outcast, an intruder—a burden. To Anthony, Henry was nothing more than a mannequin of gentility, a well-informed buffer whose task it was to seduce him into a friendship long before he had earned it. Unaware of their financial arrangement, Anthony felt certain that his mother had married Henry for his money. Why else would she spurn his father for this pretentious and boring gentleman with the pasted-on smile?

In effect, Rebecca's marriage to Henry had silenced Anthony, leaving him to sort out his tangled emotions alone. And this despite Henry's visit to his school and H.G.'s supposedly renewed interest in acting like Anthony's father. As usual, Rebecca was blind to Anthony's unhappiness, and he, in turn, chose not to tell her of his academic failings. As a result, when he returned to Stowe in October and was asked by the headmaster to leave by Christmas, the news shocked his mother. His refined manners and manly stature, along with his passion for painting and boxing, had convinced her that he was finally coming into his own. Rebecca's young friend Pamela Frankau, a gifted writer and a confidante of Anthony, had warned her of his academic trouble in the spring. But with her usual paranoia, Rebecca had seen it as Pamela's attempt, in league with Anthony, to evoke her sympathy at precisely the moment she felt settled and content. For years Rebecca had harbored fears about the limitations of Anthony's intellect, but to hear them confirmed by the headmaster of a second-rate school was more than she could bear.

H.G. had little sympathy for his son. During Anthony's visit to his father in Grasse that Christmas, H.G. wrote to Rebecca that the boy was charming but silly, immature, and naturally lazy. Anthony had told H.G. that he was through with school; he wanted to paint and was in love with a girl he wanted to marry. He begged his father for understanding, but H.G. responded by launching a diatribe against Anthony's character. Enraged, Anthony countered with his own attack, calling him selfish, duplicitous, and manipulative. He vowed that he would never again be deceived by his father's fine words and generous promises; his mother had been right about him, after all. Anthony had counted on H.G. for affection and acceptance, especially now that his mother was married. Brokenhearted and alone, he returned to London.

H.G. believed that the core of Anthony's unhappiness was his illegitimacy. He wrote to Rebecca: "[Anthony] feels he is being thwarted, apologized for and forced into an attitude of genteel atonement. The first thing needed is to restore his self-respect. I don't know what is likely to happen to him if this idea of his being an Unfortunate Accident is rubbed in much more." Ironically, H.G. concluded, "I hope he will rebel outright. That would make a man of him."

But wasn't that exactly what Anthony was doing? And had H.G. not done the same as a youth when he decided to study chemistry, dashing his mother's hope of his success as an artisan? Was H.G.'s own self-doubt so profound that it prevented him from realizing that Anthony's professed anti-intellectualism veiled his son's sadness at disappointing him? Could he not see that taking any other stance would have doomed Anthony to fight a losing battle? H.G. was a world-acclaimed genius, a literary giant; to pursue an academic or literary career would render his son a competitor, exposing him to further derision and shame.

Upon Anthony's return to London, H.G. wrote him a letter that virtually severed their ties. He had been willing, he wrote, to "concern myself with your affairs. . . . Apparently now you want to be left to your mother (with whom you have temperamentally much in common.)" Feeling powerless, H.G. had turned away just as his mother had forty years earlier. Like Rebecca, he was unable to turn insight into self-understanding or separate his own needs from those of the people around him.

No longer constrained by H.G.'s demands, Rebecca hired an eminent scholar to tutor Anthony. Although he made progress, Anthony failed the entrance test for Oxford. In the spring of 1932, Anthony fell into a deep depression, and Rebecca worried that he was suicidal. A prominent Viennese Freudian psychiatrist, Hans Sachs, confirmed her fears. Depression, he believed, was inward deflection of rage at the love object; suicide, therefore, was a form of ultimate revenge. Sachs was hesitant to initiate therapy with Anthony while he was in this state of crisis. He wrote to Rebecca in July 1932 from New York: "He is high strung to the point of danger in his emotional as well as his intellectual activity. In other words to keep him out of harm's way would be my aim more than to do positive good." Transference—that is, if Anthony were to come to regard him as a trusted father figure—would be, Sachs believed, the key to his progress. If Rebecca could not find another psychiatrist with whom he could form a satisfactory rapport, Sachs suggested that Anthony follow him to Boston, where Sachs was to assume a professorship at Harvard in the fall.

In late September, Rebecca's concern for Anthony outweighed her reluctance to let him go. With great apprehension, she and Henry accompanied him to Southampton, where he sailed for America. But Anthony and Dr. Sachs's silence during the subsequent weeks unnerved her. To compound Rebecca's anxiety, at nearly forty, she thought she was pregnant. Henry was thrilled by the prospect of a child, and for his sake, she feigned happiness. But in truth, she shuddered at the thought of the responsibility. Her forays into journalism had already set her career back, and while she had managed to produce two well-received short stories since her marriage, once again she felt cheated by the specter of motherhood. The idea of another child conjured up old rage and resentment, and yet the thought of depriving a man who had been so selflessly dedicated to her evoked profound guilt.

When the pregnancy was revealed to be ectopic, Rebecca's relief was tinged with sadness. The news had dashed Henry's hopes of ever having a child of his own. Compelled by her obstetrician to have a therapeutic abortion and a hysterectomy, Rebecca knew she had robbed Henry of the chance to be a parent forever. To make matters worse, the hysterectomy threw her into premature menopause, sapping her strength and straining her nerves, which were already stressed to the breaking point by Anthony's depression. Steady and selfless, as usual, Henry tried to console her. He whisked her off to Switzerland for a holiday in the hopes of distracting her, but even he couldn't exorcise her demons. By November, it had become clear that Rebecca could no longer function. Consumed by old fears of dependence and helplessness, she had several fainting spells; the demons seemed to be taking over. With Henry's encouragement, she checked into a sanatorium, Bad Weisser Hirsch, near Dresden, Germany.

When she had contracted tuberculosis as a young girl, Rebecca's six months at home had been a watershed; she had gained perspective on her teachers and herself, she had been free to read and study as she wished, and her long woodland walks had given her strength and confidence. Armed with that memory, Rebecca embraced the hope that the beauty of the forests, lessons in German, and daily psychotherapy would restore her health and lend insight to the root of her childhood and adolescent fears.

Rebecca knew in her heart that she had brought Anthony into the world while pinning her hopes on the illusion of H.G.'s constancy and then had abandoned him when the burden of his care thwarted her needs. She had found it easy to glaze reality with fantasy; blithely, she had blamed H.G. for Anthony's depression, washing herself clean of moral complicity. But how many times had she wished Anthony away? How many times did his very existence enrage her? And there was another question she intuited but hadn't the knowledge to ask: Did Anthony have his grandfather's (or her own) predisposition toward an intractable mental disorder?

In Henry's eyes she saw a reflection of the woman she wanted to be; his love was proof of her goodness and integrity. But the abortion, while therapeutic, resonated with her past, stoking old fires of resentment and opening the possibility of losing Henry. He deserved a child, not the terrible burden of her illegitimate son. And yet, she relished the absence of a life in her womb and the freedom from motherhood it implied. She was out of control, overcome with self-recrimination, and frightened not only that Anthony would take his life, but also that she would take her own.

Frantically, Rebecca pummeled her doctors at the sanatorium with questions, laying out Anthony's symptoms and begging them for answers, hoping to ease her anxiety and lessen her guilt. But it was a fruitless effort from the beginning. The only way out was to do exactly what the narrator of her 1928 story "There Is No Conversation" had suggested: Send a "searchlight into the uncomprehended parts of [one's] soul . . ." and look into the mirror of truth. Instinctively Rebecca sensed that the knowledge would tear her apart.

Furthermore, she was ashamed. No one other than Henry and H.G., and perhaps her American friend Fannie Hurst, knew the reason for Anthony's absence —not even her sisters. She wrote to Winnie that Roxburgh, the headmaster of Stowe, had encouraged Anthony to study art at the Sorbonne and he had taken a leave to go to Paris. Unable to relinquish her claim on victimhood, she was at war with herself. This encounter with coexistent good and evil, this "battlefield" within her mind, as she would call it, would crystallize her theory of human nature and drive her work forward.

It was six weeks before Dr. Sachs would write another letter to Rebecca. Complaining of illness and overwork, Sachs wrote "Mrs. West" a letter dated November 21, 1932, in a semi-legible scrawl:

> The strength of [Anthony's] fixation to you has not become, I believe, quite tangible to you—just because you were the object. In fact he was, even before his hostility to his father flared out, quite unable to feel interest/:sublimated love/: for any man. Men meant to him schoolboys and masters i.e. separation from you. . . . His two present occupations—painting and boxing—mark the transition. His physical health and general appearance have greatly improved since I saw him the first time. . . . I hope that Weisser Hirsch will do everything for you that can be desired.

Rebecca had informed him that she, too, had had a breakdown, and the good doctor had been gentle. But he would not let her escape the truth. She could no longer blame H.G.; Anthony's premature separation from her at boarding school was a prime cause of maladjustment. This diagnosis, however, seemed to fall on deaf ears. All that Rebecca heard was that Anthony was not going to commit suicide. Although she was soothed by Anthony's progress, she needed to hear it from him. Henry tracked him down in New York City, where he was staying with Rebecca's friend Emanie Sachs (no relation to his psychiatrist). Perhaps Anthony, also ashamed, had told Emanie that he was away on holiday and that there was no need to inform his mother. In any case, her dear friend found him not only charming but in need of no special mothering. After speaking with Anthony, Henry requested that he write his mother a letter.

Within a week, it arrived.

"We are adept at misunderstanding but I feel so much improved since this last month that I don't think I shall find it so easy to misunderstand you again," he wrote. "You are a greatly loved Pussinger though in the past I have sometimes seen you through a glass darkly."

Anthony's profession of love and forgiveness, his assumption of responsibility for his misunderstanding, and his faith in the unfolding of their relationship implicit in his quotation from Saint Paul, were an elixir to her spirit. Upon receipt of this letter, Rebecca determined that she was ready to go home; the crisis appeared to be over. At least for the moment, her faith in life was restored.

In September 1931, before the bottom had fallen out of Anthony's life and her own, Rebecca had received a letter from Virginia Woolf, publisher of Hogarth Press, a small independent company owned by her and her husband, Leonard, that published poetry and fiction along with books and pamphlets on national and international social and political issues. Woolf had put a bold question before her: "Do you think that you would possibly consent to write a letter in our Letter Series?" Rebecca, she noted, could write a letter to anyone about anything from any perspective she wished. Woolf concluded with a personal comment that was certain to flatter her: "I urge this on you not only in my capacity as publisher but as an admirer who actually drove 8 miles the other day to buy a copy of The Daily Telegraph in order not to miss your article. This is not an effort I am in the habit of making, but a proof of the great admiration with which I read your work."

The admiration was mutual. In an article in *The Bookman* written in 1929 called "Autumn and Virginia Woolf," published in 1931 as part of a compendium of essays called *Ending in Earnest*, Rebecca wrote of Woolf's genius, honesty, and courage.

Deeming Woolf's long essay *A Room of One's Own* the most important piece of feminist literature yet written, Rebecca praised Woolf's insight into notions of feminine chastity and submission, socially imposed financial dependency, and the fragility of feminine genius.

It is not surprising that Virginia admired Rebecca's literary criticism; they shared experiences and principles. As women born at the end of the Victorian era, they were part Jane Austen, that is, closeted observers of human behavior, and part Gertrude Stein, avant-garde innovators of language and culture. Their visceral experience as women in a male-dominated society and their knowledge of the feminine literary tradition rendered them keen observers of the human condition; their intellectual acuity gave them the tools with which to break the mold. In short, they lived at the nexus of old and new; fear and courage; cowardice and heroism.

Realistic assessors of their time and place, they relied on male mentors to nurture and propel their literary careers but were suspicious of the men who loved them. Aware of their extraordinary talents, they assumed the role of gadflies on the body politic, articulating the social injustices of women who could not speak for themselves.

Like Rebecca, Virginia believed that patterns of thought, individual and collective, could be deduced from the conversations and actions of ordinary people in the course of their daily lives. They both piled detail upon detail, observation upon observation, to document the organic process through which sympathies are formed and insights are revealed. The notion that life, and the literature it spawned, were governed by unfathomable mysteries was at the heart of their visions. While Virginia was a craftswoman of great economy capable of packing punch into brevity, and Rebecca had a meandering diffusive style, both found simile and symbol, analogy and allegory, essential to their writing.

Their work goes to the heart of issues that still baffle and confuse the most sophisticated twenty-first-century minds, despite scientific data that illuminate the functioning of the female brain. Do women pursue professional paths other than those of their male contemporaries because their psyches are hardwired differently? Or does the prevailing social construct determine the choices they make?

Rebecca gladly accepted the Hogarth Press assignment. She would be paid the sum of £25 upon publication and 10 percent of the royalties. Just months earlier, £25 would have been a hefty sum, equal to nearly $500 in today's currency. But by the end of 1931, England was deeply in debt; the English gold standard had been abandoned, and the pound was devalued by 20 percent. Unknown to Rebecca, the Hogarth Letters Series was proving unviable; hers would be the last letter commissioned. She began to outline her thoughts, but it would take a year before they would crystallize.

With Anthony on the path to recovery, Rebecca could devote herself to her journalism. She wrote her columns in the morning by hand, then typed them in the afternoon and mailed or delivered them to the newspapers for publication. While she loved the process of crafting essays and novels, refining her ideas and thoughts with each draft until the flow and meaning of her words reflected her intent, she found the deadlines of journalism limiting and frustrating. Nonetheless, she submitted her articles on schedule and cherished the leisure to write fiction. Henry came and went as usual, and their lives resumed an even pace.

But something had changed—Henry seemed distant and less affectionate, no longer responsive to her sexual advances. At first, she brushed her feelings aside, assuming it was just another episode of paranoia. Chastised by her friends and her sisters for being overly demanding, she wondered if Henry needed more affection than he expressed. Perhaps, beneath his veneer of compassion, Henry had resented her loss of his child; perhaps she had neglected her appearance and was no longer attractive. But her attempts to indulge him, fix her hair, revamp her wardrobe, and lose weight were fruitless. Unable to regain Henry's affection, she began to doubt his fidelity. A mutual acquaintance told her that she had seen him at a bar with a woman "dancing" on his lap. Rumors began to proliferate that her selfless husband, her father-savior, and her loving friend had a penchant for young starlets and dancers.

The scenario was painfully familiar. Her impoverished, emasculated father had betrayed her mother and their children by having serial affairs with younger women. H.G., not out of poverty but out of lust, had virtually abandoned his wife and their children for the affirmation and companionship of younger, smarter women. Now the one man she had trusted had deceived her. But, she noted, he was acting out a fantasy the opposite of H.G.'s: He was sacrificing the intellectual and faithful woman to the "mindless prostitute." No matter the fantasy or the emotional impulse, she was convinced that men were not made for constancy.

Rebecca knew that she had a choice to make. She could maintain the veneer of marriage or seek a divorce. Unlike Dorothy, Rebecca was not held prisoner by her husband's demands. Henry was neither cruel nor abusive. Rebecca had the freedom to live and work as she wished; she could profit from continuing to pool their resources. And despite everything, she valued his friendship and depended on his rational approach to Anthony to keep their relationship in balance. What was wrong with this arrangement as long as they both understood the rules? Or, better, the lack of them?

Once again, Rebecca vowed to make her way alone. The dross of her life began to slip away, and the "truth" surfaced with volcanic force. Rebecca's reason for writing had always been to understand herself, her place in the universe, the psychodynamic of the mind, and the human condition. She seized upon the letter commissioned by Hogarth as a laboratory for exploration.

She called it *A Letter to a Grandfather*. It was at once a confessional, a philosophical analysis of religion and spirituality, and an allegory for understanding the rise of totalitarianism. The grandfather to whom she wrote was fictional, but her insights were real and honest. The purpose of her letter was to share an experience intrinsic to the lifeblood of their family: an epiphany that stripped reality of illusion.

The letter has the feel and trope of poetry. Its beauty of expression, tempered by her knowledge of social and religious history, defies categorization. Slowly, she peeled away the skin of the ordinary to pierce the core of life. Musing on the meaning of acquisitive behavior, she wrote that shopping is a means of self-deception designed to ensure her safety and fool her into feeling productive. It is meant to shield those obsessed with material possessions from the onslaught of external evil. If delusion is the devil, then where is the divine?

In an attempt to examine the nature of her spirituality, she traced the evolution of church doctrine and moral philosophy through the lens of her male ancestry—architects, artists, scientists, and philosophers. Her fictional thirteenth-century ancestor, an architect, had erected an abbey just at the moment that his own faith and that of his contemporaries had begun to crumble. The Godhead and the Trinity, Rebecca explained through the voice of the granddaughter, are symbolic efforts to assume control of a senseless barbarian universe—a vestige of primitive man. Man stands alone, she concludes, and moral philosophy, literature, and nationalism assume the aspect of religion that fills the vacuum in a godless world.

She tells her grandfather of her visit to a carnival in a marketplace as an allegory for the intrinsic sadism and evil in human nature, and an extension of national character. As the hurdy-gurdy music wafts overhead, the granddaughter stops at the merry-go-round, fascinated by the tall Negro ride-master. He appears, at first, elegant and strong, dressed in an evening suit of black and scarlet, wearing a top hat, and holding a cane with a gold crook handle. As the girl watches, his eyes turn savage and his gestures become sadistic. The ride-master represents the duplicity of fascism: its seductive strength that obscures its perverse savagery. As the ride-master proves, no one can escape one's historical moment or the role one is condemned to play.

Not content to leave it there, Rebecca probes further to reveal the delusion of love. Love between men and women, as well as parent and child, much like the Godhead, she writes, is nothing more than a comforting illusion. Love cannot assuage the cruelty of the universe. Rebecca concludes that evil is within; as with individuals, so with nations. Communists in Russia and their international acolytes cannot be excused for embracing evil: "They are in love with cancer, they want the love of man for his kind to be eaten away like the love of man and woman by sadism and masochism."

Neither Virginia nor her husband could have been pleased by her allusion to Communist cruelty. As zealous socialists, they were adept at denying the ruthlessness of Stalin.

A Letter to a Grandfather depicted a future in which Rebecca and all mankind would be stripped of illusion. She had established herself as a visionary who perceived the reality of the human condition; as an observer of the political scene, she knew that her ability to see through the charade of self-determination was both rare and privileged. The European peoples, war weary, confused, and lacking the strength to endure the chaos and uncertainty of democracy and freedom, she warned, would succumb to the false divinity of dictators. The fruits of her epiphany in the context of her relationships were yet to be seen, but the thematic literary implications were immediate.

True to her prediction that the renunciation of delusion would set a person free, Rebecca had energy and time for everything. Writing her columns was just a means to an end, and her end was writing books and novels worthy of enduring.

Building on her belief in the interdependence of culture and intellectual history depicted in *A Letter,* she traced the evolution of the church from A.D. 200 to 400 in a biography of Saint Augustine. Rebecca infuses his life, some have said, with Freudian theory and autobiographical themes that obscure the context of his vision. Through him, she reasserted her spiritual vision rooted in but not defined by Christianity. While she disdained his devaluation of art and human pleasures that seem belied by the sensuality of his prose, she saw his kindred perception of human duality and frailty as the further affirmation of human evil— the source of the rise in fascism and communism across Europe. Her biography of Saint Augustine personified the vision she had presented in *A Letter to a Grandfather.*

More prolific than ever before, Rebecca could hardly get her words out fast enough. But the novel she desperately wanted to write—a dramatic portrayal of the failure of her marriage—seemed to elude her. She wanted to explore the corruption of values by power and money, and the inevitable psychological and sexual antagonism between men and women that parades as love. The new novel was to be fact stripped of illusion: Romance was a myth; marriage was a capitulation to a social and physical construct. She would title it *The Thinking Reed,* a reference to her favorite quote from Pascal's *Pensées:* "Man is a reed, the most feeble thing in nature; but he is a thinking reed. . . . If the universe were to crush him, man would still be more noble than that which killed him, because he knows that he dies and the advantage which the universe has over him; the universe knows nothing of this."

Perhaps fearful of destroying her marriage, which had reached a state of tolerable equilibrium, she couldn't summon the courage to complete it. Hoping to gain perspective and break the block, Rebecca traveled to Washington, D.C., to write articles for *The New York Times.* When she stopped in New York before her voyage home, she chose not to visit Dorothy. In 1933, masks were crucial to both Rebecca's and Dorothy's survival, and many of their friendships fell by the wayside. These were sad and lonely times for both women; neither had the capacity to empathize with the other; each preferred to borrow strength from her intellect. Yet their intellects assumed different forms of expression. Dorothy was riveted to the here and now of journalism, while Rebecca turned inward to study the psychodynamic of individuals and relationships, seeking truth and relevance through the study of biography and history.

Both were intensely spiritual beings. Rebecca saw glimpses of cosmic mysteries that proffered the hope of a better world beyond this, but she was resigned to the harsh cruelties of earthly life. Dorothy, however, while scarred by her marriage to Lewis, drew consolation from her core Christian beliefs. Individuals expressed the will of God; wisdom and salvation were gained through suffering, and despite the existence of evil in men and nations, good would ultimately triumph.

Rebecca had no such faith or optimism. The universe was indifferent to human frailty; the veil was irrevocably and eternally rent. These insights made her a brilliant writer but a lost and frightened woman, thoroughly dependent on her own intelligence and the vacillating loyalties of family and friends.

Soon, Rebecca's American feminist friend Fannie Hurst, the one woman whose mind, if not talent, was as incisive as her own, would tire of her foolish whining. Her sister Lettie, forever stunned by Rebecca's success, would tire of her constant denigration; Winnie, unable to distinguish between the woman and the mask, would throw her hands up in frustration. And while Henry would continue to be an attentive friend, he became increasingly distant and decidedly cold.

CHAPTER 8

A GOOD WIFE

A good wife, who can find? She is precious far
beyond rubies. Her husband trusts in her, and
he shall lack nothing thereby. She renders him
good and no evil all the days of her life.

—ADAPTED FROM PROVERBS 31:10–12

AUGUST 1930

At thirty-seven, Dorothy had given birth to a child. Her fear that
the baby might be defective melted into joy when she saw his face. Michael was the spitting image of Hal, with round blue eyes, red-gold hair,
and a long, narrow face. His birth made the family circle complete; if
only she were certain that she loved his father.

Between feedings, when Hal was asleep, or perhaps passed out drunk,
Dorothy's loneliness gave way to nostalgia, and with it the sense that
Michael should have been Bard's son. Dorothy would not let the fantasy
of her beautiful prince go, despite her contempt for his character and
betrayal.

On impulse, Dorothy wrote Bard a letter:

*Have you heard, Joseph, that I have a son? Somehow, I think you may
know, and I hope you are happy with me, for no one knows better than
you what his coming means to me. . . . I should so like to see you,
Joseph. I have the little snapshots of us taken on the Semmering in
June 1921. How very long ago, how very young we look—and how
very close, in memory, it seems.*

I hope you will love my little son. . . . He is so new and the world so old. When he smiles, I should be happy, and I want to weep. Please love him and be his friend.

It had been a quiet summer; life moved easily from day to day. The "long, low mountains, its dark and sun-splashed woods, its green uplands," raised her spirits and permitted her the illusion that she, Hal, and baby Michael were an ideal family. They worked; they swam; they played tennis; they dined alone or with friends. Anyone who had visited them in Vermont that summer saw a congenial couple, insulated from the realities of domesticity by two nurses, a cook, groundsmen, and a driver. This appearance of tranquillity was not accidental. It was something she cultivated to ward off her profound sense of defeat.

Hal's joy at the birth of Michael had been fleeting. The cry of a child, especially his own, was intolerable. While Dorothy would attribute Hal's emotions to selfishness, it was just as likely that the birth of another son made him sad. His memories of childhood neglect and abuse, along with the feeling of helplessness Michael's cries evoked, were the demons he had struggled against all his life—a life he wasn't certain was worthy of passing on. Perhaps, as well, there was a touch of jealousy; Michael, along with Dorothy's work, was a competitor. Surely Hal must have known how much having a child had meant to her, but his desperate need for her love compelled him to destroy anyone that got in his way—even his son. It is also possible that Dorothy's own needs had blinded her to Hal's and prevented her from understanding the depth of his loneliness.

The answers were moot; the truth no longer mattered. Dorothy moved the baby and his nurses to the farmhouse across the valley; the separation refueled her desire to find her way alone. A bond had been severed that neither she nor Hal could fully understand nor repair, and when it came time to lock up the Vermont houses for the winter, they agreed to give up their apartment in New York and move to a suburb within commuting distance to the city.

Their decision to rent a home in Westport, Connecticut, was a hard-fought compromise. Hal loathed the city, yet a manicured rendition of rural living offended his sensibilities. Dorothy, the "country girl" at heart who needed to be surrounded by natural beauty, also needed the possibility of escape. Situated on Long Island Sound, an hour and a half northeast of New York City, Westport offered the perfect solution. Frank and Esther Adams, professional associates and personal friends, owned the house. Frank was a political columnist for the *New York Herald Tribune,* as well as a poet and a scholar.

"This is partly for the baby, partly for Red . . . partly for me," she wrote to a friend. "Esther's house has an oil-burning furnace and is easily accessible to N.Y." But Dorothy was being coy. It was more than a house with a furnace. The property was called Indian Hill, and the rolling meadows and woodlands bordering the sound were visible from every window of the house. It was large enough to accommodate them all, without their having to see one another. And Westport was not just any suburb. In the 1930s, it was an affluent Protestant enclave with extraordinary public and private schools, cultural institutions, and exhibition halls. It was seen as an extension of Greenwich Village, a cradle of genius that attracted artists, writers, editors, actors, sculptors, and painters. People such as F. Scott Fitzgerald, Bette Davis, Lillian Gish, William S. Hart, and Gene Kelly lived in town. The Lewises could mingle with their peers or retreat into solitude.

They would not go to Europe together, she told her friend. "Together" was not a word they used much anymore. She would leave the baby at home with a "perfectly efficient nurse" and go to Germany and Russia for a quick trip—perhaps two months. That is, although "a couple of months away from my very little boy . . . seems brutal. Brutal I meant to me." In truth, it was not difficult to leave Michael, since the price of staying was mental atrophy.

"My brain has gone phut. That's due to domesticity—(which is unavoidable)." She needed time away on her own to sort out her problems, she continued. Besides, she lied, Hal was working quietly, and he was "crazy about [the baby]."

Dorothy had published nothing since the previous year and she was aching to get back to work. Her appetite for people and life could not be corseted in a nursery. She had to break out; she had no choice. It was a matter of survival.

But Dorothy's plans for escape were foiled by an event no one could have anticipated. On the morning of November 5, 1930, Hal, still lounging in his pajamas, received a phone call at their home in Indian Hill. As an inveterate mimic in the habit of making phony calls in perfect dialect, he erupted into laughter when a man with a Swedish accent told him that he had won the Nobel Prize. He thought it was his friend Ferd Reyer, who, much like him, was a prankster. "Oh, yeah?" he replied. "Listen, Ferd, I can say that better than you. Your Swedish accent's no good. I'll repeat it for you. You haf de Nobel Brize." The permanent secretary of the Swedish Embassy, Erik Axel Karlfeldt, was stunned. He called an American to the phone to confirm the news. Stupefied, Hal slumped back into his chair. The Nobel was a prize he had always coveted but had never dreamed of getting. And to be the first American to win the prize for literature was beyond belief.

Composing himself sufficiently to make a call, he dialed Dorothy's number in New York, where she was drumming up assignments to write articles while in Europe. For a habitual receiver of phony calls from Hal, Dorothy's response was predictably snide. "Well, I have the Order of the Garter," she quipped. But when she heard the mix of bewilderment and joy in his voice, she knew he was dead serious. Though hardly a great man, Hal was a world-class writer—this had been obvious to her from the very beginning. She was pleased that Hal, despite his self-abuse and the suffering he had inflicted on her, was finally getting his due. It had been a long time since she was proud to be Mrs. Sinclair Lewis.

Havoc ensued as the news resounded over the wires. Hal was inundated by reporters demanding interviews and photographs, and was forced to face some harsh accusations. For starters, he was seen as a hypocrite. When Hal had been offered the Pulitzer Prize in 1926 for *Arrowsmith*, he had refused the honor. He had known too much about the backroom politics at work; the jurors had first wanted to designate the award for *Main Street*, but the president of Columbia University, Nicolas Murray Butler, vetoed the decision on the grounds that the book was out of sync with the publisher's idealistic intent. With childlike glee, Hal had written a disdainful reply, debunking juried prizes that anointed the "best," and the holier-than-thou stance of the judges, confident that they could discern the merits of one book above another. In refusing to acknowledge the value of his darker satire, the Pulitzer committee, he believed, had defeated the American idealism they had set out to preserve by putting a muzzle on serious social criticism. Novelists, he predicted, would play it safe, glazing reality with a Puritanical veneer, for fear of losing the marketplace value that celebrity would bring. No one at the time had taken him seriously; his response was chalked up to opportunism. He could easily dispense with the $1,000 prize and used the moment to make a self-serving statement. But in 1930, the Nobel Prize was worth

$48,000, or $627,000 in today's currency, and a ticket to lucrative contracts. Annoyed, he faced a press that saw him as mercenary. But as far as he was concerned, they could go to hell. The prize was his and the least he could do was to pretend he had earned it.

Reminded of the days before their marriage, Dorothy and Hal wrapped themselves around the forthcoming event as if it marked a new beginning. Their bond thickened against the onslaught of international publicity and critical attention, good and bad. While their families and friends inundated Hal with telegrams and letters of congratulation, many of his colleagues in America were outright dismissive. Academics had never taken his work seriously, and members of the conservative establishments, such as the American Academy of Arts and Letters, seemed to speak with one voice: Lewis was a commercial hack who wrote novels subversive to American values and had won the award by pandering to the anti-Americanism of Europe, a belief not too far from the truth.

Most American writers were either bitter or silent. The exceptions were Eugene O'Neill, whose darkness seemed to emanate from the same place as Lewis's, and Willa Cather, on the short list of possible winners, who was disappointed but admiring of his work above the others, including Edith Wharton, T. S. Eliot, Ezra Pound, James Joyce, and Theodore Dreiser.

In Paris, the young Ernest Hemingway wrote to a friend that the prize should have gone to Pound or Joyce, but at least giving it to Lewis eliminated the "Dreiser menace." By 1930, Dreiser's literary realism had morphed into social and political radicalism. As an advocate of Soviet Communism, civil rights for American Negroes, and his own anti-Semitism, he was a menacing blight on the literary community. Hemingway and his fellow expats believed that the era of American realism and satire was over; the postwar upheaval demanded more than linear narrative; conventional notions of morality, gender, and class had been shattered. New forms of language and expression begged to be born. In their eyes, Lewis had become irrelevant.

The response from abroad was virtually nil. Only one Frenchman, Paul Morand, chose to congratulate him, and only one Englishman, his friend Hugh Walpole, offered his praise. Although the British press was laudatory, most British writers were outraged. In London, Rebecca, who held her tongue out of respect for Dorothy, would later make it clear that she thought his winning was ridiculous. She had never admired the man or his work, and if the jurors were dead set on giving it to an American, any other candidate would have been preferable.

During the intervening weeks, Hal vacillated between arrogance and humility; his neurosis had a way of bending everything to its will. He despaired that the prize would be "the end" of him. From now on, he said, he would have to produce novels up to some mythical standard, and he was certain that his best work was behind him. It hurt him to think that his colleagues agreed. But even as anxiety gnawed at his innards, Hal's lifetime of honing a persona of devil-may-care nonchalance carried him through. His crown, he knew, was thorny at best, but he saw it as revenge against his detractors and a consecration of his work bejeweled in the aura of Old World majesty. The joy of victory would never be his; no amount of glory could fill his emptiness. Salvation lay in acting the part, and with Dorothy's help, he stiffened to the task.

Her years in Europe served them well; her knowledge of international customs and protocol was an undeniable asset. For all his fame, Hal was remarkably provincial. Dorothy made him a list of professors at the University of Uppsala, Swedish writers of renown, and Swedish princes and princesses most apt to attend. She taught him how to bow and comport himself with dignity. This time it was she who played Pygmalion to his Galatea. For the moment, it seemed there was hope for their marriage after all.

Knowing he would be a representative of America, Hal surrendered to his dormant vanity and resolved to abstain from drink, practice his manners, and subject himself to the excruciating pain of electrically removing the pustules that had ravaged his face. Dorothy, too, went for an overhaul, extracting ten teeth in honor of the occasion. In bed for two weeks, nursed by her friend Rose Wilder Lane, she organized their trip and helped him with his speech. Hal agonized over every word, and she agonized with him. He wanted to be gracious, yet honest and real; it was no small task to rein in his bitterness and give American literature its due. Dorothy was keenly aware that despite every effort on his part and hers, Hal could easily act like a fool. God knows, he could get drunk and spew vulgarities at the king; the world might even applaud his fall. The question remained, would she be there to catch him?

Polished, buffed, and well rehearsed, they left Michael with Rose to supervise the nurses, and sailed for Sweden on the SS *Drottningholm* on

November 29, 1930. Ten days on the rough seas left Dorothy feeling ill, but Hal kept his promise to stay on the wagon.

If one knew nothing of Hal except for his speech, one would have a fair portrait of who he was: honest, humble, lonely, grateful for every ounce of good fortune, yet at peace with neither himself nor his profession; scathingly critical, yet effusively magnanimous, determined to speak his mind on the current state of American literature, yet poignantly aware that his moment in its mainstream had come and gone. It was his finest hour—the one time when he was fully himself. Dorothy, in no small measure, had managed to bring him there, and she must have felt the infinite joy of finally carrying him with her to the heights. From the beginning, her impulse had been to become the vehicle of his spiritual ascendancy. While Stockholm was not Mount Moriah, she had facilitated her husband's climb to the pinnacle of literary success.

When his time came to speak, he pulled his tall, lanky frame out of his seat and ascended the podium. Lamenting the irrelevance of the creative artist in a society that valued science, technology, and material wealth above letters, he assumed a wistful Wordsworthian tone. The writer, he said, was alone in a room, "assisted only by his integrity," while the world of commerce moved swiftly around him, building skyscrapers and banks, trading bonds and stocks, making motor cars and luxury goods to nourish the ever-growing lust of a consuming public. With a socialist's disdain for the great "Lords of Manufacturing," who had devised governing institutions and regulations, he mourned that the realm of literature roamed wild. There were no objective standards, no representative institutions, no social refuge, no dukes or cardinals to sing its praises or feed its soul. The academics had their bastions and universities, but "American professors like[d] their literature clear and cold and pure and very dead." Living writers were wealthy but alienated—convinced that what they produced did not matter. Graciously and generously, he honored his colleagues in America, even his enemies, whose work had been ignored or passed over by the American Academy hopelessly mired in their "doctrine of death"—Theodore Dreiser, Sherwood Anderson, H. L. Mencken, George Jean Nathan, Eugene O'Neill, Edna St. Vincent Millay, Carl Sandburg, Fannie Hurst, Edna Ferber, and Upton Sinclair, among many others. Although he was only forty-five in 1930, he spoke like an old man who was passing the torch to a younger generation, men and women under thirty who had come of age after the war and who would bring honor to American literature.

"I salute them," he said, "with a joy in being not yet too far removed from their determination to give to the America that has mountains and endless prairies, enormous cities and lost far cabins, billions of money and tons of faith, to an America that is as strange as Russia and as complex as China, a literature worthy of her vastness."

Except for a bow too far from the king, his speech to the Swedish Academy and the preceding formal festivities went off without a hitch. One can hear Dorothy's voice through his, converting his anger against the establishment into a springboard for commentary, riddled with optimism, American idealism, and faith in the future. But he spoke of his vocation as if it were an incurable disease, at once alienating him from humanity and evoking the same bitter self-righteousness he abhorred. Harcourt Brace had given the press a truncated version of the speech, distorting the underlying philosophy. Nonetheless, both he and Dorothy were hugely relieved. He hadn't stumbled or fallen dizzy with drink, nor had he, as some had predicted, goosed the princesses.

When the Lewises arrived in Berlin, the Knickerbockers gave them a Christmas party, during which Hal did a hilarious imitation of a Nobel Prize winner accepting in Swedish. But by midnight, Dorothy was doubled over in pain. The house physician at the Adlon Hotel diagnosed her condition as a ruptured appendix. What had begun as a stomachache on the ship had become a life-threatening illness requiring immediate surgery and hospitalization. Hal devotedly stayed by her side throughout her illness and then spent ten days with her in the Thuringian Forest, 155 miles southwest of Berlin, to rest. Dorothy had to postpone her trip to Russia, and instead stayed in Berlin, while Hal, proclaiming over the wireless his love for America despite his ties in Europe, promptly left for England. He saw no reason to stick around while she and her journalist friends jabbered in German about the world "situation." Besides, he was scared. He could never live up to the Nobel Prize, and the most convenient scapegoat was his publisher, Alfred Harcourt. He had arranged to meet Nelson Doubleday in London to negotiate a deal.

Finally alone in her own milieu, Dorothy set out to see what seemed like the harbinger of a new Germany. The National Socialist German Workers' Party, headed by Adolf Hitler, had just won six million votes and 107 deputies in the Reichstag, sending paroxysms of fear throughout

Europe that a fascist dictatorship was on the rise. The Allies had turned their heads as the Weimar Republic, in violation of the Treaty of Versailles, had spent hundreds of millions of dollars to sustain military operations.

When she had left three years earlier, Germany was still staggering from the human and economic losses of the war—shabby, demoralized, and entrenched in debt, dependent upon the self-interested generosity of the Americans, the British, and the French. In the winter of 1931, while it was still beleaguered with war reparations it found impossible to pay, especially now that market prices had crashed throughout the world, there was a palpable feeling of regrowth and optimism. The broad boulevards of Berlin overflowed with cafés, theaters, cinema palaces, and spanking new train stations leading to state-of-the-art undergrounds. Dorothy later wrote a series of articles for *The Saturday Evening Post* about the discrepancy between what was and what appeared to be. Parties vying for control had fractured the republic, and in order to keep it intact, the government had to pay them off, accruing hundreds of millions of dollars in deficits. Furthermore, Weimar had built a lavish cultural infrastructure to quell the Socialists and paid stipends to farmers and industrialists to silence the Communists, even as one in six people was out of work and hungry. At the same time, the German government exported machinery, food, and basic goods out of the country.

In Berlin, Dorothy witnessed fifteen thousand people crowded into the Sportpalast to hear the leader of German fascism in the north, "the wizened, club-footed and frenetic Doctor Goebbels," Hitler's right-hand man. The hall was ablaze with banners in the old imperialist colors— hooked black crosses encircled in white on a deep crimson backdrop— calculated to evoke militant nationalism. As the spectators took their seats, a brass military band boomed louder and louder and then fell to a hush as the lights grew dim. Fifty young bare-throated, white-shirted men rose at the wave of a conductor's baton. In melodic rhythm they recited exhortations of hope for a future when German men would once again be free, well fed, and unfettered by debt, and when the millions who died fighting for the fatherland would reclaim their honor through the work of the living.

To the sound of thundering applause and rolling beer kegs, the lights lifted and the music blared as shock troops stepped with military precision, ushering in "the little man with the dragging foot . . . the perverter of Nietzsche, the champion of the blond beast, the under statured and dark [Joseph Goebbels]." The spectators sprang from their seats, arms outstretched in the Fascist salute, shouting in unison, *"Heil!"*

For two hours, ignoring all the government policies that had led to the economic despair, Goebbels ranted about Germany's spiritual and financial enslavement to the rapacious victors out to "exterminate" their great nation with war reparations. He was smart, ruthless, and a great orator who passionately served a man he considered to be the Messiah. The confluence of these traits produced a mesmerizing effect; everyone sat at the edge of his seat. But what troubled Dorothy most was that those who listened, shouted, and saluted were not the street beggars or the visibly impoverished, but middle-class men and women, shabbily but neatly dressed—physicians, lawyers, and civil servants—people who by all accounts should have known better. They could have engaged in a principled fight in the best tradition of German culture and history, but had succumbed to confusion and fear. Together with the unemployed, disillusioned leftists and the young, they mistook the lust for power for the promise of a healthy and vigorous future. Truth, to paraphrase Mark Twain, was best swallowed by men who were full of optimism. Ironically they were the ones the huge Weimar bureaucracy had set out to protect and the first people to suffer once the Depression took hold. It was impossible to reconcile the gleam and wash of the city with the penury of the people, the national wealth with the economic debt. Germany, Dorothy concluded, was the "best out-fitted poorhouse on earth."

Dorothy wanted to interview the charismatic Austrian turned party leader, but despite the hospitality and support of her friends, whose contacts gave her access to people and news in and around Berlin, she was thwarted in her attempts to meet with Hitler. After three months abroad and with more material than she could use for her assignments from *The Saturday Evening Post*, Dorothy decided it was time to go home to Westport and her son. In London, Hal scavenged to find a subject for a new novel, but he was desperately unproductive, lonely, and lost. How he missed and adored her, he wrote, especially because he was "loafing—looking inside myself to see what I'm like." Wondering if he could live up to the Nobel Prize, he had wanted to stay in Europe longer in the hopes that traveling to new places would inspire him. At the last minute, however, his loneliness overtook him, and they sailed together on the *Europa,* docking on the West Side of Manhattan on March 4, 1931.

Reporters and photographers met the Lewises as they descended the gangplank. In the wake of his Nobel speech, Lewis had apparently riled old enemies and created new ones. As one observer astutely pointed out, it was easier to criticize Lewis than to deal with the Depression.

Rose had minded Michael well; he was healthy and strong despite his parents' long winter absence. At eight months, his babble had morphed into sound patterns and he was struggling to lift his lanky frame upright. As soon as everyone was settled, the family circle collapsed into its old habits. Hal was rarely at home, for many reasons, mostly trivial or fabricated, yet he never stopped declaring his unmitigated love. Dorothy was left alone to write, which meant that she was more productive but also had more time to think about her future. While she knew that her marriage wasn't working, she was not ready to let it go. Not insincerely, she, too, pledged her love to Hal in frequent letters. Perhaps, in the end, love in absentia was the best they could do. Neither truly had a home growing up, except perhaps in some shadowed corner of childhood imagination. A failing marriage was better than no marriage at all.

For Dorothy, the true reason for sustaining the relationship was Michael. When he was born, she had had one prime criterion for choosing his godparents: They must have a loving marriage. She had chosen Letitia ("Tish") and Wallace Irwin, because they were a rare couple; "courteous and friendly" to each other and "simple and worldly." They loved their children and they loved life. Michael, she told them, did not need money, fame, or social status. But neither should these be seen as signs of "disgrace" as they had been in her fundamentalist home. She wrote: "I want him to be modern, that is to say, at home in his own age, and not frightened, or paralyzed by it, but confident that man can comprehend, master, and use, anything that man can invent." No one and no system of governance was "worthy of profound reverence; that reverence should be preserved for life itself, and for those human spirits who have made life more intense and luminous." Love, a good marriage, reverence for life, and intensity of commitment to make life better—these were what she wanted for Michael. These were the ideals toward which she had striven.

As she wrote her impressions of the new Germany for her first piece in *The Saturday Evening Post*, spicing her observations with history, tradition, policy, statistics, and predictions, she realized it was exactly this perspective that the German people—the great German people—had lost. She wrote her pieces to make Americans see what comes of distorting democratic values, bartering justice and law for hero worship and pageantry. The Germans, she concluded, lacked the moral courage to face the truth. As it was for individuals, so it was for nations. She called the piece "Poverty De Luxe," and it bolstered her reputation as a thoughtful and serious journalist whose courage trumped fear and compromise.

While Hal still floundered for ideas, Dorothy spent the spring writing more articles, at ten thousand words a clip, for the *Post.* Once this work was done, however, she saw no reason to remain in Westport when she could disseminate her knowledge around the country. Another European speaking tour would turn her reputation to fame.

As summer approached, they once again moved back to Vermont, replaying the charade of a family at peace. In late August 1931, Dorothy wrote in her diary: "These days are beautiful. Hal is on the water wagon for the last five days, and, as always, never more charming, brilliant, or good tempered. It is already almost autumn. The trees are turning and the blue and gold days have begun."

September brought them back to New York, but their bohemian Village days were over. They moved into a plush new apartment on Manhattan's Upper East Side, 21 East Ninetieth Street, Carnegie Hill, home to upper-middle-class professionals and legendary private schools. As much as Hal thought Dorothy should stay at home with Michael, who was now more than a year old, she couldn't bear it. Quoting from Goethe, she wrote: "Two souls, alas, dwell in this bosom." It was a romantic metaphor for a basic truth: Her work or, by extension, her personal ambition, came first. She had to go back to Europe; *The Saturday Evening Post* had given her a platform to make her voice heard.

When she docked in England, it was as if she saw the trappings of power and the follies of her past with new eyes. She had tea with Lord Beaverbrook, who as editor in chief of the *Daily Express* continually cranked out orders like an admiral and barked into the phone as if he were trying to steer a crumbling empire. "A great play-actor is Beaverbrook," she wrote to Hal. She also saw Joseph Bard and wondered how she could have found him interesting or good-looking. For the first time, perhaps, she was able to reconcile Bard's betrayal with the reality of the man he had become. In the years since their separation and divorce, he had accomplished little; his sweeping philosophical and historical aspirations had come to naught. His sybaritic lifestyle had taken its toll; he looked dissipated and prematurely old. And, after so many years, she had lunch with Rebecca. Dorothy wrote to Hal, "Rebecca sends her love, and was nice, and looks happy for a change, and I go to dinner tomorrow with her husband who is with Schroeder, the English Bankers who are most heavily interested in Germany." She planned to milk him for information on the economy, she wrote.

It was a tribute to Rebecca's thespian gifts that she was able to fool her friend. The bottom had just fallen out with Anthony, and she was about to have her hysterectomy, now rumored to be a surgical ruse to disguise an abortion. Her life was fast being pulled from under her; yet, her veneer of gaiety remained intact. Her impulse for self-preservation ran deep, and her habit of repression had given way to the comfort of fantasy.

But then, Rebecca and Dorothy had this habit in common. Dorothy ended a letter to Hal with a paragraph that must be admired for its self-deception: "I'm having a grand time, because I like this job, and all the time I feel nice and warm inside because you and Mickey are back home and I'll see you in a short time. I love you for your funny face and funny ways. I love you period. D"

Hal sent her a letter that must have crossed hers in the mail: "Every-time [Mickey] comes back from the park and is wheeled into the hall he cries 'Mamma.' I don't think you need to worry about his remembering you when you come back." Just who was crying for "Mamma"? Hal's patience with Dorothy was running low. He was struggling to understand his place in his marriage, and, like most writers, he channeled his frustration through the medium he knew best; he was writing a new novel. It was to be the story of a suffragist. "I am going to do something that is important," he wrote to her. He would write about a woman whose "great tragedy, of course, is that she has never found any man big enough not to be scared of her." It was, in short, the tragedy of a narcissistic female whose freedom impelled her to neglect the men who needed her.

His letter greeted her at the Adlon Hotel when she arrived in Berlin. She was stunned by its clarity. Suddenly, she saw herself in an internecine struggle between her twin souls. She wrote in reply:

As you know, I should be infinitely proud if anything I might have said, or thought, or been, or felt should excite your imagination. Be-

ing the wife of an artist is in this sense disappointing. That one real-izes, and increasingly, that the artist is something enclosed in himself. All one's heart's outgoings, one's tendernesses, the sudden breaths of understanding serve a very ephemeral purpose (if any) to the artist's work. Often I think the greatest service I could do you as an artist would be to leave you—to make you free, & free from both domestic blisses & domestic responsibilities . . . and I wish in my heart very often that I could abandon the world for you. But—it's no good—I can't. The world was my first love and I have a faithful heart.

CHAPTER 9

THE RIDDLE OF THE UNIVERSE

> If during the next million generations there is
> but one human born into every generation who
> will not cease to inquire into the nature of his
> fate, even while it strips and bludgeons him,
> some day we shall read the riddle of our uni-
> verse.

—REBECCA WEST, *Black Lamb and Grey Falcon*

LONDON, 1934

High above Portman Square, Rebecca listened to the wireless as Ramsay MacDonald, the prime minister of Britain, rambled in platitudes. His efforts to assuage the fear of impending war belied reality. Adolf Hitler, the new chancellor of Germany, had suspended civil liberties and staged anti-Jewish riots; Joseph Stalin, Soviet dictator, had ruthlessly starved seven million Ukrainian peasants and purged his ranks of opposition; and Benito Mussolini, prime minister of Italy, had published his Ten Commandments of Fascism, robbing his people of basic freedoms. Paroxysms of tyranny and nationalism raged across the Continent, yet the ailing old socialist was still doing his pacifist dance.

Rebecca understood the price of peace. The poison of fascism filtered through her own life, eviscerating Henry's career and the financial sinews of their fleshless marriage. His job at Schroders hung on the thread of his distant Jewish heritage. A willing instrument of Hitler's rise, the banking baron Kurt von Schröder had become an adviser to Hjalmar Schacht, the minister of economics, and to the board of the German Reichsbank. As a reward, Hitler had appointed him to the post of SS senior group leader—a passport to his inner circle. In effect, Schröder's bank had become a microcosm of Nazi ideology. Men whom Henry had come to trust, who had run the business on standards of decency, now not only espoused the language of anti-Semitism but also cleansed their own ranks of blood-tainted Jews. Henry, who worked on the City of Berlin project, despised the bank's Nazi ties and argued with the baron's director when he dismissed his Jewish colleague. The last thing Schröder wanted was a self-righteous Jew who wouldn't keep quiet.

All over Germany, in every seat of intellectualism—Berlin, Munich, Frankfurt, and Dresden—tens of thousands of books were burned. In Berlin, Dr. Goebbels recited a dirge before every oblation: "In the name of the noble human spirit, I deliver to the flames . . ." The works of Bertolt Brecht, Albert Einstein, Sigmund Freud, Heinrich Heine, Thomas Mann, Erich Maria Remarque, and others were burned at the foot of the Reichstag. Deemed traitors and degenerates, alien journalists, or blood-thirsty Jewish intellectuals who dared to illuminate the shadows of Hitler's messianic mystique, these authors and their works were considered the enemies of blind submission. "Wherever they burn books," proffered Heine, "sooner or later they will also burn human beings."

While Hitler burned books, Rebecca wrote them. She sought the filter through which doubt gained purpose and nihilism turned to moral fortitude. Her old gods were dead. Christianity, she believed, was worse than paganism; its ethic of suffering and self-loathing squeezed the joy out of life. She believed she was not alone; there had to be others equally disillusioned. Once again, she would pin love under her microscope. If she couldn't sustain it, she would understand why.

At forty-one, Rebecca still oozed sexuality, all the more attractive with her derisive stance. She struck one male observer as a femme fatale with a "Dionysiac mane of black hair and bright eyes that always seem[ed] to hold a touch of mockery in her glance." He was right that Rebecca delighted in ridicule, but he missed the source of its fierce animation: She was sensitive to the point of paranoia. To deride was to deflect vulnerability. To write was to wield power and control. From ten in the morning until one in the afternoon, Rebecca sat in her study with a series of writing tablets, one designated for each draft of her book and a pen to suit each stage of its evolution.

If love was, as Rebecca believed, a universal agent of doom, why did she, and all humanity, crave this masochism? Her soon-to-be-published collection of short stories, *The Harsh Voice,* would establish axioms of relations between the sexes. Rebecca was certain that physical passion trumped moral principle, love, and intellectual and emotional needs; enduring love, often based on the unmet needs of one's childhood, required commitment, self-reflection, acceptance, and the practical responsibilities of creating a home—the most primal longing of human existence. The book Rebecca was now writing, *The Thinking Reed,* was to be a tour de force, a single narrative that coalesced all these ideas in the evolving consciousness of one woman.

Behind closed doors, Rebecca gathered her thoughts on the fragility of mankind. If suffering was intrinsic to the human lot, then consciousness, she implied, was the salve for pain. Only the intellect could dispel illusion.

Rebecca's new novel was a psychological comedy of manners that studied the interior landscape of men and women as they played out desire and delusion in pursuit of love. Dedicated to Henry, it was written to enable Rebecca to think her way through her marriage. Henry's sexual betrayal had poisoned her life, forcing her to face the world with a lie. She needed to understand the dynamic of his mendacity.

To that end, Rebecca presented a series of relationships, delicately engineered by a young American widow abroad, Isabelle, who some said was the thinking woman's answer to Henry James's heroine Isabel in *The Portrait of a Lady.* Within the context of social conventions, extramarital and connubial, Rebecca studied the verbal and behavioral signals that connote intent—a look in the eye, a touch of a hand, a way of walking, and the cut of a dress. Isabelle was a "manipulator" who ultimately comes clean, aware that pretense is the path toward self-destruction. In the process, Rebecca revealed the power of feminine passion, the decadence inherent in wealth, the humiliation hidden in the sanctity of marriage, and the value of salvation through self-reflection and honesty. Knowledge was the path to deliverance, but knowledge without morality was the source of gratuitous evil.

Anthony was back. His suicidal convulsions quelled, he returned to London in April 1933. His breakdown had won him his war against H.G., a stipend of £14,000 per annum, and a sizable inheritance. Immediately, he spent £300 on a handmade set of toy trains, which he hid under his bed, knowing that his mother would disapprove. Rebecca had tried to alter the terms of his inheritance so that she would become the benefi-ciary of his share of his father's estate and thereby the gatekeeper of An-thony's folly. H.G. disapproved, doubting her motives. Anthony's financial irresponsibility would remain a font of contention between An-thony and Rebecca. No matter how generous Rebecca was, Anthony's need for possessions seemed insatiable. This was a form of satisfaction she knew too well. As she had written in *A Letter to a Grandfather*, it was armor against vulnerability and a deal with the devil.

Rebecca and Henry tried to convince Anthony that his inheritance would be insufficient to support him, and counseled him to plan a practi-cal career. Anthony, pursuing the only career he had ever coveted, en-rolled in the Slade School of Fine Art, an institution that had nurtured some of the great painters and draftsmen of England. While her son's ambitions were hardly practical, Rebecca admired his paintings, espe-cially those with religious themes. But Anthony's discipline did not match his talent. Within months he dropped out; no one was permitted to question his decision. Lettie was quick to denounce Anthony's antics when she heard about them. Rebecca, as usual, protected his reputation, but she had little doubt that her habitually intrusive elder sister was right.

Sullen and recalcitrant, Anthony refused to work. He remained con-vinced that his mother had married Henry for his money, and while he hated her upper-crust social pretensions, he would have been content to feed off her funds. No matter how many times Rebecca told him that she had earned every tuppence on her own, Anthony was fixed on his moth-er's desire to do him harm by depriving him of his rightful share of her fortune. It was a tug-of-war between self-professed "victims," each of whom felt misjudged and abused. And who was to say who had suffered more? The abused child abandoned by her father and betrayed by men? Or the illegitimate son of neglectful parents? At least Anthony had lived comfortably, Rebecca reasoned. And who hadn't struggled in childhood? Angry at the happenstance of fate, neither was willing to assume the re-sponsibility that would heal themselves or each other.

As usual, Rebecca showed a stoic face; the vicissitudes of her life de-manded a mask. Henry, she wrote to her friend Fannie Hurst, was "a queer creature, naïve in some ways and full of genius in others . . . full of unusual knowledge and understanding." His position at Schroders, however, had become a "death dance," she wrote. Nonetheless, they were "getting on well." Rebecca betrayed no hint to Fannie or anyone that Henry had been unfaithful or that Anthony was anything other than "an entertaining and loveable creature." Any trouble that Anthony caused, she wrote, was due to his relationship with H.G.

After Rebecca returned from the States in the spring of 1935 to report on Roosevelt's New Deal for *The New York Times,* she fell ill. This time it was her appendix. H.G.—Jaguar as she still called him—visited her in the hospital. Quite the dandy in his well-tailored suit, he bounced into the room on his tiny feet, graceful despite his expanding girth. One might imagine him kissing her hand and sitting beside her, each welcoming the presence of an old friend. Now that H.G. had settled his financial responsibilities toward their son, their rows about Anthony were a thing of the past. For the first time since Anthony's birth, they had the luxury of enjoying each other. Perhaps they gossiped about the London literary scene and spoke about one another's work. He wanted a copy of her collection of short stories. No doubt Germany and Russia dominated their minds; both were deeply distressed about the political upheaval and disgusted by the cowardly paralysis of British politicians. But as the conversation drifted toward the personal, pretense reigned. Henry was fine, just fine, and Anthony—well, he was occupied. It is doubtful H.G. lingered over his love life, or she on the pain of her loneliness. Satisfied, they must have parted affectionately, promising to keep in touch and meet thereafter outside the hospital walls. Perhaps his visit was an act of kindness to a woman who had borne him a son—the kindness of which he had deprived Jane, regretting it only after she had died.

After H.G. left, Rebecca wrote him a note of gratitude. She thanked him for his visit and told him that the operation had left her a "trembling reed." But Rebecca was concerned about him. His mistress Odette, furious that he had tossed her out like a common hussy, had written an article about his sexual vanity for *Time and Tide.* Strictly in friendship, Rebecca offered H.G. a life raft. She was on the board of the magazine and was willing to push for a retraction on his behalf. It was a sad article because it rose from despair. Odette had dedicated five years to him and his work, isolated in the mountain town of Grasse above the Côte d'Azur, while H.G. had shuttled back and forth to Jane at will. Despite all this, Odette still felt that H.G. was the best thing that had ever happened to her. There was an element of truth in her piece that Rebecca could not deny. Ironically, it was an article she might have written herself, had she not possessed the gift of literary subterfuge. Rebecca would always have a soft spot for Odette; she was a good and generous woman whose desire for love had generated abuse.

H.G., however, refused to be ruffled. He was totally consumed by his love for Moura Budberg, to whom he had returned after leaving Odette. After a PEN club meeting in Yugoslavia, he hopped a train to meet Moura in Salzburg. Her warmth and charm completely overwhelmed him, and while she wouldn't consent to become his wife, she agreed to live with him in London.

Rebecca and Moura had much in common. Beautiful and smart, they were both fiercely independent, accomplished, and ambitious. They were intuitive and stalwart, funny and penetrating. There was one difference, however, that elevated Moura to H.G.'s long-sought "lover-shadow." She understood the primal dynamic of H.G.'s mind. Moura could play both mother and goddess, and instinctively knew how to modulate her roles. She could become "Jane" or "Rebecca" on the turn of H.G.'s whim, and he could play genius, little boy, and old fool with impunity. She could indulge his moods without feeling inferior, and thereby earn his adoration. Moura lavished her brilliance and vitality on him, and through her eyes, H.G. became all he wanted to be. It was a game Rebecca was never able to play. She had been too young, needy, and ambitious to see anyone's needs beyond her own.

Moura and H.G. had come together in maturity. Their child rearing was past, their spouses were gone, and the frenzied work of their youth was over. Moura had been the secretary and lover of Maxim Gorky for twelve years, earning her living as a translator and a British and Russian double agent. Her affair with a high-ranking British official in Russia, Robert Lockhart, and with Gorky, Stalin's literary strongman, along with her frequent unexplained absences, had made her double life apparent to those who knew her. When H.G. had returned to Moscow to visit Moura in 1920, she told him that she had been planted on him in the same way she had been planted on Gorky. He had tried to convince her that integrity was essential if she wished to remain a part of his life. But she countered disdainfully that constant hardship had taught her that surviving another day was worth any price. He left her, fearing she would sully his already tarnished reputation, only to find her again in the 1930s radiating the same emotional and intellectual magic she had more than a decade before. This time, H.G. didn't resist. Nearing seventy, he was reconciled to accepting Moura on her own terms.

By contrast, there was no magic in Rebecca's life. An affair with a surgeon, Pomfret Kilner, who had operated on her cystic breasts, had ended badly. A tryst with the Spanish count Andreas Bilbesco, whom she had first met in 1930 in Paris, also ended in disappointment. And Henry's joust with Schroders had ended in defeat. When Henry's uncle Ernest died in 1935, leaving him a hefty inheritance—£140,000 to £170,000, or approximately $775,000 in 1935 currency—both Henry and the bank found it the perfect rationale for their parting. A man of means at a time when most were impoverished, Henry withdrew to London to reinvent himself. But with time on his hands and money no object, he grew more lascivious, propositioning showgirls and even their employees—anyone who would deign to listen. Henry's growing penchant for fine wine and chocolates appeared part and parcel of his appetite for women. Rebecca began inventing methods of escape.

The prospect of a new book and the research it would require offered an opportunity to travel. In 1934, while convalescing in a hospital during an illness, Rebecca had turned the dial on the radio to find "music of a kind other than [she] sought, the music that is above earth, that lives in the thunderclouds and rolls in human ears and sometimes deafens them without betraying the path of its melodic line." They were the ominous rumblings of an event that resonated with impending disaster; sounds that dwelled in the imagination, evoking fear. The king of Yugoslavia had been assassinated on the streets of Marseille. When she dared to extrapolate the melody forward, Rebecca came to believe that war was inevitable. She saw the king's murder as revenge for the anti-Semitic policies of the Russians—revenge that took the form of retaliation against all Slavs. There was a "fountain of negativism," she would write, that sprang forth in central Europe, and the venomous spray was not merely nationalistic or racial. "Life, under any label, is the enemy," she wrote. Gratuitous evil was walking abroad.

In 1935, while Henry played the aging Don Juan, Rebecca traveled to Finland on a lecture tour commissioned by the British Council. Armed with a firsthand knowledge of Nazi and Italian fascism and cognizant of

Russia's ruthless aggression, she interviewed Finnish leaders to assess the fortitude of the fledgling democracy caught in the crosscurrents between two hegemonic dictatorships: Russia and Germany. Now, with Nazism on the rise, the country had become a target of German expansionism. Rebecca saw this looming threat as an omen of the political and moral turmoil that would plague the free countries of Europe. She planned to return to write a book about this "small nation, like a beset soul, caught between the powers of Light and Darkness."

The moment for personal concerns had passed. The political landscape of Europe was rapidly changing, and the stakes were too high to luxuriate in writing on matters of love. It was her duty, she believed, to set aside her fiction for the study of social and political history. Always the pessimist, Rebecca now became the voice of doom. If civilization were to survive, she reasoned, we must learn "the riddle of our universe." What made her think she was fit for the task? Confident of nothing except her intellect, having reached the point in her personal life when work was her only source of satisfaction, she felt impelled to seek the roots of impending disaster. In her biographical study of Saint Augustine, she had revealed him to be "the first modern man," capable of understanding the evil within the human psyche in times of political upheaval. She also found him emotionally crippled, self-doubting, and morally frail. She had studied her contemporaries and must have concluded that she was as flawed (and as worthy) as any of them. As she had written during the Great War in *The New Republic* and had reiterated in *The Strange Necessity,* Rebecca believed that objectivity in the service of art was crucial to human survival, especially during war; an artist with historical and cultural perspective could help the reader rise above daily hardships and pain.

Sheltered by gender, age, and economics from the painful realities of combat, Rebecca would use her intellect as her sword. It was to be her means of preserving democracy.

The end to another war appeared in sight. Anthony, now twenty-one, had decided to marry. At a Christmas party in 1935, attended by prominent sculptors, painters, and critics, he had met Katharine ("Kitty") Church. At first, Kitty had no interest in the gloomy, awkward young man, but he had stalked her for months until she agreed to marry him. Five years Anthony's senior, Kitty was a highborn woman of delicate beauty and a gifted painter. As the daughter of a misogynist father and an embittered, social-climbing mother, with a temperament honed by the need to survive, she was both a comrade against authority and a skilled, if blunt, instrument of salvation. Much like Rebecca at the same age, Anthony was yet to learn that no one could protect him from himself or assuage the scars of his childhood. Nonetheless, he saw Kitty as both a mother and a wife, and marriage as a means of nominal independence that would remove him from Rebecca's emotional grasp.

At their first meeting in Rebecca's Mayfair flat, Kitty was charmed by Rebecca's warmth and respect for her art. She felt unexpectedly welcome in the elegant and spacious home of her well-dressed and bejeweled future mother-in-law. Rebecca was sincere in her cordiality toward Kitty. She liked the polish of the well-bred young woman and found her pleasant to be around. But above all, she was pleased by Kitty's obvious affection for her son. Kitty was keenly aware of Rebecca's pretensions, of the way she played the grand dame with relish and ease. Nonetheless, Kitty appreciated the fine food and wine, and the gentility with which it was served. Rebecca would succeed that evening in disabusing Kitty of any sinister notions she might have had about Anthony's mother. Kitty's only wish was that the marriage would be approved by her own mother, a proud descendant of the Lyle family, known for their production of fine sweets and baking condiments. She was appalled that her daughter would marry the illegitimate son of a wanton woman.

Nevertheless, Kitty and Anthony's wedding plans proceeded. In March 1936, the wedding was performed by a justice of the peace and was witnessed by Rebecca and H.G., along with a few members of both families. Rebecca was relieved; H.G. was overjoyed. To celebrate he took them home to Easton Glebe for a lavish lunch.

The following year, Rebecca was sent by the British Council to lecture in Yugoslavia. It was there, where the Ottoman East met the Christian West, that she found the broad canvas on which to paint her drama of the pivotal moment when Nazi imperialism might mark the end of culture and civilization as she knew it. A country of disparate states whittled out of the Ottoman Empire after the Great War, Yugoslavia, consisting of Serbia, Bosnia and Herzegovina, Croatia, Macedonia, Slovenia, and Montenegro, had been a nexus of conflict for five centuries. Its history of internecine quarrels and its complex religious and political distinctions made it a perfect laboratory for observing, documenting, and re-creating Europe before the onset of war.

And so she began what can only be called a metaphysical odyssey: to discover the secrets of this violent land and perhaps reveal the course of her own destiny and that of the world. She cast herself in this effort as Everywoman, that is, every Englishwoman who dared to cross into the public sphere to contemplate the forces that determined her life. She believed, along with Virginia Woolf, that women must engage in a different kind of war than men—a war no less important for its lack of physical combat. Women's distance from the battlefield afforded them greater objectivity, the luxury of social and political analysis, and the time for self and national scrutiny.

The book was a semiautobiographical account of three trips she took to Yugoslavia at the request of the British Council—the first in 1936, which Rebecca made alone; her return in 1937 with Henry; and her final journey during the summer of 1938, after the ominous ease of the German Anschluss, reuniting Germany with Austria as the two countries had been under Hapsburg rule before the war. Political, cultural, and social commentary disguised as a travelogue, the book was based on her diaries written during these trips, in which she expressed her disappointment with her lovers and her ambivalence toward Henry, who had given her friendship but not sexual affirmation.

Throughout her tours, Rebecca remained terribly unhappy, yet she buried her sadness in the intellectual excitement of the adventure and the challenge of recording, understanding, and synthesizing all she learned and saw. In the final version of her book, Rebecca put her personal losses aside and reformulated the narrative as a husband-and-wife odyssey; male and female perspectives that enriched the thematic flow. While Henry, uncertain of the value of his wife's obsession, felt compelled to accompany her on a trip she portrayed as a seminal study of the role of culture, political history, economics, and gender in the life of a nation, for Rebecca, the journey was existential. Her distant Slavic ancestry seemed to murmur in her blood; she instinctively felt more at home in Yugoslavia than in England. Racked by loneliness and personal loss, she sought a simpler life connected to land and community. The book was an attempt to preserve the physical beauty and ancient dynamic of a kindred country on the verge of conquest, in the hopes that she might understand more about herself, human nature, and the will to survive.

As the narrator carries the reader through Croatia, Bosnia-

Herzegovina, Serbia, Macedonia, and Montenegro, Rebecca assembles a montage of facts, historical biographies, personal vignettes, and moral observations seen through the prism of social Darwinism and Freudian theory. She works like an archaeologist, unearthing the shards of Yugo-slavia's Greco-Roman, medieval, Ottoman, and Hapsburg history upon which the young nation had built its tenuous independence. A study of tribal peoples devastated by imperialism for hundreds of years who now faced the threat of fascist serfdom, Rebecca's book intended to link its past with the fomenting realities of the present, exposing the country's pulsing desire for self-determination and freedom.

For five years, from 1936 through 1941, the book, *Black Lamb and Grey Falcon,* became her obsession, consuming her mind and sapping her strength. Everything she had experienced and written before seemed a prelude to its pages. Love, God, religion, war, good and evil, artistic creation, man's place in the natural and divine universe—all rose and converged in Rebecca's mind in search of enlightenment. "Once I have done this book," she told Henry, "all my work & my life will be sim-pler."

The couple's journey (in actuality Rebecca's first) begins in Croatia, where they have secured a guide. Ironically, writes Rebecca, the Croats had assumed the racial attitudes of their oppressors, the Austro-Hungarian Empire, in their hatred of the peasants and Gypsies. Yet she sensed something hauntingly familiar in the country's topography, as if she had been there before. The contour and color of its landscape lived in her imagination, she wrote, like a private dream of a beloved home. Rebecca saw the face of her father, Charles Fairfield, everywhere, egging her on and intensifying her quest.

From Croatia they move on to Bosnia-Herzegovina, where "Rebecca and Henry" visit a marketplace filled with Muslim descendants of the Slavs who were converted by the Turks, sparking a discussion of female oppression and the lethal effects of imperialism. Calculated submission could make women free, while mindless submission is suicidal, Rebecca concludes. Women, in their acts of nourishing and begetting, play coun-terpoint to the male impulse for political machination; they are artist he-roes who enfold, caress, and humanize their men as they move ineluctably toward violence and war. Female conquest is different from male, she writes; a woman can conquer through weakness, beguilement, and sex.

But consciousness is key. Again and again, sexual metaphors of conquest and victimhood sweep through *Black Lamb and Grey Falcon*, mirroring Rebecca's own experiences, as she documented and measured the tribal leaders, peasants, and warriors who determined Bosnia's fate and created their national legacy.

In Serbia, the governing province of Yugoslavia, Rebecca exposes the dark side of femininity, wrapping it in a political framework. The wife of their guide joins "Rebecca and Henry." Her coarse manner and stereotypical mind make her a disturbing and demoralizing presence— both the epitome of female evil and the symbol of a great culture in decay. As a German nationalist, she is contemptuous of the Slavs, viewing them as barbarians useful only as Aryan slaves. Her husband is a Slavic Jew, and she eats away at his self-esteem until he, too, believes he belongs to a defective breed, evoking the contempt of "Rebecca and Henry."

In Serbia's capital city of Belgrade, Rebecca's observations move from the political to the philosophical and religious. She begins to see the deleterious effects of monarchy in the opulent display of government wealth beside the impoverished professional class. But her visit to Serbia also yields inspiration for the dominant theme of the book: sacrifice as a means of human salvation. "Rebecca and Henry" visit monasteries, one of which contains the mummified remains of Tsar Lazar, who led the Serbs to defeat against the Turks in 1389. The legend tells that Saint Elijah, embodied as a gray falcon, visited the tsar on the eve of the battle and asked him to choose earthly victory or eternal salvation. Lazar chose purification through defeat, condemning his people to five hundred years of enslavement. This legend becomes the basis of Rebecca's recurring condemnation of salvation through sacrifice, slashing Christianity at its core.

And yet, her act of condemnation is soon tempered by experience, as she moves southeast to the province of Macedonia. Even as Rebecca decries religious myth as masochistic and antilife, she encounters untainted Christian faith and devotion at her next stop, an Easter Sunday service. Unable to understand the language of the service, yet feeling the power and passion of the symphony of voices that worship there, "Rebecca and Henry" view the bishop as a conduit of hope, who lifts his flock of impoverished peasants toward dignity and spiritual transcendence. Rebecca was certain that this magical yoking of man and God that elicited prayer in search of transcendence was an important link between the simplicity of the past and the chaos of the present. And yet, she needed more.

On a vast sheep's field in Kosovo (discovered only on Rebecca's third trip), an ancient Christian rite of animal sacrifice offered the most poignant insight of her book. On the crest of a hill, overlooking the tomb of Saint George, Rebecca saw a rock covered in bloody putrescence. In the hope of conceiving children, barren women engaged in a priestly ritual of sacrificing lambs in the hopes that new life might spring from the death of innocents.

"It was a huge and dirty lie." It was dirty because it bathed infertility in sin and motherhood in the slime of gratuitous violence. "A supremely good man was born on earth, [Jesus] who was without cruelty, who could have taught mankind to live in perpetual happiness; and because we are infatuated with this idea of sacrifice, of shedding innocent blood to secure innocent advantages, we found nothing better to do with this passport to deliverance than destroy him." His crucifixion could not kill goodness. Goodness is immortal. The ethic of sacrifice, she concluded, was a theological ruse.

Her journey through this violent land had more secrets to yield before she was through. She had yet to find the principle that links what she describes as a "fundamental but foul disposition of the mind" with the evil that threatened Western Europe. For this, she looked to Montenegro, their final destination and the southernmost region of Yugoslavia, bordering the Adriatic coast. The Montenegrins are warriors who had vanquished the Turks, Albanians, Austrians, and finally their brother Serbs, who had sought to undermine their independence. But they have sacrificed human life along with their souls, she writes, trading independence for survival. Paralyzed by paranoia, they wallow in myths of self-glorification that became the means of their undoing. And yet, there were Montenegrins who wanted more: people whose lives had been destroyed by these myths who would not accept their fate unexamined.

And so the journey that began with the death of the Serbian king on the streets of Marseille ends with an old peasant woman who wanders a road that leads to the peak of the highest mountain. The Austrians have killed her husband and children; everyone she loves has been taken from her, and she depends on the goodwill of distant relatives. The woman, like Rebecca, is well fed but hungry—not for bread or gold but for meaning that might relieve the pain of her wounds. "I am not going anywhere," she tells "Rebecca and Henry" when they offer her a ride. "I am walking about to try to understand why all this has happened. If I had to live, why should my life have been like this? If I walk about up here where it is very high and grand it seems to me I am nearer to understanding it."

"If during the next million generations," muses Rebecca, "there is but one human being born in every generation who will not cease to inquire into the nature of his fate, even while it strips and bludgeons him, someday we shall read the riddle of our universe." Process, she concludes, is the path to salvation—not reason alone, but reason wrapped in imagination. It was no accident that Rebecca's redeemer was a woman, at once earthbound and ethereal. Although her weapons of inquiry were weak, wrote Rebecca, the peasant woman had refused to submit to the laws of man and nature. She embodied the consciousness of Pascal's "trembling reed," and by inference, so does Rebecca.

In the epilogue, a freestanding essay commissioned by the British Council, Rebecca applied what she learned about human nature, political and social oppression, and the longing for transcendence and salvation to bridge the imperial past with the fascist present. Nationalism and self-determination, she wrote, are birthrights. But the world did not run on reason. Hitler and Mussolini, "two embryos" in the womb of evil, propelled to power by postwar poverty, had seduced the masses with social services they had no money to sustain and had fed popular greed with the promise of military power and conquest. These demonic forces of death cultivated the tools of mass murder, and England, choking on the guilt of its Great War victory, refused to recognize their impending threat. Like Tsar Lazar in Serbia and the barren women of Macedonia, they had yielded to defeat like black lambs in the arms of priests, driven by the Christian fantasy of pleasing God with sacrifice and suicide.

Yet, she concluded, hope lies in art and reason. "Art gives us hope that history may change its spots and man will become honourable.

What is art? It is not decoration. It is the re-living of experience . . . so that its true significance is revealed. . . . If art could investigate all experiences then man would also understand life and control his destiny."

Spiritual survival lay in the courage to face and embrace the truth, and art was its handmaiden.

Written after France had yielded to Germany in what Rebecca saw as a fit of Christian martyrdom, and while German bombs were falling on London, *Black Lamb and Grey Falcon* hailed the honorable defeat of the Yugoslavians who had chosen resistance over peace through enslavement. As Rebecca watched the fires on the streets of London from high above Portman Square and listened to an aria from Mozart's *Marriage of Figaro,* she wrote of the heroism that made it possible for Greece, England, and Russia to prepare for the German onslaught. The Yugoslavians would not "buy salvation off an idiot God, they did not offer themselves up as black lambs to unsacred priests." While their leaders, willing to enslave their countrymen in exchange for peace, cowed to the fascists, ordinary citizens rose up in rebellion. They fought for their freedom, knowing they would probably die. They were the heroes who chose their destiny.

When *Black Lamb and Grey Falcon* was published in 1941, it achieved what *The Strange Necessity* had not. Hailed on both sides of the Atlantic as a masterpiece, it secured Rebecca's reputation as a serious writer. *Time* magazine called it "one of the most passionate, eloquent, violent, beautifully written books of our time." *The New York Times* described it as "the magnification and intensification of the travel book form . . . carried out with tireless percipience, nourished from almost bewildering erudition, chronicled with thoughtfulness itself fervent and poetic." In *The New Yorker,* Clifton Fadiman singled it out "as astonishing as it is brilliant. . . . It is also one of the great books of our time." Rebecca had achieved this all according to her own principles: romanticism tempered by reasoned inquiry; imagination tempered by fact and observation. The clarity of her prose and the lyrical beauty of her descriptions, along with her intent to grapple with essential issues, raised her travelogue to the level of literature.

The book sold fairly well, and although few readers could slog through its nearly 1,200 pages, its international coverage by the press influenced the debate of Allied officials. While her prejudices against Islamic culture and religion, her ignorance of Arabic language and idiom, and her pro-Serbian bias drew criticism, the majority of reviewers saw it as it was intended: a call to arms against fascism. Even today, it is considered the foremost book on Slavic history and culture and one that anticipated the Serbian-Bosnian war of 1992.

But even as Rebecca ascended to literary fame, the love and trustworthiness of those who needed her plummeted. Henry, working in the Ministry of Economic Warfare since 1938, was still massaging his ego with serial lovers. He lavished them with extravagant gifts and took them on trips to places that had recently been his and Rebecca's romantic haunts. Alternating between proud midwife of Rebecca's work and lonely, forsaken husband, he grew increasingly punitive, bedding even their mutual friends. Rebecca would later write, "Henry and I had always plenty to talk about, but I had nothing to feel about."

Anthony and Kitty, offended by Rebecca's anti-pacifist literary assault in her epilogue on the so-called effete and unpatriotic left-wing party with which they sympathized, became livid when she phoned them to say that she had bought them tickets on the *Queen Mary* to sail to America. Although Rebecca claimed that she was trying to protect them, they found her offer infantilizing and controlling. Anthony saw himself as a conscientious objector who would leave the fighting to others. Yet, he thought it was wrong to desert his country in a time of crisis. If his mother saw him as a coward, that was her problem. He would find a way to serve his country without harnessing a rifle to his chest. Rebecca understood the horror and devastation implicit in war but let him know that pacifism was not grounds for objection. Ultimately, Anthony saved face by working on a farm, which exonerated him from military duty. With this, the tension eased between them, but Anthony would never forget the moral contempt she had rained upon him.

As Rebecca had written, only part of her was sane; the other part conspired against her. And despite her riveting analysis of love, it still eluded her. "The cold truth about me is that I would have paid any price for love, and I had money in my hand and nobody would take it," Rebecca would write to a friend.

She would have to be content with the admiration of loving friends. Several months after *Black Lamb and Grey Falcon* was published, Dorothy wrote:

*[Your] book I think the greatest book published in the English lan-
guage in ten years. I have said so on numerous occasions in print. In the
hope that my words would reach your eyes. . . . Nobody but a woman
could have written that book, so personal and so scholarly, so full of
intuition and knowledge. And its epilogue is almost the only really
strong word that has been said on this war.*

*Can't you come to America? You would be a godsend here. I mean
it very seriously, and besides I miss you terribly.*

> *With all my love,*
> *Dorothy*

CHAPTER 10

THE FAITHFUL WARRIOR

I am widowed of an illusion. Because I am
tremblingly aware of the tragedy of the world
in which we live.

—Dorothy Thompson to Sinclair Lewis

BERLIN, DECEMBER 1931

As Dorothy's car rode swiftly down Wilhelmstrasse from the Adlon Hotel through the cold mist of a winter's day toward the century-old Kaiserhof Hotel a mile away, she understood why Hitler had chosen it as his headquarters. The street, named for King Frederick Wilhelm I in the mid-eighteenth century, had been the government center of the Prussian kingdom.

The expansionist vision of the soldier-king had suffused the pages of *Mien Kampf*. Hitler wanted nothing less than the resurrection of the Prussian empire; the political and military domination of Austria, Hungry, Poland, Czechoslovakia, Belgium, the Netherlands, France, England, and more—a kingdom to rival the Holy Roman Empire. He would begin by unifying Germany with the Deutsches Volk by reoccupying the territory lost to the Allies after the Great War, and restoring the purity of the Aryan race. Then he would make his move.

Finally, after seven years of waiting, she was about to meet the man who would be führer. With the expectation of garnering fifteen million votes in the March election, Hitler was ready to meet with foreign reporters. Dorothy Thompson was to be the first.

As she walked into the rococo lobby of the Kaiserhof, Dorothy was uncommonly nervous. Before she could take her smelling salts, his press attaché whisked her up to the fifth-floor hallway, where she was compelled to wait while Hitler conferred with an Italian minister. The ornately embellished decor made Hitler and his high-booted henchmen look more like thugs. On the way to his salon, the stone-faced Nazi leader walked past her with his brutish bodyguard, who resembled Al Capone.

Viscerally affected by their presence, she sensed that he and his henchmen were capable of living up to their reputation—terrorists and murderers who marauded the streets attacking their opponents.

While she waited, Dorothy had plenty of time to think. She had studied the style and substance of Hitler's speeches and knew that he had no qualms about lying in order to persuade "the masses," that he had conjured up deep-seated medieval myths about parasitic subhuman Jews to fabricate a scapegoat for the Allied victory in the Great War, and that he was prone to becoming "hysterical." Dorothy concluded that he had the mind of a manipulator and the spirit of a preacher.

She would write:

When finally I walked into Adolph Hitler's salon in the Kaiserhof Hotel, I was convinced that I was meeting the future dictator of Germany. In something less than fifty seconds I was sure I was not. . . . He is formless, almost faceless, a man whose countenance is a caricature, a man whose framework seems cartilaginous, without bones. He is inconsequential and voluble, ill-poised, insecure. He is the very prototype of the "Little Man."

As she watched and listened to the Nazi leader, the psychodrama began to unfold. Shy and cool at the outset, Hitler whipped himself into a frenzy, raising his voice to a crescendo, all the while banging his fist on the table to hammer his point. He spoke in a monologue, as if he were addressing an audience of thousands, and he seemed to be looking right through her. Cunningly shifting the focus of the meeting toward his own agenda, he sidestepped all but one of her questions. He carefully ignored queries about disarmament, foreign policy, and the details of his domestic plans, and declared that he would assume power legally, dissolve the republic and its constitution, impose a dictatorship from above, and demand strict discipline below. Dorothy was shocked to think that this great nation, this citadel of art, philosophy, and science, would voluntarily hand over its rights to a thug.

She hadn't counted on his political genius. Hitler had managed to stir class and intra-class warfare, pitting the working poor against the middle class, and international financiers and bankers against the industrialists. Feeding off the weakness of the republic, which had dissolved democratic institutions in an effort to survive; the poverty and unemployment brought about by the government's economic policies; and the humiliation suffered by the country's military when the civil authorities bypassed Germany's generals to satisfy Allied peace demands, Hitler promised the people dignity, power, conquest, and—perhaps most important—jobs.

Ultimately, Dorothy would be compelled to reevaluate Hitler, but for the moment she methodically pumped Nazi and republican officials to corroborate her views. Many journalists and citizens also saw Hitler as the quintessential "Little Man," but Dorothy's misreading was odd for a seasoned reporter. She would never rescind her judgment of Hitler, but as she observed his ascent through political propaganda and persistent sabotage of the national Right and the socialist Left, it became obvious that she had fallen victim to her tendency to project her own ideals on reality. In her personal as well as her political life, Dorothy often believed what she wished to be true.

Just before she had left for Europe, Dorothy, Hal, and Mickey had moved into their luxurious new apartment on New York's Upper East Side. Her fierce desire to escape the boredom of wife- and motherhood had made her feel overwhelmingly guilty. When she disembarked in England on her way to Germany, she had pleaded with Hal not to resent her absence. But by the time she arrived in Berlin the first week in December 1931, her guilt had given way to wistful nostalgia: "Everytime I go into the streets I'm reminded of you & our lovely early days together. My heart melts, and I long to tell you how I feel about you. But you are a funny little fellow and don't (somehow) encourage me."

She wanted to go back to Europe with Hal for a year, to recapture not only the excitement of her work, but the optimism and romance of their courtship: "I'm happier here," she wrote. "I can't help it . . . it's different. People's minds and emotions both are more complicated. The whole of

Dorothy on her return to Europe to witness the rise of Hitler, circa 1931

life is so much richer, so much thicker, and the ideal of life so much closer to my own." She was counting the days until she would see him and Mickey again.

> *I don't think about either of you more than necessary, because such a yearning possesses me when I do. I think: I will carry my boy about in my arms, for a long time, and he will smile at me, his ingratiating smile, and I will kneel and he will run to me, and I shall be happier than I am even here. And I shall kiss my husband all over his face, and feel his gentle hands and be in love.*
>
> *I kiss your heart.*

Dorothy's use of the generic "my boy" and "my husband" in the midst of intimacy is stunning. Abstractions prevail, making her desire appear more a wish than a reality.

Dorothy was a keen observer. But her perceptions of behavior outran her understanding. She loved Hal deeply on her own terms, but beyond that, she could not or would not go. Hal had told her from the beginning that he experienced life "mostly from the neck up," and she mistakenly believed that she was the same. She was learning that she had emotional needs she had not fathomed.

Shortly before Christmas 1931, Dorothy returned to New York, depressed about the state of the world yet eager to write about her interview with Hitler. The essay first appeared in a magazine and then was expanded into a book, *I Saw Hitler!*, published in 1932. It condemned both the Allies and the German Republic for Hitler's rise: the Allies for imposing "a stupid, inhumane, and impractical peace"; the German Republic for "failing to be genuinely true to its own principles."

Hal, who had been anxiously awaiting her return, was just as anxious to leave once she got there. After the turn of the year, he cloistered himself in Vermont at Twin Farms for a month, thinking the quiet and solitude would enable him to work. Dorothy's joy in seeing her son and her husband was equally short-lived. After secluding herself in her study to write her book, she embarked on a whirlwind tour of forty cities, hellbent on informing Americans about the changing landscape of German politics. In concert with Rebecca, Dorothy saw Nazism as "the apotheosis of collective mediocrity in all its political and sociological aspects . . . a complete break with Reason, with humanity, and Christian ethics that are at the basis of liberalism and democracy."

Mickey, at eighteen months, was far too young to understand why he was always being left alone with his nurse, yet he cried out in loneliness and anger. When Dorothy returned home from her tour, she wrote to Hal, who was away to points south and west with his male "secretary" cum drinking partner, doing research for his new book:

Your little son today entered your room, opened the drawer of your night table, took out a passport picture of you, kissed it, brought it over to me and said, very wisely, and quite clearly, "Papa!" He then took

it back, closed it into the drawer, and said again, but sadly, "Papa."
Before you completely melt into tears let me hasten to add that he then
turned sharply around, re-opened the drawer, extracted the picture
with an air of great firmness, and threw it into the wastepaper basket
without saying anything at all.

Dorothy, like Hal, used Mickey as a vehicle for expressing dismay at her spouse's absence. But ironically, absence was their aphrodisiac; carnal presence crushed their magic. On paper at least, the love between them never waned. They wrote to each other nearly every day, affirming their commitment and aching for the other's presence and the solace of their sacred home.

The summer of 1932, however, held none of the promise of the year before. Dorothy and Hal were rarely at Twin Farms, together or alone. When Hal was at home, he would come into their bedroom stinking drunk, smelling "like rotting weeds." In their apartment in New York, where they had separate bedrooms, Hal's nocturnal drinking was innocuous and invisible. That summer his alcoholism was reminiscent of their disastrous courtship in Berlin. But even as they grew further apart, they clung to their marriage as if it were a matter of life or death.

Hal's novel *Ann Vickers* betrays his ambivalence toward Dorothy. While the narrator admires his protagonist's ambition, energy, talent, and desire to "do good" in the world, he believes that she has bartered power for love, neglecting those who need her most. The novel is a variation of a turn-of-the-century genre, epitomized by H. G. Wells's *Ann Veronica* (1909), written in the aftermath of his affair with Amber Reeves, which traced the evolution of a rebellious young woman from socialist to suffragist to adulteress to suburban mother.

Ann Vickers is the story of a woman who has subordinated her personal life to her ambition, becoming a columnist with a national following. It was not only a portrayal of Dorothy, but also a study of the social milieu of postwar rural and urban America and the moral turpitude of the time. Hal exposed the self-denial implicit in conformity to convention, the folly of pretension, and the quiet desperation of most people's lives. As usual, he found corruption everywhere, among the powerful and the powerless, the wealthy and the poor, the famous and the infamous. Smashing the icons of marriage and parenthood, he uncovered the tension between the real and the ideal, ultimately deeming the institutions frustrating, thankless, and doomed to failure.

There is no doubt that *Ann Vickers* is a roman à clef. Dorothy's biography (intermingled with his) is altered but fully recognizable; Hal's feelings of awe and anger are evident along with his fantasies of happy endings. Dorothy's response to the book was ambivalent and restrained. Its critical reception was mixed. Some saw it as a great achievement in league with *Arrowsmith* or *Dodsworth*. Others saw it as romantic trash. The book, however, was a huge commercial success, selling 90,000 copies in its first printing and more than 133,000 in all editions. It was Lewis's first novel since winning the Nobel Prize, and the entire publishing industry, it was thought by some, would be lifted by its success. One of his critics, who slammed the book as sentimental drivel, declared tongue in cheek that its sales would pump up the whole economy. While patently absurd, his comment had a modicum of truth, considering the depth of the economic slump in 1932. At least one thing may be said for certain: The Lewis household was buoyed by its advent.

Once again, Hal's good fortune bailed out their marriage. His earnings were higher in 1932 than they had been previously or would ever be again. Samuel Goldwyn bought the movie rights to *Arrowsmith,* signing Helen Hayes and Ronald Coleman to play the leads, under the direction of John Ford. At the same time, *Dodsworth* was acquired for stage dramatization, and *Redbook* magazine bought *Ann Vickers* for serialization. Hollywood cinema was in its heyday, Broadway and magazines were flourishing, and Hal, a writer who loved movies and theater, was delighted to cash in on them all.

Nonetheless, the socialist-artist raged against paying taxes. Yelling and stomping on the floor, he unleashed a diatribe against tax policies that gave businessmen the option of staggering their earnings over several years while denying artists the same rights. But even after paying his taxes, this outcast from Sauk Centre had the means to buy what he wished. The Lewises planned an extravagant trip to Vienna in the fall of 1932. With the help of Dorothy's dear friend Genia Schwarzwald, they rented a villa in the hills above the city for the winter. It was to be a second honeymoon in central Europe, where they had fallen in love. Two-year-old Michael and his nurse would accompany them.

On August 23, 1932, they sailed on the *Europa*. While Dorothy and

Michael and his nurse went directly to Vienna to set up house, Hal went to Germany for two weeks. Once he returned to Austria and was ensconced in their mountain retreat, Villa Saurbrunn, he wrote to a friend and described their accommodations as "cuckoo-clock in aspect" and "a 'Ritz' in comfort." The beds, baths, and kitchens were wonderful and there was a beautiful garden. The views, in fact, were spectacular; they looked down into a deep valley and up to the pastoral meadows of the mountains. Hal was enchanted at first but quickly grew bored and restless. Within two weeks, he had convinced Dorothy to leave Michael with the nurse and accompany him to Italy on a walking tour. Three weeks later, they returned to the villa, but Hal stayed only long enough to finalize their plans for a grand Christmas celebration with family and friends. He then went back to Italy alone.

But even the salve of his favorite restaurants and cafés could not fill the hollow in his gut. Drowning in alcohol, he wrote to Dorothy from his hotel in Rome, pleading with her to join him. This time, however, Dorothy refused to be a pawn in his sadomasochistic game:

> *It's probably just as well I didn't go. You were cross with me and whenever I was with you I was lonely. Sometimes I don't think you see me at all, but somebody you made up, a piece of fiction, like Ann Vickers, so terribly lifelike that you almost convince me it's me, until suddenly my heart is crying outside a locked gate with the other "me" inside. I look in on the false one with you. Anyhow, I was tired in my heart, and the rest has done me good.*

In many ways, Lewis's *Ann Vickers* was prophetic. It was rumored that Dorothy was offered the editorship of *The Nation* magazine. Although she turned down this remarkable opportunity on the grounds of wanting to care for Hal and Mickey, she would soon assume the role of the "Great Woman" in which she had been cast. Like Rebecca, Dorothy was ambitious and outwardly iconoclastic, yet conventional at heart. Each needed a reliable, loving, and nurturing partner in order to feel whole. Without it, they were competent and even brilliant intellectuals, but empty and joyless shells of themselves.

Hal returned to the villa the last week in November 1932, determined to dry out. Substituting milk and candy for spirits, he became a stickler about alcohol, ridiculing visitors for the slightest indulgence. As Christmas grew near, preparations for their celebration began in earnest. They had rented an entire wing of a neighboring hotel for their guests, and hired a caterer, a butler, and a full-piece orchestra. Among their guests were Edgar and Lilian Mowrer; Frances and John Gunther and their son Johnny; Virgilia Peterson, an American journalist, and her fiancé Prince Sopeiha from Warsaw; Baroness Hatvany, the divorced Christa Winsloe, Hungarian novelist and playwright; and American novelist Marcia Davenport and her editor husband, Russell. They would even fly Dorothy's sister, Peggy, and her daughter Pamela to Vienna for the occasion. There were to be five children including Mickey, ranging in age from two to twelve, as well as a slew of nannies and day guests, such as Genia Schwarzwald, who would come and go on a regular basis. On most days, there would be as many as thirty or more people in residence in the hotel or their villa.

Then it began to rain. For ten days straight they were stuck indoors. What was to be a winter festival with skiing, sleigh riding, and fresh, crisp mountain air, became a Dionysian brawl. The children went wild and the adults grew bored, drunk, and argumentative. While Dorothy talked politics in German with her friends, Hal, sick of what he called "the situation," and not knowing a word of German, withdrew into a deep depression. Their great plan for celebration and reconciliation was a disaster, and before it was over, Hal had whirled Peggy away to Italy, leaving her daughter in the care of nannies.

The fallout was a blossoming relationship between Dorothy and Christa Winsloe. While some would see Christa as a rather pudgy and boyish Magyar past her prime, Dorothy found her face and body exquisite and her mind more agile and brilliant than any woman's she had ever known. Considered both a "man's woman" and a "woman's woman," she was extraordinarily sensitive and volatile, a trait that endeared her to Dorothy yet alienated others. And her sphere of "brilliance," as Dorothy called it, was seen by some to be limited and arcane—useless in the realm of ordinary social discourse. To Dorothy's friend Jimmy Sheean, Christa was that "goulash-woman produced on the Danube, neither an aristocrat nor an intellectual nor an adventuress, but a sort of vivid combination of them all, with a special writing talent thrown in to make it more exceptional."

After several days of partying in close quarters, Christa lingered at the foot of the stairway one evening, watching Dorothy descend. On impulse, sensing her gesture would not offend, Christa put her lips to Dorothy's breast and then kissed her on the throat. Christa was right; Dorothy did not protest. For days, Dorothy had been mesmerized by her presence and filled with a longing both familiar and intense. Christa's soft skin, full bosom, and sympathetic ear captivated her. She had been tempted before—by her English professor at Syracuse; by her suffragist colleague Gertrude Tone, for whom she still felt an erotic attraction; and by her friend Rose Wilder Lane. But none of these short-lived lesbian relationships was as powerful or soulful as this. Its power lay in its countervailing force to Hal's emotional inadequacy; in Christa's creative nature, which seemed to Dorothy superior to her own; and, ironically, in Christa's intellectual kinship with Hal.

Jimmy Sheean would later comment that he was awed by the hunger for love in a woman nearly forty, who "was by no means inexperienced, yet desperately innocent at heart, and in many ways, untouched, virginal." In a small, scrappy notebook she used as a diary, Dorothy poured out her feelings. On December 28, 1932, she wrote:

> Well then, how to account for this which has happened again. The soft, quick, natural kiss on my throat, the quite unconscious (seemingly) even open kiss on my breast. . . . What was the sudden indescribable charm in that too-soft face, and the heavy-lidded eyes. . . . Anyhow, immediately I felt the strange, soft feeling . . . curious . . . of being at home, and at rest; an enveloping warmth and sweetness, like a drowsy bath. Only to be near her; to touch her when I went by . . . "Don't go away," I wanted to say, "Don't go."

And yet, she found something weak and perverse about all the touching and kissing without consummation. "Anyway, it doesn't suit me," she wrote. "I am heterosexual. Even according to the simple Freudian definition which determines the matter by the location of the orgiastic sensation. Like Marguerite in Faust, the womb throbs—not something else, more surface. All this petting is nothing without the deep thrust to the heart of one."

While Hal was in Italy with her sister, Dorothy and some of her guests followed Christa and her ex-husband, Ladislas ("Laci") Hatvany, to his family home in Budapest. It was he, not Christa, who had wanted the divorce. Jews always return to Jews, Dorothy noted in her diary, echoing an unflattering sentiment of the time, and Laci had met a Jewish woman he wanted to marry. That was why she hadn't wanted to have Joseph Bard's child, Dorothy concluded, consoling herself with revisionist history. "He remained a sweetly assaulting male . . . and no blood relation of mine." Hal and Michael, on the other hand, felt like "blood."

All her love affairs had been based on critical relationships within her family, she mused. Dorothy would later write that her father, a lover of language, parable, and poetry, had had the greatest influence on her life. Certainly her love for Hal, Joseph, and all her male consorts and mates was fanned by their creativity. Perhaps because of his sexual restraint, she felt that Hal was more like a brother. Dorothy's desire for intimacy with women could have been a response to the loss of maternal love early in life. Perhaps Christa's desire for women had a smiliar source. She had grown up in a German orphanage for children who had lost their parents in the Great War. Christa was affectionate and seductive, but Dorothy had no reason to believe that Christa loved her. Yet she was certain that her need for Christa's friendship and presence could only be called "love."

When Hal and Dorothy returned to the villa the first week in January 1933, they were glad to see each other. She wrote in her diary, "I stood a long time in his arms, loving his familiar feel and smell, rubbing my face on his face." She bathed and put on nothing but her dressing gown, and he asked her to come to his bed. "It was awfully good," she wrote. "Especially good, with me just too tired to expect to be and suddenly it was there and wonderful."

"Darling, I didn't do anything. Did you?" Hal asked her.

"And I hadn't. And I didn't," she wrote. Her relationship with Christa, at least for the moment, had made her love him more. "It would be nice to have a new child as the end-of-the-party."

After they had closed up the villa in Semmering, Dorothy and Hal stayed for a while at a rented flat in Vienna. Dorothy had been feeling sweetly languorous since that evening in January; it was a familiar drowsiness that echoed earlier times. She wondered if she was pregnant. Was she happy? she asked herself. Dorothy had always wanted "the long-legged red-headed girl [she] had imagined Michael would be," she wrote. In any case, she wouldn't have an abortion. "My whole being rises up against that." Her shattered childhood made that a certainty—her mother's unnatural death, her sense of abandonment, and her father's betrayal through remarriage. Furthermore, she proved that she wasn't Ann Vickers; she wasn't Hal's neurotic creation, the fictional embodiment of the conniving amoral woman that fed his own fear of abandonment. As his wife and the mother of his child, she would not betray him or her principles.

Pregnancy, she felt, was both submission and empowerment.

I am not sure that having a child, actually bearing a child isn't, for a woman, the only entirely satisfactory sexual experience. It is a kind of terrible ecstasy accompanied by a feeling of great expansion and power, and terrific heightening of all impression and experience. . . . It seems to me that as my child was born I was full of agony and full of laughter. Then I remember there was an earthquake, a cosmic catastrophe; the world opened up and all the stars fell and I died. And when I woke up again, the world had never, never seemed so sweet.

In Vienna, Dorothy surrendered to her body; she read, slept, and ate cake, to Hal's great amusement. It was a quiet time, with nothing to write, no schedule to follow, and only her family to think about. But one evening she came home from an afternoon of shopping to find that Hal had ransacked the flat, breaking dishes, ripping photographs, and smashing their leased furniture. She screamed at him and he hit her. Dorothy was stunned. She vowed that it would be the last time he would hurt her. It is unknown if the incident happened before or after her pregnancy was confirmed, but shortly thereafter, she had a miscarriage. Despite her pain and anger, she was still convinced that her destiny lay with Hal. Her Methodist perception of marriage was that of a sacred and enduring covenant. Dorothy had broken it once by marrying and divorcing a Jew, and she could not bear the thought of doing it again. She would have to find consolation elsewhere.

When Hal went to London in February, ostensibly on business for *Ann Vickers,* Dorothy, Michael, and his nurse, Haemmerli, went to Munich and then on to Portofino, a harbor fishing village on the Italian Riviera, with Christa. Though the city was beautiful, all of Europe had "a smell of death," she wrote in her diary. "These years have robbed us of our Utopias. We've seen them all realized and are disillusioned with all of them. Where shall wisdom be found and where is the place of understanding? The reversion to our own hearts & souls, to the kingdom of Heaven which is within us."

The kingdom of Heaven governed those who believed, but those who did not were on their own. Despite his wealth and his culture, Hal had once again lost his way. Without a book to write and little to occupy his mind, he once again sought solace in alcohol. Gone was his tenderness, his good-natured generosity, and if not his love, the semblance thereof. To Dorothy, it was one and the same. Fundamentalist perceptions aside, she believed that all was lost.

In the course of her travels, during which she made an unexpected trip to Berlin, Dorothy did not acknowledge Hal's forty-eighth birthday. Distressed by her silence, he tried to cajole her into forgiving him with a playful letter in which he apologized, not for hurting her but for getting older. "I'm so sorry," he wrote. "I tried every way to keep from it. I skipped rope; I skied down appalling mountains; I read P.G. Wodehouse; but still I came to 4-8."

After waiting several weeks for a reply that never came, he sailed for New York alone on March 4, 1933, the day of Franklin D. Roosevelt's inauguration. Gripped by loneliness, he wrote Dorothy a letter on the deck of the steamer-freighter *American Farmer,* expressing his true feelings. "You seem to me in my mad life my one refuge and security. You see, I don't care a damn—not anymore at least—for fame and all those amiable experiences, but only (and this is not a not-too-easy contradiction) for you and Mickey on the one hand, and Freedom (whatever that empty thing may be) on the other."

Tragically, Hal was the victim of his addiction. Lucid to the point of self-disgust, he could not control his emotions. Desperately needing love but without the capacity to nurture it, he could only demand that she take him back. Soon it would be spring, he wrote, and they would return to Twin Farms. "It is true, isn't it, that there will be apple trees, and flaming lilies, and the moon over the low mountains and you and me, after dinner, sitting smoking on the terrace, and inside when it becomes chilly, the fireplace and lamplight and lots of books? Love me," he wrote, "so we can go home."

Three weeks later, she responded from Portofino.

> *My dear, my dear:*
>
> *... Hal, I couldn't write for two reasons; in the first place, in Germany, I could think of nothing but what I saw, and I was on the move from nine in the morning until twelve at night and then dropped into bed totally exhausted. The other reason is that I have never never felt so cut off from you emotionally as I have in all this time. . . . I felt as though you did not care for me any more; that last fortnight in Vienna weighed upon my memory. I felt as though our marriage was going on the rocks. And I had no emotional strength with which to pull it off. Your going back to drinking spirits was part of it. . . . I thought: I must save myself. . . . Only, and this is the truth, I do love you. I love you too terribly. I know now that it is all self deception . . . my trying to think that I could get along without you. . . . I, too, find in you the only security I have in the world. . . . We've got to go on together, forever, and be kind to each other.*

Just where did the self-deception lie? Did she love Hal or the idea of loving him?

Hal's response was equally tender. Her feeling of disconnection from him, he wrote, was partly imaginary. He blamed himself for his boredom and frustration in Semmering—his Babbitt-like, philistine ignorance of art and music, and his dislike of social intrusions, especially by Genia. The place they loved most, Twin Farms, he wrote, was only a month away, and once they were there, everything would seem like a "bad dream." She should never question his love for her. He cared deeply and always had. "You have faults. Ever know that?" he wrote. "You are somewhat too inclined to run the show, both conversationally and domestically, but as I probably am inclined also, we ought to endure that in each other so long as neither of us is mean and neither is."

Meanwhile, for six weeks Dorothy languished in the rhythm of life in Portofino with Christa. If she couldn't be with him in Vermont, she wrote to Hal, she would rather be in Portofino with Christa than with anyone else she could imagine. In the morning each would work in her separate room—Dorothy on her article about Nazism called "Back to Blood and Iron" for *The Saturday Evening Post*, and Christa on a "spiritualist" play. Then they would take a walk, have a light lunch—"the kind women living alone have, sleep for a while, work again until tea; sometimes visit a neighbor then; have our baths, dine at eight; work an hour or read, or talk, and go to bed at ten." Despite its lack of sin, she wrote, the house was charming. Dorothy had written "sin" instead of "sun," à la Freud, but catching her error, she wrote Hal, there was little of that, as well. But Christa, she continued, was "an angel." She was convinced that "every worker needed a wife."

While Dorothy reassured Hal that she wasn't "thataway," neither she nor Christa ever divulged the sexual realities of their relationship. In the postwar social environment, sexual license had surfaced as a vital response to catastrophic loss. In America and abroad, lesbian love was prevalent yet stigmatized, accepted by the intellectual and artistic elite, but condoned by neither law nor convention. To the daughter of a Methodist preacher, steeped in the proscriptions of the Old Testament, the act of making love to a woman must have seemed like a pact with the devil. And yet, loving Christa seemed beyond Dorothy's control. Many of their letters were replete with Sapphic allusions—their unabashed desire to embrace, kiss, and stroke each other. Christa, who wrote in German and English at whim, often used male pronouns when she referred to herself and Dorothy, and made sardonic references to their "amorality."

Dorothy wrote Christa several poems during the spring of 1933, but none more self-analytical and philosophical than this:

What can I do, then, with this so great love,
I being woman? There is no release
In intermingled flesh; I cannot prove
With lips and hands my love. There is no peace
For you in me, no shutter bringing rest.
These bones like yours, these too receptive thighs,
This yielding flesh, these arms, this too soft breast,
Offer you nothing, for they say who lies
With her own flesh lies with futility . . .
Rather I swear this to be true:

This love will find its form nor be less fair
Because it is incarnal as the air.

Rebecca might have called Dorothy's conflict a battle between Eros and Thanatos, or alternatively, the id and superego. Dorothy called it the tension between the "original me" and the "cultivated me." When her "original me" fell in love, it was grand, she wrote, but "it," that is, her innocent self, eventually died of malnutrition and boredom, receding into friendship. When her "cultivated me" fell in love, it was much the same. But when both aspects of her being found outlet in one person, it was "fatal," she wrote. It had happened only once before. Although she didn't specify, one can only conclude that it was with Joseph—a beautiful bisexual Jew.

Was the original "me" the God-fearing, God-loving child born of innocence and nurtured on biblical wisdom? Was her cultivated "me" outside Christian morality, expressing a longing beyond the realm of law and reason? She had always wanted to be consumed by love, as she had been by that of her father, and through him, her love of Jesus. But to be consumed by the carnal and the spiritual wrapped in the blasphemy of lesbian love—that was a hellish descent not to be contemplated. She had to deny it.

While Dorothy was riddled with frustration and guilt, Christa was at peace with her bisexuality. She wrote Dorothy several letters while she traveled to and from Germany, the common theme of which was loneliness. In one, she wrote, "Dotty darling, I feel orphaned without you and don't know what to do with myself. Downstairs I found a nice picture of you and put it on my night table as a substitute." Christa, like Hal, would have to content herself with memories and the hope of reunion. Both saw Dorothy as an anchor, a defining presence, and a tether to reality they could not sustain on their own.

Michael, too, was acting like "an orphan" or, at the very least, like someone in desperate need of a mother. His feelings, as might be expected, were primitive and unfiltered. Christa wrote that Mickey was naughty, demanding, and rebellious; the only way to calm him down was to give him anything he wanted. Miss Haemmerli, his nurse, did the best she could, but she claimed that it wasn't her burden to discipline him. Christa began to refer to him as the "wrath of god Mickey." But Dorothy was less concerned with the machinations of a three-and-a-half-year-old than with her lover, whom she deemed her "better self." In order to have a sense of fulfillment, she had to serve more "creative natures." That was at the heart of her relationships with Hal and with Christa. To complete her life, she needed to be of use to them.

Dorothy came home in May 1933. And she didn't come alone. Michael had sailed earlier with his nurse, but she was accompanied by Christa. When the two women arrived at the pier on New York's West Side, reporters questioned Dorothy about the rumors of her impending divorce. After brushing them aside, she introduced her friend as Baroness Hatvany, a fervent anti-Nazi crusader. They both vehemently opposed Hitler's rise, she said, and would assume the mission of informing the American public of what lay ahead. Christa, who wanted to write an epic play for Broadway about the coming of war, lamented the fact that she wasn't a man, while Dorothy plodded ahead, always believing that the truth would empower her.

Defiantly, Dorothy told Hal that she was going to bring Christa with her to Twin Farms. It was simple, she said; she needed her. Whether Hal knew about the sexual nature of their relationship remains a matter of speculation, but one thing was certain: Christa was another barrier to healing the wounds of their marriage. Dorothy requested that he write her a welcoming letter, and begrudgingly he did, realizing that it was his ticket to having Dorothy at home. Hal had been subjected to rumors about divorce as well, and he was anxious to put the matter to rest. Some had said that they had heard it from Dorothy, others through letters from friends. Few could have known the details of their rift, but the fact that something had changed seemed obvious to even casual observers.

The summer of 1933 was strange and disjointed. Dorothy and Hal were never at Twin Farms at the same time. He was off researching a book on the aesthetics of American culture; she remained fixed on analyzing the rise of Nazism. They continued to write to each other every day; neither could bear the thought that their marriage had failed. Both were so desperately lonely that shedding that shared dream was intolerable. They chose to perpetuate the fantasy rather than come to terms with reality. Like Rebecca and H.G., they were too ambitious, too restless, and too emotionally needy to be compatible. They each loved the image, the ideal that they had imagined the other to be, rather than the actual person. By this time, they both sensed that something essential had changed. Only one thing remained constant: Michael was left at home with his nurse.

Dorothy and Christa made a quick trip to Austria in midsummer. When they returned, Hal announced that he had bought Dorothy a house. Whether his purchase was an expression of atonement, reconciliation, or outright despair, she never liked it. Buying the house, like so many of his impulses, was spurred by fantasy. Hal, it was clear, wanted her—needed her—to become a suburban housewife. The house, a sprawling mock Tudor in Bronxville, was less than half an hour north of New York City in Westchester County. Situated in an affluent neighborhood, it was neither a country house nor a city house where she could conduct business or bring her friends. As far as she was concerned, it was the worst of all worlds. Its backyard bordered on the Kennedy property, the home of Joseph and Rose, and of the future president John. It was, nonetheless, a good place to visit Michael, and a retreat from the city, if she wished. It was there that she took Christa when the summer was over.

Hal, Dorothy, and Christa lived in Bronxville together in the fall of 1933. Hal, who was drinking again, alienated everyone, including the servants—a German cook, a French maid, a new Scottish nurse, and a butler. He had rented a penthouse apartment at the New Yorker Hotel, where he would often spend time writing and with his friends, but when he was home, he would withdraw into a private world, sipping his Scotch (surreptitiously watered down by the head servant), and reading books into the night. When he wasn't withdrawn, he would rage against anyone in eyeshot, including Christa and Michael. When Dorothy was out of town lecturing, he missed her terribly, sinking into an alcoholic stupor. Upon hearing notice of her return, he would summon his barber to the house to spruce up his hair and shave his beard. As anxiously as a lovesick child, he would wait at the front door for her taxi to arrive. Yet no sooner would he hang her coat than he would pick a fight. Dorothy would hide in the servants' quarters until he quieted down.

When Christa was alone with him in the house, she found his presence intolerable. The antipathy was mutual. To him she was a judgmental intruder, constantly vying for his wife's attention when she was home. Finally, one day, Hal threw her out. Christa would lick her wounds among friends in Virginia—ironically, the Casanovas. Hal's first wife, Grace, and her husband, Telesforo, had invited Christa to visit as a gesture of goodwill. When Hal went to Chicago to get material for his novel, Christa returned to Bronxville. During this time, Christa and Dorothy were inseparable; no one dared to invite one without the other. Christa loved to be seen as a reflection of Dorothy, and she loved the freedom that American women enjoyed. She touted American optimism and entrepreneurship. In an unpublished piece, she wrote—clearly extrapolating from her narrow experience—that while she knew there was a depression in America, she had seen no trace of it. And there was little crime, she concluded, judging by her time in Vermont, where the gardens were built without fences, open to neighbors and passersby. It was a culture built on mutual trust and respect, she declared. In the course of a mere few hundred words, Christa revealed not only her ignorance and naïveté but also the shallowness of her intellect.

When Hal returned to find Christa back in Bronxville, he was enraged. Christa wondered whom he would throw out when no one was left but himself. Upon sailing to Europe in January 1934, Christa told Dorothy that if she did not leave Red, their relationship was kaput. But she was also worried about Dorothy. "You have to separate from Red in some way . . . otherwise you'll break on me."

Throughout the fall, Dorothy had not been feeling well. Diagnosed with diabetes, she was advised by her doctor to go on a diet, one of many soon to be abandoned. But the disease and the added weight it engendered siphoned her energy and altered her moods. She started taking diet pills—Dexedrine—to keep going. She would come to depend on them more and more as her obsession to expose the true intent of the Nazis magnified. She was so committed to their downfall that she would pay any price it required, including alienating friends and acquaintances who did not share her views. One of her friends, Phyllis Bottome, commented: "She flung the whole force of her being against its ever happening in her own country. Perhaps from this moment also she lost her private life and became for the world in general, as well as for her friends, a public Dorothy."

During the winter of 1934, Dorothy found herself alone. Christa was gone and Hal was often at his apartment in New York working on a new book—a study of the architecture and business of the American hotel as an expression of America's ideal of beauty and way of life. Most of the time, however, he was on the road, visiting resorts all over the country, accompanied by his secretary and drinking partner, Louis Florey. Anguished about Michael's loneliness but incapable of staying in Bronxville, Dorothy went on another national lecture tour to speak with women about events in Europe, and began writing book and theater reviews. She was depressed, and had good reason to be. She didn't have a husband, she didn't have a lover, and as far as she was concerned, Bronxville was not her home. Furthermore, she felt helpless about Mickey, and her diabetes had begun to take its toll. When she arrived at Twin Farms, she took it all out on the servants—the garden was a mess; the carpenter was incompetent; the food was inedible.

Hal had lost interest in managing the estate, and more and more, its operation fell on her shoulders. Friends who visited them there and in Bronxville observed the "half-controlled" violence between Dorothy and Hal that would often escalate into verbal and physical fights. He would curse her, she would curse back with an acid tongue, and Hal, drunk and feeling exiled in his own home, would smack Michael "hard across the mouth," only to break into spasms of regret, deeply ashamed and loathing himself more than before. Once the greatest supporter of Dorothy's work, Hal became her biggest rival, resenting her sense of personal mission, her absence, and her neglect. Left alone for months at a time, he would drink his way into deliriousness with no one to call upon for help except the servants, Dorothy's colleague and neighbor in Vermont, George Seldes, or Dorothy's sister, Peggy, with whom he had developed a close friendship. Sometimes he remarked that he had married the wrong Thompson girl. But it was clear to her and everyone else that he still adored Dorothy.

In June 1934, Dorothy went back to Europe—sailing to England, and then on to Austria and Germany. She managed a short visit with Joseph Bard. In Austria, she spent time with Genia Schwarzwald to see how she was faring in the midst of Austria's political and economic collapse.

In January, Genia had written to Dorothy that everyone was certain that Hitler wanted war, despite his promises of peace. While individual lives would be tragically threatened because of their membership in the National oppositionist parties, her Jewish friends believed they would not be touched: "There is still an utter calm here, but the initiated know that all around us weapons abound, that no one believes Hitler's assurances of peace. The individual fates are tragic. Among my friends the Jews are the least affected; the Nationals and people of the Zentrum [militant Nationals] are the worst off, and the pacifists worse yet."

Genia and her husband, along with her Jewish compatriots and many Jews in Germany, still didn't believe that Hitler's racial policies would prevail. They were Jews, but they were Austrians and Germans first; they had fought alongside their countrymen in the Great War. At this point, the extremists on both ends of the political spectrum were the most obvious and resistant targets.

After visiting Genia, Dorothy wrote to Joseph:

Austria is terribly sad. . . . Vienna put me into a suicidal frame of mind. . . . It is terrible to see the collapse of a world where once one has lived safely and happily. It concerns me, I find, more than I had dreamed. In Vienna, particularly, the nostalgia for other times was almost unbearable. . . . But I should like to be friends with you, if that were possible. It certainly ought to be after all this time. I would like to know what you are writing and what you are doing. . . . I cannot tell you how often I think of The Mind of Europe, *and wonder whether you have utterly abandoned a manuscript, which now seems even more actual and important than it did then. If you had written it ten years ago it would have been prophetic! About my own personal life there is not so much to tell. I go off on a lecture trip or a reporting trip. I write a great many book reviews and some dramatic criticism, and some general articles. I spend a great deal of time in the country with Hal and the boy. On the whole I am happy and more happy with Hal, I think, than I have ever been.*

Having obfuscated the course of her career and the quality of her domestic life, she added: "I hate being completely out of touch with you . . . although indeed, I am I never am really out of touch with you, since these years live on in me with undiminished vividness. . . . Perhaps it is a sign of age that they seem to increase in vividness rather than diminish." Not ready to let go of her marriage, she trades one fantasy for another.

Dorothy's stay in Vienna reaped insights beyond the political.

Later that year, *Harper's Magazine* published her short story "A

Wreath for Toni," which gave voice to the human devastation of fascist infiltration and exposed the romantic idealism that heretofore was expressed only in her letters and diaries. Written with a journalist's eye for detail and the moral sensitivity of a preacher's daughter, it is the story of Anton Murbacher, a middle-class teacher and intellectual who discards religious and political tradition in the name of socialism. A dissident turned sniper who fights the fascists to save his family and countrymen, Toni becomes a hero and a martyr.

But nothing Dorothy experienced in Vienna could compare with the shocking transformation of Germany. When Dorothy had returned to Berlin in February 1933, she had witnessed Hitler's ascendance. As he had hoped, the previous March, Hitler had won fourteen million votes, constituting 37 percent of the seats and the option of forming a coalition government with the conservative Nationalist Party, the only other party besides the Communists to get substantial votes. Neither Chancellor Franz von Papen nor his successor Kurt von Schleicher had stymied the downward spiral of the economy, and, at Papen's suggestion, Hitler was appointed chancellor by President Paul von Hindenburg. Their move was an attempt to muzzle insurrection and keep Hitler under their thumb. Hitler, however, had other plans; he was designing a revolution. Dorothy had begun to hate Germany, and feared that something terrible would happen. She wrote to her friend Harriet Cohen, who was also Rebecca's friend and the woman after whom she modeled the protagonist in *Harriet Hume*, "If only someone would speak: someone in a high important place who has the ears of the world."

Now, in the summer of 1934, as Dorothy traveled west from Austria through the Bavarian countryside, she was surprised by the lack of checkpoints and border guards, as if these nations were already conjoined. The only thing that tipped her off that she had entered "Hitler's Kingdom" were the flags of "bright red with a black swastika in a white circle in the middle and sometimes they hung from the second story to the ground. They gave the streets an odd Chinese look. There were often several on one house—one for every family who lived there. They made the streets look very gay, as though there were a festival." Along with these were signs announcing the plebiscite on Sunday, August 19, to determine Hitler's right to become führer. Another American she met by chance compared Hitler's rise to a religious renewal—the Second Coming of Christ. Everyone was out in the streets parading around in brown shirts and high boots—children, workers, and ordinary citizens. She couldn't tell the difference between the civilians and the SA troopers.

She wrote in an article:

There are to be no minorities of opinion in the new Germany, and no division of loyalties. . . . Most men will wear uniforms, the badge of their membership in that secret, mystic community of blood-brothers, the German State. Women will, by preference, wear kitchen aprons and will stay at home and take care of the children, which they will gladly bear in large numbers for Germany. They will not hold political opinions—but then, neither will anyone else.

Wandering into a Hitler Youth summer camp of "six thousand boys between the ages of ten and sixteen," she was struck by the beauty of their faces and physiques, noting the huge banner stretched across the hillside, visible from every vantage point. "It was white, and there was a swastika painted on it, and besides that only seven immense black words: YOU WERE BORN TO DIE FOR GERMANY." Those words, she wrote, were antithetical to everything her father and schoolmasters taught her. "Times Change," she noted dryly.

At Twin Farms, Hal was inundated with children, but he was not impressed by their beauty. Before she had left, Dorothy had hired a Mrs. Waller and her three children to keep Michael company while she was gone. One afternoon, Hal came home to find the Waller children steamrolling through the house, sweeping both Mickey and Peggy's daughter Pamela out of their path as if they were "mere excrescences." Overcome by the rambunctious and noisy youngsters, he fired their mother on the spot, sending her and her brood off with a flick of his hand and a month's salary. He simply closed up the "old house," fired another servant, Marion, and released her with similar compensation. He called on Peggy to take care of the children.

Summing it up, he wrote to Dorothy, "Between you and me, I have had, for an undomestic gent, rather a full measure of kids heaped upon me, this summer that I meant to be tranquil. . . . I've never missed you so. I wouldn't have minded armies of kids, omitting the Wallers, if you'd been here to talk to."

Pleased with himself for weeding out the source of his son's unhappiness, he promptly left for his apartment in New York.

Dorothy had been in Austria the first week in July during Hitler's blood purge of alleged assassins, the Night of Long Knives; hundreds of SA leaders and centrist politicians were killed or incarcerated. In the event's tumultuous aftermath, Dorothy arrived in Berlin. While the outward signs of Nazi dominance were obvious, the daily workings of the city remained eerily calm. "When I reached Berlin I went to the Adlon. It was good to be there, like home. There was Fix in the bar with his shining black hair and his shining smile and his good dry Martinis. There was the manager who always remembers how many people there are in your family and what room you had last time. Oh, I was glad to be back! . . . It was all the courtesy, all the cleanliness, all the exquisite order which is Germany."

And yet, there was an undercurrent of anxiety she couldn't grasp. A journalist had told her not to make phone calls from the hotel because they were monitored. Despite his warning, she found it impossible to believe anything other than what had always been true. It was the same glaze of normalcy Genia had observed in Vienna. But how could it be? This was Berlin, nakedly real if nothing else.

Dorothy could remember sitting with her colleagues at the bar drinking vodka and beer, exchanging information and analyzing events. Partisan distortions had always been part of the official game at the Adlon, but they could easily be ameliorated by networking sources with differing views. And a correspondent could always express what he or she deemed the truth. As was her wont, Dorothy let her preconceptions eclipse the facts.

Her arrival coincided not only with the German plebiscite, but with the announcement of nominations for the Nobel Prize. Carl von Ossietzky, an indomitable anti-Nazi journalist incarcerated for his views, learned of his nomination for the Peace Prize in his prison cell. His efforts to expose the reality of German rearmament had echoed throughout the free world. To Dorothy, he was the quintessential hero—a journalist willing to lay down his life for the truth. She would help him in any way she could. At lunch with a friend in the cathedral-domed hall of the hotel, Dorothy spoke within earshot of the waiter about her scheme to smuggle Ossietzky's wife out of Germany. Her friend kicked her under the table, warning her that all the waiters reported to the gestapo. "Nonsense!" Dorothy quipped, repeating her plan a decibel louder.

The next day, August 25, 1934, the gestapo came to the hotel with an order from the highest levels of the German Reich. Dorothy had twenty-four hours to leave the country or be forcibly expulsed. If she were a German, she said, she would have gone to prison. As it was, she was going to Paris.

At the time, her expulsion was unheard of in the ranks of foreign journalists. But it was logical and almost inevitable that she would be the first to go. Any form of dissent was quickly squashed by Hitler, still smoldering from his alleged betrayal by SA troopers. After news of her book *I Saw Hitler!* hit the media in 1932, Hitler had a team of translators follow Dorothy's work, along with that of other hostile foreign authors. Her scathing commentary questioning his manhood, breeding, and mental stability, was second only to her brazen opposition of his racial policies in her articles that appeared in the American Jewish press. Dorothy's unabashed defiance in the hotel was the excuse he needed to turn her out. Citing her anti-German publications, the gestapo letter accused her of offending their "national self-respect," rendering them unable to extend "a further right of hospitality." "My offense," she wrote in *The New York Times*, "was to think that Hitler is just an ordinary man . . . a crime against the reigning cult in Germany, which says Mr. Hitler is a Messiah sent by God to save the German people—an old Jewish idea."

Ironically, her expulsion turned her into an international celebrity, a martyr to the anti-Nazi cause. Advised by the American ambassador to Germany William Dodd not to test the gestapo, she packed her bags and left the hotel the next morning to meet the train to Paris. She arrived at the station to find the entire corps of American and British press assembled in solidarity to send her off. With armfuls of American Beauty roses, a gift from the press corps, she boarded the Étoile du Nord, knowing that the Berlin she had loved, the place that had been her home and training ground, that had kindled her passion for theater and art, history, and politics, would never be the same.

Two weeks later, on the other side of the Atlantic, her welcome was equally celebratory. No longer just Mrs. Sinclair Lewis, she was Dorothy Thompson, dissident and rebel, a one-woman army against the tyrannical Third Reich. Hal stood in the shadows as Dorothy pontificated to reporters on Hitler's maniacal move toward war.

Merely by following her instincts and her staunch Methodist sense of right and wrong, Dorothy had become the voice required to awaken America to the fascist threat.

Shortly after she arrived in New York, she would begin a series of lecture tours that would carry her throughout all forty-eight states for the next eighteen months. Hal, smarting from the failure of his hotel book, *A Work of Art*, could bear neither her absence nor her prominence. He wondered "why in hell he had had to marry a Roman Senator." If he ever decided to divorce her, he said, he would name Hitler as his consignee.

PART
3

CHAPTER 11

BLOODLUST

> Let historians record that we went into this war
> stone cold sober, without one drop of blood lust
> to carry us through.
>
> —REBECCA WEST, 1940

LONDON, 1940

One Saturday evening after a long air raid, Rebecca went up to the roof of her Orchard Court high-rise to find that the bombs she had heard muffled in the shelter below had hit hundreds of buildings and homes. Waves of flames rolled through the city, blanketing London with cinders of burning wood and flesh. "We knew that this was what we must expect," she wrote, "but nevertheless it is a bitter grief, like no other, to see one's own town on fire."

As the bombs fell around her, Rebecca was wrestling with the epilogue of *Black Lamb and Grey Falcon*. The book would not be published for more than a year, but she believed that the human impulse toward self-sacrifice she had discerned on the plains of Kosovo had brought England to this moment. Rebecca was convinced that people in general, and Britons in particular, could not bear to be victorious. She believed that the Allied triumph in the Great War and the harsh sanctions imposed on Germany at Versailles had caused the British government to turn a blind eye toward German rearmament, to soften English demands for war reparations, to invest in German industry, and to diminish the strength of its own military. Ever since the fall of 1938 when Neville Chamberlain had stood on the balcony of 10 Downing Street in his black top hat and coat, raising the Munich accord on high to the roar of thousands of Londoners, Rebecca had known that the old fool had made war inevitable. Britain and France had abandoned their sworn ally Czechoslovakia to Nazi invasion, feeding Hitler's thirst for domination and nourishing his belief that the Western democracies were vulnerable and weak.

With Czechoslovakia in shambles, and their ally Poland and their African colonies under threat, England and France found themselves virtually alone. Awakened too late to Hitler's intent, Chamberlain had begun to rearm in April 1939. When the prime minister finally declared war on September 3, 1939, it was a relief. Like many of her compatriots, Rebecca felt that a veil had been lifted and the future was clear; the terrible years of suspension were over. But by May 1940 Chamberlain was compelled to resign, and Winston Churchill, among the few lone voices against German appeasement, took the helm of a coalition government.

In concert with Churchill and those few Britons who refused to be seduced by promises of peace, Rebecca and Henry had never trusted the Nazis. Rebecca had traveled widely throughout central Europe, alone and with her husband. Henry had spent most of his childhood in Germany and had been incarcerated by the Germans as a British spy during the Great War. Later, as a partner of Schroders bank in London until 1935, he had often shuttled to and from Berlin. Both had witnessed firsthand the treachery of the Reich, its racist ploys, fascist propaganda, and expansionist rhetoric. Three months after the Munich fiasco, Rebecca had fitted two rooms of their apartment in London with steel shutters so that she and Henry might have a place to eat and sleep should the bombs begin to fall.

She wrote: "It's the poisoning of the whole of life by the spread of the Nazi spirit, which is something that you come up against every day in every department of your life."

During the early stages of the war, Rebecca's American friends had tried to comfort her, but as government censorship of the mail intensified, honest correspondence became more difficult. Instead, she wrote articles for American periodicals poignantly describing the plight of Britons—that is to say, Britons of culture and a certain degree of wealth—at the outset of war.

In the January 1940 issue of *Ladies' Home Journal,* she wrote:

September 1939 was to be a haven for my husband and myself. That we had promised ourselves. We had succeeded in renting for the summer a Sussex manor house on which we had laid covetous eyes for years, two hours from London. . . . We had taken it for four months, but the first three had gone up in smoke. . . .

So September was to be a holiday, spent in eating the last raspberries from the canes in the walled garden, playing table tennis in the barn and croquet on the lawn that is shadowed by the three huge old oaks, and cutting the roses on the yew walk and dahlias on the terrace.

This exquisite tableau was marred, she wrote, by the "darkness" that had settled over Britain in late August 1939, when news of Hitler's non-aggression pact with Stalin had made the outbreak of war imminent. After nine months of playing political games with Britain and France, Russia, sucked in by Hitler's promise of dividing central and eastern Europe between them, finally sided with the Reich.

She admitted that renting the manor house, Possingworth, in the summer of 1939 had been an act of deliberate self-deception; an effort to delude themselves that living in the country would render them immune to the realities of war. But on that morning, Rebecca had laid out the newspapers on their mirror-polished mahogany dining-room table, realizing how far they had traveled from the "primitive world." Exquisitely aware of the savagery that lingered beneath the surface of life, Rebecca's fear was as intense as if she were living in a jungle where no one and nothing was safe.

Rebecca wrote to her American friend and mentor Alexander Woollcott, "I have never felt so coldly ferocious in my life, and optimistically carry a couple of linoleum knives wherever I go. . . . We do feel a wild exhilaration in what our air force has done. Really, we are the same people as the Elizabethans and doesn't it show more now that we have gotten rid of that abominable Neville!"

Within two days of the Russo-German pact, their first evacuee from London arrived—Norman Macleod, Jr., the thirteen-year-old son of her sister Winnie and her husband, Norman, a principal secretary in the Office of the Admiralty. Norman, Jr., was to stay only a few weeks, until he went to boarding school. His nineteen-year-old sister, Alison, was safe, traveling through Austria with her aunt Lettie, but to spare the younger Norman from being sent to a foster home, like nearly nine hundred thousand others, the Macleods had meticulously arranged via telegrams for his stay at Possingworth with Rebecca. Schoolchildren were labeled, addressed, and sent off by train and bus to foster homes; rushed out of school and unmonitored by medical authorities, they often took only the clothes on their back and a paper-wrapped sandwich and a piece of fruit stuffed in their pockets. Over a million children, whose parents refused to send them away but whose schools were closed, were left to run wild in the large cities. Those half-grown and half-educated, similar in age to Norman, Jr., scrounged around for any jobs they could find.

During the following weeks she and Henry would house seventeen evacuees, including relatives of their seven servants, and an ailing old housekeeper who had cared for Henry's uncle Ernest. Their attempt to black out the manor's fifty windows had proved Herculean. Each of the seventeenth-century windows had to be custom fitted with dark cloth curtains, hooked at eight points around the window frame to lie perfectly flat, in order to make them impenetrable to light. Each day Henry would travel to his office at the Ministry of Economic Warfare in London, forty miles round-trip. At night he would return in an unlit train carriage to the station, ten miles from home, and be driven in an automobile with blackened headlights through darkened roads. Every morning Rebecca would bid Henry good-bye, wondering if he would make it back home.

London was eerily silent, yet marvelously beautiful. Everyone agreed that the late summer days of 1939 were among the most glorious they could remember. The skies were bright and cloudless during the day, and when evening fell the blackouts revealed the magnificence of London in moonlight. With the closing of cinemas, theaters, and dance halls, life had become simpler, introverted, and paradoxically calm. The days were full of purposeful activity, as Londoners united in common cause, digging trenches in parks and gardens, scaffolding monuments and statues, and helping one another build outdoor bomb shelters in their backyards. Everywhere there were signs saying SMILE FOR BRITAIN, as if the proverbial stiff upper lip would carry them through. Upon returning from a trip to town, Rebecca articulated the widespread anxiety felt by her compatriots while probing the aura of impending doom. The houses were bagged with sand, and everyone carried a gas mask on his back. "Either this is the most colossal waste of resources that has ever been seen, or if it is not a waste, it is going to be hell. But indeed, in any case it is going to be hell."

In a letter to her old friend Doris Stevens in New York, Rebecca related the feminine aspect of war.

> *The defense of London is something to make a feminist smirk. The*
> *women in ARP (Air Raid Precautions) and the Services—some of*
> *them little blondes of the cutiest [sic] sort, some of them mothers [of*
> *soldiers]—and those scores of young men are superb, unthinkably so.*
> *The things that get me down are that a) the people are so much better*
> *than most of their leaders . . . and b) that people are working under the*
> *stimulus of death so much better than they worked without it. . . . I like*
> *being alive now.*

Intellect was both her strength and her shield, and from the insulation of Sussex, Rebecca had the luxury of philosophical pondering. She knew that humanity was capable of good and evil, but the exigencies of imminent attack made moral nuance irrelevant. Politicians played on the scaffolds of power while the populace grasped the immutable. Each day was a fight for survival, and each individual affected the spirit and well-being of the whole. Eight and a half million Londoners were in this together, and Rebecca found the prospect both exciting and rejuvenating. The future of Britain was predicated on the beneficence of strangers, military and civilian. Her own life, in fact, had been saved by a passerby who had shielded her from the fire of an exploding bomb as she had walked on Davey Street during a raid. If the mindless hysteria of fascism vanquished the individual, then the collective dynamic of a democratic people would give him voice.

All the while, the citizens of London, at the hub of British cultural, economic, and political life, faced possible annihilation. Thousands of commercial establishments, as well as parts of the BBC, the War Ministry, and the Ministry of Information were temporarily moved to the country. Even Churchill and his staff were evacuated to an estate in Worcestershire, a hundred miles northwest of London. But the bombs did not fall in the autumn of 1939, and Rebecca and Henry, along with the evacuees they housed in Possingworth, returned to London in November to wait the winter out. In fact, three-quarters of the evacuees returned, and daily life, initially refreshing, became painfully dull.

Whitehall, bending to popular protest, slowly began to reopen the cinemas, and while some theaters would not survive their temporary closing, those that did were lavishly attended. The pubs had never been shut, for fear of an insurrection, but the dance halls reopened to unprecedented popularity, serving as avenues for release and abandon. Everyone, it seemed, wanted to dance; since no one knew when the war would end, carpe diem became the order of the day. Rebecca and Henry, however, were of another mind. Having tasted the serenity of country life, they sought to buy a manor house that would rival the beauty of Possingworth.

Rebecca knew that this war would be different from the first. Aerial warfare would change everything. The battle would be fought on British soil, blurring the line between civilian and soldier; no one, even conscientious objectors such as Anthony, would be safe from German bombs and mustard gas, she wrote. "There was such a stillness, such a white winter of the spirit, and such a prolongation of it that death was threatened." The idea of pacifism in the face of fascist enslavement was suicidal, she wrote. Moreover, the contours of Rebecca's life were categorically different today. Twenty-five years earlier, during the Great War, she had felt helpless. Saddled with an infant and dependent on H.G., she had felt cheated of the chance to serve the Allies either as an active participant or as an influential voice in the wartime debate. While Rebecca remained on the sidelines conjuring up stories such as *The Return of the Soldier* from newspaper reports, many of her contemporaries had volunteered to be frontline nurses, such as her novelist friend Vera Brittain. The realities of war had been seared into Vera's mind as she attended the wounded and dying in makeshift hospitals on the battlefields of the Somme. Vera had been the true voice of the war; Rebecca deemed her own fiction a feeble facsimile.

In January 1940, however, Rebecca was forty-seven, Anthony was twenty-five, and she had become economically independent. Now she had both the perspective and maturity to weather the necessary suffering and sacrifice of war, Rebecca wrote to Alexander Woollcott. Although she felt like an actress showing up for a rehearsal without a part, she was certain that she would find a role. Intellectually and metaphorically, Rebecca cast herself as an objective observer, a seasoned player on the stage of war, but to Dorothy she revealed that she was confused and disoriented, barely able to keep her life together. She was optimistic, however, that both she and her compatriots would stiffen to the cause. This time, she would be armed with a reputation as a serious writer and the admiration of a husband who had given her free rein to pursue her career.

Within weeks of their return to London, Rebecca and Henry bought a country estate. Ibstone, as it was called, was an eighteenth-century manor house set high on the Chiltern Hills on ten acres of land about forty-five miles from London, overlooking seventy acres of heathland and a vast birch forest. The home was the last remaining wing of a classic redbrick Georgian mansion encircling a courtyard. Its previous owner had fallen into debt and was unable to maintain it even in its truncated form. While the house was habitable, the farmland and the barn were in severe disrepair. The barn had holes in it "big enough for a cow's head to come through," she wrote, and leaky pipes had transformed the farm into marshland. Despite all this, she was besotted. As if composing an ode to an archaeological treasure, Rebecca wrote, "The long, low building stood among laurel hedges nearly as high as itself, with a garden that tumbled down a hillside in a welter of long grasses and broken terraces." She would write to her friend Doris Stevens that the house "which is half a Regency house . . . [is] set in country so pretty it makes you cry."

Purchased from a bank, it had cost a mere £6,000 (the equivalent of $405,630 in contemporary currency). The deflation of the pound in the aftermath of the Depression along with military spending had slashed real-estate prices by one-third of their prewar value. Henry had invested his money in risky speculations, and when the stock market collapsed, he had lost it all. Rebecca and Henry decided that the safest place for their diminished funds was in real estate, a tangible asset that would serve them well should they survive the war. As an aficionado of art and architecture, Henry would have preferred a home less rural and more urbane, set close to a cultural center such as Bath, but he bowed to her wishes.

Rebecca wrote to Henry's mother, Mary, that "still everybody is broke, so I suppose we shall just be in the fashion." In truth, they would never have been able to afford the house before the war. As it was, Rebecca hustled to write radio plays in London and magazine pieces for American publications in order to defray the cost. But she was willing to do anything to keep it.

From the beginning, she had a visceral response to Ibstone. It was as if it were "something that was very precious and had been destroyed." Soon she was to understand why. "I believe my pleasure in this achievement is not realistic but the dramatization of a childhood fantasy. A sister of mine [Lettie] the other day found in an old album the photograph of the house where my mother spent the happiest years of her life, and which long ago was burned to the ground. The photograph, which I had entirely forgotten, showed a house as like my new possession as one pin to another."

"Achievement" is an interesting choice of word for the acquisition of a house. Rebecca must have felt that in buying Ibstone, she was restoring the joy of her long-dead mother's youth and with it her mother's social legitimacy after the poverty and humiliation she had suffered in the wake of her husband's abandonment. And in so doing, Rebecca was reclaiming her own. No longer was she the Dickensian street waif, the exiled Jane Eyre—she had tangible proof of a social pedigree. Those less fortunate than herself would heretofore evoke her pity or disdain, unless, of course, they were brilliant and talented. Rebecca still believed in the innate aristocracy of the intelligentsia, that is, as long as they weren't socialists or communists. Although material possessions were anathema to all she knew of the meaning of life, she believed in the necessity of worldly pleasure; much like H.G., she was convinced that natural beauty and physical comfort were essential to the sustenance of one's creative will.

While her sisters and her son would see Rebecca's purchase of Ibstone as the pinnacle of aristocratic pretension, she would later justify it in spiritual and altruistic terms: "My husband and I are not certain that any of our investments will be worth much after the war, and we have a number of people who are wholly or partly dependent on us. If need be, we and they can all pack into this house and live to some extent on what we can grow." She planned to farm more than enough vegetables from their garden to satisfy their needs, converting their purchase into a "national resource." With time, she did. The farm produced a surfeit of food. Gooseberries and plums from their garden and trees were made into jam and stored for the winter; the fruit and vegetables they could not consume, especially tomatoes and onions, were given away or sold in the market; they set to pasture two Jersey cows for milk and fourteen polled Angus bullocks and five calves for meat, and stored hundreds of bales of hay in the silos for the winter.

The renovation of the house was a luxury that the "phony war," between autumn and spring, had afforded them, along with the illusion that time was on their side. Rebecca and Henry remained in their London flat while renovations and repairs were made on the house and barn and the land was rendered fit to farm. But in the spring of 1940, after the Nazis invaded the lowlands and France fell to the Germans, the war moved ineluctably toward England. On the afternoon of September 7, 1940, German bombs began to fall; hundreds of aircraft flew up the Thames toward the center of London, leaving four hundred Londoners dead and sixteen hundred severely injured in their wake. By Monday, the ninth, four hundred more were dead. Ironically, Rebecca would once again heave a sigh of relief that after a year of nerve-racking anticipation, the war had finally begun. "I feel like a female elephant undergoing her three years of pregnancy as a result of intercourse over the radio," she wrote to Woollcott.

Immediately Rebecca went into crisis mode. The "sluttish" pace of daily life, she wrote, assumed a new countenance as she prepared to spend her nights in the building's private air-raid shelter beneath their Orchard Court flat. Unable to grasp the full dimensions of the coming devastation, she concentrated on the logistics of survival. Her first task was to purchase cheap mattresses to sling over folding chairs as makeshift beds for herself, Henry, and those of her employees who wished to stay in town. While Rebecca would be the first person clever enough to fashion these beds, the other tenants would follow in droves, making it impossible to find room to lie down if one arrived late. One of the last to make his way home, Henry would often sleep upright in a chair. But whether one was upright or prone, the noise from bombs, not to mention the crying babies, frightened mothers, and the old and infirm, made it difficult to sleep.

As uncomfortable as Rebecca and Henry were, private shelters provided by landlords were a rarity. Most London homeowners spent their nights in their backyards in dirt-covered aluminum prefabs that were neither safe nor immune to flooding. The immigrant poor, mostly Jews, who lived in the East End either were trapped in their flats or sought refuge in the Underground, where flooding and disease from lack of fresh water and latrines were rampant. Even the Orchard Court shelter would become unsanitary and overcrowded, and Rebecca was anxious to set up house in Sussex. From September to December 1940, Rebecca would periodically travel to Ibstone to check the progress of the renovations and repairs, and make certain that the laborers who sought shelter there were well fed and comfortable. Gradually the Orchard Court tenants and their servants began to notice a pattern; her excursions seemed to coincide with heavy bombings. Later she would admit that she had an uncanny aptitude for anticipating a raid, but when a friend informed her of a tide of suspicion that marked her as a German spy, Rebecca was appalled. The shock was only to be equaled by their dismay at the hate notes sent to Rebecca and Henry after they moved into Ibstone, tagging them as Jews intent on taking over the countryside, and threatening them with "elimination."

Their move to Sussex was accelerated by the escalation of bombings. The most devastating raid occurred in December 1940. Fifteen hundred fires broke out, killing nearly 4,000 people and injuring 5,200. A bomb had fallen so close to Portman Square that the dining-room furniture in their Orchard Court apartment had begun to crack. Rebecca's protestations of maturity aside, she found it intolerable to be trapped in a war zone with no easy way out. The resumption of German bombing during the day made her home in Sussex seem like a journey to the moon, she wrote. Nonetheless, Rebecca packed up supplies and traveled the dangerously unprotected country roads to Ibstone with her housekeeper and her new secretary, the classically educated and amiable Margaret Woods. Henry would remain in town until his summer holiday three weeks hence, commuting to the country on the weekends.

After five years of unrelenting research and study, writing draft upon draft of her 1,200-page manuscript, Rebecca was ill and exhausted. In truth, she hadn't been well since Germany's invasion of Czechoslovakia. The rumblings of war had played havoc with her mind and body. Pervasive anxiety, jaundice, anemia, and pain in her gut had siphoned her energy, making the process of writing nearly unbearable.

She was convinced that she had given birth to a monster that few would read, and those who did would despise—especially her pacifist family and friends on the left. Despite her controversial attacks on the moral turpitude of British character and government, its imperialist will yet flaccid foreign policy, Rebecca "would kill herself . . . rather than change or modify the truth of anything she wrote," a friend reported Henry as saying.

The strength of Rebecca's intellect was matched only by the vulnerability of her body. It was as if each fought the other for dominance. She was her book, and her book was England at war with itself—appeasement and slavery versus war and bloodshed. While revising the final draft in February 1941, Rebecca, plagued with chronic colitis and gallstones, was admitted to a hospital in Reading for surgery to remove tumors from her gut.

Rebecca's recuperation from surgery was slow and laborious, but Henry, billowed with pride in her work, was uncommonly kind and loving. It appeared he saw no contradiction between basking in Rebecca's glory and taking in lovers as a form of self-affirmation. As Rebecca's secretary Margaret typed the final draft, Henry went over the manuscript line by line, combing it for errors in spelling, grammar, and fact. Despite their estrangement, Rebecca's literary accomplishments united them. Much as Dorothy had set resentment aside when Hal was preparing to accept his Nobel, Henry jettisoned their differences to close ranks around Rebecca's work. By the time her book was published in October 1941, the Nazis had overrun Yugoslavia, and many of her friends were dead. Dedicating the book to these fallen heroes gave her little comfort; her "monstrous" tome had become a prophecy.

Simultaneously attacked as biased, ignorant, and incoherent, and praised as ingenious, penetrating, and groundbreaking, the book was a critical success. While its commercial success was less than sterling, sales were sufficient to put them back in the black within two years of purchasing Ibstone, and Rebecca was able to do what she loved most—write a novel. Not fully recuperated from her operation, she eschewed research and travel in favor of writing about political treachery in turn-of-the-century Russia. Playing on themes from her previous book—the categorical quality of male perception versus the narrow yet nuanced nature of female insight, and the politics of sexual power as a metaphor of internecine war—she inserted an idealistic young woman, Laura Rowan, into the male political world of double agents and radical revolutionaries. Laura, the daughter of a Russian mother and an Irish-English father, on a visit to her grandfather, a tsarist minister in Paris, can see what he cannot—the trickery and betrayal of his comrades and advisers—and becomes an agent of his enlightenment.

Perhaps because of her own father's duplicity, Rebecca would always be fascinated by the psychology of traitors. It was in the neurotic mind, she wrote, that one could study the "normal." This novel would be her first of several fictional attempts to examine the dynamic of the treasonous strain in her personal relationships. Rebecca would struggle with the novel throughout the war, but unable to find a resolution to this quarrel between comrades and kinsmen, she would put it aside for nearly two decades to report on the crises of the present. The world was changing fast, and she wanted to be "watching it cast off its old skin and put on a new one," she would later explain.

In September 1941, as the democracies of Western Europe engaged in an existential struggle, the PEN club, a literary and human rights organization, held its international symposium in London. Its topic, Writers in Freedom, could have been neither more apt nor more important to Rebecca, whose *Black Lamb and Grey Falcon* had augured the death of culture in a totalitarian world. Despite her less-than-optimum health, she was so moved by the prospect of participating in the discussion that she drove down to London for the day. Distilling the principles upon which her tome had been based, she presented a paper called "The Duty of a Writer." In a sense, the ideas contained in it had been brewing for twenty-five years, since she had published her piece in *The New Republic* in 1914, "The Harsh Voice," and a decade later, in *The Strange Necessity,* concluding that using the tools of science in the service of art—the union of observation and imagination, reason and romance, tradition and innovation—was the path to universal truth. But in her September 1941 speech in London, her literary and political theory would collide. Identifying the writer as a species of primitive shaman who delivered truths known only to the unconscious of his particular "tribe," she pushed the analogy into the realm of nations. The individual is to the nation as the nation is to the international community. Each nation, large or small, transitory or enduring, she said, had a unique culture that contributed to the wisdom of the whole. Together the community of imaginative writers offered "a complete vision of reality"—humanity's "absolute ideal." By denying the Nazi threat, she said, the Western democracies were all responsible for the human devastation. She implored writers to confront the problem of human evil and individual responsibility, not through political writings but through imaginative works. The deep exploration of human experience was their ultimate duty.

But even as Rebecca spoke, her Russian novel, with its quagmire of relationships and moral turpitude, was teaching her that imaginative truth was perhaps the most difficult literary endeavor of all. She was certain, however, that fostering freedom and truth, and assuming responsibility for the flowering of the young, was her duty as a writer. The challenge was to align literary theory with life. She had yet to define her role as a wife, mother, mother-in law, sister, and aunt. The everyday dynamic of relationships still unhinged her. Unlike her novel, she could not put those aside until the characters and the conflicts clarified; it was a war zone all its own.

In November 1941, her sister Winnie wrote to Rebecca thanking her for "the Great Heap of Money, or rather two great heaps." The Macleods, at least temporarily, appeared dependent on Rebecca's financial generosity; all tension dispersed, however, when they commiserated about their renegade children. While the sisters had striven to put their past behind them, their children seemed bent on repeating it. Immature, self-absorbed, and irresponsible, Anthony and Alison, Winnie's daughter, blackened their lives with anger and resentment, just as the world was palled with war. Unfortunately, neither Rebecca nor Winnie chose to see the hand each had played in forming the character of her offspring.

Anthony was talking about divorcing Kitty. Lust had trumped loyalty. No matter that his children, Caro and Edmund, were under the age of two, he blithely announced that he had fallen in love with another woman. Unbeknownst to Rebecca, Kitty had shouldered running of the farm while Anthony had gone to work at the BBC several days a week. Now nearing thirty, Anthony had fallen in love with Audrey Jones, a colleague of eighteen. Moreover, he and his "fiancée" were planning to move into the barn on their farm in Dorset while Kitty and the children packed up to leave. Given an ultimatum, Kitty, who never saw Anthony's desertion coming, was devastated. Rebecca thought her son had gone insane. Can you imagine, she wrote to Lettie, that Anthony had called to tell her the news without the least recognition that his plan was absurd? It was like something her father or H.G. would have done, she wrote. Sometimes she thought that Anthony had no autonomy; he was bound to mimic the patterns of his ancestors. As usual, she would blame Anthony's maladjustments on others; his constant need for affirmation had nothing to do with her. His illegitimacy belonged to H.G.; his motives were either mystically preordained or antiseptically genetic. Hiding her guilt from herself, she could only feel anger and contempt toward others.

Rebecca believed that the estrangement between Kitty and Anthony was linked to her son's refusal to fight in the war. As a girl, Kitty had feared and despised her father, who had nonetheless fought in the Great War and died with honor. Although Kitty's disappointment with Anthony remained unarticulated, it seeped through the cracks of their daily lives. Anthony had married Kitty for her maternal qualities; she had brought structure and focus to the aimlessness of his teenage years. But in the aftermath of his flight into farming to avoid military service, she had become increasingly demanding and controlling, critical and withholding. Too wrapped up in the farm and the children to notice, Kitty had not sensed Anthony's growing alienation. After their separation, Rebecca commiserated with Kitty, offering to help her and the children with anything they needed.

For Winnie, Alison's rebellion had an added component of shame. She had announced that she was pregnant by a West Indian man, James Hacksaw. James, she would say, was not just someone she had picked up in Piccadilly; he was the nephew of an old friend of her aunt Lettie, and the black solicitor general of Windward, the chief advocate representing the interests of the British Windward Islands to the Royal Commission. Furthermore, he was not only a gifted flutist but irresistibly handsome. While it was clear that James had no interest in her or marriage, Alison stubbornly insisted on carrying the child to term. Amid "dreadful storms of tears & grief," she told her mother that she had found him sexually exciting and had seen no reason for self-restraint. James was willing to go through with a legal ceremony to salvage the child's legitimacy, but the marriage was to be perfunctory and short-lived. No one, neither Alison's parents nor Henry, could dissuade her from having the child. Apparently Rebecca, the family expert on single motherhood, was summoned as the agent of last resort. After meeting with Alison, Rebecca wrote to her sister from Sussex: "She was completely insulated from the world, I could get no sense out of her at all, she might have been moving in a world where legs of mutton grew on trees."

Totally out of touch with reality, Anthony and Alison seemed to infantilize themselves in their quest for independence, Rebecca wrote to Winnie. While Rebecca had sympathy for Alison, and offered her a small yearly stipend as well as a sum of money in her will, it was more out of a sense of duty than love. She believed that Alison had to pay for her errors by hard work; her life was not to run smoothly on the wheels of her relatives' generosity. Through Winnie, she offered Alison advice:

> *I gather from Henry that Alison wants to give up her work for a year in order to look after the baby. . . . This is stark staring madness. If she gets out of journalism for a year, she will never get back—and the best thing she can do for the child is to make a life for herself. I made a great mistake by not sending Anthony away for the first year to some nearby place—round the corner would be best—and not getting on with my work. As it was I had to work hard later on, so that I could not give Anthony all the time he needed when he was a little older.*

Finally, Rebecca had begun to question her own decisions, if only in the context of advice to another.

When Alison and Cathy, Alison's beautiful "brown baby" girl, returned to her parents' home, Winnie was willing to assume a modicum of caretaking responsibility as long as she needn't divulge her biological relationship. But their kinship was not something anyone could see. The Macleods were an odd mix of bourgeois and bohemian. A union of like-minded professionals and intellectuals, their marriage was male dominated and family centered, with a clear division of labor. And Alison had learned the family lessons only too well. Industrious, earthy, and frugal, eschewing possessions, even when they could afford them, the Macleods had taught their children to flout the conventional, devalue the material, hone the intellectual, and defend their unique stance regardless of social cost. Norman, Jr., Winnie's son, was a gifted scientist with an academic bent whose interest in politics was secondary at best. Alison, however, was of another ilk. Outspoken and articulate, with an acerbic wit, she had only to turn the dial slightly leftward to embrace the love of a black man and the arms of the Communist Party at a time when social equality was the hallmark of the enlightened.

Socialism, entrenched in the left wing of the Labour Party, was integral to the British political scene, spearheading the push toward social equality—woman suffrage, universal education and health care, trade unions and welfare policy. But the Communist Party of Great Britain, founded in 1920, was a new organism, swept in on the wind of the Bolshevik Revolution, that promised hope for the economically disenfranchised, the socially marginalized, and the indigenous and immigrant poor. Ignorant of, or resistant to, the reality of Leninist oppression and mass slaughter, and the deprivation of the proletariat by the depraved and murderous party dictators, British intellectuals, highborn and low, espoused Marxian theory, sacrificing loyalty to kin and country to usher in a new world order through an international workers' revolution. What began as idealism often ended in thuggery. Those such as Alison, alienated but unaffiliated, were targeted by the local apparatchiks hoping to harness their discontent to their cause. Alison would later say that she was swept along. At the time, however, she would find employment and purpose as a subeditor and literary reviewer at the *Daily Worker*, an important organ of the Communist Party. Four years after Cathy was born, Alison would also find a husband. When the war was over, she and Jack Selford, the comrade who had signed her up when she was nineteen and he was an older man of thirty-one, and a widower with two sons, were married. Anthony had also flirted with Communism, but his motives appeared more personal than political, joining perhaps to defy his mother. Rebecca couldn't help thinking that everything he did was a form of revenge.

Anthony invited Rebecca and Henry to lunch at the Ritz, but bowed out at the last minute, sending Kitty in his stead. Kitty looked hauntingly beautiful, Rebecca noticed, as she waited for them in the lounge. Her blond ringlets brushed her face, catching the light. But almost immediately, Rebecca was aware that Kitty had come to punish her. Kitty defended Anthony's affair with Audrey as perfectly reasonable and mature. Rebecca at once quarreled with the idea that Anthony was at the moment "normal," and asserted to Kitty that her son's judgment had to be flawed.

"She [Kitty] then looked at me [Rebecca] with a curiously vindictive expression, and said, It's a funny thing but that's exactly what Anthony says about you." With eerie calm and self-possession, Kitty went on to tell Rebecca that her interference in their family life was totally unjustified, while Rebecca remained steadfast in her opinion that Anthony would regret abandoning his children. The sparring continued until finally Rebecca blurted out that she "wished Anthony was dead, he was evil and vile, and would bring nothing but suffering on everybody about him," and she walked out of the hotel. Henry, who was partially deaf, was unable to hear the details of their exchange. Confused and surprised by Rebecca's abrupt exit, he remained with Kitty.

Rebecca had been reluctant to tell H.G. about Anthony's break with Kitty, now that he was well into his seventies and ill. But after this abortive tête-à-tête with Kitty, she hailed a taxi and went straight to H.G.'s flat at Hanover Terrace. Sitting amid the book-lined walls of his study, H.G., with his measured rationality, was an antidote to her frenzy. Balding, loose skinned, and baggy eyed, he still gave the impression of a gentleman scholar. He raised his bushy eyebrows in surprise at Rebecca's unannounced arrival, and informed her that he already knew of Anthony's intention to divorce Kitty. H.G. told Rebecca that shortly after he had fallen ill, Anthony had barged his way into his room to give him the news. Certain that he would garner his father's support, Anthony excitedly told him about his newfound love. He didn't know that H.G.'s infidelities had not softened his opposition to divorce, especially when the marriage involved children.

Rebecca was downcast and self-flagellating; H.G. commiserated with her concern. She told him how pleased she had been with Anthony's commitment to farming and his family, and how she had come to believe that he was finally cured of his impulsivity and depression. Anthony had, in fact, written her a letter in which he had expressed pride in the life he had fashioned, declaring that he had finally come into his own. And yet, the last time she had seen him, Anthony had looked swollen and disheveled, reminiscent of his appearance as a teenager prior to one of his suicidal breakdowns. Much as H.G. had done in their early days together, he cautioned Rebecca not to be overwhelmed by her emotions; Anthony's failure was not her own. No one was guilty; all would resolve itself in time.

H.G.'s seemingly rational perspective grew out of a surprising strain of romantic naïveté. For all his intellect and mental acuity, he tended to think in broad, sweeping ideals and human stereotypes. By his own admission, he was imprisoned by his impulses, having only a vague understanding of the "mysteries" that underlay individual behavior. And for all his cataclysmic vision of humanity, he had a Hegelian faith in process that was tantamount to a belief in the divine. Until the very end of his life, when Hitler's unmitigated evil would prove his optimism wrong, he put his faith in love and in the evolution of a new socialist world order that would breed international peace. Rebecca, on the other hand, had always wrestled with God and intelligent design. Art was her path to self-transcendence, and only the artist could span the abyss through self-discipline and hard work. She had little faith in the intellect or morality of the common man.

While Rebecca's mind skillfully dived and soared, producing elegant theories and treatises, her personal life, full of distortions and treachery, gnawed like a voracious predator. Anthony, her sisters, H.G. (in fact, all her lovers), but most of all Henry, were governed by unexamined neuroses. She was the victim, never the stalker. Sadly, her lack of faith in others, which might be interpreted as the underbelly of her megalomania, hastened exactly the behavior she feared. To her unending chagrin, Rebecca craved a lover and a friend, both of which eluded her. Henry's unrestrained lust for women had long ago eroded her hope for fidelity, but he had always been her rock-solid friend. Now his confident presence seemed to be slipping away. Plagued with a duodenal ulcer, he had grown increasingly pale and thin. The prevailing remedy of a "milk diet" had a fleeting salutary effect. But more than that, this repository of classic culture and language, this touted economist and humanitarian, was losing his grasp on reality. It began with ordinary things—logistical decisions concerning the farm, and relations with the farm staff. But the more he sensed his loss of control, the more dictatorial and controlling he became. Rebecca wrote to Winnie that she was baffled by Henry's increasing forgetfulness and confusion. His mental state heightened her loneliness, and at once echoed and presaged her sense of abandonment.

The war against fascism was merely the visible battlefield between good and evil, heroism and bloodlust. Rebecca's battles were fought behind closed doors, in daily conversations, in letters and books, and in daydreams and nightmares. How should she cope with a son and daughter-in-law who shunned her? How could she give her sister and her niece psychological support, when she could not steady her own moral compass? How should she nurture a husband whose decline made him a burden and a humiliation? In sum, where could she find the emotional sustenance that would give her the confidence and strength she needed as a woman and a writer? Rebecca sensed it would be these invisible enemies that would slowly destroy her—eviscerate her vitality and creative will. As she moved through her fifties the stakes were higher, but the lessons of her youth remained the same. The way out lay in letting go of her worn-out ideals. Her marriage was tainted by weakness and betrayal. Her only son had become an adversary, and, once a source of inspiration, her sister had become a drain on her mind and pocketbook. She was unequivocally alone, and the only way forward was to embrace the reality beneath the shroud of dust that lay around her.

CHAPTER 12

GOD LUST

All those who, because they believed in and
longed for some Utopia, followed some dream
of perfection, forgot the first Commandment of
the Decalogue.

—DOROTHY THOMPSON, 1939

NEW YORK, 1935

Dorothy was imposing, buxom, and stout, yet as pink-skinned
and pretty as ever. A matron of forty-two with graying hair, riveting eyes, and a strong angular chin, she radiated confidence. She was
General Patton in skirts; "something between a Cassandra and a Joan
of Arc" with the drive of the *Titanic,* said those who mocked her. But
her friends were quick to add that she was compassionate, supremely
ethical, and all woman. In short, Dorothy had become her own feminine
ideal: "powerfully woman." In Germany her guts had made her a
star, and she had returned to a nation where stardom mattered, and
to a city that matched her appetites. Dorothy loved to eat and drink,
consumed news like liquor, and devoured culture like a famished
traveler.

New York in 1935 was a particularly good place to be, if one hungered for anything. With its thousands of shops and boutiques, restaurants and pubs—from the corner bar to the gold-laden doors of the Stork
Club—eight daily newspapers, three baseball teams, and Broadway theater in its heyday, New York was the most exciting city in the world.
"The Great White Way" seethed with people; millions of lights flickered

in tempo to the noise and tumult. The Dorsey Brothers' hit song "Lullaby of Broadway" grasped the rhythm of the number one, best-governed city in America:

Come on along and listen to
the lullaby of Broadway.
The hip hooray and ballyhoo,
the lullaby of Broadway.
The rumble of a subway train,
the rattle of the taxis,
The daffy-dills who entertain,
at Angelo's and Maxi's.

With Fiorello La Guardia flitting around the city in motorcycle sidecars and putting out fires, literal and otherwise, New Yorkers felt safe—even immune—from the political upheavals of Europe.

While London and Berlin shivered, New York glittered—a bit too much for Dorothy's taste. She could not put aside her experiences in Germany: the goose-stepping soldiers; the incarceration of dissidents and Jews; the megalomania of a dictator who had come to power as an agent of the people, only to strip them of their rights and convert a sophisticated, enlightened culture into a police state. Unlike most Americans, Dorothy saw the moral decay beneath the national façade of optimism. Her country, she believed, had embraced the hedonism that would herald its downfall. "The whole nation lived on futures, mortgaging tomorrow's wages for today's automobile or radio and the feverish turnover of goods was called prosperity," she wrote. "Our finest cities are disfigured by dark, unhealthy, crime-breeding slums. . . . We admire success and are callous to achievement." America's moral weakness, she believed, made it vulnerable not only to European fascism, but to its own.

Unemployment was down, the banks were solvent, and the economy was on an upward trend, but Dorothy believed that Americans had paid an unconscionable price. Roosevelt's New Deal, she wrote, with its public works projects and social services, had been forced down the throats of legislators; fifteen bills had been passed during his first hundred days as president. Roosevelt, she feared, was using unprecedented executive authority for what he alone deemed the public good. "That is the essence of the quarrel that many of us have with the New Deal," she would later write, "the difference between constitutional government and the kind of government that exists in dictatorships. In one there is government by law; in the other government by officials, who use their own judgment as to what constitutes 'positive and definite harm to the majority.'" But it was the minority that she was worried about. Dorothy believed that the protection of minority rights was essential to democracy. Disregarding them, as Hitler had done in Germany, "becomes the mask of Imperialism," she wrote.

Some critics claimed that Dorothy was an alarmist; that she saw a dictator under every bed. Apparently her writing was persuasive enough to convince her husband, in whose mind a fascist satire was beginning to brew. After a trip to Boston in February with four-year-old Michael to celebrate Hal's fiftieth birthday with his other son, Wells, who was attending Harvard, Dorothy, Hal, and Mickey toured Bermuda and Jamaica. With no routine or distraction, Hal became drunk and abusive. Their requisite fight and reconciliation ruined their holiday, and they returned to Bronxville earlier than planned. But when the weather turned warm and they made their annual move to Twin Farms in Vermont, Hal's novel crystallized. As usual, he meticulously laid out maps of mythical cities and developed a biography for each of his characters. Sitting alone at his desk, high in the eaves of the big house, with the blue mountain of Ascutney in the distance and acres of wildflowers and woodlands spread out before him, he wrote at a frenzied pace, finishing the novel in three months.

The book, *It Can't Happen Here*, portrayed the rise of an American dictator, a contemporary of Hitler's. A senator from the Midwest, modeled on Huey Long, he comes to power promising prosperity, employment, and military power to his people in exchange for surrendering their civil rights. Like Hitler, he manipulates his political adversaries to gain a legal majority, dissolves the constitution, and imposes martial law. America becomes a true fascist state—racist, anti-Semitic, anti-intellectual, and militaristic. Conjuring authentic, as well as fictional politicians, Lewis dramatizes the shattering of America's social and moral scaffolding. It is Hal's cleverness and literary imagination one reads, but it is Dorothy's voice that one hears, as goodness and virtue (relatively speaking) are pitted against satanic evil. Never were Dorothy's and Hal's minds more united in creative harmony than in *It Can't Happen Here.*

As Dorothy would write, "When our dictator turns up you can depend on it that he will be one of the boys, and he will stand for everything traditionally American. And nobody will ever say 'Heil' to him, nor will they call him Führer or Duce. But they will greet him with one great big universal, democratic, sheep-like bleat of O.K., Chief! Fix it like you wanna, Chief! Oh Kaaaay!" Later, when it was rumored that the blue-eyed, sandy-haired all-American hero Charles Lindbergh might run for president, she deemed him the exemplar of an anti-Semitic pro-Nazi American dictator—manipulative, messianic, and defeatist.

Dorothy, Hal, and Michael in 1932 sailing to Europe

By September 1935, Dorothy and Hal were off to Europe on the SS *Ile de France* for six weeks. By the end of October, the novel was published. In the United States, more than 94,000 copies were sold, and sales amounted to 320,000 worldwide. By 1930s standards, this was extraordinary, if not unprecedented. Hal was hailed and supped by socialists and communists, who assumed that if he wasn't a fascist, he was one of them.

In his inimitable fashion, Hal drank their liquor and ate their food, and with equal gusto, proceeded to mock their praise.

Dorothy seemed to bask in Hal's success. Once again she had reason to hope his good fortune could salvage their marriage. When Ogden Reid, president of the *New York Herald Tribune*, who had transformed his father's defunct newspaper into a viable and profitable daily, descended into alcoholism in the mid-1930s, his wife, Helen Rogers Reid, took over. Helen, whom Dorothy had known when she was the treasurer of the New York State division of women's suffrage organizations, asked Dorothy in 1936 to write a political column three times a week. The newspaper was entering a state of transition—from staunch conservatism to moderate liberalism. A thin-lipped, gray-haired, neatly coiffed woman ten years Dorothy's senior, Helen was molding the paper according to her own vision, hiring more women as reporters, columnists, and editors. It had been Helen's maverick book editor, Alabama-born Irita Van Doren, who had conscripted Rebecca to write book reviews a decade earlier. Having watched Dorothy burst into print as one of the small number of female foreign correspondents, Helen cast her in the role of teacher/translator of policy issues that affected the lives of women. Her column was to be a political primer—and a conduit of news and opinion—for the intelligent woman who did not want her facts filtered through the (often distorted, Helen believed) mind of her husband. With Hal's encouragement, Dorothy accepted the offer.

The column was a natural for Dorothy. Finally she was free to interpret the news, and there were so many things she cared about. The *Herald Tribune* boasted a prestigious assortment of voices, one of the mightiest of which would be sharing her space on alternate days: Walter Lippmann. A Harvard-educated Jew of German heritage, Lippmann had moved from being a socialist, as a founder and assistant editor of *The New Republic* and the chief editorial writer of *The New York World*, to being a right-leaning columnist for the *New York Herald Tribune* in 1931. An adviser to President Wilson during the Great War, Lippmann was a Washington insider with international connections. As an antiwar isolationist, unmoved by the plight of his kinsmen in Europe, he believed, unlike Dorothy, that European fascism was not a threat to America. His column, Today and Tomorrow, was hugely popular by the time Dorothy joined the paper. Syndicated in 250 newspapers around the county, it tended to be rigorously logical, noncontroversial, and totally impersonal. Notoriously direct, unequivocal, and passionate, Dorothy's style could not have been more different. Her voice was the perfect counterpoint to Lippmann's intellectual elitist views. While Lippmann dismissed the general public as irrational and uneducable, Dorothy saw her role as a mentor—even preacher—to the uninformed.

Before assuming her post at the *Herald Tribune,* Dorothy persuaded Hal to move to Washington for six weeks in order to soak up the political and social atmosphere. With negotiations for a movie version of *It Can't Happen Here* in the works with MGM, the buzz in Washington was that Hal was writing a new novel. He was, in fact, thinking of writing a play. Both engrossed in gathering information and mastering a new genre, Dorothy and Hal once again appeared to be the quintessential literary couple.

In March 1936, Dorothy began her three-day-a-week column, called On the Record. It was clear from the beginning that she would play by nobody's rules but her own. She would be as honest, straightforward, and accurate as she could be, but she would not be pegged as a woman's writer. While at first male readers would call her hysterical and illogical, especially when they disagreed with her, ultimately as many men as women would follow her.

Dorothy's debut column was a commentary on the corporation tax bill, a subject, she admitted, about which she knew little (Einstein didn't either, she noted, so she was in good company), but felt it was her duty to study as a student of public affairs. Her second column was a satirical political dictionary, explaining how the word "honor," for example, had been debased to mean prestige. "Defense" meant war; "unity" meant uniformity; and "truth" had become the tool of political ideology. Her third column analyzed the mechanics of statecraft, and her fourth was a diatribe against party politics as a base expression of human nature. In a thousand words, on Tuesdays, Thursdays, and Saturdays, she covered the gamut of human affairs, from domestic and foreign economic and political policy to music and theater, from personal profiles of cultural icons to the idiosyncrasies of world leaders. Toscanini's genius was as worthy of discussion as the emperor of Japan's butterfly collection. But her primary focus was political: Eight of her columns in the first three months were devoted to criticizing the Roosevelt administration. In 1936, she backed Republican Alf Landon in the presidential election.

In November 1936, Roosevelt was reelected in a landslide, winning the electoral votes in forty-six out of forty-eight states. Deflated, Dorothy spent two months abroad gathering her thoughts. She came back to New York at the turn of 1937, ready to attack. In her columns as well as in a series of speeches at Town Hall in New York, she derided Roosevelt's policies. He viewed his victory as a mandate to further impose his will, but his newest proposal, Dorothy wrote, struck at the heart of the American constitution—the division of power among the three branches of government. Roosevelt's plan, she explained, was to offer retirement with full pay to every Supreme Court justice over seventy years of age and to appoint six additional justices to round out the number to fifteen. His motive, she surmised, was to rid the court of justices who objected to his New Deal proposals. These policies, she believed, fed the vulnerability of democracy; this was how Hitler had come to power. "Once you let down the dams, once you relax in one direction, the floods sweep in." Dorothy believed that divided power was the end goal of democracy. Improvement, not perfection, was its aspiration. Perfection was an attribute of God. Clearly, she implied, Roosevelt didn't qualify. Roosevelt's proposal, known as "packing the court," ultimately fell flat, and subsequently the sitting Supreme Court came to tolerate his economic legislation.

In essence, Dorothy's columns analyzed the same issues she spoke of in conversations and public meetings, and wrote about in letters, but now she had a megaphone. Within a year her column was syndicated by eighty newspapers around the country, reaching five million readers daily. Within two years it was picked up by one hundred more. In June 1937, Dorothy received honorary degrees from six major colleges and universities, and it was rumored that she would run for the U.S. Senate from Vermont. Some of her well-connected friends were even thinking of getting her on the ballot for the presidency. "I wish they would elect Dorothy president," Hal remarked, "so I could get to write 'My Day,'" a syndicated daily news column by Eleanor Roosevelt.

Dorothy makes her radio debut on The Hour of Charm

Dorothy's voice was amplified by another five million in the summer of 1937 when she was given her own radio show by NBC, sponsored by General Electric, dubbed *The Hour of Charm* in an effort to stave off public aversion to an authoritative female voice. Introduced as the daughter of a country minister, Dorothy had thirteen minutes every Monday night during which to comment on any subject that caught her fancy, and, as in her columns, everything and everyone did. As her political diatribes grew more fiery, however, GE tried to moderate their effect by introducing her with a tune called "Love Sends a Little Gift of Roses" and signing off with a trio of young women singing "Thank God for a Garden" or "Ave Maria."

Dorothy's first radio series, *Personalities in the News,* consisted of profiles of individuals who influenced policy and events at home and abroad—from foreign officials to notable American individuals and events. The segments concerned people she admired and those she detested, individuals whose search for personal truths and national freedom was either heroic or tragic, and issues that made her doubt the validity of democratic ideals.

Much like Rebecca, Dorothy saw herself as a liberal/conservative. She was liberal in the classic sense—a believer in freedom and civil liberty under the rule of law, open to growth and innovation; she was conservative as a proponent of history, order, decency, and responsibility. Above all, Dorothy was a patriot—a woman who loved America for its constitutional ideals and who attacked anyone who violated its principles and tenets. She could quote the Federalist Papers and Lincoln's speeches by heart, and she wasn't afraid to reprimand those who transgressed. Dorothea, "a gift from God," as her Hellenic name implied and her parents intended, could heave the fire and brimstone like a preacher's daughter. It was a role, however, that didn't play well at home.

Hal's habitual postcreative slump consisted of knocking around the house in a drunken stupor, spending time in the city in his rented apartment, or traveling aimlessly with Lew Florey in search of another book idea. The movie version of *It Can't Happen Here* had been spiked on fears that it contained dangerous material that would stir international discord, and his play *The Undiscovered Country,* an exposé of anti-Semitism in New York medical schools and hospitals, had come to naught. In desperation, he was thinking of going back to his labor novel.

There was only one certainty in his life—he was unhappy with Dorothy and their life together. And not for the first time, he told her so. Dorothy's success, and his self-perceived lack of it, had estranged them. By anyone's standards, however, Hal *had* been successful; he had recently written several well-received plays, including a script for *It Can't Happen Here,* produced in eighteen cities across the country. In truth, Dorothy's work was but one factor in his discontent. He was fed up with her incessant discussion of political "situations" and especially with her attempts to reform him; he felt like a degenerative appendage in her sacrosanct universe.

Dorothy's revitalized career, and Hal's itinerant wanderings, made Michael seem like an afterthought. A journalist from *The Christian Science Monitor* visiting Bronxville to write a portrait of Dorothy "found Michael quite easily by following his voice." Michael, now almost six years old, was speaking to his violin teacher in the nursery. "You will never make me a musician," he said. "I shall be better with words; I don't like to study, so I won't. I must live my own life." Apocryphal or not, the story portrayed him as loud, definitive, and independent—traits the journalist was hoping to link with his mother. Michael Lewis was clearly being stuffed into the garments of social propriety: music lessons and long-trousered sailor suits.

Shortly after his outburst, the reporter followed him into the living room where his mother was holding court with her thirty or so luncheon guests. Totally ignored, Michael began hurling insults at them. Dorothy had been telling her audience that she was about to embark on a two-month lecture tour, which was to be her last. Now that she was a radio commentator, she said, it seemed silly to go on the road when you could stay close to home, near your husband and son. Busy touting her domestic nobility to her captive audience, Dorothy, aware of neither Michael's presence nor his diatribes, did not see him slink back to the nursery. The truth was, she didn't know how to be a mother; she had never had one. She was making up the script as she went along.

As for Hal, Dorothy chastised him for being away a lot and for taking off without telling her, but she was essentially too busy to miss him anyway. Dorothy was branching out into magazine writing. The editors of the *Ladies' Home Journal,* Bruce and Beatrice Gould, had asked her to write a monthly column on topics of her choice, targeted to a female audience. Hal's unhappiness with her was an old refrain she couldn't take seriously; early in their marriage, he had made her promise that no matter what he said or did, she would never leave him.

In a letter to Rebecca in March 1937, Dorothy told her friend of her disappointment with Roosevelt's neutrality bill (the 1937 Pittman Resolution), which continued the national policy forbidding the sale of arms or the granting of loans to nations at war, as it had during the Spanish Civil War. Dorothy would have wanted, no doubt, a more interventionist policy, given her support for the Allied cause. She believed it was an attempt to "wash his hands" of the Spanish war. It proved, she wrote, that the United States had no sense of right or wrong. Any country could be an aggressor. "I must say that I feel very discouraged about the state of the nation. . . . But perhaps, as you say of yourself, I am only a fuss-box. Red is simply fine as can be imagined."

Apparently, she was blindsided when little more than a month later Hal left her. It was a cool and rainy morning in late April 1937, just as she was planning their annual move to Twin Farms. He was standing in the arched doorway of their mock-Tudor home in Bronxville with a suitcase in hand and his raincoat collar turned up around the narrow face and thin silky red-blond hair she loved so much. He blamed it on her work, and she, in tears, was too shaken to respond. He told her that he wanted to go away by himself for a couple of years. As he turned to leave, she asked him if he wanted a divorce. He said no. Closing the door behind him, Hal, like Michael, slunk away.

It took Dorothy six days to sufficiently regain her composure to write him a letter. "When you tell me that my work has ruined our marriage, *that* statement falls on deaf ears. I *know* that it saved our marriage for the past six years. It was, for me, the outlet, the escape, from something too intense to be born[e]. Too 'devouring.'" She was speaking of his mood swings and his drinking.

"You don't know what you are like, Hal, when you are drunk," she wrote.

This restless, dynamic, overcharged, demanding personality, which is you, becomes intensified to the point of madness. It is energy completely explosive and completely off track. In our early marriage it dragged me with it, until I vomited from revolt that I couldn't control. . . . I saw it destroying something—however temporarily—which I loved with all my heart and all my mind. And it was destroying me. I didn't want to be destroyed, because I believed that I was as essential to you as you were to me. I had to keep myself—for you. And I kept myself by constant baths in the cool air of work, in the cool, impersonal, intellectual, unemotional air of an objective world.

Taking him at his word without delving deeper, she chastised him for his jealousy of her reputation, of feeling like the mere husband of Dorothy Thompson. She called it an obsession that would cease as soon as he found something satisfying to accomplish. He was a "creative genius"; she was "just a tail on an ascending comet."

"Good God, Hal, you are one of the best critics living, and you know *exactly* my worth and my limitations. So do I. I am a first rate peripatetic brain picker." As a matter of fact, she wrote, she owed a great deal of her facility with language and style to the ten years she had spent with him.

Concluding her letter with the self-righteous moralizing that was her wont, she declared, "Darling, darling, darling there's only one thing in which I am a really superior person. I have a really superior capacity to love." It was what she had written to Joseph Bard, after he had left her; it reveals a woman capable of insight, yet incapable of change. Why? Blind spots, psychological and sociological, got in the way. Both Dorothy and Rebecca seemed to share this trait. Dorothy had always used her intellect to pry open her emotional limitations. Now, as with Rebecca's, these compartments seemed hermetically sealed.

Later, she would write to Hal that her work was mere sublimation. After her love for him had become a matter of compassion and loyalty, she could use her passion only to attack frivolous causes, or turn it inward and kill herself. "What was there left for that woman except to fire at the world's injustices and stupidities for the sake of the Union League Club? Or cut her throat. You tell me the answer."

But her work was not sublimation; the Victorian ethic under which she and her contemporaries labored (in the mid-1930s, 82 percent of people polled did not believe that women should have paying jobs outside the home) had taught her that all women should put family first. She couldn't. So instead of feeling irresponsible or blasphemous for ignoring the needs of her husband and son, or believing that she had the right to a life of her own, she blamed her career on unrequited love.

Dorothy's work was the love of her life, and she was a loyal person. She didn't feel alive if she couldn't write, and neither did Hal. For him, writing was the unfolding of perception—a consuming diatribe against all forms of hypocrisy, large and small. It was frenzied creativity without a broad moral vision. But for Dorothy, her work was a divine mission; her desire to learn, write, teach, and reform was what God had created her to do. The effect, however, was a paradox of humility and arrogance, self-diminishment and hubris.

It must be recognized that Dorothy, along with her female colleagues, was moving in uncharted waters. The opportunities they had forged and the status they had achieved were unprecedented. However, as a product of her fundamentalist background, Dorothy would never escape the guilt she carried for breaking the rules and leaving her family behind. Unlike Rebecca, she could neither understand the moral "battleground" within nor find the personal courage, despite her words to the contrary, to truly validate her ambitions. Furthermore, letting Hal go would have required her, once again, to admit failure at sustaining the sacred marital union. She would adjust her expectations, but not their legal status.

Besides, Dorothy was convinced that Hal was not gone for good. And for the moment, she was right. Alternating between dependency and disgust, he did, in fact, come and go. They would attend the same dinner parties and invite each other on trips. On the surface, at least, their hostility was gone, but Hal's unhappiness lingered.

In the following months, still hoping to salvage their marriage, Dorothy would write to Hal that perhaps "*this* is a lie—a crazy bad dream, and tomorrow you will stand in the door, and the bad dream will be over." But her true concern was Michael:

> *The awful thing is Mickey. I don't dare to say it. But he seems utterly unreal to me. He doesn't seem like my child. And I don't seem any more like myself but like somebody else whom I don't know. Mickey was always you to me. Another you. But now I don't know you and I don't know him. Everything is dream-like—all the things people say to me and about me, and fame or notoriety or whatever it is. It all bounces back upon a vacuum, which is me.*

Vacuum? Not quite. Emotional disappointment, as always, fueled her work. The more unhappy she was, the more her intellect became her refuge. She wrote to Hal's son Wells, now twenty years old, that she wasn't very good at marriage. While his father had broken her heart, it had been broken before. In a sense, she wrote, she had become immune. As with Rebecca, Dorothy's discipline and ambition rescued her from implosion. Their career trajectories were the inverse of their personal happiness. While Hal disappeared into the ether, bingeing on alcohol and moving in and out of the Austen Riggs Foundation in Stockbridge, Massachusetts, in the hopes of a finding a Freudian cure for his addiction, Dorothy blazed her way to the top of her profession.

Don Wharton of *Scribner's* magazine wrote in May 1937: "Dorothy Thompson is the only woman in this country to make good as a political commentator. She is one of the very few to even try." By singling out Dorothy, Wharton unfairly glossed over Anne O'Hare McCormick. A friend of Dorothy's, Anne was the foreign correspondent for *The New York Times,* and the first woman on its editorial board. She was awarded a Pulitzer Prize in 1937, and Dorothy believed that she had earned it. She would comment that Anne had more perspective, energy, common sense, and objectivity in interpreting fact than any reporter she knew, and a gift for lucidity that gave her "real writing style." Dorothy knew that the *Times'* policy of not permitting its correspondents to be syndicated had stunted Anne's fame, while the *Herald Tribune*'s policies had served to make Dorothy a national figure.

But Dorothy's fame could not eclipse the fact that home had become a lonely place. Michael, too, had been abandoned. How was he to cope now that his father had gone, and his mother was too preoccupied to attend his needs? Hal had left Dorothy without a thought of their son, just as he had left Gracie without a thought of Wells. Dorothy cared deeply about Michael—as deeply as she cared about anyone. But she had her work and her own sanity to deal with. After Hal left, she rented a small apartment in New York City on West Sixty-sixth Street, where she spent most of her days, commuting several evenings a week to Bronxville.

Michael seemed to take matters into his own hands. By the time he was eight, he was bigger and stronger than his peers, and he used his edge to conquer his fear of irrelevancy. Unfortunately, his classmates and friends were caught in the struggle. One day, he lunged at the son of Betty and Raymond Gram Swing (Dorothy's fellow foreign correspondent in Germany) with a large knife. Later, Betty would write a letter to Dorothy suggesting that she take Michael to a psychiatrist. Dorothy recoiled. It was true, she responded, that Michael was big and strong, but he was also intelligent and imaginative. Michael's combative stance was, she continued, nothing more than an expression of pride. While he was certainly "difficult," he was neither "cruel" nor the least bit "abnormal." She went further in his defense, as if she was trying to convince herself as well as Betty:

"I know my son, much better than you think I do. I know him because I know myself, and I know his father. I know him because I enjoy a warm, affectionate, candid, and at the same time fairly detached relationship with him. We love each other."

But she wasn't detached, and she didn't know him. His teachers were baffled by the intensity of Michael's feelings. Some of his nurses at home had sought to curb his tantrums by locking him away in a closet; others had suffered his blows silently. Dorothy was roundly criticized for not staying at home, but those who knew her well were more compassionate.

They confirmed her love for him, and her sympathy for children in general. But Michael was volatile and sensitive; he had Hal's temperament, not her own. She didn't know how to help him, and her short-term solution was to shower him with money and material possessions. Michael's classmates at the Riverdale School for Boys in Riverdale, New York, were stunned by his violence and confused by his lack of parental restraint. Nothing seemed to satisfy Michael, and nothing seemed to change Dorothy's perception of him or her unwillingness to alter her lifestyle to assuage his sense of abandonment. Michael's situation was not all that different from Anthony West's. With absent parents and misguided rage, they were "poor little rich boys" alienated from their teachers and peers, and forced to compensate in expedient ways.

In desperation, Dorothy closed up their Bronxville home in early 1938, and moved with Michael to a large apartment in New York City. She enrolled him in the Collegiate School, a prestigious academy for boys on the Upper West Side. Their new, expansive L-shaped apartment occupied a high floor at 88 Central Park West with panoramic park views, a comfortable room for Michael, and an extra bedroom for Hal, should he wish to live with them. When Hal declined her offer, Dorothy helped him move across town to the Wyndham on East Fifty-eighth Street, and arranged to have their domestic help in Bronxville work for him there.

The increasingly violent and chaotic pattern of Michael's life would dramatically change when he contracted measles and double pneumonia in the summer of 1938. Everything he had known and taken for granted since birth was about to shatter.

Dorothy was relieved to find that Michael's illness was not the dreaded polio virus, but without the benefit of antibiotics, Michael's recovery from pneumonia was slow. The prevailing medical treatment for measles, horse serum, triggered allergic reactions in Michael that required adrenaline to quell. This cascade of maladies and treatments culminated in the onset of nephritis, leaving Michael weak and his doctors bewildered. In the course of extensive examinations and tests, however, a theory surfaced concerning the cause of Michael's volatility. A chorus of doctors deemed Michael's sexual development "subnormal."

Dorothy wrote to Hal, "His genitals are those of a child of four, not eight, he is overweight and the distribution of his fat indicates sub-masculinity." One eminent physician, originally from Berlin, attributed his rage to hormonal imbalances. Dorothy made it clear to Hal, however, that the biochemical underpinnings of Michael's belligerence were not sufficient to explain his behavior. She warned him that his continued neglect of Michael would have tragic results.

Michael received radiation therapy—the contemporary remedy for pituitary maladies—and Dorothy was advised to send him someplace where he could get exercise, sunlight, and warmth. The Southwest seemed a fitting place, and the Palo Verde Ranch School, in Prescott, Arizona, a school Wells Lewis had also attended, was highly recommended. Its big sky, vast plains, and massive mountains must have seemed both intimidating and exotic to an eight-year-old from New York City. Two thousand miles away from home, smack-dab in the middle of the desert with a population of five thousand, must have felt like punishing exile. Yet, Michael was neither alone—Dorothy had sent a nurse to live with him—nor uncared for. While the headmaster, Mr. Hutchinson, was sympathetic and attentive, the strangeness of his new Western lifestyle and the expectations of his teachers would prove difficult.

Michael tried hard to be happy and was anxious to please his mother. He wrote home about the trials of camping, but also of the fun of horseback riding, shooting, and tennis. At his request, Dorothy sent him a photo of his father, which he hung on his cabin wall. Michael told her how much he loved her over and over again.

Taking him at his word, Dorothy convinced herself that Michael had adjusted well. His departure set her free to travel and work, and 1938 would prove a critical year for international politics and Dorothy's effort to shape them. Armed with various "uppers," including Dexedrine prescribed by her physician, who had acquiesced when she told him that she might not be capable of keeping her rigorous schedule without them, Dorothy was unceasingly productive. In 1938 alone, she wrote 132 On the Record columns, which appeared in each of the forty-eight states, and occasionally in Canada and Australia; twelve lengthy pieces in the *Ladies' Home Journal* (with a circulation of 3.5 million); more than fifty speeches and miscellaneous articles; numerous radio broadcasts; a book about refugees, and two volumes of her collected columns from the *New York Herald Tribune*.

The Anschluss in March 1938, when Germany invaded Austria in a bloodless coup, had awakened Dorothy to the fact that the world was dealing with new kinds of movements—revolutionary and international. While her public condemnation of Germany was cold and harsh, in private she shed tears for her beloved Austria, the land of her youth, first marriage, and professional launching. She and her friend British novelist Phyllis Bottome, whom she had met in Berlin, wept in each other's arms, while Dorothy whispered between her sobs, "Our Europe is gone! We shall never see it again!"

Dorothy also worried that she would never see her Austrian and German friends again—especially the Jews and dissidents, such as Eugenia Schwarzwald, Carl Zuckmayer, and Christa Winsloe; she would offer to help each of them gain sanctuary and employment in America. But as usual, it was the larger political issue that moved her. She dug deep into the problem of international refugees; her words would penetrate the highest ranks of the government. As a result of reading Dorothy's April 1938 article in *Foreign Policy* magazine, "Refugees: A World Problem," Roosevelt organized the Evian Conference in France in July to establish a worldwide emigration and resettlement program for German Jews. While scholars now believe that Hitler would have been open to letting other countries take the Jews off his hands at that point in time, no nation, including the United States, wanted them. The conference was a total failure, and to this day Americans ponder how many people might have been saved had the countries that assembled at Evian acted.

"The results of what happened in Austria in March 1938 will not be apparent for some time to come," Dorothy wrote in the *New York Herald Tribune*. "I am firmly convinced, however, that it was the most cataclysmic event of modern history, and that as a result of it, one of two things will happen: Germany will dominate the continent of Europe, or millions of lives will be spent in another war."

Dorothy's friend Alex Woollcott, one of the many she and Rebecca had in common, would write to Rebecca that, based on her *Tribune* writing, Dorothy was ready to go across the Atlantic and "strangle Neville Chamberlain with her own hands."

In September 1938, after the Munich Conference, when England and France reneged on their treaties, abandoning the Czechs to a German takeover, Dorothy spoke at the Hollywood Bowl in Los Angeles to a crowd of more than seven thousand. Beautifully dressed and, according to Phyllis Bottome, looking lovely, Dorothy gave an impassioned speech about the individual and collective responsibility that weighed upon each American.

As Dorothy spoke to thousands of her countrymen from the cocooned safety of the Bowl, twelve thousand Jews with Polish passports living in Germany were forced to leave their homes without warning and to report to local centers. No one was allowed to take any money or any more property than they could physically carry. Among these Jews were the parents and sister of Herschel Grynszpan, a young boy of seventeen who had been sent to Paris to live with relatives in safety. The Grynszpans, along with the others, were herded onto trains by SS officers wielding clubs and whips and dumped in a small Polish town, penniless and without contacts. A drenching cold rain fell on the refugees; they eventually found shelter in the ruins of an old Polish army base. When Herschel received a postcard from his sister telling him about their forced exile and the appalling conditions under which they were living, he grew profoundly depressed. After sending a postcard to his family, apologizing for what he was about to do, Herschel gained entry to the German Embassy in Paris and shot and killed the German attaché Ernst vom Rath.

After only one radio broadcast on behalf of Herschel Grynszpan, Dorothy raised $40,000 from her listeners to pay for his legal defense. "They are holding every Jew in Germany as a hostage," she said. "Therefore, we who are not Jews must speak out." For this she would become the object of hate mail that would brand her as both a Jew lover and an anti-Semite. Her answer would always be the same: Prejudice against any minority was un-American.

This one act by an angry, desperate teenage boy was exactly what the Nazis were waiting for, providing them justification for Kristallnacht. During the Night of Broken Glass, on November 9, 1938, 7,500 Jewish shops were destroyed; thousands of Jewish homes were burned in Vienna and Berlin, along with 1,500 synagogues. It was estimated that 2,000 to 2,500 Jews were killed in the process, but Grynszpan's life, largely through Dorothy's efforts, was spared for the time being. Although he was convicted two years later, he was never brought to trial. Late in the war, he would die alone in a German prison.

In recognition of her efforts, Dorothy was appointed president of American PEN and elected to the American Academy of Arts and Letters. "Too many honors," she complained. And one is inclined to say that she was right. Dorothy could sway millions, illuminate and alter conditions several thousand miles and a continent away, and help save the life of one desperate boy, but she was unable to fulfill the emotional needs of her young son. Hal would agree. Mincing no words, he later wrote: "The strangest aspect of your great brilliance, your power to analysis masses and men outside yourself, is that you never—almost never—analyze your motives, or your feeling and relationship toward anybody near you."

Hal's words echoed those of H.G., who after praising Rebecca's literary gifts, wrote, you are "a little disaster of a girl who can't even manage the most elementary trick of her sex." While their expressions differ, the meaning was the same.

On December 6, 1939, Michael wrote a letter to Dorothy from Palo Verde describing the Thanksgiving celebration at the ranch and thanking her for the decorations she sent. He also asked if he might come home for Christmas. The fact that his spending the holidays at home was not an assumption—that he had to ask his mother for permission, one week into December—reflects the degree to which Dorothy had lost touch with her personal life.

What Michael sensed, but could not articulate, Dorothy unabashedly shared with her readers in the *Herald Tribune*. In a column she had written in 1938, she explained that her personal life was of secondary importance in the "revolutionary world." She explained: "There are people about me whom I love—tenderly and furiously. Yet something comes between us. What comes between us is the whole of society. The nucleus, myself, my husband, my child, the people dependent upon us and our friends, should somehow tie up and be part of a larger collective life, be integrated with it through and through."

But Michael was just one boy, not a larger collective, and her flesh and blood, not an abstract social concept. He needed her and insisted on being part of her life. Totally disillusioned by the moral frailty of democratic leaders, and repelled at the thought of another devastating war, Dorothy found Hal's self-pity and Michael's sniveling insipid. Nonetheless, Michael did come home. He spent the holidays alone with her in

Vermont, since his half brother Wells decided to remain in New Orleans where, thanks to Dorothy, he had an internship on New Orleans's *Times-Picayune*. On tour with a play and totally immersed in his work, Hal wrote Michael a letter five days before Christmas, one of the two extant. It is funny and sardonic in his inimitable way, yet detached—almost abstract. It could have been written to any young child. It seems as if someone, most likely Dorothy, had reprimanded him for not acknowledging Michael at Christmas.

Dear Michael:

If you will go flipping about the country by aeroplane, dipping down to inspect the North Pole or the Grand Canyon or Thayer's Store from time to time, how can I catch up with you with Christmas presents? I sent you a couple of books to the Palo Verde Ranch, and probably they will be awaiting you when you get back.

One of them is a dairy. No, it's a diary, not a dairy. I'm never quite sure about the spelling of those two words, but anyway, what I sent you wasn't a set of cows, with Murphy and Stub, done up in cellophane and red ribbon, hanging about their necks. Not at all. It is a book, in which to write daily what you have done, so that some time you can look back and remember whether it was William Zimple you had a fight with on the 7th of March, or Dousweiler Fishcake. . . . [By the time you finish the diary] in 1941, you will be a very profuse author and (I hope) writing both my novels and your mother's columns, so that we may devote ourselves to bridge and the crossbreeding of catnip plants.

Anyway, love and Merry Christmas,

Daddy

While portraying the prospect of domestic harmony, Hal withheld the truth—one that Dorothy knew and feared would damage Michael's already fragile sense of security. Hal had fallen in love with an eighteen-year-old actress, Marcella Powers, whom he had met in summer stock a year earlier. He was thrilled, if somewhat deluded, to have a young woman dependent upon him and by his side. He had needed Dorothy to keep him straight and had hated her for it. And not realizing he had asked the impossible, he hated her for letting him down. His revenge was to become someone else: the controlling mother she was to him; the loving father he never had. With Marcella, it was he who held the reins of power. She was his Pygmalion—a delicate, sylphlike "woman-child" he could shape according to his ideal vision. She was so inexperienced and needy that he succeeded in convincing himself she would never stray. Her youth, beauty, and devotion to him inspired him to write a novel, *Bethel Merriday*, and plays in which he cast them both in starring roles. In effect, he created a fantasy world in which he was the writer, director, and leading man.

Through Hal's lawyers, Dorothy was notified in the spring of 1939 that he wanted a divorce. When the news of their impending split became public, Walter Lippmann abandoned his rational persona, gleefully knocking Dorothy off her pedestal. He wrote to a female friend:

Did you ever realize how much Dorothy is like the Statue of Liberty? Made of brass. Visible at all times to all the world. Holding the light aloft, but always the same light. . . . Capable of being admired, but difficult to love.

My sympathies, and this is not pure male prejudice, are with Sinclair Lewis, who took to drink and then to the Riggs Sanatorium. You know, when I think of it, being moralized over by a woman who has made a mess of two marriages seems to me to be the height of impudence.

Hal's lawyers informed Dorothy that he wanted to give her Twin Farms and the property, now valued at $150,000, as well as the Bronxville house, valued at $50,000, of which she was already the sole owner.

Crestfallen and feeling, not for the first time, cheated and abandoned, Dorothy sat in her empty apartment, surrounded by the park and the wide expanse of New York City, writing a letter to Hal:

If you think [our relationship is] wicked—go ahead and divorce. I won't oppose it. I also won't get it. For God's sake, let's be honest. You left me, I didn't leave you. You want it. I don't. Go and get it. . . .

You are happy. Happier, you write, than you have been in years. I
congratulate you. I am glad that you are happy. I happen not to be. I
am not happy. I am not happy because I have no home; because I have
an ill and difficult child without a father. Because I have loved a man
who didn't exist. Because I am widowed of an illusion. Because I am
tremblingly aware of the tragedy of the world we live in. . . .

Give me Vermont. I want to watch the lilac hedge grow tall and the
elm trees form, and the roses on the gray wall thicken, and the yellow
apples hang on the young trees, and the sumac redden on the hills, and
friends come, and your two children feel at home. Who knows? Maybe
some time you might come home yourself. You might go a long way
and do worse. As a matter of fact and prophecy—you will.

Disillusioned by marriage and motherhood, and feeling powerless to
influence a world on the brink of war—a war she had seen coming for six
years—Dorothy wrote a column for the September 1939 issue of *Ladies'*
Home Journal, once again pouring out her heart to her faceless, invisible
readers. She entitled it, "If I Had a Daughter."

I would tell her that she has to choose. I would tell her that if she
feels in herself some talent for the development and expression
of which everything else is worth the sacrifice, to go ahead and
develop it, but to know that the development will cost her a great
deal. Marriage is a union—it is not a league of two separate sovereign states, it is not two orbits in a common sky; and I would tell
her that making a successful marriage is, by and large, a full-time
job for most women. . . . Society, at this moment, has a greater
need of good mothers than it has of more private secretaries, laboratory assistants, short-story writers, lawyers, social workers and
motion-picture stars. [It is more important] to produce a fine man
than it is to produce a second-rate novel, and fine men begin by
being fine children.

Intuitively, Dorothy finally understood the price she had paid for her
career, but she had made her decision long ago. To stay at home with Hal
and Mickey would have been tantamount to suicide. If she was "widowed of an illusion," it was her perception of herself. She was not the
superior moral being she had thought she was, and in breaking the rules,

she, too, had given up "the best things that life had offered" her. Unwittingly, and with the purest of intent, she had become a cold brass beacon of freedom, and lost the capacity to touch those she loved. Like Rebecca, Dorothy was deemed an androgynous creature, with "masculine" tastes and ambitions. Out of sync with their time, yet deeply, longingly feminine, neither knew how to be a woman.

CHAPTER 13

FRACTURED

> Destiny cares nothing about the orderly presen-
> tation of its material. Drunken with an exhilara-
> tion often hard to understand, it likes to hold its
> cornucopia upside down and wave it, while its
> contents drop anywhere they like over time and
> space.
>
> —REBECCA WEST, *A Train of Powder*, 1955

BUCKINGHAMSHIRE, 1944

In the calm of the English countryside, in the safety of Ibstone, Rebecca sat among her silks and satins drinking her morning coffee and
reading the papers. While contemplating events from afar, she roiled
with outrage. The war had reached epic proportions. The Allies were
battling on two fronts. The Germans and the Japanese had vowed to
fight to the finish; Russia had repelled the German invasion; Hungary
was about to surrender; there were rumors that the Nazis had sent millions of dissenters, Jews, and Gypsies to the gas chambers; and Yugoslavia had become a political pawn in an Allied deal. The world had gone
mad; the old order was in ruins.

As she reviewed the events of the previous year, Rebecca was pained
by thoughts of death and betrayal; the personal and the political seemed
inextricable. In May 1943, Churchill's military advisers convinced him to
back the duplicitous Tito, a slippery Soviet puppet, over Mihajlović,
whose stewardship, Rebecca believed, had held the promise of a free and
independent Yugoslavia. She saw Churchill's act as an expedient move
against Germany that betrayed her beloved Yugoslavian people. Re-

becca insisted that Churchill had a personal vendetta against the peasant Serbs, because, as she wrote, they were "non-Blenheim born." Once again the Yugoslavians had become enslaved to an oppressive hegemony. Hadn't they paid their pound of flesh when hundreds of thousands had died attempting to thwart the Nazi takeover two years earlier? It was the final tragic blow against an ancient, freedom-loving people. In a strange leap of logic, Rebecca conflated this political perfidy with her sister Lettie's conversion to Roman Catholicism. It had been "savagery" on a lesser scale, she wrote; Lettie had rejected their family's "pioneer Protestantism" for the sake of a dogmatic theocracy. That, too, she believed, was an attack on human liberty.

As much as the surreal magnitude of Allied war casualties pained her, it was the ordinary death of her dear friend Alexander Woollcott that cut to the quick. It was he who had given her hope and confidence, opening the door to financial independence after her flight to America to escape the talons of H.G. As both her mentor and advocate among the American literati, Alex had been a countervailing force to the vengeful slurs of her spurned lover. His untimely death from heart failure had silenced a voice of encouragement, admiration, and reassurance she had come to trust and depend on. His passing heightened her loneliness, as those related by blood and law had begun to feel like a band of conspirators. Rebecca wrote in her diary, "I have had wonderful friends all my life; people who owe me nothing; it is the people closer to me who have failed me."

A descendent of musicians and wordsmiths, Rebecca had come to see her life as an opera—a clash of desire, expectation, and conscience, riddled with pain and tragedy. The death of Alex and her pervasive loneliness were the latest permutation of her sense of victimhood. Again, she feared that a malevolent force was in control. As she wrestled with the demons that stalked her, was she finally the author of her own libretto? Or was she still the unfortunate target of a sadistic maker? Whatever the answer, this vision permeated her relations with people and her perception of politics.

The year 1944 promised more death and deceit. Anthony was mired in his plans to divorce Kitty. His love for the BBC reporter Audrey Jones ("himself at 18," according to Kitty) was deemed pure fantasy by everyone except Anthony. More than anything, Rebecca feared the impact of his leaving on his three-year-old daughter, Caro. The girl was lithe and beautiful like her mother; his leaving would crush her innocence. While Rebecca stewed, Kitty was stoic. Anthony was not without blemish, Kitty told Rebecca; she had caught him in lies about their finances. But she admitted that she, too, had been at fault; her careless criticism of his behavior and writing had alienated him. She had been too immersed in the household to see it coming, she said. Besides, it stood to reason that Anthony would stray; he had married her when he was so young.

Distraught by Anthony's irresponsibility and rashness, Rebecca tried to inject a voice of reason. In a letter she said to him, "I wish you'd remember that the excitement and support you seek will probably—for you—never be found except in your own work." He should not expect it to come from places outside himself. With the irony of one who had broken all the rules, she advised him to curb his sexual impulses, because relationships require permanence for the sake of the children. But Anthony, inured to her hypocrisy, had a theory of his own. He blamed his inconstancy and quest for constant affirmation on his illegitimacy, specifically on his villainous aunt Lettie, who had insisted on concealing his father's paternity—a fantasy promulgated by H.G. Rebecca was convinced, in turn, that blaming Lettie was a convenient cover for his own inadequacy. Adding another log to the fiery interchange, H.G. believed that if Anthony would enlist in the army, as he should have done in the first place, all would be resolved. For their part, Winnie and Lettie had lost hope long ago that there would ever be a resolution. They deemed Anthony hostile from birth and Kitty a self-righteous, insensitive fool. But this endless cacophony of voices drowned out the reality: A young family was in dissolution, and no one could help them.

At the age of seventy-seven, H.G. was fighting another battle—one of personalities as much as disease. His health was failing, and as he sat among his books in his study on Hanover Terrace, rumors of his impending death swirled. Eager to gain control, his sons, Gip and Frank, had taken it upon themselves to tell him that he was dying of liver cancer. They believed it was their moral responsibility, considering his lifelong quest for the "truth." Appalled by their impudence and suspicious of their knowledge, not to mention that she believed H.G. to be an inveterate liar, Rebecca went to see H.G. for herself. She wrote in her diary that he was "pitifully miserable and afraid. He told me that he hated his illness and complained that the doctor wouldn't tell him exactly when he was going to die, in a way that made me realize that he really minded terribly about his dying." Rebecca felt deeply protective, as if he were her child, and went back to Ibstone to walk the woods and weep. He was, now and always, exactly what he had told her he was: not the Jaguar he had pretended to be, the puffed-up image of a powerful predator, but a lonely man who craved kindness and company. One senses that Rebecca's tears were as much for the demise of his image as they were for the man. She knew she had wasted too many years of her youth fighting a phantom.

Although Anthony had warned Rebecca that he would never forgive her if she attempted to interfere, she called their longtime friend and physician Dr. Horder, who had attended H.G. throughout his illness. He said that the sons' story was nonsense. Horder had told Gip that H.G.'s liver was "enormously enlarged," but when Gip had asked him for the worst-case scenario, he responded that it might be cancer, but "there are absolutely no clinical symptoms of cancer at the present moment." Despite all this, Gip had told H.G. that he had only twelve months to live—a total fabrication. Later, said Dr. Horder, he had received a note from either Gip or H.G., asking him not to call again. Horder was heartbroken.

Saddened and confused, Rebecca visited H.G. again, only to find him delirious and delusional. Was it fear or true mental deterioration? Had the cancer spread to his brain? She concluded that the answer was beside the point. H.G. needed a friend, and her task was to comfort him. She would have thought that Moura, his live-in companion and lover of eleven years, might offer him consolation. But Rebecca was convinced that even now the cagey, double-faced Moura was using him. Callous and uncaring, she lounged around smoking and drinking his brandy, while the poor soul anguished in limbo.

H.G.'s illness and looming death brought Rebecca to a new level of consciousness, reviving her curiosity in the inscrutable. Believing that there were "mysteries" one could not fathom, she wondered if death was ultimately meaningless; if there was something more important than physical life.

But despite her philosophical musings, Rebecca held tight to the petty vacillations of earthly life. Anthony continued to defy her understanding. He seemed "queer . . . fat and animal," someone alien to her family and to the man he might have been. He made her ill at ease, and she didn't trust him. Unlike his father, Anthony didn't deserve her friendship; his overt hostility had stripped him of his claim on comfort. It is true, she wrote in her diary, that H.G. had subjugated and abused her, isolating her from her friends, and wreaking vengeance upon her after she had left him. But ultimately she saw him as a good man, mired in his past and trapped in his neuroses. She must have somehow harbored doubts about her own integrity and sensed that her demands on their relationship had been unreasonable. Only if her "affection is real and living" would her behavior make sense. Yet she was far from ready to forgive Anthony for being the insufferable offspring of their extraordinary, if less than sacred, union.

While Rebecca felt certain that Anthony would distort everything she said, she wanted to "get it straight" about her relationship with H.G. before the old man died. She poured out her heart in a letter to their son. First of all, she wrote, it was important for him to understand that she had sent him away to boarding school when he was three for financial reasons; she could not depend on H.G. to provide for them. Second, Jane Wells was not who she appeared to be. Jane was, she wrote, a "wicked woman," who had a vice akin to drugs or liquor. Rebecca explained, "Unfortunately her madness fitted in with H.G.'s not at all uncommon complex—which was to sacrifice women he found attractive to the Virgin-Mother." Jane, as the pure soul in his female universe, manipulated H.G. by cultivating a façade of loyalty and caring, while selfishly going off and leaving him in the hands of his mistresses.

Rebecca continued, "[After Jane died], it really was as if a shadow had been lifted from his character." She and H.G. had become "good friends" with a "deep affection" for one another. In fact, he had asked her to marry him, but "he still [was not] sane about any matrimonial matter. He was mad in a particular kind of way as you and I are in our way." Besides which, she was not interested in "sharing the throne" with Odette or Moura. "The story of H.G. and me ... was ... tragic and pitiful," she concluded. She ended her missive by underscoring her prime reason for writing. She admonished Anthony that having children with different people "lets the prowling devils of the psyche come to their own. . . . H.G. suffered, it split him."

But what then was her explanation for Henry's philandering? Was his, too, a matter of survival? Unlike H.G. and Anthony, Henry had no children, yet still "the devil prowled." Her theory had always been that men were hardwired for infidelity; their polygamous impulse was part of their Darwinian quest to spread their seed. If Rebecca was not Henry's Virgin Mother, she was certainly Henry's feminine ideal. And ideals, no matter their species, did not make good lovers. Henry required the conquest—the banality of seduction—to affirm his manhood. After fourteen years of marriage, Rebecca still didn't understand his psychic terrain. He seemed to have no core; he was a kaleidoscope of personalities. He could be kind, sweet, and paternal, or he could withdraw into reverie, a prisoner of his own fantasy world. But lately he insisted on playing another role: an old man. Henry was much too young to be acting old, and yet, he was inexplicably irrational, inappropriate, and dependent. Was it just his need for emotional reassurance, or did it mask something deeper?

Rebecca put thoughts of Henry's psyche aside for the concrete concerns of money and war. She was "tormented by the fear that H.G. might have left some more money to Anthony, and that it would be wasted, Kitty would have none." But her real fear was that she and Henry, with their diminished funds, would have to support Kitty and the children for the rest of their lives. Claiming that her health was poor, Rebecca worried that she would never be able to stop working. Hate, vengeance, and evil hovered like demons over her universe of innocent victimhood—the familiar recitative of her personal opera.

But the Allied war against the evil Third Reich seemed mercifully clear-cut. On June 6, 1944, the second front was opened. "Everything is tangled up with the Second Front," she wrote. But Rebecca feared German retaliation.

The American and British forces launched an unprecedented amphibious operation on the northern coast of France under the command of General Eisenhower. Over the span of twenty-four hours, nearly 176,000 troops were put ashore at Normandy between Cherbourg and Le Havre, protected by 9,500 aircraft and 600 warships, far outnumbering their German counterparts. Within days the beachheads were linked and the Allies were approaching Rome from the south, eating away at the Vichy control of France, and pummeling Berlin with bombs. From the east, Russian troops pushed through Finland and the Soviet "Fatherland" on their way to Warsaw. But within a week, despite or because of these Allied victories, Rebecca's fears of reprisal materialized.

Germany began launching V-1 rockets, long-range twenty-five-foot-long unmanned missiles, at England. Eight thousand were fired, and

2,500 reached London. Their buzz and crash terrorized Londoners, killing more than five thousand and injuring nearly sixteen thousand. More than a million houses were destroyed or damaged, along with schools, churches, and hospitals. While Rebecca remained out of the range of fire, her sisters were in the heart of it. Lettie, the director of the medical office in London, was frantically trying to maintain medical services. Rebecca worried that she would have a nervous breakdown. Winnie chose to attribute Lettie's "insanity" to her Roman Catholicism and feared for her own family's lives. She pleaded with Rebecca to find a farmhouse near Ibstone where they could ride out the war. Rebecca quickly found one, moved in some appliances and old furniture, and, by some glitch in wartime law, was able to rent it to Winnie for one dollar.

Following each Allied move closely from her perch north of London, Rebecca was relieved in October when the Nazi sweep through eastern Europe was nearly done. Northern Africa would soon be liberated. But despite having suffered more than a million casualties since the Allied invasion in June, the Germans refused to surrender. They continued to bomb British civilians with the updated V-2 missile, while in turn, the Allies bombed German cities. In desperation, the Germans cranked up their cremation efforts in the camps, and their remaining troops, exhausted and demoralized, launched ineffective counterattacks against the Allies.

In mid-December the Allies almost lost the war; in a carefully coordinated counteroffensive, the Germans launched a massive attack against the Americans in the Ardennes Forest in Luxembourg, catching them by surprise. As deaths mounted in the dense forests of Ardennes, many deserted, and morale sank; soldiers felt they had been abandoned to die. But eleven days later, in a masterful move by an American general, George Patton, from the south, and with the help of British reinforcements, the Ardennes offensive was ended. In the course of the attack, later dubbed the "Battle of the Bulge" because of the configuration of American troops, nineteen thousand lives were lost. It was an Allied victory that might have easily ended in defeat. Although it was a tactical triumph for the Germans, they would never recover from their losses.

The Allies dropped four thousand tons of bombs on German cities, including, in mid-February 1945, Dresden. Rebecca would later condemn this raid that was believed to have killed thirty-five thousand civilians as one that would forever remain a stain on Allied wartime conduct.

The American general George C. Marshall blamed it on the Russians' desire for revenge; Churchill denounced it; Rebecca, still fuming from Churchill's betrayal of Yugoslavia, denounced him as a conspiratorial dissembler with civilian blood on his hands.

Now certain of victory in Europe, the Allies met at Yalta in February 1945 to plan their strategy in the Pacific.

By the end of March, the worst seemed to be over, and Dorothy and her loving husband of two years, Maxim Kopf, a gifted and cosmopolitan painter from Czechoslovakia, felt it safe to visit their friends in England. On March 29, 1945, Rebecca and Henry met them in London. Rebecca wrote in her diary that they had dinner together and a "wonderful talk." Dorothy, she wrote, had even brought her a silk nightdress—an unthinkable wartime luxury in Britain. While the British economy had collapsed during the war, the American economy, spurred by the production of wartime materials, had held its footing. Rebecca had never met Max before, but she immediately took a liking to him. Physically large and charismatic, Max was a force of nature who instantly lit up the room— the complete opposite of the intellectual and restrained Henry.

Two days later, Dorothy and Max visited Ibstone. Henry picked them up at the station and gave them a tour of the gardens and the house. Dorothy was thrilled to see photos of Anthony and his family. The last time she had met him was as a child of eight. To see him now—a tall and husky brown-eyed and dark-haired man of thirty with a family of his own—made her realize how much she hungered to be a part of Rebecca's life. Unlike Rebecca, Dorothy had few women friends; her work as a journalist drew her toward men, and in truth, she liked them better. But Rebecca was different. She had that same spark of independence; the same insatiable curiosity; the same intense desire for success as herself.

The two couples had much in common. The men were multilingual cosmopolitan connoisseurs of art and culture, who had been incarcerated during the First World War; the women, now friends for twenty years, had much to commiserate about—their troubled sons, the emotional trials of their genius fathers, and their attempts to juggle their professional commitments and family obligations. Together, the four of them probed the political dynamic of what might be postwar Europe among the Allies, and the Allied stance toward the nearly defeated Nazi regime.

Later that week, on April 4, 1945, Rebecca and Henry met Dorothy and Max in London at Piccadilly for tea, introducing them to several of their literary friends. Afterward, Rebecca and Henry strolled toward Hyde Park. With the Allies swiftly closing in on the Germans, the park was dizzy with celebration. They walked for hours amid "much smoke and flare," with "hyacinth blue" searchlights casting beams across the grass and trees. It was an "enchanting scene," Rebecca wrote in her diary, and quite a contrast to the somber ambience of the expressionless figures who had lined the benches, inhaling the last smell of roses before the darkness set in during their stroll nearly six years earlier.

As if on cue, in sync with the ending of war, Anthony, no longer the "conscientious objector," went back to Kitty. Bent on teaching him a lesson, Kitty was initially cold and withholding. But it wasn't long before she took him in. Rebecca could see their reunion only as her loss. "Kitty has taken him from me," she wrote in her diary. To feel betrayed by her daughter-in-law, to see her as a competitor when Anthony's search for happiness had been so elusive, was telling. It is as if Rebecca felt that only she could be the agent of her son's well-being; her reaction speaks of guilt for work undone. More and more, she seemed the maestro of her own defeat.

Soon Rebecca's paranoia would resurface with a vengeance. There were rumors that she and Henry, simultaneously with other "titans" of industry and finance, had invested part of their vast fortune, that is, £3,500,000, in the Yugoslavian economy in order to sustain Colonel Draža Mihajlović, an anti-Nazi, anti-Communist Serbian official. Of course the charges were pure idiocy, she wrote—they barely had enough money for themselves and their dependents, let alone the Serbs—but she feared that the Communists would target them. Rebecca was sick with diarrhea and felt like she was dying. She believed that spies had infiltrated their home; their housekeeper had created an atmosphere of trouble, and it led Rebecca to believe that she and her husband were part of a larger conspiracy. She wrote to Doris Stevens that the "mildest possible laxative" that she had been taking for years had been making her sick. She told Doris that if she heard either Henry or she had committed suicide or accidentally died, she would know why.

Nonetheless, there was reason to celebrate. Churchill and Truman declared May 8, 1945, V-E Day, the official end of the war in Europe. Events in Germany had quickly come to a close. On April 30, Hitler had committed suicide in his rat hole of a bunker beneath the lavish marbled halls of his chancellery; a day later, in another pathetic hellhole beneath the chancellery, the bodies of Goebbels, his six children, and his wife were found poisoned to death. Although Grand Admiral Karl Dönitz, Hitler's designated successor, had vowed to keep fighting, he surrendered all German land, sea, and air forces to the Allies at General Eisenhower's headquarters at 2:41 A.M. on May 8, 1945.

At 3 P.M. that day, Churchill spoke on the flag-draped balcony of the Ministry of Health, as throngs of people jammed Whitehall for blocks, from Trafalgar Square to Buckingham Palace. The big red lion, symbolic protector of generals and soldiers, had been carried down Whitehall from Trafalgar Square, painted on all sides with the slogan, THERE'LL ALWAYS BE AN ENGLAND. Two hours earlier, there had been a Thanksgiving service at St. Paul's Cathedral, and the pubs were packed with singing, beer-drinking Britons.

Churchill's speech was bittersweet:

> Today, perhaps, we shall think mostly of ourselves. Tomorrow, we shall pay a particular tribute to the heroic Russian comrades whose prowess in the field has been one of the grand contributions to the general victory. The German War is, therefore, at an end. ... We may allow ourselves a brief period of rejoicing, but let us not forget for a moment the toils and efforts that lie ahead. Japan, with all her treachery and greed, remains unsubdued. ... We must now devote all our strength and resources to the completion of our task, both at home and abroad. Advance Britannia! Long live the cause of freedom! God save the King!

For the moment, Rebecca and Henry did indeed rejoice. At 9 P.M., as King George VI and Queen Elizabeth, in the company of Churchill, stood on the balcony of Buckingham Palace waving to a crowd of millions, Rebecca and Henry and their friends raised their glasses at Ibstone to toast the Allied victory. Dorothy Thompson was among them. Always the astute observer, Rebecca noted that there was something different about her. She seemed awkward, almost embarrassed, about her newfound success. Yet Dorothy masked her feelings behind strong—even aggressive—remarks, self-righteous and raw. Rebecca noted that she had liked Dorothy better when she had something to fight against—her unhappiness with Red and her lack of recognition. Perhaps it was because she saw in Dorothy what she disliked in herself: dissemblance and self-sabotage. It was troubling to see it so clearly in someone she had admired for so long.

The next day, reality set in. Rebecca knew that Churchill was right; hard work lay ahead. It would take years and millions of pounds before England would recover from the war. Much of London was in ruins, and Rebecca and Henry had not been untouched—a bomb had decimated their Orchard Court high-rise in Portman Square. She was certain that there would be little economic relief for years to come. Unemployment was rampant; housing and food were in short supply; inflation was high. Rebecca tried her best to bring in money. She financed the writing of her long-abandoned Russian novel, *The Birds Fall Down,* by engaging in what she called "contentious journalism," mostly about Yugoslavia, and by preparing articles for *The New Yorker,* whose editor, Harold Ross, had become her newest admirer. But they were now dependent on her savings, and she was not earning enough money to sustain their lifestyle. Henry's term at the Ministry of Economic Warfare had expired with the return of exiled governments, and he had nothing to do—a dangerous situation for a man whose lust for women outweighed his pocketbook and his self-esteem. She urged him to write about his wartime experiences, promising to pass his work on to her contacts in the States. He resisted.

But her thoughts went beyond Henry and Britain to the political future of Europe. Rebecca worried about the spineless stance of the British government toward the Soviets, and her fears had been confirmed by Churchill's expressed gratitude. She wrote to her friend Doris Stevens, "We have the falling sickness as we had it before Munich. Just as we couldn't stand up straight then before Germans so we can't stand up straight before Russia. The Right generally and Left Wing journalists— the rank and file of the Left are different—would lie down in the gutter if Stalin said he'd like it." Alienated from the Left because of her anti-communism, she'd offended most of *The New Yorker*'s readership. Lord Beaverbrook's *Evening Standard* was willing to publish her, but otherwise her journalistic pickings were small. Ever a bundle of paradoxes, Rebecca delighted in her role as flamboyant maverick, while resenting the rejection of the Left; she seemed to want it both ways—intellectual autonomy and popular acceptance.

The end of the war did nothing to improve family relations; it was to be a difficult summer. Lettie had to be flown back to London from Ireland during her holiday, unable to walk because of an infection in her legs. Henry's ulcer was back and he was growing thin. Rebecca, no longer believing that he was employable, found him modestly useful around the farm. Even so, his feeble attempts at farm management made her worry that he was working too hard; his hearing had deteriorated to the point that he would need "an instrument." Anthony and Kitty had bought a house in London near Maida Hill—one that they could neither afford nor repair. Anthony was still working at the BBC news service as an editor, and Kitty was getting ready for an exhibition of her work at Lefevre Galleries on Bond Street. But their relationship seemed to be coasting; none of their old patterns had changed. Caro had, indeed, lost her innocence, but perhaps it was all for the good, Rebecca mused. In time, it would have happened anyway. Rebecca worked hard to repair her relationship with Anthony and Kitty, which had deteriorated during their separation; she desperately wanted to be part of her grandchildren's lives.

The economic upheaval of her family reflected postwar Britain at large. The people were desperate for new leadership. Rebecca believed that Churchill had been a hero of grand proportions during the war, but England needed a leader for a new era who wasn't rooted in eighteenth- or nineteenth-century thinking and could move the country forward. She voted for the Labour Party that summer, in the hope that ministers such as Herbert Morrison and Ernest Bevin, who had proven tough in domestic affairs, would have the courage to stand up against the Soviets. In July, Churchill was ousted in a landslide victory for Clement Attlee, his deputy prime minister under the wartime coalition government. As it turned out, Attlee and his ministers would ameliorate Britain's postwar economic problems, but he and Ernest Bevin, whom he appointed as his foreign secretary, would not stem the tide of Soviet domination in Eastern Europe or the Balkans.

That September, Rebecca was among those paid the highest honor. When *Time and Tide,* a British literary magazine, published the names of authors blacklisted by the Nazis, she was on it. Soon this mark of prestige would breed an extraordinary opportunity.

In December 1945, *New Yorker* editor Harold Ross, whom Rebecca considered her partner in thought, offered her a carte blanche assignment. He had been more than pleased with Rebecca's articles on Yugoslavia, and one on the trial and conviction of the British war traitor

William Joyce. Ross singled out the latter article's psychological insight and Rebecca's erudite understanding of the nuances of British law. "Please write any story you want for us, fact or fiction," he wrote, and asked her if she would be willing to write book reviews. Ross had thought about asking her to go to Nuremberg to cover the last two months of the war trials, but he had already made arrangements with their Paris correspondent, Janet Flanner, a literary journalist and novelist living in Paris among the American expatriates. Flanner, however, would prove unsuited to its spartan rigor, and within weeks, Ross asked Rebecca to take her place. Beaverbrook's *Daily Telegraph* also contracted her to cover the trials, but later she would admit that her agreement with them was only an attempt to maintain relations with the British press. Going to Nuremberg was an opportunity to further study the psychodynamic of treason, but, as she would later note, her motives were even more complex and personal:

> I had been living the scrambled life which English conditions had precipitated during the Second World War, which meant that I had seen my county's way of life go from an orderly pageant through a familiar landscape to a gallant forced march through a landscape that became unrecognizable. . . . I left England to go to the Nuremberg Trial of the Nazi leaders with a sense of relief. . . . The occasion was clear-cut. Hitler's armies had been defeated and his lieutenants were to be tried for their crimes.

But her experience would prove her expectations wrong. Rebecca had left one theater of the absurd for another. "To begin with," she would write, "I was surprised by the physical ruin I found. . . . I knew not such a scene in England. . . . I found myself looking down on hollow square holes dug out of the earth, which were full of wriggling like anglers' bait, foundations of buildings were being grabbed out of the ground and the heavy trucks had the withered jaws of old women."

Although Nuremberg was only three or four hours away from London by plane, it had taken Rebecca nearly a week to arrive. Stymied by protocol, misinformation, and countless other glitches in communication, she finally managed to fly there on an official Royal Air Force convoy with several members of the press on July 23, 1946. It wasn't until a Tuesday morning in the eighth month of the trial proceedings that Rebecca set foot in the courthouse.

When Rebecca entered the Palace of Justice she was certain that she had been thrust into "a man's world" of petty bureaucratic military officials who seemed to have nothing better to do than torture the international press with innumerable checks of credentials and passes. Total chaos and inefficiency prevailed in the dark corridors of the Palace, where it was virtually impossible to read—let alone detect irregularities in—their documents. The labyrinthine web of officialdom seemed a bizarre waste of time and personnel.

It had been nearly two years since the American, British, and Russian foreign ministers had met in Moscow to decide how to punish the major Axis officials for crimes committed during the war. Among the alternatives set forward were summary executions of high-ranking officials or the establishment of an international legal forum, which would reflect Western principles of justice and individual accountability. While the Russians called for immediate summary executions, perhaps to cover up their own mass killings of civilians, the British and the American ministers were wary of its long-term implications as international precedent. The idea of revenge as punishment was anathema to the principles on which their governments were founded, but the complexities of establishing an international court of justice, never attempted before, seemed overwhelming.

Nonetheless, as an Allied victory appeared certain, consensus prevailed: Eschewing the potential quagmire of a civilian court, which they believed would give the defendants rights and means of appeal to which they were not entitled, the Allies decided to establish a military tribunal in Nuremberg. After the death of Franklin Roosevelt in April 1945, President Truman, who passionately believed in the concept of an international military court, appointed Robert Jackson, an eminent jurist and an associate justice of the Supreme Court, as the chief prosecutor of the tribunal. Jackson would become the architect of its legal structure and the mastermind of its proceedings, thereby enabling the trial to begin seven months after V-E Day, on November 20, 1945.

The International Military Tribunal, an invention that was unique in its mission and scope, consisted of a panel of eight judges, two (one judge, and one alternate judge) appointed from each of the four Allies, the United States, United Kingdom, France, and Russia, as well as prosecuting teams of five to twelve members, who agreed to pursue convictions on behalf of the newly formed United Nations. Conducted in four languages by lawyers trained in four different legal systems, the trial accused the defendants of plotting and waging aggressive war, using slave labor, looting occupied countries, and abusing and murdering civilians, especially the Jews, and prisoners of war. With the understanding that "perfect justice" could never prevail, the Allies agreed to conduct the trial according to the highest possible legal standards, establishing a precedent for all international forums that would follow.

Each of the twenty-four defendants (three were tried in absentia), the most primary of whom was Hermann Göring, the commander of the Luftwaffe, the German air force, was given a defense lawyer of his choosing, and the court appointed interpreters to translate the proceedings. Decisions would be made by a majority vote of the four judges. On issues that were evenly divided, Lord Justice Geoffrey Lawrence of Great Britain would make the deciding vote. The decisions of the International Military Tribunal would be final; they could not be appealed by either the defense or the prosecution.

Rebecca's arrival in July 1946, eight months after it convened, coincided with the final days of the trial and the rendering of the prosecutors' summations. She arrived feeling, and looking, tired, haggard, and gray—an apt visage in a devastated landscape. The city was rubble, she would write, and the buildings that remained were twisted and broken. The working people of Nuremberg, shrouded in gloom, waited for their trams, while the Americans, well dressed and full of pleasantries, whizzed by in their jeeps. But Rebecca was careful to note that the Americans were neither sadistic nor jovial, just busily engaged in the intricacies of occupation. Members of the press corps, some of whom had been there from the beginning, were lodged several miles outside the city in a Victorian villa built by the Farber family, manufacturer of pencils. The accommodations spoke of incredible wealth, with spires and turrets, marbled halls and grand staircases, gold-encrusted frescoes and vaulted corridors. It seemed to Rebecca "an old-fashioned opera-set," marked by the cruel ousting of its most recent owners, descendants of a wealthy Bavarian landowning family. Rebecca would see the opulence of this fantastical compound of pavilions, mansions, and gardens, as symptomatic of "a mania that was to force their country to the edge of an abyss." Now the mansion had the aura of a "haunted house," justly punished by the presence of shabbily dressed international journalists racing down its corridors, at once mocking its architecture and reporting "the last convulsion of a German crime."

But something else was dangerous to civilized adults, emanating not from the Germans but from their occupiers: an untamed aura of illicit sex.

The American and British judges and prosecutors—lonely, bored, and trial weary from the eight-month ordeal—were housed in villas in another sector of town. One of two American judges assigned to the international tribunal, Francis Biddle, had the luxury of his own Victorian villa that had been the property of an ousted Bavarian manufacturer, replete with gardens, rows of pines and birches, rolling lawns and pavilions, and a domestic staff still managed by the wife of the banished industrialist, who had insisted on remaining in their ancestral home. Rebecca and Francis had first met in the early 1920s during one of Rebecca's early trips to New York, and then again in 1935, when they were reintroduced by Rebecca's friend Doris Stevens. Eyeing each other across the courtroom, they reacquainted themselves during a recess. It had been twelve years since they had seen one another; she found him as dashingly handsome and aristocratic as ever, while he wondered why this brilliant, attractive woman had "let [herself] go," and lost no time telling her so. After Rebecca inquired about his wife Katherine, and he touted the literary and historical merits of *Black Lamb and Grey Falcon,* they parted.

To his delight, however, within days of their meeting, Rebecca had colored her hair and revamped her wardrobe (thanks to the help of the sisterhood within the press corps who had quickly rallied around her). Sensing something in her demeanor that radiated a loneliness and sexual frustration consonant with his own, Francis sent a note to the press quarters inviting her to a formal dinner at his personal headquarters, the Villa Conradi. That night, only three days after her arrival, Rebecca and Francis became lovers. The chemistry between them was immediate and intense, but it is interesting to contemplate the other variables that might have come into play. Francis was a great admirer of H. G. Wells; perhaps he thought of making love to his onetime mistress as a conquest in itself.

Francis's wife, Katherine, was a good and loving woman, but ultimately uninspiring, he would tell Rebecca. A proficient writer who had dedicated his life to legal procedure and had worked his way up the government hierarchy to attorney general under Roosevelt, Francis—confident, worldly, and intellectually agile—awakened Rebecca's sexuality. After so many years of having "put the shutters up . . . he made me take them down," she wrote. He grounded her; she lifted him; it was a perfect pairing of mind and body, exiled in a cocoon of time and geography.

Francis truly "saw" Rebecca. He recognized that her persona of cleverness was compensation for her innate shyness, masking her self-doubt and uncertainty. Neither the beguiling child-mistress of H.G. nor the desperate young woman seeking confirmation in serial lovers, Rebecca had gone to Nuremberg as a journalist in search of information and understanding, work and remuneration. And yet, exactly when she thought it was no longer possible to feel love for a man, after so many years buried in Henry's icy adoration, she felt cherished and free.

Both eager for the pleasures of the moment, they dived uninhibited into intimacy. Their dinner date, which extended through the weekend, continued for ten days thereafter, as she accompanied him to lunches, dinners, parties, and on romantic walks through the gardens and woodlands surrounding the city of Nuremberg. Their colleagues understood, no doubt, the nuances of their companionship, but so many were engaged in similar liaisons, there was a professional honor code—if not leak-proof, it was well guarded. Using her room in Francis's villa (not coincidentally chosen for its erotic art) as her office, Rebecca edited and organized her notes on the trial. She and Francis often discussed and exchanged impressions, filling in spaces in each other's memories and formulating theories.

As Rebecca had planned, she left Nuremberg for London during the first week in August, expecting to stay at home while the court was in recess preparing the final judgments. Initially conceived as a chance to gain perspective on the trial and the physical and economic devastation of Nuremberg, along with an opportunity to write an article before returning for the last two days of sentencing, her trip home now had an added dimension: to test her feelings for Francis in the framework of home and family. Greeted by Henry, Anthony, and Kitty, and—to her extreme irritation—her sister Lettie, she was bathed in compliments. After fewer than two weeks abroad, Rebecca, they commented, looked lovely and well—better than she had looked in years. Amused by their response and holding her secret tightly, she arrived at Ibstone ready to work. She unpacked her photographs and her notes, relishing the idea of sharing them with H.G. before she returned. It had been several weeks since she had seen him, and despite her happiness with Francis, her affection and concern had not diminished. Even as Francis wrote her adoring letters about the "murmur of [her] spirit," she realized that it was only the absence of Francis's wife and the suspension of practical realities that had made their romantic liaison possible. Nonetheless, she counted her feelings as honest and as real as any she had ever known.

A drawing of H. G. Wells as a sad and broken man,
much as Rebecca saw him at the end of his life

On the morning of Tuesday, August 13, 1946, Rebecca awakened nervous and trembling, instinctively attuned, as always, to the rumblings of imminent trouble. Agitated beyond reason and unable to work, she asked Henry to drive her three miles out to the head of the valley in the hopes that the walk back home would clear her mind. But Henry greeted her at the front door with the news that Marjorie Wells, H.G.'s daughter-in-law, had called to say that H.G. had died. Marjorie said that he had been dressing for tea, and had suddenly fallen back dead. Rebecca had had no inkling that he had remained in his room for two weeks, too weak to go out. And yet, he had looked so well that his death had taken his family by surprise. Nonetheless, they assured her that his end had been peaceful. H.G. would be cremated at Golders Green Crematorium, as had been his wife, Jane.

Like all such news involving the death of those loved and long ill, his passing was not unexpected so much as crushingly finite. It marked the end of possibility and the beginning of a necessary reconciliation with the past. Ironically, H.G.'s friend J. B. Priestley, novelist, essayist, and social commentator, remarked in his eulogy, "This was a man whose word was light in a thousand dark places. . . . When he was angry, it was because he knew, far better than we did, that life need not be a sordid, greedy scramble." As she listened, Rebecca must have snickered; she knew too much to accept this image of moral purity, and must have wondered if Priestley had truly known the man apart from his work. But when Priestley spoke of the twinkling and mischievous blue eyes of her onetime lover, his habit of enclosing "droll little drawings" in his letters, his inventing "uproarious family games," and his high-pitched voice that had never lost its "Cockney impudence," the "Great Prophet of Our Time" that Priestley eulogized once again became the lovable man she knew.

Rebecca struggled to concentrate on her writing, but her emotions rebelled, thrusting her backward in time. Should she have married H.G., as his family now wished she had done? What would her life have been like? Had marrying Henry been the right decision? What had she gained by her marriage and what had she lost? And now, Francis. Would their affair last beyond Nuremberg, or was it just another recipe for disappointment and pain?

Her conclusions seemed to surprise her. Rebecca was glad she hadn't married H.G. She would not have had a literary career, and being his wife would have been tantamount to being the curator of a museum. And yet, she mused, they had loved each other to the end. It was not H.G., she realized, but Henry who had ruined her life. It was he who had cut her down sexually in her prime, eroding her confidence as a woman, making her feel old and unwanted, and compelling her to seek affirmation elsewhere. In the end, Rebecca decided that she didn't care about the hurt that might ensue from her affair with Francis; it would be worth the price. She was lonely to the core.

Rebecca was glad that her absence had fanned Francis's desire. His letters that he sent to her at Ibstone were rhapsodic declarations of love: "I believe in prayer when you are at my side, for you live behind appearances, and open possibilities I had never shared." Their love, he insisted, would thrive "even in the wilderness" of their domestic lives. It was as if both Francis and Rebecca saw their affair as their last chance to transcend what seemed the irrevocable commitments of their youth.

But on August 16, when she returned home from H.G.'s cremation, a letter had arrived from Francis; the "wilderness" to which he had alluded had begun to encroach. Appearing overwhelmed by responsibility, yet denying its hold on him, he told her that they would not be able to take a holiday "till the show is over." But clearly her presence meant a lot to him, a consoling aspect of his life in Nuremberg. Exercising the power of his office, he asked her to name her preference: should he send his plane to pick her up in Paris, or would she prefer that he take his plane to visit her. He said he longed for a "few days of dragon flies and meadow sweet," and thought there was little chance that Katherine would come over since his son was ill (he had contracted malaria during his tour of duty in the Pacific). Perhaps reflecting the stench of death at the trial, Francis felt pursued by a deadening despair. He wrote that he dreamed of her more than ever.

Dragonfly—a predacious insect with enormous eyes, sensitive antennae, and legs adapted for grasping its prey. No doubt it was a sexual allusion, but it was also Rebecca's perceptive darting eyes that entranced him, he would say; her ability to see beyond the surface of people and events to the heart of things. He would also call her his bird of paradise. But one needn't consult a dictionary for his meaning. Rebecca was his woman, his captive bird on this island of Nuremberg, that made this hellish trial a bright, sensual, and joyous thing.

But three days later, his wanderlust was eviscerated by the possibility that Katherine might be planning a visit. He thought that they should meet in Paris, since it was "much more anonymous, much easier to arrange. . . . I do think the villa is unwise now." He thought Katherine smelled "a water rat," he continued, an ironic epithet considering that "rat," a play on Henry's "Rac," was his pet name for her. "She knew you were here ten days, she knows what an attractive creature you are." He also intimated that one of his colleagues' wives might have informed Katherine of their affair. Nonetheless, he wrote that he was hungry for her—the sound of her voice, the dart of her eyes, the funny things she said, that make him "come alive and stay alive."

It was beginning to sound all so familiar—the hiding, the dissembling. It was like H.G. and Jane all over again. And yet, Rebecca was unwilling to let Francis go. She decided to test his feelings by pulling back into formalities, thus offering him the opportunity for retreat. But her efforts threw him into a panic. He chastised her for doubting the integrity of his love, yet he ended his next letter on a cautionary note:

"We shall have to suspend things—if you can—for a while, perhaps for a week or so—until I hear finally from Katherine. . . . Farewell my dear, stupid, enchanting and rather magnificent rat."

While at home, Rebecca had sent one of Francis's letters to her sister Winnie, the expert handwriting analyst of the family. At first not revealing the identity of the writer, and then concocting a story about her "misapprehension" of his marital status, she wrote a letter to Winnie, thanking her for her insights:

When I had known him in America he had a very plain and disagreeable wife, who disliked him extremely and did everything to persuade his friends that he was superficial and worthless and she was a fountain of sweetness and moral worth. She was a hypochondriac and neglected his household and two children (one of whom died, she did not call the doctor when he had a septic throat) and had a sinister female friend, 20 years older than herself whom she insisted on having to live in the house. She was also extremely extravagant.

Rebecca went on to tell her that after the birth of their second son, Katherine had moved out of their bedroom for eighteen months in order to punish him for the pain she had suffered—further echoes of H.G. and Jane. "He is highly intelligent, not noticeably masochistic. I cannot make out what he is at." But she was deceiving herself. Although Rebecca would fly back to Nuremberg for the "final show," that is, for the reading of the verdicts, she was already sensing that their affair was over.

As if planning for a future without Francis, and longing to escape the dull, dreary rhythms of Henry and another claustrophobic winter at Ibstone, she wrote a letter to Dorothy on August 31, 1946, asking for her help:

> *My dear Dorothy,*
>
> *I am going to cast myself on your mercy. I have had an emotional upset, which has left me horribly aware of the fact that in some ways my life has been a failure. The death of H.G., who devoured my youth and bullied me, and was so much made for me that to the last he glowed when I came to see him, helped to rub that in. The worst of the life I live here is that it drives me back on the fundamentals, which are gaunt. I would do anything to have a month or two in America. . . . I haven't got the guts to say to Henry that I just want to go.*

Rebecca asked Dorothy to fabricate some "vague reason—or if there is some political event [she] could attend—or just an invitation would do." She wished that she had decided to live in America when she had the chance; she hated the dreariness of English life. Once in New York, she planned to stay with Emanie Arling.

It was a pathetic letter that would impel anyone to whom it was addressed to seek avenues for Rebecca's escape, but she wrote to Dorothy knowing that she had the fire and the clout to get the job done. Rebecca chose well; Dorothy wasted no time. She wrote to Harold Ross asking him to commission Rebecca to write articles that would enable her to travel around the country a bit. His response was enthusiastic, mentioning that he had already offered her the opportunity to write, in addition to the longer pieces, book reviews, but that he could easily assign her stories that would keep her busy for two or three months. Rebecca immediately agreed, informing Henry of the offer.

Dutifully, not knowing what to expect from Francis, Rebecca returned to Nuremberg for the final days of the trial. Upon her arrival, Rebecca wrote a letter to Henry, who knew that she would be staying with Francis. He had sent a car for her, she wrote, with orders to take her to Villa Conradi. It was 9 A.M., and Francis was still at the courthouse, having worked all night. When he finally arrived, she was "alarmed" by his appearance. Since she had left, "he seemed to have aged and looked extremely ill." Perhaps it was the stress of formulating the judgments, but he looked as if he had a fever. "I have had to content myself [long] in a house with copies of the judgment lying about which I must not open. . . . Francis says he will fly me to Northolt [an airport just outside London proper], he will go on to see Wheeler-Bennett [his friend from Oxford who had assisted the British prosecution during the trial]." Rebecca promised to send Henry the particulars of her return ten days hence.

As she had promised, Rebecca wrote to Henry to inform him of the date and time of her arrival at Northolt. Francis, among the fortunate few who had access to a government plane, flew with Rebecca to England at the appointed time, only to find that Henry, confused by the timing of her commitment to Ross in New York and busy with his latest sexual conquest, never showed up. Compelled to make the hour-and-a-half drive to Ibstone, Francis was already blank-eyed and poker-faced. His perfunctory telephone call the next day from Oxford left Rebecca cold. Francis visited her one more time at Ibstone before going to Paris and on to the States. He assumed a lighthearted, affectionate tone that made her hopeful their relationship might continue, but after he left for home, she never heard from him again. Rebecca wrote in her diary, "Katherine has got him."

But, perhaps, Rebecca never had him. She had been playing against a force too powerful to foil—his ambition, which could not withstand the publicity of a sex scandal. Moreover, his correspondence with Katherine during the trial reveals the same perverse voyeurism employed by Jane. Katherine knew all about his affair with Rebecca and took pleasure in Rebecca's ensnarement and her husband's apparent duplicity; Rebecca never knew that she was a familiar pawn in their marital chess match. Nor did she seem to know that Katherine, his dull, clinging, hypochondriac of a wife, was an acclaimed poet who dallied with the literary elite, a consultant in American letters to the Library of Congress, and a member of the American Society of Poets, among other prestigious literary associations. Or if she did, she dismissed the value of Katherine's work, seeing her only as the "enemy" in her quest for happiness. Like Jane and Kitty, Katherine was just another inept and manipulative wife who could not satisfy her man.

But in the end, one cannot truly be certain that Francis's love for Rebecca was the mere dissemblance of a lonely man. Perhaps his letters to Katherine were diversionary attempts to allay his wife's fears and diminish the rumors. Later, Rebecca would compare their affair to the 1945 Noël Coward/David Lean movie, *Brief Encounter,* in which the doomed romance between two strangers who meet by chance in a train station transforms their humdrum lives into a wildly passionate adventure. But, like the middle-aged woman in the film, Laura Jesson, Rebecca goes home to her husband—her sweet and doting, if dotty, Henry. But unlike Laura, Rebecca had already planned her escape.

Rebecca's account of the trial process, culminating in the reading of verdicts, was later published in two parts in *The New Yorker.* While they were elegant essays strewn with poetic allusions to classical English literature and Greek mythology, they were more like philosophical treatises on the human potential for good and evil than reportage. She portrays the proceedings as an old-fashioned morality play with the sinners parading across the stage, indistinguishable from one another except by language and national garb. All are guilty; none is morally pure by virtue of their collective humanity. Ultimately, she concludes, it is a matter of perspective and degree.

Using her extraordinary powers of observation, Rebecca captures the look and feel of the proceedings. She understands the psychology of each defendant, judge, prosecutor, and petty official as he performs his task; the aura and stench of impending death; and the imprisonment of all in an ugly time warp of human history each would as soon forget. She documents the shame of some, the arrogance of others, and the madness of one. She describes the tension in the courtroom as a tug-of-war between those who know they will die and those who defend and judge them. The accused want to stop time, she writes, while the others want to leave the war and return home.

"It is possible that [the accused] never think directly of death or even imprisonment and that there is nothing positive in them at all except their desire to hold time still."

Each of the twenty-one defendants present is at once an individual and part of a community, she observes. And as the trial wears on, each seems to lose his individuality. And yet, there prevails a hierarchy of status and righteousness among them, determined by self-perceptions of intelligence, guilt, and former rank within the Reich. As her eye roves over the prisoners in the dock, she exposes their stances and posture, the

arrogance, humility, "madness," and the abrasiveness and charm familiar to observers of everyday life.

Those who believe they are innocent sit among the accused as if by a
mere accident of fate: Hermann Göring, commander in chief of the German air force; Hjalmar Schacht, head of the Reichsbank and Hitler's economic minister; and Albert Speer, Hitler's chief architect and, later, his
minister of armaments and war production. They appear to despise the
others, deeming them a breed apart—deserving of punishment by dint
of crimes, cowardice, and betrayal of the Reich. Schacht, who cannot
seem to bear the sight of his codefendants, sits cross-legged facing the
interpreters' stand as if his innate superiority renders him equal to the
appointees of the court.

But it is her penetrating description of Göring that echoes the para-
doxical and multifaceted analogies that riddle all her work:

> He is, above all things, soft. He wears either a German air-force
> uniform or a light beach suit in the worst of playful taste, and
> both hang loosely on him, giving him an air of pregnancy. He has
> thick brown young hair, the coarse bright skin of an actor . . . and
> the preternaturally deep wrinkles of the drug addict; it adds up to
> something like the head of a ventriloquist's dummy. His appear-
> ance makes a pointed but obscure reference to sex. . . . Sometimes,
> particularly when his humor is good, he recalls the madam of a
> brothel.

Ironically, she writes, the judges, who may not be the social or political superiors of the accused in ordinary life, reign from a platform above,
entrusted with exacting justice on those who fidget and giggle and pose
in the dock below. The difference is, of course, that as the victors, they
have inherited the impossible task of neutrality within the confines of the
law. They have assumed the mantle of authority, and they consciously
strive to earn their position with unwavering focus and disciplined ad-
herence to the rules established by the international court, yet she questions their ability to succeed.

The Americans, she observes, are less formal but just as disciplined as
their British counterparts; the Russians, reflecting their government's
disdain for the trial and presumption of German guilt, offer a strange
visage in military regalia amid a trial meant to transcend the rules of the

battlefield; the French, while elegant and dignified, lack the passion and fire of their counterparts, having anticipated the German move toward European dominance since the Franco-Prussian War in 1870.

Rebecca seems to snicker at the Americans and the Brits, to whom all seems new, for embracing the process as if it had never happened before. It is clear, she writes, that the story is as old as punishing the Jews for the crucifixion of Christ—a strange allusion fraught with moral turpitude, considering this is the sole mention of Jews in her piece and that she omits any reference to the millions of documents blatantly describing the Nazi war crimes against them.

Documenting the political pas de deux of the British prosecutors, attorneys general Hartley Shawcross, appointed by the new prime minister Clement Attlee, and David Maxwell Fyfe, Churchill's appointee under the coalition government during the war, she notes their warm relations with their American colleagues, whom they deeply admire. The best of them, she believes, is Robert Jackson, who presents a masterful summation—civilized, incisive, and pertinent—during which he points his forefinger at defendants in the dock as he recites the crime for which each was accused. Stunned by his vitriol, some of them mumble as if in a dream, others giggle, and some stiffen, while the Hitler Youth leader with "the soul of a governess," responsible for the deaths of hundreds of thousands of children, takes off his earphones and lays them gently on the ledge before him, refusing to listen.

Rebecca concludes her piece with an ode to German flowers in the gardens of the cottages that stand where the rubble of the city ends.

> It is difficult not to conclude that a people who so love flowers must love all beautiful and simple things. . . . Unquestionably there is a German mystery, and certainly it needs to be solved, and a continued critical relationship with the American and the British people, such as has begun at Nuremberg, would help toward a solution. Such a relationship, however, needs the sanction of force.

Rebecca writes that as she left the courthouse, she took one last look at the prisoners as they exercised in the open courtyard. Like many of the accused, she, too, was immersed in private reverie. Probing the complexities of human nature, she scanned the grounds, unable to discern between the condemned and the men who guarded them. Both appeared lifeless, numbed by unexpressed frustration and rage, and profoundly, irreconcilably bored.

Published after Rebecca's final return to Ibstone in the midst of grieving for the love affair that may never be, her second article, "The Birch Leaves Falling," is an autumnal ode to the passing of the great German culture and a rumination on the paltry tools of those who documented its fall and those who judged the perpetrators of its demise. Repetitive and dreamlike, philosophical and lyrical, and once again riddled with literary and mythical allusion, it seems to meander, much like her perception of the trial itself, without form or purpose. Alluding to Göring's suicide the night before he was to be hanged, she writes, "The door at the back of the dock shut on the last of the prisoners, who had worked their confusion by showing a heroism to which they had no moral right, proved that it is not true that the bully is always a coward and that not even in that respect is life simple." All was for naught; the cyanide flowed, the judgments were read, and the sentences were pronounced. Rebecca expressed her sadness not for the doomed lives of the defendants so much as for the human capacity for evil. She wrote:

> It is not exactly pity that takes one. One would not alter the sentence of death. The future must be protected. The ovens where the innocent were baked alive must remain cold forever; the willing stokers, so oddly numerous, it appears, must be discouraged from lighting them again.

And yet, she wonders if all their efforts to eradicate the cruelty and the violence and those who wrought it would not prevent their recurrence in a new form. Would the people of Germany once again grow desperate through hunger, disease, and poverty? And would their desperation give rise to a new regime, more repressive and evil than the Nazis?

Nine years later, a new version of her account would be published in a book entitled *A Train of Powder,* a compendium of her articles covering the British and German trials and a racist lynching trial in the American South. While the dominant theme remains the same—all are guilty; neither the victors nor the vanquished are free of moral, even legal condemnation—she carries her observations further, universalizing the human impulse toward evil and the struggle for human dignity even in the face of death.

While references to the suffering of the Jews by name are noticeably absent from her *New Yorker* pieces, she mentions them twice in her revised book version in proper context and with sympathy. Yet in the name of objective journalism, her commentary exudes a moral cowardice that defies understanding. In an attempt to elucidate the nature of man, she dispels notions of good and bad, right and wrong, guilt and innocence, eviscerating standards of personal accountability and unbiased justice.

In neither account does she write that Francis Biddle, her aristocratic and "highly intelligent swan," and his predacious bird of paradise made love at the villa the night before the verdicts were read, hoping to quell the horror of the next day's events, or that they could not let go of their romantic fantasy. Waiting for government transport to England, they spent the following eight days of that glorious Bavarian fall walking the familiar terrain of the villa, and traveling to the city of Prague, relishing the beauty of its bridges and waterways, its urban architecture and adjacent farmlands, and its orchards and gardens—playing out the final recitative of their ill-fated opera.

CHAPTER 14

IHR KAMPF

> To beat the Nazi revolution we have got
> to jump ahead of it, or be dragged after it
> in chains.
>
> —DOROTHY THOMPSON TO
> WENDELL WILLKIE, 1940

NEW YORK CITY, 1940

Propped up on pillows, nightgown rumpled, head scarf askew, Dorothy scoured the morning news like a bloodthirsty hound. It was column day. Her eyes scanned the pages to get the lay of the land as she tossed five newspapers one by one into a heap on her half-empty bed. Finding her prey, she zeroed in for the kill. Sometimes it was a speech; sometimes it was a book. It could be a declaration or a well-founded rumor—anything that could serve as a lodestone, a strike point, a warning. Her weapon was often a democratic ideal articulated by the Founding Fathers a century and a half earlier, or a quote from the Bible that would enlighten the path ahead.

Her breakfast of toast and prunes jiggled on the bed as she cast orders to her three secretaries and her maid: "Get me that quote from the Federalist Papers. More coffee, please. Don't forget to pick up Michael. I need stockings for the dinner tonight." She commanded like a general; she had better charge ahead or she would be forced to retreat. The enemy was not those who dared to differ; the enemy was time. And a shot could come from any direction—a call from Michael, a letter from his headmaster, a telegram from a desperate friend up the street or three thousand miles away, another threat from Hal intent on divorce. But the worst blow was a countermand from her staff. No personal allowances were made; they would perform without question or they were out. Dorothy demanded no more of them than she did of herself.

She was a quick and lucid writer. Once her ideas coalesced, composing her column was a forty-five-minute project, after which it was hand-delivered by one of her staff to the *Herald Tribune* offices. She had typewriters scattered throughout her apartment on Central Park West, and there were signs over each of them that read GOD PROTECT US FROM TRAITORS AT HOME AND TYRANTS ABROAD.

At forty-seven, Dorothy was still remarkably pretty—silver-haired, she emanated the same peaches-and-cream radiance of her youth. She was a fulsome and magnificent animal. Dorothy had put her loneliness to good use. With the help of "uppers," such as Dexedrine and other stimulants prescribed by her doctor, along with barbiturates to lull her to sleep, she could write three columns and dozens of letters per week, broadcast her ideas to millions via radio, telephone informants in Washington and abroad, attend numerous dinners surrounded by men, and then go home alone, calming herself to sleep with pills and poetry late into the night. Her life had purpose; she was convinced that she had been created to inform and reform the world, and her vision was simple: world unity moving in sync with the mightiest of forces—the ethical commandments of a Christian God.

Unlike Rebecca, who doubted everything and felt a kinship with the devil, Dorothy believed she could pinpoint the devil's surrogates on a map. And in 1940, he wore many faces. She had come to see that isolationists were among them. As a columnist for the right-leaning *New York Herald Tribune*, she was assumed to be a supporter of the Republican candidate for president, Wendell Willkie. Early on, she had considered the tall, handsome, and rugged utilities executive to be the sole candidate with the charisma, intelligence, and levity to take on Roosevelt. When she had first met Willkie in the spring of 1939, she was so impressed that she told Helen Reid, "If the politicians won't nominate Wendell, believe me, Helen, we can elect him ourselves! I'll go into the street and get the people to elect him!" The businessman turned Wall Street lawyer, Democrat turned anti–New Dealer, would challenge Roosevelt's interventionist and populist bent with his free-market, pacifist, America-first thinking. Dorothy's reasoning was that after eight years of Roosevelt, who may have been the right man at the right time to lift the nation out of the Depression, now was the moment to infuse the government with new blood. Moreover, Dorothy believed that Roosevelt was tired, and there were rumors emanating from Congress that his heart was ailing. No president before him had run for a third term of office, and despite the fact that Europe was at war, and the nation under threat, the time had come to think of America's domestic interests, rather than those of Britain and its allies, an ocean away.

Dorothy's enthusiasm for Willkie vacillated as the campaign wore on, and her trips abroad had the effect of confusing rather than enlightening her. But of one thing she was certain: Western democracy must be preserved, and she was committed to being an agent of its sustenance.

From March through May 1940, she toured Italy and France, visiting the pope in the Vatican to enlist his voice in a plea for peace in Europe, then continuing on to Paris, where she met her old friends and colleagues Jimmy Sheean of the *Chicago Tribune* and his recent bride, Diana (Dinah) Forbes-Robertson, and Edgar Mowrer, now the Paris bureau chief of the *Chicago Daily News*, and his wife, Lilian. They were convinced along with Dorothy that the nine-month-old "phony war" was about to end. On May 10, Dorothy awakened to find that Germany had invaded Holland, and thousands of French troops had been ordered to the eastern front. Her crisis instincts ignited, she followed the troops northeast to Nancy and, after securing permission from the French government and marshaling an entourage of reporters and photographers, visited the Maginot Line on the German front along the Alsatian border. In her fashionable gabardine suit and brimmed hat, equipped with obligatory hiking boots, Dorothy descended hundreds of feet into an air-conditioned tunnel of France's largest fortress, ten to fifteen miles deep and sixty-two miles long, from which the French hoped to repel the Nazi onslaught. To Dorothy's astonishment, a soldier signaled her to fire one of his 75 millimeter guns. She would later record, "Ten times, in the roar, trying to keep my thoughts together, I began counting them; one [shot] for the Czechs, and one for the Poles, and one for the Norwegians and one for the Dutch, and then in the noise I lost track."

Despite the fact that the French government had spent years of planning and building this state-of-the-art fort, which housed and supplied thousands of men with food, fuel, telephone lines, artillery, and ammunition, the Germans managed to find its weak point. They broke through at the junction between the French and Belgian fortification systems. Amid the ensuing chaos of Dunkirk, Dorothy managed to sail home.

After witnessing the might of the Germans and the vulnerability of the Allies, Dorothy concluded that Roosevelt's charisma and good intentions were not enough. He lacked the aggressive leadership commensurate with the crisis. Roosevelt was "tired and defeatist," she wrote. Willkie was her man; he was exactly what America needed: an executive president.

On the evening of May 28, 1940, after Denmark, Norway, and the Netherlands had fallen to the Nazis, and France was in chaos, Dorothy attended a black-tie dinner at the Waldorf. When it was over, she invited Julian Bach, a young editor at *Life,* and a small group of others, back to her apartment on Central Park West, a place that had become synonymous with gatherings of the intellectual elite. Later, Bach would recall that the times were "unbelievably dark . . .":

> The one land army of Europe had been smashed, the nakedness of the democracies had been revealed, so to speak, there was nothing between the Nazis and the sea. . . . [Dorothy] was standing in front of her fireplace with one arm on the mantel and she spoke about the situation, democracy and the war—so magnificently that we all had our handkerchiefs out all of the time. . . . I kept thinking of the Lion of Lucerne [a sculpture of a lion carved into a cliff in Switzerland, commemorating the Swiss soldiers slaughtered during the French Revolution]. . . . She had a large body—big-boned—she wasn't a fat woman—she was a picture of strength, like the feminine version of a football tackle.

Following the surrender of France on June 22, 1940, Dorothy would offer an explanation in her column, On the Record, in the *Herald Tribune.* "The democratic ideal," she would tell the readers of her column, "which started as a noble and heroic conception, as an attempt to liberate human beings, and offer them the opportunity to develop and perfect themselves . . . has degenerated away from the idea of self-perfection through effort, away from the idea of equal and cooperative endeavor, into the idea of self-interest. The pursuit of happiness . . . has become the pursuit of pleasure." In short, she wrote, democracies no longer bred nobility of purpose in its citizens, nor encouraged the pursuit of happiness beyond hedonism.

Two weeks later, after Willkie had won the nomination at the Republican National Convention in Philadelphia, which she deemed a lackluster event, devoid of vision or inspiration, she wrote him a letter:

> *The reality is [that there is an ongoing] world revolution. The world revolution means that, both as between classes of society and as between nations, the entire system of production and distribution is being challenged. This revolution arises out of the fundamental revolution which has taken place in the sphere of science and technology, whereby a world of limited possibilities has become a world of unlimited possibilities.*

The world, she believed, was moving away from capitalism and isolation, the principles for which Willkie stood. Most important, she admonished Willkie, the locus of power had shifted to America—Britain was now an outpost of the English-speaking world. But Britain's security was vital to the protection of the United States and North America. She believed that we would have to fight the whole of Europe were we to lose them. America must fight to ensure the survival of Great Britain, she concluded, even if it means war.

Our times, she continued, called for a supranational entity that would foster political and economic cooperation among nations and the sharing of manpower in times of war. It was as if she wanted Willkie to be someone else—Roosevelt, perhaps?

After the Willkie campaign lost popular support and funding during the spring, Dorothy flew to Europe to survey attitudes and ground conditions. Upon her return to the States in October, she visited Roosevelt, finding him surprisingly vigorous, magnetic, and courageous. A week later, with full knowledge of the repercussions, she announced her conversion in her column in the *Herald Tribune*. Firmly she stated that she was not against Willkie, who was a fine and capable man with good values, she was *for* the president. She had criticized him and his administration many times in the past five years but believed that despite his errors, he had moved the country in the right direction. Our basic institutions were intact, she wrote, and we were relatively prosperous. Unlike his opponent, Roosevelt was a man of government experience and intimate knowledge of world affairs. He had spread the prestige of America throughout the world, had worked for hemispheric unity, and had brought the nation together. He was a man who had earned the confidence of his countrymen, and he was ready to govern now. Many readers were shocked by Dorothy's editorial, and many canceled their subscriptions to the *Herald Tribune*.

The editors and her fellow columnists at the paper were totally at odds with her views; rumblings of hostility began to surface. Walter Lippmann, a self-appointed adviser to Willkie, declined to take a stand, disguising his disillusionment by declaring that the role of the commentator was beyond political bias. Irita Van Doren, who was having an affair with Willkie, was doing her share to keep him fired up and ready for the challenge. The pro-Republican bent of Helen and Ogden Reid was well known, and their friends, Henry and Clare Boothe Luce of Time-Life, were equally convinced of Willkie's superiority to Roosevelt.

Clare, an avid partisan, even challenged Dorothy to a verbal duel. Dorothy, fearing that Clare's beauty, style, and cool rhetoric would override the substance of the debate, refused to appear with her on the same stage. Nonetheless, they blasted each other from afar. When Clare intimated that Dorothy's hotheaded conversion to Roosevelt was due to menopausal symptoms that had clouded her brain, Dorothy attacked her as an empty-headed, supermodel society lady who took on causes as often as she changed her hats. These highly publicized contests of wit were promoted as a heroic battle of female warriors, "two blond Valkyries on the prows of opposing ships of state." Wounded when the media cast their exchange as a "catfight," Clare remarked, "Men can disagree violently and the press will acknowledge the possibility of a reasonable difference of opinion. If women disagree, it immediately becomes a catfight, a fingernail-scratching or hair-pulling contest." A playwright, unused to the stings of the male-dominated press, Clare vowed never to participate in a debate with a woman again. However, in 1942 she would make a successful run for Congress against a wide field of male contenders and became the Republican U.S. congresswoman from Fairfield County, Connecticut.

Despite Dorothy's gracious rhetoric toward Willkie, privately she believed that electing him would mean inviting fascism into the White House. She told Edgar Mowrer, now back in the States, that Willkie's campaign and the Nazi campaign in America were parallel. She was more right than perhaps she knew. Hans Thomsen, chief of the German Embassy in Washington, was writing home in the summer of 1940 that Charles Lindbergh, a man of "moral superiority" and the "most important of them all" against the Jewish element in America, was "a mortal enemy of Roosevelt." Lindbergh would wait to see if "Willkie will be able to avoid the bondage to Jewry." Lindbergh requested that German authorities put pressure on Willkie's sister, the wife of Commander P. B. Pihl, assistant U.S. naval attaché in Berlin, and a woman of pro-German sympathies, to sway her brother to their cause. Whether or not it was his sister's doing, Willkie was turning emphatically toward isolationism.

On the evening before the presidential election, November 4, 1940, the Democratic State Committee of New York sponsored a national extravaganza over live radio to rally the public in support of Roosevelt. The event began with Mayor La Guardia at Carnegie Hall in New York City, moved to Hollywood with an array of screen celebrities, and then on to Washington, where Secretary of State Cordell Hull awaited his cue.

From there the broadcast moved to Hyde Park, where Roosevelt, sitting by the fireside in the library with his family, set himself above the political fray. Speaking the warm, humble words of an ordinary American, although with decidedly patrician overtones, and pitting the dark climes of European despotism against the sunny skies of American peace and freedom, Roosevelt affirmed his faith in the wisdom of the electorate. It was the elegant and lofty monologue of a gifted politician who had already decided to sway the populace toward war.

Turning back to Carnegie Hall, the narrator introduced Dorothy as an outstanding personality of America who has won international fame as a champion of democracy and the American way of life. In a voice that was feminine, yet resolute and steadfast, Dorothy called for the defeat of Willkie and the reelection of Roosevelt for a third term. Citing statistics from the National Industrial Council on jobs and prosperity, Dorothy refuted Republican claims of Roosevelt's economic incompetency. Portraying the war abroad as an ominous threat to American democracy, she implied that FDR was a man of peace but capable of commanding a war. Dismissing the claims of those who feared a third presidential term, she deemed the prospect unprecedented but not unconstitutional. No candidate, she said, can bring about national unity and strength alone. It is "we the people" who can unite against evil. Roosevelt, she concluded, governs in the great tradition of Lincoln. Speaking in her British lilt with upper-crust vowels (an affectation some found irritating) she never dropped her ladylike demeanor or her passionate partisanship. It is easy to see how her combination of voice, breadth of knowledge, and supreme confidence might have struck some as arrogant, but FDR could not have had a more capable advocate.

Portrait of Dorothy, circa 1940s

Frances Fineman Gunther, a struggling novelist and wife of John Gunther, would deem her speech the most exciting performance by a woman she had ever heard. Dorothy, Frances believed, was a born orator.

Compelled to create a persona of strength and sustain it at any cost, Dorothy had developed an overriding need to control the events and people around her. The flip side, of course, was a kind of megalomania—a neurotic belief in her capacity to effect change. Perhaps neurotic narcissism is the mind-set of every reformer, but it is also a means of disconnecting one's intellect from one's emotions. If her childhood loss required a suit of armor, it also left an emotional void. Dorothy needed both someone to love, nurture, and control, and someone who could resist and fight against her. This was evident in her relationships with Bard and Lewis, but nowhere is it clearer than in her stance toward her son.

In 1940, Michael, still at Palo Verde Ranch in Arizona, was ten years old. For the moment, Dorothy had succeeded in persuading him to stay out west by having Mr. Hutchinson, the headmaster, buy him a horse at her behest. The fact that this gift coincided with the premiere of a play she had written (which unfortunately failed after a week) and an impending trip to Europe defies coincidence. Michael, however, already desperate for an excuse to leave the ranch, fell off the horse and, seeing it as his final symbolic failure, became depressed. In a letter to his mother, he wrote that he was not certain that he wanted to come home for Christmas, thinking perhaps that she might come "out here." But there was one thing he made clear: "Mother, I am not happy in this school. . . . I could go to Collegiate School [the school in New York that he had attended before he became ill]. The boys are nice to me there. Write as soon as you can. Love, Micky."

Home seemed as elusive to him as it was to Dorothy and Hal. And Dorothy didn't know how to realize the purpose of her life while tending to the needs of her child. Once again, she hid behind idealized abstractions.

Against the backdrop of the European war, and the fascist subjugation of women, she gave a speech entitled "The Changing Status of Women." She called for a second feminist movement, different from the competitive individualism of the first, that would foster the creative and noble aspects of life, male and female.

As if attributing her personal choices to a larger overriding force, she said, "all women are and must be individualists. . . . The individualism of women lies in the deep desire of every mother to produce a child who shall surpass its parents in excellence and in opportunities; who shall be a good human being and a free one."

To avoid offering mere vagaries, Dorothy proposed, as was her custom, a sweeping five-point plan, advocating a resurgence of family, cooperation among unspecified social forces, and government projects to enhance housing, working conditions, education, and public resistance toward a dictatorial, militaristic state.

In words that reached far beyond women's issues, she urged her audience "to have a showdown with one's self," and to define one's core values. But where was Dorothy's showdown with herself? Perhaps her answer was both consistent and obvious. Despite her loneliness, Dorothy cared more about the world outside her family; she was convinced that her own humanity was best achieved in the public realm. She would go only so far in helping Michael achieve it for himself, and one can discern her disappointment in not producing a child capable of surpassing her.

Dorothy's words reflect her rich grasp of history and literature, and her ability to transcend the turmoil of the present to articulate universal ideals. And yet, she could not find the words to inspire her son; she managed only to alienate him. Dorothy, like Rebecca, who was about to dazzle the world with her magnum opus, *Black Lamb and Grey Falcon,* was haunted by this seemingly insurmountable failure. The best each could do was to attribute the intractability of her son to some alien gene pool within her child's father.

In August 1940, Dorothy wrote to a friend that she was "as near a nervous breakdown . . . as I've ever been in my life." While she would chalk it up to some vague "household catastrophe," others would attribute it to the hormonal aftermath of a hysterectomy, the pressure of her work, and her loss of contact with her friends in Europe, trapped in the belly of a raging war. Her doctor, along with her friends, would try to encourage and cheer her. "You must learn to conserve your resources," wrote her doctor. "You have a responsibility not only to your friends but to the world." By the fall, Dorothy would be back in stride.

On November 5, 1940, President Roosevelt won a third term in office by a little less than five million votes. (In 1936 he had enjoyed a margin of eleven million.) Dorothy felt that her efforts on his behalf had been justified, and while she knew she was about to lose her job at the *Herald Tribune,* she had won access to the president. Later, he would write her a letter of gratitude, quipping, "You lost your job, but I kept mine—ha ha!"

Bitter about Dorothy's political apostasy, despite her profound admi-

ration for her analytic and rhetorical skills, *Herald Tribune* publisher
Helen Reid, anticipating Dorothy's response, asked her not to write on
political issues. Feeling muzzled, Dorothy wrote a letter to Helen in
early January 1941, "I think we shall be happier divorced. . . . I feel an
unbridgeable hostility in the *Tribune*." She knew she had to go, and while
she appeared stoic at the time, telling Roosevelt not to worry, that she
had not incurred any financial loss, Dorothy also knew that she had lost
a platform from which to crusade for America's role in preserving European democracy.

Without missing a beat, Dorothy gained a new arena for her voice.
While those at the *Herald Tribune* doubted a syndicate would ever top
their record of selling her tri-weekly column to 196 papers—some 7.5
million readers—Bell Syndicate quickly sold On the Record to 200
newspapers with a combined circulation of 9 million. Among the liberal
newspapers in the syndicate, the *New York Post* and *The Washington
Times* were the most important. New York was the most populated, and
Washington the most influential city in America. It was true that Dorothy had lost no money, and her readership had increased, but she had lost
something she valued more: There was no one and nothing to push
against. Although she continued to be a passionate interventionist, she
was now one voice among many, easily drowned out by the crowd. The
learned and savvy intellectuals who wrote for the *Herald Tribune* had
kept her sharp, current, and controversial and brought out her best.

And so, Dorothy kindled a blaze of her own. On June 22, 1941, as
Germany, declaring its failure to observe the pact, invaded Russia, she
wrote a column calling on the American people to cast off their lethargy
and support their allies abroad. To champion her belief that ordinary
working-class Germans remained sufficiently Christian to feel repug-
nance at Hitler's social policies, and desired, above all else, the freedom
to choose honorable employment to sustain their families, Dorothy
formed an organization called the Ring of Freedom.

Predicated on moral, quasi-religious principles that Dorothy called
"the Ten Articles of Faith," which affirmed the equality and interdependence of individuals, regardless of their socioeconomic status, the Ring
of Freedom was a voluntary service network that employed existing social organizations in cities around the world to translate credo into action
by gathering and warehousing tangible goods to be distributed to the
peoples of Europe after the war. Dorothy would call this "a people's

war" against totalitarianism to rouse America's "instincts of heroism and service." She hoped her efforts would counter "Lindberghism" and the antidemocratic forces within the America First Committee, but she feared that her response had come too late.

Within weeks of the creation of the Ring of Freedom, a committee of prominent New Yorkers who believed in her cause honored Dorothy with a dinner held in the Grand Ballroom of the Waldorf-Astoria, attended by three thousand people. Its purpose was to launch "the Dorothy Thompson Defense Fund," in support of democracy. Isadore Lipschutz, a Jewish diamond dealer, gave her a check for $5,000, promising to raise $25,000 more among his friends. Called to the podium, Dorothy recited her Ten Articles of Faith, a product, she said "of eighteen years of gradual, slow, dawning experience, plus the torrential cataract of the experience of the last two years."

*Dorothy launches her "Defense Fund" at
the Waldorf-Astoria in New York in 1941*

President Roosevelt sent a telegram hailing Dorothy as a friend of democracy and the American people, but it was Churchill's telegram that was the most unexpected and moving. It read, "She has shown what one valiant woman can do with the power of a pen. Freedom and humanity are grateful debtors." Within weeks of the dinner and Churchill's praise, Dorothy flew to England for a monthlong tour of civilian and military operations. Her mission: to gain a visceral sense of England at war after the fall of France, and to test the validity of her interventionist cause. Rhetoric aside, even Churchill was worried that Britain might not make it through. Dorothy was wildly popular, perhaps more than she knew, in British society and among the press.

In fact, Dorothy's reputation had long preceded her visit in July 1941; James W. Drawbell, an editor of the *Sunday Chronicle* of London, had been reprinting her articles for ten years, and for him and his publishers, her acceptance of their sponsorship during her trip to London was a bit of a coup. Dorothy received one of the most enthusiastic receptions ever accorded an unofficial visitor, well beyond what she and the *Sunday Chronicle* had anticipated. At Dorothy's suite at the Savoy, Drawbell was compelled to hire a staff of secretaries, point men, chauffeurs, and public relations people to coordinate the onslaught of invitations to speak, visit, and dine. Queen Elizabeth received her; Winston Churchill complimented her on the accuracy with which she had foreseen the development of the war, and she was invited to address committees in the House of Commons.

What Britons saw was a bright, beautiful face with a ready smile; a woman of intellect, capable of cold analysis and profound compassion; and a comrade in arms who encouraged and inspired both ordinary citizens and high officials. In her speeches, Dorothy imbued her words with personality and passion—and the more she witnessed of the Britons' dignity amid hardship, the more inspired she became. There was immediate reciprocity between her and the British public that surprised them and gave them hope.

In November 1941, Dorothy's domestic war of wills finally came to an end. Before she had left for England, Hal had pleaded with her for a divorce; besides reiterating her profound loneliness and disappointment in their marriage, Dorothy had blithely countered that her trip to England during the Blitz might settle the matter "in a more thorough manner."

Hal, still cultivating the delusion of marrying Marcella, wanted to be free. He demanded in the name of sanity and generosity that she let him go. But it was only when Hal threatened never to see Michael again that she finally capitulated. In a letter to her stepson, Wells, she wrote, "I think your father is the goddamndest fool of a great man anybody ever knew."

Always the survivor, Dorothy bought a townhouse in Turtle Bay, at 237 East Forty-eighth Street, near the East River in midtown Manhattan. A commanding general at home, touted by Roosevelt in Washington, hailed in Britain as a compatriot, and read daily by millions of Americans, Dorothy was beginning to believe the myths that flourished around her. The townhouse "was a veritable command post," she told *Look* magazine. It was a mildly ironic metaphor, but only mildly, now that Dorothy's quest for international influence had become a reality. She wanted to step up her "operations," equating her efforts with those of a commander in chief. In celebration of her reaching her aspired status, somewhat tongue in cheek, she commissioned the design of colored glass panels inlaid on the front door depicting herself in heroic medieval dress as writer, speaker, and hostess. The irony of her noble stance and elegant accommodations, given her past, was not lost. Her choice of house motto, prominently displayed in Latin, *Gallus in sterquilinio suo plurimum potest,* translated as "The cock crows best on his own dunghill."

But Dorothy's professed humility did not prevent her from fomenting a fierce social agenda. In a memo to Bill Paley, president of CBS, she laid out her vision of the role of radio during wartime. In essence, it was a call to use radio news and entertainment as a form of propaganda. She believed drama, music, and news must eschew the pleasurable and concentrate on the heroic: Casualty lists must be announced by those capable of instilling pride in sacrifice and hatred of the enemy; the trade unions must devise dramas that imbued industrial life and science with patriotism and honor. In sum, the radio must be a source of "power, vigor, beauty, humor, affirmation."

Meanwhile, Michael had returned from Arizona. Now eleven years old, he had been enrolled by Dorothy in Riverdale School for Boys, a private school located in the Bronx, just north of Manhattan. A friend of Michael's, Denis Fodor, the son of Marcel, Dorothy's colleague and mentor during her early days in Austria, remembered that during a visit to their Forty-eighth Street brownstone, he had seen Michael sneaking a shot of liquor from the unlocked bar. While somewhat unusual, he thought it naturally in sync with the family habit, considering his father's notorious drinking and his mother's escalating indulgence. Michael's homecoming seemed to have solved nothing. He still wondered how much his mother cared about him, even more so now that his father was out of the picture, but she was so wrapped up in her push for universal freedom that he just felt like a burden. Michael's fear of abandonment was so intense, for example, that he worried his mother would forget to come to commencement ceremonies at his school, and he asked the headmaster's office to give her a special call.

Sometimes, Hal's first wife, Grace Hegger Casanova, would invite Michael for the weekend at their country home. The women seemed to have adopted each other's sons. For Dorothy, the curly haired, blond Wells, idealistic and brilliant, was beginning to feel like the son Michael never would be. While as yet unarticulated, Dorothy's disappointment with Michael was evident. Like Rebecca with Anthony, Dorothy had begun to think that her son was uneducable and lacked the capacity for higher cognitive function. Whether right or wrong in her assessment, neither woman would take responsibility for her son's frailties, vaguely chalking them up to the absence of his father and random genetics— beliefs that would bind them in years to come.

Meanwhile, however, Grace delighted in Michael's presence—he was a "fearless swimmer"—and fraternal resemblance to Wells, who was serving in the European theater as an army officer. Upon divorcing Hal, Dorothy would remember Grace's comment that he was neither a husband nor a father—solely a writer. Upon hearing of Dorothy and Hal's divorce, Rebecca would write that both seemed otherworldly, more like aurorae borealis—spontaneous explosions of diaphanous iridescence swirling across the darkened horizon, in obeisance to a primal mystical force. Rebecca wasn't surprised that their marriage had imploded. Hal and Dorothy's friend Jimmy Sheean would concur. He later wrote that it was a pity that the greatest novelist and the greatest journalist married. "Such things ought not to happen."

On the night of December 8, 1941, Michael and Denis Fodor returned from a movie to find Dorothy's townhouse ablaze in lights and Dorothy alone and crying. Despite the years of anticipation, the reality seemed to devastate her, remembered Denis. Michael asked her if someone had died. No, she answered, repeating it several times, as if in a daze. The country was at war. Dorothy would blame the war on Washington's failed negotiations with Japan, and urged the readers of her monthly column in the *Ladies' Home Journal* to make it "a war of liberation," and not "antiquated imperialism."

In the spring of 1942, Dorothy took a leading role in the anti-Nazi propaganda campaign. Bill Paley agreed to let Dorothy broadcast a series of talks via shortwave radio, in the hope of fostering a German insurgence from within. In fluent German, acquired during her years as a foreign correspondent, she addressed her remarks to "Hans," a fictional Everyman who represented the ordinary German worker; a family man with simple needs and good Christian values, who she believed was appalled at Hitler's atrocities. Unlike true Nazis, the workingman not only felt guilt, she believed, but also secretly hoped that Germany would lose the war. She believed that like workingmen throughout the free world, his prime goal was economic security close to home, not in the strange faraway cultures of a sprawling Nazi empire. In tandem with composing her talks, Dorothy collected them for a book, published for an English-speaking audience and augmented by an introduction that would trace the history of the German people and probe the cultural forces within the country's psyche.

Based on painstaking research, the validity of which would later be confirmed by rave reviews from German expatriates and American scholars, Dorothy's book examined the history, philosophy, social structure, and culture of Germany. As much an effort to influence policy as to convince the German worker to see himself as an agent of freedom, her book asserted several overarching principles, some of which she would later recant: She proffered that "complete military defeat would be the most salutary thing that could happen to [Germany] . . . open[ing] the gate to a new rational idealism." Citing Wilson's Fourteen Points, she asserted the need for "national interdependence." Just as the world must collaborate "to help us defeat the German Devil," we must strive for a "universalism to help us construct a new German order"—a confederation of interdependent national states under a supranational organ to promote order and eradicate war.

Dorothy was on top; she had hit her stride, and she had hit it on her own. Critics might disagree with her analysis, but they honored her conclusions. Moreover, she had convinced Paley that the radio was an important instrument of war. In the spring and summer of 1942, Dorothy would claim a media victory as a participant in yet another shortwave broadcast to Europe, also in German, in concert with two leading theologians. Again her intent was to awaken the ethical and religious consciousness of the ordinary German to the desecration of human life, and incite his will to overthrow Hitler's Third Reich.

Dorothy had been honored by her peers, the president, the queen of England, and Winston Churchill, and she was beginning to think that her success was indeed enough. But that summer, as she launched a key component of her Ten Articles of Faith, the Land Corps, converting the area surrounding Twin Farms in Vermont into an agricultural training ground for up to two thousand high school and college students, a man walked into Dorothy's life, taking her by surprise.

Maxim Kopf was an Austrian-born political dissident who had become a citizen of Czechoslovakia and escaped prison amid the chaos of Hitler's occupation in 1938. Fleeing to France, he was imprisoned again, this time as an enemy alien during the Russo-German Pact of September 1939. But during the upheaval after the Allied declaration of war, he once again escaped, making his way through Europe and sailing to the South Seas. A painter and sculptor, he lived off the paltry income of his crafts for four years. Immigrating to the States in the summer of 1941, with the help of Jan Masaryk, the foreign minister of Czechoslovakia and his government in exile, he was sent to Twin Farms in the hope that Dorothy, known as a sympathetic defender of foreign exiles, might take him in.

With the intent of commissioning a portrait of Michael, who was now withdrawn from the Riverdale School for Boys and was provisionally enrolled in the Putney School in Vermont, a progressive academy for "gentleman farmers," Dorothy offered Maxim a one-week stay with room and board, though she initially resented the intrusion on her privacy. But soon Dorothy would replace Michael—temperamentally unsuited to portrait sitting—as his model. Fascinated by Maxim's background and character, as well as the virile, muscular physique of this tall and exotic stranger who had dedicated his life and art to Christ in gratitude for his freedom, Dorothy came to enjoy his company and their time alone. Max painted Dorothy once, and not quite getting it right (she looked like George Washington!), stayed to paint her again. The weeks passed and they became lovers; when it came time for him to leave, neither could let the other go.

But Dorothy would have to marshal all her clout, money, and energy to keep him. Max was married. Although his marriage to a Czech-born Jewish actress, Lotte Stein, had been one of convenience—she had gained an American passport and he a place to lay his head—Lotte was reluctant to give Maxim up without some compensation. When Dorothy naïvely sent her a letter declaring her love for Max and demanding a divorce, Lotte knew she held the means by which to blackmail the eminent Miss Thompson. Sensing disaster, Dorothy hired Louis Nizer, lawyer to celebrities and astute defender of the libeled and famous. Nizer managed to broker a deal, rumored to have cost Dorothy $30,000, for the return of the letter and a Reno divorce. In truth, the divorce "deal" would be only a down payment. She must have known it would be her responsibility to support Max. His subsistence wages would no longer suffice as the husband of a world-renowned journalist.

Dorothy was thrilled to have found a man who had used his trials to hone his spirit; beautiful Bard had grown greedy and undisciplined in the midst of plenty, while Hal, unable to bear the burden of his gifts, preferred the oblivion of drink and delusion. Max was a man of strength and integrity, both anchor and sail, friend and enabler, with whom Dorothy could reclaim her faith and find refuge. For the first time, perhaps, she could stop running.

Nonetheless, Dorothy would caution Max that she spelled trouble in any man's life. She warned him that he might become a casualty of her fame. She was enslaved, she explained, to the brute whim of the public and yet, she assured him, she knew that she must persevere. Max replied that he loved everything about her—mind, spirit, and body—and promised never to be an impediment to her career or way of life.

Dorothy and Max were married a year after their meeting, on Wednesday, June 16, 1943, at the First Universalist Church near Twin Farms in Barnard, just north of Woodstock in eastern Vermont. The church was a far cry from the fundamentalist Methodist church of her upbringing, but at forty-nine years old and twice divorced (Max was fifty-one and had been divorced three times) she sought sanctification, not purity.

After attending the wedding, Zuckmayer would comment that Maxim exuded strength and the worldliness of a well-traveled man of good humor, dedicated to his art. After his tumultuous years in exile, he knew the difference between marriage and safety, but he believed that Dorothy loved him and he had found a home. "Both of them suffered from something unfulfilled, from a hardly conscious never expressed longing for home."

The longing for home is what had brought Dorothy and Hal together and, the promise unfulfilled, had driven them apart. So, too, Rebecca and Henry would hang on to Ibstone as a sacred symbol of their primal desire for "home," even as they drifted apart.

The twenty wedding guests were friends from New York and Boston. They included Dorothy's doctor from New York; authors; singers; friends and neighbors; Dale Warren of Houghton Mifflin, whom Dorothy would call "the best friend any woman ever had"; a Polish friend of Maxim's; Dorothy's sister and brother-in-law, Peggy and Howard Wil-

son; and Michael, home from the Putney School, who was already cultivating a strong bond with his surrogate dad. Sadly, Dorothy's friends in
Europe, trapped by war, were absent.

On the vast lawns of Twin Farms after the ceremony, facing Mount
Ascutney, the guests stood to toast the bride. Round and voluptuous in
her silk print dress, she seemed uncommonly small and feminine next to
her expansive new husband, as she graciously accepted their good wishes.
No longer the slim young woman with her effete Semitic prince in the
Viennese church, plagued with guilt at forsaking her father's faith, or the
stalwart bride of a literary genius whose future well-being lay heavily on
her shoulders, she was the mature, accomplished, and besotted bride of a
loving, generous man, as sensitive and vulnerable as he was strong, as
gay and bawdy as he was solemn and religious. Dorothy knew she had
found the man she "ought to have married in the first place."

Dorothy and Maxim after their church wedding, June 16, 1943

The wedding feast had kept Dorothy's cook frantic for a week. She had prepared a gourmet buffet of luscious casseroles, enormous cakes, and platters of cookies. The salads were composed of greens and vegetables from the garden, and the wedding punch was lavishly spiked. Dale Warren had carried fourteen lobsters all the way from Charles Street in Boston (along with several wedding presents), and the guests ate and conversed to the tunes of Zuckmayer's guitar.

Soon the party became a saturnalia, with Maxim and Zuckmayer wrestling half-naked on the lawn, and then falling into a serpentine dance led by Dorothy's friend and live-in research assistant, Budzi, the Polish renegade who had had the distinction of introducing the couple. While several guests slurped caviar by the spoonful, Peggy and Howard Wilson, exercising the Methodist restraint of Dorothy's youth, sat silently on the sidelines. Their perspective ran contrary to Dorothy's belief that while her marriage to Maxim may have crossed the line of decorum, she had not renounced her fundamental faith in God. Certain of her righteousness, Dorothy bathed in the joy of her most cherished marriage.

She had never had much fun being married, she wrote to Wells Lewis, now an army lieutenant on tour in North Africa, who had heard the news from Hal. She told him that she felt as if she and Max had known each other forever, and she feared that her vacuous smile might erode her edge. But the foibles of humanity promised to keep her sufficiently sharp. In fact, the remainder of 1942 as well as 1943 would prove more challenging than she might have liked.

A photographer and journalist from *Look* magazine, Benny DeVoto, whom Dorothy had permitted into her townhouse in the hopes of fostering the career of her émigré interior designer, would deem her a hypocrite. While Dorothy preached material sacrifice to the middle-class public, DeVoto described each room and piece of furniture in his article, concluding that she lived in utter luxury.

When Dorothy protested in a personal letter, he responded by attacking her impulse to live a life of excess, while preaching public restraint and espousing fundamentalist religion. Furthermore, he countered that excessive materialism such as hers was often the guise of wealthy fascists and those isolationists whose "liberal philosophy" required their patronage. Perhaps this was an allusion to Dorothy's previous alignment with the Willkie crowd. He concluded by attacking the fundamentalist

Methodism of her youth, suggesting that had she been born a Catholic, she might have been less reformist and more charitable, as well as more tolerant of human imperfection.

Perhaps unknown to Dorothy, his comments about religion were those of a man who had grown up with a Mormon father and a Catholic mother and who had rejected both faiths; DeVoto's words carried an ironic twist, tinged with a smidgen of guilt.

Regardless, the myth of the pious spendthrift Dorothy had so carefully crafted had begun to crack. And the discrepancy between her private life and public persona would become more and more clear to those around her, even as she kept it hidden from herself.

One of the most hurtful betrayals would come from her journalist and novelist friend Phyllis Bottome, who wanted to publish an article revealing the intimacies of Dorothy's relations with Joseph Bard and Sinclair Lewis. While Phyllis saw it as a gift to Michael that would enable him to glimpse the humanity of his parents, Dorothy thought it nothing less than libel. If Phyllis didn't withdraw it from publication, warned Dorothy, she would take legal action. Phyllis, confused by her scorn, nonetheless spiked it. She retorted that the "old Dorothy" would have understood. It was this accusation that stung her most.

All in all, her latest incarnation as a public intellectual was a boon to Dorothy's career. In November 1943, Paul Brooks of Houghton Mifflin told Dorothy that she had a blank contract "for any book you want to write, big or small." She was thinking about doing one about her father. Meanwhile, however, as the war appeared to be moving toward Allied victory, the Germans were cranking up the crematoriums at the death camps. Though the extent of the horror was unknown to the general public and suppressed by the popular press, the question became how to salvage the remaining Jewish population of Europe and bring them to safety.

Dorothy reached out to help many of her friends from Austria and Germany to immigrate to the United States. Some were political dissidents, but most were either Jews or in jeopardy because they were married to Jews. As conditions grew worse, more and more Jews sought asylum in the British-run mandate of Palestine. Realizing for the second time that the Jewish refugee problem was a matter of international concern, Dorothy assumed the mantle of advocate for the formation of a

Jewish state. She attacked the problem as she had earlier refugee issues—focusing on the German mind as well as domestic policy and politics—with a mix of passion and instinct, scholarship and statistics. In a series of talks before the American Zionist Emergency Council at the New York Public Library, she surveyed the post–World War I history of the British policy toward its colonies in the Middle East. While granting some quasi-independence, she explained, they had shrewdly governed their oil resources, balancing their own interests against those of the large Muslim populations throughout the colonies. London's ambivalent policy toward the Jews, she asserted, was clearly a means of counterbalancing the strength of burgeoning Arab national aspirations that threatened Britain's own power structure, permitting it to "divide and conquer." Seeing no hope for a change in British policy, Dorothy encouraged the Zionists to take the reins and demonstrate to the British that the loyalty of the Palestinian Jews contributed to their military might and economic strength.

"The question is no longer whether there should be a Jewish home and a Jewish nation in Palestine," she said. "There *is* one. It exists." There must be two separate spheres of sovereignty divided between Arabs and Jews, she insisted—as was definitively implied by the 1917 British Balfour Declaration. In one of the most graphic, impassioned, and poetic pleas for accepting the reality of Jewish nationhood, she declared, "For this, tens of thousands of teachers and students have unburied the language of the Bible and Talmud, exhumed it from the dust of antique books, and made it a living, spoken tongue. For this, tens of thousands of youths from the ghettos of Europe have broken their backs upon the stones of Palestinian roads, and under burning skies lifted their songs."

Moving on to the philosophical and psychological to lay out her case for Jewish nationhood, she probed the basis of anti-Semitism. At its root, she said, is the fact that the Jews have no country. "It haunts the mythology of primitive-minded Christians. . . . If the Jews are a people without a country, doomed to wander the face of the earth, must that not be a punishment for some dreadful sin? Did not the Jews of the Sanhedrin crucify Christ? . . . So runs the myth, nor stops to think that Jesus of Nazareth was born in the very womb of Jewry, descendant of the great religious and philosophical line of Amos and Isaiah." She went on to relate the history of the struggle for Jewish survival, from the Spanish Inquisition to the ghettos of Nazi Germany. She even cited the fears of Jews in free nations that a Jewish state would stir up anti-Semitism in their own. She saw it all—the mythological, the sociological, and the psychological underpinnings of anti-Semitism, and asked, how could a democracy deny Jews their right to a homeland without destroying the ideals of democracy itself? The Jews needed to become a state among states in order that all people might work together in an increasingly interdependent global world.

The most self-transcendent tenet of her argument was her validation of the Jewish concept of the Messiah. "Perhaps," she mused in a later speech, "the Messiah is not a person but a mind, a concept that will re-create the world. Perhaps the Messiah is in you—in all of you together, when you put the enormous talents and wisdom of your race to work to demonstrate to the world how a social order can be created in which there is freedom and order, individual rights and community well-being." She ended her speeches with two challenges to the Zionists: Preserve your people and your commandments, and join with those of all faiths to forge a "path out of our present darkness."

One can only imagine the thunderous applause that followed in a reading room of that hallowed hall of scholarship and learning. Rarely, if ever, had a Christian made such a masterful argument for the inherent virtue of the Jewish people and the necessity of Jewish statehood. Like all her idealistic rhetoric, no matter how honestly expressed and deeply felt, this, too, would be tested in the years to come.

While Dorothy wrote a letter to Churchill pleading the case for providing British supplies to the Jews in Palestine in the name of Balfour's promise, in early December 1943 the prime minister had his mind on the entire European theater. As she spoke in New York, Churchill was meeting with Roosevelt and Stalin in Tehran, negotiating the end terms of the European war. In exchange for the continued Russian domination of Poland and Yugoslavia, Stalin pledged to join the Anglo-American forces in a two-front war through southern France and into the heart of Germany.

By mid-December 1943, Dorothy began to calculate the value of her voice. She would refuse to accept less than $7,000 for a speech. Unwittingly, she had become a cottage industry; she was also bent on making

100 acres of the 360 surrounding Twin Farms into a commercially viable business. In collaboration with the County Soil Conservation Service, she supported a small herd of cattle; another herd of sheep, mainly for clearing and fertilizing; and one thousand chickens for laying eggs as well as hundreds of others raised and sold for poultry. Much like Rebecca's farm at Ibstone, this was Dorothy's small-scale effort to supplement wartime food production. Dorothy's farm would become an object of great admiration by Rebecca, as well as another source of comradeship between them.

Beginning in January 1943, when the Allied leaders had convened in Casablanca and resolved to demand "unconditional surrender" of Germany and Japan, Dorothy had been outraged by their ruthlessness. By November, while her rage had not diminished, it was infused with sobriety.

In a letter to Wells, now on duty in France, she wrote:

> *I'm taking the war awfully hard. And often, often, a terrible fury possesses me, that maybe all the people who lead us won't be good enough to make it worthwhile. . . . If anyone in a position of great power just appealed consistently and exclusively to the noblest and most creative instincts in "mankind"—he could release a power that few believe exists. And even if he were crucified he couldn't be stopped.*

While neither she nor Rebecca thought much of the human race, Dorothy believed in its salvation through leadership and sacrifice. That is to say, that Christ need not have died in vain. Rebecca, however, saw the suffering of Christ as a destructive delusion; as she had written in *Black Lamb and Grey Falcon*, moral insight belonged to few, and moral influence to even fewer.

In 1944, Michael was not invited back to Putney. A letter from his English teacher summed up the attitude of the faculty: "I have never seen anyone write more naturally and easily. I have never seen a larger vocabulary for a child his age. But his writing goes from the brilliantly original to the most hackneyed pulp with no sign of discrimination on his part."

At her wit's end in her attempts to curb Michael's inability to conform to conventional academic demands, she enrolled him in the Valley Forge Military Academy in Pennsylvania. While at first he was entranced by the dignity and virtue of military rigor—after all, America was at war, and his half brother Wells was fighting in North Africa—Michael quickly lost his enthusiasm. For the moment, however, Dorothy chose to ignore his pleas to come home.

Dorothy continued to fear that the fate of the German people would be devastating. She insisted to her friends and to anyone who would listen that the Germans were victims of circumstances—that most Western societies would have reacted the same way toward a despotic demagogue under similar conditions. Her words fell on deaf ears; friends accused her of outright treason. Even John Gunther and William Shirer had learned not to broach the subject. The British Foreign Office, which counted Dorothy as both an important friend and "a dangerous enemy," would firmly denounce her views.

At a Manhattan debate in the late spring of 1944 among Dorothy; Mark Van Doren, a poet and critic, and the brother of Carl; Rex Stout, the leftist novelist; and Louis Fischer, a Stalinist who wrote for *The Nation* magazine; Dorothy blatantly spelled out her view, alienating not only her colleagues but many in the audience. Paralleling Rebecca's position, Dorothy stated that the Allied nations, which had traded with the Germans after World War I, and had been quick to forgive them their debts, had enabled Hitler's rise to power as much as the Germans had. While she evoked vociferous accusations from the audience of exonerating the German people of guilt, others in the crowd viewed Mark, Rex, and Louis as bloodthirsty avengers.

In early August 1944, when Hitler's generals revolted, Dorothy said it proved that there was resistance within the Reich.

Meanwhile, the United States was once again preparing for a presidential election and a possible fourth term for Roosevelt. FDR made it clear that he wanted her support. Despite having great doubts about his health and ability to live out his term, Dorothy agreed to campaign on his behalf. Roosevelt, of course, was notorious for cajoling support from all kinds of celebrities—from Hollywood stars to writers and journalists—and Dorothy had worked her magic before. She took her role seriously. Through Roosevelt's speechwriter Robert E. Sherwood, she cautioned him not to permit the Republicans to bring him down.

"They know he is tired and he has had times of great discouragement," she wrote. "Beg him to ignore them and to put himself on a level so sovereign, so far above, that they seem like ants and bedbugs in comparison." Sherwood later remarked that most of the good ideas for Roosevelt's campaign had come from Dorothy.

On October 20, 1944, Dorothy gave a speech on behalf of the president that denigrated the Republican candidate Thomas A. Dewey, governor of New York, as one who didn't understand the Soviet Union, which she believed would be the true postwar threat. For twenty years, she said, the Russians had feared the destruction of their state. And history proved them right—they were invaded by Poland and lost Finland. "[The] Russian mind is haunted by the past." She said that Russia's part in the war had been heroic, but negotiations must be done by those with experience and informed judgment. She dismissed Dewey as "frivolous."

On election eve, November 6, 1944, after the president had given another of his folksy speeches from his hearth in Hyde Park, Dorothy once again dazzled her friends in a live radio broadcast from Carnegie Hall, bringing them to tears with her impassioned words. John Gunther wept, he wrote in his diary, along with Dinah Sheean and Janet Flanner.

Roosevelt won, but it was a close call—25.6 million votes to Dewey's 22 million. In terms of electoral votes, however, it was a landslide—432 to 99. The tired president had earned the chance to finish his work, but Dorothy was exhausted. She wrote in her diary that she was losing her own struggle to proffer a humane peace settlement toward the Germans. "In the public prints I am entirely isolated."

Even her colleague Walter Winchell had betrayed her publicly. In one of his columns, he quoted a flippant remark that Dorothy had made at a party: "The intellectual level of America is so low that I am moving to Germany for good," as if it summed up her political views. Awestruck, Dorothy sent him a personal letter, not only accusing him of lying, but also implicitly castigating him for his cowardice. He, who had denied that the free world was appeasing Hitler and had refused to recognize that the Jews of Europe faced extermination, had dared to frame her as a traitor? No matter what she said, her words were distorted. The German people *were* better than the Nazis, she believed, but to stuff them all into the militant Prussian stereotype was to brand them all as complicit racists. The "race theory about the Germans . . . makes me sick to my stomach."

But all this repartee would seem like idiocy in the face of what was to

come. Just one week after the election, she would receive news that
would crush her.

Wells Lewis was dead. He had been shot in back of the head by a German sniper in Bruyères, France, on his way to the Ardennes. When she
received the news on November 13, 1944, Wells had been dead for two
weeks, since October 29, while Dorothy had been campaigning for
Roosevelt.

At 9:15 on the evening of the thirteenth, Dr. Cornelius ("Connie")
Traeger, her personal physician, called John Gunther to tell him that
Dorothy had received the news of Wells's death. John wrote in his diary
that he had spoken with Max, who said, "I have her now under alcohols
but she loves you so much, you should come over."

"Dr. Traeger," recorded John, "bought some Amatol [a barbiturate]
and we went."

> Dorothy in tears. Sobbing. Could not broach. And Grace had
> been in icy hysterics. Snob to the end. "Why did they have to take
> an aristocrat like Wells? Why couldn't the cheap riffraff die?"
> Also, "The Goddamned little fool of a son of a bitch to get him-
> self killed!" I wondered what it would do to a) Michael b) Red.
> Red en route to Chicago. We tried to fix a wire to stop the Cen-
> tury. Couldn't. D. couldn't bear it that he should hear of it from a
> reporter. So she called her sister Peggy and asked her to meet him
> in the A.M. D. sobbing and sobbing. Then: under control, "He's
> dead just as his life should be beginning."

Michael had looked to Wells as a model of manhood, and it is difficult to know how he felt when he heard about his death from a friend
at school. Aside from his grief, and perhaps the ensuing guilt of his own
survival, there might have been some ambivalence. He was alone, but
he was also unique—the sole remaining son of his mother and his father. Hal's reaction was as icy as Grace's, yet free of snobbism. Marcella
Powers, now living on her own, had heard the news through a mutual
friend and telegrammed Hal, but it was only when Dorothy's brother-
in-law Harold Wilson phoned him that he acknowledged Wells's death.
Always the satirist, regardless of his feelings, Hal quipped, "Oh *good*
for you, you're the one who got to tell it! All day everyone has been
trying to tell me—the newsboy, the bootblack, the cigar counter man,

the desk clerk, everyone's been trying to tell me. But great, great! You're the one who got to tell it." According to his biographer Mark Schorer, Hal became quiet and philosophical, thinking about all the other fathers in America, Germany, and Japan to whom such news was broken.

And yet his obvious pride in Wells's literary and journalistic accomplishments contradicted his cool veneer. Surely he was deeply saddened. But as usual, his sadness morphed into a sword; he attacked Dorothy for staging a publicity stunt by canceling her morning radio broadcast. More and more, he seemed a bitter, lonely, and tragic figure, alienating everyone who might have cared.

Carl Zuckmayer would write Dorothy a letter of condolence that approaches the truth of Dorothy's feeling for Wells: "I know what it means to you. I know you lost a son—for you were more than a mother—and a friend, and the hope and care for a young brilliant rising life." He told her that he was desolated by the suffering of war. It seems to take the lives of "the best and the bravest," making him feel helpless and ashamed.

Dorothy would reply without self-censor or restraint to the one friend she knew would understand:

> Dear Zuck,
>
> Your letter was so full of affection and understanding that I answer it, leaving aside many others, to express my gratitude. . . . He was the most blessed by the Gods and yet unfortunate child I have ever known. He had superlative good looks and talents and a most superlative brain, and was torn between two gifted and bitterly quarrelling parents. I know that because I loved him and he loved me, he felt a security with me that he had found nowhere else, and out of that grew a very great influence that I had over his whole development. In some ways he was closer to me than to Michael, since a maternal possessiveness and exaggerated sense of responsibility seems to divide us from our own children. . . . He was in a most intimate, complicated, and infinitely comforting way something of my own. I make myself recriminations, that I did not do more—do something active and positive, to get him out of the hell in which he had fought

uninterruptedly for two years but neither my own convictions nor his would allow me to. My grief is in every cell, and I do not even want it assuaged. It is part of me forever and it is what remains to me of him.

Dorothy's response to the death of Wells was as to the loss of a soul mate and literary heir. She had come to love him as her own, and Wells had become the son Michael would never be. But her expression of grief rose to the universal and the theological. Dorothy's perception of human effort was couched in helplessness before the machinations of government, human nature, and God's will, while Rebecca's beliefs were premised on an inscrutable and punitive divine force, necessitating powerful, even aggressive, intervention in human affairs, political and personal. Dorothy was merely an instrument; Rebecca was the compensating source.

Dorothy felt betrayed by her own idealism, but her passion to preserve democracy and freedom by advocating American intervention in the European war had been paramount. If she did have, as she wrote, a great influence on Wells's life, she must have felt that it was she who had inspired his patriotic entry into the armed forces. It was the height of irony that her struggle to influence the course of the war resulted in such profound personal loss.

She had lost not only a son in the war but beloved friends as well— Genia Schwarzwald had died in Zurich in 1940, Helmuth von Moltke had died in a Nazi death camp, and Christa Winsloe had been shot by a madman posing as a Nazi in the south of France in 1944.

Dorothy's desire for a humane peace for the German people turned into a fiery resentment of Anglo-American policy. "All that is really needed now is the re-opening of the gas chambers and crematoria— perhaps with American boys manning the furnaces." She was glad that all her friends were dead, for it proved, she concluded, that the Allies had assumed the amoral barbarism of their enemies.

In April 1945, when Roosevelt died, Dorothy and Max were overseas— first in London where they had visited Rebecca and Henry, and then in Jerusalem to await Hitler's personal demise and with it the end of the Third Reich.

By the time the Japanese surrendered, there were 70 million people dead, 5.7 million Jews had been cremated in death camps or shot, most major German cities were in rubble, 30 percent of Polish and 20 percent of Yugoslavian urban centers were shattered, and two-thirds of the cities in Japan were devastated. Dorothy was certain that the end of the world was near—that the human race would be consumed in a fiery apocalypse that would rid the world of evil and allow it to rise up cleansed and pure. Rebecca, however, was just as certain that human cruelty and cosmic indifference would prevail. Yet in the event that Dorothy's glorious conflagration might come to pass, Rebecca would have been the first to jump into the holy pyre.

Max, Dorothy, Michael, and dog, circa 1943

After V-J Day in August 1945, Carl Zuckmayer observed that Dorothy's grief over the death of Wells "hurt her to the core. . . . This was the first time I saw her broken, even her boundless courage and spirit seemed broken. Her innate sense of security was shaken. . . . In this spirit rather than in the joy of victory she experienced Germany's defeat. The bombing of Hiroshima, Japan's capitulation, and VE Day was [*sic*] celebrated brutally and noisily in the streets of the cities."

Kampf ended in disillusion, but there remained Max to love and comfort her, and Michael, as alien to every cell of her being as Wells was consonant, to nurture into manhood.

PART
4

CHAPTER 15

NO EXIT

> We might stretch as far as we could to the right,
> to the left, to the sky, to the ground, but we are
> bound to our place in the universe.
>
> —REBECCA WEST, *A Letter to a Grandfather,* 1933

NEW YORK, MARCH 1947

When the SS *Queen Elizabeth* sailed into New York harbor on Tuesday, March 25, 1947, it was a relatively balmy fifty degrees, at least twenty degrees warmer than it had been when Rebecca had left Southampton, England, six days earlier. Her trip to New York had been delayed nearly two months as she struggled with a bout of bacterial pneumonia. Weak, listless, and unable to work, Rebecca had felt caged in by circumstances beyond her control. Her illness had been compounded by the harshest winter on record, a coal shortage, continued food rationing, and financial worries.

Ibstone had become a prison. In September 1946, Rebecca had thrown herself on the mercy of Dorothy to fabricate some vague pretext—the promise of writing assignments, anything—to justify her leaving home. The deterioration of Henry's mental and physical health, H.G.'s death, Rebecca's rejection by Biddle, and the prospect of another dreary winter in Buckinghamshire had made her desperate for the vibrancy of New York's intellectual and social climes. Dorothy had easily succeeded in marshaling Harold Ross, the editor of *The New Yorker,* to her cause; Rebecca's coverage of the trials at Nuremberg and the British wartime traitors had been critically acclaimed. She had broken new ground, raising journalism to a form of literature with her keen observations of the evil inherent in human nature, and her storyteller's eye for people and relationships. Ross offered her an open opportunity to write book reviews and any other articles of her own choosing.

Rebecca's journey aboard the most luxurious ship afloat, paid for by Ross, felt like a well-earned holiday. The rolling waves and fresh salt air she inhaled reading on the deck wrapped in a shawl made her forget the winter she had left behind. Now that the war was over and the ships had relinquished their military role, they had become lavishly staffed and stocked seafaring hotels, ferrying travelers to and from Europe in record numbers. When the *Queen Elizabeth* docked, Rebecca pushed her way through the throng of two thousand passengers to present her papers to the immigration officers. If only she could make her way down the gangplank, she would find herself in the welcoming arms of Dorothy and her close friend Emanie, and on her way to three months of freedom.

After two hours of waiting, "an act of saintliness" on the dock, Emanie and Dorothy whisked Rebecca off to the St. Regis, a residential hotel at the corner of Fifty-fifth Street and Fifth Avenue in midtown Manhattan. It was lunchtime when Rebecca finally settled into her dingy two-room suite, furnished more like an office than a hotel room. Exhausted from her trip and not quite well, Rebecca was nonetheless delighted by the bouquets of flowers sent by friends and colleagues. She adjusted her dress and makeup and rushed off to a restaurant, already an hour late for a luncheon. Ross, a young associate of his from *The New Yorker,* Dorothy and Emanie, and her old friend John Gunther were already sipping cocktails when she arrived.

John had missed Rebecca's landing at the dock, despite having carefully searched the crowd for Dorothy, and had left for the restaurant to await their arrival. Six martinis and much raucous laughter later, John would confide to Rebecca his increasing despair in the face of his son Johnny's brain tumor; she would, in turn, tell him of Henry's illnesses, his chronic ulcers, and his steady descent into dementia. In the days and weeks succeeding this first tête-à-tête, Rebecca and John, thrown together by chance and choice, would commiserate, cultivating a friendship that had long lain fallow.

John and his wife, Frances Fineman, had been divorced for years; Frances had proven unstable and manipulative. Her unfulfilled aspirations as a writer had made her bitter and jealous of her husband's success despite the fact that she had been integral to his work. In short, she had been a hellish companion. While neither John nor Rebecca sought to resurrect their romantic liaison, they had great affection and admiration for each other. It had been Rebecca who, when they became lovers in 1924, had steered him away from fiction writing, and by 1947 John had earned renown with his Inside books—meticulously researched accounts of the political and social structures of Europe, Asia, and America, filtered through the lives of government officials and ordinary citizens. Only ten days earlier, John had completed his ambitious fourth book in the series, *Inside U.S.A.* John had intended this book to be a balanced and unbiased "political guidebook" to democracy in action, a mirror to America at its coming of age as a world power. His yet-to-be-published 975-page tome was both an ode to American ideals and its human and industrial potential, and a diatribe against the low moral standards, materialism, ignorance, and vulgarity of its politicians and its people. He painted a society prone to violence and waste, run by special interests and driven by materialism.

During this trip, John and Rebecca would spend many hours together; each was lonely and in need of a sympathetic ear. Their conversations grew in scope, progressing from the personal to encompass their views of American government and politics, and the moral character and values of its people. It would become clear to Rebecca that her vision of America was consonant with John's. Trapped in the moment, neither could have foreseen that America was on the brink of a great explosion of creativity and prosperity.

Echoing John's views, Rebecca wrote to Henry (careful to omit the gaiety of her lavish lunch with her friends) about a dinner in her honor at Emanie's new apartment on the evening of her arrival: "Nobody seems at all happy here. There is a désouvré feeling about everybody." And yet, "the bright, clean, untroubled look of the streets is something beyond anything. And the feeling there isn't a bit of bomb-damage anywhere is wonderful too." Americans, she implied, despite having come through the war relatively unscathed, were spoiled and malcontent. New York had the air of "a flimsy stage-set," she wrote. At least the problems of the English were real.

Rebecca's subsequent letters to Henry were riddled with more complaints, small and large—the quality and cost of food and clothing; the weather; the caliber of service at the hotel; the insensitivity of her friends and acquaintances; the superficial knowledge and perspective of Americans; their hedonistic bent and mindless frivolity; their dearth of ideas; and their lack of philosophical, religious, and ethical underpinnings. To Rebecca, New York seemed like a godless place: "I do not in practice like a community where nobody is Christian. It is two-dimensional. And if people don't believe in Christianity, they believe in anything else you tell them." Given her profound contempt for organized religion and Christian "mythology," this was at the very least a confirmation of its ethical validity.

Rebecca's hope for escape appeared a foolish delusion. Discontent followed her everywhere. Conscious or not, her distaste for America served several purposes: It assured Henry that he wasn't missing anything, thereby assuaging her guilt for leaving him in the midst of a deep freeze and relentless snow; it sustained her sense of war-ravaged superiority; and it helped her prepare herself for her inevitable return.

Out of her milieu, Rebecca was unusually volatile; undisciplined by compelling work, except for writing a few minor articles for Ross, she was producing nothing. Everything seemed a prelude to disaster. Vacillating between self-pity and unrestrained activity, she wrote to Henry that her life in New York was truly "odd." She seemed to stumble rather than steer her way through life, a mode of being that heightened her innate anxiety. Pains in her back and severe digestive disorders compounded her lingering pneumonia. And, she wrote, she had been feeling out of sorts for several days. At the behest of John, Dorothy, and her new friend, the novelist Marcia Davenport, a tall and elegant woman with a coarse face, Rebecca had gone to see a doctor at Yale University, who discovered that an abscess had formed around a stitch left after the removal of a tumor from her bowel in 1941.

Then, suddenly, in a remarkable change of mood, she wrote Henry that she had defied the doctor's advice to rest and had attended a meeting of the Refugee Defense Committee on Long Island. She and Dorothy had held a press conference, after which Rebecca had given a half-hour lecture.

But the dinner that followed, she wrote, was an "outrage." At the center of the conversation was Russia. "The atmosphere here is hysterical to the last degree—they are all either so pro-Russia that they would blow up the Capitol or they hate Russia as the Germans hated England in the last war. It's insane—and it's a fantasy, it doesn't relate to life."

Dorothy, she noted, was one of the worst; she wanted to draft the refugees from Eastern Europe as soldiers to fight against the Soviets. Rebecca thought her old friend was "rather silly just now, tired and worried."

As usual, her observations were astute. Dorothy was worried that her relationship with her son had become a war of wills. Everything she had taught him about hard work and excellence, the fine line between independence and conformity to expectation, had come to naught. She had reenrolled Michael, now seventeen, in the Collegiate School, but his behavior and lack of academic performance made it clear he would not stay long. He fought with his classmates, was insolent to his teachers, and took it out at home on Max, ironically the one man who loved him like a father and made him feel safe. Michael was angry—angry that the only token of his real father's love was an allowance of forty dollars a month; angry that his mother was preoccupied with her new husband, her friends, and her work; angry that Max was a stranger—worse, a foreigner—who he felt feigned fatherhood and had the audacity to share his mother's bed; angry that his half brother and role model Wells had deserted him in death. Without friends, siblings, or a place in the life of his parents, he felt isolated and alone. To make matters worse, he had difficulty concentrating in class and couldn't keep up with his work. The boy had taken to drifting off in a world of his own.

An eminent psychiatrist, the son of a friend of Dorothy's, suggested that Michael be confined to an institution. He said that Michael's shock at realizing he had to be institutionalized would motivate him to cooperate with the doctors and take responsibility for himself. Even if he were to be confined, however, the psychiatrist was sorry to say that the outlook appeared grim. Terribly saddened and unwilling to acquiesce, Dorothy looked for another solution. At the suggestion of another friend, she wrote to a history professor at Loyola College in Baltimore, Maryland, asking him to find a companion/tutor for Michael who could be with him on weekdays. In effect, wrote the professor, Dorothy wanted to hire "an older brother" for her son. While he was initially doubtful of fulfilling her request, he was, to his surprise, able to find a young man, just out of the armed forces, who would be willing to stay with Michael every day from 7 A.M. to midnight, if necessary. Dorothy, either too ashamed to tell Rebecca or finding her preoccupied and unsympathetic, had kept her silence about this latest crisis with her son. She sensed that regardless of their level of intimacy, she would appear to Rebecca much like the other New Yorkers she had met—childish, self-absorbed, and unreliable.

Outside this collective mania, providing relief from the small-minded people Rebecca was meeting in New York, there were still some heroes, she assured Henry—the loneliest and most courageous of whom was John Gunther. The doctors had now informed him that his seventeen-year-old son, Johnny, was dying; his brain tumor had morphed into a glioblastoma, the most deadly and incurable form of brain cancer. They would try to remove some of it, to give him a few months of respite, but after that, Johnny would quickly descend into coma and death. Rebecca found this "terribly bitter," she wrote to Henry, although it is interesting that Rebecca made no mention in her correspondence of Johnny's extraordinary valor in the face of the disease. Perhaps her failed relationship with Anthony was a barrier to empathy. Dorothy, however, was highly attuned to the family's pain; Johnny was exactly the same age as Michael and had attended some of the same schools. A year earlier, when Frances had asked Dorothy to pray for a miracle, knowing that she was a woman of faith, Dorothy had responded with a magnificent letter to John:

> I do not know whether the fervent passionate prayers for that miracle, prayers which are silently breathed in this household moment after moment, can directly influence or change the mystery of life and death. But I feel sure that the waves of love that emanate toward you and into the universe . . . contribute to sustain you all. Life, John, through all its transmutations must be eternal. That was my childhood faith. It is now my faith and the conviction of my mind. Whatever comes to Johnny will be a miracle. Whatever comes will be a great renewal of life. God and nature do not waste their gifts nor concentrate so disproportionate a share of them upon so beautiful a mind and soul as Johnny's in order to whimsically destroy them.

After Johnny died in June of that year, the notion of death as eternal life, however, would strike John as meaningless. True to her fundamentalist vision of human imperfection and divine resurrection, as John wrote in his diary, Dorothy would attempt to console him, somewhat perversely, by writing "He's still alive!" In response he wrote that it was "small comfort to a) Johnny b) F. and me, c) the world he might have served." But strange as it seems, Dorothy would go even further: "He might have been an idiot! He might have been a murderer! He was a scientist; he might have found the way to destroy mankind!"

What could have prompted this kind of comment? The answer might have been that while her own son was very much alive, he was, as she often noted, perfectly "useless."

UNINTERESTED IN THE "miracles of the afterworld," at least for the moment, Rebecca settled for earthly pleasures. Despite being surrounded by sadness and plagued by illness, she had a social calendar that looked like the who's who of New York's literary, intellectual, and theatrical world. During those three months, she dined with the Cass Canfields; the E. B. Whites; Irita Van Doren; several *Herald Tribune* columnists; Communist intellectuals; Time-Life editors; Henry and Clare Boothe Luce (whom she admired for, of all things, her passionate commitment to Catholicism); John Chamberlain, journalist and editorial writer for *Life* (a good and honest man); Edmund Wilson, the editor of *The New Republic* (who seemed to have a new bride each time she saw him); the "old" and abrasive gossip columnist Elsa Maxwell; along with theatrical stars, such as Ruth Gordon, Katharine Cornell, and John Gielgud. She insisted to Henry, however, that she was having a terrible time and couldn't wait to come home. She "hated being away so long" and longed for "my tulips. And the Spring generally."

Her experience in New York reached the height of absurdity, however, when Max Beaverbrook, her old beau who had "done me a mortal injury and inflicted on me a supreme humiliation" turned up in her hotel room unannounced, after learning she was ill and in New York. He acted as though "he were a tender and loving friend. . . . I looked up at him with astonishment. I could not fit it in with the drunken, lying, cheating little vagabond I had learned to see him as." While all this had occurred twenty-odd years earlier, she was still, she wrote to Henry, "frozen with rage."

Rage and contempt, in league with death and illness, had darkened her escape from Ibstone in March. Although it was now mid-May and the sun was finally shining, the promise of warmth did not assuage her discontent. She complained to Henry, "American people don't seem as interesting as Europeans . . . [and] the place is sick, sick, as we are not in Europe. Needless to say my interview with Max made me feel what undeserved luck I had in meeting you." Here her guilt seemed to have reached its peak, culminating in an outright lie. But her hunger for home had reached genuine intensity: "God prevent me from ever having to live here. The slowness, the incompetence, the talk," she would write in a letter that followed.

As the weather turned and her illness lifted, Rebecca, who had done mere piecework since her arrival, finally sat down with Ross (who had, with characteristic generosity, been footing her bills for more than a month) to hash out ideas for a serious article. Rebecca had read in the news about a forthcoming trial in Greenville, South Carolina, related to the alleged murder of a white taxi driver by a Negro man, and his subsequent murder by a mob of thirty-one white vigilantes. While she worried that she was becoming a bit too "typecast" as a courtroom-obsessed journalist, it was the one assignment that seemed to excite her. She sensed that, like the trials at Nuremberg, the Greenville trial would be a fascinating study of social prejudice and crime. While the cultural barriers might have loomed as insurmountable to those more cautious and less confident than she, Rebecca was undaunted. She had never lived in the South, had no direct knowledge of southern life and mores, and had little understanding of the realities of black and white relations in a locale deeply entrenched in the legacy of slavery. Nor did she know the nuances of American law. She was entering foreign territory.

Totally dependent on her ingenuity and powers of observation, along with her intuitive sense of human nature, she waltzed into Greenville on May 20, 1947, looking exactly like what she was—a bona fide misfit. The inhabitants had a knee-jerk antipathy toward northerners, but a foreigner with ladylike airs and a strange highfalutin accent—she might as well have been from Mars. The advantage of her ignorance, however, was her untainted eye. It rendered her vision universal.

Rebecca would compare Greenville's climate to the only European referent she knew: the hot cities in the plains of Spain. And yet, the ethic of the people could not have been more different, she noted. The citizens of Greenville were vigorous and hardworking; there were no long, soporific lunches laced with wine, or lazy afternoon Spanish-style siestas. Rebecca reveled in the sounds of Greenville's streets—the laughter of children playing with joyous abandon, and the chorus of voices that emanated from the local Baptist church. It echoed the Easter Sunday service she had witnessed in Macedonia and reminded her of an opera by Verdi. The courtroom, too, had the air of an opera, with its warring factions, diversity of social status and race, and, she would write, the hierarchy of its citizenry all functioning within the law. Continuing a theme that had permeated her previous writing and correspondence, Rebecca would name the *New Yorker* piece "Opera at Greenville."

A gifted manipulator and trained actress, Rebecca immediately ingratiated herself with the townspeople—defendants, family and friends of the plaintiff, and reporters—by expressing sympathy and respect. Three days into the trial, having gained entry into the inner circles of the press and the law, Rebecca had already begun to write her article. She was in constant touch by cable and mail with Ross in New York, giving him a sense of the place, the people, and the legal proceedings; she jauntily signed her name "Rebecca Magnolia," or "Rebecca Lou." He was delighted not only by her wit, but also by her ability to master the cultural and legal ambience of the event. And when she needed help understanding an arcane legal point, he was the conduit between her and an expert.

"Opera in Greenville" was first published as an article in *The New Yorker* in June 1947, and in 1955, in her book *A Train of Powder*, as a companion piece to her coverage of Nuremberg. The most striking insight one may deduce is that exactly what made Rebecca's personal relationships so disingenuous and multifaceted, would become the tools with which she ascertained the complex truths of this particular social and legal quagmire. As in her coverage of Nuremberg, Rebecca saw both the cinematic panorama of places, people, and events and the microscopic nuances of personality and attitude in the facial expressions, body language, and behavior of the people involved. "Opera in Greenville" reads like a twentieth-century morality play, a finely honed drama in which the "sinners" interact and collide against the ethical backdrop of Christian virtue. Bursts of light, shadow, and color splash onstage, as Rebecca's vision shifts from judge to jury, from defendants to defense lawyers, from plaintiffs to prosecutors, from press to townspeople. At root, Greenville was the site of a clash between southern whites and blacks. But once Rebecca trained her eye on them, finer distinctions proliferated: white federal officials, northern whites, southern white city and state government employees, white defense and prosecuting attorneys, the white northern press, the black local press, the white judge, the all-white jury.

Just as her eyes saw everything, her body registered every quiver of emotion and circumstance. Rebecca's visceral response to the late-May South Carolina heat, and the vacillating swings of pummeling rain and relentless sun, are as textured as her response to the unbridled rage of the defense lawyers and the extreme—perhaps overcompensatory—rationality of the judge. The distinction in the piece between law and justice is omnipresent, as is the pervasive distortion of racial law and biblical scripture to justify criminality. Rebecca revealed that racial prejudice corrupted even the finest minds, eroded democratic institutions, and perverted the essence of biblical scripture. If there was now one implacable touchstone in Rebecca's mind, it was Christian morality. It was this, she believed, that would ultimately save humanity.

Just as Dorothy had been certain that the Christian roots of the German worker would trigger an insurgence from within, Rebecca had come to believe that the prevailing social atrocities in the South could not go unnoticed. For the moment, though, she saw no way out of the moral darkness. Within the social framework of Greenville in 1947, justice could not reign. The ultimate acquittal sparked a moment of "orgiastic joy" by the defendants and their supporters, she wrote, predicting that the exoneration of the white defendants would ignite a fever of killings and lynchings that would spread an infection throughout the region. But by the time *A Train of Powder* was published in 1955, she knew she had been wrong.

In the book she would write, "The lynching trial in South Carolina and its sequels were symptoms of abating disease.... There was a strange and dramatic tempo to be felt at the Greenville trial, wickedness itself had been aware of the slowing of its pulse. The will of the South had made its decision, and by 1954 three years had gone by without a lynching in the United States."

Before sailing home on the SS *Queen Elizabeth* on June 11, 1947, from New York, the eminent Ms. Magnolia delivered her twenty-thousand-word article to Ross's office in New York. In a note attached to the draft of her essay she quipped that it was a tome barely shorter than *War and Peace*.

The critics would deem the article brilliant, and Ross would later say that it was the one piece in his twenty-six years as editor of which he was most proud. Yet, sadly, Rebecca's professional victory had done little to relieve her chronic discontent; no sooner was she home than she began complaining again. All Rebecca could think about was how "loathsome a time [she] had in New York. . . . It was like being ill among savages," she wrote to her sister Winnie.

And once again, Rebecca would commiserate with Winnie about how much Alison and Anthony were alike: They didn't understand the effect of their actions on others, they each expected everyone to cater to their financial needs, and they couldn't discern between those who loved them and those who didn't. She mourned the fact that Gip Wells had given Anthony permission to write a biography of their father, along with four suitcases of unsorted and unread letters. Although Anthony had signed an agreement that no personal matters would be mentioned, and the literary executors would probably make him keep his word, she couldn't help thinking that Anthony's fantasy of H.G. as a devoted father, and of her as an incompetent, jealous, and injudicious mother, would distort his vision. To her relief, there was an ensuing tussle between Anthony and the Wells family that would result in his returning the letters and renouncing his claim on a definitive biography.

Rebecca would soon learn that Anthony and Kitty were moving again. Their children constantly ill with colds in London, they were planning to sell their house and use the proceeds to buy a home in Tarrant Hinton, Dorset, nearly one hundred miles to the southwest, near the coast. Their restlessness evoked both her sympathy and disdain. Anthony seemed to be withdrawing from society and into himself, which had always been a sign of depression and a prelude to implosion. It was a dangerous move. Her own attempt to escape reality in her youth had been a destructive delusion. And she was still paying the price.

By the fall, the troubles of her past were making their way into her home. Rebecca had been seduced against her better judgment into permitting photographers and journalists from the Time-Life office in London to interview her in Ibstone for a *Time* cover story. She instinctively believed that their motives were less than honest; they had stayed for hours asking impudent questions and requesting old photographs of her and H.G. To get rid of them, she put on her coat and hat and told them she was going out. Before leaving, they asked for her permission to interview her old friend and secretary Margaret Hodges, her friend

G. B. Stern, and her sister Lettie. Reluctantly, Rebecca had given them permission.

Within weeks, one of the researchers at work on the piece in New York leaked to John Gunther the fact that their writers were inserting into the story a paragraph about Rebecca's affair with H.G. and Anthony's parentage. Earlier Rebecca's agent A. J. Peters had been reassured by the London office that they would omit anything personal. Clearly it was a breach of their agreement, and it explained why they hadn't sent her a prepublication proof. John had tried to exert pressure on Henry Luce but had gotten nowhere. John would write to Rebecca that it was Dorothy's hand-delivered note to Henry Luce that saved the day. "It was done from deep in Dorothy's fine bowels, and when D. writes a letter from her stomach or parts below, it is really something to stir a statue."

In a letter of gratitude to Dorothy, Rebecca recited a litany of complaints: She was "desperately" overworked, Henry was ill, as was her sister Lettie, and the lack of petrol was "tormenting." With her usual histrionics, she wrote that, had the article appeared, "I simply could have cut my throat. You know how dreadful my life is in many ways, and what a constant anxiety Henry's worsening health is."

In November 1947, her book *The Meaning of Treason,* which included edited versions of her *New Yorker* articles on the renowned British traitors William Joyce and John Amery, as well as articles on the trials of others less well known, was published in America two years earlier than in Britain. In order to make the book palatable to a larger and more diverse readership, Rebecca dropped her original conceit of Irishman as alien and alien as traitor in reference to Joyce, instead raising the book's theme of treason to a universal plane. She suffused her text with philosophical, moral, and legal discussion, explaining to her recently redeemed ally and friend at the *Evening Standard,* Max Beaverbrook, who had not only tried to help her with the "*Time* business" but had published edited versions of her treason articles in his newspaper, that the study of treason "is valuable not only to the historian but to everybody else who wants humanity to survive." She wrote that the point of the book was to examine the implications of treason in regard to the cruel treatment of modern prisoners of war whose motives might be genuinely patriotic, and the psychological axiom "that treason is an attempt to live without love of country, which humanity can't do—any more than love of family."

But that was mere intellectual rationalization. Integral to the articles contained in the book was Rebecca's passion to understand the factors that create motives for treason—socioeconomic class, personal aspirations and loyalties, and religion. To Rebecca, Joyce and Amery were "revolutionaries" who both loved and hated order; they were men worthy of compassion—martyrs who had sacrificed their lives for the sake of personal and political principle, however misguided. This attitude tells us more about Rebecca's vision of herself than that of her subjects—in particular, her willingness to sacrifice everything for social and moral validation.

In November, Harold Ross wrote to Rebecca that *Time* magazine and *The Saturday Review of Literature* had decided to do a cover story on her book. The combined attention was having, he wrote, "the effect of a size 9 atomic bomb. . . . I noticed in a Sunday newspaper some book editors had picked *The Meaning of Treason* as one of the 10 best books of the year." Even before Christmas the book had sold more than twenty-five thousand copies. To top things off, Rebecca had been offered her second honorary degree, this one from Wellesley College. They could find no American woman worthy of the honor. The first had been conferred by Smith College. Considering Rebecca had not attended college, this was a confirmation of brains and credentials, or as she and H.G. might have said, of the aristocracy of the intelligentsia.

The *Time* cover story appeared on December 8, 1947, fronted by a picture that depicted Rebecca exactly as she would have wished to be seen—as a graying, curly haired, middle-aged woman with a Roman war helmet chicly askew on her head, a pencil protruding from behind her ear, and a cup of tea held daintily in her hand. The article inside portrayed her much the same way, as a courageous warrior-journalist whose years of experience had sharpened her tongue and fighting spirit, while never eclipsing the propriety of her stance. The article negated the nastiness of *Time*'s original intent and gave a boost to her image.

Rebecca's reputation on both sides of the Atlantic had never been more solid. In January 1948, the feature editor of the *Evening Standard*, Herbert Gunn, wrote to his boss, Max Beaverbrook, that her series of stories was going well. "I hear her name discussed more than any other writer these days."

Less than a year later, on March 20, 1948, Rebecca sailed once again on the *Queen Elizabeth* for New York. It would be a quick sprint across the Atlantic; she would return to Southampton ten days later. As Ross had predicted, *The Meaning of Treason* and her articles in *The New Yorker* had had an explosive effect on her reputation, culminating with an honor never before bestowed on a foreigner: The Women's Press Club granted Rebecca their award for excellence in journalism.

Before she left, she and Henry had argued; Henry had claimed that in the interest of her having a good rest, she ought to remain in the States through the political conventions ending in late July. Rebecca had refused on the grounds that she had changed her plans once and would not bother the travel agent again. It was clear that Henry was quite content to be alone at Ibstone, enjoying the freedom her absence implied. Perhaps Rebecca would have preferred being at home, but more likely she worried about the devilry Henry might incur. Deliberate or not, he had a mischievous bent. He had become increasingly impulsive and erratic, and his driving had become dangerous to himself and others. It had been a long time since she could trust him to be on his own—even with the servants.

Once again, Rebecca's New York social calendar flourished with famed literati. Unfortunately, it did not include Dorothy, whose unabashed jealousy—an enduring theme of their friendship— would occasion a remonstrative letter questioning the sincerity of her feelings, as if Rebecca were a wayward lover. After writing a preface to the book by Yale science and humanities professor Evelyn Hutchinson, her new friend and compatriot, and dining with Emanie and her old Socialist friend Ben Stolberg, Rebecca left by train for Washington, D.C.

The Women's Press Club awards were scheduled for the evening of April 3, 1948, at the Statler Hotel. It was the newest and grandest hotel in Washington, and perfectly suited to Rebecca's tastes. Its neoclassic architecture and solid mahogany furnishings were a far cry from the stage-set accommodations she had encountered in New York, although, as usual, she complained to Henry about the hotel's food and staff. Nonetheless, the ceremony was intoxicating, even for Rebecca, as she took her seat at the high table alongside President and Mrs. Truman, several cabinet members, and the other seven awardees, including Ingrid Bergman for theater; Helen Rogers Reid (Dorothy's nemesis and Rebecca's newest admirer) for public service; Representative Margaret Chase Smith for politics; and Jean Stafford for literature. Truman presented Rebecca with the award, calling her "the world's best reporter."

As the president, diplomats, cabinet members, and awardees looked on, the Women's Press Club enacted a political satire of the coming conventions, at which Truman would stand for reelection. The president, known for his wry sense of humor, took the burlesque in stride.

ONCE BACK IN BUCKINGHAMSHIRE before the conventions, Rebecca felt impelled to defend her friend Dorothy from insults by Hal Lewis that he ungraciously included in a congratulatory letter he wrote to her on the publication of *The Meaning of Treason*. Dorothy, Red observed, had resorted to screaming her pro–civil rights and anticommunist views and appeared more strident and abrasive than ever. Rebecca responded, "You are unjust. Dorothy is tuned into a different wavelength from yours, but to me she doesn't scream."

But in truth, perhaps Dorothy was screaming. Stripped of her New York journalistic platforms, first the *Herald Tribune* in 1945 and the *Post* in 1947, she was writing freelance columns in periodicals, her monthly column in *Ladies' Home Journal*, and in large-circulation newspapers via her syndicate. She wrote letters to government officials in the hopes of influencing foreign policy, but it was a futile task; most replies were polite, but uninterested; she was poignantly aware that her opinions and requests no longer carried the clout they had enjoyed during Roosevelt's terms in office. Dorothy was still occasionally asked to speak in public, but not with the same regularity or remuneration as before. If she had the appearance of "screaming," her frustration was understandable. That is, of course, unless you were Hal Lewis.

Her latest "screams," however, had been channeled toward a new worldwide political organization against a nuclear confrontation with Russia. Dorothy's project was an organization called WOMAN—World Organization of Mothers of All Nations—a steering committee for organizing a mass movement of women to effect peace through already existing organizations.

In a form letter to prospective members she had sent out the previous fall, she had written, "To this end we have prepared two things: A Manifesto, called *A Woman's Manifesto*, which we wish to have introduced before any and every organized group of women, and, if they respond to it, adopted. . . . It is a rather monumental statement of Woman's attitudes toward war," and second, a statement outlining a plan to effect their goals. They would target organizations and individuals in all the countries involved, as well as government diplomats at the United Nations, and prepare a petition to bring before the UN Security Council. Later deemed to have played into the Soviet ruse to establish Communist domination through the semblance of peace, both her grand vision and the organization would die on the vine.

In early 1948, the Communists had taken over the Czechoslovakian government. In March, Jan Masaryk, the Czech foreign minister and lover of Dorothy's friend Marcia Davenport, was found dead in a courtyard in Prague. It was unclear if he had been pushed or had committed suicide, but everyone who knew him assumed the latter. His death would mark the end of Czech independence. For Rebecca and Dorothy, it was a painful loss. Henry had worked with Masaryk on Central European policy during the war, and they had become good friends. Masaryk had also been instrumental in getting Max asylum in the States.

Rebecca had written to Dorothy before Masaryk's death, saying, "Well everybody told us that Czechoslovakia was handling Russia beautifully. It's time they started trusting you and me, President and Vice-President of the Pessimists' Club."

Rebecca was planning to return to New York in early June 1948. She would be covering the political conventions for the *New York Herald Tribune* and its syndicate, as well as for London's *Evening Standard*. The Republican convention was scheduled for June 21–25, and the Democratic convention for July 12–15. The Progressive Party convention would follow two weeks later, July 23–25. She and Dorothy would be attending all three.

In a rare coincidence of decision making, all three parties met in Philadelphia. Dorothy had taken the liberty of reserving their rooms in advance at the Drake Hotel, anticipating that politicians, delegates, and reporters would inundate the city. She wrote to Rebecca, "If you have never covered an American national convention you have no idea how wearisome it can be. Philadelphia will be hot as hell. But the Republican convention, at least, will be very exciting. I hope that the moment the first one is over, you will come with me to Vermont, where you shall do exactly as you please."

As Dorothy had predicted, the conventions were momentous and full of surprises, some of which she had not anticipated. She was right about the weather, as well.

Many seasoned American journalists chose to stay away from the hall during the first two days of the Republican convention, preferring to watch the preliminary activities on television in the second-floor press lounge, where there was air-conditioning and free beer. Rebecca, unprepared for the chaos, hurtled into its vortex. She wrote to Henry that her first days in Philadelphia were beyond imagination. "Life completely broke down," she wrote in despair. The elevator was defunct, the telephone service was poor, room service was impossible, and there were long queues downstairs for food. She had to wait in line for her mail, transportation for the press was unannounced and out of the way, the heat was intolerable, and taxis were scarce, forcing her to walk miles back to the hotel dripping with sweat or in the pouring rain.

Aside from such inconveniences, Rebecca's most pressing problem was that in order to meet her deadlines for the American and British newspapers, she had to write two articles a day—the deadline for the American press was eight at night, and for the English press it was half past two in the morning. The convention meetings were geared to American time zones, so that while her colleagues were resting and showering, she had to sit for hours at her typewriter knocking out copy.

She wrote to Henry: "Dorothy was of great use to me, but she was slow in moving and cannot get round nearly as fast as I can and she is getting appallingly deaf. Had I not been with her she would have missed a great deal as she misheard a great many of the instructions, and I was very happy about that. She was the most delightful and sweet-tempered companion."

The Republican convention, among the first to be televised, had its comical moments. The presence of cameras changed everything; the nominating process had morphed into a stage drama. One reporter remarked that the delegates "were in fact like a studio audience." In one of her articles for the *Herald Tribune,* Rebecca commented on the absurdity of the technological intrusions. "You fill up the hall with all these monstrous instruments that come between the audience and the speakers," and just as the drama reaches its highest pitch, the observer can neither see nor experience it.

On the second day of the Republican convention, to Dorothy's surprise, forty-six-year-old Thomas E. Dewey, governor of New York, was nominated for the presidency on the third ballot. Governor Dewey, who had been attorney general of New York City, where he was nicknamed

"Gangbuster" for his success in reining in the Mafia, had run in the Republican primary in 1940, but had lost to Wendell Willkie. He had managed to win the Republican nomination in 1944 by accepting New Deal policies, while attacking many of Roosevelt's cabinet and officials as corrupt, inefficient, and pro-Communist. He had garnered 46 percent of the popular vote, only to be defeated by Roosevelt.

In 1948, the first election since 1932 not to have a true incumbent, the press relished the backroom politics as Taft and Dewey jockeyed for the top Republican slot. Those who wrote for magazines, assigned to cover the newspaper reporters, offered a unique perspective. Their job was to critique the critics. One in particular, from *Time* magazine, had been tracking Rebecca. He would write: "Miss West, her face hidden behind dark glasses to protect her from the glare, stood on a table to watch the Dewey demonstration. Her convention reports read a little like an eye witness account by a visitor from Mars who had read a guidebook before coming." The townspeople of Greenville, South Carolina, might have concurred with this observation, although this time Rebecca's "untainted eye" was not an asset to her vision.

It was true that Rebecca wrote like a foreigner—although to call her writing the work of an alien might have gone too far. Since her only framework was British and European elections, her observations about American politics tended to be off the mark. But Rebecca sensed this, and once she admitted it, that awareness set her free. Most of her coverage was social commentary rather than political analysis. Her articles resembled her pieces in *Time and Tide* in the 1930s—more like critical essays geared toward magazine readers, rather than straight news or feature articles. Her ultimate conclusions were irrefutable: Substance didn't matter in politics; imagery trumped everything.

The British press was lukewarm about Rebecca's articles. Herbert Gunn of the *Standard* thought them "readable." For Rebecca, however, her coverage of the convention felt like a victory akin to her lynching trial coverage in South Carolina. As a foreign observer, she had found a human angle at once uniquely American and universal.

In late June, Rebecca went with Dorothy by train to Twin Farms to await the start of the Democratic convention. "It was an allnight journey here," she wrote to Henry, "and we landed in a quaint old wooden town among beautiful rounded hills covered with woods."

After a twenty-five mile drive we came to Woodstock, a beautiful village of white Georgian houses built round a village green, set in country like the Lake District in England or the fertile parts of Montenegro. After five miles of the worst road I have ever been on in a civilized country we got up to this house, which is incredible. It is actually bigger than Ibstone, but does not look so for it is low and rambling. It is a very old farm, which Dorothy has altered—and she has a positive genius for architecture and everything to do with a home. . . . She is also a marvelous gardener, and knows every plant in the garden, which is just as I would love Ibstone to be, very tidy and full of flowering shrubs that are perfectly pruned—all of these she herself planted herself. . . . Her workroom made me very envious; it is a huge place with desks and bookcases. The garden goes down in terraces to the valley, and I believe there is a fine view of the mountains.

Rebecca and Dorothy at the Democratic National Convention, 1948

The Democratic convention two weeks later was just as crowded, hot, disorganized, and combative as the previous one, but in its evocation of the old Civil War North–South divide, it had a distinction all its own. Truman was nominated on the first ballot, but then all hell broke loose in its aftermath. Minneapolis mayor Hubert Humphrey addressed the convention urging his party to "get out of the shadow of states' rights and to walk forthrightly into the bright sunshine of human rights." His anti–states' rights agenda and the subsequent insertion of a strong civil rights plank into the platform provoked southern anger, prompting the entire delegation from Mississippi and half the Alabama delegates to walk out of the convention. These and other discontented southerners, who had already begun to slip away from the party, would call themselves "Dixiecrats" and were determined to hold their own convention in Birmingham, Alabama, to nominate a states' rights candidate. Anti–big government, segregationist, and socially conservative, the Dixiecrats would nominate Governor Strom Thurmond of South Carolina for president. His campaign would run on the slogan "Segregation Forever!" Rebecca and Dorothy, as might be expected, were appalled.

Rebecca remained in Philadelphia after the close of the Democratic convention, closeting herself in the Bellevue-Stratford Hotel, where she had moved to write her article for the *Herald Tribune*. The next morning, she and Dorothy caught the train at Princeton Junction for New York, and Rebecca went straight to the *New Yorker*'s offices to proofread her piece. She wrote to Henry that Dorothy had taken her bags over to Grand Central Terminal so they could catch the midnight train to Vermont. "It is wonderful to be with her—she is the one American I know who is not scatterbrained. She is easy and sweet and wise. If she wouldn't drink Scotch she would be perfect."

A week later, Rebecca and Dorothy were back in Philadelphia attending the first Progressive National Party convention. While the nominating process lacked the complexity of the previous two, the candidate, his platform, and the delegates who attended provided just as many fireworks. Henry Agard Wallace had left his editorship of *The New Republic* to run for the presidency. He had been vice president under Roosevelt during his first three terms of office, but in 1943, embarrassed and worried about Wallace's socialist leanings, Roosevelt stripped him of his responsibilities and replaced him with the little-known but competent senator from Kansas City, Harry Truman, with the blessings of the Democratic Party.

For the first time, Wallace was campaigning on his own; he could no longer hide in Roosevelt's shadow. He would either prove himself worthy or be thrown to the wind, and after witnessing a press conference,

Rebecca was certain it would be the latter. She would write that "It was as if [Wallace] had heard a great deal about sabotage as an admirable thing from his far-left friends and being an absent minded man began to sabotage himself." He also became increasingly evasive in his answers, or boldly stated facts that weren't true.

Furthermore, she was certain that the convention was Communist controlled. Wallace's people would resist, she thought, because they were "soft people," enfolded in skin that neither he nor anyone else could contain. But the Communists who were running the show were hard-nosed and skilled men and women.

Dorothy agreed with Rebecca that Wallace was a tool of Moscow, but she would blame the importation of an American strain of Communism on Truman. Dorothy believed that Communism was a virus activated by the war. Regardless of the cause, however, she was so appalled by Wallace's views that at another press conference, she asked him point-blank about his Communist connections. Her colleagues silently admired her courage, including her most vociferous detractor H. L. Mencken, and yet she seemed increasingly out of touch with the times; her tight-laced classical liberalism seemed a nineteenth-century anachronism. Her colleagues had begun to publicly shame her. When a New York newspaper published a photograph in which she looked obese, Dorothy ran straight to her personal lawyer Louis Nizer and asked him to file a suit, which, of course, he wouldn't. "Politically," remarked one of her friends, "she was like a great ship left stranded on the beach after the tide had gone out." Clare Boothe Luce advised her to drop her column in the *Ladies' Home Journal*, but Dorothy said that she needed the money.

Yet it had been Clare, among others, who had been eager for Dorothy to run for president just a few short months earlier. Jimmy Sheean had been the most avid of all. John Gunther would write in his diary that Jimmy's eyes flashed "a positive sulphuric blue fire" at the possibility. Clare was to nominate her, wrote John, "and the speech that D. will make will sweep her in. Trans-valuation of values. A woman as president, who believes in peace, who lost one son in a war, and who has another of military age. I listened goggle-eyed."

Dorothy had longed for a statesman with substantive ideas, yet she feared that the breed was extinct. No matter who would be elected, international peacekeeping would remain her prime concern. Her solution for maintaining a balance of world power was a supranational organization that would act to curb nationalist uprisings—the source, she believed, of both world wars, and now the trouble in the Middle East between the Arabs and the Jews. She predicted that Zionism implied perpetual war. Jimmy Sheean agreed. "The Zionist adventure bodes very ill indeed," Dorothy wrote to Jimmy Sheean, referring to Israel's self-declaration of statehood.

When she voiced these views in articles, Dorothy was labeled an anti-Zionist and an anti-Semite. To those organizations and people who deemed her such, she would counter with more nuanced responses. While her predictions would be prescient, she hadn't counted on the will of Jews to fight for a homeland.

ON JULY 29, 1948, Rebecca sailed for Southampton on the RMS *Queen Mary,* along with nearly two thousand other passengers. While she was still on the dock waiting to board, a reporter from *The New York Times* asked her a loaded question. What were her impressions of the three conventions? She responded, I did not think that the conventions were ridiculous at all, but did think that the Progressive Party had a "definite fascist tendency."

Her attacks on Wallace in the *Herald Tribune* and *Evening Standard* would cut even deeper; so much so that she began to receive letters accusing her of being a lying, anti-Democratic, anti-Semitic, and anti-Negro troublemaker. Ross would also receive letters, consoling her by saying, "If you mention any race at all, you're going to be accused of that." Rebecca would become, in fact, the target of forces beyond the extreme Left. Doris Lessing would write, "Orwell was a target and so was Rebecca. It must have been hard to stand up to it, W. particularly as she was sensitive and hated being considered negligible, yet she did, standing by her guns."

Rebecca and Dorothy were certainly pessimists about foreign policy, which occupied their minds and suffused their correspondence after the war. The fate of the Jews was of prime importance.

And yet, it is difficult to know what Rebecca felt about the Jews. There seemed to be a discrepancy between her humanitarian views and her feelings for Jews as individuals. While her public stance was pristine, in her private correspondence she would often remark that Jews were ugly, cagey, generally offensive, and dishonest. They were, she would write, "another breed—set apart." Ironically, Rebecca, who had hated the Nazis, was inclined toward racist and ethnic generalizations based on anecdotal evidence. Her perception of the Jews, the Germans, the Americans, the Roman Catholics, and earlier, the Serbs and Croatians, were unabashed stereotypes, determined by transient exposure and superficial knowledge. This tendency, consonant with others of her time, including Dorothy, would mar the brilliance of her work. It is worth mentioning in reference to her essays about Nuremberg that she never referred to the Jews by name.

Did Rebecca know that during the war, Dorothy had made it clear in her columns, speeches, and articles that she believed it was, in fact, the responsibility of Christians to speak for the Jews, because as victims of Nazi persecution, they could not effectively speak for themselves? Dorothy had deep respect for the Jews and Judaism. But anti-Semitism in America and abroad was still omnipresent, and Dorothy's biggest test was yet to come. An independent, self-determining political entity, the Jewish state was categorically different from an ancient people with an abstract set of ideas.

Rebecca had planned to return to New York in September, but an injury had delayed her trip. She wrote to her friend Doris Stevens that she was relieved to be held up in England because her family was in such a bad state—both of her sisters were ill and also in financial straits. To make matters worse, Winnie's daughter Alison was once again on the brink of a breakdown. The doctor advised that she be hospitalized for rest and treatment, concerned that the twenty-eight-year-old had "a tendency to become a lunatic." In the Fairfield tradition, Rebecca and her sisters believed that madness and genius were inextricably linked, but they all agreed that Alison was too mad to achieve anything.

Rebecca also saw trouble brewing with her granddaughter, Caro. When Anthony, Kitty and the children had come from Dorset to visit at Christmastime, she found Caro, now seven, beguiled by her own beauty, self-absorbed, and narcissistic, and as a result, "a bit of a bore—and it is something unknown in our family; I feel it's most dreary." Five-year-old Edmund, however, could not have been more different. He was loving, sensitive, and kindhearted, yet gregarious; he enjoyed being at Ibstone with Rebecca and Henry, savored the serenity of the woods, and was fascinated by adult conversation. But it was Anthony who had finally given her cause for pride. He had just turned in the manuscript of his first novel. After reading it, Rebecca called it "his prize," and told everyone she knew that they would like it, too. Perhaps it was her prize as well, and certainly something that sprang from the Fairfield and Wells gene pool.

Published in 1949 in London as *On a Dark Night* and as *The Vintage* in 1950 in the United States, the novel told the story of a privileged middle-class lawyer, Wallis, a prosecutor at one of the criminal war trials in Germany. Based largely on Anthony himself, Wallis is a former painter and highly self-indulgent. He comes to symbolize the liberal humanist thrust into the midst of war who is compelled to reexamine his values and motives. His death is a catalyst toward self-examination in his afterlife and a confrontation with the meaningless hedonism of his youth. Wallis says, "Man is nothing but the sum of his thoughts and actions," and by extension, the sum of his animal appetites. Ultimately, he realizes that one cannot escape responsibility for one's past or the realities of the human condition.

It was no wonder Rebecca was proud. The resemblance of Anthony's first novel to the form and substance of hers cannot go unnoticed. The nexus of the specific and universal; the examination of moral and social issues against a historical backdrop; the search for universal truth; and the story cum morality play are thematically akin to her fiction and nonfiction. Rebecca might have wondered if Anthony had truly confronted his past, but at the moment, it was irrelevant. The important thing was that he was struggling with the moral issues she hoped would lead to maturity. It was an extraordinary victory for her lost and troubled son—if only on paper.

By the turn of the year, in January 1949, Rebecca was in love again. Or she thought she was. The loneliness of tending the needs of a sickly, unreasonable man, incapable of reciprocity, had become overwhelming. And so she sought a relationship with someone who might be more capable and responsive—the features editor at the *Evening Standard*, Charles Curran. But when she made a verbal allusion to their becoming more than colleagues, he spurned her. His Roman Catholic vows, he stiffly countered, would prohibit him from committing adultery. The following day she wrote Charles a letter, rationalizing her behavior and altering the facts to suit her ends:

I am very fond of you and have from the first felt an untroubled af-
fection for you. . . . I have lived a completely celibate life for eighteen
years. I don't mind doing so; I prefer it. If at any time in that period
men have made advances to me of an insolent kind I have not even
become hysterical. I have remained completely wooden, in a way that
has often been regarded as most insulting. . . . In the last few years I
have liked some men. . . . I have felt like that before. I assumed you
either had a happy relationship with someone or like me had chosen to
forget about sex.

I hated you last night when you talked about sex, when you talked
again and again about lust. You were repudiating it, but you were so
much aware of it that you practically felt it. . . . I am frightened of
you. It sounds insulting and a revocation of what was good, but I don't
want to see you. In the night I lay and thought of you as a part of the
darkness. You aren't that, but that's the way you have made me see
you. You aren't evil but at this moment, I feel you in league with evil.

Even at fifty-six, Rebecca's demons still prevailed. The forces of evil
continued to stalk her. She believed she was doomed to live a loveless
life; Charles's or any man's rejection seemed the work of the devil. Her
childhood abandonment by her father still made each rejection satanic. It
was the evil of inexplicable duplicity that she mourned:

Not with the tears that burning scald,
Not with the tears that youth had seen.
But with the anguish of a Soul
that finds its twin has faithless been.

While Rebecca had written this remarkable poem when she was eight
years old, her anguish lingered, and sadness remained.

FOR ANTHONY WEST AND MICHAEL LEWIS, abandonment had
become the stuff of alchemy. They were converting pain to hunger; inherited talent to personal success. As Anthony was finally rising above
his past, Michael was beginning to find his calling. At nineteen, he was
realizing that the chiseled face, redheaded good looks, tall physique, and

verbal gifts he had inherited from his father were his ticket to a career in the theater. Michael had his father's gift for mimicry and a burning desire to succeed where his father had failed. When he received his acceptance to the Royal Academy of Dramatic Art in London, he was ecstatic. Rebecca's response to the news was to invite him to Ibstone as soon as he was settled and able. She wrote to Dorothy that Michael was coming in two weekends hence, "when my nephew [Norman, Jr.], and his best friend—both science instructors in the RAF and crazy on the stage—will be here. I will ask the very brilliant young star of the Rep over for Sunday lunch, and together we will do our best. Look forward to seeing Mike quite selfishly because I think he is of good value and I love the look of him."

Musing on the effect of H.G. and Hal on the academic fortunes of their sons, Rebecca continued:

It is odd how an erratic father makes it impossible for a son however clever he is and however much he likes study and mixing to go through a University. The boys don't trust authority with a double take. First, they distrust authority because their father was the earliest form of authority they knew, second, the erratic father is always attacking authority and the side which loves him backs him up. I had precisely that trouble with Anthony, who would NOT go through Oxford, which was really the place for him.

Once again, Rebecca was massaging the facts to suit her ego. Anthony had been failing at school in everything but English, and despite diligently preparing for the entrance exam, he had failed to earn a place in the class.

Rebecca tried to console Dorothy about her dwindling opportunities in journalism. "I know you must be feeling depressed, at the same time I do not believe that anybody can keep us down. We are too good workmen." Her home life, however, was a hell of its own. "Henry has been passing through a phase of confusion and depression and living here has been like being shut up in a black box." Rebecca coped by going to London occasionally and working on articles for the *Evening Standard* and *The New Yorker* to "break down the awful isolation which keeps on being imposed on me, although I know it is the last kind of work I should be doing. I should be writing books before the night co-meth. But still . . ."

By early February, Rebecca was reaching out to Charles Curran again, feeling that she had gone too far in her condemnation. And yet, she was strangely unaware of what had motivated either her attack or her need to forgive him. She acknowledged that there was a misunderstand-ing, and that he had mistaken sexual desire for long-term possession, a sexual rendezvous for a committed relationship. But in a letter to Winnie, she wrote her true feelings:

"I have made it up with Charles Curran, after having given him hell. He really is hopelessly perverted; he cannot understand a normal life in which you respond to the needs of the people around you." If he had truly adhered to Roman Catholic principles, he would have made "gentle concessions."

Learning, perhaps through Michael, that Dorothy was planning to travel through Germany in early summer, Rebecca wrote to her suggest-ing that she and Henry might join her. Rebecca would claim that it was Henry's idea—that he thought it would be more fun if they were to travel together. But there was an underlying sense of desperation she knew Dorothy would immediately discern. And she did.

They were to leave during the last week in May; Rebecca and Henry would arrive several days early in Frankfurt, spend time in Berlin, then travel to Nuremberg and environs to visit with friends, before meeting Dorothy in Munich.

During the three months prior to the trip, Rebecca's realization that she should, in fact, be writing books took hold. She began a novel about her childhood called *Cousin Rosamund*. (Later it would become the first volume in the *Cousin Rosamund* trilogy and be renamed *The Fountain Overflows*.) She also started writing a series of articles about the mysteri-ous murder of Mr. Setty, a British used-car dealer, for *The New Yorker*. His murderer, Mr. Hume, had been born illegitimately, like Anthony. It was a true story that Rebecca would transform into a philosophical in-quiry into crimes against humanity, family life, and the meaning of evil.

Rebecca had not only renewed her friendship with Charles Curran, the heretofore personification of evil, but had elevated him to her dearest and most compassionate confidant. Ironically, her change in attitude toward him might have grown out of her respect for his unyielding prin-ciples. The death of Alex Woollcott and an overblown misunderstanding with Harold Ross, who was now sick and ailing, had left a vacuum of trust and confidence in her life; she needed a rational sounding board and an enabler, and women seemed unable to fill the role. She would write to Charles that his influence was a source both of strength and of distress— her need for him made her reluctant to defy his opinions. His voice would pervade her personal and professional life.

In mid-April 1949 Rebecca became despondent about her own journalism career, and sought advice from Charles. "I cannot do journalism anymore. I have not the nerve or hand for it. I only like writing my crazy novel [*Cousin Rosamund*], which is crazy." She didn't much care about bad reviews so much as low revenues. "I am living in a madhouse, and that is why I can't keep on the plane of cheerful, normal observation, on which you write journalism. I have to retire into fiction, which is, as you have found, a completely air-tight container."

Charles responded that he had not reprinted her *New Yorker* article in the *Evening Standard* "brilliant as it was (and it was brilliant, some of it was as good as anything you have ever written) [it] was not arranged, in my opinion, so as to make things easy for the uninformed reader. All readers are stupid, ignorant, lazy. I've learned that, if nothing else in newspapers offices, and now I take it for granted. But you don't."

As yet unaware of the depth of Henry's illness and his dependency on her, Charles told Rebecca to reorganize her life so that she was free to work on fiction; to sell the house or get someone to manage it, and to stop being a safe haven for psychopaths. Charles also explained to Rebecca that she suffered from public misconceptions about her personality and attitude: "Why, when I first met you, I expected to see what? A caustic, bitter, twisted woman with a tongue like broken glass, fierce, mocking, inhuman. I was astonished at the difference between you and the you I had been told about. . . . It took me five minutes to decide that it was rubbish." Her image, he wrote, was marred by female stereotypes of impulsivity and unpredictability. He found her, however, "attractive, stimulating, exciting, with any amount of wit, temperament, grace" and chided her for undervaluing herself.

Charles was straightforward and uncensored in his criticism and praise, yet also compassionate and encouraging. He understood who she was, and he took her seriously. Had they become lovers, he might not have become a moral touchstone in her life. This had proven true with H.G., Max Beaverbrook, and Francis Biddle. Rebecca had needed their emotional sustenance and affirmation of her femininity too much to with-stand their criticism, valid or not. Any withdrawal of desire or affection would feel tantamount to abandonment, leading one to conclude that perhaps her marriage to Henry had been saved by its asexuality. Until he was consumed by illness, he was her "knight," her savior, and her friend.

Dorothy, who had just been in London to visit Michael and to recon-nect with friends, must have reiterated her own despondency about work prospects. Rebecca asked Charles if he would give her some assignments. Charles spared no words. Although he would comply with her wishes, he wrote:

I find it easy to be coldly dispassionate about female popes—Dorothy Thompson, Elsa Maxwell, Louella Parsons, Hedda Hopper, etc. They are all the same. Large, shapeless, sexless chain-smokers, with high shrill, never-ending voices. Like sea lions crossed with peacocks. They kill off husbands like dispatch riders killing off horses. They talk about Prime Ministers by their first names (which they call given names; they refer to "The Column" as though it were the Blessed Sac-rament; they know something to the detriment of everybody and never shut up). . . . Most of them are professional anti-Fascists sick for the glorious 30s, when they doped about Hitler & Mussolini & what Goe-ring said to Princess Colonna when he found her in bed with Ciano. They're dead but they won't lie down.

So you're going to Germany with one. My poor Rebecca.

Rebecca did not defend her friend. Perhaps she was beginning to be-lieve he was right, and she had always believed that except for the rarefied few, among whom she included herself, women were always inferior to men. Her response, therefore, was sharp and indifferent: Most American women, Rebecca maintained, talked too much as they got older.

Upon Rebecca's return to England, after five weeks of travel with Henry and Dorothy, she wrote two letters, one to Margaret Hodges, her former secretary, and one to Doris Stevens, her American friend, docu-menting the events of the trip along with her observations and concerns. Each individual in her constellation of friends and family had a distinct role. Taken as a whole, they provide diverse visions of Rebecca's life that reveals loyalty to no one. Dorothy was a colleague whose political interests and parenthood issues coincided with her own; Doris Stevens was an old friend with whom she gossiped, and in whom she confided to a limited degree; Pamela Frankau, the young novelist with whom she spent time in the south of France with Anthony when he was a child, served as a conduit of information from her son; Winnie was both a sister and a limited confidante, but one she clearly saw as less sophisticated and intelligent than herself; Henry was a friend in need, but a constant burden. Her former secretary, Margaret Hodges, remained an ally with whom she could speak frankly.

In the letter to her, Rebecca wrote:

> *My main worry is Daddy [Henry]. He has twice been in Germany during the past year, and it has not been good for him. There is something in him which has always knuckled down to the Germans and he is doing it all over again. But the particular complication is that he has fallen madly in love with a German woman called Countess Dönhoff. She is a little dark woman of forty, very good-looking and most unpleasant. . . . She is a liar of the maddest kind. . . . I went with Henry and Dorothy Thompson for five weeks from May 22nd. It was frightfully interesting. . . .*
>
> *But it was difficult. For one thing, the Germans were so awful about me. It was ironic. Dorothy Thompson is very much on her way out in America as a writer, she has largely lost her position as a columnist and is never heard on the radio. But the Germans had heard of her and not of me, and I can't tell how delicately it made me feel. . . .*

Apparently, the Germans had inundated Dorothy with flowers while completely ignoring Rebecca and Henry. In Hamburg, their final stop, where the Press Center gave them a reception, Rebecca was not even invited to sit on the platform, but worst of all, Dorothy received the press award she had been given in Washington, two years earlier. She felt dethroned.

> *This was hard to bear. But what was harder to bear was that both Dorothy and Daddy are deaf, Dorothy far worse than Daddy. Going through Germany was a wild comic strip in consequence. . . . Daddy is so rude and disagreeable to people, our Daddy, that you would not*

believe it. He is good to me when I am ill, but on the other hand his disregard of my convenience and his refusal to let me have a word in the order of our daily life is becoming utterly extraordinary. And his lack of common sense . . .

The burden of Henry apart, Rebecca saw people and circumstances as reflections of herself. If her companions' actions were shameful or embarrassing, especially if one happened to be a woman, she denigrated the importance of the event and its participants. With some frequency, Rebecca would return to the primal scene of her childhood as a way of making sense of events in adulthood. Rebecca's emotions were still frozen in the past, when Lettie was her father's favorite and would soon become her mother's pride and source of strength.

Rebecca's letter to Doris Stevens further disparaged Dorothy: After buffering her remarks with initial praise, calling her a "heavenly companion, she was as sweet and as good as can be," Rebecca wrote, "Dorothy is incredibly unobservant. This is partly because she is deaf. Partly because she just floats in a coma half the time, thinking her own thoughts. We found that she didn't see through people to the most extraordinary degree. People would turn up who were the rawest Nazis and imperialist Germans, and she just wouldn't notice the clues."

But Rebecca's perceptions were also limited. She had missed clues to Anthony's intentions to publicize his novel by naming her and H.G. as his parents. When she and Henry had visited Anthony and Kitty at their home in Dorset the previous Christmas, Anthony had promised not to defy her wishes to keep H.G.'s paternity a secret. Her reasons had been the same as they were with the *Time* article—the publicity would derail her career, and there was no reason to alienate the Wells family, which deserved their privacy and her continued goodwill. She told Anthony, however, that he was free to reveal her identity as his mother. Anthony countered that it would be healthy to acknowledge the truth, and while he did not understand her decision, he would abide by her wishes.

In early September, when Charles Curran called to say he had received a press release about Anthony's novel at the *Evening Standard*, identifying her and H.G. as Anthony's parents, Rebecca was shocked. The revelation of her son's paternity conjured up old fears, resentment, and shame. Anthony refused to relent; Rebecca felt betrayed. Anthony wrote to Henry that Rebecca had tried to keep him away from H.G. and cheat him of his inheritance. She had always been jealous and paranoid, and this latest ploy was a flagrant attempt to rob him of legitimacy. Determined to minimize the damage, Rebecca called Anthony's editor, Douglas Jerrold at Eyre and Spottiswoode, an old friend of Henry's at Oxford, who said that Anthony had assured him that "no one would take exception." Feeling duped, his editor resolved not to have it mentioned again in advertisements related to the book. Like Rebecca, Gip and Margaret Wells were distraught about the invasion of their privacy.

Rebecca silently probed her son's motives. Was his declaration of ancestry an effort to validate his birth? Was it a self-healing catharsis? Or was it an attempt at retribution?

Once again, Rebecca tried to reason with Anthony, knowing he would not believe a word she said. In a letter, she explained her relationship with H.G., and H.G.'s with him, hoping to dispel his distortions. It was the same story she had told him many times. Denying his accusations of deliberate malice, she reminded him that he was only ten years old when she and his father had separated, and the reality of their relationship had been beyond his understanding. When he finally reached an age at which he could comprehend its complexities, Anthony had chosen to move away to the country. It seemed to her that during the past fifteen years, he had spent too much time fabricating fantasies about his parents and their relationship to him and to each other. "I can't even convey to you that you are living in a dreamland."

By late fall, Anthony was on his way to New York. He told Kitty and Rebecca that his intent was to "scout out" professional opportunities. He would either return home or call for Kitty and the children. But neither Kitty nor Rebecca heard from him for months, save for £200 that he sent Kitty. A resourceful investigator, Rebecca contacted her friends to track him down. As expected, he had gone to live with Dorothy for a few months at her townhouse in New York, until he got settled. When Emanie had gently probed Dorothy for her reactions, Dorothy said that she had found him quite polite and charming, and very positive about Rebecca. When Anthony went to see Harold Ross, Ross wrote to Henry:

> *I get a great kick out of Anthony because I can see so much of Rebecca in him and talking to him. And also, I like to be helpful to strangers in a strange land, or even a fairly strange land.*

The principal thing I have to report at the moment is that Anthony is working on Time, *and has been since the fourth day after his arrival here. . . . He said that he hadn't told anyone about it, because he assumed that if Rebecca heard that he got connected with the* Time *outfit, she'd be pained. . . .*

The only other fact I have to report is that Anthony is considering taking a place in Connecticut. . . . Taking a residence in Connecticut is also normal, and as inevitable as taking a job at Time. *Anthony is making the usual start of a young writer coming to New York.*

Referring to the disagreement over the publicity, Harold wrote: "There is no question that Anthony is distressed at all the fuss."

There was also no question that Ross was being protective of Anthony; he later said he had admired his guts and his work, and he worried about the young man's financial status. Ross wrote that it was logical that the publication of his novel would cause a stir, and that Anthony was "originally, an innocent party." Nonetheless, he insisted that he wouldn't form "any opinion about any of the details of this situation. My attitude is that I will just stand by and be helpful, if possible." Clearly, Ross had befriended him. John Gunther and his new bride, Jane Perry Vandercook, younger than Anthony and interested in the arts, had done the same. Rebecca was no doubt jealous of his relationships and fearful that her friends would take his side against her. Pamela Frankau, Anthony's friend and Rebecca's ersatz spy, confirmed that this was, in fact, Anthony's intent.

Adding to Rebecca's worries was Kitty. Anthony finally wrote her to invite her to come to the States with the children for a visit, but he told her that he no longer loved her and wanted a divorce. Rebecca did not hear from her for ten days, and she feared the worst.

Rebecca wrote to Charles Curran, who had encouraged her to see Anthony, explaining why she could not.

"H.G. did not care a button for him. He had in fact not a shadow of real affection for any of his children. They were rivals and he would not admit their existence."

The wife of his oldest son confirms this, she wrote. Embellishing the facts to alleviate her guilt, she painstakingly related Anthony's adolescent failures, his disappointments, and details of his nervous breakdown and his marriage to Kitty.

But, in a rare moment of self-examination, she wrote:

I don't know what sort of character could have stood up against this. I have stood up against a horrible life, a terrible childhood and a ghastly adult existence, because fundamentally I'm not aware of myself. When I catch sight of myself in a mirror I'm always surprised to know I look like that, I have the same sort of nescience about my own character and destiny. Anthony has had much happiness that I never had, he had amusing friends to grow up with and wonderful holidays as a child, and complete freedom in his late teens and twenties while I was a bullied drudge, but he has had in these ways more than I had to bear, and he is passionately aware of himself and his own destiny.

Admitting that she might have been responsible for ruining Anthony's life by permitting his illegitimacy, she wrote, "There is nothing to do but leave him alone with his fantasies and let reality triumph over them if it can."

It was not until late January 1950 that Rebecca discovered the real reason for Anthony's flight to America. After he begrudgingly returned the four suitcases full of letters given to him by the Wells family to write H.G.'s biography, she learned that Marjorie Wells, Gip's wife, had been mistaken when she told Rebecca that H.G. had destroyed all the letters he had written to her.

Rebecca wrote to Charles, "Today the letters arrived. I went over them very carefully and I found the explanation of the whole dreadful business." She related how she and H.G. had corresponded, quarreling incessantly about Anthony's education and his academic performance. She had found many letters "which referred to Anthony with indifference and hostility." When she had urged H.G. to pay more attention to Anthony's needs, he had responded that he wasn't worth taking trouble over. In response, she told H.G. that he "begrudged every penny he had spent on Anthony."

"This must have affected Anthony as nothing on earth could have affected him," she concluded. "Anthony, who is vain, had a fantasy that H.G.'s interest in me had been only temporary and evanescent and that it was in him that H.G. was truly interested. He told me in so many words when his father was so very ill in 1944. It was not an altogether amiable fantasy, but it was what he lived by and to read this paragraph must have struck him to earth."

The publicity, she explained, was meant to punish her; Anthony had learned that he hadn't had his father's love in the way he had imagined, and it was she who had revealed this to him. It had also been Anthony's way of punishing H.G. for loving Rebecca deeply, not, as he had thought, as a transient sexual partner.

"There isn't anything to be done about this, ever. I can't feel any anger any more at what he has been doing; I see that it is a harsh and cruel reaction to suffering, but I can't blame him for that, the suffering must be so extreme. And obviously I will to the end of time be the last person to set this right."

Rebecca had concluded that both she and Anthony were trapped by their past, the casualties of an error that would follow them for the rest of their lives.

CHAPTER 16

DESCENT TO GLORY

> I am confident to the depths of my mind and
> soul that this life is but a preparation for a new
> life . . . in which will be of more love, and of
> greater love. . . . I find no despair whatsoever in
> contemplating that like all that lives in this
> world of the flesh, I, too shall leave it.
>
> —DOROTHY THOMPSON TO A DYING FRIEND

TWIN FARMS, 1950

Michael's first year at the Royal Academy in London was over, and Dorothy's swashbuckling prince, as rash as he was handsome, would be traveling through Europe for the summer. Six-foot-two, sporting a red mustache and the air of an Englishman, Michael's allure, she was certain, outmatched his naïveté. Dorothy's advice to her son was rife with cliché; Polonius could not have said it better. Don't drink, don't hang out with bad company, stick to beer and wine, be thoughtful of your hosts, keep track of your money, and beware of "wolves, male and female."

Dorothy and Rebecca had been commiserating about their sons, each ensconced on opposite sides of the Atlantic. Dorothy felt pity for these children of "too famous" parents. An absent father and a domineering mother (although she wasn't one, implying that Rebecca was—"the Medusa head"—no less) are bound to make any child feel inadequate. Add to that their sons' native volatility and fantasies of abandonment, and you've got a recipe for lifelong trouble.

Michael and Anthony, however, had ideas of their own, and couldn't wait to cut loose from their overprotective, undersensitive mothers. Unfortunately, Anthony was nearly thirty-five and the father of two by the time he woke up to the fact that he had married his mother. Michael, at twenty, had only begun to find his way among women. Neither woman trusted her son's instincts or judgment; each concluded that her son was too neurotic and damaged to survive on his own.

Without the anchor of family or friends, Anthony had been living in Dorothy's townhouse on Forty-eighth Street while navigating the shoals of New York City. Although they hadn't seen much of each other—he was working and she was lecturing—they cultivated a domestic relationship amounting to a negotiated truce. The last thing Anthony wanted was someone looking over his shoulder, telling him what to do. Dorothy, of course, felt somewhat responsible for Anthony and informed Rebecca about his attitudes, comings and goings, and accomplishments, to the extent she knew of them. Dorothy had read his novel *A Dark Night* and had found the book written by someone "remarkably talented" and "not afraid to tackle the fundamental matter of guilt." A serious effort to confront existential questions, it reminded Dorothy of Dante's *Inferno*. She told Rebecca that she was much better at dealing with other people's children. Too emotionally invested in Mike, Dorothy could see only his shortcomings in relation to hers or Hal's. Forced to be both his mother and father, she vacillated between indulgence and restriction.

As usual, Dorothy's salvation was her writing, and postwar Europe and the Middle East were providing much fodder for her provocative pen. After the creation of the State of Israel in 1948, Dorothy had turned away from it. In an article in *Commentary* magazine in March 1950, called "America Demands a Single Loyalty: The Perils of a Favorite Foreign Nation," Dorothy painstakingly wrapped her case against Zionism in political history and sets forth its dangers to the integrity of American society and the international community. She saw the Jews as "alien invaders" of Palestinian land—radical terrorists who had adopted the tactics of their Nazi oppressors by devastating defenseless Palestinian people, stripping them of their ancestral land and livelihood, and rendering them impoverished refugees. She saw the Jews of Israel not only as power-seeking imperialists, but as international agitators who conspired to create a perfidious fifth column in America and Europe. To a degree, Dorothy viewed American Jews the way the Nazis had, as a demonic force seeking to dominate U.S. foreign policy.

Blind to the impact of her words, Dorothy wrote that she was offended by the reaction of the American Zionist community to her comments. Anti-Zionism, she asserted, is often equated unfairly with anti-Semitism. Israel's leaders and their policies, she said, must be open to criticism, like those of any other nation.

In cool response to her article in *Commentary*, American immigration historian Oscar Handlin wrote, "American foreign policy outside of war is subject to open debate—in the same way domestic policy is; it is formulated through free discussion, open exposition of diverse opinions, leading to realistic compromises. American Jews are subject to the same rules and must go through the same legal channels as every other minority."

Dorothy's facts were anecdotal, and her interpretations were so damning as to not be taken seriously.

As usual, her private life brought little consolation. While Michael's concerns were more carnal and mundane, they were just as controversial. He wanted to get married, but at age twenty, one year short of reaching majority, he was still subject to his mother's rules and sense of realism. Michael had fallen in love with a Catholic Frenchwoman, Bernadette Nansé, who was studying English in London while working as an au pair. They had met shortly after Michael had arrived at the home of the reputed double agent Moura Budberg, the well-known lover of H. G. Wells and Maxim Gorky, and the object of Rebecca's lifelong disdain. Moura's flat served as a salon where gin-guzzling iconic intellectuals shared their tattered memories and exchanged ideas. Depending on the day of the week, Monday or Wednesday, she hosted her Soviet comrades or her conservative British friends. It's difficult to know where Michael or Bernadette fit into Moura's world, except that Moura had great admiration for Dorothy and took pleasure in matchmaking. For Michael, it was love at first sight of this pretty, feminine, and, above all, practical young woman. He sensed she would rein him in and keep him grounded. If the relationship between the two seems familiar, it is because it could be read backward to Red and Dorothy and laterally to Anthony and Kitty. Could Michael, as Anthony, have fallen in love with his mother?

For the moment, the question was moot. Dorothy would not permit him to marry, and she believed that his rebellious philandering made him a prime candidate for intense psychiatric help. Michael responded by making appointments with her chosen physician and never showing up, and by once again spending the summer traveling through Europe. He was, however, agreeably tethered to one port of call—meeting his step-father Max in Spain and touring its architectural and artistic landmarks. All agreed that Michael's penchant for travel would be an asset in view of his less than conventional academic career.

Max proved to be a friend and role model—a disciplined artist and self-educated, cultured man. If he was a bit rough around the edges and his manners less than proper, he made up for it with his compassion and sensibility. Michael found him to be more of a father than Sinclair Lewis ever was. Earlier that spring, Red had invited Michael for a summer Alpine walking tour, but at the last minute, he had called it off, telling Dorothy that he was in no mood to "entertain" him. Dorothy wrote to Rebecca that she could not believe he used that word when referring to his own flesh and blood.

But Dorothy could be equally detached from the life of their son, and as if in compensation, she often intertwined personal experience with cultural commentary. Throughout her career, even in her column, On the Record, she meshed the two. In May, she launched a diatribe against the growing deterioration of American culture in an address to a meeting of the U.S. Chamber of Commerce, attended by Bess Truman. Americans have become, she said, "grossly materialistic, conformist and lacking in ideals and purpose." Furthermore, she said, perhaps thinking of her marriage to Red, the family, which had historically provided the most basic form of education, was slowly deteriorating; the divorce rate was almost the same as the marriage rate.

Speaking of divorce, there was one fermenting within the walls of her home. Anthony, who recently had moved into the top floor of her townhouse, seemed to have tremendous guilt about deserting his children. And yet, Dorothy wrote to Rebecca, for some reason, he had been "charming when he is gay" in the last few weeks. Dorothy told her that Anthony was looking for a home in Stonington, Connecticut, a New England fishing village that had become a fashionable summer resort. She added that she was frustrated by her descending public image. "As a result of championing Arab refugees, and . . . refusing to follow along on the Jewish attitude on the German question, which is one of pure revenge, no matter what the consequences for the west. I am now . . . being systematically boycotted by every Jewish agency in the United States." She doesn't back down, she wrote. But she doesn't fight back, either.

"Jews . . . ruthless[ly] exploit you when they can," she continued, "and especially exploit your feelings of sympathy and charity, and kick you all the harder in the teeth if you cease to be of use to them, or draw back a little on being exploited."

Ensconced in Twin Farms and with new help to keep it going, Dorothy felt it to be a place apart, but that didn't stop her from lashing out against the State Department's stance toward Russia. Fearing Russia's unbridled expansionism, she wrote that any military action taken in Europe by the Red army or satellite armies should be considered an act tantamount to war against the United States. Dorothy's bleak picture of world affairs prompted the Cleveland *Plain Dealer*, one of her Bell Syndicate subscribers, to drop her column. While Dorothy augured cosmic destruction, Maxim, home from Europe, painted a radiating scarlet resurrection—a rising golden-bodied Christ with penetrating eyes and an expression at once "stern and serene."

By summer's end, Dorothy felt helpless in the face of the continuing disappointments of her family and friends, and the political affairs of Europe and America. With cultivated narcissism, she still grasped at the illusion of authority, working double time as if her efforts alone could prevent her personal world and international relations from falling apart. Nonetheless, her usual myopia prevailed close to home. Much like Rebecca, it was easier for Dorothy to worry about some large-scale catastrophe than those that were happening under her nose. For quite some time, she had been blind to the fact that Jimmy Sheean's mind was fracturing. Always swaying in sync to some "mystical force" he neither understood nor governed, he had been prone to breakdowns and seizures, often alienating people while in their throes. Dorothy had long ago taken him under her wing, but his emotional and financial dependency had increasingly become a problem. Furthermore, Anthony had disappeared from under her watch "without a trace," and Michael was lonely and disoriented without Bernadette, whose visits to his flat had become less frequent in deference to Dorothy. Seeking respite from personal chaos in her concern for the continuing Arab-Israeli conflict, Dorothy planned a trip to the Middle East in November.

As the end of the year approached, Michael, emotionally distraught, accepted his father's invitation to visit him during Christmas in Rome, while Bernadette spent the holidays with her family in Paris. But despite his good intentions, Michael sabotaged his visit by not showing up at his father's home until late afternoon on Christmas Day. Having spent the night in bed with a prostitute, he arrived at his father's door disheveled and hungover. When Red saw him, he refused to let him stay, telling Michael that he was free to go back to London where he could engage in whatever he wanted to do without hurting anyone's feelings. Stung by the rebuke, yet not sufficiently ashamed to ask his father for a ticket to Paris to see Bernadette, Michael called his mother in New York. She frantically tried to wire him money and ultimately succeeded, but in the process of engineering Michael's return to the States, Dorothy suffered a bout of nervous exhaustion severe enough to land her in the hospital. As Max told Jimmy Sheean's wife, Dinah, Dorothy was "cracking up" with worry about Michael's self-destructive bent. Dorothy's state of mind would further deteriorate when news of Red's death reached her just as she was packing up to leave the hospital for home.

Her housekeeper called to tell her that Red had died in Rome at a Catholic clinic. His death at the clinic was ironic, Dorothy wrote to Rebecca, considering Red was an "old defiant Atheist"; his last words, uttered to an attending nun, were, "I am happy. God bless you."

She ordered her servants to keep the radio off and not to tell Michael, who waited at home in her townhouse in New York. She wanted to tell him herself and try to soften the blow when she returned that afternoon. Despite all this, she told Rebecca that upon hearing the news, Michael's "legs seemed to crumple under him, he dropped into a chair, his face in his hands, said, 'My God, my God' half a dozen times and then said, 'I suppose I killed him.'" In an attempt to shake him out of his "self-dramatization," Dorothy explained that his father had always been self-destructive, and his health had been deteriorating for more than a year.

Jimmy, who visited the family shortly after Red's death, had the mystical sense that "evil [was] at work." Mike was shooting off tension by presenting random dramatic readings to the guests, Dorothy was again anxious beyond consolation, and Max seemed totally helpless, sitting mute on the library sofa.

Dorothy wrote to Rebecca, she "guessed that Mike both felt himself somehow doomed to follow in his father's footsteps in this regard [alcoholism], and justified by the fact that his father's fame and the honor was accorded to him despite it." She went on to say that no one in her family had ever been an alcoholic (a debatable fact), and Red would never admit he was.

At Dorothy's behest, Michael agreed to psychological testing. Her hope was that they could somehow pull him out of his alcoholism once they knew the facts. She reported to Rebecca that the doctors saw "a trace of psychosis but serious character disturbances. . . . Everything is uneven including intelligence. . . . It is prodigiously high in some categories and almost moronic in others. Very mature powers of abstract ideation, where numbers are not involved, and incapacity, almost, to balance a checkbook or make the right change. (That's one thing, at least, that a French bourgeois wife could supply!)"

In some ways, this report merely confirmed what she already knew. The discrepancy among his cognitive abilities, as well as his impulsivity and lack of organizational skills, would now be considered attention defict/hyperactivity disorder. Many with these symptoms, male and female, are highly intelligent but are often labeled "lazy," as was Michael—a tag that creates tremendous frustration and erodes self-esteem. If undiagnosed, they often try to escape or relieve their anxiety through self-medication with alcohol or drugs. While ADHD is a hard-wired, lifelong condition that cannot be outgrown, a "genius," such as Red Lewis, might cultivate the capacity to override its effects or harness its creative upside to a task. But Dorothy feared that Michael was not of that caliber. She wrote to Rebecca that the "discerning boy" hoped he wasn't another "Elliott Roosevelt," the alcoholic ne'er-do-well son of Eleanor and Franklin, totally dependent on family funds. Michael worried that no one would want him for who he was, apart from his father's name.

It is interesting that Dorothy chose to confide in Rebecca. But in truth, she had few intimate female friends. Moreover, she had few friends she believed savvy enough to understand and reflect upon the psychodynamic of her family as a whole and as individuals. Dorothy felt a kinship with Rebecca, an extraordinarily talented and ambitious writer whose son was also the issue of a brilliant man bent on self-destruction. While Rebecca had many female friends, as well as her compassionate and sensitive sister Winnie, she seemed to derive strength and knowledge from helping those with less acute perceptions; her observations became the raw data, the scientific bases for her fictional characters.

While presenting a stoic face to an inquiring world, Dorothy unabashedly admitted to Rebecca, "Red's death hit me, and regardless of Michael, far, far harder than I would ever have dreamed. For Red, with all the suffering he inflicted on himself, and on those closest to him—with all his hunger for love, and his perverse capacity to throw it into the ashcan—was the single greatest experience of my life—rather the way some people felt about World War I. (Painful but glorious.)" Their love affair was indeed a war entered into when Dorothy was still naïve enough to believe that Red could be conquered.

> *The truth is that I loved him, in the early days of our marriage excru-ciatingly. (I think that word is correct.) No one ever, before or since, had the capacity to hurt me so, and I fear that is one of certain sign of love. No one ever gave me such an utter sense of failure, as a woman. And no one ever awakened in me to such depths of pity. And, quite objectively, it is as though another peak has fallen. . . . The horizon seems to me flatter and duller, while mediocrity, enthroned as the God of Democracy, produces the century of the common man.*

By mid-February 1951, encouraged by her family and friends, and knowing that work was her emotional salvation, Dorothy summoned the strength to tackle the essential foreign policy issue of the day—U.S. Cold War strategy. In a letter to Senator Robert Taft of Ohio she attacked it as unrealistic, one-dimensional, naïve, and wasteful of manpower and treasure. She questioned the validity of funding a standing army of three million, ready to send arms, food, and soldiers to every noncommunist country wherever and whenever a "fracas breaks out, between states, or within states, today in Korea, tomorrow in India." Without power or resources, she wrote, with an air of disdain she would have never expressed to Rebecca, "[European countries] are falling back on the nostalgic convention of superiority of European culture. The Americans are rich barbarians. The Russians are poor barbarians. Europe is finished—but it is still a museum. . . . If the museum is not blown up, then, in the long run, a humanizing influence may emanate from the cradle of civilization." She advocated the formation of "small, highly armed very well paid, well-screened and thoroughly reliable professional armies" and taking diplomacy out of the "'deep freeze.' We are heading towards war—and like the last one for no clarified purpose—except to punish Sin." As usual, her comments were a conflation of politics and Christian morality.

Dorothy's interest in the Middle East did not flag under the weight of a flattened horizon. Bent on recapturing a peak, she promulgated her cause on the radio. The Middle East is a very important part of the world, she told national radio show host Mary Margaret McBride. "It's the source of almost the whole oil of Europe: in Iran and Iraq and Saudi Arabia." "I'm simply amazed by Arab women. Egyptian girls are now getting secondary and university education." But broadcasting the advances of dictatorial oil-rich countries did not sit well with the American Zionist Council, whose members flooded her lectures armed with mimeographed material that refuted the arguments she proffered in her columns.

As the fencing continued, Dorothy decided to combat the "organized interests" by forming a policy institute called the American Friends of the Middle East (AFME). (She was advised not to use the words "Arab" or "Islamic" to avoid a backlash.) One of her first acolytes was General Dwight D. Eisenhower, now the supreme commander of the North Atlantic Treaty Organization. While he agreed wholeheartedly with her points of view, he declined to participate because of his workload as NATO commander. His endorsement, however, intensified her commitment to parity between Palestinians and Israelis. The support of a top American military officer added a patina of legitimacy to Dorothy's otherwise beyond-the-pale point of view.

Closer to home, Dorothy was fighting a losing battle alone, without an organization behind her or a top general by her side. Michael was determined to wed Bernadette. Marrying a woman of another culture and class challenged every axiom of marital harmony and longevity Dorothy held true—except one. Michael was happy only when he was with Bernadette, and except for some idealized notion of "the way things ought to be," who was she to object? She told Rebecca that she was smart enough to know she couldn't choose her son's wife. Besides, no one could have predicted that her marriage to Max would bring either one of them enduring happiness. While Dorothy had painstakingly climbed the journalistic hierarchy, Max was a self-educated man who had always lived at the edge of society. His artistic talent was his only claim to legitimacy, and his passion for visual images was the antithesis of her life lived in words.

Finally, with many "misgivings," Dorothy gave Michael permission to marry "Benny." As if to proclaim his manhood publicly, he married

Bernadette on June 20, 1951, his twenty-first birthday, on a mountaintop in Woodstock, Vermont. This was the first Roman Catholic wedding in the family since the Reformation, Dorothy later quipped, finding the pomp of its rituals and liturgy alien after the spartan Methodist church ceremonies of her youth.

On Dorothy's fifty-eighth birthday, less than three weeks after handing Michael over to Benny, perhaps inspired by the hope of her son's salvation through marriage and Catholicism, she called for her organization WOMAN to convene "an international pilgrimage of women, to the spot where two conflicting powers meet each other in the most dangerous tension—that ruined, battle-scarred city of Berlin." She believed it might "spark a universal act of conversion." It would be, she decided, a solemn festival, opening with Beethoven's Ninth Symphony (the composer himself was a Roman Catholic dedicated to individual freedom and dignity) and closing with multilingual speeches honoring the ideals of compassion and humanism. It would represent a female principle that could rise above the fray of conflict, harmonizing the peaceful aspirations of the Soviet bloc countries with those of the West.

Perhaps Dorothy's vision was too good to be true, or perhaps, more cynically, her reputation preceded her. Her affiliation with the Arab cause seemed to make all her proposals, no matter how apolitical, appear suspect. Her alignment with dictators against democracy in the Middle East caused some, most importantly Eleanor Roosevelt, to think that her calls for peace were a ruse consonant with Soviet propaganda.

Roosevelt wrote to a friend,

At a time when Soviet-inspired and directed "peace movements" are seeking to infiltrate and maneuver women's groups in various parts of the world, and especially in Germany, it is essential for all women's organizations to be on guard and to be precise in the positions they take in order to avoid being used in behalf of false peace propaganda.

Roosevelt quotes Dorothy's comments, noting that "the United States, United Kingdom and France are bracketed with the Soviet Union as equally of bad faith. . . . The proposed round-the-world flight and an International Women's Congress in Berlin open wide the door for Communist manipulation."

Dorothy would blame the lack of cohesive support for her project on the ignorance of most women and the willingness of professional businesswomen to align with male attitudes toward militarism. Roosevelt, now the chair of the UN Commission on Human Rights, would subsequently denounce Dorothy, as well as her organization and its mission, on the floor of the international forum Dorothy had always seen as the vehicle for world peace. In response to a letter in which Dorothy questioned the legitimacy of her claims, Roosevelt declared, "The only practical answer for the forces of peace is strength and unity to deter aggression."

Although Dorothy might have agreed with her before the death of her stepson Wells and the death of millions during the war, she had now assumed the unaccustomed role of a pacifist. She must have asked herself, how could an idea so deeply entrenched in Christian virtue and fundamental American values be so disparaged?

Resigned to the fact that the pilgrimage to Berlin would never take place, Dorothy wrote to Jane Hayford, the chief executive of WOMAN, that she was a liability to its cause. Her very presence, she wrote to another board member, was a liability "because my highly heretical views on American policy past and present are extremely well known."

But her "heretical views" were beginning to cause more than trouble. They were costing her money and influence. The Washington *Star*, already refusing to print her anti-Zionist On the Record columns, threatened to suspend her contract permanently. It was one thing to lose her voice in New York, but if congressmen in Washington couldn't read her, it would be tantamount to a gag order. Writing for small-town newspapers, which is to say, those without perspective or power, would be equivalent to writing in a key-locked diary.

Expressing her bitterness at her increasing irrelevance, Dorothy told an interviewer from the *Ladies' Home Journal* that she had sacrificed her health and her looks to her career in journalism. Repeating a sentiment that had resonated from her first days as a reporter, she said that it was nature—"things living, and growing, birds, trees, the sky, water, flowers, wild and domestic animals"—that pleased her most. "I am an unreconstructed country woman."

Her home at Twin Farms was beginning to have a distinctive allure for Dorothy as her taste for public expression waned. Furthermore, she wrote to a friend, her robust confidence was starting to deflate. "I am not fitted (or fitted anymore) for my profession—chiefly because what interests me (or arouses my speculations) does not interest the public, and I am not sure of anything, an attitude not allowable for a communicator."

The public outcries against her views were becoming increasingly vitriolic. Walter Winchell, a national gossip-mongering radio broadcaster, said that Dorothy was doing official propaganda for the Arabs. During a spring 1952 trip to Israel and Tehran, Syria had decorated her with a medal for contributing to U.S. and Arab friendships. The Zionists accused her of accepting bribes from Arabs to express their views. Downtrodden but still bent on speaking her truth, she deemed herself "a bubble of protest mass." She hoped to dissolve the mass before it fossilized by changing the party in power.

As usual, Dorothy went straight to the top to get the job done. When Adlai Stevenson threw his hat in the ring as the Democratic candidate for president in August 1952, Dorothy offered to be his adviser. The soft-spoken cerebral governor of Illinois accepted her services, calling Dorothy "the best informed American on Europe." Like Dorothy, he was a writer and idealist with superior intellectual understanding. At a campaign rally, someone remarked that Stevenson was "the thinking man's candidate." Stevenson quipped: "Thanks, but I need a majority to win."

As one of his speechwriters, Dorothy told Stevenson that a categorical vision of foreign policy, one that sees things as "good and evil," enervated the chance for diplomacy. Tutoring him on the methods of "good leadership," knowing that he didn't have the battlefield experience of his opponent, she told him, "The weakest thing that Ike has said is his flat statement, 'America cannot stand alone.'" Politicians, she insisted, need to project courage and confidence. "That leader is strongest who speaks to the soul, for the soul often knows and believes what the mind rejects. Besides there are more souls than minds." She mourned that the Zionists were "trapping" both Stevenson and Eisenhower. "My contention (and experience) are supported that the ZOA is the only political pressure group in this country that no candidate dares to buck," she wrote to Stevenson. "So the canonization of Israel (the only state in history to have been canonized at birth) goes on."

But even as she publicly endorsed Stevenson, she confided to Jimmy less than a month later that she thought he would lose the election. She was right. In November, Eisenhower won in a landslide. Dorothy wrote to Jimmy that she was not surprised by Stevenson's loss. "We frontal lobe people like you, Adlai, and to a lesser extent myself is that . . . we think a different kind of mind and approach indicates lack of intelligence or intellect."

Privately, Dorothy's friendship with Jimmy had put her in a bind. Jimmy was a part owner of Twin Farms. He had bought the "guest house" two years earlier, before his marriage to Dinah fell apart, but now the federal government was threatening to confiscate his income in payment for back taxes. For Jimmy, losing the house shattered his dream for happiness; for Dorothy, Jimmy's default marked the end of her delusion that she could mix mortgage sharing and friendship. Coincidentally, the income from her columns was dwindling, and for the first time she thought about putting Twin Farms on the market.

Consoled by Max, she vowed to put more time and energy into her relationships with family and friends. And cultivating Rebecca's friendship was among her most important priorities. Early in November, when Dorothy had met Anthony by chance, she wrote to Rebecca and Henry, eager to share what she thought was good news. "This was in late fall and [Anthony] seemed terribly glad to see me—astonishingly so—and told me of his forthcoming marriage." Just before Christmas, Dorothy and Max had been invited to Anthony's wedding reception at a friend's home. But after that, he had again disappeared without a trace, leaving them to wonder if the event had taken place without them.

In January 1953, Henry and Rebecca went to New York. In celebration, Dorothy gave them a dinner party at the Eldorado Club, at 300 Central Park West. It was their first visit to the States since Michael had married and since Red had died. When Harold Ross had died a year earlier, Rebecca had wondered out loud why she hadn't gone back to New York to see him or her other friends. Their visit would be an attempt to make amends for their neglect. Hoping to promote provocative conversation, Dorothy invited an international crowd with diverging views: eminent Russians (one of them a Jew), a Romanian official, newspaper editors such as Helen Reid of the *Herald Tribune* (who canceled several engagements to attend), and a "bona fide" Prussian.

In a letter she sent befor their visit, Dorothy wrote to Rebecca and Henry that they were precious friends. What she meant was that they were not only sympathetic and understanding, but their views about the

Jews and the Middle East were as intense as hers. Rebecca had been labeled an anti-Semite in the wake of a series of articles in the *Evening Standard* about the Mosleyite fascist uprising in London. Turning Nazi racism on its head, she had written to Dorothy that one must subscribe to the Herrenvolk (master race) theory assumed by the Zionists, or they would try to bring you down. She deemed them duplicitous, ungrateful, and unjust.

As in the States, postwar antipathy toward the Jews, emanating from the establishment of Israel and its perceived expansionism, had taken hold in Britain, especially among the right-wing groups such as Oswald Mosley's British Union of Fascists. While many Americans and Brits held these views, Dorothy and Rebecca bore the brunt of public criticism as well-known voices in the media.

Dorothy went further than Rebecca. Injustice had to be righted or what was the reason for living? She believed she was put on earth to help God perfect the world, and she was certain that the Jews would, if not restrained, greedily consume the land and peoples of the Middle East. But Dorothy was also an American whose guiding principles were those of the founders—freedom of expression and equality under the law. Perhaps these sacred beliefs, along with her discussions with Rebecca and their friends in New York, gave her the courage to approach Churchill, who was once again the Conservative prime minister of Britain.

She wrote to him: "I have become convinced that the Jews, phenomenally brilliant individually and especially in the realm of abstract thought, are collectively the stupidest people on earth. I think it must come from cultural inbreeding—perhaps physical inbreeding also—in a desire to retain a homogenous, in-group society in the midst of 'aliens.' [Criticism of Israel is] not anti-Semitic," she concluded, but since the majority of Jews are Zionists, they were inextricably linked.

The only consolation amid this dirty quagmire of political accusations was her marriage to Max. He wrote to Dorothy, as they prepared for their move to Twin Farms, that July 1953 marked their tenth anniversary. "One thing is sure, I love you so much, more than ever, and send you my heart." But with her typical myopia, Dorothy didn't see how lonely Max was without her—even when she was physically present. She wrote to Rebecca that she was frustrated; she was "overwritten" and "overworked."

Later in the summer, Dorothy complained to Rebecca that she had virtually been supporting Mike and Benny since they had moved in with

them in the spring. Mike, who had signed a contract with a summer theater in Wisconsin, lived on his father's money and the small wages he
earned. Fortunately, Benny was a wonderful cook and helped around the
house by doing the shopping and making them dinner. Dorothy had
been looking for a cook to work at Twin Farms, but, she said, "Appli-
cants want preposterous wages and conditions nobody can meet. I loathe
the proletariat." They were "the worst slave drivers in history." She
would like to simplify her life by selling her house, but she still loved
Twin Farms. Totally unaware of Henry's increasing dementia and his
constant philandering, Dorothy concluded, "Well, we love our husbands
and they us, which is a very great deal."

Dorothy's retreat from public life had begun, but Bruce and Beatrice
Gould of the *Ladies' Home Journal* still hammered her with requests to
write columns. Realizing she no longer had the influence or the energy,
Dorothy declined. She had also decided not to go on any more lecture
tours, but money pressures prompted her to amend her decision; she became highly selective. Her thoughts seemed to revert toward a simpler,
more idealistic era that had prevailed in America, or at least to her fantasy of America during her childhood.

More and more, Rebecca became Dorothy's confidante. She wrote to
her as to no one else, as if she were writing entries into an uncensored diary.
The public interest in the life of Sinclair Lewis, she told her, had heightened
with the years. His first wife, Grace, seemed to be capitalizing on the public's curiosity by writing a book that sentimentalized their relationship, and
his young mistress Marcella, acting like a widow, had divorced her husband
after Hal's death. Dorothy told Rebecca that she had never been happy with
Hal and admitted that she had contributed to their breakup. She had not
been willing, however, to go through psychoanalysis just to figure out *his*
neurosis. There was much speculation about Red's sexuality, she wrote, but
she assured Rebecca that he was "thoroughly heterosexual." The problem
was, she said, "Something frustrated his capacity to love at all."

With these confessions off her chest, she was relieved to move on to
the intellectual crux of their relationship: British and American foreign
policy. Reiterating the objections to American policies she had written to
government officials, Dorothy declared that she was against the Korean
War; the only way to stop Communism was through diplomacy, and
while she didn't like McCarthy, she didn't like the Communists, either.

One senses that as Dorothy aged, she sought to grasp the Holy Grail—

the elusive essence of Christian virtue. Her hunt in youth had been for a good story; now it was for a sense of purpose—or, perhaps, to prove that she still had one. It seemed that no matter how many times she said she was professionally washed up, and that beauty and love were all she cared about, in reality, neither could suffice. Nature was a divine gift, not a raison d'être. Even her sister, Peggy, told her to stay home and keep out of harm's way, but still she pushed, hoping to make enough noise to stir the conscience of the "unconverted." But to do that, she needed money, and she needed funding independent of the Arab countries in order to preserve her guise of objectivity. Her goal was to take a trip to Egypt without the support of the Egyptian government. In July 1954, she wrote to John Wheeler, Francis Biddle's friend in the British foreign office and her wartime confederate, who was now the head of a wealthy foundation. She told him she would be going to Cairo, Alexandria, and the Suez Canal Zone in August, where she would have "exceptional privileges in reaching important people." Whether he funded her or not is unclear. What mattered was that she went, no matter how she got there. In doing so, she became the symbol of anti-Zionist propaganda and a target of American Zionists. Vowing, as she had to Stevenson, that the strongest person is one who can stand alone, she defiantly held her ground in public lectures and letters to the State Department. Six months earlier, when Dorothy had corresponded with John Foster Dulles, the U.S. secretary of state, she wrote, "I greatly fear that one day the present suppressed resentments will flare up, not only into anti-Zionism but anti-Semitism here." It was the other side of Red's question in his book *It Can't Happen Here,* and the inverse of her pre-1948 views. She and Red had always known that American ground was fertile for anti-Semitism, but this time it really would be the fault of the Jews, along with those Christians who let them have their way.

AS THE CHRISTMAS HOLIDAYS APPROACHED, Dorothy mused on the substance and purpose of journalism. Immersed in thoughts of the consecration of human life and its ethical and humanitarian implications, she remarked that journalism encompassed "the teachings of Jesus Christ regarding the operation of cause and effect in the spiritual life of the individual and the community." Furthermore, she had aligned herself with the "universal cosmic and creative force" of "altruistic love." In times of despair, she drew strength from her rural Methodist upbringing. As the year progressed, the mundane exchange of insults between her and the Jewish community escalated. It seems ironic that even as the media as well as her editors silenced her voice, the Jews found it weighty and influential. Embroiled in controversy, she once again eschewed fact for philosophy: "The element in the Bible that has most shaped my thinking is its concern with justice, and the evolution of the idea of justice, from the primitive concept of 'an eye for an eye and a tooth for a tooth,' through its association with mercy, to, in Christ, the concept of reconciliation in a blazing triumph of altruistic love."

The *Toledo Blade* dropped her column.

Ever persevering, Dorothy continued to write On the Record. In 1955, three mornings a week, as she had done for nearly two decades, she wrote from nine in the morning until one in the afternoon, insisting to all who asked that she needed the money. Her efforts would find new justification when Michael announced that he and Benny were going to have a baby. While Dorothy had protested early in their marriage that she should be "counted out" of their domestic affairs, she continued to send them small sums of money to supplement Michael's floundering theatrical career. Her grandson John-Paul Sinclair Lewis was born on July 30, 1954, two weeks early. Having wanted to witness the child's birth, Dorothy was thoroughly disappointed that Benny had "jumped the gun" without her, nearly having the baby in a restaurant. Upon hearing news of the birth, Dorothy raced up to Poughkeepsie in her car through summer rainstorms to see the baby. She was besotted.

Michael, in summer stock at Hyde Park in rehearsals for *My Three Angels,* had missed the birth by a few hours, but the whole family gathered shortly thereafter for the christening at a Catholic Church near their home in Barnard, Vermont. Dorothy wrote in a letter to a friend that, much like the wedding, "The Christening ceremony astonished my Protestant mind. . . . Protestant ceremonies concentrate on dedicating the child to God, but the devil is very present in the Catholic, being exorcised in many points of the ritual. I think it all very pre-Christian and pagan." Attitudes such as these must have set the foundation for her less-than-optimal relationship with her daughter-in-law. Just as Dorothy had refused to recognize the domineering nature of her parenting, she never recognized the controlling aspects of her relations with Benny. While Dorothy believed she had always been perfectly selfless in her dealings, Benny would remember her as bossy and intrusive.

In the fall of 1954, shortly after the birth of John-Paul, Michael was cast in a romantic comedy by Noël Coward set in late nineteenth-century France called *Quadrille*. Alfred Lunt, who both directed and starred in the play, cast Michael as an overbearing Nazi-like Frenchman. Michael's arrogant demeanor, hunched-over frame, and potbelly seemed to fit the part. While Alfred deemed his performance as quite good, Alfred's wife, Lynn Fontanne, also a cast member, saw Michael as more trouble than he was worth. His constant drunkenness and mood swings seemed to throw the whole ensemble out of kilter, defying the standards of theatrical discipline and responsibility toward one's colleagues. Unbeknownst to him, Michael's participation in the play as the "second Frenchman" would be the highlight of his career.

Meanwhile, Benny wasn't the only one who chafed at Dorothy's criticism. Her friend Emanie would write to Rebecca that Dorothy had called her a "fool" too often to let it slip by. Although Emanie knew she had to forgive her, and even acknowledged that she might have been right, she had gotten "too much of that sort of thing in my childhood to take it with aplomb."

It was clear that the diminution of her column subscriptions and speaking engagements was affecting Dorothy's ability to sustain their lifestyle, so she began pushing sales of Max's paintings. She wanted to keep Twin Farms, and to continue to travel on behalf of AFME, but she knew her funds, and therefore her independence, would run dry if she didn't at least go through the motions of putting Twin Farms on the market. By assigning an exorbitant price to the property, she hoped to hang on to it a little bit longer.

Throughout 1955, Dorothy worked to bring the aims of her Middle East organization to fruition, upping the ante as she went along. Once again publicly denouncing the Jews as "alien invaders of Palestine," calling for Arab repatriation, and warning American politicians who sought election not to be cowed by Zionist pressure groups, she continued to alienate readers and editors, not to mention the American Jewish community.

Even her friends were noticing her self-righteousness. In January 1956, Emanie wrote to Rebecca that she found Dorothy's arrogance all too familiar. She, too, had witnessed her imperious attitude. "All things I hate in women," she wrote. Dorothy acted as though she were "Mrs. God" who knew everything about children and motherhood. Emanie, who had a daughter of her own, thought that Dorothy had little capacity for self-reflection or understanding of spontaneous emotions. "The NERVE," she shouted on the page.

While all this was transpiring behind her back, a new challenge moved front and center demanding her attention. During the spring and early summer of 1956, world peace was threatened by a new conflagration—Gamal Abdel Nasser's ascent to power as president of Egypt and his nationalization of the Suez Canal. Originally a gateway for protecting British and French colonies in Asia and Africa, the Suez was controlled by the British and had become the conduit through which nearly two-thirds of Europe's oil flowed. Convinced that the canal afforded him control of the Arab world and Europe, Nasser was given military support by the Soviet Union and Communist bloc countries, who shared his goals. As tensions escalated, the British tried to persuade the United States under President Eisenhower to fight alongside them, but to no avail. Eisenhower wanted to sustain peace through diplomacy. A secret alliance was formed among Britain, France, and Israel, whose self-interests momentarily coalesced. Their combined strategy was ultimately thwarted, however, when the Eisenhower administration, fearing a wider war, threatened to side with Egypt, promising to unleash catastrophic economic sanctions on Britain if the alliance did not relent. Ultimately, the pressure of the Soviets and the United Nations on the allies forced their withdrawal from the Sinai in March 1957. While Britain and France had failed to gain control over the canal, Israel had preserved its border with Egypt and gained the right to navigate its ships through the Strait of Tiran.

Dorothy was exasperated, but her lack of a platform from which to air her views compelled her to seek personal channels. During the Suez crisis she wrote to Rebecca, "The world has found no substitute or equivalent for force. . . . There is no international body capable of adjudicating in any dispute. . . . I do not know whether anything the West might have done would have changed the course of events, but I do know we are absolutely obtuse about Arab psychology. We are light years removed from contact with the Arab mind."

To remedy that ignorance, Dorothy went on a three-month tour to Athens, Jerusalem, and Tangier in the fall. On her return, she received a letter from Jack Wheeler, editor of Bell Syndicate. In a letter dated December 22, 1956, Jack gave Dorothy a straightforward ultimatum. She must resign from AFME and make up her mind if she "is a newspaper woman or a propagandist for the Arabs!" She resigned from the AFME.

She angrily wrote to a colleague at the American- and Saudi-funded organization that she was

> *apparently to report the facts only provided they don't step on Israeli, Zionist, British or French toes. . . . I had a three hour talk with Nasser. I've reported it in five columns straight with comments to follow. I suppose they will call that scoop propaganda. They wouldn't if I had bagged an interview with Khrushchev. . . . The Canal crisis, insofar as it involves Britain and France will, I feel confidant, straighten out. Not Israel so easily. Israel wants war.*

She was quick to add that they also wanted dominance. The analogy was complete; the Jews were, in effect, the Middle Eastern Nazis.

While Jimmy's adoration of Dorothy's moral and spiritual integrity was unshakable, he confided in John Gunther that Dorothy was "right in the broad, simple principles," but had "an uncanny faculty for being wrong in the short run. She gets lost in day-by-day news."

It is hard to disagree with him. Dorothy had so many unassailable principles that one cannot imagine they could veer in the wrong direction. But they not only went against the mainstream, they seemed to defy gravity with her airy idealism, making her into a modern-day Sisyphus, compelled to roll a great rock up the mountain every day, only to find it at the bottom each morning. Some would call her Cassandra, the seer who could predict the future but not alter it. But Dorothy preferred comparisons with Joan of Arc. Given that she was willing to go up in flames rather than change her views, the latter does indeed seem closest to the truth.

In 1957, having been encouraged by the Bell Syndicate to stay on, Dorothy continued to write her columns as usual, along with her monthly essays in *Ladies' Home Journal*. Now her editor at Houghton Mifflin, Dale Warren, presented Dorothy with a proposition that would magnify her voice and draw upon the loyalty of her *Journal* readers: a memoir in the form of essays about her past, deriving lessons from her experiences that readers could apply to the future. It was a look back, a critique of the soulless present, and an exercise in letting go.

In title and in content, the book was intentionally reminiscent of *The Courage to Be*, written by her friend Paul Tillich, a Protestant theologian, and published in 1952. Writing in a more personal, less philosophical, tone, Dorothy sought to take women on her journey from past to present, acknowledging the sociological, moral, and spiritual changes of the past half century. Entitled *The Courage to Be Happy*, the book was her means of self-examination and affirmation in the hope of inspiring others. Like her column in the *Ladies' Home Journal*, it was a thinking woman's guide to contemporary living.

With the ghost of Sinclair Lewis lingering nearby, Dorothy writes about "geniuses": who they are, what they demand of themselves, and what they have demanded of her. She writes that, for some reason, "It has been my fate during much of my life to be mixed up in one way or another with geniuses. . . . I am the bread and milk, never the caviar. I am the pick up [the decanter], never the wine. I am not the subject of an ode but the object. . . . I am not the lightning. I am the lightning rod." Either Dorothy was trying to be clever or humble or both. Books had been written and inspired by her—to wit, *Ann Vickers* and *It Can't Happen Here*. Paintings had been made of and enabled by her—Max's prototypical portraits of Dorothy radiate throughout his work. Her conclusions also seem specious; for example: "They are more likely to drive others to suicide than commit it themselves." Lewis had slowly poisoned himself to death; Max's nervous system was far more fragile than her own; and one could name numerous friends who were self-defeating, if not outright self-destructive—Jimmy Sheean, Christa Winsloe, Rebecca West, and Jan Masaryk, to name just a few. The fact that she excluded herself from the pack, while at the same time defined genius as obsession with one's work to the exclusion of everyone else, is the most obvious hole in her argument. Although perhaps not on the highest rung of the hierarchy, Dorothy certainly acted like a genius. Self-absorbed, selfish, and obsessed in search of fame—or at least influence—she might as well have been one. Perhaps the one distinction both she and the reader can make is that whatever she did, she did in the name of God. To her that made all the difference.

Moving toward the present, she triumphantly declares her joyful acceptance of old age. She sees it as freedom from ambition for worldly recognition and the competitiveness necessary to accomplish it. She looks ahead to the luxury of reveling in love for her grandchildren, without the responsibility for their welfare; the cherishing of her mate in old age without the fears, bitterness, and jealousy of her youth—his face, the comfort of his presence, and their sharing of the mundane pleasures of food, friends, and places; the acceptance of each other in a "ripened marriage." But her sense of "letting go" is perhaps the most poignant of her messages. "All my life I have had what one might call an unhappy love affair with the world—its charms and achievements; its wars, revolutions, injustices. Now I know that the world got along without me for a long time and will do so again. Once I was very eager to reform my fellow men and their institutions. Now I am more concerned to understand them." She wants to live in the present, because the future, even if painful, will be short. "Today is precious," she writes.

"Love" is the raison d'être of life, she concludes. Not love of humanity, which even in the abstract she doubts she loves, but singing the praises of things as they are.

> The Bible is the greatest book ever written because it contains the most penetrating observations of the operations of natural law, the greatest warnings of what happens to men who defy it, and the most certain promises of happiness to those who accept and cooperate with it. . . . No, the world is not in chaos. Men are in chaos . . . because of disobedience, because of opposition to accepting their place in the natural order.

Dorothy writing at her desk, ca. 1957.

Her book culminates with one last attempt at personal exoneration. She respects all Americans, she writes, regardless of origin, faith, or race, but she staunchly demands respect for her own opinions. To respect opinions of others, one must first respect one's own. Dorothy's final chapter is an ode to America—its national riches, its gifted and courageous political founders, and its hardworking, God-fearing pioneers.

Her last words are both self-defining and self-transcendent: "I believe in God. This is my loyalty oath."

Although the book would be read as inspirational, her proclamation of "loyalty" to America and her belief in God, which she saw as inextricable, would be her final rebuke to those who saw her as anti-Semitic, racist, and, therefore, un-American. When it was published in the fall of 1957, the reviews were solid, and the sales were good.

Paul Brooks, editor in chief of Houghton Mifflin, remarked that her book "is not exciting publishing. On the other hand, I see nothing against it. *The Courage to Be Happy* has certainly done as well as I expected, probably better. She seems to have established a public for this kind of thing quite apart from her earlier—and I guess now defunct—following as a political commentator." Dorothy wrote to Dale Warren, "I was disappointed in the review in the *New York Times* book section. . . . It's a magnificent testimony to my character—of the 'whether you agree with her or not' variety, but it seems to be my fate to always be judged as a conscience and a character, rather than as a mind and as a writer."

By the turn of the year, with the weight of the past off her chest, and her loyalty pledged to God and country, Dorothy felt she no longer had anything to lose. In an address to an anthropological organization about anti-Semitism, racism, integration, and white superiority, she presented both sides of the anthropological research on the future of Negroes. She came down on the side of those who saw categorical immutable differences between Negroes and whites, noting, "The rate of syphilis, illegitimacy, [and] crimes created in sexual passion is higher among negroes than any other part of the American population. I defy anyone to name *one single* distinguished American Negro!" Once fastidious about statistics and history, she had succumbed to distorting them to suit her vision.

Relieved that now all her public work was completed, she turned her attention back to her personal affairs. Dorothy's book had taken her into the next stage of life. In an effort to simplify her life, and unburden herself of material possessions, Dorothy made the decision to sell the big house at Twin Farms and move into the smaller one. Simultaneously, she sold the townhouse on Forty-eighth Street and moved into a seven-room co-op at 25 East End Avenue, overlooking the river. She found the apartment pretty, but it felt cramped for space. Dorothy wrote to Rebecca, "I feel rather ghostly about it all, but I know it's prudent. But two moves in a year is worse than a fire."

Dorothy continued that she "has heard several good things by Anthony suggesting he is maturing." She reported with obvious disappointment that "Michael is playing off Broadway. He's gifted but still thinks acting is imitation. He now has two sons. John-Paul is a sprite, a delicate Ariel. I think he'll be a ballet dancer. The baby [Gregory] has the look of a Junior Executive. But perhaps a wish dream for *one* business man in the family."

Despite Dorothy's philosophical reconciliation, the stress of the past few years had begun to take a physical toll. Not only had she lost some of her robust girth and the pink radiance of her youth, she also looked "somehow thyroid—her eyes are a bit popped out," according to her friend Emanie. And regardless of her generous declarations about Anthony's new maturity, Dorothy "had nothing positive to say about him; in fact, she said quite the contrary." Little did Dorothy know her two friends were gossiping about her. In view of what she thought about humankind, however, she would not have been surprised.

Time seemed to speed up, and her epigram "Today is precious" assumed greater meaning. During the first week of March 1958, after having visited the little house at Twin Farms to survey the renovations, Max slipped outside an inn in Hanover, New Hampshire. It was about ten-thirty in the evening when he caught his foot on the running board while descending from the jeep, falling flat on his face on the icy ground. Managing to get up, he staggered across the street, his face covered in blood. Later, he couldn't remember the accident. He was advised to remain in bed for two weeks.

Their seasonal move to Twin Farms, by now an end-of-May ritual, was rendered more difficult than usual by their need to vacate the big house and its surrounding property to make way for its new owners. The emotional "ghosts," as she had put it, infused the process of transferring deed and possessions with memories, aspirations, and regret, perhaps even guilt, about not reconciling aspiration with reality. Twin Farms was supposed to have been "home"—a vehicle to carry the feelings of her childhood into the present as a gift to her husband Hal and their child. It never was. One might say that the reclamation of this ideal was the thrust of her private life.

Shortly after Michael and Benny had married, Dorothy had expressed to Michael her hope to preserve the house for him, but the prospect was not practical, and Michael was not interested. Michael's unhappy childhood memories were enough to make him refuse her offer. Although Dorothy was resigned to the necessity of the sale, the process was emotionally devastating, making her vulnerable and needy. "Letting go" in the abstract proved far easier than in fact. Max, who so easily embraced her trials as his own, was equally overwhelmed. Four days after they arrived back at the farm for the season, Max had a heart attack. At first, doctors at Mary Hitchcock Memorial Hospital in Hanover, New Hampshire, thought it was gastric thrombosis, a blood clot in the intestines, but tests revealed cardiac infarction—a heart attack. For the moment, his prognosis looked good. With a blood thinner and rest (the conventional protocol of treatment in the fifties), Max's blood pressure normalized. But Dorothy's own blood pressure exhibited wide swings, consonant, she noted, with "worry, overwork, or anxiety." She looked forward to a visit from Michael and his family, who would be staying at a nearby farm while he was playing summer stock. Sadly, their own house was off-limits to guests in deference to Max's need for tranquillity.

But within weeks, Max was dead. On July 7, 1958, at three o'clock in the morning, as Dorothy sat in a hotel room near the hospital, the call came. Seeking words of consolation, she had been reading passages from the Gideon Bible, mysteriously coming to rest on a section of a psalm entitled Koph: "I cried with my whole heart, hear me O Lord. . . . I cried unto thee." Numb with shock, Dorothy felt no pain and shed no tears. Her first instinct was to make arrangements and notify her family and friends. She sent out one hundred telegrams announcing his death. FUNERAL HERE THURSDAY. PRAY FOR ME—DTK. Max was to be buried one day after her sixty-fifth birthday at the pinnacle of beauty of a Barnard summer.

In a letter to Rebecca and Henry, Dorothy described her feelings at the funeral.

There was no question of what would be done because Maxim and I had often talked about our funerals in the way people do who think of it as a remote question. There was no "funeral," in the usual sense, and no "lying in state." Maxim's body was buried in fresh pale gray pajamas, a set he especially liked. No one touched his face with those cosmetic treatments he abhorred. I had seen him less than half an hour after his death. With his lips slightly parted and his color unchanged, he looked exactly, except for his closed eyes, like the self-portrait he had painted in 1944—years younger and strangely innocent. . . . God to Maxim was Life—all of it—and Christ the Redeemer, who would understand [everyone] even . . . pagans.

Dorothy's memory of the funeral was a mystical kaleidoscope of events.

I remember almost nothing of the burial services, except that it was a brilliantly beautiful day. I saw our friends against a background of trees, and masses and masses of flowers around the evergreen blanket that covered his body, upon which was just one spray of flowers—of the rare and lovely showy lady's slipper, the wild orchid, that a neighbor had brought me that very morning. It was as though Maxim had planned it all himself, as he always planned my perennial birthday party, which had not been celebrated the day before. I had not the slightest sense of his being in the ground, but a powerful sense of his presence, felt, also by others. This I felt with extreme intensity as, after the service, I turned, with my son, and walked away. I literally saw him walking slightly ahead of me, with the air of one who would say that it had been a sweet party and gone off well.

The service too, was as we had agreed for each other. Father Green

of the Woodstock Episcopal Church (it is a high church) read the beau-
tiful, beautiful prayer for the dead, which is common with few changes
to the Catholic and Protestant ceremonies.

We have taken a great boulder of blue limestone from the fields to
head his grave, upon which will be engraved only: Maxim Kopf. Pres-
ently mosses, ferns and little flowering plants will grow over all of it
by the face with his name. He adored stone and the silent life of stone;
he had a sculptor's hands, and no piece of polished granite would be
appropriate.

Despite her professed calm, Dorothy was unhinged. It wasn't supposed to have happened this way. She had assumed that they would die
simultaneously and so had no sense of the toll of Max's death, even after
the fact. She could still see him and hear him, prodding her, chastising
her, protecting her. Those were the gifts he gave and price she paid for
losing him, she wrote to her friends Bruce and Beatrice Gould. "The
extent of my grief is in exact proportion to the extent of the joy that I had
from and through him," she wrote to another friend.

Dorothy believed that Max was still protecting her, even from herself. And while it was too late to make up for time lost at home with him,
six weeks from the day that Max died she finally summoned the courage
to do what she should have done two years earlier.

Dorothy quit her column On the Record in the *Herald Tribune*. Her
last column was published on August 18, 1959. She no longer wanted
the constant pressure of working against deadlines, but more important, she said she had lost faith in the power of the medium to influence
people. In truth, Dorothy had lost faith in her power to persuade. To
commemorate her and her colleagues' place in the history of journalism,
she set to work on a book Max had always encouraged her to write—a
memoir of her life and times. Dorothy wanted to be remembered for
her intellect, for her capacity to observe, analyze, and interpret, not just
for her spiritual qualities. But the question remained: Did she have the
energy and clarity to carry it out? She was not sleeping, and she was
devastated by grief, which was so intertwined with guilt that it was difficult to separate one from the other. She not only mourned Max's death,
but also regretted the constant distractions she had created in their lives.
Writing her column, which necessitated meeting with secretaries and
strangers, had robbed them of so much time and intimacy. For fifteen

years, Max had offered her unprecedented happiness, and she had not returned it.

On January 22, 1959, Dorothy wrote in her diary: "Journalism was only a means to an end—to see, to learn, if possible to be. The means swallowed the end and the search for freedom became a (voluntary) slavery. I find today that the 'success' I had means nothing to me whatsoever. I wonder what exactly went wrong."

Dorothy was starting to feel out of place in the world. She made the decision not to return to New York; she found the anonymity of the city corrosive. She kept the little house at Twin Farms for summering and moved to an apartment in Hanover for the winter, where she would have access to Dartmouth library—"the second best university library," she declared. She wrote to Rebecca and described her pleasantly furnished duplex apartment:

I have a sitting room, a study-dining room, kitchen, bedroom, bath and dressing room on one floor, and I keep it all tidy, if not immaculate, in less than an hour's work, which I rather like. I get my own tea and toast breakfast, and snack lunch, and dine directly for the evening at one of several excellent inns or restaurants. But I cannot feel at home in the place or anywhere else, even here where I spend at least four days a week. Oh, Rebecca, Maxim was home.

Meanwhile, Michael and his career were quickly sinking. Dorothy's sympathetic publishing friends were propping him up without his knowledge. But it was he who had begun to prop her up, lecturing her as she had him when he was a young man. From his apartment on Central Park West he wrote:

I feel that work is your "salvation," if you will forgive the cliché and that without it you like myself tend to brood, turn inward, toward self-pitying rage and drink far too much. The times that Bernadette and I have spoken to you on the phone have, I'm afraid, revealed in your voice the unmistakable evidence of "one Scotch too many," and far from wishing to sound like a censorious young squirt, I cannot help thinking what endless evenings alone in Hanover, with no

other company save Traudle [the maid] might lead to. . . . Make
no mistake about Traudle—her relation to you is one of dollars
and cents.

Michael was right. A death wish had overtaken her, and Traudle was
no friend. Dorothy had begun to notice that her "insides [were] not
working well." In late November 1958, Dorothy had abdominal
surgery—her colon was blocked by polyps; the doctors had to cut out
twenty-four inches. She wrote to Rebecca and Henry, "I don't think I
pity myself; I am just fed up with me and absolutely drained of talent,
ambition, ideas—absent of all indignation, which has kept me going
when all else has failed!"

She could not sustain her "obsession with [the] book." She had become aware of the possibility that the project was a self-manufactured
goal that provided a reason for living and wondered if it had been just an
excuse for quitting her column. Yet, she sensed that she would not live
long and "the thought is not unwelcome. . . . With Maxim's death I lost
my guts—literally."

It took Dorothy seven months to cry. On February 3, 1959, she wrote
in her diary, "I woke up this morning and suddenly burst into sobs. I do
not feel well—in fact I feel very unwell indeed. There are days when I
do not want to go on anymore and this has been one of them."

Despite her doctor's assurances that she was all right, Dorothy continued, she felt "sick and bloated." Nonetheless, she wrote, "I cannot
face the possibility of another operation."

Michael and Bernadette no longer visited Dorothy. Their two sons,
John-Paul and Gregory, now four and one, required unrestricted open
space to play and explore, Michael explained, and the little house at Twin
Farms with its precisely orchestrated gardens was not the place for them.
Dorothy adored her grandchildren and saw them as her link to a future
she could not grasp and dared not imagine. But to be robbed of them
through the whim of her son, who could articulate but not feel her despair, evoked blind anger.

In a letter to Dorothy, ostensibly about her behavior but in substance
a settlement of old scores, he laid out a litany of offenses. Michael expressed her neglect of him as a child when she was writing her columns;
her unwillingness, even as an adult, to take his judgment or interest in

foreign affairs seriously; her constant denigration of his intellect, education, and character both in private and in public; and her dismissive attempts to restrain his self-destructive drinking habits. He was tired, he wrote, of covering up his hurt.

> *In many ways, you have changed; become bitter, hyper-critical, intolerant. This is not my sole opinion, I regret to say, I have heard it time and again from your friends. "What's wrong with Dorothy? I went over there the other day and she bit my head off." Most of them realize as I do, that the enormous pressures of your work are bound to erupt, but people, to coin a cliché, are human.*
>
> *I only hope you believe this is not written in any but a sincere, filial, and loving vein.*

M.

Two weeks after her sixty-sixth birthday in July, Dorothy had a heart attack. And then another, and a third. After the third, Dorothy refused to go to Mary Hitchcock Hospital, where Max had died. She had too many bad memories.

In August, Dorothy wrote to Rebecca and Henry: "I think everything that has happened to me physically since then was due to losing Maxim. He spoiled me so and nothing is so wonderful as being spoiled. Very healthful."

Dorothy stayed in another local hospital for four weeks, permitted to see only family—that is, Benny; Michael never came. Those who spoke with her concluded that Dorothy no longer wanted to live. Throughout the month of September, Dorothy recuperated at Twin Farms. In an act of self-discipline, only possible with the imminent threat of death, she gave up smoking. But she felt very slow and unproductive. She was still attempting to write her memoir, but the blood pressure medicine, she complained, was clouding her mind. She was "drowning in drugs." Her walking was restricted to seven stairs once a day, and she was counseled by her physicians to sleep a lot. The doctors believed that the attacks were not due to thrombosis that constricted the blood vessels of the heart, and therefore they thought her heart would repair itself. The following months would test their theory.

Michael continued to drink heavily. And like his father, he was a vulgar and abusive drunk. Bernadette and Dorothy were easy targets for his anger. The reasons for Michael's drinking began to emerge after the Lunts cast him as a policeman in the revival of a play called *The Visit*. He was quite successful in the role, but he fought with everyone, including the cast, and was once again on the brink of losing his job. Dorothy wrote to Rebecca that he had "a sort of longing for the gutter," perhaps implying that it was all too proper for the inferior heir of his genius father. To complicate matters, during the summer of 1959, Michael had fallen in love with an English actress named Valerie Cardew, who had followed him during the tour of the play. Word was that Valerie was a "sex pot." Michael had always had affairs—everyone knew it, even his wife. But by the spring of 1960, Michael had left his wife and his children. After hearing the news, Dorothy slipped on a rug and broke her ribs.

As she recuperated Dorothy found the quiet of Hanover unnerving, and she made little progress on her book. After her first heart attack, she turned away from it to focus on her column in the *Ladies' Home Journal*. On April 30, 1960, the magazine published her essay "May I Tell You About My Heart Attack?" The article, written in her usual vein of educating women within a personal context, was not really about herself. She had done some research, informing the reader about the psychosomatic and physical roots of heart attacks, the process by which the damage takes place, the various kinds of attacks, the personalities prone to its dangers, and the various protocols or remedies—medicinal, nutritional, and physical—prescribed in their aftermath. It is clear that she wrote to inform her readers, not to gain their sympathy. And regardless of her true feelings, which she readily shared with friends, Dorothy presented a persona of optimism and faith, appearing certain that reason would triumph over ignorance. Perhaps her experience with politics had taught her that public pessimism did not pay.

Privately, she once again confided to Rebecca about Michael: "It is his heartlessness about other people that drives me crazy." When I had that heart attack last July [he] was awfully upset, but what he said was, 'If Mother should die, I would be sunk.' He is the protagonist in all his dramas. . . . If I had my life to live over I would be damned careful by whom I had a child, and I would not choose a genius or a near-genius, and certainly not a drunkard."

Rebecca, who had had a painful experience with Anthony, when he publicly accused her of neglect, consoled Dorothy that she, too, had been disappointed and hurt by her son, but it was something all mothers had to do and bear up against.

In December, Dorothy decided to get her financial house in order. Her taxable estate totaled $408,607.13. One-half of it would go to Michael, and the other half to his wife Bernadette Nansé. Her sister, Peggy, would net $2,500, as well as her jewelry, clothes, and furs. She would bequeath her books and papers to Syracuse University, but not the literary rights or the copyrights. She appointed Morgan Guaranty Trust Company as trustee, and one-half of her literary works to Michael, and the other half to her grandons, John-Paul and Gregory Lewis. Upon the death of Michael, she wrote in her will, the taxable estate would pass to John-Paul and Gregory—at twenty-one in quarterly payments, and then outright at twenty-five.

As a refuge from her constant fights with Michael, Dorothy sought consolation with her friend Tish Irwin, whose husband had died recently and who had been chosen at Michael's birth as his guardian. Realizing that she was no longer able to live alone, Dorothy agreed to spend the winter of 1960 with Tish in Washington, D.C., but as soon as she arrived, she fell ill and spent six weeks in bed. During her visit, Dorothy began to cough up blood. The doctors had been wrong; her heart refused to heal. She was sick, and she knew it, but she chose to brush aside thoughts of death as she prepared to spend Christmas with Benny and her grandsons in Portugal. Bernadette had gone to Lisbon, where her sister lived, with her two sons, hoping to reinvent her life.

Tish put Dorothy on the train back to White River Junction in Vermont, knowing that she was "a frail and sick old lady." Before Dorothy left for Europe, she had lunch with Dinah Sheean at the Cosmopolitan Club in New York City. Dinah would later say that she had been overcome by sadness to see someone who had been so majestic and vital looking crippled and emaciated—like a toothless corpse walking toward her grave.

The woman who had been touted as an "Amazon Queen" and a modern-day Joan of Arc, who had always felt "embarrassingly healthy," had been reduced to a pathetic skeleton. Her friends who saw her in New York found her "unrecognizable."

As Jimmy Sheean, Dinah, and Michael gathered at Idlewild Airport to send Dorothy off to Lisbon, she appeared weak and confused, seeming not to know who they were. But as they bade her farewell, Dorothy went forward, undaunted. She dived through the doorway to catch her flight.

CHAPTER 17

OBSESSION

Art is the bulwark. Art will stand against the
barbarians. Art gives us hope.

—REBECCA WEST

IBSTONE, BUCKINGHAMSIRE, 1951

Obsession for power was everywhere. Those who were victors in
war wanted more; those who were defeated wanted the illusion of victory; those who never had it vied for it; and some who had earned it were
suddenly stripped of it. But those who lusted after power weren't just
nations and their leaders; they were ordinary people who desperately
wanted to reclaim their lives. The cataclysm had passed; the tectonic
plates of power had shifted, and people craved "normalcy." Justice, however, seemed driven by retribution, while law and truth were often left to
scurry behind.

On pleasant mornings, Rebecca would rise early, cook herself some
breakfast, and eat it on the terrace overlooking the gardens and the forest
beyond. In front of her were black and white tiles that led to a stone stair-
case flanked by twin sphinxes, handpicked for her amusement. Both were
of seductive and rebellious women—dual aspects of femininity: narcissism and martyrdom—Madame Pompadour and Madame Du Barry.
The beauty of the plantings, woodlands, and busts served as a backdrop
for the contemplation of her inner landscape. By the turn of her head
from left to right, the entire aspect of femininity lay before her. Of late,
the unfortunate Du Barry, whose life had ended on the blade of the guil-
lotine, felt most kindred. Rebecca felt powerless.

As spring had turned to summer, Anthony had made it clear that he would not return home. He had rejected Kitty and Rebecca, and with them, England. Unable or unwilling to send money to his wife and children, leaving them with debts they could not repay, Anthony wittingly let them dangle on his blade, knowing his mother would catch them as they fell. To Rebecca, Anthony's leaving echoed her father's abandonment of her own family—stealthy, irrational, and irresponsible. And just as her father's desertion had never ceased happening, Anthony's departure kept turning in her head. What had she done to bring this about? Was it an act of retribution for some injustice she wrought? It was the Gordian knot she had to cut.

Rebecca didn't have obsessions—she was obsessive. She reviewed, analyzed, and dissected a problem, squeezing its innards till it no longer pained. Once it was eviscerated, she let it go. But, more often, her obsessions found new life in her work, opening doors to insights and helping her forge paths uniquely her own. She jokingly called it the Racgeist— a clever merging of Henry's pet name and her worldview.

For now, Anthony's absence plagued her. He became the reason for everything she couldn't accomplish, for every stricture that bound her. The time she wasted on filling out his tax forms; the money she spent in doing so; the need to write commercial pieces to support Kitty and the children, forcing her to choose journalism over art; the books she couldn't write or finish; the friends in America she couldn't visit. In short, Anthony was, she wrote to Doris Stevens, "a total loss, he has spoiled my work and my friendships, he is the worst thing that ever happened to me. And to have to feel that about one's own child is something that hurts unspeakably. . . . He is like some horrible dwarf in a fairy tale."

Overwhelmed by sadness and guilt, she asked herself why she hadn't inspired love in Anthony. She had given him so much when he was a child. All those years she had spent worrying about him and his schooling; encouraging his art; guarding his health; compensating for the indifference and neglect of H.G.; finding a physician to analyze his rage and placate his pain; accepting his need to marry, to father children, and even to live out the war years on a farm—all this had yielded nothing. Rebecca had done everything she could, and it hadn't been enough. Did the answer lie in a force beyond her control? Anthony was so much like H.G., gifted and restless, enervated by commitment, always searching for that someone who could make him whole. It had been going on for generations, as demonstrated by her own father, Wells's father—all these men of genius at war with themselves and the women around them. Perhaps it was a pattern so deeply ingrained, it was impossible to change. Perhaps, Rebecca thought, she was merely the casualty of a predetermined law.

Then there was Kitty. Anthony had been right; his mother would cushion Kitty's fall. At first, Rebecca mourned her son's desertion of his wife like a kindred spirit. A gifted painter, Kitty would have to sacrifice her career to Anthony's whim. But it didn't take long for Rebecca to realize that Kitty was not only impervious to assault, she was hopelessly unworldly and naïve. She seemed to harbor no resentment toward Anthony, thinking "it quite natural for him to leave her and the children on [Rebecca's] hands." Furthermore, Kitty knew nothing about money and was extravagant beyond her means. She sent the children to expensive boarding schools and sustained a lifestyle dependent on Rebecca and Henry's generosity. While Kitty was verbally effusive in her gratitude, she appeared insensitive and greedy. It was as if Kitty knew that she and her children were all Rebecca and Henry had left. They were pawns in her audacious chess game, and Kitty instinctively relished her power.

The children were indeed precious to Rebecca, and especially to Henry, who had none of his own. Caro, now ten years old, was beautiful—graceful and lithe like her mother. She loved music, and Rebecca was certain she would become a dancer. But there was something shallow and narcissistic about her, Rebecca believed. Caro radiated beauty but nothing more. Edmund, at eight, was different. He was keenly aware and curious; his fine mind made him an observant and adventurous companion. He was open to people and new experiences, responsive and affectionate. Rebecca craved the closeness of her grandchildren, but their mother knew nothing about fostering relationships. She had hated her own father as a child and now had little contact with her mother or her sisters. Instead of embracing the affection Rebecca and Henry offered to her and her children, Kitty seemed to recoil in fear, as if their love would make her vulnerable to their manipulation.

From Kitty's point of view, this was nothing new. In truth, she had never liked Rebecca or her conspicuous materialism. Furthermore, Rebecca had been far too intrusive in their marriage, telling them where and how to live, especially during the war. Rebecca had treated her and Anthony like children, as appendages of herself.

And yet, when Anthony had left Kitty for his eighteen-year-old female BBC colleague, and had threatened to evict her and the children from the farm, it had been Rebecca who had implored H.G. to leave Kitty money in his will, and who had tried to console her during their separation. And now as Rebecca was turning her life inside out to keep her daughter-in-law afloat, Kitty chose to bring up the children in isolation. Rebecca lamented that Caro and Edmund would have no generational continuity with family or friends. She had always sensed that there was something strange about Kitty, but now she could put her finger on it: She was stupid. She wrote to Doris Stevens that she was a woman "thirsty in her own desert"—a greedy and manipulative fool.

On the surface, Anthony was doing well in New York. He was writing reviews for *Time* and articles for *The New Yorker,* and was freelancing for other literary magazines, such as *Flair* and *The Spectator.* He had published an impressive first novel to respectable reviews and was editing another. Although Anthony had not told his mother that he had moved out of Dorothy's townhouse to an apartment in Connecticut, Rebecca knew where he was and what he intended to do, thanks to her secret network of friends. Or at least she thought she did. Dorothy had written to Rebecca that Anthony appeared to feel guilty about leaving the children but had confided in her that he had no intention of returning to Kitty. Harold Ross wrote that Anthony was visibly upset by the break with his family. Some of her friends said he was maturing; others said that he was lost. All claimed that he looked just like Rebecca and agreed that he was charming and talented.

In fact, Anthony was enraged at his mother. It was she, he believed, who was responsible for all his heartache and lack of success—as a writer, a biographer, a husband, and a father. It was her twisted sense of love and morality that had thwarted and blackened his every move. As he would later write, "The truth of how things were between my mother and myself was that from the time that I reached the age of puberty, and she came to the point of a final rupture with my father, she was minded to do me what hurt she could, and that she remained set in that determination as long as there was breath in her body to sustain her malice." Kitty, whom he saw as an emasculating taskmaster, was tossed on the pyre like a minor demon, easily sacrificed in his search for freedom. His guilt lay only with the children, the true victims of this play for power.

Few were privy to Anthony's feelings toward Rebecca, and if they

were, no one was willing to tell her. His apparent success in New York
brought her a sigh of maternal relief, along with a spasm of jealousy.
Rebecca was certain that her American friends preferred Anthony to her.
Seeming to believe in a Cain and Abel prototype of relationships, Rebecca felt that if Anthony was admired, she was out of favor. One simply
implied the other. Obsessed by a desire for affirmation and loyalty, as if
anticipating Anthony's accusations, she wrote letters to her American
friends in her own defense. Offering a litany of his possible slurs on her
character, she wrote that Anthony's antipathy toward her was neurotic.
She was wont to add that, despite all this, "He is brilliant and writes like
an angel."

In the wake of Anthony's exodus to America, Rebecca wrote an essay
called "Goodness Doesn't Just Happen." When she was young, she
wrote, she was rebellious, but she always believed that people were good
and human nature was perfectible. Rebecca now realized that love and
law must prevail in order to preserve goodness in society. She believed
that there was a God but that she could not relate to him through established religion. "I hope I am working a way toward truth in my writing.
I also know that I must orientate my writing towards God for it to have
any value." Rebecca instinctively knew that she lacked the tools, the
mind-set, to foster relationships with her family, even if she didn't know
why. She had to work hard in the only way she could—through her
writing—if she was to transcend the vicissitudes of daily life. Her understanding that St. Augustine believed there was a God, had taught her that
the "higher law" toward which she strove must be divine. But Rebecca's
God remained an abstraction—a force not grounded in Church doctrine. And yet it was a God for whose salvation she hungered.

Secretly, or at least, unknown to anyone but Henry, her hunger for
divine consolation had overtaken her. In the wake of Anthony's leaving
and Kitty's subsequent emotional and financial demands, Rebecca had
experienced mysterious signs—ominous visions—during her visit to
France in the summer of 1950. At Amiens Cathedral in France, Rebecca
had prayed to a statue of Christ carved in gold into a tree trunk. It was
"most impersonal, most personal," she wrote to her English friends at
Yale, Margaret and Evelyn Hutchinson. She prayed that Christ do
"something to make her life more livable." In the aftermath of a dream
and a vision that had propelled her into a new realm of being, she met a

Franciscan monk in the street in front of their hotel who remarked that she looked as though she needed help and should become a Catholic. She told him of her devotion to the Orthodox Church, originating with her admiration for the Slavs, and he answered, "But I am a Slav and I am content to be in the Catholic Church, it is a Universal Church, it is where you ought to be." Rebecca said, "Do not forget me." He told her he would pray for her.

Despite Rebecca's outright contempt for her sister Lettie's devotion to Catholicism, her horror at Anthony's threat to convert while at St. Piran's, and her long-held belief that the suffering and atonement of Christ was nothing more than a primitive human delusion, she told Margaret and Evelyn that she was preparing for conversion.

In less than eighteen months, however, Rebecca had a change of heart. Although she had found herself in the midst of intolerable misery, feeling like "the victim of a poltergeist of bad luck," Rebecca nonetheless had decided that she could not become a Catholic. She wrote to the Hutchinsons: "Though I am sure there is the right magical process of art in ritual and worship, for me to become a Catholic means a constant and degrading contact with priests who are homosexuals sublimating their troubles in intellectual pretensions which produces something worse than homosexuality."

Neither magic nor the consolation of ritual would suffice, it seemed, to transcend her distaste for homosexuality and intellectual posturing. Perhaps the thought of subjugating her beliefs to Catholic doctrine scared her away.

By early December 1951, Rebecca's losses had multiplied. Harold Ross was dead of lung cancer. Rebecca had known that he was ill with pleurisy, but hadn't been informed that his disease was life threatening. Ross's successor and friend William Shawn told her that he had withheld the details of Ross's debilitation "because right to the end [she] meant so very much to [him.]" It was another terrible void in her life—"a preoccupying misery."

Ross had edited her work with his head and his heart, and had been a kind, generous, and inspiring mentor, much like Alex Woollcott. His death was another instance of people—men—who had abandoned her without warning. "Why the hell did I not hop a boat to go to New York when I heard from Ross that he would have liked to see me? Why, come to that, am I not in New York doing the dramatic critical job that the *New York Herald Tribune* offered me?" she wrote to Doris Stevens. The answer was simple and always the same: "Because of Anthony."

When Kitty and the children visited Anthony in Connecticut in July 1951, he made it clear for the second time that he no longer loved her and he wanted a divorce. His sprawling seven-room apartment, littered with feminine furnishings, had left Kitty wondering if he was living with someone. Later that fall, Dorothy wrote to Rebecca that she had met Anthony by chance, and he had announced his intention to marry Lily Emmet, a nineteen-year-old student at Radcliffe with a New England pedigree and Irish ancestry. Like Kitty, Lily had a hostile relationship with her parents, but unlike Kitty, she was warm and understanding. Raised by a nanny, Lily knew what it meant to grow up deprived of parental warmth. Rebecca learned from Kitty that Anthony's plan was to get an American divorce, thereby freeing him from responsibility, while keeping Kitty tethered to a dead marriage in Britain.

At Kitty's request, Rebecca helped her to assemble the documents necessary to apply for a divorce. Kitty's intent was at once selfless and calculated: to protect Anthony from prosecution in America, where he might be accused of bigamy, and to open the door to the possibility of a future marriage for herself in Britain.

The following May, Rebecca accompanied Kitty to the divorce proceedings in London. The judge was sickened by Anthony's letters, which he read aloud in court. He denied Anthony access to the children without Kitty's presence and consent. Afterward, Rebecca took Kitty to lunch and bought her a new sweater and a jumper. Anthony's marriage to Kitty had ended as it had begun—through rebellion against female control. Feeling tossed out, and sick at heart, Rebecca returned home to Henry.

In April 1953, Dorothy wrote to Rebecca:

I went to the cocktail party and there were Anthony and his bride right back by motor from their wedding, and looking like anything but a wedding party—the gal in a sports dress and Anthony in a pink shirt—rather breathless and saying they had just decided that morning to be married that day. Anyhow they avoided the chi-chi. She is very young without looking very young, very tall—taller than

Anthony—handsome in a way with, I thought, a rather coarse mouth and something of a smoldering look. I do hope they won't smolder each other to suffocation. I know so few of the younger set that I really know little at all about her, except that hers is a "good" family, by which I mean in or on the periphery of the social registry.

After learning the news, Rebecca would write, "Anthony's in love with a girl of nineteen, of whom I think with pity every time he comes to mind." She thought, however, that the marriage might have a chance, if they were not to have children. He was a good father as far as it went, she would say, but he clearly lacked the tenacity to carry it through.

Henry, Rebecca, and her beloved dog Albert
on the terrace at Ibstone, circa 1950s

But Ibstone, she wrote to her sister Winnie, was giving her the "psychological horrors." It wasn't that the house was expensive to run, but the problem was hiring competent help. There were the gardeners who required constant supervision, of which Henry was incapable.

In April 1953, Rebecca escaped to Paris alone. She wrote to Charles Curran that she had left Ibstone because two of their secretaries had gone "mad" on them, and Henry either wasn't aware of it or was unable to admit it. She described her relationship with her husband as exasperating.

I wish I could stay here for good, though I miss Henry very much. I like him as a companion, but the impossibility of living an orderly life with him is driving me nuts. . . . I realize that I have spent quite a lot of time . . . keeping Henry from doing things that would have led him to jail or to bankruptcy court. . . . I sit here in Paris and feel that I have got damned little out of life and have been monstrously prevented from using my gifts.

By the spring of 1953, Rebecca's relationship with Henry had further deteriorated. She could no longer trust him. His incompetence and lack of sexual restraint with other women had proved incorrigible. Later she would write that it was his infidelity that had weakened her faith in God. "For many years I never realized that though he was not sleeping with me he was sleeping with every other woman who would listen to him. But for me it was a choice between believing in him or believing in nothing."

Rebecca was sixty years old. It was a time of reckoning. There were losses she could not reconcile—Anthony, her grandchildren, and a husband who defied understanding. Henry had become, like Anthony, a drain on her time and creative energy. She was too old to begin again, and too young to throw in the towel. Did she dare to confront him? She risked losing everything. Now, at least, she had the semblance of a proper marriage and home. Realizing, once again, that her only hope was her work, she sought to complete the first part of her ambitious trilogy—a series of semiautobiographical novels that would begin with her childhood and move through the war years.

The first volume, entitled *The Fountain Overflows,* was an attempt to mine her past in search of the woman she had become. Her intent was the same as Dorothy's in *The Courage to Be Happy,* but in fictional form. In the hopes of raising her personal story, as she did her journalism, to the level of art, Rebecca would portray her family as a microcosm reflecting the social and political landscape of Edwardian Britain. Her trilogy would be soaked in the betrayal of her father—a sensitive and loving man and a gifted writer, yet deeply flawed. Rebecca was determined to dissect and delineate the effects of her father's abandonment on her mother, herself, and her sisters. She sought to come to terms with his loss, and to deduce insights into human nature both universal and transcendent.

Every failure and assault, personal and political, past and present, that Rebecca endured crescendoed into overwhelming resentment that alternately stymied and fired her imagination. The powerful feelings she confided in her letters and diaries would become the soil out of which her fiction and nonfiction would grow, and *The Fountain Overflows* is no exception. Her fictional family is a violent battlefield on which each member stakes his ground and establishes his identity.

Clare Aubrey, the narrator's mother, becomes the mouthpiece of disillusionment. She represents the paltry attempts of men and women, lovers, siblings, and friends to translate abstract feelings into true acts of kindness: "This is the worst of life, that love does not give us common sense but is a sure way of losing it. We love people, and we say that we are going to do more for them than friendship, but it makes such fools of us that we do far less, indeed sometimes what we do could be mistaken for the work of hatred."

Presented through the lens of the daughter Rose, a surrogate for Rebecca and perhaps all young women who struggle to find their own identity, the rituals of family life and the vicissitudes of events and fortune are portrayed as both unique and universal, no less true for their subjectivity. As the novel moves toward conclusion, Rebecca, through Rose, confirms her vision of humanity as a plaything of cosmic, historical, and social forces. Rose, she writes, cannot extricate herself from its thrust; she is "swept on by a strong flood of which [she is] a part," exonerating Rose, and thereby Rebecca, of personal responsibility.

Absorbed in her work, consumed with dissecting the treachery of her childhood, Rebecca had little patience for her husband.

Throughout most of April 1953, Rebecca's letters to Henry from Paris were matter-of-fact—a diary of events and visits. But only days before she returned to England, she threw him a bombshell, echoing her words to Charles Curran: "It seems to me often that you like to provoke me into having to make violent protests against what you do, by proposing to do things which are obviously absurd. But in any case, I simply cannot stand this violent and disorderly life we seem to have been forced to live, I cannot bear it."

There is no record of the conversation that ensued upon her return. But the day after she arrived home, Rebecca wrote a letter to Dorothy complaining about managing the affairs of Ibstone, which primarily fell on her shoulders. She concluded, "Still I love Henry, which is something and something again." For the moment it appeared that Rebecca had chosen reconciliation.

In the same letter, she mentioned that she had met French philosopher Raymond Aron, "an ugly little Jew," yet the "most brilliant man now living." He believed, she wrote, that the United States would continue to have trouble with McCarthy and his interrogations of suspected Communists. Rebecca had written four articles on the investigations, herself, but she said that left-wing publications such as the *New Statesman* had told so many lies to the public that Britons were convinced the rule of law in the States had been totally suspended.

Rebecca's articles were published in the London *Sunday Times* and reprinted in *U.S. News and World Report* in May 1953. The buildup of Soviet power had been among her deepest concerns since the end of World War II. Disillusioned by the will of Britain or America to stand up to Stalin, Rebecca, like Dorothy, was obsessed with the idea of a Soviet Communist takeover from within. McCarthy's interests appeared parallel to her own.

Senator Joe McCarthy of Wisconsin, she wrote, was just a typical politician, trying to gain status within the Republican Party. His personality was such that he had evoked the fear of many who had been involved in the underground American Communist movement. She asserted that he and the House Un-American Activities Committee were doing their country a service because during Roosevelt's terms in office, the movement had been swept under the rug, for the sake of Russia's involvement in the war. McCarthy was, she insisted, not a dictator. He had no power. But the threat of Communist infiltration was real.

Rebecca evoked the ire of the liberal historian Arthur Schlesinger, who, along with many Democrats, admired Roosevelt and the New Deal, opposed unregulated capitalism, and agreed with the radical left-wing candidate for president in 1948, Henry Wallace, that the United States should seek coexistence with the Soviet Union. Labeled a "Harvard Communist," Schlesinger sought to separate the Democratic Party from the Far Left, which was truly engaged with Soviet agents, eschewing Rebecca's claim that he was using the party as a vehicle for propagation.

Rebecca wrote to Dorothy that she had been infuriated when she received a letter from "a creature called Arthur M. Schlesinger, Jr., whom I know only as a mediocre historian with a lamentable prose style. This letter was a vomit of insults. Apparently the creature cannot read, and he accused me of having written a defense of McCarthy on lines of which there is no trace in my article."

Rebecca would write Schlesinger a long and contemptuous letter in defense of her point of view, which resulted in a public feud, ultimately reconciled with the help of their mutual friend John Gunther.

Much like Dorothy, Rebecca felt betrayed and misunderstood by American intellectuals and the press. Her political ostracism only compounded her sense of personal failure and despair. In a letter to Doris Stevens she confided her sadness and her feeling that Ibstone was the epicenter of it all. Like Dorothy, Rebecca felt that her home had become a reminder of aspirations unfulfilled. Ibstone held too many bad memories for her and often its beautiful setting seemed a mockery.

Rebecca believed, but could not prove, that Anthony, who had flirted with Communism in his youth, was wrapped up in a Communist conspiracy to bring her down. Increasingly paranoid, she was certain that Communists were stalking her. "May all our enemies fry in hell," she wrote to Doris.

Unaware of Rebecca's contempt or suspicion, Kitty continued to write friendly letters. Their relationship was an emotional chess game, but it is difficult to discern who was in control. Was Kitty still on Anthony's side? Was Anthony masterminding her moves? During one of Kitty's ritual summer visits to Anthony in Stonington, Connecticut, she wrote that the comments she had heard about her McCarthy articles were mostly positive. She continued:

> *The children had a heavenly time. Lily is really an extremely nice girl though untidy to a degree almost incredible. As she is practically their age + gave her entire time to entertaining them, you can imagine how nice it was for them. Imagine a big sister who never scolds one but drives one to pools + beaches + riding schools in an enormous Packard whenever Daddy is too busy + produces lovely presents + teaches one to play the recorder + is never too busy sweeping or washing up to have time to play chess or "Monopoly" or whatever one feels like.*

Rebecca found it strange that Kitty liked Lily. But then, Kitty was surprised by her own feelings, too. Ultimately, Lily would prove to be less a threat than an asset. Anthony had found the way back to his children through Lily's youth and temperament. It was a victory no one could have predicted, least of all Rebecca, but perhaps it was also a testimony to Kitty's desire to hang on to Anthony on any terms he demanded. As Rebecca had predicted, she was proving to be the frightful specter of Jane.

Upon Rebecca's return to Ibstone from Paris, her relationship with Henry seemed to move from intolerable to nonsensical. His behavior followed no pattern she could discern, and he appeared more and more out of sync with reality. In November, she wrote to Charles Curran, her confidant in all things male and marital, relaying an account of a recent conversation with Henry. If things grew more complicated and difficult later, she wanted Charles to know the background:

> *He said something that suddenly made me conscious that he was very unhappy. He has always had a feeling that there isn't enough room for him in any house where we have lived. . . . It appears that he had a terrible grievance against me because I have not prepared the library for him. This is a huge room on the other side of the house. It all came out: he has resented it for years that I would do nothing to clear a lot of furniture out of it.*

She had told him that he was capable of doing it himself, she said.

> *[He had] not a touch of gratitude for what I do for him, which seems to me not inconsiderable. My first instinct was, of course, simply to walk out on him. . . . But I can't leave him. . . . I am really fond of him, and want to protect him; though I was quite aghast at the cold selfishness he showed. I always have put him before my work, and I didn't ever fail him. . . . He really regarded me with something like hatred. I had a queer feeling that he had turned the corner that something I had dreaded from about three years after I had married had at last happened. I shouldn't be surprised if he gave me a bad time, and if after a year or two he slung me out.*

The "something" she intuited was Henry's feeling, valid or not, that he had been "unmanned." Had his sense of emasculation preceded their marriage? Or had her dedication to her work and her constant criticism made him feel neglected and inferior? The fact that he had a penchant for barmaids and dancers spoke to his feelings of inadequacy. The origins of his impulses are difficult to know, but what is certain is that Rebecca had contempt for those less intelligent and capable than her, and the renovation of the library never came to pass. It was another grievance buried beneath the surface of marital propriety, and another instance in which Rebecca had unwittingly sacrificed someone she loved to her obsession for work. Whatever neurosis Henry had brought to their marriage, the fact is that she had never put his needs or anyone else's first. From this point on, except on rare occasions, Rebecca and Henry would each travel alone. They seemed never to be in the same country at the same time.

Rebecca wrote to Charles Curran, "I feel I am in some extraordinary zoo, circus, freak-show of a destiny, can't get clear." The idea of divine manipulation, the puppet show metaphor she conceived in the 1920s during her relationship with H.G., seemed to reemerge in moments of psychic confusion, along with a heightening of paranoia.

That paranoia had begun to spread to her reputation as a journalist. She complained to Doris that she hadn't received any writing assignments from newspapers since the publication of her articles about Communism in March. Her income had been nil. She had been forced to dip into her savings in order to help Kitty, and would soon become totally dependent on Henry's money. If anything happened to that money, they would be penniless. She had recently been given an assignment from the *Daily Telegraph*, but otherwise nothing. "Furthermore, the people in the *Sunday Times* who loathed my articles have been spreading the story that I am insane, asylum insane, and am not safe to employ or know." While her inquiries to the editors of the *Telegraph* and the *Times* would later dispel these fears, the idea that there was a conspiracy to thwart and punish her continued to haunt her. She believed that even her sisters were in on it.

For several weeks in November, Winnie had "invaded" her home. Transported by ambulance, she was in a state of exhaustion from gastric flu and near death; she had not eaten anything, was sixty-six years old, and had high blood pressure. Rebecca was certain, however, that Winnie was hysterically faking an illness. She wrote to Doris:

She lay and gave a marvelous imitation of an octogenarian who had had a stroke—on complicated motives of jealousy. She resented my career as a writer; she resented it on her own account and on account of her witless Communist daughter. For three solid weeks she kept me running up and downstairs, and we had a nurse and my sister's husband living here, which made a household far beyond the powers of my staff, which is old and considerably iller than my sister. . . . But I wonder if anyone ever had such devastating personal relations as mine. I have always been devoted to this sister, and her hostility to me—The nurse said, "You're the cause of this illness—your sister wants attention, she feels you've always had it, and she loves upsetting your work and your household," and that was that—was a blow to me. My other doctor sister was as useless as she has always been. . . .

All my life, so far as I can remember, I have had a terrible time largely owing to people's determination to punish me for having such a wonderful time.

In a letter that followed, Rebecca would write that Winnie had decided that she had cancer of the stomach and wouldn't be dissuaded. "I can hardly bear this, for it is all so unlike her. She was the love of my life and she might as well be dead for all the resemblance she bears to her delightful self."

Rebecca needed to get away from Ibstone if she was to get on with her work. In December 1953, stymied on her way to completing *Cousin Rosamund,* she decided to turn her attention toward finishing a collection of essays covering the Nuremberg trials and the lynching trial in Greenville, South Carolina. Once again, she wrote to Dorothy that she "hunger[ed] and thirst[ed] for America." But come the spring of 1954, Rebecca would settle for Paris. She went to France for a month to work on her trilogy and *A Train of Powder.* The betrayal of trust, personal and societal, documented in the lattter was to Rebecca's mind tantamount to murder.

As soon as she returned to England in the fall, her sisters were clawing at her again. She wrote to Doris that Winnie

is now half-lunatic, and wholly devoured by jealousy and hatred of me. I dare not go see her. She falls into a state of hysterical collapse at

*the sight of me. The other is such a monster of selfishness and cruelty
that I weep with fear when I have to go and see her. She has now retired
from her medical job, and is devoting herself to the task of becoming
a great writer who will outshine me, with such childish candor and
avowed malice that I feel not only sorrow but shame. I am terribly
lonely. I have put too much into my marriage, I have sacrificed my
friends, and as you know there was a barrier between me and friendship, people have always had an odd fear and suspicion of me, to my
husband, and Henry is old before his time. But worse than loneliness
is the lack of pleasant memories I have.*

Lonely, haunted by her past, and unable to cope with the present, she
found her only hope lay in escape, or at least in the illusion of it.

In October 1954, Rebecca wrote to Dorothy that she was coming to
New York during the second week of December, and asked if it would be
possible to spend two weeks sleeping in "Mike's old room." She had been
asked "to do a stint for *Ladies' Home Journal.*" In a rare gesture of family
holiday togetherness, she noted that Henry would join her later, and they
would move to a hotel. They would spend Christmas and New Year's in
America, and then head back to England toward the end of January.

The word leaked to Anthony that his mother would be coming to
town, possibly through their mutual friend John Gunther. Perhaps in
an effort to assuage his anger, Anthony wrote Rebecca a letter in early
December.

In a tone both affectionate and sincere, Anthony apologized for not
writing sooner, but explained that he had been sick with pneumonia in
November and that he and Lily had had to move into a new house, which
they were working hard to renovate. It was difficult to describe his life,
he continued. "Lily comes from a large family part Bostonian and part
Newport. The Bostonians are cousins of the Henry James family, anyway they're all very literate and very anglophile. . . . All nice and admirable people." He seemed intent on impressing his mother with Lily's
pedigree and implying that he had married into a family of wealth. He
continued:

*John Gunther and [his wife] Jane are great friends. . . . We go to New
York two days a week to do my editing for Harpers, then back here to*

work. We have a tiny cottage in the middle of the woods, 12 miles from
the sea, no other houses in sight and the nearest shop eight miles away.
Deer come up to the house in hard weather and it's all very pleasant
and beautiful. I hope you'll come and stay with us here soon. I'm sure
you'll like Lily and the way we live. I heard a rumor that you might be
here, at Christmas or soon after, I wish it were true.

Yours always, Anthony

Rebecca did not know that she and Anthony were moving on a parallel course. He, too, was mining his past to find his identity. He had begun to write a fictional account of his childhood with the purpose of coming to terms with his relations with his mother and father. It was something that he was compelled to do in order to survive, Lily would later say.

Rebecca did not visit them at their home, but in August 1955, Anthony and Lily came to England. Though they were staying with Kitty and the children, who now lived in Dorset, they drove three hours northeast to visit Rebecca and Henry at Ibstone. During the long drive, Lily asked Anthony if was going to tell his mother about his new book, urging him to do so. He didn't answer. Upon arriving, Lily's impression of Ibstone, no doubt colored by Anthony's and Kitty's descriptions, was of ostentatious wealth. Henry and Rebecca seemed to enjoy their roles as "Lord and Lady of the Manor," she said, and exuded an air of moneyed aristocracy. Lily's impressions would contradict those of Rebecca's relatives who knew the house intimately. Her nephew Norman Macleod would later say that the house was "comfortable but far from lavish. It is hard to believe that anyone coming there would see it as over-the-top opulent or anything like that." It is possible, however, that Rebecca and Henry put on a show sufficiently credible to the inexperienced twenty-two-year-old wife of their renegade son.

But the pretense cut two ways. Choosing to avoid confrontation, Anthony, when asked by his mother about his latest work, portrayed it as a "light novel," brushing it off with nonchalance. Either his visit to Ibstone was a Machiavellian attempt to soften the blow of the book's family revelations or a true desire for rapprochement in the aftermath of his emotional and literary catharsis. In any case, Rebecca would experience their visit as an affectionate reunion, during which she and Henry warmly welcomed Lily into the fold. Encouraged by the success of the visit, Rebecca and Henry reciprocated by driving down to Dorset. To their joy, it seemed as if the family bonds were not only repaired but also renewed. Before Anthony and Lily left England for America, Rebecca and Henry invited them to dinner at the Ritz and gave them a belated wedding gift of £200, or $6,500 in today's currency. It was a lavish gift by anyone's standards and symbolic of the magnitude of their happiness.

August and September seemed to slide by as Rebecca worked on the second volume of her trilogy and *A Train of Powder* in tandem, while preparing a spring lecture series at Yale. At the end of September 1954, she and Henry boarded a train to Leicester, in the East Midlands, to visit her nephew Norman Macleod, now a doctor of philosophy in chemical engineering, who was teaching at the university there. As their visit came to an end, Rebecca grew despondent. She had received a devastating phone call.

Most likely, it was Charles Curran who had told her that Anthony had published a novel about a man's struggle for self-definition as the bastard son of a famous actress and a writer who had denied their parentage. Clothed in fiction, the book explored the role that each of Anthony's parents had played in determining the course and vision of his life. Objective truth played no part in its intent or effect, and Rebecca viewed the roman à clef as a malicious assault on her character and integrity.

As Norman stood on the station platform with Rebecca and Henry awaiting their train home to Ibstone, his aunt appeared in shock. "She could hardly talk," he later said. Referring to Anthony, she would subsequently write in her memoir that "inflicting pain, it is the only real happiness he knows."

Anthony's book *Heritage* belongs to the genre of "a young man's journey toward moral consciousness," akin to Salinger's *The Catcher in the Rye,* the publication of which preceded his book by four years. Like Salinger's, Anthony's book examines the inherent corruption of human nature from an adolescent perspective and observes its impact on relationships and social institutions. But transported in time and place to Edwardian England after the First World War, in the midst of great social upheaval, and infused with the fluidity of European culture, its complexities heighten and intensify. *Heritage* is Salinger meets George Bernard Shaw meets Rebecca West. Like Shaw, the narrator grasps the animal "life force" that transcends human will, and the seductive schemes of men and women to fulfill it. He understands, as well, the behavioral and lingual signs of "class" and sees the rapidly changing social complexion in the aftermath of the Industrial Revolution and the Great War. Like Rebecca, the narrator articulates his romantic sensibility in his descriptions of natural, human, and architectural beauty, both rural and urban, and his awareness of the subtleties of facial expression and physical demeanor that reveal character and breeding. Much like his mother's, Anthony's prose is lyrical, his ear for dialogue acute, and his longings both sensual and transcendent. He unabashedly craves fulfillment of his animal drives, delights in the pleasures of food and sex, and yet yearns for insight into the human condition that would set him free to live an autonomous, purposeful life.

There is, however, a story within his story intended to damn Rebecca's reputation. Anthony's choice of the name Richard Savage as his fictional surrogate and protagonist exposes an undercurrent of hostility that was well known to the British reading public. A brilliant eighteenth-century English poet, Savage had claimed to be the bastard son of landed aristocrats reared by a succession of poor foster parents. Obsessed with proving his noble birth, Savage publicly exposed his mother as an adulterous liar who had cheated him of his birthright and inheritance. He was unable to unearth sufficient documentation, however, and succeeded only in evoking the ire of his alleged mother, who used the platform of her social station to persecute and destroy him. Although, as Anthony would later say, employing the name of Richard Savage was "like taking up a bludgeon to do what a stiletto would have done more neatly," the violent stroke of his pen left no doubt of his aim.

Anthony portrays his mother-surrogate Naomi Savage, a gifted actress, as the shifting face of cosmic evil, and idealizes his father-surrogate, Max Town, an eminent author, as the rational, honest, and loving victim of viciously scheming women. In essence, Naomi becomes a force of "creative destruction" that reveals the true nature of each character and frees them all from delusion and dependency.

With time, Naomi's persona cracks, and she starts to become more approachable, protective, and giving. Richard senses her sincere desire to give him the stable rooted existence she had never provided. Yet, abruptly, his mother leaves her new husband, Colonel Arthur (a stand-in for Henry), the lord of a vast country estate, without warning. When

Richard returns from an abortive and yet instructional holiday with his father in London, he finds the colonel alone and bereft. In a scene that redefines Richard as a mature independent man, he explains to the colonel that his mother is bigger than any role anyone could provide. She must constantly explore aspects of herself in order to feel fully alive. It is a moment of reconciliation, and perhaps forgiveness, as he realizes that her leaving has liberated him to find his way.

The book was an extraordinary accomplishment, and one that Anthony could not have written if he had still been married to Kitty. Lily's unconditional love and understanding implicitly gave him permission to plumb the intricacies of his emotions and bring them to resolution, at least on paper. Unfortunately, the book would set into motion a venomous war of wills and words that would deny both Anthony and his mother any possibility of escape.

With the publication of *Heritage,* Anthony made it clear to Rebecca that she could no longer evade her responsibility for his pain. The tragedy is that she might have stopped the emotional devastation the novel wrought with simple honesty. There is evidence in her earlier letters to her friends and family that she understood the unintentional consequences of her son's birth, the effect of her poverty, ambition, and marriage, and his many illnesses, on Anthony's emotional life. She might have acknowledged what she had often told others: She had done her best within the personal and financial constraints she had. She didn't. She countered his "lies" with a set of her own. Frozen in time, Anthony's perceptions were those of a child, paralyzed by the emotional damage inflicted by his parents. Objective reality aside, Anthony's bizarre portrayal of his mother was testimony to the distorted image she communicated to her son, intentionally or not.

Implicit in his message was that no matter how emotionally crippled Rebecca was, it was her moral obligation to assume responsibility for her actions. Ultimately it came down to her psychic integrity or his, and her decision was all too evident. Again and again Rebecca chose self-delusion and hatred, surrounding herself only with those who would justify her stance.

Dorothy had tried to keep Rebecca honest; she was characteristically willing to sacrifice friendship for what she deemed to be true. In response to a letter in which Rebecca called *Heritage* Anthony's "latest performance" and "the end of a main strand in my life," Dorothy replied that a son may have "ambivalent feelings about his mother, but a mother would do herself incalculable harm if she hated her son." She must learn to "humor and forgive" Anthony. And later, "Stop having fits, and stop being wounded in your respectability. You are not, you never have been, and you never will be 'respectable.'" Dorothy saw Anthony's depiction of Naomi Savage as a gifted woman whose motherhood and role as a "squire's lady" had not squelched her desire to live out her destiny as a great artist. Feeling betrayed, Rebecca responded in another letter that when Michael had been in trouble in London, Dorothy's feelings had been dramatically different. It was a battle that Dorothy knew she could not win.

Rebecca wanted to set the record of her relationship with Anthony straight, but a public denunciation was out of the question—that would only bring attention and legitimacy to the book. Instead, she attacked Anthony through correspondence, writing to anyone who might be sympathetic.

To Charles Curran, she wrote: "I could not feel more astonished and horrified if he had in fact raped some children. This is something fundamental, something related to ties of the flesh that you can't argue out of existence. It is as if I told you that because my eldest sister Letitia was hideously cruel to me as a child I was poisoning her slowly with arsenic."

The analogy was telling, revealing both the depth of her hatred toward her sister, never before expressed, and categorizing both Lettie and Anthony as existential threats. In short, she acted as though Anthony had murdered her.

Anthony was, in turn, pulling out all the stops. He made desperate attempts to have the book published in Britain. Rebecca received requests from an agent at Warburg offering to leave out selected passages if she wrote a preface to the book. She wrote to Dorothy that "It must be the lot of few mothers to be blackmailed by their sons. I sent a message that if the publisher published I would sue, and I have heard no more."

She told Charles Curran that she never wanted to see Anthony again. "I would not know what to do if I met him."

Winnie did her best to console and advise Rebecca, despite her illness and depression: "Life is a piteous mist of error, & death or dreadful storm of terror. . . . I hope & pray & believe this storm will pass—I am very far from minimizing the dangers. . . . I tell you this, because there is a great need for calm—don't say one unnecessary word or do an unnecessary thing."

Hoping to prevent an irreparable break, Lily, too, would write Rebecca a letter. While she would exonerate herself from moral responsibility by claiming it was none of her business, she wanted to assure Rebecca, "in case you have any doubt, that Anthony was not, while writing *Heritage,* and is not, motivated by feelings of animosity towards you. The book grew to be what it is as much by accident as by design, and I know that Anthony loves and respects you deeply. . . . He always spoke of you as a magnificent, passionate, gifted creature, whom he felt privileged to have as a parent." She offered their hands in friendship, and invited Rebecca to their home in Connecticut.

Rebecca would later remark that the letter made her vomit.

Doris was the most supportive of her friends, and received Rebecca's gratitude and love in return. Doris denounced Anthony's book as an aesthetic failure that defeated its own purpose. "Be comforted, dearest. Those who know and love you know what a fine generous person you are. . . . Maybe your darling monster will be one, too, some day!"

To Dorothy and Rebecca's shock, however, Emanie, an officer of the New York chapter of PEN, had invited Anthony to be the guest of honor at one of their meetings. Pamela Frankau wrote to Rebecca in good faith: "The boy [Richard Savage] isn't in the least like the Anthony I know. Naomi is, to me, an attractive, exasperating, sympathetic creation. But not, to me, Rebecca; maybe a third cousin, if that. I knew H.G. only slightly. Max Town doesn't remind me even of the little I knew." Upon reading the letter, Rebecca would remark to Charles Curran that Pamela was "a moral imbecile."

Dorothy, trying to make up for her alienating letter to Rebecca, wrote to her in February 1956, demanding her forgiveness and offering an account of the book's reviews:

I received your letter in the south, where I was speaking, not vacationing. But if mine to you was "rude and silly"—which I am capable of being at times, though unwittingly my feelings were simply because Naomi did not remind me of you at all. . . . [Yet] Max Town was completely recognizable as Wells. But never say you won't speak to me again, because I won't let you not. I am absolutely devoted to you, not because you are superb writer (though it helps) but because of a few unique kindnesses, in one of my worst moments with Michael.

Subsequently forgiven for her transgression, Dorothy was the first to link the book to a political motive. Rebecca concurred. She was convinced that Anthony had not written the book alone, discerning differences in style in various sections that documented her belief he was part of a Communist plot to destroy her. Furthermore, Rebecca wrote, Anthony had recruited Beaverbrook to plead the case for its publication in Britain. "Anthony had poisoned his mind against me." She concluded that "the aim of the persons who stirred all this up was not to get the book published but to give a jerk on the noose round my neck. . . . Somebody's after me, sister, and I know quite well as you do who it is likely to be." Reconciled by a case of twin paranoia, the two women slipped back into bonds of affection.

While her private affairs were beyond her control, Rebecca fought to polish her public persona. Henry called upon one of his undergraduate friends, London journalist Beverly Nichols, to attend and report on the celebration of their twenty-fifth wedding anniversary in the Dorchester Hotel on Park Lane, in the heart of fashionable Mayfair. Appearing in the January 19, 1956, issue of *My World*, Nichols's account said, "'This,' I thought, 'is civilization,'" touting the lavish display of flowers, food, and wine:

It is time that you met our hostess. The name by which she is known throughout the English speaking world is Rebecca West, and if there are any living women of keener intelligence or of more passionate integrity, they have not made themselves known to me. . . . She looked radiant, in an enchanting dress that billowed out in pale silky tones. Henry combines the exquisite manners of one's ideal Oxford don with an almost frightening comprehension of European economics. Moreover, he has a wit that is like a very subtle dry wine; it stimulates but it does not shock. . . . The guests, of course, were shared, but it was Henry who made the little after dinner speech which made each feel that he, or she, was the guest of honor.

Rebecca and Henry were portrayed as the quintessence of gentility, elegance, and sensitivity, and their marriage a model of perfection. Their complementary gifts and styles coalesced to enhance and enrich the lives of their family and friends.

And perhaps it was an amazing stroke of luck when the January 1956 issue of *Good Housekeeping* published an interview with Rebecca that had been conducted by one of its contributors, Nancy Spain, in the summer of 1955, before Anthony's book was published. Or was it the product of a well-timed phone call from her agent to the editor?

"Hatred is sterile, love is fruitful," said Rebecca, many years ago. But what a remarkable woman it is, who can so live out her epigrams. . . . No wonder they say that Rebecca West is the greatest reporter in the world. . . .

Rebecca is smallish and coy, with a great sense of humor, a great gift of the gab and an honest love of a good girl's gossip. Her mind may be full of matters of political significance at breakfast-time, but by dinner she will certainly be wondering what she has to wear, and whether she needs a new hair-do. When she walks in the garden she will talk to you on five subjects at once: two profound and three trivial. . . . When she laughs, she will throw herself against the sundial to laugh. And then the tears run down her cheeks. (And how many women do you know who really laugh?)

The article depicts Rebecca as a brilliant but humble, intellectually facile yet feminine, down-to-earth woman exquisitely sensitive to natural beauty. With all these qualities, along with a sense of humor both sincere and infectious, she appears the paragon of womanhood.

Massaging her image was one thing, but deflecting the impact of the book's emotional devastation on her health was another. In her unpublished memoir, she would write:

In that year I went into University College Hospital to have my gallbladder out, and a few days later got pancreatitis, not of the harmless kind that occasionally follows that particular operation, but the kind which often kills. I was so *savaged* by it that it was six or seven weeks before I was discharged from hospital. I was not in a fit state for this ordeal. The witch-hunt Anthony had started up with his book, *Heritage,* was still in full cry.

Scheduled to present a series of literary discussions as the Terry lecturer at Yale in the spring of 1956, Rebecca feared that her presence would damage the reputation of the university. She cabled her friend Evelyn Hutchinson that she would understand if Yale were to cancel the lectures. Upon being reassured of Yale's delight in welcoming her as their guest, Rebecca and Henry flew to the States to oblige. Whatever Henry's resentments, he had seen her through a difficult time, proving once again his affection and friendship.

The lecture series would be published in a book entitled *The Court and the Castle* the following year. Rebecca, echoing and refining the theories she articulated in her 1928 book *The Strange Necessity,* defines a great work of art as one that must "change the aspect of reality, [giving the audience] an experience of the order which breaks up the present as we know it, transforming it into the past and giving us a new present." Nearly thirty years had passed since *The Strange Necessity* was published, and she had earned the hard-won perspective of one who has witnessed the distortion of classical works by critics who twist their meaning to suit their ideology. She writes, "The long life-span of literature is a source of danger, for though it gives the writer a many-branched and deep-rooted tradition to uphold him, it also gives time for his readers to repeat these [interpretive] tactics to the point of success." Through repetition of these distorting interpretations, she suggests, the content of a work of art becomes not what the artist intended. She writes, for example, "The practice of misreading the character of Hamlet, and hence the significance of the play, has been carried on by generation after generation of persons interested in the play on widely different levels, all over the world."

Ironically, Rebecca's analysis of Hamlet's character is obviously influenced by her contemporaneous feud with Anthony. Turning the conventional interpretation of Hamlet on its head, she seems to infuse her hatred for her son into her reading. "It is true that he was sensitive and thoughtful and melancholy," she writes, but "he was cruel as well as sensitive, impulsive as well as thoughtful, and though melancholy he was coarse as any barroom drunk." She portrays young Prince Hamlet not as naïve and indecisive, but as a disobedient son, a duplicitous lover and friend, and a heartless murderer who destroys human souls along with their beings. Once again, Rebecca blurs the line between reality and literature, seeking, perhaps, consolation in the universality of familial betrayal and the pernicious evil that may lie beneath a mask of fidelity.

In March 1957, Rebecca went to Cannes in the hope of finishing the second volume of her trilogy. In a letter to Henry, she wrote "I MUST GET THIS BOOK OFF MY CHEST. It is something I must do, for my own work, the Racgeist, and for the sake of our relationships with our friends the Goulds and the Ginzbergs." Perhaps because they were not only her friends but her editors, Rebecca wanted to prove that she was not the evil figment of Anthony's imagination and that her creativity had not been exhausted by his assault. It was to be, in essence, her semiautobiographical response to his, and proof that she was capable of making sense of her past. Like Anthony, Rebecca needed to write the book in order to survive—to pick up the pieces and go on with her life.

The Court and the Castle was published by Yale University Press in 1957, and that same year *The Fountain Overflows,* the first volume of her fictional memoir, was published by Macmillan in London. *The Court and the Castle* was highly regarded in American and British academic circles, and *The Fountain Overflows* was ranked number five that year in British fiction best sellers.

In May 1957, Rebecca flew to Paris to accept the cross of the French Legion of Honor. It had been awarded to French nationals and foreigners, both women and men, from its inception in 1867, to honor those whose work was consonant in furthering the principles and ideals on which the republic was founded. When Rebecca received the news, she was delighted. In a letter to Henry she revealed her belief that she deserved it and that the literary world had finally caught up with reality. "It will be lovely to have the Legion of Honour, I own it frankly." Gaining international recognition for her work with a prestigious award was exactly what she needed after all the years of emotional turmoil. She considered it a boon to her public image.

BY THE SUMMER, Rebecca found Winnie totally irrational. She wrote to Winnie's daughter, Alison, that her mother talked nonsense. She saw Winnie as a vigorous woman eviscerated by a lack of nutrition and a surfeit of emotional distress. "She is really suffering from the silt-ing up of a lifetime's frustrations and disappointments—which are no-body's fault I know, but painful to her."

To Rebecca's chagrin, Winnie got into a "frenzy" about a silver star Rebecca wore on her coat (perhaps her Legion of Honor pin), and would point to any object in her possession and accuse her of having paid a for-tune for it. Winnie's son, Norman, Jr., would later say that his mother disdained anything that spoke of wealth. She believed that leading a vir-tuous life implied thrift. It wasn't that she didn't appreciate beautiful ob-jects; she would rummage at flea markets to her heart's content. She just believed that no one should buy expensive items when they were new. It was part of the legacy of poverty resulting from their father's abandon-ment and one that she shared with Lettie: the fear that at any moment she might be penniless, and that economic survival required constant vigi-lance.

Along with her disgust at Winnie's frugality, Rebecca continued to criticize her succession of psychosomatic illnesses. In August, Rebecca wrote to Winnie: "Now for Heaven's sake drop this impersonation of a dotty old lady who is unaware of the way the world conducts its busi-ness." Unfortunately, Rebecca did not yet know that Winnie was in the throes of cerebral arteriosclerosis.

In December, she responded with compassion to Dorothy's news of selling their townhouse in New York because of Maxim's illness. Hiding the details of her recent phlebitis and subsequent thrombosis, she re-ferred to her condition as "a long and dreary illness" that responded to injections of vitamin B_{12}. Moving on to her writing, she revealed that she had managed to do a "fair copy of the sequel to *The Fountain Overflows* [*This Real Night*]." She did not mention her reservations about publish-ing it in her lifetime and fears of her sisters' reactions. In response to a comment by Dorothy that Anthony was maturing, she replied that she hadn't "seen any signs of it." Anthony and Lily, she wrote, had come to England on their way back from a world trip for *The New Yorker*, but she did not see them. "They have left a mess behind, and there will be no good outcome."

She couldn't tell Dorothy, for fear of adding to her troubles, that she was ill and frustrated with her work, and that her family demands were constantly increasing. Lettie had presented her with financial problems, as had her daughter-in-law. She was certain that no one was capable of living the life she was forced to endure.

Fortunately, however, her public reputation flourished as film producers sought the rights to convert her books to screenplays and television networks pursued her for interviews.

The summer of 1958 marked the third year since Rebecca and Anthony had had any form of contact. It was one thing to harbor hatred for someone three thousand miles away, but Rebecca's animosity toward her family now invaded her home. Paying no heed to poet and novelist Vita Sackville-West's warning upon the publication of *Heritage*, "If one gets an obsession about malice, and allows it to grow, it gets into the beams of one's life like the death-watch beetle ticking away in the roof of an ancient church," she continued her quest to rout Anthony from her life.

Concomitantly, Rebecca's desire to rid herself of the burden of Henry's mental and emotion distortions would remain unarticulated, but the hurt and shame they evoked poured out onto the pages of her memoir:

During the ten years before his death, I used to say to myself, "I wish he would die, I wish he would die. I wish he would die." I would lie in bed and say it to myself, watching the line of light under the door between my room and his, a line itself a sign of abnormality and crazed waste. He never switched off his lamp when he was in bed, he went to sleep and it would be alight in the morning if I had not got up and gone into his room to turn it off. He would be lying on a mountain of pillows, his mouth wide open, his spectacles on his nose, the traveling-clock he had taken from the bedside table cast down somewhere in the quilt, as if he wanted to keep close by him the time that now was running away from him after he had squandered it all his life, I would think of the awful thing that had happened that day, there was always something, and I would take off his spectacles and the clock, which would record that the hour was anything between midnight and four in the morning. By the time he went to hospital I was taking two Soneryls and two tranquillizers every night but I hardly ever slept except between five and eight. I would go back to bed, thinking, "I wish he would die."

The beetle was no longer just in the gables; it had invaded Rebecca's body. During the summer of 1958, Rebecca had a heart attack, along with two vascular spasms. These, too, she would blame on Anthony, writing to the Goulds that neither she nor Ibstone would ever be the same again.

That same July, Maxim died, and Henry became Rebecca's ambassador to Dorothy. He wrote letters and visited Twin Farms, sending their love and condolences and trying to lift her spirits, while obfuscating the reality of Rebecca's illness.

In September 1958 Winnie began showing such pronounced signs of dementia that even Rebecca could not ignore them. Rebecca felt sorry for her and believed that death would be merciful. She noted that, as usual, Lettie expressed great resentment toward and lack of sympathy for her younger sister. And, emblematic of her estrangement from Henry, Rebecca wrote that he should not cut his travels on the Continent short to return home if she were to die.

But even as she was devoured with hatred, she was once again honored, this time to the highest order in her native land. In late November, Rebecca accepted the royal honor of Dame Commander of the British Empire. The decoration was totally unexpected and certainly uncoveted, she wrote to a friend. "I never sought to be teacher's pet and Bloomsbury loathed me." But to her nephew Norman she revealed that after years of being tortured by Anthony, "conventional respect means something." If her sisters harbored jealousy or suspicion as to the legitimacy of the honor, as Lettie was rumored to have, Rebecca never learned of it, and both offered their unrestrained congratulations.

In fact, Lettie and her grandson, Edmund, accompanied Rebecca and Henry to the ceremony on February 14, 1959, at Buckingham Palace. The luncheon offered Rebecca the rare opportunity to speak at length with the queen and Princess Margaret. Afterward, dressed for the occasion with a custom-made black hat, coat, and skirt, she approached a dais, and, according to protocol, curtsied and took two steps backward. The queen, in turn, leaned over the table and pinned a cross and a steel star to her chest. The queen offered gratitude for her "good work," although Rebecca would wonder if she even knew what she had written. Nonetheless thrilled, Rebecca shook her hand, curtsied, and began moving backward toward the door. But in an unusual break with custom, the queen, lowering her voice, told Rebecca how much she had enjoyed their conversation during lunch. Rebecca relished this personal touch most of all.

In the summer of 1959, Rebecca once again retreated to Cannes to work. But with the end of the second volume of her trilogy in sight, she suddenly pulled back, not yet ready to bring the story of her sisters into adulthood. She wrote in a notebook, "If I can do this, I can do anything. But I fear I can't." Lettie had taken offense at the portrayal of the oldest sister, Cordelia—a narcissistic, self-aggrandizing, and delusory girl—in *The Fountain Overflows*. And while Rebecca had denied the similarities, it is clear from her letters and memoir that she did, in fact, intend the resemblance. Perhaps, while Lettie and Winnie were still alive, Rebecca feared revealing too much. Not yet having the emotional distance to convert truth to art, she chose silence.

In the fall, Rebecca learned from Bruce Gould that Michael Lewis had left Bernadette. In early December, she wrote a letter to Dorothy offering her sympathy and understanding.

> *My heart goes out to you. There is nothing so bad in life. I remember a Yug [Yugoslavian] saying to me once that there are some sorrows, which are of God and some, which are not, and this is one of those which are not, it seems a denial of divine purpose. . . . In any case, don't make your tragedy worse by giving into the sense of guilt, which is the occupational hazard of motherhood. . . . Its an idiotic trick we have—all we mothers.*

Rebecca, however, still blamed Anthony's treachery on H.G. and their collective fame.

> *The other day we went down and stayed with my daughter-in-law who broke to us the unpleasant news that Anthony never writes to her about the plans he has made for the children's future. . . . The effect of those plans is to take the children away from Kitty—who has handled all the real business of bringing them up. It's a cad's trick; and immediate[ly] I heard the horrid details I felt abased. . . . Mike and Anthony [have the same need] for a gimmick that will make them as much noticed by the world as their parents were. Anthony has as his gimmick his hatred*

of me, and his incessant moralizing. Mike has gone in for the beatnik
gimmick. This is an odd pitfall that we couldn't have foreseen. Let us
not beat our breasts, we will only spoil our elegant contours and do no
good.

Linking their personal misfortunes to the universal plight of women,
and invoking Dorothy's help in changing social expectations, she continued:

Oh, I do wish this hadn't happened to you. It does no good to say so;
yet that I feel this means that I love you dearly, and like me you love
to be loved. Well, you have my love. . . . It is a feminist work we have
to perform. In the past women subscribed to the legend that the mother
was always wrong, and gave themselves up to the sense of guilt. We
have got to refuse to go under. . . .
I wish we could see each other. I will try and get this book done
quickly if my spiritual exercises succeed. I am tempted at that to
go and get some sunshine in South Africa and do a few articles on
Apartheid.

Rebecca would not finish her book, or rather, would not deem it suit-
able for publication, but she did go to South Africa at the turn of the year.
Determined to get as far away as possible from Henry and Ibstone, she
leaped at an offer from *The Sunday Times* to embark on a three-month
tour, beginning in January 1960, to write about the status of apartheid
and the brewing unrest among the black population. This time Henry
had done the unimaginable. He had taken up with one of the secretaries
who were living in their home. The woman, Lorna Yedell, whom Rebecca deemed a psychopath and later learned had a habit of becoming
emotionally involved with her employers, had convinced Henry that she
was in love with him. Playing one against the other, Lorna would belittle
Henry to Rebecca and Rebecca to Henry in the hopes of instigating marital discord sufficient to lead to divorce. Upon Rebecca's departure,
Lorna formulated for Henry a list of grievances against Rebecca, which
he then parroted to Rebecca in a letter. Discerning the true source of the
complaints Rebecca exposed Lorna as a manipulative, gold-digging ad-
venturer and Henry as an egocentric, love-hungry, gullible fool.

In a series of letters across six thousand miles, they exchanged the most intimate and honest thoughts of their thirty-year marriage. From Johannesburg, Rebecca wrote Henry a letter that could have been written to Anthony or even H.G. Once again, everyone else's feelings were measured in terms of their effect on her work:

My dear Ric, I feel utter despair over your letter. . . .

If you had not done this unpardonable thing of letting a lunatic adventuress in to sabotage my life, I would by now have gone on to the next book which is fully covered by the first draft, and This Real Night *would have been finished by now. I would have known peace of mind and body, which seems entirely unattainable now.*

I really do not know what to do. I am devoted to you. Ibstone House is run entirely to suit you, and I seem to myself a good deal to do with its running. We live the life you want to live and I have never grudged any sacrifice which seemed likely to make you happy. I have not done enough for you but I have done what I can. Nothing seems worth while any more. Your letter is free from any sense that you may have defects which make life with you difficult, and it is singularly free from any trace of gratitude. What is apparent is that anybody who comes in to the house is put above me, is considered capable of passing judgment on me, and if the judgment is adverse, I am supposed to accept it.

Henry, blindsided by Rebecca's despair, self-righteousness, and rage, deemed the situation a series of misunderstandings. Rebecca shot back that she no longer trusted him, and felt no "pleasure in sharing with you the things I enjoy. . . . You are right outside the limits of normality. I am considering what can be done." She signed it "R," omitting her usual declaration of love.

And yet, before returning home, she pledged her love:

I am willing to start again and I am glad to do so, because I love you. But I could not go through such an ordeal again. I say this knowing that there are many ways I have fallen short of what I ought to have been to you, and there is no hope that I will ever repay your goodness

*and generosity to me. All the same I could not go through anything
like this again.*

Much love, my dearest. Rac.

But the truth was out. Henry needed love that Rebecca could not—
would not—give him, and he was willing to get it any way he could, including undermining her work and her femininity, and desecrating their
marriage. Rebecca would soon find out that Henry was suffering from
cerebral arteriosclerosis, the same disease as Winnie. But in some ways,
Henry was more himself than ever before. No longer restrained by convention, he coveted the life he needed, and acted upon it. He, like Anthony, had hurt Rebecca most with his honesty. She had deprived them
both of emotional sustenance and her physical presence, which they desperately needed, and so they had sought revenge, sometimes wittingly
and sometimes not. The phantom that stalked Rebecca had once again
taken human form. Angry, but also sad and ashamed, Rebecca was forced
to confront her self-serving deceptions.

This episode of domestic betrayal eerily evokes the plot of Ibsen's
play *Rosmersholm,* from which Rebecca had taken her name. As a young
woman and H.G.'s mistress, she had played the part of the iconoclastic
invader of conventional domesticity who supersedes a wife as lover, intellectual companion, and confidante. Now in her late sixties, she found
herself prey to a vulturous invader who sought to dethrone her and become Henry's young lover, enabler, and liberator.

Shortly after Rebecca's return home from South Africa, Winnie died.
Rebecca was devastated. She remembered the older sister who had protected and nursed her, and the beautiful young girl with the musical voice
who had recited poetry, igniting her own love of literature. Rebecca refused to believe that the old woman who had become an invalid and a
recluse, who had slid into a world of fantasy and shunned reality, was the
sister she had adored. She mourned the girl Winnie was, and the artist
she might have become. It was the denial of her gifts, she believed, that
had robbed Winnie of salvation.

Less than a year later, in January 1961, Dorothy died in the wake
of her fourth heart attack, while visiting Bernadette and the children in
Lisbon.

In mid-February Rebecca wrote a letter to her and Dorothy's mutual friends Bruce and Beatrice Gould, remembering Dorothy in the same wistful tone she had Winnie, wondering what might have been:

I expect you feel as I do about the death of Dorothy. She was part of the shoreline of life, like the Maine coast or the cliffs of Dover, and it is not possible she should have gone. I had known her for forty-one years and I remember her as a singularly composed girl in her twenties, whom nothing—it seemed—could disconcert. I didn't reckon with Josef Bard and Red and Mike! I was glumly happy when Maxim turned up and concerned when he died—and I had been distressed about her, was thinking of her often during the last few months, when my troubles have been thick upon me. With concern I heard of her death on the radio and wondered what she was doing in Lisbon. Two days afterward I got a letter from her asking us to go out to Lisbon. A piteous, piteous letter. The comfort was that she knew she couldn't get well unless she rested and with the family situation as it was she couldn't rest. There were grateful words about Bernadette, and friendly words about you—she was disturbed about the cutting down of her work for the Journal, but felt, I think, that she really could not have gone on doing all she used to do for you. I would have loved Dorothy if she had had no virtues, but she had many, including courage, and this last letter of hers is full of that. Her courage made her well aware of where she was—"there is nothing the matter with my heart except that it is broken." So I am really not sorry for her sake that she has gone, but for her sake only.

Rebecca sought salvation through her art, but Dorothy, while grateful for earthly pleasures, found true salvation through her faith in God.

In a letter to Michael dictated to her friend Alice Tarnowski shortly before her death, Dorothy wrote: "I leave to you, your loved ones, and my grandchildren the memory of my love for you all; the wonders and beauties of this earth and universe that have given me so much joy; the solace of faith in a superhuman purpose and design; and the delights of art and of great minds."

Unlike Rebecca, Dorothy had faith that her love would sustain those she would leave behind, and that God would be her source of redemption. Yet both women reveled in the beauty of nature, in the joys of intellect, and in the value of art. Perhaps it was these commonalities that had nourished their friendship through the emotional swings of pain, loss, illness, and professional success and decline throughout four decades. Their friendship would die with Dorothy, but the story is not yet complete. Rebecca would live and work for another twenty-two years.

EPILOGUE

When Dorothy landed at the airport in Lisbon on December 21, 1960, Bernadette barely recognized her. She was shocked to see this once-robust figure now so haggard and drawn. But Dorothy's desire to celebrate Christmas with Bernadette and her grandchildren and the old thrill of foreign travel were a potent elixir. She had loved Lisbon when she stopped there on her way to England in 1940, during the London Blitz, deeming it a wonderful city to live and die in. And she looked forward to savoring her time with officials at the U.S. Embassy, exchanging memories of the tragic devastation of Europe during the war, and views of future U.S. relations with Europe and the Soviets.

Once the holidays were over, however, Dorothy deflated. On the morning of January 2, 1961, Dorothy, unable to breathe, summoned Bernadette to her hotel room. She immediately took Dorothy to the British-American hospital in Lisbon. When the physicians deemed her condition "grave," Michael, rehearsing *The Visit* with the Lunts in New York, flew to her bedside. After four days, Dorothy's health seemed to buoy, and Michael returned to New York. The officials from the embassy who visited her in the hospital found her vibrant, talkative, witty, and charming, describing her as propped up on pillows like a queen on a throne, curls wrapped up in a scarf over her head, welcoming guests and directing nurses with a royal sweep of her hand. She stayed in the hospital for three and a half weeks, and impatient to get back home, checked out on January 30, in defiance of her doctors' orders. Back in a hotel room, after dismissing Bernadette and her grandsons, and ordering a full-course Portuguese dinner, she suffered her last heart attack. The next morning, Bernadette found her doubled over in bed, the half-eaten dinner by her side and the handset of the telephone off the hook. She apparently fell as she had reached out to summon help.

It was said that when he heard the news, Michael drank nine brandies in succession.

There was a funeral service at a small English church in Lisbon attended by a handful of relatives and friends. Dorothy's body was then shipped to Vermont and placed in a vault in Woodstock, until the earth was thawed enough to accommodate burial. On a cold, wet morning in May 1961, she was laid to rest in the Barnard village graveyard next to Maxim beneath the blue granite stone she had chosen for him. At her request, she was buried in the "cheapest" coffin available, and in her nightgown, without adornment or embalmer's makeup. There was a simple graveside service—the recitation of the Lord's Prayer and two Psalms—concluded without a eulogy. A large gathering of family and friends attended the burial, including Michael; her sister, Peggy, and brother-in-law, Howard Wilson; her local neighbors and friends; and Vincent Sheean. Vincent would remark that it was like "saying good-bye to a lifetime." On the flat headstone were imprinted the words DOROTHY THOMPSON—WRITER. At the foot of her grave, as she requested, lay a basket of lilies.

MICHAEL LEWIS DIED at age fifty-five in 1985 of Hodgkin's lymphoma. He had continued his lackluster career as an actor and struggled with alcoholism. Those who witnessed his performances deemed him self-conscious and histrionic. At his best, he was considered a skilled character actor. Like his mother, he preferred classical theater and Shakespeare to contemporary experimentation in postmodern expressionism. After marrying Valerie Cardew, he had fathered another child, a daughter named Lesley, who would grow to resemble her grandmother so much that she would turn heads on the streets of New York. In 1970, Michael quit the stage for three years and retreated to Twin Farms to wrestle with his drinking problem. Sadly, the heavy burden of being the son of Sinclair Lewis and Dorothy Thompson, along with the familial tendency toward alcoholism, finally defeated him. Dorothy had been right. He had inherited enough of his father's genius to coast on his gifts but neither the discipline nor the drive to convert his raw talent to accomplishment. Michael left behind his first wife, Bernadette, and their two sons, John-Paul and Gregory, along with Valerie and their daughter, Lesley.

IN THE TWENTY-TWO YEARS succeeding Dorothy's death, Rebecca wrote or completed seven more books: *The New Meaning of Trea-*

son in 1964; *The Birds Fall Down* in 1966, which marked the completion of a novel she had begun in 1944; *1900,* in 1982, a personal memoir linked with political, social, cultural, and scientific history; *This Real Night* and *Cousin Rosamund,* the final two volumes of her semiautobiographical fictional trilogy published posthumously in 1984 and 1985, respectively; *Sunflower,* in 1986; and, finally, *Family Memories* in 1987, an interpretive autobiography that begins with her parents, moves into her school years, and ends with a biographical tribute to the youth of Henry Maxwell Andrews, in which she ironically called her marriage "the most important thing in my life." She had written more than twenty-five books in all, along with hundreds of articles in British and American publications.

After his tryst with the secretary Lorna, Henry began a succession of affairs with friends, employees, and prostitutes. His was a quick but horrible death from cancer and kidney disease; on his deathbed he accused Rebecca of robbing him of his share of Ibstone. At the very end, calling out the name of his latest mistress, he tenderly kissed her. When Rebecca told him she was his wife, Henry turned away in disgust. The memory of this final rejection, she would write in an unpublished memoir, would haunt her for the rest of her life. Henry died on November 3, 1968, two days after their thirty-eighth wedding anniversary. Rebecca's animosity toward him was mitigated by her knowledge of his mental disease, which had probably been escalating for thirty years, but it took her nearly a decade to forgive his deceit and blows to her dignity.

Shortly after Henry's death, Rebecca found a record of his undisclosed wealth hidden in securities that he had hoarded away to justify his complaints of penury and continual demands for funds. She also found Henry's desk a "mausoleum of my illusions," she wrote to Emanie, "stuffed with stupid, vulgar albums of photographs of naked women, and dirty books." She felt duped by her own naïveté and angry that she did not even have the luxury of hating him, knowing he was "mad."

As Rebecca entered her eighties, she, too, showed symptoms of madness. What had begun as a gloomy and paranoid turn of mind became a full-blown sickness in the last years of her life, akin perhaps to the incurable mental illness attributed to her father. Her ability to compartmentalize her actions and deny their moral implications—and even her Manichaean sense of the universe—can be seen as emotional and philosophical manifestations of her desperate attempts to cope with the invisible and unconquerable demons that threatened her sanity.

After six years of complete estrangement, Rebecca and Anthony had a tentative rapprochement in the mid-1960s, but neither would ever trust the motives or actions of the other. After selling Ibstone shortly after Henry's death, Rebecca moved to a flat in Kingston House, at the edge of Hyde Park, where she lived alone. At night she would often imagine Anthony, who had returned to London, in the courtyard garden outside her window lying in wait to attack and kill her. According to her unpublished memoir, he had told her he would torture her until the day she died, and she never doubted Anthony's intent or his ability to keep his promise. Sometimes the specter of Henry would stand beneath the garden trees, classically handsome and perfectly groomed as he had been in his youth, evoking both her love and resentment. More and more, her bifurcate universe of good and evil deteriorated into a world of treacherous demons that hounded and tortured her. Frustrated by the nagging difficulties of aging—weight gain, loss of muscle, arthritis, and increasing immobility—she nonetheless continued to write books and reviews, read voraciously, watch television, go to the cinema, and accept visits from family and friends. While some would find her ornery and bitter, others would enjoy her warmth and generosity. Those close to her would say that she never lost her sense of humor or her flirtatious whimsy, but during the last two years of her life, Rebecca's memory lagged along with her energy.

In the autumn of 1982, she fell and broke her hip. The surgery to repair it was a success, but she remained bedridden and sedated. To those who visited, she spoke of H.G. as a wonderful companion but a lost cause as a lover or husband. She called Anthony a "wicked boy" whom she loved despite his hatred of her. Her perceptions of reality became frighteningly dissonant and chaotic, and she often descended into delirium. According to her secretary Diana Stainforth, near the end Rebecca would often call out to Henry for help, wondering aloud why he had deserted her. In the final days of her life, in search of consolation and absolution, she summoned a Catholic priest to her bedside. It was an act as full of pathos as irony—the final gesture of a spirit who had sought the divine, yet was filled with doubt and contempt for Christian doctrine. Forever hoping that her work would lead her to God, she found the ultimate uncertainty of its worth and the loneliness of death too much to bear. Rebecca West, née Cicely Isabel Fairfield, contracted pneumonia and died on the morning of March 15, 1983, nine months short of her ninety-first birthday.

Rebecca outlived Henry by fifteen years, her sister Lettie by five years, and Winnie by twenty-three. By the time she grew ill, most of her friends had died, and she was dependent on those she hired—secretaries, housekeepers, and nurses—to care for her on a daily basis. To the end, the children of friends, Justin Lowinsky and Merlin Holland, along with Winnie's children, Alison and Norman, Jr., and his wife, Marion, remained devoted to her and to easing her pain. Rebecca would leave the majority of her estate to Norman, Jr., perhaps thinking of him as the son she never had, and to Alison, her friend and confidante in her old age, a generous share. Her granddaughters, Caroline and Sophie, were also remembered in her will, as were some of her employees and friends of later years.

Her funeral service was held at Saint Martin-in-the-Fields Church in central London, whose halls had honored many of Britain's illustrious literary and cultural figures. Bernard Levin, journalist, broadcaster, and loving friend, recited a eulogy in which he called her a seeker of truth, a fine journalist, and the author of books equal to those of the greatest minds of the twentieth century. Refusing to be buried beside Henry in the valley they had overlooked from their terrace at Ibstone for twenty-eight of their thirty-eight years together, or in Highgate Cemetery in London along with her mother and sisters, Rebecca chose to be interred nearly an hour's drive from Ibstone, in Brookwood Cemetery near Woking in Surrey, alongside other figures that dominated the artistic, political, and academic culture of Britain. There, apart from her family, among the flowering rhododendrons, azaleas, and bluebells, surrounded by stately pines and oak trees, Rebecca found her rest. Anthony attended neither the church service nor the burial, deeming his presence "inappropriate."

True to his promise, Anthony had continued to torture her while she lived, and, after her death, he set out to destroy her public image. He published numerous articles about his mother's neglect, and the 1984 British edition of *Heritage,* printed within a year of her demise, included a scathing new introduction. Anthony's final book, *H. G. Wells: Aspects of a Life,* is a sympathetic and forgiving portrait of his genius father's literary and political life and loves. His mother makes a minor but contemptuous cameo as a neglectful, duplicitous, and self-serving woman insensitive to the needs of her lovers, husband, sisters, and friends.

Anthony Panther West died of a stroke at his home in Stonington, Connecticut, on Sunday, December 27, 1987, only four years after his mother. He was seventy-three years old. He left behind his first wife, Kitty Lyle West, and their two children, Dr. Edmund West and Caroline Duah, and his second wife, Lily Emmet West, and their two children, Sophia and Adam West.

JUDGED BY THE Victorian standards of *The Cult of True Womanhood*, the lives of Dorothy Thompson and Rebecca West were "ashes." Even if Dorothy was pious, in the loosest sense of the term, she was neither pure and submissive nor domestic. Lusty, arrogantly self-righteous (even in the service of God), and domestic only with the help of servants, Dorothy would have found true womanhood tantamount to suicide. Eighty years earlier, Dorothy's grandmother and her generation of Victorian women had pierced the myth of female purity. Grandma Grierson had played by the rules only to be deserted by her "black Scot" free-thinking, union-organizing husband. She had learned her lessons too late, and was determined to balance the scales. She had even been willing to risk her daughter's life in order to do so. Margaret Thompson, Dorothy's mother, paid the price, as did Dorothy's father, Peter, Dorothy, and her two siblings. Dorothy, in turn, had tried to right the scales by sloughing off the constraints of the myth in ways her mother and grandmother could never have imagined, and her husbands and her son paid another sort of price, equally devastating, if tinged with modernity. Feeling neglected and abandoned by a woman whose primary loyalty was to self-realization, they were felled in the path of her consuming ambition.

Rebecca experienced the sacrifice of her mother's life in the name of virtue as similarly abhorrent. She could not witness the treachery of her father or the ensuing diminishment and poverty of her mother without rage and a deep and abiding inability to trust men. Unlike Dorothy, who put her life in the hands of God and, through this faith, into the hands of men, Rebecca always held back, fearing not only vulnerability, but also psychological, even physical, death.

Equally deprived of security in childhood, equally courageous and ambitious, the two women viewed their lives through a moral prism that determined the value of all their relationships and their own accomplishments. While Rebecca was clearly the more gifted and successful of the two, it was Dorothy who was ultimately able to reconcile her failures and her frailties with the sheer joy of living. Her faith enabled her to believe that the good she had done would survive her.

Rebecca, eschewing her mother's piety, chose to see life as a disorderly confluence of events ungoverned by an anthropomorphic God yet suffused with great mysteries. She put herself in the center of her own ethical universe, declaring the dogma of Christianity a ruse, and sacrifice in the name of virtue a sham. And yet, it was as if she had an unrequited love of God that she hungered to consummate all her life. It was this hunger for divine sanctity that drove her writing, converting it into a holy and inviolable obsession. The more that people and relationships disappointed her, the more piously she struggled to complete her work. It was her only vehicle of controlling a universe that appeared increasingly senseless and self-destructive. And while she succeeded beyond her imagination, her literary accolades were never enough to satisfy her craving for affirmation. Rebecca was always mourning what might have been—what she might have accomplished, had it not been for H.G., for Anthony, for her sisters, for Henry.

Rebecca had tried her best to balance the scales, codifying her quest in universal terms in her novel *The Judge*, with the words "Every mother is a judge who sentences the children for the sins of the father." And, consciously or not, Rebecca made Anthony pay, intiating the hostility that would diminish both their lives. The lesson is, perhaps, that the scales cannot be righted; one must live reasonably and compassionately within the constraints of one's time, and dare to create and transcend within the time-honored moral traditions of Judeo-Christian society. In short, one cannot break the rules without paying the price.

Rebecca addressed these issues in *The Strange Necessity*, which set forth her belief that innovation must be built on a knowledge of and respect for the past. Tradition must be both preserved and modified to accommodate new challenges and opportunities. In this book and in others, a recurring theme is that one must have standards by which to measure one's life; an ethic and a purpose that transforms and justifies it. Finding the standard, while embracing the vicissitudes of life, she believed, was a never-ending process.

Rebecca and Dorothy not only surpassed Victorian expectations, they transcended gender. They assumed the affect and costume of the moment, but never the substance. Ironically, they invented new female prototypes while appearing to conform to prevailing convention. And they fabricated the narrative of their lives as they went along, understanding the prevailing convention and ironically wanting to win it on its own terms. They hungered to be loved and cherished according to Victorian myth, even as they rejected the myth, and the men who embraced it rejected them.

Dorothy left the world, thinking—knowing—that death would liberate her soul and sanctify her life. She was right when she told Hal that she was a "peripatetic brain picker," while he was a genius whose work would be remembered long after he was gone. Her own literary legacy did not extend beyond her death. But what does survive is her Christian ethic of hard work and honesty, and her belief in divine salvation and the importance of revering the principles of the Founding Fathers. They remain as testimony to her character and abiding sense of public service.

Rebecca was never certain that good would triumph over evil, or that "triumph" was integral to the human condition. Her view of human nature was as much cerebral as it was intuitive, and she understood the necessity of doing battle against evil, internal and external, if one were to survive at all. If life was a battlefield, too bloody to bear, she would cope by making it into a "stage set." Objectifying her self and reality was essential to withstanding both daily vicissitudes and the act of creation. The brilliance of her writing lay in splintering and compartmentalizing aspects of her psyche and suffusing her characters with conflicting ideas and goals, then moving them around like pieces on a chessboard and watching them struggle as their stories unfolded. Her writing was at once an act of creation and self-preservation, providing catharsis while protecting the integrity of her mind. Ultimately, it was truly Rebecca's art—her writing—that saved her. And upon reading her books and essays, one may conclude that art holds enough divinity to save the world.

Rebecca and Dorothy were delusory when it came to love. They projected idealized stereotypes onto their men, and demanded more of them than any man could fulfill. Given their emotional deprivation as children, and their impulse toward social legitimacy, there was no amount of piety for Dorothy, or psychoanalysis for Rebecca, that could compensate for the emotional damage they caused and incurred. And the men they chose—Joseph Bard, Sinclair Lewis, H. G. Wells, and Henry Andrews— were equally crippled. For Dorothy, to love was to mother, be it her husbands or her son. And to be a mother was to teach, discipline, and—by definition—control. Dorothy ultimately survived in a marriage not because she came to understand its dynamic, but because she finally found a man she believed could take care of himself. More than God, it was Dorothy's marriage to Max that saved her, but she would not have separated the two.

Rebecca in her mid-seventies

It's likely that Rebecca never really loved anyone, not only because her expectations were too high, but also because she simply didn't know how. One may say of her what she said of Saint Augustine in *Black Lamb and Grey Falcon:* "He loved love with the hopeless infatuation of one who, like King Lear, cannot love." When H.G. told her that despite her brilliance she didn't know the basic wiles of womanhood, he hit upon the truth. In fact, within the context of contemporary gender expectations, neither Rebecca nor Dorothy knew how to be a woman. Smart, ambitious, and driven to succeed, within their contemporary gender stereotypes, they were more like men. As for Rebecca, without Henry's friendship, she would have been lost, but without his perfidy, she would not have been as lonely or embittered.

Anthony West at seventy years old

Rebecca's relationship with Dorothy was at once special and typical. They were drawn together by ambition, a consonant political and social vision, and an extraordinary sense of historical mission. Later, their friendship was intensified by emotional loss, the blessings and curses of fame, and the resonance of their relationships with literary geniuses and their troubled sons. While Rebecca had many female friends, Dorothy had few whom she trusted or deemed capable of understanding herself, her family, and her needs. But while Dorothy measured her friends by their emotional generosity, Rebecca's touchstones were practical and intellectual. She demanded loyalty and preferred women of intelligence and those with connections to power. Just as Rebecca's vision of reality, past and present, was kaleidoscopic, her judgment of people was forever changing according to her immediate needs, moods, and self-perception. She could diminish her sisters, or squash her dearest friends, with a direct reprimand or a spate of contemptuous gossip. The hallmark of her friend-ships was inconsistency: She dismissed Doris Stevens as a bore in the 1940s and then loved her in the '50s, was mesmerized by the youth and freshness of Pamela Frankau in the 1930s and saw her as a moral idiot in the '50s, was enamored of Emanie Sachs in the 1940s and saw her as a traitor in the '50s, and alternated between cursing and admiring Charles Curran as a man, editor, and politician throughout his life. Dorothy was no exception. In the wake of the deaths of many of her friends, including Dorothy, Rebecca wrote a letter to Jimmy Sheean on Christmas Day 1963 after having read his book *Dorothy and Red*.

Referring to her old friend, she wrote,

I've never loved, or even liked anybody who had such a great big flaw running down the center of them. . . . Dorothy had not the faintest un-derstanding of what I was up to. She never knew what I was thinking or feeling, she hadn't the faintest idea of where my mind was going, she was, for instance, completely baffled by The Court and the Cas-tle. *It was as if she had deliberately chosen, when buying a house, not to live in the same district as myself. . . . We had no common ground, she didn't know what I was or what I did, and . . . all the same I was still deeply fond of her. It seemed mysterious and the mystery seemed, if I can use the word without being Wagnerian myself, sacred. . . . There was no contact, but there was love.*

AND SO THE STORY HAS come full circle. These women must be honored for their accomplishments at a time when self-realization re-quired superhuman tenacity and grit. While the conflict that existed within them lives in all those whose aspirations exceed the social expecta-tions of their time and place, the distortions their ambitions engendered in their personal relations are uniquely their own. Sitting on high, from the lofty perspective of twenty-first-century readers, we cannot truly grasp the anguish of their struggle or the depth of their pain, but we can learn from their attempts to right the scales of injustice of previous generations by punishing their own. Understanding both their dissonance and their folly holds the promise that with time, each new generation will be better able to confront the danger that lies beneath personal ambition.

ACKNOWLEDGMENTS

When I was a student at the Columbia University School of the Arts, a teacher of mine said that writing a biography was akin to running a small company. The truth of that statement has resonated throughout the six years I have struggled to bring this project to fruition. I would amend it by stating that my "company" was large and global, extending through time and space—through generations of ancestors and descendants of my remarkable subjects. It has required marshaling the talents of an infinite number of specialists—from editors to editorial assistants, librarians to archivists to researchers, from photographers to photo-imaging technicians, from permissions experts to permissions lawyers. I have imposed on the generosity of my friends, fellow biographers, and my dear spouse. My humility has no bounds. I have stood on the shoulders of giants, peers, and those who love and inspire me.

My giants:

Peter Kurth, whose research and insights contributed to my understanding of Dorothy Thompson and her family, and whose generosity has served as a role model for my helping others.

Carl Rollyson, whose Rebecca West scholarship made him a resource to draw upon, reckon with, and set the standard by which I would measure my own.

Victoria Glendinning, who had the distinction of meeting and earning the trust of Rebecca West, and whose insights and research have been invaluable.

And all the Thompson and West scholars who preceded me, gathering and sorting letters and documents, and making their work and commentary available to those who would try their hand at making sense of the lives of these complicated and extraordinary women.

My gratitude to:

McIntosh and Otis Literary Agency, and the Thompson/Lewis Estate; Norman Macleod and Helen Macleod Atkinson, co-executors of the West Estate.

A special thanks to librarians and students who have taken the time to help me in my research: Letters, photos, and documents: Nicolette Dobrowlski, Mary Ann Hinton, Debbie Olson; Burt Helm; Melissa Antonucci, Alison Greenlee.

I thank the following libraries for giving me help and access to letters in their collections and, where appropriate, permission to publish them: Harry Ransom Humanities Research Center, The University of Texas at Austin; British Library Department of Manuscripts; The Library of Congress, Manuscript and Audio Collections; British Library of Television and Film; FDR Library, Hyde Park; Houghton Library at Harvard University; House of Lords Record Office, Library Service; The Rare Book and Manuscript Library of the University of Illinois at Urbana-Champaign; University of Chicago Library; The Columbia University Rare Book and Manuscript Library; Pierpont Morgan Library; The New York Public Library; Princeton University Library, Special Collections; The Lilly Library of Indiana University; Beineke Rare Book and Manuscript Library, Yale University; John Gunther Papers, Special Collections Research Center, University of Chicago Library; Dorothy Thompson Papers, Special Collections Research Center, Syracuse University Library; Dorothy Thompson Collection, Special Collections Center, Syracuse University Library; Women United for the United Nations Records, Schlesinger Library, Radcliffe Institute, Harvard University; Manuscripts Division, Department of Rare Books and Special Collections, Princeton University Library; scholars at the International Rebecca West Society, from British and American universities, whose published and unpublished papers and presence have broadened my scope of knowledge, enriched my understanding, and encouraged my work.

I wish to express my appreciation to the following people who took precious time away from their own work and responsibilities to speak with me: Marion and Norman Macleod; Helen Macleod Atkinson; Diana Stainforth; Victoria Glendinning; Lily West; Arthur Schlesinger, Jr.;

Alison Macleod Selford; George Weidenfeld; John-Paul Sinclair Lewis; Margaret May ("Peggy") Thompson Wilson; Jane Gunther; Lolo Sarnoff; Stephen Graubard, Lois Wallace.

This book represents a veritable symphony of voices, even as the responsibility rests with me.

I offer a special debt of gratitude to Elizabeth Sheinkman, my literary agent, who first believed in my project and gave me the opportunity and encouragement to shepherd it to completion, and to Susanna Porter, my editor at Ballantine/Random House, who never lost interest in my project or the hope that it would flourish and fulfill its promise.

I would also like to thank the women and men whom I have never met for their long hours assisting the editor, copyediting, designing the book cover, the format, and the type font: Priyanka Krishnan along with Nancy Delia, the production editor, and her staff who labored to assemble it into the wondrous finished product on the shelves and electronic devices that you hold in your hands today.

The list of editorial and research assistants who helped me throughout these years is long but redolent with energy and talent. Each brought her special skills and knowledge to the task, yet earned her respect as a teammate: Vanessa Mobley, Julie Gracius, Anika Weiss, Kate Foster, Greer Martin, Abigail Rasminsky, Mary Dalton-Hoffman, Dana Burnell, Courtney Williams, and Gloria Phares who eased me through the permissions process, and a special thank-you to Emily Adler, who insured the integrity of the manuscript and embraced it as if it were her own, and to Abigail Santamaria whose research, editorial skills, and affection carried me through to the end. All of those who have assisted me throughout the years are professional writers, editors, translators, or consultants who earn the freedom to pursue their true passions by helping others follow theirs. I salute them.

I would also like to thank Ryan Bailer for his technical acumen. It was he who unstuck many a gadget, stationary and mobile, and managed to set me free to resume my self-torture, which is to say, writing.

Most of all, there are no words sufficient to express my gratitude to my husband, Roger. His extraordinary mind, passion for history, and love of life have lit up many a dark day, filled me with courage, and given me the confidence that hard work and faith would bring this book to fruition.

NOTES

NAMES

AMS	Alison Macleod Selford
AW	Anthony West
DT	Dorothy Thompson
HA	Henry Andrews
HGW	H. G. Wells
ML	Michael Lewis
RW	Rebecca West
SL	Sinclair Lewis
WFM	Winifred Fairchild Macleod

LETTERS AND DOCUMENTS IN SPECIAL COLLECTIONS

IU	Indiana University
PML	Pierpont Morgan Library
SU	George Arents Research Library, Syracuse University
UT	McFarlin Library, University of Tulsa
YU	Beinecke Rare Book and Manuscript Library, Yale University

EPIGRAPHS

ix **"Only part of us is sane"** RW, *Black Lamb and Grey Falcon: A Journey Through Yugoslavia in 1937* (New York: Viking Press, 1941), 1102.

ix **"I love life because"** DT, *The Courage to Be Happy* (Boston: Houghton Mifflin, 1957), 121.

INTRODUCTION

xiii **"The attributes of True Womanhood"** Barbara Welter, "The Cult of True Womanhood: 1820–1860," *American Quarterly* 18, no. 2 (Summer 1966): 152.

GEMINI

3 **"One spoke of Berlin"** Peter Gay (quoting Carl Zuckmayer), *Weimar Culture: The Outsider as Insider* (Westport, Conn.: Greenword Press, 1968), 132.

6 **"Buy a new wardrobe"** Dale Warren, "I Remember Dorothy," *Courier* 4, no. 2 (Summer 1964), Peter Kurth's research, courtesy of Peter Kurth.

7 **"Rebecca's in town"** scene from Rebecca's arrival and Dorothy's party, and information for chapter, based on various letters and diaries including: Eileen Agar

collection, SU; DT to JB 1/6/27, 1/19/27, 1/25/27; DT, European Diary, SU. DT to Phyllis Bottome, January, 1927; RW, unpublished memoir; RW to Gordon Ray, July 30, 1973; and books and articles including: Carl Zuckmayer, *A Part of Myself,* pp. 340–41; Dale Warren, "I Remember Dorothy"; Robert Boyce, ed., *French Foreign and Defense Policy, 1918–1940;* Ken Cuthbertson, *Inside: The Biography of John Gunther;* Robert W. Desmond, *Crisis and Conflict: World News Reporting Between Two Wars, 1920–1940;* Julia Edwards, *Women of the World: The Great Foreign Correspondents;* Charles Fisher, *The Columnists;* Peter Gay, *Weimar Culture: The Outsider as Insider;* Anton Gill, *A Dance Between Flames: Berlin Between the Wars;* Peter Kurth, *American Cassandra: The Life of Dorothy Thompson;* John McNamara, *Extra! U.S. War Correspondents in Action;* Lillian T. Mowrer, *Journalist's Wife;* Joseph Roth, *What I Saw: Reports from Berlin, 1920–1923;* Anna Maria Sigmund, *Women of the Third Reich;* Hedda Adlon; *Hotel Adlon, Berlin: The Story Behind the Legend* (Wilhelm Heyne Verlag, 1998); Sigrid Schultz Collection, Wisconsin Historical Society.

11 **"something no other woman has been"** DT to Phyllis Bottome, ca. early 1920s, unpublished MS, SU.

11 **"picked them for their brains"** DT to George Seldes, December 13, 1938, SU.

CHAPTER 1 / BECOMING REBECCA

19 **"When winds and showers"** GEN MSS 240, series 2, box 5, folder 128, G. Evelyn Hutchinson Papers, YU.

21 **"loneliness to loneliness"** RW, *Family Memories,* (New York: Penguin, 1989), 10.

22 **The real story, uncovered recently** Julian Moore, presentation at Rebecca West in London: The Fourth Biennial Conference of the International Rebecca West Society, September 19, 2009, from notes of Norman Macleod.

24 **By the time Cicely was born** Description of Richmond upon Thames from Ben Weinreb and Christopher Hibbert, eds., *The London Encyclopedia* (London: Macmillan, 1995), 665–67.

25 **"I had a glorious father"** RW, *The Fountain Overflows,* 274.

28 **Bert found solace in the "mystery"** HGW, *Tono-Bungay* (New York: Oxford University Press, 1997), 29.

32 **While Maud was entranced** AW, *H. G. Wells: Aspects of a Life* (New York: Random House, 1984), 9.

33 **As was to become his pattern** HGW, *Ann Veronica: A Modern Love Story* (New York: Harper and Brothers, 1909); and HGW, *The New Machiavelli* (New York: Harper and Brothers, 1909).

35 **"This callousness should teach"** RW, "An Orgy of Disorder and Cruelty," *The Clarion,* September 27, 1912, in Jane Marcus, ed., *The Young Rebecca: Writings of Rebecca West 1911–1917* (New York: Viking Press, 1982), 99.

35 **"the most exquisite beauty of person"** RW, *Time and Tide,* in Marcus, *Young Rebecca,* 4.

35 **In this case, she asserted** RW, "The Divorce Commission: A Report That Will Not Become Law," *The Clarion,* November 29, 1912, in Marcus, *Young Rebecca,* 126.

37 **In 1912, when Wells published** RW, "Review of *Marriage* by H. G. Wells," *The Freewoman,* September 19, 1912, in Marcus, *Young Rebecca,* 64–70.

38 **"walk of the matador"** Rollyson, *Rebecca West,* 41.

39 **"She had a fine broad brow"** HGW, *H. G. Wells in Love: Postscript to an Experiment in Autobiography,* ed. G. P. Wells (Boston: Little, Brown, 1984), 94.

40 "You're a very compelling person" HGW to RW, February 1913, YU.

42 "Dear H.G." RW to HGW, June 1913, series 1, box 18, folder 905, YU.

42 "How can I be your friend" HGW to RW, June 1913, GEN MSS 239, YU.

43 "You are as wise as God" HGW to RW, ca. early July 1913, series 1, box 18, folder 905, YU.

44 **By 1913, thanks to government** Regina G. Kuzel, *Fallen Women, Problem Girls: Unmarried Mothers and the Professionalization of Social Work 1890–1945* (New Haven, Conn.: Yale University Press, 1993), 50–56.

45 **but also as "confederates"** Gordon N. Ray, *H. G. Wells and Rebecca West* (New Haven, Conn.: Yale University Press, 1974), 33.

45 **to maintain the "legend"** HGW to RW, 1914, series 1, box 18, folder 910, YU.

46 **intrinsic to his "double life"** HGW to RW, January 14, 1914, YU.

46 "I am radiant this morning" HGW to RW, August 5, 1914, YU.

46 "great man" HGW to RW, August 4, 1914, YU.

47 "Citizen for the Age of Peace" HGW to RW, August 3, 1914, YU.

47 **H.G. had tried to anticipate** Ronald Steel, *Walter Lippmann and the American Century* (New York: Vintage Books, 1981), 68.

48 "detach us lovers a little more from the nursery" HGW to RW, August 20, 1916, YU.

49 "criticism must break down" RW, *Henry James* (Port Washington, N.Y.: Kennikat Press, 1968), 98.

49 "great man" ... "I am in the most miserable state" RW to S. K. Ratcliffe, February 4, 1916, PML.

CHAPTER 2 / BECOMING DOROTHY

50 "black Scot" Kurth, *American Cassandra*, 17.

51 "He took my hand" DT, memoirs, SU.

52 "plugged the flow, sealing in the poisons" DT, memoirs, SU; Marion K. Sanders interview with Peter Willard Thompson, October 23, 1970: Kurth, *American Cassandra*, 19.

52 **All abortions, either surgical** Leslie J. Reagan, *When Abortion Was a Crime: Women, Medicine, and Law in the United States, 1867–1973* (Berkeley and Los Angeles: University of California Press, 1977).

53 "crackling with starch and reeking of cleanliness" Elizabeth [Peggy] Thompson Wilson, "Goodbye, Little Angel," unpublished MS, SU. See also Peter Kurth, *American Cassandra: The Life of Dorothy Thompson* (Boston: Little, Brown, 1990).

54 "gift of God" DT, railway diary, November 20, 1935, SU.

55 "fallen in love" DT, memoirs, SU.

56 "I was exposed" DT, railway diary, January 14, 1936, SU.

58 "poor but proud" Fanny Butcher, *Many Lives, One Love* (New York: Harper and Row, 1972), 20–21.

58 "Aunt" and "Auntie" DT, railway diary, December 11, 1935, SU.

58 **cultivate her "feminine" virtues** DT, unpublished MS, SU.

58 "Also they kept telling me I was pretty" DT to Vincent Sheean, April 13, 1950, series 2, box 3, SU.

58 **at the same time she felt** Barbara Miller Solomon, *In the Company of Educated Women: A History of Women and Higher Education in America* (New Haven, Conn.: Yale University Press, 1985).

59 "the epitome of all worldliness" DT to Christa Winsloe, December 21, 1935, SU.

60 "capacity to meet life," Kurth, *American Cassandra*, 36.

60 **"make people love [her]"** From advice to "Organizers" and annual report (1917) of the New York State Woman Suffrage Party, Foley and Laidlaw collections, Schlesinger Library, Radcliffe College.

62 **"something of the kind was fated"** DT to Ruth Hoople, February 10, 1922, SU.

63 **"still kindled our hopes and aspirations"** DT, *The Developments of Our Times* (De Land, Fla.: John B. Stetson University Press, 1948).

63 **"Since you are obliged to earn your own living"** Quoted in Eugenia Schwarzwald, "Eine Journalistin," n.d., SU.

64 **"on space"** DT to Ruth Hoople, February 10, 1922, SU.

64 **"democracy, socialism, nationalism were all assuming new, strange forms"** DT, Europe diary, n.d., SU.

64 **"inside track"** DT to C. B. Wade, March 23, 1951, box 2, folder 4, SU.

64 **"For the first time since leaving"** Ibid.

65 **"There has never been anyone like"** Rose Wilder Lane to DT, January 21, 1928, Herbert Hoover Presidential Library.

65 **"heartbreaking"** Kurth, *American Cassandra*, 59.

66 **"I believe being happy doesn't count"** DT to Beatrice Sorchan, December 9, 1920, box 35, folder 1, SU.

66 **"good strong coffee," "bad sour wine"** Kurth, *American Cassandra*, 62.

66 **"he as a news-collector"** DT to Rose Wilder Lane, September 14, 1921, SU.

67 **"Nowhere are capital and labor"** DT, "Agitation of Karl Grows at Hungary," MS, SU.

67 **"a thunder bolt" . . . "not only at first sight"** Vincent Sheean, *Dorothy and Red* (Boston: Houghton Mifflin, 1963), 24.

67 **"His hair lay on his head"** DT, "The Tulip Box."

68 **"Your charm for me is"** DT to Joseph Bard, April 3, 1927, box 1, SU.

68 **"something imaginative, kindling, kind"** DT to Joseph Bard, January 27, 1926.

68 **"He is a gentle and remote soul"** DT to Rose Wilder Lane, July 15, 1921, SU.

68 **"accomplished flirt" . . . "a national pastime in Hungary"** Louis Untermeyer, *Bygones: The Recollections of Louis Untermeyer* (New York: Harcourt, Brace, and World, 1965), 82.

69 **"Back again in this hot and smelly town"** Joseph Bard to DT, September 1, 1922, SU.

69 **"radiantly pretty" . . . "all woman"** Kurth, *American Cassandra*, 79.

69 **"Sometimes I want love"** DT to Rose Wilder Lane, September 23, 1921, SU.

69 **"If I had [children]"** DT to Rose Wilder Lane, September 14, 1921, SU.

70 **"the relations between men and women"** DT to Gertrude Tone, n.d., ca. 1922, SU.

70 **"I have humbled myself before you"** Joseph Bard to DT, August 18, 1922, September 9, 1922, August 20, 1922, and undated, SU.

70 **"I have in me the capacity"** DT to Joseph Bard, December 16, 1926, unsent.

71 **"[Joseph was] not an unkindly soul"** RW to Vincent Sheean, December 25, 1963, Houghton Mifflin Company archives, Houghton Library, Harvard University.

71 **"perfect bliss"** DT to Joseph Bard, January 8, 1936, railway diary, SU.

71 **"ahead at Journalism"** DT to Rose Wilder Lane, September 3, 1921, SU.

71 **"Delirious with love"** DT, January 8, 1936, railway diary, SU.

71 **"had so little time together"** DT to Joseph Bard, January 27, 1926, SU.

72 **"back into a semi-homosexual state"** DT to Joseph Bard, January 1927, SU.

72 **"If I have a friend with whom I can work"** Kurth, *American Cassandra*, 97.

72　**"If you find the"** DT to Joseph Bard, January 25, 1927, 50.

73　**"starch his prick"** Agar, Eileen, and Andrew Lambirth, *A Look at My Life* (London: Methuen, 1988), 55–56.

73　**"And on top of that you *planned*"** DT to Joseph Bard, January 25, 1927, SU.

73　**"A real woman can be two things"** Ibid.

74　**"Byronic"... "irresistible"** Agar and Lambirth, *Look at My Life*, 65–66.

74　**"his head [was] overfed and his heart starved"** Ibid.

74　**"suffering for [him]"** DT to Joseph Bard, January 14, 1926, SU.

75　**"I am sending this boy of mine"** DT to Eileen Agar, July 12, 1927, box 1, SU.

75　**"Curious... how I believed"** DT to Joseph Bard, January 29, [1920s], SU.

CHAPTER 3 / THE TRINITY

77　**"a classic set-up"** AW, "Life with Auntie Panther and H. G. Wells," *The Observer*, January 4, 1976.

78　**Freudian theory, which had as many** Misha Kavka, "Men in (Shell-)Shock: Masculinity, Trauma, and Psychoanalysis in Rebecca West's *The Return of the Soldier*," *Studies in Twentieth Century Literature* 22, no. 1 (Winter 1998): 151–71.

78　**It was Freud as well** Sigmund Freud's writing on shell shock, *Collected Papers*, vol. 5, ed. James Strachey (New York: Basic Books, 1959), 83–87; and Ben Shephard, *A War of Nerves: Soldiers and Psychiatrists in the Twentieth Century* (Cambridge, Mass.: Harvard University Press, 2001), 110.

78　**"When one is an adult"** RW, *The Return of the Soldier* (New York: George H. Doran, 1918), 79.

79　**"Every mother is a"** *The Judge*, frontispiece.

79　**"a stout, generous, lively"** Virginia Woolf to Ottoline Morrell, July 18, 1922.

79　**"an ill-conceived sprawl"** Ray, *H. G. Wells and Rebecca West*, 123.

80　**"pitched"... "sort of place"** AW, "Life with Auntie Panther and H. G. Wells."

81　**"terrible trouble"** Ibid.

81　**"She's my mother"** Author's interview with Norman and Marion Macleod, June 2009.

82　**"It seems to me that almost"** HGW to RW, 1922, series 1, box 21, folder 965, YU.

82　**"He treated me"** RW, diary of war years, April 5, 1944, UT.

82　**"I do love some sort"** HGW to RW, series 1, box 21, folder 965, YU.

84　**"I'm not really a Jaguar"** HGW to RW, March 1923, series 1, box 21, folder 966, YU.

84　**"I don't think it just"** HGW to RW, March 21, 1923, box 21, folder 966, YU.

84　**"Will you ask"** HGW to RW, March 1923, YU.

85　**"Rebecca was always making excuses"** Author's interview with AMS, May 13, 2006.

85　**"I shall miss you so much"** AW to RW, n.d., ca 1924, series 2, box 105, folder 980, YU.

86　**It was "gorgeous"** RW to WFM, November 2, 1923, IU.

87　**"Jewess of the most opulent oriental"** RW to Letitia Fairfield, February 8, 1924, IU.

88　**"I love America and I loathe it"** RW to SL and Grace Casanova, December 9, 1923, SU.

88　**"I have been in three places"** RW to WFM, November 2, 1923, IU.

89　**"hounded by a malevolent fate"** RW to WFM, n.d., ca. mid-1920s, IU.

89　**something "evil" inside her** RW, autobiographical memorandum, January 28, 1958, YU.

89 **"a gothic angel"** RW to Harold Ross, August 25, 1947, New York Public Library.

90 **"If it wasn't for Anthony"** RW to Fannie Hurst, June 12, 1924, Harry Ransom Center, University of Texas at Austin.

91 **"not murdering Jane"** HGW to RW, March 21, 1923, YU.

91 **"body slave"** HGW to RW, August 3, 1924, YU.

91 **"some way of dealing"** HGW to RW, 1924, YU.

92 **"There Is No Conversation"** RW, *The Harsh Voice: Four Short Novels* (Garden City, N.Y.: Doubleday, 1935), 145.

93 **Rebecca's affair with Max** RW, manuscript notebook, UT.

93 **"animals we would be free to"** Rollyson, *Rebecca West*, 115.

94 **Anthony would later write** AW, "My Father's Unpaid Debts of Love," *The Observer*, January 11, 1976.

95 **"Dear Mr. Wells"** AW to HGW, ca. June 1920, GEN MSS 105, box 22, folder 980, YU.

CHAPTER 4 / RESURRECTION

96 **"Marriage is the triumph of imagination over intelligence"** Commonly attributed to Oscar Wilde; sometimes attributed to Samuel Johnson.

96 **"It was a vitally important element"** Sheean, *Dorothy and Red*, 13.

97 **"first rate peripatetic brain picker"** DT to SL, April 29, 1937, SU.

98 **"I don't even know you, Mr. Lewis"** Sheean, *Dorothy and Red*, 29.

98 **"pretty brutally"** Mark Schorer, *Sinclair Lewis: An American Life* (Minneapolis: University of Minnesota Press, 1963), 488.

100 **"When I was beginning"** DT to Peggy Wilson, October 12, 1927, SU.

102 **"If he would sit still so that life"** RW, "Sinclair Lewis Introduces *Elmer Gantry*," *New York Herald Tribune*, March 13, 1927.

102 **"To see Dorothy"** DT to Arthur Lyons, April 17, 1939, SU

103 **"creative marriage"** DT to Joseph Bard, January 27, 1926, SU.

103 **"the little Lanvin taffeta"** DT diary, September 21, 1927, box 4, Diaries 1920–1928, SU.

105 **"I know you fondly dream"** Dorothy's sonnet, December 25, 1927, Sheean, *Dorothy and Red*, 81.

108 **shouting "at the top"** Sanders, *Dorothy Thompson*, 141.

108 **"go to for strength"** Schorer, *Sinclair Lewis*, 502.

CHAPTER 5 / DESCENT

113 **Descend, so that you may ascend** Saint Augustine, *The Confessions of St. Augustine* (New York: P. F. Collier and Son, 1909), 58.

114 **"I am thinking of making"** RW to Fannie Hurst, n.d., ca. early 1920s, box 241, folder 6, Harry Ransom Center, University of Texas at Austin.

114 **"the source of my troubles"** RW to Fannie Hurst, ca. 1927, Harry Ransom Center, University of Texas at Austin.

114 **"I am entirely convinced"** Ibid.

116 **"The only thing against Uncle Wells"** RW, *The Strange Necessity* (London: Virago Press, 1987), 199–200.

117 **"So is this book a sham"** HGW to RW, August 1928; Rollyson, *Rebecca West*, 101.

118 **"It means we have neglected"** HGW to RW, January 1, 1930.

118 **"I am afraid you've got"** RW to HGW, December 1930, series 1, box 21, folder 973, YU.

118 **"He was in fact almost ineducable"** RW's correspondence with Gordon Ray, October 30, 1973, PML.

120 **Hugh Walpole of** *The New York Times* Hugh Walpole to RW, September 26, 1928, YU.

120 **"Fiction and poetry"** RW, "The Novelist's Voice," September 14, 1976, Radio 4, BBC recording reference T 37283.

120 **"It's more your stuff"** HGW to RW, September 13, 1929, YU.

121 **"European ambassador"** Richard Roberts, *Schroders: Merchants and Bankers* (London: Macmillan, 1992), 181.

122 **"bluer than blue"** . . . **"a knack for making you feel"** Carl Rollyson interview with June Head Fenby, who overheard Rebecca's comments, Rollyson, *Rebecca West*, 139.

123 **"sides but no back"** Ibid.

124 **"loving delight"** HA to RW, May 10, 1930, GEN MSS 105, series 1, box 2, folder 24, YU.

124 **"If I had no happiness"** RW to S. K. Ratcliffe, October 30, 1930, YU.

124 **"heaven and hell"** RW to HA, January 12, 1930, YU.

124 **Rebecca did, nonetheless** Author's interview with Norman and Marion Macleod, November 2009.

124 **"who adored her baby so"** Letitia Fairfield to HA, Manuscript Collection, IU; Rollyson, *Rebecca West*, 148.

126 **"I have never known anybody so"** RW to Douglas and Mia Woodruff, November 9, 1968, Douglas Woodruff Papers, Georgetown University Library.

126 **Later, H.G. would write** HGW, *H. G. Wells in Love*, 161.

127 **"body slave"** HGW to RW, August 3, 1924, YU.

127 **"[Rebecca] invited herself to tea"** HGW, *H. G. Wells in Love*, 113.

127 **On November 1, 1930** For further wedding observations see C. Patrick Thompson, "The New Rebecca West," *New York Herald Tribune*, February 7, 1932, UT.

128 **"proper backdrop"** Rollyson, *Rebecca West*, 147; assorted newspaper clippings.

CHAPTER 6 / RENAISSANCE

130 **"Show me a woman married to"** DT to Helen Woodward, October 9, 1930, series 2, box 1, SU.

131 **"What can you carry in a caravan"** DT, honeymoon diary, May 29, 1920, SU.

132 **"You are . . . a bread pudding"** Ibid., June 8, 1928.

133 **"Bad temper is the most destructive of human faults"** Ibid., August 2, 1928.

136 **"[Hal] had been drinking terribly again"** DT, diary entry, February 13, 1929, SU.

137 **"I want to understand all manner"** Ibid.

137 **"I can really do nothing for him"** Ibid.

138 **"stay more or less forever"** Sheean, *Dorothy and Red*, 121.

140 **"one-and-only earthly edition of paradise"** SL to Alfred Harcourt, February 15, 1930, in SL, *From Main Street to Stockholm: The Letters of Sinclair Lewis, 1919–1930*, ed. Harrison Smith (New York: Harcourt, Brace, 1952), 285.

141 **"Ponce de Leon's country"** DT to Joseph Bard, August 20, 1930, SU.

141 **"the most delightful little house"** Sanders, *Dorothy Thompson*, 158.

143 **"A woman must be gravid"** Sheean, *Dorothy and Red*, 170.

143 **"This is barbarous and utterly unworthy"** Ibid.

143 **"Bring in the child"** Ibid., 171.

CHAPTER 7 / A COLD WIND

144 **"A cold wind blew past me"** RW, *A Letter to a Grandfather* (London: Hogarth Press, 1933), 7.

145 **"No words can express"** UT.

145 **"she [had] sold herself into bondage"** Carl Rollyson, *The Literary Legacy of Rebecca West* (San Francisco: International Scholars Publications, 1998), 88–89.

146 **"I must say"** RW to WFM, February 15, 1931, IU.

146 **"the whole of London"** Louise Morgan, "Rebecca West: Who Eats Her Cake and Has It Too," *Everyman,* November 5, 1931.

148 **"[Anthony] feels he is being thwarted"** HGW to RW, December 31, 1931, series 1, box 21, folder 973, YU.

148 **"concern myself with your affairs"** HGW to AW, April 14, 1932, series 1, box 21, folder 974, YU.

148 **"He is high strung to the point"** Hans Sachs to RW, July 1932, YU.

150 **a "searchlight into"** RW, "There Is No Conversation," *The Harsh Voice,* 145.

151 **"The strength of [Anthony's] fixation"** Hans Sachs to RW, November 21, 1932, YU.

151 **"We are adept at misunderstanding"** AW to RW, n.d., UT.

152 **"Do you think that you would"** Virginia Woolf to RW, September 18, 1931, GEN MSS 105, YU.

154 **"mindless prostitute"** Several manuscript notebooks containing draft versions of RW's memoirs, UT.

156 **"They are in love with cancer"** RW, *Letter to a Grandfather,* 35.

157 **"Man is a reed"** Pascal's *Pensées* from the frontispiece in RW, *The Thinking Reed* (London: Hutchinson, 1936).

CHAPTER 8 / A GOOD WIFE

159 **"A good wife"** Jules Harlow, *Siddur Sim Shalom: A Prayerbook for Shabbat, Festivals, and Weekdays* (New York: Rabbinical Assembly, United Synagogue of America, 1985), 725.

159 **"Have you heard, Joseph"** DT to Joseph Bard, August 20, 1930, SU.

160 **"long, low mountains"** Ibid.

161 **"This is partly for the baby"** DT to Helen Woodward, October 9, 1930, series 2, box 1, SU.

161 **"perfectly efficient nurse"** DT, "The Baby in the Kitchen," in *Courage to Be Happy,* 83.

161 **"a couple of months away"** Lingeman, *Rebel from Main Street,* 351.

161 **"My brain has gone phut"** DT to Helen Woodward, October 9, 1930, series 2, box 1, SU.

162 **"Oh, yeah?"** Schorer, *Sinclair Lewis,* 539.

162 **"Well, I have the Order"** Ibid.

163 **"Dreiser menace"** Ibid., 544.

165 **"assisted only by his integrity"** (and subsequent quotes) SL, "The American Fear of Literature," ed. Mark Schorer, in *An American Primer,* ed. Daniel J. Boorstin (New York: Penguin, 1985), 847–62.

167 **"the wizened, club-footed and frenetic"** DT, "Poverty De Luxe," *The Saturday Evening Post,* May 2, 1931, 6–7, 150–52.

167 **"the little man with the dragging"** Ibid.

168 **"best out-fitted poorhouse on earth"** Ibid.

168   **"loafing—looking inside myself"** SL to DT, February 12, 1931, SU.

169   **"courteous and friendly"** DT to Tish and Wallace Irwin, November 26, 1930, series 2, box 2, folder 1, SU.

169   **"I want him to be modern"** Ibid.

170   **"These days are beautiful"** DT, diary, August 24, 1931, series 4, box 2, SU.

170   **"Two souls, alas, dwell in this bosom"** DT quoting Goethe, "Something Must Happen," *The Saturday Evening Post.*

170   **"A great play-actor is Beaverbrook"** DT to SL, November 10, 1931, series 2, box 4, SU.

171   **"Rebecca sends her love"** Ibid.

171   **"I'm having a grand time"** Ibid.

171   **"Everytime [Mickey] comes back from the park,"** SL to DT, November 8, 1931, SU.

171   **"I am going to do something that is important"** SL to DT, November 21, 1931, SU.

171   **"As you know, I should be infinitely proud"** DT to SL, December 1931, series 3, box 4, SU.

CHAPTER 9 / THE RIDDLE OF THE UNIVERSE

173   **"If during the next million generations"** RW, *Black Lamb and Gray Falcon*, 1013.

174   **"In the name of the noble"** Amos Elon, *The Pity of It All: A History of Jews in Germany: 1743–1933* (New York: Metropolitan Books, 2002).

174   **"Wherever they burn books"** Piers Brendon, *The Dark Valley: A Panorama of the 1930s* (New York: Alfred A. Knopf, 2000), 186.

174   **"Dionysiac mane of black hair"** Derek Patmore interview with RW, *Sunday Referee*, March 12, 1933, UT.

176   **"a queer creature"** RW to Fannie Hurst, October 30, 1933, Harry Ransom Center, University of Texas at Austin.

177   **"trembling reed"** RW to HGW, 1934, series 1, box 21, folder 975, YU.

177   **had written an article** Odette Keun, "H.G. Wells—The Player, Part 1," *Time and Tide*, October 18, 1934, House of Lords Records Office.

178   **"lover-shadow"** *H.G. Wells in Love*, 61.

179   **When Henry's uncle Ernest died** Carl Rollyson, *Rebecca West: A Life* (New York: Scribner, 1996), 181.

179   **"music of a kind other than"** RW, *Black Lamb and Grey Falcon*, 2.

179   **"fountain of negativism"** Ibid., 1083.

179   **"Life, under any label"** Ibid.

180   **"small nation, like a beset soul"** Brian Hall, "Rebecca West's War," *The New Yorker*, April 15, 1996.

180   **"the riddle of our universe"** Ibid.

183   **"Once I have done this book"** RW to HA, May 15, 1938, in Bonnie Klime Scott, ed., *Selected Letters of Rebecca West* (New Haven, Conn.: Yale University Press, 2000), 166.

185   **"It was a huge and dirty lie"** Ibid., 826, 827.

185   **"fundamental but foul disposition of the mind"** Ibid., 831.

186   **"I am not going anywhere"** Ibid., 1012.

186   **"If during the next million generations"** Ibid., 1013.

186   **"two embryos"** Ibid., 1113.

186   **"Art gives us hope"** Ibid., 1127–28.

187   **"buy salvation off an idiot God"** Ibid., 1145–46.

187   **"one of the most passionate"** *Time*, November 11, 1941, 94.

187 **"the magnification and intensification"** Katherine Woods, "Rebecca West's Brilliant Mosaic of Yugoslavian Travel," *The New York Times,* October 26, 1941.

187 **"as astonishing as it is brilliant"** Clifton Fadiman, "Magnum Opus," *The New Yorker,* October 25, 1941, 88–90.

188 **"Henry and I had always plenty"** RW, unpublished memoir, 1927, courtesy of AMS, 36.

188 **"The cold truth about me"** Hall, "Rebecca West's War," 80.

189 **"[Your] book, I think"** DT to RW and HA, October 12, 1942, GEN MSS 105, box 16, folder 823, YU.

CHAPTER 10 / THE FAITHFUL WARRIOR

190 **"I am widowed of an illusion"** DT to SL, 1938 or early 1939, SU.

191 **"When finally I walked into"** DT, *I Saw Hitler!* (New York: Farrar and Rinehart, 1932), 13.

192 **"Everytime I go into the streets"** DT to SL, December 3, 1931, series 3, box 4, SU.

192 **"I'm happier here"** Ibid.

193 **"I don't think about"** Ibid.

194 **"a stupid, inhumane, and impractical peace"** DT, *I Saw Hitler,* v–vi.

194 **"the apotheosis of collective mediocrity"** DT to Raoul de Roussy de Sales, July 20, 1942, Peter Kurth's research courtesy of Peter Kurth.

194 **"Your little son today entered your room"** DT to SL, February 1932, series 3, box 4, SU.

194 **"like rotting weeds"** Sheean, *Dorothy and Red,* 193.

196 **The book, however, was a huge** Schorer, *Sinclair Lewis,* 583.

197 **"cuckoo-clock in aspect"** Sheean, *Dorothy and Red,* 195.

197 **"It's probably just as well"** Schorer, *Sinclair Lewis,* 576.

198 **"goulash-woman produced on the Danube"** Sheean, *Dorothy and Red,* 220.

199 **"was by no means inexperienced"** Ibid., 214.

199 **"Well then, how to account for"** DT, diary, December 28, 1932, series 4, box 1, SU.

199 **"Anyway, it doesn't suit me"** Ibid.

200 **"He remained a sweetly assaulting male"** DT, diary, January 2, 1933, SU.

200 **"I stood a long time in his arms"** Ibid.

200 **"It was awfully good"** Ibid.

200 **"Darling, I didn't do anything"** Ibid.

200 **"It would be nice to have"** Ibid.

200 **"the long-legged red-headed girl"** DT, diary, January 7, 1933, SU.

201 **"My whole being rises up"** Ibid.

201 **"I am not sure that having"** Ibid.

202 **"a smell of death"** DT, diary, January 4, 1933, SU.

202 **"These years have robbed us"** DT Diary, January 5, 1933, SU.

202 **"I'm so sorry"** SL to DT, February 12, 1933, Peter Kurth's research, courtesy of Peter Kurth.

202 **"You seem to me in my"** Ibid., February 18, 1933.

202 **"It is true, isn't it"** Ibid., March 4, 1933.

203 **"My dear, my dear"** DT to SL, March 25, 1933, SU.

203 **"bad dream" . . . "You have faults"** SL to DT, April 3, 1933, Peter Kurth's research, courtesy of Peter Kurth.

204 **"the kind women living alone"** Combined from DT to SL, March 26, March 30, and n.d., ca. March 1933, SU.

204 **"What can I do, then"** Holograph, SU.

205 **"original me" "cultivated me"** DT to Christa Winsloe (unsent?), "Sunday," 1933–1934, SU.

205 **"Dotty darling, I feel orphaned"** Christa Winsloe to DT, April 14, 1933, series 1, box 27, SU.

205 **"wrath of god Mickey"** Christa Winsloe to DT, n.d., series 1, box 27, SU.

206 **"better self" . . . "creative natures"** DT to Christa Winsloe, n.d., "Sunday," ca. 1933–34, SU.

208 **"You have to separate"** Christa Winsloe to DT, undated, Syracuse, series 1, box 27, SU.

208 **"she flung the whole force of her being"** Phyllis Bottome, manuscript, series 4, box 8, pp. 16–17, early 1930s, SU.

209 **"hard across the mouth"** Brendan Gill, *Here at the New Yorker,* (New York: da Capo Press, Inc., 1997), 65.

209 **"There is still an utter calm here"** Genia Schwarzwald to DT, January 7, 1934, series 1, box 27, SU.

210 **"Austria is terribly sad"** DT to Joseph Bard, January 7, 1935, SU.

210 **"I hate being completely"** Ibid.

211 **"If only someone would speak"** DT letter, March 18, 1933, in *A Bundle of Time: The Memoirs of Harriet Cohen* (London: Faber and Faber, 1969), 174–78.

211 **"Hitler's Kingdom"** DT, "Good-by to Germany," *Harper's Magazine,* December 1934, 43–51.

212 **"There are to be no"** DT, "Room to Breathe In," *The Saturday Evening Post,* June 24, 1933.

212 **"six thousand boys"** DT, "Good-By to Germany," *Harper's Magazine,* December 1933.

212 **"mere excrescences"** SL to DT, August 15, 1934, SU.

212 **"old house"** Ibid.

212 **"Between you and me"** Ibid.

213 **"When I reached Berlin"** DT, "Good-by to Germany."

214 **"national self-respect" . . . "a further right of hospitality"** Sanders, *Legend in Her Time,* 381.

214 **"My offense,"** DT, "Dorothy Thompson Tells of Nazi Ban," *The New York Times,* August 26, 1934.

215 **"why in hell he had had to marry a Roman Senator"** Schorer, *Sinclair Lewis,* 619.

CHAPTER 11 / BLOODLUST

219 **"Let historians record"** RW, "The First Fortnight," *Ladies' Home Journal,* January 1940.

219 **"We knew that this was"** RW, "Housewife's Nightmare," *The New Yorker,* December 14, 1940, p. 59.

220 **"It's the poisoning of"** RW to Irita Van Doren, Library of Congress manuscript, 1938.

220 **"September, 1939 was to be"** RW, "The First Fortnight."

221 **"I have never felt so coldly"** RW to Alexander Woollcott, May 22, 1940, Houghton Library, Harvard University.

222 **"Either this is the most colossal"** RW, "The First Fortnight."

223 **"The defense of London"** RW to Doris Stevens, November 19, 1940, GEN MSS 239, box 3, folder 100, YU.

223 **Eight and a half million Londoners** Interview of RW by Derek Hart, December 3, 1969, BBC recording reference LP 32883, NSA 195491.

224 **"There was such a stillness"** RW, *Black Lamb and Grey Falcon*, 1115.

225 **"big enough for a cow's head"** RW, "Housewife's Nightmare," p. 52.

225 **"The long, low building"** Ibid.

225 **"which is half a Regency house"** RW to Doris Stevens, November 19, 1940, GEN MSS 239, box 3, folder 100, YU.

225 **Purchased from a bank** Rollyson, *Rebecca West*, 201.

225 **"still everybody is broke"** RW to Mary Andrews, February 10, 1940, box 2, folder 33, YU.

226 **"something that was very precious"** RW, "Housewife's Nightmare," p. 52.

226 **"I believe my pleasure"** Ibid.

226 **"My husband and I"** Ibid.

227 **"I feel like a female elephant"** RW to Alexander Woollcott, n.d., Houghton Library, Harvard University.

228 **"would kill herself"** John Gunther, diary of 1941 London, December 4, 1941, add. 2, John Gunther Papers, University of Chicago.

230 **"watching it cast off"** Bernard Levin interview with RW, December 4, 1981, British Library Sound Archives, MT recording reference 40868-BBC TLN48/379K417.

230 **"a complete vision of reality"** RW, "The Duty of the Writer," 1941, in *Writers in Freedom: A Symposium Based on the XVII International Congress of the P.E.N. Club*, ed. Herman Ould (New York: Hutchinson, 1942), 20–24. Shortly thereafter, RW would be elected president of International PEN.

231 **"the Great Heap of Money"** WFM to RW, December 20, 1940, GEN MSS 105, box 12, folder 528, YU.

232 **"dreadful storms of tears & grief"** Winifred Macleod to RW, n.d., ca. early 1940s, GEN MSS 105, box 12, folder 528, YU.

232 **"She was completely insulated"** RW to WFM, 1940s, IU.

233 **"I gather from Henry"** Ibid.

233 **beautiful "brown" baby girl** Author's interview with Norman and Marion Macleod, June 7, 2007.

234 **Anthony was at the moment "normal"** RW to Dr. Glover about AW's "bad mental state," ca. mid-1940, GEN MSS 105, box 22, folder 981, YU.

234 **She [Kitty] then looked** Ibid.

234 **she "wished Anthony was dead"** Ibid.

236 **"milk diet"** RW to Mary Andrews, 1940, GEN MSS 105, series 1, box 2, folder 33, YU.

CHAPTER 12 / GOD LUST

238 **"All those who, because they"** DT, "It Was Bound to Happen," On the Record, *New York Herald Tribune*, September 1, 1939.

238 **"something between a Cassandra"** "Cartwheel Girl," *Time*, June 12, 1939.

238 **"powerfully woman"** DT, *Dorothy Thompson's Political Guide: A Study of American Liberalism and Its Relationship to Modern Totalitarian States* (New York: Stackpole Sons, 1938), 92–97.

239 **"The whole nation lived"** DT, "A Nation of Speculators," speech at the Union League Club, April 25, 1937.

240 **"That is the essence of"** DT, On the Record, *New York Herald Tribune*, September 22, 1937.

240 **"becomes the mask of Imperialism"** Ibid., September 27, 1937.

241 **"When our dictator turns up"** DT, "Ruffled Grouse,"On the Record, *New York Herald Tribune,* February 17, 1937.

243 **"honor," for example** Ibid., March 20, 1936.

244 **"Once you let down the dams"** DT, "Our Constitutional Crisis: Two Views," speech to League for Political Education, March 10, 1937, New York Public Library.

244 **"I wish they would"** Margaret Case Harriman, "The It Girl—II," *The New Yorker,* April 27, 1940, p. 27.

246 **"found Michael quite easily"** Marjorie Shuler, "Expedition to Olympus," *The Christian Science Monitor,* December 24, 1935.

247 **"I must say that I feel"** DT to RW, March 10, 1937, GEN MSS 105, box 16, folder 823, YU.

248 **"When you tell me that my work"** DT to SL, April 29, 1937, SU.

248 **"You don't know what"** Ibid.

248 **"creative genius" . . . "just a tail on an ascending comet"** Ibid.

248 **"Good God, Hal"** Ibid.

249 **"Darling, darling, darling there's only one thing"** Ibid.

249 **"What was there left for that"** DT to SL, late 1930s, Peter Kurth's research, courtesy of Peter Kurth.

250 **"*this* is a lie—a crazy bad dream"** DT to SL, late 1930s, Ibid.

250 **"the awful thing is Mickey"** Ibid.

250 **"Dorothy Thompson is the only woman"** Don Wharton, "Dorothy Thompson," *Scribner's,* May 1937.

251 **"real writing style"** DT, *Personalities in the News,* sound recording, RWA, 2287 B2, 1938, LOC.

251 **"difficult" . . . "cruel"** DT to Betty Swing, April 21, 1938, series 3, box 3, SU.

251 **"I know my son, much better"** Ibid.

252 **"subnormal"** DT to SL, n.d., ca. 1939, SU.

254 **"Our Europe is gone!"** Phyllis Bottome, reflections on DT, IX, 8, p. 21, SU.

254 **"The results of what happened in Austria"** DT, *Let the Record Speak* (Cambridge, Mass.: Riverside Press, 1939), 152–57.

254 **"strangle Neville Chamberlain"** Alexander Woollcott to RW, February 21, 1938, in *The Letters of Alexander Woollcott,* ed. Beatrice Kaufman and Joseph Hennessy (New York: Viking Press, 1944), 206.

255 **looking lovely** Phyllis Bottome, September 1938, series 9, box 8, at page 22.

255 **"They are holding every"** DT, *Let the Record Speak,* 256–60.

256 **"Too many honors"** DT to Pearl Buck May 10, 1938, Schlesinger Library, Radcliffe College.

256 **"The strangest aspect of your"** SL to DT, January 28, 1939, Peter Kurth's research, courtesy of Peter Kurth.

256 **"a little disaster of a girl"** HGW to RW, ca. early July 1913, series 1, box 18, folder 905, YU.

256 **On December 6, 1939** ML to DT, December 6, 1939, series 3, box 3, folder 7, SU.

256 **"revolutionary world"** DT, "The Dilemma of the Liberal," 1938, Peter Kurth research, courtesy of Peter Kurth.

257 **"Dear Michael"** SL to ML, December 20, 1939, series 3, box 2, SU.

258 **"Did you ever realize"** Walter Lippmann to Helen Armstrong, February 13, 1938, Walter Lippmann Papers, Sterling Memorial Library, YU.

258 **"If you think [our relationship is] wicked"** DT to SL, circa 1938, unsent, SU.

259 **"If I Had a Daughter"** DT, *Ladies' Home Journal,* September 1939, SU.

259 **"widowed of an illusion"** . . . **"the best things"** DT to SL, circa. 1938, unsent, SU.

CHAPTER 13 / FRACTURED

261 **"Destiny cares nothing"** RW, *A Train of Powder* (Chicago: Ivan R. Dee, 1955), 250.

262 **"non-Blenheim born"** RW, diary of war years, June 6, 1944, UT.

262 **"savagery"** . . . **"pioneer Protestantism"** Ibid.

262 **"I have had wonderful friends"** Ibid.

262 **"himself at 18"** Kitty West to RW, 1944, GEN MSS 105, box 22, folder 985, YU.

263 **"I wish you'd remember that"** RW to AW, n.d., ca. 1944, GEN MSS 105, box 22, folder 979, YU.

263 **"pitifully miserable and afraid"** RW, diary of war years, June 6, 1944.

264 **"enormously enlarged"** . . . **"there are absolutely no clinical symptoms"** Ibid.

264 **"queer . . . fat and animal"** Ibid.

265 **"affection is real and living"** Ibid., April 5, 1944.

265 **"get it straight"** RW to AW, 1944, PML.

265 **"wicked woman"** Ibid.

265 **"Unfortunately her madness fitted"** (and subsequent quotes) Ibid.

266 **"tormented by the fear"** RW, diary of war years, June 6, 1944, UT.

266 **"Everything is tangled up"** Ibid., April 5, 1944.

268 **"wonderful talk"** RW, journal, March 29, 1945, series 3, folder 58, UT.

269 **"much smoke and flare"** (and subsequent quotes) Ibid., April 4, 1945.

269 **"Kitty has taken him from me"** Ibid., March 30, 1945.

269 **There were rumors that she** RW to Doris Stevens, April 5, 1945, GEN MSS 239, box 3, folder 100, YU.

269 **"mildest possible laxative"** RW to Doris Stevens, May 12, 1945, GEN MSS 239, box 3, folder 100, YU.

270 **THERE'LL ALWAYS BE AN ENGLAND** A patriotic war song. Melody and text by Ross Parker and Hugh Charles, 1939.

270 **"Today, perhaps, we shall think mostly of ourselves"** Winston Churchill, "End of the War in Europe," May 8, 1945, broadcast, London and House of Commons.

271 **"contentious journalism"** RW to Doris Stevens, February 10, 1945, GEN MSS 239, box 3, folder 100, YU.

271 **"We have the falling sickness"** Ibid.

272 **"an instrument"** RW to Mary Andrews, December 1945, box 2, folder 34, YU.

272 **When *Time and Tide,* a British literary magazine** *Time and Tide,* September 22, 1945, UT.

273 **"Please write any story you"** Harold Ross to RW, December 17, 1945, GEN MSS 105, box 13, folder 612, YU.

273 **"I had been living"** RW, notes for Nuremberg, UT.

273 **"To begin with"** Ibid.

274 **"a man's world"** Ibid.

274 **It had been nearly two years since** Information on International Criminal Court and Nuremberg provided by William Shawcross, journalist, author, and the son of the chief British prosecutor, Hartley Shawcross.

275 **"an old-fashioned opera-set"** RW, *Train of Powder,* 23.

275 **"a mania that was to force"** Ibid., 24.

275 **"haunted house"** Ibid., 25.

276 **"the last convulsion"** Ibid.

276 **"let [herself] go"** Francis Biddle to Katherine Biddle, July 30, 1946, box 19, SU.

277 **"put the shutters up ... he made me"** Rollyson, *Rebecca West*, 249.

278 the **"murmur of [her] spirit"** Francis Biddle to RW, September 1946, GEN MSS 105, series 1, box 6, folder 140, YU.

279 **"This was a man whose"** (and subsequent quotes) J. B. Priestley, September 16, 1946, Golders Green Crematorium, House of Lords Records Office; Beaverbrook Papers, personal correspondence, Hist 184 C 323.

280 **"I believe in prayer"** Francis Biddle to RW, August 10, 1946, GEN MSS 105, series 1, box 6, folder 140, YU.

280 **"till the show is over"** Francis Biddle to RW, August 16, 1946, GEN MSS 105, series 1, box 6, folder 140, YU.

280 **bird of paradise** Ibid.

280 **"much more anonymous"** Francis Biddle to RW, August 19, 1946, GEN MSS 105, series 1, box 6, folder 140, YU.

281 **"We shall have to suspend things"** Francis Biddle to RW, August 21, 1946, GEN MSS 105, series 1, box 6, folder 140, YU.

281 **"When I had known him"** RW to WFM, 1946, MSS, IU.

281 **"He is highly intelligent"** Ibid.

282 **"My dear Dorothy"** RW to DT, August 31, 1946, SU.

282 **"vague reason—or if there is some political event"** Ibid.

282 **"he seemed to have aged"** RW to HA, mid-1946, GEN MSS 105, series 1, box 2, folder 35, YU.

283 **"Katherine has got him,"** Rollyson, *Rebecca West*, 254.

284 **"It is possible that [the accused] never think"** RW, "Extraordinary Exile," *The New Yorker,* September 7, 1946, 35.

285 **"He is, above all things, soft"** Ibid., 34.

286 **"It is difficult not to"** Ibid., 46.

287 **"The door at the back of the dock"** RW, "The Birch Leaves Falling," *The New Yorker,* October 26, 1946, 103.

287 **"It is not exactly pity"** Ibid., 98.

288 **"a highly intelligent swan"** RW, "Extraordinary Exile," 38.

CHAPTER 14 / *IHR KAMPF*

289 **"Get me that quote"** Gleaned from documents and letters about how DT worked, as well as Peter Kurth's interview with the childen of Jimmy and Dinah Sheean.

290 **GOD PROTECT US FROM TRAITORS** Geoffrey C. Ward, "Wonder Woman," *The New York Review of Books,* August 16, 1990.

290 **"uppers"** Author's interview with Jane Gunther and Peter Kurth, July 29, 2002.

290 **"If the politicians won't nominate"** Sheean, quoting Helen Reid, 1948, *Dorothy and Red,* 282.

291 **"phony war"** DT, *Listen, Hans* (Boston: Houghton Mifflin, 1942).

291 **"Ten times, in the roar"** DT radio broadcast, reprinted in *Current History,* June 1940.

292 **"tired and defeatist"** DT to Paul Block, June 7, 1940, SU.

292 **"unbelievably dark"** Peter Kurth interview with Julian Bach, May 9, 1987, Peter Kurth's research, courtesy of Peter Kurth.

292 **"The democratic ideal"** DT, "Opportunity in Crisis: Thoughts After the Fall of Paris." *The Washington Post,* June 17, 1940.

293 **"The reality is [that there is an ongoing] world revolution"** DT to Wendell Willkie, 1940, series 2, box 8, SU.

294 **"two blond Valkyries on the prows of opposing ships of state"** Sanders, *Dorothy Thompson*, 261.

294 **"catfight"** Shadegg, *Clare Boothe Luce: A Biography* (New York: Simon and Schuster, 1970).

294 **"Men can disagree"** Ibid.

295 **"moral superiority"** Hans Thomsen, Documents on German Foreign Policy, July 20, 1940.

295 **No candidate, she said** DT, campaign speech for FDR, November 4, 1940, Library of Congress, RWB 7351 B1-4.

297 **"out here"** ML to DT, 1940, series 3, box 3, folder 9, SU.

297 **"Mother, I am not happy"** Ibid.

297 **"all women are"** DT, "The Changing Status of Women," 1940.

298 **"to have a showdown with"** Ibid.

298 **"as near a nervous breakdown"** DT to Mr. Meyer, W. Weisgal, August 10, 1940, SU.

298 **"You must learn to conserve"** Connie Traeger to DT, August 5, 1940, box 29, folder 1, SU.

298 **"You lost your job"** John Gunther, *Roosevelt in Retrospect: A Profile in History* (New York: Harper, 1950), 36.

299 **"I think we shall be happier"** DT to Helen Reid, January 1941, Peter Kurth's research, courtesy of Peter Kurth.

299 **Predicated on moral, quasi-religious principles** DT to Tom Lamont, October 1, 1941, series 2, box 1, SU.

299 **"a people's war"** DT to Congressman Mundt, June 2, 1941, series 2, box 1, SU.

300 **"instincts of heroism"** DT to Tom Lamont, October 1, 1941, series 2, box 1, SU.

300 **"Lindberghism" and the antidemocratic** DT to Tommy Dix, June 2, 1941, series 2, box 1, SU.

300 **Called to the podium** "Dorothy Thompson Asks a New Society," *The New York Times*, May 7, 1941.

301 **"She has shown what one"** Winston Churchill, 1941, UT.

301 **"in a more thorough manner"** Kurth, *American Cassandra*, 338.

302 **"I think your father"** DT to Wells Lewis, n.d., ca. January 1942, Grace Hegger Lewis Papers, Harry Ransom Center, University of Texas at Austin.

302 **"was a veritable"** Kurth, *American Cassandra*, 340.

302 **"The cock crows best"** DT, early 1942 MS, series 9, box 8, SU.

302 **"power, vigor, beauty, humor, affirmation"** DT to Bill Paley, December 11, 1941, series 2, box 1, SU.

303 **"fearless swimmer"** Grace Casanova to DT, June 25, 1941, series 1, box 7, folder 6, SU.

303 **"Such things ought not to happen"** Sheean, *Dorothy and Red*, 256.

303 **"a war of liberation" ... "antiquated imperialism"** DT, "This War and the Common Sense of Women," *Ladies' Home Journal*, April 1942.

304 **Based on painstaking research ... "complete military defeat"** DT, *Listen, Hans*, 62–80.

305 **Nizer managed to broker a deal** Louis Nizer, *Reflections Without Mirrors* (Garden City, N.Y.: Doubleday, 1978).

306 **"Both of them suffered"** Carl Zuckmayer, *Aufruf zum Leben: Porträts und Zeugnisse aus bewegten Zeiten* (Frankfurt: S. Fischer Verlag, 1995).

306 **"the best friend any woman"** DT to Dale Warren, n.d., SU.

307 **"ought to have married"** Sheean, *Dorothy and Red*, 289.

308 **live-in research assistant, Budzi** Hermann Budzislawski, whom Dorothy had sponsored during the war, was later exposed as a Soviet partisan who had distorted the information he had relayed to Dorothy to conform to Communist Party line. As a result, some of her wartime writing had made her appear a "fellow traveler," instead of the fiercely anti-Soviet advocate she was.

309 **"for any book you want"** Paul Brooks to DT, November 3, 1943, Houghton Library, Harvard University.

310 **"divide and conquer"** American Friends of the Middle East Steering Committee, "Statement of Aims," May 1951, box 191, folder 8, Clare Boothe Luce Papers, Library of Congress.

310 **"The question is no longer"** DT, "There Is Only One Answer," speech to the American Zionist Emergency Council, New York, 1943, New York Public Library.

310 **"For this tens of thousands"** Ibid.

310 **"primitive-minded Christians"** Ibid.

311 **"Perhaps ... the Messiah"** DT, "Jews in the Family of Nations," speech, 1943, New York Public Library.

312 **"I'm taking the war awfully hard"** DT to Wells Lewis, December 10, 1943, Grace Hegger Lewis Papers, Harry Ransom Center, University of Texas at Austin.

312 **"I have never seen anyone"** Putney School to DT, April 1943.

314 **"They know he is tired"** DT to Robert E. Sherwood, October 17, 1944.

314 **"Beg him to ignore them"** Ibid.

314 **"[The] Russian mind"** DT, speech to Democratic National Committee, October 20, 1944, Library of Congress.

314 **"In the public prints"** DT, diary, February 1945, series 4, box 1, SU.

314 **"The intellectual level of America"** DT to Philip Wylie, July 20, 1945.

314 **"race theory about the Germans"** DT to Philip Wylie, March 16, 1945.

315 **"I have her now under alcohols"** Maxim Kopf, quoted in John Gunther's diary, November 12, 1944, box 2, add. 2, John Gunther Papers, University of Chicago.

315 **"Dr. Traeger"** Ibid.

315 **"Dorothy in tears"** Ibid.

315 **"Oh *good* for you"** Schorer, *Sinclair Lewis*, 722.

316 **"I know what it means to you"** Carl Zuckmayer to DT, November 12, 1944, series 1, box 34, SU.

316 **"Dear Zuck"** DT to Carl Zuckmayer, November 16, 1944, DLA Marbach.

317 **"All that is really needed"** DT, untitled MS, SU.

319 **"hurt her to the core"** Zuckmayer, *Aufruf zum Leben.*

CHAPTER 15 / NO EXIT

323 **"We might stretch"** RW, *Letter to a Grandfather*, 42.

324 **"an act of saintliness"** RW to HA, March 25, 1947, GEN MSS 105, series 1, box 2, folder 36, YU.

324 **Six martinis and much raucous** Box 2, add. 11, John Gunther Papers, University of Chicago, March 22, 1947. See also John Gunther, *Inside U.S.A.* (New York: Harper and Brothers, 1947).

325 **"Nobody seems at all happy here"** (and subsequent quotes) RW to HA, March 25, 1947, GEN MSS 105, series 1, box 2, folder 36, YU.

326 **"I do not in practice like"** RW to HA, April 1947, GEN MSS 105, series 1, box 2, folder 36, YU.

326 **New York was truly "odd"** Ibid., March 25, 1947.

326 **"The atmosphere here is hysterical"** Ibid., April, 1947.

327 **"an older brother"** Harry Kirwin to DT (quoting DT back to her), September 24, 1947, series 3, box 2, folder 6, SU.

328 **"terribly bitter"** RW to HA, April 21, 1947, GEN MSS 105, series 1, box 2, folder 36, YU.

328 **"I do not know whether the fervent"** DT to John Gunther, August 2, 1946, box 40, add. 11, John Gunther Papers, University of Chicago.

329 **"He's still alive!"** John Gunther diary, July 30, 1947, University of Chicago.

329 **"small comfort"** Ibid.

329 **"hated being away so long"** RW to HA, April, 1947, GEN MSS 105, series 1, box 1, folder 36, YU.

329 **"done me a mortal"** . . . **"he were a tender and loving friend"** Ibid., May 1947.

330 **"American people don't seem"** Ibid.

330 **"God prevent me"** Ibid., May 13, 1947.

331 **Rebecca would name** RW, "Opera in Greenville," *The New Yorker,* June 14, 1947, 31–65.

331 **"Opera in Greenville" was first published** RW, *A Train of Powder* (Chicago: Ivan R. Dee, 1955), 81–123.

332 **"orgiastic joy"** RW, "Opera at Greenville."

332 **"The lynching trial in South Carolina"** RW, *Train of Powder,* 113–14.

333 **"loathsome a time [she] had in New York"** RW to WFM, 1947, IU.

333 **Although Anthony had signed** RW to WFM, 1947.

334 **Within weeks, one of the researchers** RW to Herbert Gunn, November 30, 1947, *Evening Standard* microfilm 250, Beaverbrook Papers, House of Lords Record Office.

334 **John would write to Rebecca** John Gunther to RW, December 7, 1947, GEN MSS 105, box 9, folder 335, YU.

334 **hand-delivered note** DT to Henry Luce, November 25, 1947, SU.

334 **"It was done from deep in"** John Gunther to RW, December 7, 1947, GEN MSS 105, box 9, folder 335, YU.

334 **"I simply could have cut my throat"** RW to DT, November 26, 1947, series 11, SU.

334 **In November 1947, her book *The Meaning of Treason*** RW, *The Meaning of Treason* (New York: Viking Press, 1947).

334 **"is valuable not only to the historian"** RW to Max Beaverbrook, December 4, 1947, Personal Correspondence, History 184, C 323, Beaverbrook Papers, House of Lords Record Office.

335 **"the effect of a size 9 atomic bomb"** Harold Ross to RW, December 9, 1947, GEN MSS 105, box 13, folder 614, YU.

335 **"I hear her name discussed"** Herbert Gunn to Lord Beaverbrook, *Evening Standard* microfilm H250, Beaverbrook Papers, House of Lords Record Office, January 6, 1948.

336 **Rebecca had refused on the grounds** RW to HA, March 1948, series 1, box 3, folder 37, YU.

336 **The Women's Press Club awards** Linda Charlton, "Dame Rebecca West Dies in London," *The New York Times,* March 16, 1983.

337 **"You are unjust"** RW to SL, 1948, box Wells-1, folder w-210-1A, H. G. Wells Collection, Rare Book and Special Collections Library, University of Illinois at Urbana-Champaign.

337 **"To this end"** DT, "A Woman's Manifesto," September 7, 1947, series 11, box 2, folder "Jan–Dec 1947," SU.

338 "**Well everybody told us**" RW to DT, February 28, 1948, SU.

338 "**If you have never covered**" DT to RW, February 19, 1948, GEN MSS 105, box 16, folder 823, YU.

339 "**Life completely broke down**" RW to HA, mid-1948, GEN MSS 105, series 1, box 2, folder 34, YU.

339 "**Dorothy was of great use**" RW to HA, June 1948, GEN MSS 105, series 1, box 2, folder 142, YU.

339 "**were in fact like a studio**" "The Press: Covering the Convention," *Time*, July 5, 1948.

339 "**You fill up the hall**" RW, *New York Herald Tribune*, June 25, 1948.

340 "**Miss West, her face,**" "The Press: Covering the Convention."

340 "**readable**" Herbert Gunn to Lord Beaverbrook, November 16, 1948, *Evening Standard* microfilm H250, Beaverbrook Papers, House of Lords Record Office.

340 "**It was an allnight journey**" RW to HA, July 13, 1948, GEN MSS 105, series 1, box 2, folder 37, YU.

342 "**get out of the shadow**" Hubert Humphrey, Democratic National Convention, 1948.

342 "**It is wonderful to be with her**" July 17, 1948, YU.

343 "**It was as if [Wallace] had heard**" RW, *New York Herald Tribune*, July 23, 1948.

343 "**soft people**" "Rebecca West Says Communists Controlled Wallace Convention," *New York Herald Tribune*, July 25, 1948.

343 "**Politically**" . . . "**she was like**" Sanders, *Dorothy Thompson*, 330.

343 "**a positive sulphuric blue fire**" John Gunther Diary, July 30, 1947, box 2, add. 11, John Gunther Papers, University of Chicago.

344 "**The Zionist adventure**" Jimmy Sheean to DT, February 13, 1948, American Embassy in Cairo, Peter Kurth's research, courtesy of Peter Kurth.

344 **I did not think the conventions** "Queen Mary Sails with 1,987 Aboard," *The New York Times*, July 30, 1948.

344 "**If you mention any race at all**" Harold Ross to RW, September 14, 1948, GEN MSS 105, series 1, box 13, folder 615, YU.

344 "**Orwell was a target**" Rollyson, *Literary Legacy of Rebecca West*, 181–82.

345 "**another breed—set apart**" Ca. 1940s, box 3, folder 37, HA Papers, YU.

345 **Rebecca had planned to return** RW to Doris Stevens, September 29, 1948, GEN MSS 239, box 3, folder 101, YU.

345 "**a tendency to become a lunatic**" WFM to RW, October 2, 1948, GEN MSS 105, box 12, folder 528, YU.

345 "**a bit of a bore**" RW to Doris Stevens, December 29, 1948, GEN MSS 239, box 3, folder 101, YU.

346 "**Man is nothing but the sum**" AW, *On a Dark Night* (London: Eyre and Spottiswoode, 1949).

347 "**I am very fond of you**" RW to Charles Curran, January 26, 1949, UT.

347 "**Not with the tears**" RW, Childhood Poetry, G. Evelyn Hutchinson Papers, YU.

348 "**When my nephew**" RW to DT, January 24, 1949, SU.

348 "**It is odd how an erratic**" Ibid.

348 "**I know you must be**" Ibid.

349 "**I have made it up with Charles**" RW to WFM, February 5, 1949, IU.

350 "**I cannot do journalism anymore**" RW to Charles Curran, April 14, 1949, UT.

350 "**brilliant as it was**" Charles Curran to RW, April 17, 1949, GEN MSS 105, YU.

350 "**Why, when I first met**" Ibid.

351 "**I find it easy**" Ibid.

352 **"My main worry"** RW to Margaret Hodges, July 30, 1949, Carl Rollyson Papers, UT.

353 **"heavenly companion"** RW to Doris Stevens, July 29, 1949, GEN MSS 239, box 3, folder 101, YU.

354 **"no one would take exception"** RW to Emily Hahn, January 26, 1952, IU.

354 **"I can't even convey"** RW to AW, September 16, 1949, GEN MSS 105, box 22, folder 979, YU.

354 **"I get a great kick"** Harold Ross to HA, March 8, 1950, GEN MSS 105, box 13, folder 617, YU.

355 **"originally, an innocent party"** Harold Ross to RW, March 21, 1950, GEN MSS 105, box 13, folder 617, YU.

355 **"H.G. did not care a button"** RW to Charles Curran, November 6, 1949, GEN MSS 105, box 7, folder 216, YU.

356 **"I don't know what"** Ibid.

356 **"Today the letters arrived"** RW to Charles Curran, January 31, 1950, UT.

CHAPTER 16 / DESCENT TO GLORY

358 **"I am confident"** DT to Annie Schwarzenberg, December 2, 1953, series 2, SU.

358 **"too famous"** . . . **"the Medusa head"** DT to RW, March 18, 1950, GEN MSS 105, box 16, folder 813, YU.

359 **"remarkably talented"** Ibid.

359 **"alien invaders"** DT to Benjamin H. Freedman, September 19, 1955, SU.

361 **"grossly materialistic"** DT, May 2, 1950, speech at the Annual Meeting of the Chamber of Commerce of the United States.

361 **"charming when he is gay"** DT to RW, May 9, 1950, GEN MSS 105, box 16, folder 823, YU.

361 **"As a result of championing"** Ibid.

362 **"Jews . . . ruthless[ly] exploit"** Ibid.

362 **"stern and serene"** DT to Carl Zuckmayer, July 21, 1950, Zuckmayer estate, DLA Marbach.

362 **"without a trace,"** DT to RW GEN MS 105, box 16, folder 823, October 15, 1950, YU.

363 **"an old defiant Atheist"** DT to RW, January 14, 1951, GEN MSS 105, box 16, folder 824, YU.

363 **"legs seemed to crumple"** Ibid.

363 **"evil [was] at work"** Dinah Sheean to RW, January 20, 1951.

363 **"guessed that Mike both"** Ibid.

364 **"a trace of psychosis"** DT to RW, January 23, 1951, GEN MSS 105, box 16, folder 824, YU.

364 **"discerning boy"** Ibid.

364 **"Red's death hit me"** Ibid.

365 **"The truth is"** Ibid.

365 **"fracas breaks out, between states"** (and subsequent quotes) DT to Senator Robert Taft, February 17, 1951, series 2, box 3, SU.

366 **"It's the source of almost"** *Mary Margaret McBride Show,* February 19, 1951, sound recording, Library of Congress recording reference LWO 15577 147A.

367 **"an international pilgrimage"** DT to Clare Booth Luce, July 10, 1951, Clare Booth Luce Papers, box 191, folder 8, Library of Congress.

367 **"At a time when Soviet-inspired"** Eleanor Roosevelt to Mrs. William Barclay Parsons, December 21, 1951, Peter Kurth's research, courtesy of Peter Kurth.

368 **"The only practical answer"** Eleanor Roosevelt to DT, January 23, 1952, Schlesinger Library, Radcliffe College.

368 **"because my highly heretical views"** DT to Vilma Mönckeberg, January 7, 1952, series 2, box 4, SU.

368 **"things living, and growing"** DT interview with Richard Pratt from *Ladies' Home Journal*, folder January 1952, SU.

368 **"I am not fitted anymore"** DT to Margaret Boveri, June 13, 1952, SU.

369 **"a bubble of protest"** DT to William Yale, July 29, 1952, Peter Kurth's research, courtesy of Peter Kurth.

369 **"the best informed American"** Adlai Stevenson to DT, August 5, 1952, SU.

369 **"The *weakest* thing"** DT to Adlai Stevenson, August 16, 1952, SU.

369 **"That leader is strongest"** Ibid.

369 **"my contention"** September 25, 1952, Peter Kurth's research, courtesy of Peter Kurth.

370 **"We frontal lobe people"** DT to Jimmy Sheean, November 16, 1952, series 2, box 4, SU.

370 **"This was in late fall"** DT to RW, April 23, 1953, GEN MSS 105, box 16, folder 824, YU.

370 **precious friends** DT to HA and RW, GEN MSS 105, box 16, folder 824, YU.

371 **"I have become convinced"** DT to Winston Churchill, January 22, 1953, Peter Kurth's research, courtesy of Peter Kurth.

371 **"One thing is sure"** Maxim Kopf to DT, February 27, 1953, SU.

371 **"overwritten" and "overworked"** DT to HA, April 23, 1953, GEN MSS 105, box 16, folder 824, YU.

372 **"Well, we love our husbands"** Ibid.

372 **"thoroughly heterosexual"** Ibid., June 30, 1953.

372 **"Something frustrated his capacity"** Ibid.

373 **"exceptional privileges and meet"** DT to John Wheeler, July 8, 1953, series 2, box 5, SU.

373 **"I greatly fear that one day"** DT to John Foster Dulles, October 26, 1953, SU.

373 **"the teachings of Jesus Christ"** DT to Donald P. Costello, December 29, 1953, series 2, box 5, SU.

373 **"universal cosmic and creative force"** DT to J. H. Shrader, December 30, 1953, SU.

374 **"The element in the Bible"** DT to Dr. LeRoy E. Smith, January 12, 1954, series 2, box 5, SU.

374 **"counted out"** Carl Zuckmayer, *A Part of Myself* (New York: Harcourt Brace, 1966), p. 217–22.

374 **"jumped the gun"** DT to Agatha Young, August 5, 1954, Letters to Agatha Brooks Young, Berg Collection, New York Public Library.

374 **"The Christening ceremony astonished"** DT to Norman and Katherine Littell, August 25, 1954, Peter Kurth's research, courtesy of Peter Kurth.

375 **"fool" . . . "too much of that"** Emanie Arling to RW, October 31, 1954, GEN MSS 105, box 5, folder 77, YU.

375 **"alien invaders of Palestine"** DT to Benjamin H. Freedman, September 19, 1955, series 2, box 6, SU.

375 **"All things I hate"** Emanie Arling to RW, 1956, GEN MSS 105, box 5, folder 79, YU.

376 **"The world has found no substitute"** DT to RW, September 25, 1956, GEN MSS 105, box 5, folder 79, SU.

376 **make up her mind** DT to John Wheeler, December 8, 1956, SU.

377 **"apparently to report the facts"** Peter Kurth's research, courtesy of Peter Kurth.

377 **"right in broad, simple"** Vincent Sheean to John Gunther, September 13, 1952, box 39, John Gunther Papers, University of Chicago.

378 **"It has been my fate"** DT, *The Courage to Be Happy*, 42.

378 **"They are more likely to drive"** Ibid., 46.

379 **"All my life I have had"** Ibid., 117.

379 **"Today is precious"** Ibid., 118.

379 **"The Bible is the greatest book"** Ibid., 122.

380 **"I believe in God"** Ibid., 183.

380 **"is not exciting publishing"** Paul Brooks to Lovell Thompson, June 2, 1958, Peter Kurth's research, courtesty of Peter Kurth.

380 **"I was disappointed in the review"** DT to Dale Warren, n.d. ("Sunday"), ibid.

380 **"The rate of syphilis"** DT speech, January 15, 1958, series 2, box 6, folder January 1958, SU.

381 **"I feel rather ghostly"** DT to RW and HA, December 10, 1957, box 16, folder 825, YU.

381 **"has heard several good things"** Ibid.

381 **"somehow thyroid"** Emanie Arling to RW, February 2, 1958, GEN MSS 105 box 5, folder 81, YU.

381 **"had nothing positive"** Ibid.

382 **"worry, overwork, or anxiety"** DT to Grace Peat, June 13, 1958, series 2, box 6, folder June 1958, SU.

382 **"I cried with my whole heart"** Psalm 119:145–46.

383 **"There was no question"** DT to RW, August September 25, 1958, GEN MSS 105, box 16, folder 825, YU.

383 **"I remember almost nothing"** Ibid.

384 **"The extent of my grief"** DT to Nancy Astor, September 2, 1958, series 2, folder 7, SU.

385 **"Journalism was only a means"** Sanders, *Dorothy Thompson*, 353.

385 **"the second best university library"** DT to Jack [Alexander?], July 22, 1958, series 2, box 7, SU.

385 **"I have a sitting room"** DT to RW, July 21, 1959, GEN MSS 105, box 16, folder 825, YU.

385 **"I feel that work is your 'salvation'"** ML to DT, October 31, 1958, series 3, box 3, folder 9, SU.

386 **"insides [were] not working well"** DT Diary, February 3, 1959, SU.

386 **"I don't think I pity myself"** DT to RW and HA, December 4, 1958, GEN MSS 105, box 16, folder 825, YU.

386 **"obsession with [the] book"** DT, diary entry, January 31, 1959, series 4, box 1, folder "Diaries 1950–60," SU.

386 **"the thought is not unwelcome"** Ibid.

386 **"I woke up this morning"** Ibid., February 3, 1959.

386 **"I cannot face"** Ibid., February 5, 1959.

387 **"In many ways, you have changed"** ML to DT, January 22, 1959, series 3, box 3, SU.

387 **"I think everything that"** DT to RW and HA, August 26, 1959, GEN MSS 105, box 16, folder 825, YU.

387 **"drowning in drugs"** ML to DT, February 9, 1960, SU.

388 **"a sort of longing"** DT to RW, December 1, 1959, SU.

388 **On April 30, 1960** DT, "May I Tell You About My Heart Attack?" *Ladies' Home Journal,* April 1960.

388 **"It is his heartlessness"** DT to RW, December 1, 1959.

389 **"a frail and sick old lady"** Kurth, *American Cassandra,* 464.

CHAPTER 17 / OBSESSION

391 **"Art is the bulwark"** Television interview, *The Life and Work of Rebecca West,* December 12, 1981, British Museum, recording references M 40865 or TLN 48/379K417.

392 **"a total loss, he has spoiled"** RW to Doris Stevens, December 8, 1951, GEN MSS 105, series 1, box 3, folder 103, YU.

393 **"it quite natural for him"** RW to Doris Stevens, September 24, 1952, GEN MSS 239, series 1, box 3, folder 104, YU.

394 **She wrote to Doris Stevens** RW to Doris Stevens, January 15, 1954, GEN MSS 239, series 1, box 3, folder 107, YU.

394 **"thirsty in her own desert"** RW to WFM, August 29, 1950, MSS, Lilly Library, IU.

394 **"The truth of how things were"** AW, *Heritage* (New York: Random House, 1955), 1.

395 **His apparent success in New York** Doris Stevens to RW, September 24, 1952, GEN MSS 239, series 1, box 3, folder 104, YU.

395 **"He is brilliant and writes like"** RW to Jane and John Gunther, November 6, 1952, UT.

395 **"I hope I am working a way"** RW, "Goodness Doesn't Just Happen," in *This I Believe,* ed. Edward P. Morgan (New York: Simon and Schuster 1952), 187–88.

395 **St. Augustine believed there was a God** *Living Writers,* December 1, 1971, interviewer Hugh Kay, British Film Institute.

395 **most impersonal, most personal** RW to Margaret and Evelyn Hutchinson, fall 1950, G. Evelyn Hutchinson Papers, YU.

396 **"But I am a Slav"** RW to Margaret and Evelyn Hutchinson, 1950, G. Evelyn Hutchinson Papers, YU.

396 **"the victim of a poltergeist of bad luck"** RW to Evelyn Hutchinson, June 22, 1955, G. Evelyn Hutchinson Papers, YU.

396 **"because right to the end"** . . . **"a preoccupying mystery."** RW to Doris Stevens, December 8, 1951, GEN MSS 105, series 1, box 3, folder 103, YU.

396 **"Why the hell did I not hop a boat"** RW to Doris Stevens, December 8, 1951, GEN MSS 105, series 1, Box 3, Folder 103, YU.

397 **"I went to the cocktail party"** DT to RW, April 23, 1953, GEN MSS 105, series 1, box 16, folder 824, YU. A justice of the peace in Stonington, Connecticut, had married Anthony and Lily; author's interview with Lily Emmet West, July 2006.

398 **"of whom I think with pity"** RW to Doris Stevens, September 24, 1952, GEN MSS 239, box 3, folder 104, YU.

398 **"psychological horrors"** RW to WFM, October 1, 1952, MSS, Lilly Library, IU.

399 **I wish I could stay** Ibid.

399 **"For many years I never"** RW's unpublished memoir, 1927, courtesy of AMS.

400 **"This is the worst of life"** RW, *The Fountain Overflows* (New York: Viking Press, 1956), 303.

400 **"swept on by a strong flood"** Ibid., 313.

400 **"It seems to me often"** RW to HA, April 26, 1953, GEN MSS 105, box 3, folder 40, YU.

400 **"Still I love Henry"** RW to DT, April 30, 1953, Syracuse.

401 **"most brilliant man now living"** Ibid.

401 **Rebecca's articles were published** Her articles were printed in *The Sunday Times* and reprinted in *U.S. News and World Report* in May 1953. In 1953, upon his second term as senator from Wisconsin, McCarthy was made chairman of the Committee on Government Operations, which included the Permanent Subcommittee on Investigations. It wasn't until 1954 that his reputation suffered because of his tactics. He wasn't censured until December 1954. Rebecca would come to think that his cause was good, but his techniques were wrong.

401 **"a creature called Arthur M. Schlesinger"** RW to DT, June 16, 1953, SU.

402 **Ibstone held too many bad** RW to Doris Stevens, October 17, 1953, GEN MSS 239, box 3, folder 106, YU.

402 **"May all our enemies fry"** RW to Doris Stevens, January 17, 1953, GEN MSS 105, box 3, folder 105, YU.

402 **"The children had a heavenly time"** Kitty West to RW, GEN MSS 105, box 22, folder "1953," YU.

403 **"He said something that suddenly"** . . . **"not a touch of gratitude"** RW to Charles Curran, November 10, 1953, UT.

403 **"[He had] not a touch of gratitude"** Ibid.

404 **"I feel I am in some"** RW to Charles Curran, April 9, 1953, UT.

404 **"Furthermore, the people in the"** RW to Doris Stevens, November 23, 1953, GEN MSS 239, box 3, folder 106, YU.

405 **"She lay and gave a marvelous"** Ibid.

405 **"I can hardly bear this"** RW to Doris Stevens, March 5, 1954, GEN MSS 239, box 3, folder 107, YU.

405 **"hunger[ed] and thirst[ed] for America"** RW to DT, December 5, 1953, SU.

405 **"is now half-lunatic"** RW to Doris Stevens, October 4, 1954, GEN MSS 239, box 3, folder 109, YU.

406 **Lonely, haunted by her past** The anxiety and loneliness of creativity has been well documented in Ernest Becker, *The Denial of Death* (New York: Free Press, 1973); and Sandra M. Gilbert and Susan Gubar, *The Madwoman in the Attic: The Woman Writer and Nineteenth-Century Literary Imagination* (New Haven, Conn.: Yale University Press, 1979).

406 **"Mike's old room"** RW to DT, October 25, 1954, SU.

406 **"Lily comes from"** AW to RW, December 15, 1954, GEN MSS 105, box 22, folder 979, YU.

407 **he was compelled to do in order** Author's interview with Lily Emmet West, January 16, 2003.

407 **"Lord and Lady of the Manor"** Carl Rollyson, *Rebecca West: A Saga of the Century* (New York: iUniverse, 2009) 262.

407 **"comfortable but far from lavish"** Author's interview with Norman and Marion Macleod, June 2009.

407 **"light novel"** Rollyson, *Rebecca West: A Life*, p. 300.

408 **"She could hardly talk"** Ibid.

408 **"inflicting pain"** RW, unpublished memoir, 1927, courtesy of AMS, 44.

409 **"like taking up a bludgeon"** AW, "Mother and Son," *New York Review of Books*, March 1, 1984.

410 **"latest performance"** RW to DT, 1955, SU.

411 **"ambivalent feelings about his mother"** Rollyson, 305; DT to RW, November 11, 1956.

411 **"I could not feel more astonished"** RW to Charles Curran, November 21, 1955, UT.

411 **"It must be the lot"** RW to DT, 1955, SU.

411 **"I would not know"** RW to CC, November 21, 1955, UT.

411 **"Life is a piteous mist of error"** WFM to RW, September 20, 1955, GEN MSS 105, box 12, folder 533, YU.

412 **"in case you have any doubt"** Lily Emmet West to RW, 1955, GEN MSS 105, box 22, folder 985, YU.

412 **"Be comforted, dearest"** Doris Stevens to RW, November 11, 1955, GEN MSS 105, box 16, folder 285, YU.

412 **"The boy [Richard Savage] isn't in the least"** Pamela Frankau to RW, 1955, GEN MSS 105, box 8, folder 285, YU.

412 **"a moral imbecile"** RW to Charles Curran, November 21, 1955, UT.

412 **"I received your letter"** DT to RW, February 14, 1956, GEN MSS 105, box 16, folder 824, YU.

413 **"Anthony had poisoned his mind"** RW to DT, 1955, SU.

413 **"'This,' I thought, 'is civilization'"** Beverly Nichols, *My World*, January 19, 1956.

414 **"Hatred is sterile, love is fruitful"** Nancy Spain, "Rebecca West," *Good Housekeeping*, January 1, 1956, 36–37.

414 **"In that year"** RW, unpublished memoir, 1927, courtesy of AMS, 25.

415 **"change the aspect of reality"** (and subsequent quotes) *The Court and the Castle*, 5–6, 11.

416 **"I MUST GET THIS BOOK"** RW to HA, n.d., likely March 25, 1957, box 3, folder 46, YU. The book would be published posthumously, in 1984, as *This Real Night*, followed by the third volume, *Cousin Rosamund*, in 1985.

416 **"It will be lovely to have"** RW to HA, May 1957, Hotel Gray d'Albion, Cannes, France.

417 **"She is really suffering"** RW to AMS, summer 1957, IU.

417 **the fear that at any moment** Author's interview with Norman and Marion Macleod, June 8, 2009.

417 **"Now for Heaven's sake"** RW to WFM, August 26, 1957, IU.

417 **"a long and dreary illness"** (and subsequent quotes) RW to DT, December 15, 1957, SU.

418 **"If one gets an obsession about malice"** Vita Sackville-West to RW, February 8, 1950, GEN MSS 105, box 15, folder 700, YU.

418 **"During the ten years before his death"** RW, unpublished memoir, 1972, courtesy of AMS.

419 **And, emblematic of her** RW to HA, September 4, 1958, HA Papers, box 3, folder 45, YU.

419 **"I never sought to be teacher's pet"** RW to Nicholas Bentley, January 4, 1959, UT.

419 **"conventional respect means something"** RW to Norman Macleod.

420 **"If I can do this"** RW, notebook, UT.

420 **"My heart goes out to you"** RW to DT, December 6, 1959, SU.

422 **"My dear Ric, I feel"** RW to HA, January 30, 1960, GEN MSS 105, series 1, box 3, folder 47, YU.

422 **and felt no "pleasure in sharing"** Ibid., February 1, 1960.

422 **"I am willing to start again"** Ibid.

424 **"I expect you feel"** RW to Beatrice and Bruce Gould, February 13, 1961, box 13, folder 6, Bruce and Beatrice Blackmar Gould Correspondence, Princeton University.

424 **"I leave to you, your loved ones"** DT to ML, December 6, 1960, series 3, box 2, folder 3, SU.

EPILOGUE

427 **When Dorothy landed** Sanders, *Dorothy Thompson*, 397–98.

428 **"saying goodbye to a lifetime"** Sheean, *Dorothy and Red*, 325–27.

429 **"the most important thing"** RW, *Family Memories: An Autobiographical Journey* (New York: Viking Penguin, 1988).

429 **After his tryst with the secretary** RW, unpublished memoir, 1972, courtesy of AMS.

429 **a "mausoleum"** RW to Emanie Arling, January 16, 1969, UT.

430 **her secretary Diana Stainforth** Interview with Diana Stainforth at Conference of the International Rebecca West Society, 2003, Mercantile Library, New York.

431 **Rebecca outlived Henry by fifteen years** Author's interviews with Norman and Marion Macleod, September 17, 2003, and June 7, 2007.

432 **Anthony Panther West died** Wolfgang Saxon, "Anthony West, Critic and Author; Wrote Essays for *The New Yorker*," *The New York Times*, December 28, 1987.

434 **"peripatetic brain picker"** DT to SL, April 29, 1937, SU.

435 **"He loved love with the hopeless"** RW, *Black Lamb and Grey Falcon*, 828.

437 **"I've never loved, or even liked"** RW to Vincent Sheean, December 25, 1963, Peter Kurth's research, courtesy of Peter Kurth.

SELECTED BIBLIOGRAPHY

Adcock, St. John. *The Glory That Was Grub Street*. London: Sampson Low, 1928.

Agar, Eileen, and Andrew Lambirth. *A Look at My Life*. London: Methuen, 1988.

Angoff, Charles. *The Tone of the Twenties and Other Essays*. South Brunswick, N.J.: A. S. Barnes, 1966.

Augustine, Saint. *The Confessions of St. Augustine*. New York: P. F. Collier and Son, 1909.

Balfour, Michael, Leonard Graham, and Julian Frisby. *Helmuth von Moltke: A Leader Against Hitler*. London: Macmillan, 1972.

Baughman, Judith S., ed. *American Decades: 1920–1929*. New York: Gale Research, 1996.

Becker, Ernest. *The Denial of Death*. New York: Free Press, 1973.

Bell, Ann Olivier, ed. *The Diary of Virginia Woolf*. Vol. 5, *1936–1941*. London: Hogarth Press, 1984.

Bell, Quentin. *Bloomsbury*. London: Weidenfeld and Nicolson, 1968.

Beschloss, Michael. *The Conquerors: Roosevelt, Truman, and the Destruction of Hitler's Germany*. New York: Simon and Schuster, 2002.

Blair, Karen J. *The Clubwoman as Feminist: True Womanhood Redefined, 1868–1914*. New York: Holmes and Meier, 1980.

Blumenthal, Ralph. *The Stork Club: America's Most Famous Nightspot and the Lost World of Café Society*. Boston: Little, Brown, 2000.

Boyce, Robert, ed. *French Foreign and Defense Policy, 1918–1940: The Decline and Fall of a Great Power*. London: Routledge, 1988.

Braun, Hans-Joachim. *The German Economy in the 20th Century*. London: Routledge, 1990.

Brendan, Piers. *The Dark Valley: A Panorama of the 1930s*. New York: Alfred A. Knopf, 2000.

Bridenthal, Renate, Atina Grossmann, and Marion Kaplan, eds. *When Biology Became Destiny: Women in Weimar and Nazi Germany*. New York: Monthly Review Press, 1984.

Brinnin, John Malcolm, and Kenneth Gaulin. *Grand Luxe: The Transatlantic Style*. New York: Henry Holt, 1988.

Brittain, Vera. *Chronicle of Friendship: Vera Brittain's Diary of the Thirties 1932–1939*. Edited by Alan Bishop. London: V. Gollancz, 1986.

———. *Testimony of Youth*. New York: Penguin, 1933.

Brome, Vincent. *H. G. Wells*. London: Longmans, 1951.

Bulman, David, ed. *Molders of Opinion*. Milwaukee: Brace, 1945.

Butcher, Fanny. *Many Lives, One Love*. New York: Harper and Row, 1972.

Canetti, Elias. *The Play of the Eyes*. Translated by Ralph Manheim. New York: Farrar, Straus and Giroux, 1986.

Cannadine, David. *The Decline and Fall of the British Aristocracy*. New York: Vintage, 1999.

Chase, Ilka. *Past Imperfect*. Garden City, N.Y.: Doubleday, 1942.

Chesler, Ellen. *Woman of Valor: Margaret Sanger and the Birth Control Movement in America*. New York: Simon and Schuster, 1992.

Cockin, Katharine. *Women and Theatre in the Age of Suffrage: The Pioneer Players, 1911–1925*. New York: Palgrave, 2001.

Cohen, Debra Rae. *Remapping the Home Front: Locating Citizenship in British Women's Great War Fiction*. Boston: Northeastern University Press, 2002.

Cohen, Harriet. *A Bundle of Time: The Memoirs of Harriet Cohen*. London: Faber and Faber, 1969.

Conrad, Barnaby. *Name Dropping: Tales from My Barbary Coast Saloon*. New York: HarperCollins, 1994.

Cooke, Alistair. *Six Men*. New York: Knopf, 1977.

Cooper, Diana. *Trumpets from the Steep*. Boston: Houghton Mifflin, 1960.

Cowley, Malcolm. *The View from 80*. New York: Penguin, 1982.

Crawford, Cheryl. *One Naked Individual*. New York: Bobbs-Merrill, 1977.

Current Biography 1940. New York: H. W. Wilson, 1940.

Cuthbertson, Ken. *Inside: The Biography of John Gunther*. Chicago: Bonus, 1992.

Davis, Tracy C. *Actresses as Working Women: Their Social Identity in Victorian Culture*. London: Routledge, 1991.

Department of Commerce and Labor, United States of America. *Marriage and Divorce 1867–1906: Part 1, Summary, Laws, Foreign Statistics*. Westport, Conn.: Greenwood Press, 1978.

Derrida, Jacques. *Archive Fever: A Freudian Impression*. Translated by Eric Prenowitz. Chicago: University of Chicago Press, 1996.

Desmond, Robert W. *Crisis and Conflict: World News Reporting Between Two Wars 1920–1940*. Iowa City: University of Iowa Press, 1982.

———. *Tides of War: World News Reporting 1931–1945*. Iowa City: University of Iowa Press, 1984.

Dickson, Lovat. *H. G. Wells: His Turbulent Life and Times*. New York: Atheneum, 1969.

DiFonzo, J. Herbie. *Beneath the Fault Line: The Popular and Legal Culture of Divorce in Twentieth-Century America*. Charlottesville: University Press of Virginia, 1997.

Donell, Alison, and Pauline Polkey, eds. *Representing Lives: Women and Auto/biography*. New York: St. Martin's Press, 2000.

Dove, Richard. *He Was a German: A Biography of Ernst Toller*. London: Libris, 1990.

Drawbell, James Wedgwood. *Dorothy Thompson's English Journey: Record of an Anglo-American Partnership*. London: Collins, 1942.

Drucker, Peter. *Report from Atlantis: "Hemme and Genia."* New York: Harper and Row, 1979.

Dubois, Ellen Carol. *Feminism and Suffrage: The Emergence of an Independent Women's Movement in America 1848–1869*. Ithaca, N.Y.: Cornell University Press, 1978.

Dunbar, Janet. *Mrs. G.B.S.: A Portrait*. New York: Harper and Row, 1963.

Eaden, James, and David Renton. *The Communist Party of Great Britain Since 1920*. New York: Palgrave, 2002.

Edel, Leon, and Gordon N. Ray, eds. *Henry James and H. G. Wells: A Record of Their Friendship, Their Debate on the Art of Fiction, and Their Quarrel*. Urbana: University of Illinois Press, 1958.

Edwards, Julia. *Women of the World: The Great Foreign Correspondents*. Boston: Houghton Mifflin, 1988.

Elon, Amos. *The Pity of It All: A History of Jews in Germany: 1743–1933*. New York: Metropolitan Books, 2002.

Fadiman, Clifton, ed. *I Believe: The Personal Philosophies of Twenty-Three Eminent Men and Women of Our Time*. New York: Simon and Schuster, 1939.

Ferguson, Niall. *The War of the World: Twentieth-Century Conflict and the Descent of the West*. New York: Penguin, 2006.

Fisher, Charles. *The Columnists*. New York: Howell, Soskin, 1944.

Fleming, Nicholas. *August 1939: The Last Days of Peace*. London: Peter Davies, 1979.

Foot, Michael. *The History of Mr. Wells*. Washington, D.C.: Counterpoint, 1995.

Frederiksen, Elke P., and Martha Kaarsberg Wallach. *Facing Fascism and Confronting the Past*. Albany: State University of New York Press, 2000.

Freud, Sigmund. *Collected Papers*. Vol. 4. Edited by James Strachey. New York: Basic Books, 1959.

———. *Collected Papers*. Vol. 5. Edited by James Strachey. New York: Basic Books, 1959.

———. *Delusion and Dream*. Boston: Beacon Press, 1956.

Friedrich, Otto. *Before the Deluge: A Portrait of Berlin in the 1920s*. New York: Harper and Row, 1972.

Fromkin, David. *A Peace to End All Peace*. New York: Henry Holt, 1989.

Gabler, Neal. *Winchell: Gossip, Power, and the Culture of Celebrity*. New York: Vintage, 1995.

Gaddis, John Lewis. *The Cold War: A New History*. New York: Penguin, 2005.

Gaines, James R. *Wit's End: Days and Nights of the Algonquin Round Table*. New York: Harcourt Brace Jovanovich, 1977.

Gale, Maggie B., and Clive Barker, eds. *British Theatre Between the Wars: 1918–1939*. Cambridge: Cambridge University Press, 2000.

Gay, Peter. *Weimar Culture: The Outsider as Insider*. Westport, Conn.: Greenwood Press, 1968.

Gelernter, David. *1939: The Lost World of the Fair*. New York: Free Press, 1995.

Gilbert, Sandra M., and Susan Gubar. *The Madwoman in the Attic: The Woman Writer and Nineteenth-Century Literary Imagination*. New Haven, Conn.: Yale University Press, 1979.

Gill, Anton. *A Dance Between Flames: Berlin Between the Wars*. London: John Murray, 1993.

Glendinning, Victoria. *Rebecca West: A Life*. New York: Knopf, 1987.

Glinert, Ed. *A Literary Guide to London*. London: Penguin, 2000.

Goebbels, Joseph. *The Goebbels Diaries: 1942–1943*. Translated by Louis Paul Lochner. Garden City, N.Y.: Doubleday, 1948.

Goldman, Emma. *Anarchism and Other Essays*. New York: Mother Earth Publishing Association, 1910. Reprint, New York: Dover, 1969.

Gordon, Linda. *Woman's Body, Woman's Right: A Social History of Birth Control in America*. New York: Grossman, 1976.

Gorham, Deborah. *Vera Brittain: A Feminist Life*. Toronto: University of Toronto Press, 1996.

Gottesman, Irving I. *Schizophrenia Genesis: The Origins of Madness*. New York: W. H. Freeman, 1991.

Griffiths, Dennis. *Plant Here the Standard*. London: Macmillan, 1996.

Gunther, John. *Death Be Not Proud: A Memoir*. New York: Perennial Classic, 1965.

———. *Fragment of Autobiography*. New York: Harper and Row, 1962.

———. *Inside U.S.A.* New York: Harper and Brothers, 1947.

———. *The Lost City*. New York: Harper and Row, 1964.

———. *Roosevelt in Retrospect: A Profile in History*. New York: Harper, 1950.

Haining, Peter. *The Day War Broke Out—3 September 1939.* London: W. H. Allen, 1989.

Hammond, J. R. *H. G. Wells and Rebecca West.* New York: St. Martin's Press, 1991.

Harris, Carol. *Women at War: In Uniform 1939–1945.* Gloucestershire, UK: Sutton Publishing, 2003.

Heilbut, Anthony. *Exiled in Paradise: German Refugee Artists and Intellectuals in America, from the 1930s to the Present.* New York: Viking Press, 1983.

Hoffmann, Peter. *Hitler's Personal Security: Protecting the Führer, 1921–1945.* New York: Da Capo Press, 2000.

Holroyd, Michael. *Works on Paper: The Craft of Biography and Autobiography.* Washington, D.C.: Counterpoint, 2002.

Hurst, Fannie. *Divorce As I See It.* London: Noel Douglas, 1930.

Jennison, Peter S. *The History of Woodstock, Vermont.* Woodstock, Vt.: Countryman Press, 1985.

Johnson, Paul. *Modern Times: The World from the Twenties to the Eighties.* New York: Harper and Row, 1983.

Kaltenborn, Hans V. *Fifty Fabulous Years.* New York: G. P. Putnam's Sons, 1950.

Kaplan, Robert D. *Balkan Ghosts: A Journey Through History.* New York: St. Martin's Press, 1993.

Kaufman, Beatrice, and Joseph Hennessy, eds. *The Letters of Alexander Woollcott.* New York: Viking Press, 1944.

Kiernan, Kathleen, Hilary Land, and Jane Lewis. *Lone Motherhood in Twentieth-Century Britain.* Oxford: Clarendon Press, 1998.

Kluger, Richard. *The Paper: The Life and Death of the "New York Herald Tribune."* New York: Knopf, 1986.

Klurfeld, Herman. *Winchell: His Life and Times.* New York: Praeger, 1976.

Koch, Stephen. *Double Lives: Stalin, Willi Münzenberg, and the Seduction of the Intellectuals.* New York: Enigma Books, 1994.

Kracauer, Siegfried. *From Caligari to Hitler: A Psychological History of the German Film.* Princeton, N.J.: Princeton University Press, 1966.

Kroeger, Brooke. *Fannie: The Talent for Success of Writer Fannie Hurst.* New York: Times Books, 1999.

Kunkel, Thomas. *Genius in Disguise: Harold Ross of "The New Yorker."* New York: Carroll and Graf, 1995.

Kurth, Peter. *American Cassandra: The Life of Dorothy Thompson.* Boston: Little, Brown, 1990.

Kuzel, Regina G. *Fallen Women, Problem Girls: Unmarried Mothers and the Professionalization of Social Work 1890–1945.* New Haven, Conn.: Yale University Press, 1993.

Labon, Joanna. "Come in from the Cold War: Rebecca West and Storm Jameson in 1930s Europe." In *Women Writers of the 1930s: Gender, Politics, and History,* edited by Maroula Joannou. Edinburgh: Edinburgh University Press, 1999.

Laqueur, Walter. *Weimar: A Cultural History, 1918–1933.* New York: G. P. Putnam's Sons, 1974.

Large, David Clay. *Berlin.* New York: Basic Books, 2000.

Larsen, Egon. *Weimar Eyewitness.* London: Bachman and Turner, 1976.

Lee, Judith Yaross. *Defining "New Yorker" Humor.* Jackson: University Press of Mississippi, 2000.

Leffler, Melvyn P. *The Specter of Communism.* New York: Hill and Wang, 1994.

Lehmann, John. *The Year's Work in Literature, 1949.* London: Longmans, Green, 1950.

Lesinska, Zophia P. *Perspectives of Four Women Writers on the Second World War: Gertrude Stein, Janet Flanner, Kay Boyle, and Rebecca West.* New York: Peter Lang, 2002.

Lewis, David Levering. *The Portable Harlem Renaissance Reader*. New York: Viking, 1994.

Lewis, Peter. *A People's War*. London: Methuen, 1986.

Lewis, Sinclair. *Arrowsmith*. New York: Harcourt Brace Jovanovich, 1972.

———. *Babbitt*. New York: Grosset and Dunlap, 1922.

———. *Elmer Gantry*. New York: Harcourt, Brace, 1927. Reprint, New York: Penguin, 1967.

———. *From Main Street to Stockholm: Letters of Sinclair Lewis, 1919–1930*. Edited by Harrison Smith. New York: Harcourt, Brace, 1952.

———. *It Can't Happen Here*. New York: Doubleday, Doran, 1935. Reprint, New York: Penguin, 2005.

———. *Main Street*. New York, Harcourt, Brace, 1920. Reprint, New York: Penguin, 1961.

———. *The Man from Main Street: A Sinclair Lewis Reader: Selected Essays and Other Writings, 1904–1950*. Edited by Harry E. Maule and Melville H. Cane. New York: Random House, 1953.

Lingeman, Richard R. *Sinclair Lewis: Rebel from Main Street*. New York: Random House, 2002.

Longmate, Norman, ed. *The Home Front: An Anthology of Personal Experience, 1938–1945*. London: Chatto and Windus, 1981.

Lucas, John. *Budapest 1900: A Historical Portrait of a City and Its Culture*. New York: Weidenfeld and Nicolson, 1988.

Macleod, Alison. *The Death of Uncle Joe*. Woodbridge, UK: Merlin Press, 1997.

MacMillan, Margaret. *Paris 1919: Six Months That Changed the World*. New York: Random House, 2001.

Manent, Pierre. *The City of Man*. Translated by Mark A. LePain. Princeton, N.J.: Princeton University Press, 2000.

Mann, Carol. *Paris Between the Wars*. New York: Vendome Press, 1996.

Mann, Klaus. *The Turning Point*. New York: Marcus Wiener, 1984.

Marcus, Jane, ed. *The Young Rebecca: Writings of Rebecca West 1911–1917*. New York: Viking Press, 1982.

Marcus, Steven. *Representations: Essays on Literature and Society*. New York: Random House, 1975.

Marx, Samuel. *Queen of the Ritz*. Indianapolis: Bobbs-Merrill, 1978.

Marzolf, Marion. *Up From the Footnote: A History of Women Journalists*. New York: Hastings House, 1977.

Matthews, Anne, Nancy Caldwell Sorell, and Roger J. Spiller, eds. *Reporting World War II*. New York: Library of America, 1995.

May, Elaine Tyler. *Great Expectations: Marriage and Divorce in Post-Victorian America*. Chicago: University of Chicago Press, 1980.

McCullough, David. *Truman*. New York: Touchstone Books, 1993.

McNamara, John. *Extra! U.S. War Correspondents in Action*. 1945. Reprint, New York: Books for Libraries Press, 1973.

Meyer, Mathilde Marie. *H. G. Wells and His Family as I Have Known Them*. Edinburgh: International Publishing, 1956.

Michaelis, Karin, with Lenore Sorsby. *Little Troll*. New York: Creative Age Press, 1946.

Moorehead, Caroline, ed. *Selected Letters of Martha Gellhorn*. New York: Henry Holt, 2006.

Moran, Charles. *Churchill at War, 1940–45*. New York: Carroll and Graf, 2002.

———. *Churchill: The Struggle for Survival, 1945–60*. New York: Carroll and Graf, 2006.

Morris, Sylvia Jukes. *Rage for Fame: The Ascent of Clare Boothe Luce.* New York: Random House, 1997.

Mowrer, Lilian T. *Journalist's Wife.* New York: Grosset and Dunlap, 1940.

Nicolson, Nigel, ed. *Harold Nicolson: Diaries and Letters.* Vol. 2, *The War Years, 1939–1945.* New York: Atheneum, 1967.

———, and Joanne Trautmann, eds. *The Letters of Virginia Woolf.* Vol. 3, *1923–1928.* New York: Harcourt Brace Jovanovich, 1977.

Nizer, Louis. *Reflections Without Mirrors.* Garden City, N.Y.: Doubleday, 1978.

Orel, Harold. *The Literary Achievement of Rebecca West.* London: Macmillan, 1986.

Ray, Gordon N. *H. G. Wells and Rebecca West.* New Haven, Conn.: Yale University Press, 1974.

Reagan, Leslie J. *When Abortion Was a Crime.* Berkeley and Los Angeles: University of California Press, 1977.

Reintjes, Monique. *Odette Keun: 1888–1978.* Amsterdam: Monique Reintjes, 2000.

Riley, Glenda. *Divorce: An American Tradition.* New York: Oxford University Press, 1991.

Roberts, Andrew. *A History of the English-Speaking Peoples Since 1900.* New York: HarperCollins, 2007.

Roberts, Richard. *Schroders: Merchants and Bankers.* London: Macmillan, 1992.

Roiphe, Katie. *Uncommon Arrangements: Seven Portraits of Married Life in London Literary Circles, 1910–1939.* New York: Dial Press, 2007.

Rollyson, Carl. *Beautiful Exile: The Life of Martha Gellhorn.* London: Aurum Press, 2001.

———. *The Literary Legacy of Rebecca West.* San Francisco: International Scholars, 1998.

———. *Rebecca West: A Life.* New York: Scribner, 1996.

———. *Rebecca West and the God That Failed.* New York: iUniverse, 2005.

———. *Rebecca West: Saga of the Century.* New York: iUniverse, 2009.

Rose, Phyllis. *Parallel Lives: Five Victorian Marriages.* New York: Vintage Books, 1984.

Rosenberg, Rosalind. *Beyond Separate Spheres: Intellectual Roots of Modern Feminism.* New Haven, Conn.: Yale University Press, 1982.

Ross, Ishbel. *Ladies of the Press: The Story of Women in Journalism by an Insider.* New York: Harper and Brothers, 1936.

Roth, Joseph. *What I Saw: Reports from Berlin, 1920–1933.* New York: W. W. Norton, 2003.

Russell, Bertrand. *Divorce As I See It.* London: Noel Douglas, 1930.

Sanders, Marion K. *Dorothy Thompson: A Legend in Her Time.* New York: Avon Books, 1974.

Schmalhausen, Samuel D., and V. F. Calverton, eds. *Women's Coming of Age: A Symposium.* New York: Liveright, 1931.

Schofield, Mary Anne. *Marking the Frontiers of World War II with "Stabilized Disorder": Rebecca West Reads St. Augustine.* Edited by John Doody, Kim Paffenroth, and Robert P. Kennedy. Lanham, Md.: Lexington Books, 2006.

Schorer, Mark. *Sinclair Lewis: An American Life.* Minneapolis: University of Minnesota Press, 1963.

Schuschnigg, Kurt. *My Austria.* New York: Knopf, 1938.

Schweizer, Bernard. *Rebecca West: Heroism, Rebellion, and the Female Epic.* Westport, Conn.: Greenwood Press, 2002.

Scott, Bonnie Kime. "Rebecca West's Traversals of Yugoslavia: Essentialism, Nationalism, Fascism, and Gender." In *Women's Studies in Transition: The Pursuit of Inter-*

disciplinarity, edited by Kate Conway-Turner, Suzanne Cherrin, Jessica Schiffman, and Kathleen Doherty Turkel. Cranford, N.J: Associated University Presses, 1998.

————, ed. *Selected Letters of Rebecca West.* New Haven, Conn.: Yale University Press, 2000.

Sebba, Anne. *Battling for News: The Rise of the Woman Reporter.* London: Hodder and Stoughton, 1994.

Shadegg, Stephen. *Clare Boothe Luce: A Biography.* New York: Simon and Schuster, 1970.

Shakespeare, William. *King Lear.* New York: Washington Square Press, 1993.

Shapiro, Yonathan. *The Road to Power: Herut Party in Israel.* Translated by Ralph Mandel. Albany: State University of New York Press, c1991.

Shawcross, Hartley. *Life Sentence: The Memoirs of Hartley Shawcross.* London: Constable, 1995.

Shawcross, William. Unpublished manuscript, including material concerning the Nuremberg Trials, London.

Sheean, Vincent. *Dorothy and Red.* Boston: Houghton Mifflin, 1963.

Shepard, Ben. *A War of Nerves: Soldiers and Psychiatrists in the 20th Century.* Cambridge, Mass.: Harvard University Press, 2001.

Shirer, William. *The Rise and Fall of the Third Reich.* New York: Simon and Schuster, 1960.

————. *20th Century Journey: A Memoir of a Life and the Times.* New York: Simon and Schuster, 1976–1990.

Sigmund, Anna Maria. *Women of the Third Reich.* Richmond Hill, Ontario: NDE, 2000.

Smith, David C., ed. *The Correspondence of H. G. Wells.* 4 vols. Brookfield, Vt.: Pickering and Chatto, 1998.

Solomon, Barbara Miller. *In the Company of Educated Women: A History of Women and Higher Education in America.* New Haven, Conn.: Yale University Press, 1985.

Speer, Albert. *Inside the Third Reich.* New York: Macmillan, 1970.

Stec, Loretta. "Dystopian Modernism vs. Utopian Feminism: Burdekin, Woolf, and West Respond to the Rise of Fascism." In *Virginia Woolf and Fascism: Resisting the Dictators' Seduction,* edited by Merry M. Pawlowski. Houndsmills, UK: Palgrave, 2001.

Steel, Ronald. *Walter Lippmann and the American Century.* New York: Vintage Books, 1981.

Swinnerton, Frank, ed. *The Journals of Arnold Bennett.* Baltimore: Penguin, 1954.

Tarner, Evelyn. *An Easter Cantata in Song: "Lift Your Voices."* Chicago: Tabernacle, 1969.

Taylor, Ronald. *Berlin and Its Culture: A Historical Portrait.* New Haven, Conn.: Yale University Press, 1997.

Taylor, Telford. *Munich: The Price of Peace.* Garden City, N.Y.: Doubleday, 1979.

Thompson, Dorothy. *The Courage to Be Happy.* Boston: Houghton Mifflin, 1957.

————. "Dorothy Thompson Imagines the Horror of a World Controlled by Adolf Hitler." In *In Our Own Words: Extraordinary Speeches of the American Century,* edited by Robert G. Torricelli and Andrew Carroll. New York: Kodansha International, 1999.

————. *Dorothy Thompson's Political Guide: A Study of American Liberalism and Its Relationship to Modern Totalitarian States.* New York: Stackpole Sons, 1938.

————. *I Saw Hitler!* New York: Farrar and Rinehart, 1932.

————. *Let the Record Speak.* Cambridge, Mass.: Riverside Press, 1939.

————. *Listen, Hans.* Boston: Houghton Mifflin, 1942.

————. *My Husband, Maxim Kopf: The Artist in the Twentieth Century.* New York: Praeger, 1960.

————. *The New Russia.* New York: Henry Holt, 1928.

————. *Refugees: Anarchy or Organization?* New York: Random House, 1938.

————. *The Tulip Box.* Holograph, Special Collections Research Center, Syracuse University.

————, and Phyllis Bottome. *The Depths of Prosperity.* New York: George H. Doran, 1925.

Thompson, Lawrence. *The Greatest Treason: The Untold Story of Munich.* New York: William Morrow, 1968.

Tillich, Paul. *The Courage to Be.* New Haven, Conn.: Yale University Press, 1959.

Tone, Andrea. *Devices and Desires: A History of Contraception in America.* New York: Farrar, Straus and Giroux, 2001.

Tyrer, Nicola. *They Fought in the Fields: The Women's Land Army: The Story of a Forgotten Victory.* London: Sinclair-Stevenson, 1996.

Untermeyer, Louis. *Bygone: The Recollections of Louis Untermeyer.* New York: Harcourt, Brace, and World, 1965.

Van Doren, Carl. *Sinclair Lewis: A Biographical Sketch.* New York: Kennikat Press, 1969.

Villard, Oswald Garrison. *The Disappearing Daily: Chapters in American Newspaper Evolution.* New York: Knopf, 1944.

Voss, Frederick S. *Reporting the War: The Journalistic Coverage of World War II.* Washington, D.C.: Smithsonian Institution Press for the National Portrait Gallery, 1994.

Wallace, Diana. *Sisters and Rivals in British Women's Fiction, 1914–39.* Basingstoke, UK: Macmillan, 2000.

Ward, Sadie. *War in the Countryside, 1939–1945.* London: Cameron Book, 1988.

Ware, Susan. *Letter to the World: Seven Women Who Shaped the American Century.* New York: W. W. Norton, 1998.

Weinreb, Ben, and Christopher Hibbert, eds. *The London Encyclopedia.* London: Macmillan, 1995.

Wells, Catherine. *The Book of Catherine Wells.* Freeport, N.Y.: Books for Libraries Press, 1971.

Wells, Frank. *A Pictorial Biography.* London: Jupiter Books, 1977.

Wells, H. G. *Ann Veronica: A Modern Love Story.* New York: Harper and Brothers, 1909.

————. *Experiment in Autobiography.* 2 vols. London: Faber and Faber, 1934.

————. *H. G. Wells in Love: Postscript to an Experiment in Autobiography.* Edited by G. P. Wells. Boston: Little, Brown, 1984.

————. *The New Machiavelli.* New York: Harper and Brothers, 1909.

————. *The Time Machine.* London: William Heinemann, 1895. Reprint, Sandy, Utah: Quiet Vision Publishing, 1999–2000.

————. *Tono-Bungay.* London: Macmillan, 1909. Reprint, New York: Oxford University Press, 1997.

West, Anthony. *Heritage.* New York: Random House, 1955.

————. *H. G. Wells: Aspects of a Life.* New York: Random House, 1984.

————. *On a Dark Night.* London: Eyre and Spottiswoode, 1949.

West, Rebecca. *Birds Fall Down.* New York: Viking Press, 1966.

————. *Black Lamb and Grey Falcon: A Journey Through Yugoslavia in 1937.* New York: Viking Press, 1941.

———. *The Court and the Castle*. London: Macmillan, 1958.

———. *Cousin Rosamund*. London: Macmillan, 1985. Reprint, New York: Penguin, 1987.

———. *Ending in Earnest*. Garden City, N.Y.: Doubleday, 1931.

———. *The Essential Rebecca West: Uncollected Prose*. Pittsburgh, Penn.: Pearhouse Press, 2010.

———. *Family Memories: An Autobiographical Journey*. Edited by Faith Evans. New York: Viking, 1988.

———. *The Fountain Overflows*. New York: Viking Press, 1956.

———. "Goodness Doesn't Just Happen." In *This I Believe*, edited by Edward P. Morgan, 187–88. New York: Simon and Schuster, 1952.

———. *Harriet Hume: A London Fantasy*. New York: Doubleday, Doran, 1929.

———. *The Harsh Voice*. London: Jonathan Cape, 1935. Reprint, Garden City, N.Y.: Doubleday, 1935.

———. *Henry James*. London: Nisbet, 1916. Reprint: Port Washington, N.Y.: Kennikat Press, 1968.

———. *The Judge*. London: Hutchinson, 1922. Reprint, London: Virago, 1980.

———. *A Letter to a Grandfather*. London: Hogarth Press, 1933.

———. *The Meaning of Treason*. New York: Viking Press, 1947.

———. *My Religion*. Edited by Arnold Bennett. London: D. Appleton, 1926.

———. *The New Meaning of Treason*. New York: Viking Press, 1964.

———. *1900*. London: Weidenfeld and Nicolson, 1982. Reprint, New York: Crescent Books, 1982.

———. *The Real Night*. London: Macmillan, 1984. Reprint, New York: Viking Press, 1985.

———. *Rebecca West, a Celebration: Selected from Her Writings by Her Publishers with Her Help*. New York: Viking, 1977.

———. *The Return of the Soldier*. London: Nisbet, 1918. New York: George H. Doran, 1918.

———. *Selected Letters of Rebecca West*. Edited by Bonnie Kime Scott. New Haven, Conn.: Yale University Press, 2000.

———. *The Sentinel: An Incomplete Early Novel*. Edited by Kathryn Laing. Oxford: Legenda, 2002.

———. *St. Augustine*. London: Peter Davies, 1933. New York: D. Appleton, 1933.

———. *The Strange Necessity*. New York: Doubleday, Doran, 1928. Reprint, London: Virago Press, 1987.

———. *Survivors in Mexico*. Edited by Bernard Schweizer. New Haven, Conn.: Yale University Press, 2003.

———. *The Thinking Reed*. London: Hutchinson, 1936.

———. *A Train of Powder*. New York: Viking Press, 1936. Chicago: Ivan R. Dee, 1955. London: Macmillan, 1955.

———. *Woman as Artist and Thinker*. Lincoln, Neb.: iUniverse, 2005.

Whitman, Walt. *Leaves of Grass*. Brooklyn, N.Y.: Rome Brothers, 1855.

Wolfe, Peter. *Rebecca West: Artist and Thinker*. Carbondale: Southern Illinois University Press, 1971.

Wollheim, Richard. *Sigmund Freud*. Cambridge: Cambridge University Press, 1990.

Woolf, Virginia. *A Writer's Diary*. New York: Harcourt Brace Jovanovich, 1953.

Wordsworth, William. "Ode to Duty." In *The Oxford Book of English Verse: 1250–1900*. Edited by A. T. Quiller-Couch. Oxford: Clarendon Press, 1900.

The World's Best Short Stories of 1930: Sixteen Stories Selected by the Editors of Leading American Magazines. New York: Minton, Balch, 1930.

Yagoda, Ben. *About Town: "The New Yorker" and the World It Made*. New York: Scribner, 2000.

Ziegler, Philip. *London at War*. New York: Knopf, 1995.

Zuckmayer, Carl, *A Part of Myself*. New York: Harcourt Brace, 1966.

————, and Dorothy Thompson. *Second Wind*. Translated by Elizabeth Hapgood. New York: Doubleday, 1940.

CREDITS

Pg 296 Dorothy Thompson Papers, Special Collections Research Center, Syracuse University

Pg 300 Sueddeutsche Zeitung Photo/Lebrecht

Pg 307 Elli Marcus/Time & Life Pictures/Getty Images

Pg 318 Photo by Elli Marcus. Photo published with permission from the Marcus family. Dorothy Thompson Papers, Special Collections Research Center, Syracuse University

Pg 341 Lisa Larsen/Time & Life Pictures/Getty Images

Pg 379 Alfred Eisenstaedt/Time & Life Pictures/Getty Images

Pg 398 Dezo Hoffman/Rex USA Rebecca West papers 1986.002. Department of Special Collections and University Archives, McFarlin Library, University of Tulsa, Tulsa, Oklahoma.

Pg 435 Horst Tappe/Lebrecht Music & Arts

Pg 436 Stanley Devon/The Sunday Times/NI Syndication

TEXT CREDITS

Grateful acknowledgment is made to the following for permission to reproduce both published and unpublished material:

Alfred Music Publishing Co., Inc.: Excerpt from "Lullaby of Broadway" (from "Gold Diggers of 1935"), words by Al Dubin, music by Harry Warren, copyright © 1935 (Renewed) by WB Music Corp. All rights reserved. Used by permission of Alfred Music Publishing Co., Inc.

A. P. Watt Ltd: Excerpts from the letters of H. G. Wells. Used by permission of A. P. Watt Ltd on behalf of The Literary Executors of the Estate of H. G. Wells.

Commentary: Excerpts from "Do Israeli Ties Conflict with U. S. Citizenship? America Demands a Single Loyalty" by Dorothy Thomas from *Commentary*, March 1950, copyright © 1950 by Commentary, Inc. Used by permission of Commentary.

Estate of Eileen Agar and Joseph Bard: Excerpts from letters written by Joseph Bard, copyright © Estate of Eileen Agar and Joseph Bard. Used by permission.

Estate of Rebecca West: Excerpts from both published and unpublished documents and letters by Rebecca West. Used by permission of the Estate of Rebecca West.

Jane Perry Gunther: Excerpts from the John Gunther papers. Used courtesy of Jane Perry Gunther.

Houghton Mifflin Harcourt Publishing Company and Hogarth Press, a member of The Random House Group Ltd: Excerpts from *The Letters of Virginia Woolf*, Vol. II, 1912–1922, copyright © 1976 by Quentin Bell and Angelica Garnett and excerpts from *The Letters of Virginia Woolf*, Vol. IV, 1929–1931, copyright © 1978 by Quentin Bell and Angelica Garnett. Used by permission of the Houghton Mifflin Harcourt Publishing Company and Hogarth Press, a member of The Random House Group Ltd.

McIntosh and Otis, Inc.: All previously published Dorothy Thompson letters and papers, copyright © 1963, 1974, 1990, 1991, 1998 by John Paul Lewis, Gregory Lewis, and Lesley Lewis; all previously published Sinclair Lewis letters and papers, copyright © 1952, 1963 by Melville H. Cane and Pincus Berner, Executors of the Estate of Sinclair Lewis; all previously unpublished Dorothy Thompson, John Paul Lewis, Gregory Lewis, and Lesley Lewis letters and papers; all previously unpublished Sinclair Lewis letters and papers, copyright © 2011 by the Estate of Sinclair Lewis, administrator De Bonis Non, J. P. Morgan Chase Bank; all previously unpublished Michael Lewis letters and papers, copyright © 2011 by The Estate of Michael Lewis, Eugene Winick, Administrator C.T.A. All material used by permission of McIntosh and Otis, Inc.

Viking Penguin, a division of Penguin Group (USA), Inc., and SLL/Sterling Lord Literistic, Inc.: Excerpts from *Black Lamb and Grey Falcon* by Rebecca West, copyright © 1940, 1941 and copyright renewed 1968, 1969 by Rebecca West. Used by permission of Viking Penguin, a division of Penguin Group (USA), Inc., and SLL/Sterling Lord Literistic, Inc.

INDEX

ABOUT THE AUTHOR

Susan Hertog was born in New York City and graduated from Hunter College. After earning her M.F.A. from Columbia University, she became a freelance journalist and photographer. She is the author of one previous book, *Anne Morrow Lindbergh: Her Life*. She lives in Manhattan with her family.